The Wizard of Oz
FAQ

The Wizard of Oz FAQ

All That's Left to Know About Life According to Oz

David J. Hogan

APPLAUSE
THEATRE & CINEMA BOOKS
An Imprint of Hal Leonard Corporation

Published in 2014 by Applause Theatre & Cinema Books
An Imprint of Hal Leonard Corporation
7777 West Bluemound Road
Milwaukee, WI 53213

Trade Book Division Editorial Offices
33 Plymouth St., Montclair, NJ 07042

Except where otherwise specified, all images are from the author's personal collection.

The FAQ series was conceived by Robert Rodriguez and developed with Stuart Shea.

Printed in the United States of America

Book design by Snow Creative Services

Library of Congress Cataloging-in-Publication Data

Hogan, David J., 1953–
    The Wizard of Oz FAQ : all that's left to know about life according to Oz / David J. Hogan.
        pages cm. — (FAQ series)
    Includes bibliographical references and index.
    ISBN 978-1-4803-5062-5
1. Wizard of Oz (Motion picture : 1939) I. Title.
    PN1997.W593H64 2014
    791.43'72—dc23
                                                                    2014015040

www.applausebooks.com

For Judy Garland, the greatest entertainer of the 20th century,
whose gifts have captivated millions

Contents

Acknowledgments

No book writes itself, and nobody writes a book completely alone, either. My thanks to the following people for special help, expertise, and all-around encouragement: Margaret Borst, Ronald V. Borst/ Hollywood Movie Posters, David Harnack, Ian Hogan, Mark Thomas McGee, Mark A. Miller, Ted Okuda, Mark Turner, and Bob Villard.

Special thanks to designers Michael and Anna Snow and to Marybeth Keating, Jessica Burr, Gary Morris, and the other creative people at Applause.

Introduction

Magic Enough for Everybody

". . . and to the young in heart we dedicate this picture. . . ."
(from the opening epigraph to *The Wizard of Oz*)

Metro-Goldwyn-Mayer released fifty-two films in 1939. At that time, the studio represented the gold standard among Hollywood production companies and prided itself on movies of consistently high quality. Although some of its pictures were less expensive than others, all of them were "class" entertainment.

Many of the MGM fifty-two for 1939 have fallen into obscurity; even golden-age film buffs aren't likely to summon much enthusiasm for screenings of *Burn 'Em Up O'Connor* or *Society Lawyer*. On the other hand, many of the year's MGM releases are available and very well liked today: *Tarzan Finds a Son!* and *At the Circus*; *Ninotchka* and *Goodbye, Mr. Chips*; *Babes in Arms* and *Another Thin Man*; *The Adventures of Huckleberry Finn* and *Idiot's Delight*.

One release that is particularly well recalled, *Gone With the Wind*, wasn't an MGM movie at all. The studio's distribution arm placed *GWTW* into theaters, but Selznick International produced the picture.

Of all the films produced by MGM for release in 1939, one has achieved special status.

For reasons that we'll discover, *The Wizard of Oz* endures. Planning and film-ing demanded great effort, and MGM's many employees took up the challenge.

Movies are complicated endeavors comprised of numberless elements. From the beginning, movies have been a collaborative art form involving anything from a handful of people to many thousands. In the studio era as MGM knew and practiced it in 1939, experts from every imaginable discipline were on the lot, on salary. They waited for instructions and were eager to offer their own ideas. Moreover, if particular sorts of people were not already on the lot, they would be there tomorrow.

A movie must appear seamless, but every film is really a puzzle constructed not just from pieces of film (or digital bits), but from the efforts of countless

This beautiful title card heralds an American movie masterpiece.

people we never see. They whip up a torrent of effort and imagination, synchro-nizing their work and directing it to a single goal.

Oz represents studio-system collaboration in its highest form. Everything meshed: screenplay, direction, and performances; cinematography, art direc-tion, and sets; costumes, makeup, and special effects; music, songs, and danc-ing—all of these are peerless.

The better part of a century has passed since *The Wizard of Oz* first played on theater screens. Existing now in the rear-view mirror of hindsight, *Oz* looms larger than ever before. For various reasons, it continues to speak to us. As with any other movie or similarly immersive experience, *The Wizard of Oz* is a single movie—and an infinite number of movies. In its most basic form, *Oz* is a physical thing that was born as 35mm film stock spooled on reels. It later found its way onto 16mm, and finally made the leap into the various digitized media we know today. All of those comprise Version #1. The *other* versions of the movie are the ones that each of us creates when we watch and absorb Version #1. MGM and Victor Fleming and all the others that labored on *The Wizard of Oz* assembled the template that the rest of us have worked with for seventy-five years. Because we naturally bring our own experiences, prejudices, and expectations to the film (as to any film), we become co-creators of *Oz*. Every one of those versions is unique. Moreover, the acts of co-creation are evolutionary as well as ongoing:

the version of *Oz* you created at age six isn't the same as the one you created at fourteen or at thirty-five, or seventy. *The Wizard of Oz* has lived because *we* live.

Our shared authorship of the movie has led to some illuminating bursts of individual creativity. Later in the book we'll look at such things as fan fiction and the plentitude of rumors that swirl around *Oz*; here, we will note the reasonably uncommon but intriguing assertion that, at film's end, the camera pans down from Dorothy's bedside to the floor, revealing a pair of ruby slippers. Ah, Dorothy's adventure wasn't a dream after all. It was real!

The claim periodically shows up in discussion threads on *Oz*-centric Web sites, where viewers insist that they saw that final image. Most of the claimants add that they saw this version only once, implying that a conspiracy is afoot, as if the image inadvertently reveals a profound secret that mysterious forces later expunged. These people are positive about the slippers under the bed—and why not? They are co-creators of the movie. They want Dorothy's journey to be real, so they make it real.

A phenomenon like this suggests that *The Wizard of Oz* lives on not just as an artifact, but also as a physical, biological entity, powered and transmuted by the brains of millions. That a film enjoys that kind of life is remarkable because so few markers of popular culture can stride across decades and maintain their vigor, let alone increase and augment it. Time diminishes so much of the past. People and things that carried real weight when *Oz* was new are now just wisps of vapor. Who remembers Walter Winchell, the *New York Graphic*, or the Bendix wringer-washer? What became of the national preoccupations with Brenda Frazier, mah-jongg, Dale Carnegie, and *One Man's Family*? Those people and things have found places in the minds of historians and a few nostalgists, but they are no longer parts of the national consciousness. They didn't become timeless because they never deserved to be.

The real issue may be, of course, that Americans generally have a very low regard for things past, but that's a concern for another kind of book. The fact is that *The Wizard of Oz* came onto the American scene as a movie and became an individually personalized institution. It is an irresistible engine that has transported millions of viewers to a fabulous place. Once there, each of us manipulates it, via imagination, to suit our wishes and needs. (Salman Rushdie has said, for instance, that there might be no better person for us to "fill up" with our individualized hopes than the pathetically hollow Tin Woodman.)

Based on an astonishingly imaginative book, the movie's own inventions are no less wonderful. We hum the songs' melodies and we know the lyrics by heart. We murmur dialogue along with the cast. We cannot wait to see what happens next even though we *know* what's going to happen next. We are enchanted and swept away, every time.

These ongoing combinations of joyful and interpretative responses suggest that *The Wizard of Oz* is art (or, ominously, Art). Like a lot of art, it pleases many. Like true art, it inspires differences of opinion and serious debate. Some argue, for instance, that Dorothy's ruby slippers transform and "empower" her. Others insist that the slippers do not make Dorothy more powerful at all, but simply affirm the person Dorothy has always been. Other intellectual responses claim the movie as a celebration of matriarchy, the inner goddess, girl power, or plain femaleness. Some viewers think about the story and find representations of imperialism, fascism, and the misleading relationship of perception to power. Others react with dismay to the seeming surrender embodied in Dorothy's relieved, "There's no place like home!" (More about this in chapter 19.)

Because of the film's particular focus on totems the likes of the slippers, the Witch's broomstick, crystal balls, and Glinda's wand, some observers regard *Oz* as almost atavistic in its symbology: as keenly calculated primitivism disguised as a fairy tale. Others take a vaguely similar tack, but in literary terms, venerating Dorothy as a descendant of Beowulf, another resolute hero who absorbs bizarre punishments while pursuing a plainly mythic quest adventure.

Many people accept *The Wizard of Oz* as a celebration of the Christian qualities of kindness, mercy, and responsibility to others. On the other hand, Dorothy's self-reliance, which allows her to succeed when the essential impotence of the all-powerful Wizard leads only to dashed hopes and dismay, encourages factions that hail *Oz* as a disavowal of organized religion, or even of God Himself.

Intellectualized responses to the film are fun to consider, and they are important to an understanding of whom and what we are. Unavoidably, though, a significant part of the appeal of *Oz* lies in what we know about the career and private life of the film's star, Judy Garland. Seldom happy with herself, unlucky in love, and in a perpetual state of exhaustion, she searched for but never found the peace achieved by Dorothy. Some biographers have claimed that *Oz* haunted Garland's life, and that Dorothy Gale became Judy's unwelcome doppelgänger. There's something facile about that kind of thinking, and something unkind, as well, because it implies that Garland had no inner resources. Better, perhaps, to acknowledge the poignancy of the Garland-*Oz* connection this way: it is *we* who are haunted. Just as hindsight has let the movie grow larger, our awareness of what transpired in Judy Garland's short life has encouraged us to assign to her more unhappiness and ambivalence than she may have been willing to accept. Judy remained grateful to *The Wizard of Oz*, and acknowledged its importance by invariably speaking of it with fondness and adopting its key song as her lifelong signature tune. Let's be willing to accept that *Oz* was a gift to Garland instead of a burden. Dorothy's life can exist in our minds as a kind of alternate lifetime for Garland, with the happy conclusion we've always suspected Judy deserved.

Emotions frequently drive us, and *The Wizard of Oz* plays cleverly on a broad range of them: love and longing; friendship and responsibility; adventurousness and apprehension; delight and dread; triumph and disappointment; kinship and abandonment—even the feared finality of death. The story's dark moments are terrifying, and the happy ones are as deeply satisfying as a morning in June. The film provides a heroine whom we love and adore, and supporting characters that alternately amuse, puzzle, charm, and appall us.

None of that would matter as much as it does if the film had not "worn well." Although film grammar has evolved considerably since 1939, the visual aspects of *The Wizard of Oz*—not least the sweeping, moving camera eye—capture our attention and grip it tight. Above all, the movie creates an environment that, although wildly fantastic, has a subtle internal logic. Somehow, all of the place's joys and madness make perfect sense, and we can't imagine it *not* existing.

What a fabulous achievement.

But as we'll see, the making of *The Wizard of Oz* was neither calm nor tidy. Some elements of casting, particularly the central role of Dorothy, were difficult. Many people wrote and massaged the screenplay, and numerous directors found themselves hired, dismissed, or replaced. Fantasy was a tough sell in 1939, and on top of that, the picture was going to be shot in Technicolor, which was expensive and, frankly, a pain in the ass.

The songwriters insisted on a new kind of integration of song and story. Virtually everything on screen was created from scratch, with extraordinary imagination and great expenditures of time and money.

Then there were new challenges that no film had ever faced. Just how, for instance, do you create a winged monkey and make him fly? And what does he wear? What does a Tin Woodman sound like? Dorothy had better be the most appealing girl that ever lived. Where are we going to find her? How does she think and what does she say? She'll have to be one of a kind *and* just like the rest of us, all at once.

What does an angry apple tree look like? And have we ever hatched a human being from an egg before?

Remember that business with the poppies? Well, we're going to need about seven truckloads of them, and they can't wilt beneath those hot lights. Got any ideas?

How are we going to pull off a journey from the dull plains of Kansas to the sinister parapets of a witch's castle, and then back again to Kansas? How do we design the trip so that it's utterly fantastic yet rooted in an honesty that audiences will recognize and embrace?

The questions must have seemed endless. This book answers them and many others, exploring along the way *Oz* history, relevant events that came after 1939, and oddities not discussed in other books about the film. You will get a sense of the gifts and personalities of many who worked on the picture in front of the camera and behind it, on-set, in executive offices, and in studio workshops.

The Wizard of Oz attracted enormous audiences and splendid critical reaction, but lost money because it had cost a great deal to make. The film was a financial disappointment, a prestige picture that hurt MGM's bottom line. In that regard, the movie defied the expectations of its creators. *Oz* defied expectations in other ways, too, by achieving a life far more enduring and grand than any that might have been imagined by Louis Mayer or anyone else at the studio. Lacking the alternate existences provided by TV rights, home video platforms, and streaming, Hollywood films of the 1930s were here-and-gone product.

Important pictures might play at big-city houses for weeks, but got just two or three days when they made their way to neighborhood theaters. If you missed a movie, you missed it. Few films of the era enjoyed studio re-releases, and even those that did were usually away from screens for five or ten years. Yet here we are, well into the 21st century, and *The Wizard of Oz* is as available and as beloved as any movie ever made.

The Wizard of Oz was a risky and expensive project, and the teenage Judy Garland had to bear the greater part of its weight herself. Fortunately, her supporting cast was brilliant.

The film's continued success is a grand act of defiance that's been welcomed by countless millions of people. Many big-budget Hollywood movies from the golden age are paragons of imagination and collaboration. A relative few that satisfy popular taste also attract the intelligentsia. The one that takes us to Oz and back is peerless. Given its craft, beauty, and humanity, the movie is easy to adore. But we also believe in it. *The Wizard of Oz* touches our hearts and sparks our thinking, and we long to return to it, again and again.

David J. Hogan
Arlington Heights, IL

The Wizard of Oz
FAQ

Ars Gratia Artis

The Little City Called MGM

MGM began in 1924, when New York–based Loew's Theatres boss Marcus Loew purchased a Los Angeles production company named for its founder, Louis B. Mayer (see "In Focus: Louis B. Mayer," this chapter). Because Loew's already owned Metro Pictures and Goldwyn Pictures, the new entity was Metro-Goldwyn-Mayer. It established itself in Culver City, near Los Angeles. Although the Culver City facility had been established by Sam Goldwyn, the founder of Goldwyn Pictures, Mr. Goldwyn wasn't directly involved in the creation of MGM; he had been eased out of his own company in 1922, and functioned thereafter as an independent producer.

Carving a Place in Hollywood

MGM rose to real industry dominance in the 1930s, under the hands-on stewardship of Louis Mayer and with the financial resources of Loew's. The studio had made fine films during the '20s, but its golden age took hold a decade later, with high-quality releases as dissimilar as *The Big House* (1930) and *Trader Horn* (1931); *Tarzan the Ape Man* and *Red Dust* (both 1932); *Dinner at Eight* and *Bombshell* (both 1933); *The Thin Man* (1934); *Mad Love* and *Mutiny on the Bounty* (both 1935); *Rose Marie*, *Fury*, and *San Francisco* (all 1936); *The Good Earth* and *Captains Courageous* (both 1937); and *Love Finds Andy Hardy* and *Boys Town* (both 1938). By 1938–39, filmgoers and the industry recognized MGM as the most prestigious of all movie studios.

MGM was one of Hollywood's Big Four; the others were 20th Century-Fox, Paramount, and Warner Bros. Fox and Paramount worked in the MGM vein, producing sophisticated comedies, dramas, and musicals marked by glossy production values and beautiful, very popular stars. Alone among the Big Four, Warner Bros. cultivated a gritty, streetwise sensibility. Somewhat less prosperous than its three main rivals, Warner elevated character actors like James Cagney and Paul Muni to star status, and carved a niche with gangster melodramas and other "social problem" films, elaborate musicals that had an affinity for the concerns of working people, and hilariously anarchic cartoon shorts.

The industry's "minor majors" were Universal (horror thrillers, musicals, and westerns), Columbia ("common man" comedies and melodramas, edgy romances, and westerns), and RKO (comedies, horror thrillers, and adaptations of provocative literary works). The other minor major, United Artists, had set itself up as a distributor that would also produce films. Sophisticated comedies, adult drama, and handsome costume pictures dominated UA output.

Of the minor studios, Walt Disney Productions was unique because it was thoroughly dominated by the vision of one person. It produced only short- and (after 1937) long-form cartoon animation and had no distribution arm. Its films were booked into theaters by Columbia, United Artists, and, after 1936, RKO (the last, like MGM, Fox, Paramount, and Warner, controlled its own exhibition via ownership of a nationwide theater chain).

Hal Roach Productions became a significant minor studio via silent and talking live-action comedy shorts starring Laurel and Hardy, Charley Chase, Our Gang (the Little Rascals), Thelma Todd and ZaSu Pitts, and other stars that had become audience favorites. Roach began to release the occasional feature in the early 1930s. It eliminated two-reel shorts altogether in 1936 and made increasingly ambitious feature comedies and dramas. Pathé, and later MGM, distributed the Roach product.

The other important minor studio was Republic, home to peerless technical craftsmen and quick, capable directors who occupied themselves with formulaic but very well-executed westerns and serials.

Then there were the so-called Poverty Row or Gower Gulch operations, tiny outfits often headquartered near Gower Street in Hollywood. The most active of these studios were Monogram and Producers Releasing Corporation (more familiarly known as PRC). These two essentially imitated whatever sorts of pictures played well for the larger studios, only with minuscule budgets; writers and directors that were tired, untalented, or just disinterested; and young players who might be on their way up and veteran players who were definitely on their way down.

Monogram, PRC, and even Republic were beneath contempt as far as MGM was concerned, but there were numerous other production companies (one hesitates to call them studios) that existed even lower on the Hollywood ladder; Mascot, Tiffany, Chesterfield, and Educational were among the more prominent of the lot. Additionally, a very few poverty-stricken but ingenious indie companies produced and distributed "black cast" films, in all genres, to the nation's segregated, "colored-only" movie houses.

Below these were shoestring independent producers inhabiting a substratum from which issued pure and unabashed exploitation dealing with wild youth, unwanted pregnancy, marijuana, sex hygiene ("birth of a baby" films could always find an audience), and women romanced by gorillas. No legit distributors handled this product, which was peddled to the nation's independent neighborhood theaters on a screen-by-screen basis, and aggressively promoted via local radio and newspapers, and even with flyers posted to telephone poles.

So then, Hollywood in the 1930s was a big, variegated business run, variously, by self-educated immigrants, Ivy Leaguers, bootstrappers, knockaround guys, and sleazeballs. There was room enough for plenty of players, and the one that sat atop all the others was MGM. One or another of the town's major studios could certainly have made *The Wizard of Oz*, but none could have equaled the imagination and sumptuousness mandated by Louis Mayer and MGM, and made possible by the studio's wealth and human resources.

MGM's movies always looked good, but not all of them were true "A" pictures. Although MGM produced a heavy slate of expensive, prestige films, it relied (like the other majors) on smaller pictures for quick, profitable turn-arounds that helped finance the "important" projects. MGM did B-level dramas, romances, and crime pictures, as well as profitable, lightweight series like the Andy Hardy and Maisie movies. The studio's second-tier releases had strict budgets and were dependable earners. And then there was the MGM short-subject unit, which provided Loew's theaters with additional audience-luring product and functioned as a training ground for promising actors and behind-the-camera personnel.

MGM's Physical Plant and Staff

MGM's facilities sprawled across 185 acres of Culver City real estate. At peak employment during World War II, the studio had some four thousand on-site employees (many hundreds more worked at MGM film exchanges located in every major American city and at offices abroad). The physical plant had thirteen miles of paved roads and six distinct lots, distinguished as follows:

Lot 1 was on forty-four acres that held twenty-eight immense, hangar-like sound stages and most of the studio's permanent buildings, nearly two hundred of them. The executive office building was on Lot 1, as well as the publicity department, casting, special effects, sound, and the commissary (which fed nearly three thousand people every working day). Numerous craft and industrial buildings were on this lot, and were served by a dedicated rail line.

The studio music library was on Lot 1; likewise, art, wardrobe, film processing, and projection.

Lot 2 occupied thirty-seven acres developed during the studio's rapid expansion in the '20s. Here you'd find the animation department (by 1939, the home of Tom and Jerry), along with an elaborate prison set and various false-front buildings and streets that suggested the Colonial era, the American Victorian period, a New England town, and New York streets and waterfront.

A jungle exterior with a sixty-three-million-gallon lake and an enormous, painted-sky cyclorama dominated sixty-five-acre **Lot 3**. The lot also had a grouping of Colonial-era buildings, an old-European street, and three Old West streets and facades (including a ghost town).

Lot 4 took up five and four-tenths acres dedicated to a working zoo and parking for Lot 3.

If you needed things that go, you went to **Lot 5**, seven and eight-tenths acres taken up with horse stables and corrals, as well as a wealth of working transportation: automobiles old and new, carriages and wagons, a variety of train engines and train cars, and various complete and partial aircraft.

Lot 6, at six acres, held the studio nursery, which cultivated living trees, flowers, bushes, and ground plantings. Nursery staff also maintained sod.

Although located in Culver City, MGM was itself a small city, with its own fifty-man police force (including a pair of plainclothesmen) headed by Chief Whitey Hendry. He protected studio property, including its stars, and worked with area police forces to manage potential scandals. The studio had a fire department and a post office. There was a florist shop, a foundry, and a commissary; a barbershop, a sanitation unit, and a small zoo. One could also find a lumberyard, a carpentry shop, an upholstery shop, a stable, a plastering shop, a bakery, a welding shop, plus a complement of electricians, painters, and costume patternmakers. The wardrobe department held 150,000 costumes dispersed among fifteen warehouses.

A dedicated power plant that could have supplied twenty-five thousand households provided electricity.

The studio employed machinists, engineers, hair stylists, dialogue and drama coaches, and a small army of laborers. The artists, sculptors, cosmeticians, and various assistants in the MGM makeup department were capable of preparing as many as twelve thousand players in a single ten-hour day.

Salaried elocution coaches, dance instructors, equestrians, fencing experts, swimming instructors, and singing teachers instructed young contract players (and any veterans that needed some brushup).

A certified schoolteacher was on-set daily to ensure (in theory) that child players received the state's minimum requirement for schooling. According to state law, child actors were to receive their schooling in one-hour blocks throughout the day. Not surprisingly, the law was flouted at the studios, where irregularly scheduled fifteen- or twenty-minute breaks for school were typical, and usually allowed only if a technical chore, such as resetting the lights, meant that the young star wasn't needed on-set anyway.

A film lab on the studio premises processed between 150 million and 200 million feet of release prints each year. Executives could easily view daily footage in any of twenty-two screening rooms.

MGM's massive library of recorded music held about four million songs, instrumentals, and scores. A research library that never locked its doors was handy when you needed to know, for instance, how many buttons a 17th-century fusilier wore on his uniform. Research staffers handled five hundred queries a day.

A massive cache of furniture and props comprising more than a million items was maintained on-site, and negatives and other film stock were stored in a dedicated vault.

"Talent" employees other than actors included salaried directors, cinematographers, editors, and readers (underpaid college grads who evaluated plays, novels, and other works that might be suited for film). There were art directors, set designers, special-effects specialists, and camera operators; focus pullers, sound recordists, and composers; publicity people, secretaries, and sound editors; comptrollers, accountants, and bookkeepers; attorneys and other legal staff; stunt coordinators, drivers, studio security, and maintenance. There was a small army of executives, too: senior, junior, and in-between.

Dozens of screenwriters were on salary, and many more cycled in and out as freelancers.

Making It Pay

Not surprisingly, MGM's overhead was enormous. A brigade's worth of salaried employees (there were about four thousand of them at the time of *The Wizard of Oz*) mandated a weekly "nut" that could be met only if the studio ran nearly 365 days a year and released, on average, a movie a week, annum after annum. (During 1938–39, in fact, MGM averaged sixty feature films a year.) Sixty percent of MGM output was "A" product that reflected well on Mr. Mayer, and that perpetuated the carefully cultivated MGM image. Leo the Lion dated to 1924 (the first Leo came from Port Sudan, Africa), his noble head framed by a mission motto, in Latin: *ARS GRATIA ARTIS*: art for art's sake. The sentiment was only partly true, and a little pretentious, too, but Mayer and his lieutenants liked to think they wholeheartedly believed it. For added luster, executives had the unofficial MGM motto: "Do It Right, Do It Big, Give It Class."

Besides feature films, MGM produced animated cartoons (the first "Tom and Jerry" cartoon was made in 1939) and short subjects encompassing travelogues, comedy, mini-musicals, sports, and general-interest mini-documentaries. Much in the manner of a present-day sports franchise, the studio constantly signed and groomed young players who showed promise. In most cases, careers didn't pan out as the youngsters might have hoped, but by paying novices very modestly, the studio ensured that it never suffered financially. Many newcomers endured "working" tests in the studio's short subjects. As we'll see, a pair of very young contract players, Deanna Durbin and Judy Garland, had just that sort of opportunity in an MGM short produced in 1936. MGM had a farm team, and at one time, Deanna, Judy, and hundreds more whose names are now obscure, played on it.

MGM functioned with six-day workweeks; a purposeful redundancy of directors and producers, tech personnel, and support people; as well as "more stars than there are in heaven." By the time that production #1060, *The Wizard of Oz*, was put on the schedule in 1938, the studio had staff directors the caliber of Victor Fleming, Clarence Brown, and Jack Conway, as well as top screenwriters. The finest craft and tech people were on the lot, as well as three cynically effective senior executives who served Mayer directly: Eddie Mannix (general studio operations), Howard Strickling (publicity), and Howard Dietz (advertising).

The roster of contract players was broad and remarkable. Although the studio and the entire industry had been rattled by the tragic 1937 death of the beloved Jean Harlow, other MGM stars still twinkled: Clark Gable, Robert Taylor, and Mickey Rooney; Greta Garbo, Joan Crawford, and Norma Shearer; Robert Montgomery, William Powell, and Spencer Tracy. Even character players the likes of Marie Dressler, Wallace Beery, and Lewis Stone had been elevated to star status.

Because of its tremendous human and material assets, MGM continually pursued shooting, editing, publicity, and exhibition of multiple films. The sound stages hummed with activity year-round; simultaneous with the production of *The Wizard of Oz*, for instance, were *A Christmas Carol, Ice Follies of 1939, Idiot's Delight*, and *Out West with the Hardys*.

Besides efficiencies of scale, MGM prospered because it distributed its own films—to its own theaters. Any theater with "Loew's" in its name was owned by MGM's parent company, and was thus a guaranteed venue for MGM product. By controlling production, distribution, and exhibition, MGM and the other vertically integrated studios—RKO, Paramount, Warner Bros., and 20th Century-Fox—had a street-level stranglehold on the business. Universal, Columbia, and Republic, as well as the Poverty Row outfits, owned no network of theaters, and thus were engaged in continual struggle to book their films onto theater screens.

A storm cloud appeared on MGM's horizon in 1938, when the Department of Justice looked at the vertical integration—production, distribution, and exhibition—of MGM, Fox, Warner, Paramount, and RKO—and filed an antitrust complaint that the government subsequently pursued in fits and starts. But with wartime, Washington had to deal with more important things, and besides, motion pictures were invaluable morale boosters. MGM and the others got a reprieve.

The Decline

New stars like Gene Kelly, Esther Williams, Van Johnson, Elizabeth Taylor, and Margaret O'Brien established themselves at MGM in the 1940s. Wartime exigencies, though, forced MGM to reduce output by a third, to about thirty-five releases a year. The studio was spending less money than before, but saw a concomitant drop in income.

American moviegoing peaked in 1946, when MGM showed a profit of $18 million. The sum was impressive, but a key MGM competitor, Paramount, saw profits of $39 million the same year. There was trouble in paradise. After 1946, overall movie attendance slumped, partly because of a temporarily stagnant postwar economy, and partly because the glossier studios, particularly MGM and Paramount, had been slow to pick up on the public's new interest in reality-based movies. (Warner Bros. and RKO had long cultivated their gritty voices, and by the close of the 1940s, Columbia and United Artists were following the trend. Even genteel 20th Century-Fox had good early-postwar success with tough films noir.)

Just as MGM's box office began to suffer following World War II, the Justice Department's ten-year-old antitrust suit was resolved in a May 1948 U.S. Supreme Court ruling that forced MGM and the other vertically integrated studios to divest themselves of their theaters. Because lesser studios had been at a competitive disadvantage, the divestiture ruling was proper, but nevertheless spelled doom for the classic Hollywood studio system, for without guaranteed exhibition and control of playdates, the vertically integrated studios could no longer pursue production schedules as aggressively as in the past. It was the war-years scenario all over again: production (and exhibition) had to be slowed and income diminished.

Another reprieve arrived in the form of musicals, many created for MGM by producer Arthur Freed and such directors as Vincente Minnelli and Stanley Donen. However, the cost of film production was rising, and increasing numbers of Americans stayed home nights to watch television. MGM profits fell alarmingly after 1950, and the studio cut loose a lot of its salaried talent in 1952. Film stars began to establish their own production companies, which weakened every studio's hold on actors. To address these and other changes, and to justify their overhead, Universal, Columbia, and Warner Bros. prepared for lucrative moves into television production and distribution. MGM, though, lagged behind.

Spiraling budgets and too many box-office duds in the 1950s further weakened MGM, and paradoxically encouraged the studio to believe that its salvation lay in continued production of lavish and expensive releases.

The studio began to sell off its physical assets in the 1960s; the back lots fell into the hands of real estate developers, and a great deal of priceless historical material, particularly decades of interoffice memos and other paper records, was crushed, pulped, burned, and buried in a landfill. In 1970, MGM pursued a rather embarrassing public auction (see chapter 19), and watched as independent producers became the engines that moved the industry. A succession of corporate owners and investors (including Ted Turner, Giancarlo Peretti, and Kirk Kerkorian) leveraged the MGM name for use in mergers and for a Las Vegas hotel-casino venture that sucked money out of MGM like a vacuum cleaner. Still more owners came and went. A 1981 merger with United Artists (perpetrated in order to acquire UA's film library) created MGM/UA, but the company was no longer a studio in the traditional sense. In 1986, workers removed the letters "MGM" from the façade of the MGM Tower.

Today, the James Bond films, the *Lord of the Rings/Hobbit* franchise, and other series help maintain MGM's distribution presence. The company has no studio, no back lots, no sound stages, and no contract players. It shares a Century City skyscraper with HBO, ABC, 20th Century-Fox, and SunAmerica (an investments firm formerly known as AIG-SunAmerica). In 2010, MGM submitted a bankruptcy reorganization plan. The company came out on the other side and now finances and co-finances ten to twelve films a year. Although that's not necessarily discouraging, the aggressive glory that was Louis B. Mayer's MGM is now *artis quae est in memoria*: art that lives in memory.

In Focus: Louis B. Mayer (1884–1957)

Film historians agree that the production chiefs of the great Hollywood studios of the 1930s and '40s—most of them Jewish immigrants—"invented" America by offering to a mass audience visions of an idealized nation that the studio bosses had imagined and dreamt about while youngsters in Europe. From their dreams came movies that celebrated a uniquely upbeat Americanism. In the quasi-fictional America embraced by

millions, life was defined by strong families and other sturdy relationships, and devotion to church and community, as well as by courtesy, law and order, and personal and political moderation. This on-screen America was populated and led by white Anglo-Saxon Protestants, and even when the USA reeled beneath the Depression, and teetered on the edge of armed revolt, Hollywood assured us that everything was fine and good, and that with patience and a little faith, and some good humor, too, we'd soon be back to normal.

Of all the men that became studio heads during Hollywood's golden age, none were as successful, or as fervently devoted to movie-myth America, as Louis B. Mayer, the longtime production chief of MGM. Although not born in America, he was a self-created creature of bedrock American values. Short, bespectacled, and barrel-chested, Mayer nurtured talent and made great movies. He earned untold millions for Loew's Inc., MGM's parent company, and turned ordinary actors (and even some non-actors) into wealthy paragons of stage-managed desirability.

Louis B. Mayer was a onetime scrap dealer who became a film exhibitor, and finally the lord and master of Metro-Goldwyn-Mayer, Hollywood's greatest studio. During his prime in the 1930s and '40s, Mayer was the highest-paid executive in America.

Mayer's feelings for his stars and for movie audiences were contradictory. He thought he respected order and fairness, but even when on his best behavior he regarded his stars as fortunate children, and gave audiences movies designed to be free of ambiguity. When Mayer was on his bad behavior, he intimidated and even struck underlings, and suspended ungrateful stars, or exiled them to second-rate films. He connived with his top executives to protect the studio's image all the time, even when the lapses and crimes committed by stars and other valuable employees had to be covered up.

Louis B. Mayer also okayed The Wizard of Oz, which isn't just a great movie but a high point of the American imagination. MGM's Oz was a titanic collaborative effort marked by craft, intelligence, and pure, real wonder. It is perfectly and gorgeously delightful. Mr. Mayer made that happen, so although he wasn't the nice man he wished to be, he fashioned himself into a great entertainer and storyteller, and a cultural figure of huge importance.

Louis B. Mayer was born Eliezer Meir, or possibly Baer, in Dumier, Ukraine (not far from Kiev), in 1884. The day was July 12, but Mayer later claimed to have been born on July 4, 1885, to suggest that, although Russian, he had been destined to thrive in America. Symbolism meant a lot to Mayer, who settled with his abusive father and a loving mother in New Brunswick, Canada, near Maine, in the early 1890s.

Mayer labored for years in his father's ship-salvage and scrap metal business, and then left for Boston in 1904. He married, moved to Brooklyn, and set himself up as a junk dealer. By this time, Eliezer Meir was Louis B. Mayer; the B stood for Burt, but the middle name was shortly anglicized to Burrell. Back in Boston, Mayer took a risk by purchasing run-down Boston-area burlesque houses and nickelodeons. He bought his first one in 1907, and by 1913, Mayer and partner Nathan Gordon owned theaters not just in Boston, but throughout New England.

Mayer established a film-distribution corporation in 1915. When the company earned $500,000 as the New England distributor of D. W. Griffith's sensational *The Birth of a Nation* (1915), Mayer pondered how things might work out if he distributed not just pictures by others, but films he produced himself. Very early in his career, then, Mayer understood that true power in the movie business came from a three-step ladder incorporating production, distribution, and exhibition.

He took a modest step into production, working steadily during 1915–17 with Mary Miles Minter, a thirteen-year-old who had piqued Mayer's professional interest. American film production had been centered in New York and environs, but the allure of yearlong sunshine and a variegated landscape in Los Angeles caused Mayer to move his operations there in 1918. Louis B. Mayer Productions was run by Mayer and an unusually able young executive named Irving Thalberg. In 1924, Mayer joined exhibitor Marcus Loew to form what became Metro-Goldwyn-Mayer. The company was created in order to supply product to the Loew's Theaters chain. Paramount, RKO, Warner, and 20th Century-Fox had similar sorts of vertical integration, but none pursued it as aggressively or as prestigiously as MGM.

As MGM developed and grew, Mayer indulged his good qualities (a capacity for hard work and faith in his instinct for what made good popular entertainment) and his bad ones, too (impatience, imperiousness, preoccupations with his diet and health, and a condescendingly paternal relationship with his stars).

Mayer's best asset was his devotion to sophisticated, essentially wholesome films with appeal to families, but particularly to women, who typically decided for the entire family which movies to see. Mayer had been spooked by the Fatty Arbuckle scandal of 1922, which threw all of Hollywood in a bad light and encouraged interference from opportunistic politicians, church groups, chambers of commerce, and other busybodies. Mayer's smartest decision, and his gift to film history, was his devotion to a quality product created by people of quality. He'd been born poor and had wrestled scrap. He'd gotten into the movie business during the rough-and-tumble nickelodeon era, and he'd seen more than one film career derailed by scandal. He resolved that MGM was going to elevate the entire industry.

It did.

Mayer's politics and artistic vision were deeply conservative, but within those self-imposed boundaries, he was immensely creative. He had a solid general grasp of story structure, characterizations, and "message." His talented young right-hand man, Irving Thalberg, possessed the education necessary to deal with the specifics of what Mayer saw in broad terms. Thalberg died young in 1937, which was a blow to Mayer personally and professionally. Thalberg's absence also encouraged Mayer's autocratic nature. MGM's product and image were simply unparalleled during the 1930s and most of the '40s, but after the war, Mayer's boss, New York–based Loew's Inc. president Nick Schenck, became concerned with a postwar fall-off of profits. In 1947, and without informing Mayer beforehand, Schenck hired screenwriter-turned-producer Dore Schary to be chief of MGM production. Schary was a progressive who believed that movies must teach as well as entertain. He had had an on-again off-again relationship with MGM as a writer and supervising producer going back a decade, and now—although subordinate to Mayer—he had considerable executive power. Schary's first project, a grim, character-driven war picture called *Battleground*, had originated at RKO (where Schary had been in charge of production), but that studio had had doubts about the realism promised by Schary, particularly the notion that not every moment of World War II had been awash in gung-ho heroism.

Mayer had an almost instinctive antipathy for Schary, and his negative feelings were intensified by *Battleground*, which he advised Schary not to make. However, Schary did make it, and even had the *chutzpah* to cast MGM's boy-next-door marquee draw, redheaded Van Johnson, as a combat-weary dogface who struggles with his platoon to survive the Battle of the Bulge.

Battleground became a major hit of 1949, and by then even Mayer could see that his days were numbered. Schary knew that the government-mandated forced divestiture of theaters owned by MGM and other big studios would change the whole complexion of the business, and he wasn't completely unaware of the potential threat posed by television. With all of that, plus an eagerness to dramatically increase the studio's production slate, Schary took MGM in a direction quite different from the one pursued by Mayer. Schary favored intense "ripped from the headlines" dramas, often shot in black and white on modest budgets and cast with mid-level stars, and even newcomers. During 1949–51, Schary put through tough, uncompromising pictures about mental illness (*Dial 1119*), criminal forensics (*Mystery Street*), the human price of war (*The Red Badge of Courage*), illegal immigration and exploitation of workers (*Border Incident*), race prejudice (*Intruder in the Dust*), and the psyches of criminals (*The Asphalt Jungle*). By present-day standards, these and other Schary projects were "modern movies" with intellectual sophistication and no qualms about allowing audiences to wrestle with difficult ideas. Louis Mayer hated Schary's movies.

Schary shepherded a useful amount of profitable fluff and spectacle through the MGM machine (*The Yellow Cab Man, Neptune's Daughter, Annie Get Your Gun, Father of the Bride, Summer Stock, King Solomon's Mines*), but Mayer knew that his rival's real devotions lay elsewhere. Finally tiring of Schary, and pricked by his own pride, Mayer offered a bluff "resignation" to Nick Schenck in June 1951. Schenck shocked Mayer by accepting it, and so the man who had been the highest-paid executive in America found himself removed from the company he helped create.

Although the nominal chairman of the Cinerama Corp., Louis Mayer was effectively out of the picture business. He busied himself with Republican politics (expressing admiration for Sen. Joseph McCarthy) and noted that while Universal (by that time, Universal-International) was forging new paths in television production, MGM wasn't doing the same. Further, the studio suffered miserable box office during 1952–55, and profits plummeted. Mayer perceived an opening, but his complicated and clumsy attempt to regain power by manipulating the MGM board during 1956–57 failed. Even if he had somehow succeeded, Mayer wouldn't have lived long enough to enjoy his victory. He'd been feeling tired since the summer of 1956, and although his wife and doctor knew he had leukemia, the news was kept from him. Louis Mayer died on October 29, 1957.

But in 1956, before Mayer's death, Loew's Inc. president Joseph Vogel dismissed Dore Schary. Louis Mayer didn't exactly have the last laugh, but if he'd been looking for satisfaction, he may have a found a morsel.

2

The Real Wizard of Oz

L. Frank Baum and His Many Creations

Lyman Frank Baum was born in Chittenango, New York, near Syracuse, in 1856. A number of things about Baum's early life seem significant in retrospect. His father, Benjamin, made a fortune in oil, and the Baums lived on a handsome estate called Rose Lawn. Benjamin was an entrepreneur who traveled frequently, leaving the boy with his strong-willed mother, Cynthia Stanton Baum; two older sisters; and three brothers. (Three other siblings died before Lyman was born.) The relationship of Benjamin and Cynthia was strong and loving; Benjamin's frequent absences did nothing to damp the pair's fervor for each other.

Although Benjamin Baum was frequently away, he was attuned to his son's personality and interests. When Frank was fifteen, Benjamin gave him a printing press. A bit later, he enjoyed, and funded, Frank's early experiments with theater. (Benjamin Baum's investments included a number of live theaters and opera houses.) Frank enjoyed and respected actors, and envied their ability to travel to new places by becoming other people. He eventually became general manager and, later still, the owner of the family's theaters.

Frank was homeschooled, but when Cynthia and Benjamin came to feel that Frank needed a life that was more physically active, the boy was sent to military school. Frank objected to the perfunctory regimen of the place, and instead of thriving, his health failed. He returned home and was allowed to follow what interested him.

As a boy, Baum was enchanted by the outdoors. He developed a sense of distance and scale, and revered the life and beauty nature provided. Science also absorbed his attention; he was curious about why and how things happened in the natural world. The cyclone that destroyed the town of Irving, Kansas, on May 30, 1879, profoundly impressed Baum. The storm killed eighteen people and injured sixty. Witnesses reported that a farmhouse lifted from its foundation whirled "like a top."

In practical terms, Baum's interest in nature encouraged him to explore the care and breeding of chickens. As a young adult, he created and published a poultry magazine, and his first book, *The Book of Hamburgs*, was a guide to that breed of chicken. It was published in 1886, the year Frank turned thirty.

Frank had formed a Shakespearean troupe as a younger man and taught himself to be a playwright. An early work, *The Maid of Arran*, was well received. He met Maud Gage around 1880 and fell in love. Maud was a bright and determined young woman from a wealthy Fayetteville, New York, family; she and Frank married in 1882.

Maud's mother was Matilda Joslyn Gage, a vocal champion of women's rights. Maud shared her mother's convictions, so it may have been inevitable that Frank came to support the suffrage movement. He was impressed by the minds of the women he knew, and by women's general resilience. He was especially moved by the physical bravery and mental toughness of women who fought to make homes in the harshness of the American plains. Baum's Dorothy has Maud and Matilda's resiliency, Frank's optimistic turn of mind, and Frank and Maud's strength of character. With all of this, Baum's Dorothy is heavily disguised biography and autobiography. She wasn't just a character to Baum; she was the embodiment of what he most admired about himself and the women that sustained him.

Frank's health, never robust, began to decline in the 1880s, and only grew worse when subordinates badly mismanaged the finances of his theaters. Another family business, Baum's Castorine (the product was a machine lubricant), dated to 1879, and faltered following the death of Benjamin Baum. The whole enterprise had to be sold in 1888, after a minor employee stole and gambled away a great deal of the firm's money. The employee killed himself, and nothing remained to be recovered.

Frank was a bit of a dreamer; the hardheaded pragmatist was Maud, who suggested that the two of them test their fortunes in the Dakota Territories. They settled in Aberdeen, South Dakota Territory, in 1888. They opened a quality-merchandise general store, but because drought had beaten up the local economy, the store was lost in 1890.

All right, a career in retail didn't work out. How about journalism? When the local newspaper, *The Dakota Pioneer*, came up for sale in 1890, Frank and Maud bought it and changed the name to the *Aberdeen Saturday Pioneer*. But too many area farms were struggling, and many went into foreclosure. Locals had no disposable income, so the *Aberdeen Saturday Pioneer* went into bankruptcy and folded in 1891.

That same year, the Baums moved from South Dakota to Chicago, a rapidly growing metropolis that had put the memory of the awful citywide fire of 1871 behind it. Baum occupied himself during the next few years with a variety of vocations: he was a reporter with the Chicago *Evening Post*, a traveling salesman of china, and a window dresser. A man made of tin highlighted one of Baum's Chicago window displays.

Baum was an indefatigable storyteller. He scribbled whimsical story and character ideas even when on the road, and told stories aloud to children at home in Chicago. He had maintained his contacts with Chicago journalists, who encouraged his storytelling. In 1897, Way & Williams published Baum's

Printings of L. Frank Baum's book dated 1900 to 1902 were titled *The Wonderful Wizard of Oz*. Editions from 1903 onward dispensed with "Wonderful." W. W. Denslow did the cover art and all interior illustrations for this first Oz novel.

Mother Goose in Prose. The book expands upon twenty-two of the venerable rhymes, effectively turning them into short stories with background information about key characters that the original rhymes barely hint at.

Baum's follow-up, *Father Goose: His Book*, appeared in 1899 and became the year's best-selling children's book in America. *Father Goose* is particularly significant because it marks the first pairing of Baum and illustrator W. W. Denslow; the two would collaborate on *The Wonderful Wizard of Oz* just a year later.

Denslow was an extrovert who enjoyed calling attention to himself. He was hearty, even forward, with other people, and although he and Baum weren't temperamentally well suited as collaborators, each valued the abilities of the other. The great success of *Father Goose: His Book* encouraged a Baum-Denslow follow-up, *Songs of Father Goose*.

Baum Goes to Oz

Oz had been percolating in Baum's mind for some years. He had amassed notes about the place and the creatures that inhabited it, and he'd been telling versions of the tale, in bits and pieces, to neighborhood children. He knew that Denslow could create vivid, appealing illustrations. The *Father Goose* books were good, but they were derivative; Baum was eager to publish a book that was wholly his own.

Baum titled early drafts *The Fairy Land of Oz*, *The Land of Oz*, *The Emerald City*, and *From Kansas to Fairyland*. Finally, he and his publisher, Geo. M. Hill Company, agreed on the title. *The Wonderful Wizard of Oz* was published in 1900. (In all printings from the 1903 edition onward, the book's title was shortened to *The Wizard of Oz*.)

In that first Oz novel, the Kansas scenes are very brief. More significantly, Dorothy's adventure in Oz is not a dream. Oz is a real place, and the cyclone carries her there.

The Scarecrow, Tin Woodman, and Cowardly Lion are generally resolute and well equipped to handle adversity. Dorothy and her friends are threatened not just by the witch, but also by a variety of other antagonists.

Dorothy has the circle of a good witch's kiss on her forehead, an identifier with mythic, heroic overtones. (Victor Fleming biographer Michael Sragow likens this to the forehead scar carried by J. K. Rowling's creation Harry Potter.)

Baum thought carefully about the wishes of his fictional protagonists and cleverly thwarted them during the group's first meeting with the Wizard. Dorothy sees a Great Head. The Scarecrow sees a beautiful woman. The Tin Woodman sees a monster, and the Cowardly Lion sees a ball of fire. Dorothy's vision of a Great Head isn't unreasonable, but that vision is better suited to the Scarecrow, who searches for brains. The Tin Woodman (heart) should see the beautiful woman, and the Cowardly Lion (courage) should confront the monster. (Of course, all of that would mean that Dorothy would see a ball of fire, which doesn't allow a reasonable thematic interpretation.)

In keeping with unexpurgated fairy tales and other traditional children's literature, Baum's book contains some unsparing violence, most graphically when the Scarecrow swings his axe to decapitate a wildcat that's been chasing a mouse. (A nation of friendly field mice figures prominently in the book.)

Baum's Wicked Witch of the West is a relatively minor character, a pigtailed troll with an eye patch who sends wolves, crows, and bees against the traveling friends, as well as her Winkie army. The pursuit ends when the winged monkeys accost Dorothy and her friends. The Lion is captured, and (in another very violent moment) the Scarecrow and Tin Woodman are literally pulled to pieces.

At the castle, the Witch puts Dorothy to work, à la Cinderella. When the Witch takes one of the silver slippers, Dorothy is angered and douses her with a bucket of water.

The grateful Winkies repair the Scarecrow and Tin Woodman. The humbug Wizard awards the gifts of heart, brains, and courage, and tells Dorothy he will return her to Kansas via hot-air balloon, which he'll pilot over Oz's great desert. As in the MGM adaptation, the balloon breaks free of its moorings before Dorothy can clamber into the basket (she's been looking for Toto), and the Wizard takes off alone.

In protracted sequences that MGM eliminated, Dorothy and her friends must subsequently travel to the Quadling Country, home of the helpful witch, Glinda. Before they get there, they must deal with Hammerheads, belligerent trees, people made of china, and a giant spider. Finally, the winged monkeys carry the group the rest of the way to Glinda.

After "three taps" of the slippers (retained for the MGM movie), Baum's Dorothy is returned to Kansas. The silver slippers have vanished from her feet, but there's no doubt that Oz, and Dorothy's adventure, is real.

Much of the appeal of the first Oz book is rooted in W. W. Denslow's imaginative and sure-handed illustrations. Denslow worked in black and white; color was added at the printing stage.

Denslow's conception of Dorothy as a rather tiny little girl surely helped to encourage Louis Mayer, some thirty-eight years later, to seek Shirley Temple to play the part in the MGM film. Contrary to what one might expect, Baum and Denslow never collaborated again; the illustrator developed a rather proprietary interest in Dorothy and the rest of Baum's *Oz* characters, and had his own ideas, which didn't always tickle Baum. He and Denslow split up after the first Oz adventure—though they remained connected because Denslow brazenly created his own Oz books to compete with Baum's. John R. Neill illustrated the subsequent thirteen Oz books written by Baum.

Baum wrote books other than those involving Oz and used a variety of pseudonyms. As "Capt. Huey Fitzgerald," Baum wrote the Sam Steele adventure series; "Edith Van Dyne" got credit for books in the Aunt Jane's Nieces series; "Laura Barcroft" wrote the Twinkle and Chubbins stories; and "Suzanne Metcalf" was the supposed author of *Annabel*.

Success inspired Baum to resume his role as a theatrical producer. Many of his shows lost money, and *Fairylogue and Radio Plays*, a 1908 traveling show that combined film and live performers, was very expensive and was another money loser.

Baum declared bankruptcy in 1911. He had had to allow (and distance himself from) a film version of his first book the year before, in order to pay off debt. His Oz books were hugely successful, but his stage shows had lost too much money. That same year, the Baums moved to a quiet California town called Hollywood. There, they built a handsome frame house that they called Ozcot. In 1913, Baum and partners and founded the Oz Film Manufacturing Company. This entity would produce four Oz films. (See next chapter.)

Baum was barely past sixty in 1918, when his always-dodgy health left him altogether. He died in May 1919, just sixty-two years old.

Like most people, Baum was a bag of contradictions. He was tenderhearted and kind, and respected the humanity and individuality of children. (He and Maud had four of their own, all boys: Frank Joslyn, Harry, Robert, and Kenneth.) But he also had an unreasoning, genocidal hatred of the Sioux Indians, an unappetizing prejudice that frequently revealed itself in his editorials for the *Aberdeen Saturday Pioneer*. He loved the simple pleasures of nature, but was also absorbed in the complexities of politics and Theosophy (see chapter 2).

In the end, Baum was a brilliant and devoted storyteller. He wrote more than fifty novels, scores of short stories, and two hundred poems. In addition, he wrote for many of his numerous stage productions. After more than a hundred years, Baum's Oz books remain in print not simply because they are good, but because people want to read them. Baum struggled for much of his adult life to make a commercial go out of this enterprise or that. The fact that he succeeded with the Oz stories, in his own lifetime and far past it, certainly isn't ironic, nor is it unexpected. Baum cared deeply for Oz and its marvelous inhabitants, but that's almost immaterial. Baum is gone, and he took his personal feelings with him. The books remain. We are enchanted with them today, in no small part because, once upon a time, a movie studio called Metro-Goldwyn-Mayer became intrigued with a little girl, a cyclone, and a land called Oz.

Important 19th-Century Precursors to Baum's *The Wonderful Wizard of Oz*

L. Frank Baum's *The Wonderful Wizard of Oz* is a singular achievement that, unavoidably, found inspiration in earlier works. No work of art is wholly discrete, of course. To the contrary, part of the nature of art is to build on what has come before, and to offer implicit (and sometimes explicit) elaboration and comment on those things. Art is an ever-expanding circle of reactions to culture: unending and inevitably self-referential. Dorothy's adventure was shaped not only by Baum's immense imagination, but also by writers and events that preceded him.

During the first third of the 19th century, a significant proportion of children's fantasy literature from England, the Continent, and America took from classic myth, scripture, and fairy tales. These works encouraged children to be pious and do good turns for others. Conservation, frugality, and cooperation were common themes. In all of that, and in their activist sort of conservative Christian thought, they reflected the immense influence of John Bunyan's 1678 parable for children and grown-ups, *Pilgrim's Progress*. The themes remained even when "plot" (as in Johann David Wyss's *Swiss Family Robinson*, 1812) and magical reality (James Kirke Paulding's *A Gift from Fairy Land*, 1838) became pronounced. (*Swiss Family Robinson* wasn't widely read in English until 1879—close enough in time to the publication of *The Wonderful Wizard of Oz* to be included as a probable influence on Baum.)

Religious conservatism in children's fantasy literature didn't completely die out in the 19th century, but it did experience an inexorable diminishment. Ironically, the very nature of fantasy, vis-à-vis Christian doctrine, helped open the door to doubt; literary historian Nicholas Royle has described the genre's "sense of strangeness," which, according to Victorian religious thinking, "ought to remain secret and hidden." As we'll see below, the doors to "dangerous" thought had opened by mid-century, with successive authors pushing the doors wider and wider.

Illustrators began to establish their importance in the 19th century, as well, particularly after 1850. The power and commercial success of William Mulready's illustrations for William Roscoe's *The Butterfly's Ball and the Grasshopper's Feast* (1824), for instance, helped to begin the now-long-standing melding of prose and art in children's books. Charles Tenniel, whose illustrations for Lewis Carroll's *Alice's Adventures in Wonderland* (1865; see below) eventually became timeless, established that fanciful stories were only enhanced by imaginative, complementary artwork. Writer-illustrator Edward Lear composed inspired nonsense verse, including the much-loved "The Owl and the Pussycat," a story that's part of Lear's popular 1871 book *Nonsense Songs, Stories, Botany, and Alphabets*. Two very early appearances in book form of work by illustrator Arthur Rackham are Shafto Justin Adair Fitzgerald's *The Zankiwank and the Bletherwitch* (1896) and Maggie Browne's *Two Old Ladies, Two Foolish Fairies, and a Tom Cat* (1897). Charles Robinson found immense popularity with his illustrations for Robert Louis Stevenson's *A Child's Garden of Verses* (1895) and Eugene Field's *Lullaby Land* (1897).

None of this was lost on L. Frank Baum, whose collaboration with artist W. W. Denslow helped make the Land of Oz indelible (and also propelled Denslow's later, solo career as an interpreter of Oz).

In a turn that has important reverberations in Baum's *The Wonderful Wizard of Oz*, numerous non-fantasy children's books of the 19th century revolve around orphans that band together; or lost or displaced children who discover their inner resources and defeat adversity.

Here are some 19th-century children's books that anticipate various elements found in *The Wonderful Wizard of Oz*:

1835–37: *Fairy Tales Told for Children* by **Hans Christian Andersen**—This seminal collection of adapted and original fairy tales (originally published in three installments) includes "The Princess and the Pea," "The Little Mermaid," "Thumbelina," and "The Emperor's New Clothes." Besides their value as imaginative literature, the stories promote a healthy skepticism of authority and suggest that young children (frequently girls) can find their way in difficult circumstances.

1846: *Book of Nonsense* by **Edward Lear**—Nonsense poetry; the book gained little attention, but Lear's whimsical rhymes finally became popular in the 1860s and were widely published. One very successful follow-on was Lear's *Laughable Lyrics* (1877).

1848: *Midsummer Eve: A Fairytale of Loving and Being Loved* by **Anna Maria Hall**—a handsome gift book by an Irish historical novelist and writer of children's books; Irish life and character fascinated Hall, and *Midsummer Eve* is just one of numerous examples of her ability to show equal appreciation for Catholic and Protestant Irish life—something that caused her books to be relatively unpopular in her own country. *Midsummer Eve*, though, found a wide audience outside of Ireland.

1855: *The History of Sir Thomas Thumb* **by Charlotte M. Yonge**—An elevated fairy tale combining the Brothers Grimm, folktales, and Arthurian legend.

1862: *Goblin Market* **by Christina Rossetti**—an ambitious and sophisticated variant of the fairy tale, told in verse. Two young sisters resist the goblin men, who try to tempt them into bad behavior. • *Alice's Adventures Underground* **by Lewis Carroll**—Carroll's first "Alice" book, written in longhand and presented by Carroll to his inspiration, young Alice Liddell.

1863: *The Water-Babies* **by Charles Kingsley**—The author was a correspondent of Charles Darwin, and this book is a fantasy about a little boy who goes backwards in evolution when he misbehaves and forward when he acts as he should.

1865: *Alice's Adventures in Wonderland* **by Lewis Carroll**—Carroll's elaboration on *Alice's Adventures Underground* is a milestone of intellectual fantasy that intrigues children and challenges grown-ups. Young Alice goes "down the rabbit hole" to a peculiar world of metaphoric characters, and real menace.

1868–71: *At the Back of the North Wind* **by George MacDonald**—Originally a magazine serial, this theological fantasy concerns a boy named Diamond, who befriends the North Wind and rides on her back as she goes about her blustery business. The North Wind promises the boy that she knows a far better world than Diamond's, which the boy sees only after he dies. MacDonald was a Congregational minister.

1870: *Twenty Thousand Leagues Under the Sea* **by Jules Verne**—Built on the success of Verne's *Journey to the Center of the Earth* (1864), this science-fantasy novel was devoured by bright youngsters and was important in the development of stories of remarkable, dangerous adventures in exotic locations.

1872: *Through the Looking Glass and What Alice Found There* **by Lewis Carroll**—The continuation of Alice's alternate-reality adventures. • *The Princess and the Goblin* **by George MacDonald**—Young Princess Irene and her nurse-maid, Lootie, defy a scheme of the underground-dwelling goblins to take over the upper world of humans. A sequel, *The Princess and Curdie* (1883), involves murderous clergy and a helpful monster.

1876: *The Hunting of the Snark, an Agony, in Eight Fits* **by Lewis Carroll**—A droll, linguistically elastic quasi-follow-on to Carroll's own "Jabberwocky," as ten companions, armed only with forks and their wits, set out to bag the legendary snark.

1881: *Wood Magic: A Fable* **by Richard Jefferies**—A young boy in the British countryside encounters talking animals as he explores and learns about nature.

1882: *The Day Boy and the Night Girl* **by George MacDonald**—An evil witch manipulates the lives of two stolen children by keeping the boy in sunlight and the girl in gloom. Happenstance exposes the boy to the night and the girl to day. Buoyed by each other, they escape the witch and marry.

1883: *The Adventures of Pinocchio* **by Carlo Collodi** (real name: Carlo Lorenzini)—A semi-realistic interpretation of fairy-tale style, concerning the title character, a wooden marionette who leaves his creator-father, Geppetto, only to be lured into seemingly endless danger. The picaresque, frequently grim and violent narrative is stuffed with lies, bad decisions, various disfigurements, petty crime, and, finally, redemption, when Pinocchio does good and is turned into a real boy. • *Treasure Island* **by Robert Louis Stevenson**—Although not a fantasy, this landmark children's novel is important because, like Baum's *The Wonderful Wizard of Oz*, it's preoccupied with a child who functions admirably in a challenging adult world.

1888: *Four Ghost Stories* **by Mary Louisa Molesworth**—A collection of supernatural tales. Molesworth followed it with *Uncanny Stories* (**1896**).

1889: *The Blue Fairy Book* **by Andrew Lang**—This important British collection of fairy tales mined the Brothers Grimm, the *Arabian Nights*, and other sources. Lang edited twelve "Fairy Books" between 1889 and 1910. The others by Lang that preceded the 1900 publication of *The Wonderful Wizard of Oz* are *The Red Fairy Book* (**1890**), *The Green Fairy Book* (**1892**), *The Yellow Fairy Book* (**1894**), and *The Pink Fairy Book* (**1897**).

1894: *The Jungle Book* **by Rudyard Kipling**—Fanciful stories about the East Indian wolf-boy Mowgli and other characters, and the various animals he meets. As with Baum's later Cowardly Lion, Kipling's animals have human characteristics, and a grasp of right and wrong. Kipling continued in the same vein with *The Second Jungle Book* (**1895**).

1895: *Lilith: A Romance* **by George MacDonald**—Epic fantasy with an "afterlife" theme in which a bibliophile meets a ghost; the beautiful Princess Lilith; and the Little Ones, children who are not permitted to grow up. Only through considerable sacrifice does the librarian bring peace to the Little Ones, and to himself—via the sleep of death.

1897: *Blown Away: A Nonsensical Narrative Without Rhyme or Reason* **by Richard Mansfield**—A cyclone carries Beatrice and Jessie to a strange new place inhabited by odd people and peculiar creatures. In the book's preface, author-publisher Mansfield wrote, "This book contains no sarcasm, satire, or cynicism. It was written as a purely childish and innocent pastime. It hides no sting. It was never intended for publication. . . . It relates no story. It has no point, policy, or purpose. If the author harbored any design, it was to entertain some young people during a lengthy journey. It was then tossed aside and forgotten. It should *not* have been disturbed. Alas! It cropped up one day by the seashore—a rainy day. The author read these pages to a number of small boys who could not escape. The smallest and least intelligent boy was amused. He bore out the promise of his childhood by becoming a publisher."

1898: *Dream Days* **by Kenneth Grahame**—A story collection that includes **"The Reluctant Dragon,"** the tale of a brilliant dragon; St. George; and the young boy who brings them together in a faked battle that encourages the local townsfolk to accept the dragon. The story suggests that, with reasoned mediation (the boy), rapprochement between the establishment (St. George) and intellectualism (the dragon) is possible, and desirable.

1899: *The Story of the Treasure Seekers: Being the Adventures of the Bastable Children in Search of a Fortune* **by E. (Edith) Nesbit**—The six Bastable children come to the aid of their widowed father and recapture the family fortune. This influential children's book emphasizes the courage of children against daunting circumstances.

A Note About Children's Books That Came Later

The immense popular success of *The Wonderful Wizard of Oz*, and Baum's many sequels, was pivotal to a subsequent explosion of fantasy literature for children. The very existence of some of them may have helped encourage MGM to pursue a film version of *Oz*. The years 1900 to 1940 brought the publication of *The Tale of Peter Rabbit* (Beatrix Potter, 1902), *Peter Pan* aka *Peter and Wendy* (J. M. Barrie; 1904, play; 1911, book), *The Wind in the Willows* (Kenneth Grahame, 1904), and *A Little Princess* (Frances Hodgson Burnett, 1905). Success also came to *Raggedy Ann Stories* (Johnny Gruelle, 1918), *Raggedy Andy Stories* (Gruelle, 1920), *The Story of Dr. Dolittle* (Hugh Lofting, 1920), *Raggedy Ann and Andy and the Camel with the Wrinkled Knees* (Gruelle, 1924), *Winnie-the-Pooh* (A. A. Milne; 1927) and *The House at Pooh Corner* (Milne, 1928), *Mary Poppins* (P. L. Travers, 1934), *The Hobbit* (J. R. R. Tolkien, 1937), *The Sword in the Stone* (T. H. White, 1938), *Ben and Me* (Robert Lawson, 1939), and *A Traveller in Time* (Alison Uttley, 1939).

After World War II, many children's writers attempted to duplicate the immersive magic of Baum's fantasy world: J. R. R. Tolkien (*The Lord of the Rings*), C. S. Lewis (the Narnia series), Madeleine L'Engle (*A Wrinkle in Time*), and Roald Dahl (*Charlie and the Chocolate Factory*). More recently, we've seen J. K. Rowling (the Harry Potter adventures), Rick Riordan (the Percy Jackson series), Lloyd Alexander (the Chronicles of Prydain series), Angie Sage (the Septimus Heap series), Suzanne Collins (the Hunger Games series), and so many others that "young adult fantasy" has become one of publishing's most significant and profitable categories.

Is Baum's Oz an Allegory?

For many years, some academics and historians have insisted that L. Frank Baum's *The Wonderful Wizard of Oz* isn't "just" a children's book. The frequently made claim is that the book expresses very sophisticated financial and political ideas. However, supporters of the idea can't agree as to whether Baum did this purposely or unconsciously.

In a 1964 article published in *American Quarterly*, cultural historian Henry Littlefield proposed that the first Baum book is an unconscious political allegory encompassing many things, including abused factory workers (the Tin Woodman) and struggling farmers (the Scarecrow), and the gold standard and Baum's apparent desire for "available money" via unlimited coinage of silver and gold (Dorothy's silver slippers). Littlefield also saw links to the failed Populist movement of the 1890s and the shortcomings of the Democratic-Populist presidential candidate for 1896, William Jennings Bryan (the Cowardly Lion), chicanery of the evil lords of business and finance (the Wicked Witch), an impotent federal government (the Wizard), and even the harsh landscape of Kansas (a state that was a hotbed of Populist politics).

Other quarters insisted that the Yellow Brick Road is a clear endorsement of the gold standard, and noted that "Oz" is the abbreviation for ounce, which is how we value gold and silver. More recent theorists, some of them preoccupied with imagined conspiracies, assert that the "Tin" of "Tin Woodman" is an acronym for (Individual) Taxpayer Identification Number, never mind that the TIN program wasn't introduced until 1996. (Other, non-political interpretations encompass support for atheism [the Wizard is a fraud] to feminism [the two most assertive characters, Dorothy and the Witch, are female].)

According to Henry Littlefield, Baum was furious because American labor had been led on, and then thrown to the wolves, by Populist politics. Some academics were, at the least, favorably intrigued by Littlefield's thesis. L. Frank Baum's great-grandson, on the other hand, labeled it "insane."

In 1991, a Baum scholar named Michael Hearn annihilated Littlefield's theory by revealing that his own research showed that Baum was neither Democrat nor Populist, and that, to the contrary, he was demonstrably sympathetic to Republican concerns of his day. Hearn's claim made the theory of Baum's populism an impossibility.

Incredibly, Littlefield responded by confessing, "there is no basis in fact to consider Baum a supporter of turn-of-the-century Populist ideology."

Still, Littlefield may have been on to something, if only because Baum had been a journalist, and an astute observer of politics and current events. Baum's 1902 theatrical adaptation of *The Wizard of Oz* satirizes Populism, so maybe that first book isn't propounding a Populist point of view after all. Then again, Baum's Witch of the South grasps the power potential of the silver slippers, which suggests to Rogers State College history professor Quentin P. Taylor that this "good" witch represents the American South, which mounted great support for Bryan in 1896. Taylor also posits that the various impotencies of the Scarecrow, the Tin Woodman, and the Cowardly Lion (which are shown by Baum to be partly self-inflicted and partly the result of the Wicked Witch and other demeaning power players) are illusory. The characters have plenty of intelligence, heart, and courage—all they need is an advocate to encourage them.

That advocate is Dorothy, whom Taylor views as a symbol of the good-hearted American common man. And when good people band together, they become stronger and more capable of change than they could be as individuals. Allegory or not, that notion is certainly clear in Baum's handling of the tiny mice of Oz, who coalesce in gratitude for the Tin Woodman's having decapitated a frightful cat with a single swing of his axe; later, the mice rescue the Lion from the initiative-sapping poppy field.

Theories continue on this path. The China people (who live behind a great wall) represent the real-world China that was then being exploited by monied Western interests. The green of Oz is symbolic of the ambivalent effects of American greenbacks at home and abroad. The enslaved winged monkeys are stand-ins for America's Plains Indians, and a great spider (slain by the Lion) is a metaphor for trusts and other unregulated industry. The abused Winkies, who represent the immigrant Chinese exploited by American railroads and other businesses, rejoice in the death of their oppressor.

With special ingenuity, Prof. Taylor suggests that when Baum's Dorothy loses her silver slippers in the desert, she's giving life and animation to the free-silver movement, which shriveled rapidly after the 1896 election.

None of these divergences of interpretation is unreasonable. Art should be provocative and it should stir debate. Baum's first Oz book has certainly achieved that, and suggests that there really can't be a right or wrong in such debates, just other avenues to explore.

Baum and Theosophy

The author of *The Wonderful Wizard of Oz* had an interest in theosophy, an egalitarian study of comparative religion, and of ways in which doctrine from many faiths might be incorporated into a wide and embracing view of God (or gods) as manifest in every aspect of the natural world. More closely aligned with Eastern religions than Western ones, theosophist thought holds that all religions came from a single, ancient source grounded in true wisdom. Further, a mystically inspired evolution of the individual is possible, and ultimate personal evolution is marked by total knowledge.

Theosophy with a capital T was brought to the fore by Helena Blavatsky (née von Hahn) and two associates in New York City in 1875. Blavatsky and her followers founded the Theosophical Society, to espouse a philosophy characterized by critics as based in the occult (Blavatsky was a proponent of spiritualism, reincarnation, Atlantis, and personal "auras"). Proper instruction, Blavatsky said, will prepare people to accept the existence and teachings of mystical intermediaries that represent the Spiritual Hierarchy. The Hierarchy is "hidden" in the sense that the spiritual perfection of its members cannot be comprehended by the less evolved.

The Theosophist goal was for humanity to rid itself of anxiety and embrace the evolutionary process in order to achieve a full understanding of the carefully engineered workings of the cosmos. Nothing, however, can be accomplished without an earthly agent, such as, say, the Theosophical Society.

Blavatsky died in 1891, and the Society shortly fell into argument, and accusations of misapplied knowledge and various perfidies—proving that people are indeed underevolved.

L. Frank Baum probably picked up his interest in Theosophy from his mother-in-law, Matilda Gage, who was an active follower, Baum and his wife, Maud, were admitted into the Chicago branch of the Theosophical Society September 4, 1892.

The Wonderful Wizard of Oz—and, by extension, the 1939 MGM move—may indeed have Theosophist underpinnings, and Baum may have been a proselytizer. If he was, though, he was a subtle one, managing details and themes of his story so that they might be absorbed by readers unconsciously, while remaining clear to fellow Theosophists, particularly those that might wish to utilize *The Wonderful Wizard of Oz* in Theosophist instruction.

Here are some elements of Dorothy's adventure that are shared by the first Oz novel and the 1939 film:

- Glinda is a mystical intermediary who becomes Dorothy's guide.
- The Yellow Brick Road is the path to enlightenment.
- The Scarecrow longs for what Helena Blavatsky called "head-learning," which, although necessary for personal growth, is valueless without "soul wisdom."
- As Dorothy pursues her adventure, she employs thought, feeling, and will—attributes Theosophists call the threefold flame.
- Key characters in the tale are female, which jibes with Theosophy's interest in recognition of the gifts of women.
- The Wicked Witch of the West is evil, but a broader view suggests that she is the chief impediment to Dorothy's attainment of full knowledge. Once free of the Witch, Dorothy will have a clearer path to enlightenment.
- Dorothy destroys the Witch with water, an element that Theosophists link to one's chakra (physical or spiritual energy).
- When Dorothy clicks her heels three times, she invokes the Trinity, a basic element of Christianity, which sprang, according to Theosophists, from a single, ancient source of wisdom.

The MGM movie does not include a striking section of the book: Dorothy's time in China Country, during which she expresses a desire to take one of the china people home with her. The china person doesn't think that's a good idea at all; Theosophists mark this interlude as Baum's statement against American imperialism.

Amusingly, though, a favorite element of the Oz mythos that does *not* appear in the book is the rainbow, an invention of lyricist E. Y. "Yip" Harburg and one that nevertheless finds favor with Theosophists—some of whom may assume it came from Baum—because the rainbow can be looked at as a horizontally "stepped" bridge to true knowledge, a goal of every Theosophist.

Again, the rainbow isn't part of Dorothy's adventure as created by Baum. The takeaway, then, is that symbols and messages aren't always where you expect them to be, but often where you imagine them.

The White City and Oz

In 1893, L. Frank Baum and much of the nation were fascinated by the World's Columbian Exposition, also known as the Chicago World's Fair. The Exposition was officially dedicated in the fall of 1892, and opened the following May, as a celebration of the 400th anniversary of Christopher Columbus's voyage to the New World. (The presidential election of 1892 caused the fair to open to the public a year late, during the *401st* anniversary instead.) By besting New York, St. Louis, and Washington, D.C., to be chosen as the Exposition venue, Chicago demonstrated that vibrant life, art, and commerce existed not just on the East Coast, but also in the heartland, on the edge of the great prairie.

The fair was calculatedly traditional *and* forward-looking, much of it designed by Burnham and Root, a Chicago architectural firm headed by sales genius Daniel Burnham and architect David Root. B & R had become prosperous with designs for neoclassical mansions demanded by Chicago's *nouveau riche*. More significantly, David Root drove B & R to increasingly sophisticated commercial designs that incorporated steel frames that took buildings to unprecedented heights. Root's vision culminated in Chicago's ten-story Rand-McNally Building, which began construction in 1889. By relieving exterior walls of load-bearing responsibility, B & R took early steps toward what we know as modern skyscrapers.

David Root died in 1891, but his vision and commitment to innovation were carried on by his partner. Daniel Burnham gave commissions to leading architects from around the country to design some two hundred neoclassical buildings spread over six hundred acres at Chicago's Jackson Park. Although the Exposition structures had the appearance of stone, they were intended to be temporary, and were made mainly of wood, plaster, and lath. The predominant color was white, which encouraged fairgoers to dub the site "The White City."

George Westinghouse won the bid to illuminate the fair, and he did so in grand fashion, placing eighteen thousand miniature lights of red, white, and blue on the twenty-two-foot Tower of Light. Illuminated fountains that dotted the grounds sent spouts of multihued water skyward. An inventor named George Ferris was represented by his great wheel, and one exhibit displayed an early movie camera.

None of these wonders were lost on L. Frank Baum. In his first Oz novel, he described the Emerald City as a dazzling place of "brightness and glory" that dominates the horizon with "a beautiful green glow." Ozites appeared "happy and contented and prosperous."

Unfortunately, there is well-concealed trouble in Oz, not least that the Wizard who dominates the city is a fraud.

How does this relate to the White City that Baum witnessed in Chicago? The beauty parallels are obvious, but Baum was more interested in suggesting the essential hollowness of Oz—an intriguing construal of the false-front, temporary buildings that dominated the Exposition.

Baum had already been a victim of economic contraction in South Dakota, so it's not difficult to imagine his reaction to the Panic of 1893, an economic depression spurred by reckless railroad expansion and speculation that developed in parallel to the White City. Baum's Emerald City is a beautiful place, but because the Wizard is a fraud, the city's prosperity exists only because the residents have been *told* that it exists.

L. Frank Baum had an expansive imagination that reflected reality. Because of that, his Emerald City and the 1939 film adaptation have roots in six hundred acres of Chicago real estate, where a make-believe city dazzled all who saw it.

The Famous Forty

Only the first Oz book, *The Wonderful Wizard of Oz* aka *The Wizard of Oz*, was published by the Geo. M. Hill company; subsequent volumes written by L. Frank Baum were published by Reilly & Britton, except for the last two, which were published by Reilly & Lee. That company published the remainder of what are collectively called the Famous Forty: all the authorized Oz novels published through 1963.

For reader convenience, each of the Famous Forty is noted in the list below with "FF." Because the list notes the first book under both of its titles, you'll come up with forty-one FFs, if you're counting.

by L. Frank Baum:
* *The Wonderful Wizard of Oz* (1900; FF)
* *The Wizard of Oz* (1903 edition; FF)
* *The Marvelous Land of Oz* (1904; FF)
* *Ozma of Oz* (1907; FF)
* *Dorothy and the Wizard of Oz* (1908; FF)
* *The Road to Oz* (1909; FF)
* *The Emerald City of Oz* (1910; FF)
* *The Patchwork Girl of Oz* (1913; FF)
* *Tik-Tok of Oz* (1914; FF)
* *The Scarecrow of Oz* (1915; FF)
* *Rinkitink in Oz* (1916; FF)
* *The Lost Princess of Oz* (1917; FF)
* *The Tin Woodman of Oz* (1918; FF)
* *The Magic of Oz* (1919; FF)
* *Glinda of Oz* (1920; FF)

by Ruth Plumly Thompson (an established children's author who was engaged by Reilly & Lee to continue the *Oz* series):
* *The Royal Book of Oz* (1921; FF; originally attributed to L. Frank Baum)
* *Kabumpo in Oz* (1922; FF)
* *The Cowardly Lion of Oz* (1923; FF)
* *Grampa in Oz* (1924; FF)
* *The Lost King of Oz* (1925; FF)
* *The Hungry Tiger of Oz* (1926; FF)
* *The Gnome King of Oz* (1927; FF)
* *The Giant Horse of Oz* (1928; FF)
* *Jack Pumpkinhead of Oz* (1929; FF)
* *The Yellow Knight of Oz* (1930; FF)
* *Pirates in Oz* (1931; FF)
* *The Purple Prince of Oz* (1932; FF)
* *Ojo in Oz* (1933; FF)
* *Speedy in Oz* (1934; FF)
* *The Wishing Horse of Oz* (1935; FF)

by Frank Joslyn Baum (the oldest of L. Frank Baum's four sons):
* *The Laughing Dragon of Oz* (1935; this unauthorized Whitman Big Little Book brought a lawsuit from the L. Frank Baum estate.)

by Ruth Plumly Thompson (cont.):
* *Captain Salt in Oz* (1936; FF)
* *Handy Mandy in Oz* (1937; FF)
* *The Silver Princess in Oz* (1938; FF)
* *Ozoplaning with the Wizard of Oz* (1939; FF)

by John R. Neill (an authorized *Oz* illustrator who turned to writing):
* *The Wonder City of Oz* (1940; FF)
* *The Scalawagons of Oz* (1941; FF)
* *Lucky Bucky in Oz* (1942; FF)

by Jack Snow (a print and radio journalist and lifelong *Oz* fan):
* *The Magical Mimics in Oz* (1946; FF)
* *The Shaggy Man of Oz* (1949; FF)

by Rachel R. Cosgrove (an *Oz* fan who became a prolific adult novelist after her *Oz* novel, which was her first book):
* *Hidden Valley of Oz* (1951; FF)

by Jack Snow (cont.):
* *Who's Who in Oz* (1954; this is a non-fiction reader's guide)

by Dick Martin (a professional illustrator and designer):

- *The Visitors from Oz* (1960; this book is a redrawn rewrite of *Queer Visitors from the Marvelous Land of Oz*, a 1904–05 newspaper comic strip written by L. Frank Baum and illustrated by Walt McDougall. It is not one of the Famous Forty.)

by Eloise Jarvis McGraw and Lauren McGraw Wagner (a graphic artist and daughter of Eloise Jarvis McGraw):

- *Merry Go Round in Oz* (1963; FF; the last of the Famous Forty)

by Ruth Plumly Thompson and the International Wizard of Oz Club (the preeminent *Oz* fan organization, founded in 1957):

- *Yankee in Oz* (1972)
- *The Enchanted Island of Oz* (1976)

by Eloise Jarvis McGraw and Lauren Lynn McGraw (Lauren McGraw Wagner; see above) (cont.):

- *The Forbidden Fountain of Oz* (1980)

by Dick Martin (cont.):

- *The Ozmapolitan of Oz* (1986)

3

Not in Kansas Anymore

Oz Stage and Film Adaptations Before 1939

With their colorful, and very popular, characters; unique settings; and fabulous plots, the *Oz* books were ideally suited to adaptations to stage and film.

The Wizard of Oz (1902; stage production)

A musical adaptation, with book and lyrics by L. Frank Baum, and music by Paul Tietjens and A. Baldwin Sloane, and produced by Fred Hamlin, opened at Chicago's Grand Opera House in June 1902. Librettist Glen MacDonough (*Babes in Toyland*) wrote some gags to punch up Baum's work, and collaborated with the director, Julian Mitchell, on script rewrites.

The principal players were Anna Laughlin (Dorothy), Dave Montgomery (Tin Woodman), and Fred Stone (Scarecrow). Arthur Hill played the Cowardly Lion, a character reduced to insignificance by Mitchell and McDonough. Good witch Locasta (as she was called during the Chicago run of the play) was portrayed by three actresses: Ella Gilroy, Doris Mitchell, and Romayne Whiteford. Mitchell and McDonough's rewrite eliminated the Wicked Witch altogether.

Although Toto is with Dorothy during the musical's Kansas scenes, he fades into the background once the action moves to Oz. Dorothy interacts with a new character, Imogene the Cow (played by Edwin J. Stone). Baum gave Dorothy a last name (Gale) and added King Pastoria, the rightful ruler of Oz; Tryxie Tryfle, a waitress from Kansas; Sir Wiley Gyle; a poet named Sir Dashemoff Daily; General Riskitt; and Cynthia Cynch, a madwoman who is noted in some sources as having been named Lady Lunatic. Although Dorothy remains the familiar character that grounds the story in a bit of reality, her role as an instigator of the plot is much reduced. Instead, considerable attention is given to King Pastoria and various royal intrigues.

Baum remained enamored of the poisonous poppy field of his novel, but realized that, on stage, Dorothy and the others could not be rescued by an army

Actor Dave Montgomery played the Tin Woodman—here called the Tin Man—in producer Fred R. Hamlin's 1902 stage production, *The Wizard of Oz*. Original Oz author L. Frank Baum wrote the show's book and lyrics.

of friendly field mice that come to the rescue in the book. As an alternative, Baum created the snowstorm, a clever stroke that was retained by the 1939 film.

The Chicago production was a test of the property's viability for Broadway. Because the show was an immediate hit that ran for twelve weeks, it was quickly slated for a New York run.

The Wizard of Oz (1903; stage production)

In a follow-on to the successful Chicago tryout of 1902, *The Wizard of Oz* opened in January 1903 at New York's Majestic Theatre (then owned by newspaper mogul William Randolph Hearst), where it enjoyed a run of 293 performances during 1903, and 1904–05 (Occasional revivals appeared into the 1930s.) The Chicago cast members repeated their roles, though Locasta/Glinda was by now written out of the story.

During the course of the show's run, literally dozens of songs cycled in and out. Originals encompassed a variety of styles: Irish, minstrel, pseudo-martial, and other forms. L. Frank Baum worked with Paul Tietjens, and Nathaniel Mann, to co-write about a dozen songs, but many more were created by other hands: Vincent Bryan, Glen MacDonough, James O'Dea, and A. Baldwin Sloane. During the course of the run, a handful of songs were lifted from other, earlier shows, such as *Ziegfeld Follies of 1907* and *The Swedish Chef*.

Subsequent touring companies active through 1911 brought the Broadway version to cities and towns across the USA. The musical continued to be revived, off and on, for the next twenty-five years, and is occasionally revived today. A music CD was released by Hungry Tiger in 2003, and the show was mounted with a full orchestra by the Canton (Ohio) Comic Opera Company in 2010.

The Wonderful Wizard of Oz aka The Wizard of Oz (1910; film production)

In 1908, L. Frank Baum mounted *Fairylogue and Radio Plays*, a touring stage show that featured Baum as a storyteller. The production lost a great deal of money and left Baum with many creditors. One of them was the Selig Polyscope Company, a Chicago firm that had created the film footage shown on screens behind Baum during the tour. (Selig created an industry precedent when it departed Chicago in 1909 to establish the first permanent movie studio in Los Angeles.) In order to pay what was owed to Selig, Baum agreed to allow the company to film the first *Oz* novel. Central to the agreement was that Baum would have no creative involvement. Selig's *The Wonderful Wizard of Oz* is a thirteen-minute short written and directed by Otis Turner. Dorothy was played by child actress Bebe Daniels, who later became a popular leading lady of the silent and early sound eras.

Following the death of the Witch, the Scarecrow (Robert Z. Leonard) is installed as the king of Oz. (In the early sound era, Leonard directed *Dancing Lady* and *The Great Ziegfeld*.) The Cowardly Lion (an actor in a full-body suit) looks remarkably like *Oz* illustrator W. W. Denslow's squat creation.

The Wonderful Wizard of Oz (1910) was the first adaptation of Baum's world to the screen. Dorothy was nine-year-old Bebe Daniels, who became a leading lady in silent and early talking pictures. She later moved to England, where she conquered the stage, radio, and television. The Scarecrow, Robert Z. Leonard, was a successful producer-director from 1913 to 1957.

Dorothy and the Scarecrow in Oz (1910; film production)

This is the second Selig Polyscope *Oz* adaptation and the second time that L. Frank Baum was prevented from creative involvement. Otis Turner returned to write and direct what is essentially a continuation of adventures from the first novel. With the Witch having been melted in the previous film, Dorothy (Marcia Moore) and her friends are free to approach the Wizard with their wishes. Conflict is provided by an earthquake and the Mangaboos.

The Land of Oz (1910; film production)

This Selig Polyscope short was released just a month after *Dorothy and the Scarecrow in Oz*. As with that film, Otis Turner wrote and directed, and Marcia Moore played Dorothy. The film includes reasonably ambitious military sequences featuring General Jinger, which encouraged Selig promotional material to emphasize not only the adventure's "scintillating comedy" but also "spectacle worthy of the best artists in picturedom."

The Tik-Tok Man of Oz (1913; stage production)

Baum's musical adaptation of *The Wizard of Oz* had been a hit on Broadway in 1910, and the writer hoped he could catch lightning in a bottle a second time. March 1913 brought L. Frank Baum's musical, *The Tik-Tok Man of Oz*, to the Majestic Theatre in Los Angeles. He wrote the book and lyrics; music was by Louis F. Gottschalk, who became vice president of Baum's Oz Film Manufacturing Company a year later. James Morton played Tik Tok, with Frank Morton as the Shaggy Man and Fred Woodward as Hank the Mule. *The Tik-Tok Man of Oz* was very popular in L.A. but didn't travel well, and never reached Broadway.

Baum's Oz Film Manufacturing Company; 1913–15

In 1913, after living in Los Angeles for two years, Baum and his new partners, composer Louis F. Gottschalk and the Uplifters (a Los Angeles businessmen's club) founded the Oz Film Manufacturing Co. Baum and Gottschalk brought the creativity; the Uplifters brought the money. The enterprise lasted two years, making a variety of features and shorts that included four five-reel (approximately fifty-minute) Oz adventures: *The Patchwork Girl of Oz* (1914), *The Magic Cloak of Oz* (1914), *The New Wizard of Oz* (1914), and *His Majesty, the Scarecrow of Oz* aka *The Scarecrow of Oz* (1914). One indication that Baum and the others felt that not all was going smoothly is that *The Magic Cloak of Oz* (aka *The Witch Queen*) was cut to three reels before release. In any case, each of these Oz films failed commercially. Following five non-Oz short films, the Oz Film Manufacturing Company went out of business in 1915.

Executives from the Oz Film Manufacturing Company gather for a company portrait. Co-owner L. Frank Baum is seated, left. Numerous box-office failures limited the firm's life span to 1913–15. Note the "OZ" logo at top center.

The Poor Little Rich Girl (1917)

Although not an official (or authorized) part of the Oz canon, this feature-length fantasy helped itself to many elements from the first Baum novel. A lonely little rich girl (played by twenty-five-year-old Mary Pickford) is ignored by her parents, and seems to have no friends or peers. During a feverish slumber, she imagines three adults in her life as fanciful friends: a huntsman, an organ grinder, and a talking donkey. The friends set out on a quest adventure to find the Land of Happy Children. Along the way, they encounter floating heads, a humanoid spider, and other peculiar creatures. In a nice bit of timing, a wizard offers to help the group. In the end, Gwendolyn learns that her parents love her after all, and that her home has been the Land of Happy Children all along.

Key *Wizard of Oz* screenwriter Noel Langley seems to have been inspired by *The Poor Little Rich Girl*, particularly by the unpleasant household servants that intrude themselves into Gwendolyn's life, much as Miss Gulch does to Dorothy during the movie's opening Kansas sequence. In a forest, Gwendolyn and her friends are directed by a pair of magic signs that say, "Follow" "Your nose"— much as Langley's Scarecrow offers antic directions to Dorothy. Gwendolyn pines terribly for her mother, as Langley's Dorothy longs for Aunt Em.

The Poor Little Rich Girl is imaginative and more brisk than one might imagine. The movie is part of the National Film Registry.

The Wizard of Oz (1925)

A bright-eyed, long-nosed silent-era film comic named Larry Semon mounted his most ambitious project yet in 1925, a seventy-two-minute Chadwick Pictures adaptation of Baum's *The Wizard of Oz*. Semon had been a prolific and reasonably popular screen actor for ten years before that, and he stretched himself on this project, acting as star (three roles), director, and co-writer. His scripting partners were Leon Lee and Frank Joslyn Baum (L. Frank Baum's son), who is credited on screen as L. Frank Baum Jr.

The film is recalled today mainly because of its relative closeness in time to the later MGM movie, and because the Tin Woodsman [*sic*] is played by Oliver Hardy. Hardy took two other roles, as well: a farmhand and a Knight of the Garter. This veteran actor from Georgia had worked with many screen comics, including Larry Semon, during the previous decade. He was an accomplished "heavy" in comedy shorts and occasional features, but his body of work to date didn't suggest the enormous stardom he began to achieve in 1927, after independent comedy producer Hal Roach teamed him with British-born comic Stan Laurel. For the remainder of his life, and beyond, Hardy would be beloved and world famous as half of Hollywood's best-ever comedy team.

Semon cast himself as a Kansas farmhand, the Scarecrow, and (in the film's framing device) an elderly toymaker. Semon's very pretty wife, nineteen-year-old Dorothy Dwan, took two roles: Dorothy and Oz's Princess Dorothea. Vital to the plot is that Dorothy had been spirited to Kansas as an infant and abandoned there—a scheme by the corrupt rulers of Oz to remove her from Oz's political equation. In other words,

The 1925 movie version of *The Wizard of Oz* was the first big-scale treatment of the story. This is Larry Semon, the film's producer, director, co-writer, and star.

Dorothy and Dorothea are the same person. Oz is real, and so is Dorothy's adventure there.

The film has no Wicked Witch, but general-purpose actor Otto Lederer snarls nicely as Ambassador Wikked, and Josef Swickard lives up to his billing as Prime Minister Kruel.

Fifty-three-year-old Charlie Murray played the Wizard. In this version, the character is a "medicine-show hokum hustler" and a toadie to the prime minister. Murray was a longtime vaudeville player who'd begun his career in childhood. He got into movies in 1912 and worked steadily in shorts and features until 1938. From 1912 to 1915, Murray starred in a series of Keystone one-reelers as "Hogan," a boozy Irish layabout. Some of the titles suggest what the character was all about: *Hogan's Wild Oats*, *Hogan's Aristocratic Dream*, *Hogan's Annual Spree*, and *Hogan's Mussy Job*.

Spencer Bell, the black actor cast as the Cowardly Lion, was—in the tedious and humiliating Hollywood tradition of the day—billed as "G. Howe Black." In the early part of the story, he's an indolent farmhand called Snowball who, once in Oz, is dragooned by the Scarecrow into impersonating a lion. Predictably enough, Snowball's lion is a cowardly one. In other movies, Bell played porters, servants, and a shoeshine boy, as well as characters called Snowflake and Suntan. Such were the opportunities for black actors in the 1920s!

As noted, Semon's adaptation is significant because the Oz adventure is no dream, but very real. The film is also important because of its emphasis on the Kansas farmhands who assume other roles in Oz, or already have peculiar counterparts there. These characters (called Zeke, Hunk, and Hickory in the 1939 film) are not part of the original Oz mythos.

Semon's version is essentially a tale of palace intrigue, with Kruel and Wikked plotting with Lady Vishuss (Virginia Pearson) to take control of Oz in Princess Dorothea's absence. Wikked is finally undone when the Scarecrow dumps enormous flower urns onto his head at the very moment that Wikked gets the best of Prince Kynd (Bryant Washburn) in a climactic sword fight.

Many sequences, particularly the Scarecrow's encounter with a lion in a dim tunnel, have the style and danger of the famed Mack Sennett comedies (the lion is real, and just inches from Semon). When Spencer Bell, half in and half out of his Cowardly Lion disguise, spies the big cat crouched above the Scarecrow's head, he tries to run but can't because his feet are stuck fast with fright. His subsequent flying leap through an opening in the side of a mountain is very similar to Bert Lahr's later crashing exit from the Wizard's palace. (And a big hand for the stuntman, who executed an endless series of rolling somersaults that takes him all the way down the mountainside.)

Larry Semon began his show business career in the grind of vaudeville and eventually became a gag writer for Vitagraph, a prosperous player in the then New York–based American film industry. Semon was in front of the camera by 1915, working almost exclusively in Vitagraph shorts and enjoying steadily increasing popularity. He settled on a mild, white-faced persona—an innocent adrift in an often hostile world.

Semon left Vitagraph in 1923 to co-found Chadwick Pictures. He got into features in 1925, when he directed and costarred with his future wife, Dorothy Dwan, in *My Best Girl*. Semon and Dwan followed up with *The Wizard of Oz*, but because Semon allowed the film's budget to get away from him, Chadwick reeled financially.

Chadwick was out of business by 1928, the same year Semon appeared on screen for the last time. He returned to vaudeville and other stage work, but died later in 1928, when he was just thirty-nine years old.

Semon's *The Wizard of Oz* is available on stand-alone DVD (with a fine new score by Robert Israel), and has been included in various commemorative *Wizard of Oz* box sets.

An Adventure in the Land of Oz (1925)

This stage presentation played with Larry Semon's movie (see above) at the Forum Theatre in Los Angeles.

The Magical Land of Oz (1928)

The Jean Gros French Marionettes headlined this ambitious production that played America's Chautauqua circuit.

The Land of Oz (1932)

Dorothy (Maryruth Boone) enlists "Nick Chopper" (Fred Osbourn), the human version of the Tin Woodman, to help battle the sorceress Mombi (Sissi Flynn) and General Jinjur (Louise Ringland). Various dancers and other background roles were filled by the Meglin Kiddies, a revolving troupe of talented child actors, selected and schooled by dancer/impresario Ethel Meglin, a former Ziegfeld Girl and the director of this short. Association with the Meglin Kiddies gave early professional experience to Judy Garland, Shirley Temple, Jane Withers, and Mickey Rooney, as well as to future Our Gang players Jackie Cooper, Dickie Moore, Darla Hood, and Scotty Beckett.

The Wizard of Oz (1933)

New York–based animator-producer Ted Eshbaugh is a footnote in cartoon history. He was active throughout the 1930s, seems to have occupied himself with other things for a few years, and returned to animation (briefly) in 1945. A rowdy, obnoxious show-off named Goofy Goat, Eshbaugh's 1931 stab at creating a continuing character, went nowhere. Most of his shorts are one-offs, and while competent, they're not outstanding. However, Eshbaugh contributed something very important to the Oz mythos with his 1933 *Wizard of Oz* cartoon short: he designed an ingenious visual distinction between the Kansas scenes, which are in black and white, and the Oz sequences, which are in two-strip Technicolor. It seems virtually impossible that this cartoon—and its clever innovation—never crossed the radar of anybody who would later be connected with the MGM movie. It's a good bet, then, that Ted Eshbaugh deserves credit for one of the most well-liked aspects of the 1939 classic.

Like nearly all of the Eshbaugh cartoons, his *Wizard of Oz* is dominated by music and has virtually no dialogue. (The cartoon's opening credits cite "Col. Frank Baum," who was Baum's son, as the writer. Earlier, the younger Baum had co-written Larry Semon's 1925 *Wizard of Oz* feature comedy.) Music is by that future stalwart of the Warner Bros. animation unit Carl Stalling, working in his familiar allusive style; when Dorothy meets the Scarecrow, for instance, Stalling gives us a few bars of the bucolic "Comin' Through the Rye."

Dorothy's friends are the Scarecrow and the Tin Woodman; the Cowardly Lion has no role in this interpretation of the Oz universe. And instead of L. Frank Baum's "little old man, with a bald head and a wrinkled face," Eshbaugh's long-bearded wizard is a combination magician and sorcerer, clad in a peaked cap adorned with a star (that might as well be a pentagram), and looking very much like the demented sorcerer Rotwang in Fritz Lang's 1927 science-fantasy classic, *Metropolis*. He forces hens to lay egg after egg, and chases Dorothy and her friends around for a while.

The two-strip Technicolor is agreeable enough, but Eshbaugh worked in the then-popular "bigfoot" character style, which has not aged well, and he forced the characters to provide all the movement within the frame; the animation camera rarely pans.

Eshbaugh's *Oz* ran aground on copyright issues related to the Technicolor Corporation and didn't see commercial release until 2009.

Besides standard cartoon fare, Eshbaugh produced music-heavy promotional films that include *The Sunshine Makers*, a 1935 cartoon for Borden dairies; and *The Wonder Bakers at the World's Fair*, a 1939 Wonder Bread cartoon that screened at the 1939 New York World's Fair. Eshbaugh did at least two 1935 cartoons for KOOL cigarettes (in which penguins who make the popular cigarette on an icy KOOL assembly line deliver a butt to the Statue of Liberty, who lights up with her torch).

Shortly after, Eshbaugh collaborated with New York's Van Beuren animation studio to create RKO's "Rainbow Parade" cartoon series, which were filmed in Technicolor.

Oz University (1936)

Sarah Pierce directed this Technicolor short capturing the University of Michigan's freshman pageant, sponsored by the school's Women's Athletic Association. The show was loosely inspired by L. Frank Baum's 1904 novel,

The Marvelous Land of Oz, with residents of Oz having magical visual access to U of M students.

Land of Oz (1938)

An unfinished animated cartoon produced by Kenneth McLellan and Maud Gage Baum.

Oz on the Radio Before 1939

From the 1920s until the late 1940s, a radio set was a central item in American homes, much as the TV/home theater/home entertainment center is dominant today. Simple, crystal set receivers of the early '20s got dodgy reception from the few operating commercial stations, and listeners had to wear headphones, but people were nevertheless thrilled to have music and voices in their homes. Before the '20s were out, radio had established itself as a permanent part of the American scene, and became a true titan in the 1930s. News, music, drama, comedy—all of that was available daily via table models kept in kitchens and bedrooms, and ornate floor models that presided over living rooms and parlors.

The first *Oz*-related radio broadcast happened just as the medium was on the verge of breaking out:

Topsy Turvy Time (1926)

Originating from Chicago's WMAQ, this Monday through Friday children's show was broadcast during 1926–27. Sometime in 1926, host Russell Pratt (an announcer-pianist who was known as the Topsy Turvy Time Man) did a read-aloud serialization of Baum's *The Land of Oz*. WMAQ aggressively promoted the program with on-air contests and prizes, and urged kids to join the Topsy Turvy Club and wear the membership pin.

No audio from *Topsy Turvy Time* is known to have survived.

The Wizard of Oz (1933–34)

This NBC radio program starring twelve-year-old Nancy Kelly as Dorothy originated from Milwaukee's WTMJ. The show was licensed from L. Frank Baum's widow, Maud Gage Baum, and sponsored by Jell-O, which offered four softcover "Little Wizard Stories" books as listener premiums. Production was supervised by WTMJ staffer Donald Stauffer, who was simultaneously directing the weekly *March of Time* radio program. *The Wizard of Oz* was broadcast as three fifteen-minute segments each week (Monday, Wednesday, and Friday) from September 25, 1933, to March 23, 1934. Stories were adapted from the first six Baum books.

Nancy Kelly had a successful career as an adult actress, and is best recalled today as the hapless mother of the fiendish little girl in the 1956 film *The Bad Seed*. Others in the cast were Bill Adams (Scarecrow), Parker Fennelly (Tin Woodman), and Jack Smart (Cowardly Lion). Other roles were taken by Agnes Moorehead (who became a member of Orson Welles's *Mercury Theatre* radio program a few years later) and Ian Wolfe.

The narratives could be unintentionally amusing because references to Jell-O were awkwardly worked into the scripts. No audio of the show's twenty-six episodes survives.

The Wizard of Oz (1930s)

Exact dates are unknown, but at some time in the 1930s, *The Wizard of Oz* was dramatized on the radio by writer-director John Elkhorn. Music was provided by Charles Paul and His Munchkin Music Men. Early in 1931, when Paul was the orchestra leader at the Valencia Theatre in Jamaica, Long Island, a teenage girl from a wealthy Long Island family became infatuated with him. She was sent by her parents on a European tour intended to cool off her ardor. During the voyage home, the girl fell for a pair of male passengers and vanished after the ship docked. And, no, the girl's name wasn't Dorothy.

Alice, the Bard, and Snow White

MGM's *The Wizard of Oz* imitates no other film, but the studio did take a general kind of inspiration, and absorbed some cautionary lessons, too, from a few Hollywood fantasy films that preceded *Oz*. At issue was the moviegoing public's tolerance for fantasy.

American movie audiences of the late-Depression era enjoyed fantasy when it was reality based and expressed in romantic pictures about wealthy, funny "swells" or in lively musicals. What we now understand to be movie fantasy—*The Hobbit*, *Harry Potter*, *The Hunger Games*—wasn't at issue in the 1930s because studios never thought about it, except as something suitable for small children, and best offered as seven-minute cartoon shorts, at that. Horror, a cousin to fantasy, had become lucrative at Universal, and although other studios did their imitations, the whimsy of magical other worlds was found mainly in books and storybooks. But very occasionally, when a recognized literary property might be translated into a prestige film release, Hollywood took a risk with fantasy.

Paramount's *Alice in Wonderland*, a 1933 adaptation of Lewis Carroll's *Alice's Adventures in Wonderland* and *Through the Looking Glass* (1865/1871), was a hugely ambitious production from Paramount, the Hollywood studio established, via merger, in 1914, and that was second only to MGM in gloss and prestige. Director Norman Z. McLeod had experience with comedy, via cartoons, live-action shorts, and features dating to 1921. By 1933, he had had recent success with star comic Leon Errol (*Finn and Hattie*) and the Marx Brothers (*Monkey*

If not for the great box-office success of Walt Disney's *Snow White and the Seven Dwarfs* (1937), MGM might never have made *The Wizard of Oz*.

Business and *Horse Feathers*). McLeod had a pleasing sense of the absurd and handled actresses effectively. He seemed a reasonable choice to helm *Alice*. (McLeod was at his peak later, from the late 1930s to the mid-'50s, when he scored with *Topper*, *The Secret Life of Walter Mitty*, *The Paleface*, and *My Favorite Spy*. He ended his career in television in the early 1960s.)

Scripters Joseph L. Mankiewicz and William Cameron Menzies were faithful to the Alice books in many aspects, and the film is rich with fancy. However, the studio's decision to be slavishly faithful to John Tenniel's famed illustrations put some twenty stars into heavy makeup or face-covering full-body costumes. Except for their voices, most of the stars—other than winsome Charlotte Henry, as Alice—were unrecognizable. Of course, by 1933 Hollywood filmmaking was a star-driven enterprise; when audiences went to see Cary Grant in *Alice*, they expected to *see* Cary Grant—not an enormous Mock Turtle (a full-body costume) that merely sounded like Cary Grant. The pattern was repeated with Humpty Dumpty (W. C. Fields), the Cheshire Cat (Richard Arlen), and Tweedledum and Tweedledee (Jack Oakie and Roscoe Karns, respectively). As the White Knight, handsome Gary Cooper is unrecognizable with bald cap, putty nose, and false whiskers. Some players, such as Edna May Oliver (the Red Queen), are costumed but show their (more or less) real features. But too many of the film's stars were deeply disguised.

The picture feels heavy and deliberate, and because Alice expresses no particular desire to return home or even to accomplish anything (she's mainly curious about what's going on), there's no dramatic tension. The guest stars show up in a series of unconnected scenes that work against development of a narrative. Sets are marvelously ambitious, but because the camera moves almost not at all, *Alice* becomes a unique paradox: a visually sumptuous movie that has very little visual excitement. The whole adventure is generally more bizarre than engaging. Paramount spent heavily on promotion (and even wrangled the cover of *Time* magazine), but *Alice in Wonderland* flopped at the box office.

The Hollywood community noted the picture's failure, of course, and the prospects for future live-action fantasy did not look good. Nevertheless, in 1935 Warner Bros. grabbed for "prestige" with a lavish adaptation of Shakespeare's *A Midsummer Night's Dream*. The picture was a curious melding of late-16th-century fantasy and romantic comedy, and the distinctly American performance styles of Warner stars Jimmy Cagney, Joe E. Brown, Dick Powell, Hugh Herbert, and Olivia de Havilland. Adapted with laudable fidelity to Shakespeare by Charles Kenyon and Mary C. McCall Jr., and sumptuously staged by co-directors Max Reinhardt (who had triumphed with the play on Broadway) and William Dieterle, *A Midsummer Night's Dream* mainly raised the ire of critics and was a box-office dud. Cagney is a wonderfully antic Bottom, and his presence usually ensured good box office, but *Dream*'s 133-minute running time probably didn't help. In any case, the failure looked like just another bullet in the heart of film fantasy.

Then came Walt Disney's *Snow White and the Seven Dwarfs* (1937). This animated cartoon was Disney's first feature-length production and his first major appropriation of an established fairy tale. *Snow White* turned out to be not just a stupendously lovely film, but also a surprise box-office success that changed the whole complexion of Hollywood.

Certainly, it was a coup for Mr. Disney, a onetime animator who began producing cartoon shorts in 1922 and introduced a little fellow called Mickey Mouse in 1928. During the ten years separating that first Mickey cartoon, *Plane Crazy*, and the general release of *Snow White*, Disney produced more than 160 cartoon shorts that included one-shots and many that elaborated on Mickey's adventures, introducing such characters as Minnie Mouse, Daisy and Donald Duck, Goofy, and Pluto. Nearly all of these shorts were enthusiastically received upon release, and some went on to stand the test of time as classics of short-form animation: *Steamboat Willie*, *The Skeleton Dance*, *Flowers and Trees*, *The Three Little Pigs*, *The Mail Pilot*, *The Mad Doctor*, *Pluto's Judgment Day*, *Thru the Mirror* (starring Mickey, in a clever riff on Carroll's *Alice's Adventures in Wonderland*), and *The Old Mill.*

Not surprisingly, Disney was an astute executive, and he realized early in the 1930s that there was no real growth potential in a production slate made up exclusively of shorts. The animation units at other studios were just that: units that helped the bottom line but that were minor parts of the studios' overall output and business plans. On top of that, Disney had no distribution arm and released his cartoons through United Artists, which naturally demanded a fee for the service. (Disney rectified that in 1953, when he created the Buena Vista Distribution Company.)

Walt Disney began thinking about a feature-length animated cartoon in 1933, which was intriguing all by itself, and a bit of a shocker, too, because Disney informed his staff that the new film would *not* star Mickey Mouse. What, then, could Walt possibly have in mind?

Well, it wasn't *Snow White*, at least not right away. Disney had wanted to do a feature-length animated version of *Alice's Adventures in Wonderland*, and even put the project into preproduction in 1931, only to pull the plug when Paramount announced plans for the live-action version discussed above. After that, he considered popular humorist Will Rogers for a combination cartoon-and-live-action feature based on Washington Irving's "Rip Van Winkle"—but Paramount had tied up that property, too. Walt kept thinking. He liked a Victor Herbert operetta, *Babes in Toyland*, but was preempted by Hal Roach, who turned it into a feature-length Laurel and Hardy vehicle in 1934. (Disney eventually got to all three of his early choices: the animated feature *Alice in Wonderland* was released in 1951, and a live-action musical version of *Babes in Toyland* was done in 1961 [it's one of the studio's weakest films]. Disney never did a "Rip Van Winkle" theatrical film, but the story was included with Irving's "The Legend of Sleepy Hollow" [a tale Disney brought to the screen as a half-hour cartoon in 1949] on a 1963 Disneyland Records release.)

Well, what about *Snow White*? Disney had once thought he might do the story as a cartoon short; now he reconsidered. The "Snow White" fairy tale was familiar to him, and to most Americans, as a 19th-century product of the Brothers Grimm, but those writers had not created it, only embellished a much older tale. Disney saw the story's dramatic possibilities, and envisioned comic ones, too. The fairy tale had been adapted for film as early as 1902. Numerous short and feature-length versions followed (more than a few were bunched in the years 1916–17), from companies based in New York, New Jersey, and, later, Los Angeles. One of the earliest film studios, Thanhouser Company of New Rochelle, New Jersey, produced a significant version, *The Legend of Snow White*, in 1914. A later adaptation called *Snow White* was produced by Educational Films in 1916 and ran nearly two hours. At least two silent versions came from France. Just as Walt Disney began outlining his version, animator Max Fleischer cast the inimitable Betty Boop in *Snow-White*, a 1933 cartoon short featuring music by singer-bandleader Cab Calloway.

Disney was particularly struck by *Snow White*, a Famous Players/Paramount version from 1916. He had seen the movie while a kid newsboy in Kansas City, and had never forgotten petite, dark-haired Marguerite Clark as Snow White. Disney's fondness for that film, as much as anything else, moved him to mount his own adaptation.

It soon became clear, though, that an ambitious, feature-length cartoon was going to be very expensive. Walt's very capable top executive, his brother Roy, grew alarmed at the costs of staff expansion and uncontrolled overtime pay. By 1936, even the holder of Disney's line of credit, Bank of America, expressed nervousness. When Disney's distributor, United Artists, asked for more rights to the property than Walt was willing to grant, he dumped UA and signed a distribution deal with RKO, even though UA was in a position to help mitigate what had become enormous production costs.

Walt pressed on, and when *Snow White and the Seven Dwarfs* had its Hollywood premiere shortly before Christmas 1937 (young Judy Garland was in the audience), and went into general release three weeks later, audiences swooned and critics raved. Even staff animators and story men who had doubted their boss's sanity were shamefacedly exultant. Audiences loved Snow White and her relationship with the charming, keenly delineated seven dwarfs that become her protectors. The wicked queen is a marvelous figure, and Snow White's rescue-with-a-prince's-kiss, while paternalistic, was well liked in 1937–38. The glowing assessment from the *New York Herald Tribune* was hardly atypical; the paper insisted that *Snow White* "belongs with the few great masterpieces of the screen."

The film is a triumph for many reasons, but two of them are particularly important. First is the technical artistry, which is astonishing. When this writer saw the movie for the first time on a big screen, during a 1975 re-release, tears came to my eyes—not because of the sentimental story (I was, after all, a young adult), but for the film's impeccable craft and the sheer gorgeousness of the images. Director David Hand marshaled the studio's human and artistic resources brilliantly; *Snow White* is a visual feast, alternately light and airy, and dark and terrifying. On the pictorial level alone, the film is dazzling and thoroughly inspired. In this, *Snow White* has more than a passing resemblance to MGM's *The Wizard of Oz.*

The other reason for the piquancy of Disney's *Snow White* is the film's subtle yet compelling reflection of the world into which the movie was released: great nations still struggled to recover from economic calamity, and the globe seemed to shrink daily as clouds of war gathered in Europe and Asia. That Disney's protagonist is a young, vulnerable woman provoked a primal, familial response in adults and children in 1938; Snow White, like Judy Garland's Dorothy, is a dear, sweet girl who, although defended by staunch (and amusing) friends, faces terrors that most of us can only imagine. Audiences desperately wanted to defend her.

Innocent Snow White's antagonist, a glamorous, irredeemably wicked queen, provided MGM with an early template for its own Wicked Witch, and demonstrated the on-screen power found in a contrast of good and evil. "Heigh Ho," "Whistle While You Work," "Someday My Prince Will Come," and other splendid songs proved that music was a congenial partner to fantasy.

A skilled voice cast led by Adriana Caselotti contributed hugely to unique, likable characters that were simultaneously whimsical and rooted in reality.

(Caselotti is heard in *The Wizard of Oz* when she says, "Wherefore art thou, Romeo?" in response to the Tin Woodman's "If I Only Had a Heart.") The technical achievement of *Snow White* inspired MGM and *Oz* producer Mervyn LeRoy to equal or exceed it.

Then there was the way in which Disney's gamble paid off. He had lavished $1.5 million on his feature-length cartoon, a sum that was hefty for a live-action feature of the day and simply unprecedented in animation. As noted, not all of his closest advisers and finance partners were completely on board, so the film's 1937–38 gross of $3.5 million, and $6.5 million by mid-1939, was an enormous vindication of Walt's instincts. ($6.5 million is the equivalent of $108 million in 2013 dollars.)

MGM, and all the rest of Hollywood, had been shown that what they'd assumed was kid stuff might be for grown-ups, too.

4

There's No Place Like Home

MGM Acquires Oz

We forget today that MGM's decision to do *Oz* as a musical was extraordinarily risky. First, of course, was that this would be an expensive and time-consuming project with no guarantee of easy profit. Another consideration, and one that weighed heavily on Louis Mayer, was that previous film versions of *Oz* had been financial failures. Then there was this: *Oz* would be unlike any other musical film of the day, with no backstage story, no chic creatures in gowns and tails, and no high society or (as in the Warner Bros. musicals of the '30s) explicit invocations of the Depression. MGM's *The Wizard of Oz* would be pure fantasy.

MGM's New York chief, Nick Schenck, had no affinity for fantasy and was sure that his studio's version of *The Wizard of Oz* would be a disaster. (Schenck had considered adapting *The Wizard of Oz* to film as early as 1924.) But because Louis Mayer had been worked on so effectively by Mervyn LeRoy, the project's producer; and by Arthur Freed, a songwriter who had been promoted to associate producer, Schenck allowed himself to be persuaded. But later, the boss of bosses reconsidered. Mervyn LeRoy remembered, "Schenck wanted to stop the picture. He thought I was ruining the company, spending too much money. I remember I told him, 'Mr. Schenck, I wish I had three and a half million [dollars], I'd buy it from you. It's going to be worth more than that!'"

By the late 1930s, the film rights to Baum's *Oz* novels were owned by independent producer Sam Goldwyn, who had purchased them from Baum's son, Frank Joslyn Baum, on January 26, 1934, for $40,000. The deal came after four months of negotiation and the younger Baum's clearance of rights. Goldwyn thought that his popular contract player, entertainer Eddie Cantor, was ideal for the role of the Scarecrow. Goldwyn envisioned comic actor W. C. Fields as the Wizard and had a couple of unlikely candidates to play Dorothy: Broadway actress Helen Hayes (age thirty-three) or silent star Mary Pickford (age forty).

Goldwyn wanted to shoot *The Wizard of Oz* in three-strip Technicolor. The film would be a major one, but Goldwyn was unable to get it off the ground until 1936, when twelve-year-old Marcia Mae Jones made a splash (in a downbeat role) in *These Three*, a drama about two spiteful young girls who ruin the reputations of a pair of female schoolteachers. By 1937, though, it was apparent that Jones was going to be locked into supporting roles, and Goldwyn scratched her from his list.

A 1937 MGM idea for a series of *Wizard of Oz* theatrical cartoons was abandoned when research suggested that adults wouldn't be interested. Nevertheless, the property continued to intrigue the studio. In February 1938, Sam Goldwyn was persuaded to sell the rights to MGM's parent company, Loew's Inc., for $60,000. *Daily Variety* noted the sale in a February 24, 1938, story, adding, "Metro . . . has assigned Judy Garland to the role of Dorothy."

MGM gave the Baum family a separate payment of $40,000. (The studio laid its claim to *The Wizard of Oz* just in time: Walt Disney had been casting around for an animated follow-up to his 1937 smash, *Snow White and the Seven Dwarfs*, and had sent his brother Roy to inquire about the rights to Baum's *Oz*, unaware that the property was now held by MGM. Years later, in 1954, Disney purchased the rights to twelve of Baum's Oz books—the first one was not among them—and intended to present *The Rainbow Road to Oz* as Disney Studio's first live-action musical. That film was never made, and although Walt Disney died in 1966, the company held onto its book rights. Disney's live-action *Oz* film finally appeared in 1985, as *Return to Oz*.)

Producer Mervyn LeRoy

Louis B. Mayer's closest professional associate, and MGM's seemingly indispensable creative voice, was executive Irving Thalberg. He had joined the studio in 1924, and brought intense focus and an unremitting work ethic to the development of sleek, commercial properties. Slight, good-looking, and always impeccably dressed, Thalberg was the personification of the ideal that Mayer wanted as the studio's executive core. The younger man was well educated and erudite, and when he married MGM star Norma Shearer, he entered the ranks of Hollywood royalty. Thalberg was a feverish worker, but was never a healthy man, and his frailness finally caught up with him. When he died in 1936, he was just thirty-seven years old.

Mayer was deeply shaken by Thalberg's death, and taken aback by the 1936 departure of another *wunderkind*, producer David O. Selznick, who left MGM to pursue independent production. (There was an uncomfortable sidebar to this because Selznick had been married since 1930 to Irene Mayer, Louis Mayer's daughter.) Like Thalberg, Selznick had good commercial instincts mated with what Mayer considered a "classy" sensibility. But Selznick was eager to produce the long-awaited adaptation of Margaret Mitchell's wildly popular 1936 novel, *Gone With the Wind*. He valued his autonomy, but he also understood the expense of mounting a project as ambitious as *GWTW*. He needed outside money, and accepted when MGM offered $1.25 million and the services of Clark Gable in return for distribution rights and half the net profits.

Producer Mervyn LeRoy (left) and Victor Fleming join Judy in Munchkinland. LeRoy had wanted to direct *Oz* as well as produce it, but Louis Mayer felt that both jobs would simply be too much to manage. Little Olga Nardone (foreground, left) looks up at LeRoy; the tallest female Munchkin player in this photo (right) is Nita Krebs, who (like Nardone) played a villager as well as one of the Lullaby League.

Mayer had grown accustomed to the intelligence and passion of Thalberg and Selznick, and wanted to carry on this tradition of bright young men at his side. Mayer finally decided that former Warner Bros. producer-director Mervyn LeRoy, thirty-seven, who had come to MGM at the beginning of 1938, had the story sense and practical experience needed to fill the right-hand-man role. Experience was particularly important to Mayer. He selected LeRoy to produce *The Wizard of Oz*. Although Arthur Freed's ambition had been acknowledged with his assignment as (uncredited) associate producer, Mayer wanted an older hand to backstop Freed.

In a *New York Times* piece, LeRoy reflected on the unique and layered task he faced. "A bigger job than merely creating something unreal descended upon us all," he said. "[It was] the task of putting realism into the fantastic."

MGM gave *The Wizard of Oz* production number 1060, a number of no particular importance other than that it designated a project mounted by the world's greatest film studio.

At that time, a typical "important" MGM picture was shot in eight weeks and was budgeted at about $1.5 million (the equivalent of $25 million in 2013 dollars). "Small" MGM projects were shot in three to four weeks. Because of the unique challenges presented by *The Wizard of Oz*, MGM and LeRoy set the budget at $3.7 million. (That was generous, as the final cost to MGM was $2.8 million.) *Oz* was a fantasy, a complete environment that would have to be created from scratch. There would be no quick, dollar-saving tweaks to standing sets; no easy trips to and from the MGM costume department; no pickup of songs already available to the studio; and no casting from among MGM contract players only. This was going to be difficult and different. Eight weeks to shoot? Not likely. In the end, *Oz* required a twenty-two-week shoot, which came after Loew's Inc. had entertained on-again off-again thoughts about *Oz* for twenty-four years before entering into a year of concentrated development and pre-production.

LeRoy was given a salary of $6,000 a week. (The average U.S. wage in recession-year 1938 was sixty-three cents an hour. Assuming a sixty-hour week, the average American worker grossed $37.80.)

From the start of the project, LeRoy dedicated himself to capturing the spirit, if not every detail, of the Baum novel. The book, and the follow-ons written by Baum and others, remained very popular, and had an active fan base with numerous concerns. A Canadian reader, May H. Hedemark, wrote to LeRoy, asking that Toto not speak in the film; in *Tik-Tok of Oz*, Baum's eighth Oz book, Toto reveals that he can talk, and he's positively chatty in Baum's *The Lost Princess of Oz*. Readers also asked that character designs follow those set down by original illustrator W. W. Denslow. LeRoy noted those comments, and many others, but you have to wonder how May Hedemark would have reacted upon hearing associate producer Arthur Freed's early description of Dorothy: "An orphan in Kansas who sings jazz."

In Focus: Mervyn LeRoy (1900–1987)

Although Mervyn LeRoy became one of Hollywood's most successful producers, he was, at heart, a director. Like many executives who rose to prominence during Hollywood's golden age, he had to struggle as a youth. LeRoy was born in upper-middle-class San Francisco in 1900, but his parents' divorce, and the 1906 earthquake that destroyed his father's department store, meant that Mervyn would spend his childhood in reduced circumstances. He was a street-corner newsboy at twelve, and later juggled that job and work with a theatrical stock company. He became a cheeky, confident performer, adept at imitations, songs, and patter. LeRoy found work in vaudeville before he was sixteen, and toured the tough and demanding national circuit for nine years. Sometimes he was The Boy Tenor of the Generation; other times he was The Singing Newsboy. When he hooked up with a young pianist named Clyde Cooper, LeRoy took the stage as part of LeRoy and Cooper, Two Kids and a Piano.

LeRoy won a bit part in a 1923 movie shot in Fort Lee, New Jersey, and then followed the latter part of the industry's exodus to Hollywood. His cousin was producer

Jesse Lasky, who helped LeRoy get work as a Hollywood wardrobe handler. After that, LeRoy dyed and processed film, punched up scripts with jokes, gained invaluable technical knowledge as an assistant cameraman, and did more bit parts, too.

Ambitious, and knowledgeable about the business on both sides of the camera, LeRoy directed his first movie, *No Place to Go*, for independent producer Henry Hobart in 1927. *No Place to Go* was a romantic comedy, but if one thing characterizes LeRoy's subsequent career as a director, it's his refusal to be identified with just one genre. He had a particular affinity for crime films, and directed three gems starring the rapidly rising Warner star Edward G. Robinson: *Little Caesar* (1931), *Five Star Final* (1931; with Robinson as a crusading tabloid editor), and *Two Seconds* (1932).

One of the six Warner features LeRoy directed for release in 1932, *I Am a Fugitive from a Chain Gang*, still hammers audiences with its bleak fatalism. LeRoy also was comfortable with earthy, talented Warner leading ladies the likes of Joan Blondell (*Gold Diggers of 1933*, 1933), Ann Dvorak (*Three on a Match*, 1932), and Glenda Farrell (*Hi, Nellie!*, 1934). He got back to comedy, too, guiding the outsized talent of Joe E. Brown in *Broadminded* (1931).

At MGM, LeRoy directed *Tugboat Annie* (1933), an enormously successful teaming of character stars Marie Dressler and Wallace Beery, but his 1934 marriage to Doris Warner—the daughter of Warner Bros. co-owner Harry Warner—brought LeRoy back to the Warner lot. He became a producer there in 1936, and returned to MGM as a director-producer in 1938. LeRoy had put a young actress named Lana Turner under personal contract in 1937, and when he returned to MGM, he brought the untutored but promising starlet with him. Lana was just seventeen at the time, and as LeRoy's star rose at MGM, so did hers. From the beginning of his association with the studio, then, LeRoy brought more than just creative talent; he brought an ability to sniff out box-office potential, in stories and actors.

LeRoy remained active as a director after *Oz*, producing his own projects and bringing intelligence and gloss to commercially important pictures in many genres: *Waterloo Bridge* (1940), *Johnny Eager* (1941), *Madame Curie* (1943), *Thirty Seconds Over Tokyo* (1944), *Little Women* (1949), *East Side, West Side* (1949), *Quo Vadis* (1951), and *Million Dollar Mermaid* (1952). He skillfully directed films adapted from stage plays *Mister Roberts* (1955), *The Bad Seed* (1956), *No Time for Sergeants* (1958), and *Gypsy* (1962). LeRoy also helmed an alternately violent and sentimental whitewash of J. Edgar Hoover and the FBI, *The FBI Story* (1959).

LeRoy became an independent producer late in his career; his final producer credit is *Moment to Moment* (1965), a film that's also his last director credit. However, LeRoy went behind the camera one last time to direct, without credit, parts of John Wayne's simplistic Vietnam adventure, *The Green Berets* (1968). (The assignment, for which LeRoy wanted no credit, came as a request from Jack Warner, who worried that star-director Wayne was out of his depth. LeRoy traveled to Fort Benning, Georgia, and directed the scenes that featured Wayne—which is to say, the greater part of the film.)

In his final years after retirement, LeRoy missed the business discipline and product clarity of the studio era he'd known so well. Obviously unmoved by the many superior American films that began to be made after the mid-1960s, LeRoy wrote in his 1974 autobiography, "Nowadays movies aren't made by great creative minds, but by a cartel of businessmen on the one hand and a haphazard group of young and undisciplined rookies on the other. Too many directors today make movies that puzzle and offend and confuse the audience. They seem to equate bafflement with art."

That's a statement of a corporate-minded filmmaker—and LeRoy, after all, spent his career being mindful of the buck while successfully negotiating the line separating art from commerce. He regarded movies as product that had no excuse to be anything but the best.

Associate Producer Arthur Freed

When *The Wizard of Oz* went into production at MGM in 1938, the project's neophyte (and uncredited) associate producer, Arthur Freed, was forty-four years old. While he'd already made a mark in the industry as a lyricist, Freed realized that real power lay with producers. He told Louis Mayer that he was the fellow to produce *Oz*. He'd read the Baum books as a boy, and felt he had an understanding of how to work with writers and a director to structure the whimsical material. But Mayer wanted a more experienced hand at the helm, so Mervyn LeRoy was hired to produce *Oz*, with Freed allowed to run a great deal of the day-to-day producer's chores.

Freed had a feel for economical narratives and emotional nuance. He also was a keen evaluator of actors. Besides advocating for Judy Garland, Freed wanted Buddy Ebsen as the Tin Woodman and May Robson as Auntie Em. Ebsen was cast (although, originally, as the Scarecrow), but Robson was never seriously considered.

Freed envisioned futurist designer Norman Bel Geddes as a key contributor to production design, and mentioned Vincente Minnelli (who had been a successful costumer for the stage) as costume designer. Neither of those ideas panned out; neither did Freed's suggestion of Herman Mankiewicz as chief screenwriter, although Mank did contribute, as we'll see.

Freed's musical background gave him more clout in that area. He selected E. Y. Harburg as the lyricist, plus two others who did not contribute to *Oz*, Ira Gershwin and Dorothy Fields.

As we'll see, Freed's best and most active contribution to *Oz* was development of the script. He insisted that the script have an emotional center, for without one, *Oz* would be little more than a good-looking curiosity.

In Focus: Arthur Freed (1894–1973)

Because he was a lyricist, Freed was essentially a storyteller, and the stories he told between 1925 and 1937 (many done in collaboration with songwriter Nacio Herb Brown) included "You Are My Lucky Star," "Singin' in the Rain," "You'll Never Know," "You Were Meant for Me," "Broadway Melody," "All I Do Is Dream of You," "Good

Morning," "Beautiful Girl," and dozens more. In October 1938, just as director Richard Thorpe was about to begin shooting *The Wizard of Oz*, Freed sold Louis Mayer on doing a movie version of a popular Rodgers and Hart Broadway musical, *Babes in Arms*. The vehicle was ideal for Judy Garland and Mickey Rooney. Mayer was so enthused by the idea that he instructed Freed to move from the music department to the Irving G. Thalberg Building, the administrative heart of MGM. For Freed, this was an enormous elevation of status. Very shortly, he was a producer, and *Babes in Arms* was his first assignment.

Freed's experience with *Oz* had been extraordinarily useful to him because he emerged from the project unafraid of big, ambitious assignments. He became a full producer in 1939 with *Babes in Arms*, and later headed an MGM musicals unit that helped keep the studio afloat in the late 1940s and '50s. So successful was this studio within a studio that it was referred to on the lot and throughout the industry as the Freed Unit.

Arthur Freed was born Arthur Grossman in South Carolina in 1894, and grew up in wealthy surroundings in Seattle. His father was an art dealer, and there were eventually eight children, most of whom pursued music as a profession. Arthur had an exclusive prep-school education and then entered the music business the hard way, working as a song plugger and piano player before becoming a performer in vaudeville. He produced modest musical shows, managed theaters, and began to see success as a lyricist in the early 1920s. Freed was taken on as a lyricist by MGM in 1928.

The studio kept him very busy during the next ten years, profiting enormously from songs that were used repeatedly in MGM movies and for sales of sheet music. Freed understood how the business worked; he wasn't a rebel. He liked to work within the system and bend it to his will with sheer competence. He once remarked, "Don't try to be different. Just be good. To be good is different enough." He had no patience at all with mediocrity. As the film industry evolved, Freed evolved with it, anticipating audiences with lavish pictures that were also invariably surprising.

No studio of the time did musicals better than MGM, and MGM musicals were synonymous with Arthur Freed. After achieving producer status immediately after *The Wizard of Oz*, Freed proved himself with *Babes in Arms*, *Strike Up the Band*, *Cabin in the Sky*, *Meet Me in St. Louis*, and *Ziegfeld Follies*. Those are beautifully crafted entertainments, but Freed really hit his stride after World War II and thrived throughout the 1950s. Movie musicals were a venerable form dating to the beginning of the sound era; Freed refined and reinvented the genre, and created what amounted to the last great burst of Hollywood musicals. One of his pictures, *Singin' in the Rain* (1952), is rightly celebrated as one of the finest American films ever. Freed had many other postwar triumphs: *The Pirate*, *Easter Parade*, *On the Town*, *Take Me Out to the Ball Game*, *Show Boat*, *Royal Wedding*, *Silk Stockings*. Two Freed productions, *An American in Paris* (1951) and *Gigi* (1958), were awarded the best picture Oscar.

The bitter paradox of Freed's latter-day MGM output is that the films found critical and box-office success at a time when the studio was struggling—and not very well—to adjust to the changing relationships of stars and studios, and new expectations of postwar audiences.

The gifts that propelled Freed to power and artistic success were his flair for negotiating studio politics, dogged self-promotion, and unshakable confidence. He loved and cultivated orchids—an unexpected avocation for a man who was neither soft-spoken nor subtle. He could be stern, but because he had begun on the purely creative side of the business, he showed patience to exacting directors like Vincente Minnelli, Stanley Donen, and George Sidney and encouraged Gene Kelly, Fred Astaire, Cyd Charisse, Van Johnson, Judy Garland, and many others to stretch as performers.

There are many reasons why pictures from the Freed Unit are widely watched and enjoyed today; the most important is Arthur Freed himself.

E Pluribus Unum

Assembling the Cast

When casting of *The Wizard of Oz* began in 1938, studio casting director Billy Grady had access to 120 leads and character players under contract to MGM. (Even more actors—253—had been on the lot when young Judy Garland was signed in the fall of 1935.) The contract actors were available for whichever projects they might be suited to. Audiences were encouraged to identify certain stars as MGM players (such as Robert Taylor and Greta Garbo), and to take enjoyment from the studio's roster of hardworking character actors. MGM contract player Frank Morgan, for instance, was cast in twenty-five pictures between 1935 and his 1939 appearance as the Wizard. Morgan and other contract players brought personal and stylistic continuity to the MGM product, and were living reminders of the high quality on which the studio prided itself. This was the case at other studios, too: for instance, Warner Bros. had cultivated George Raft, James Cagney, Bette Davis, Ann Sheridan, and others as stars (Bogart's rise would begin a year or two later), and the likes of Frank McHugh and Allen Jenkins as character men. Small studios followed the same system. For example, Republic developed John Wayne and Gene Autry as stars, and had contract supporting players, like Gabby Hayes, that became popular. Even Monogram, a small but aggressive Poverty Row studio, crafted star images for such contract players as Rex Bell and Tim McCoy.

MGM had plenty of ingénues on the lot, but who had the star potential needed to carry off Dorothy and *The Wizard of Oz*? At the end of January 1938, Arthur Freed sent casting suggestions to Louis B. Mayer. Although Mervyn LeRoy, Nick Schenck, and other MGM executives thought first of Shirley Temple as Dorothy, the only reason Freed was enthusiastic about *Oz* was Judy Garland's presence at MGM. Before anyone else, Freed realized that this young contract player was ideal for the Dorothy role.

Musical arranger Roger Edens, another early booster of Garland, realized Temple was hopeless as a singer. To be sure, little Shirley sang in her films, but she got by on charm and cuteness—certainly not on her vocalizing, which was enthusiastic but amateurish.

In Focus: Shirley Temple (1928–2014)

The Wizard of Oz attracted large audiences and compiled a healthy gross during its first release in 1939–40. It would have shown a profit right away except that it had cost so much to make.

Shirley Temple would have brought a marquee name to *Oz*, but her performance style lacked the sophistication the role of Dorothy demanded.

If reigning child star Shirley Temple had played Dorothy—something that had been a vague possibility—*Oz* could have enjoyed a greater gross, or it may have earned less. It might have come to television in the 1950s as just one more title in a larger package of old MGM releases. Today, a Shirley Temple *Oz* might be a Technicolor curiosity in a DVD box set highlighted by Shirley's earlier, more popular movies.

None of this is a knock on Shirley Temple. She was a peerless child star with brilliant instincts as a performer. She was warm, bright-eyed, and thoroughly enchanting. The trouble is that if she had been cast as Dorothy, she would have been ten years old during the shoot and eleven when the film was released.

Through no fault of her own, little Shirley Temple would have been past her prime.

The peak of her career, 1934–37, was brief, but encompassed a staggering seventeen films. Between 1935 and 1938, Shirley was America's number-one box-office star—bigger than Gable, bigger than Harlow—bigger than anybody. During an American decade crippled by the Depression, Shirley brought immense profits to 20th Century-Fox, and was praised by no less a personage than President Roosevelt for buoying the spirits of millions of moviegoers.

Shirley Jane Temple was born in Southern California in 1928. Gertrude Temple was the archetypal stage mother, pulling two-year-old Shirley around to auditions, where the tiny child was accepted into the Meglin Kiddies dance and movie troupe, and, in 1942, hired for Universal short subjects. (The first of those, *Runt Page*, was released before Shirley's fourth birthday.) Between 1932 and 1934, Shirley had bits, often uncredited, in a half dozen features from major studios and independent filmmakers, and featured roles in more than a dozen one- and two-reel short comedies produced by low-rent Educational Films. In 1934, Temple broke through at Fox with *Stand Up and Cheer!*

That one was followed by a deluge of tailor-made vehicles that brought enduring stardom: *Little Miss Marker, Baby Take a Bow, Bright Eyes, The Little Colonel, Curly Top, Captain January, Poor Little Rich Girl* (in which Shirley danced with Jack Haley), *Dimples,*

Wee Willie Winkie, *Heidi*, and others. Shirley mugged, sang, and danced; she laughed, pouted prettily, and cried on cue. She was remarkable.

As she approached ten, her legs became a little longer and her adorable head seemed not as large as before. She was no longer a baby, and audiences apparently had trouble reconciling themselves to that. 20th Century-Fox's splashy fairy-tale fantasy "answer" to *The Wizard of Oz*, *The Blue Bird* (1940), was shot when Temple was eleven. Adapted from Maurice Maeterlinck's 1908 stage play, the movie is extraordinarily handsome but perhaps too earnest for its own good. Shirley played a selfish and ungrateful little girl (from some indeterminate nation in 19th-century Europe) who becomes a better person after a series of magical encounters in the past and the future, including meetings with her departed grandparents and yet-to-be-born younger sister. Despite Temple and fulsome Technicolor (which is bookended by sequences in black and white), *The Blue Bird* laid an egg at the box office.

Temple became a beautiful teenager, co-starring with adult stars in "A" pictures, and taking the leads in glossy Bs from RKO, Columbia, and independent producers. Her best from these years are *I'll Be Seeing You* (1944), *The Bachelor and the Bobby-Soxer* (1947), and *Fort Apache* (1948).

Shirley retired from acting in 1949. During her career she had earned over $3.2 million (more than $50 million by today's index), but discovered that her parents had squandered all of it but $28,000. After a brief marriage to soldier-turned-actor John Agar, Temple became Mrs. Shirley Temple Black in 1950. She headlined a pair of television anthology series, *Shirley Temple's Storybook* and *Shirley Temple Theatre*, during 1958–61, and then developed an interest in Republican politics. She was named the U.S. delegate to the United Nations in 1969. Later, she was U.S. ambassador to Ghana (1974–76) and ambassador to Czechoslovakia (1989–92).

Temple had a happy and successful adult life. For her, "America's sweetheart" was just an interlude. She told *Time* magazine in 1967, "I always think of her as 'the little girl.' She's not me."

Judy Garland as Dorothy

As Metro-Goldwyn-Mayer prepared for the August 1939 release of *The Wizard of Oz*, the studio's publicity machine churned out countless posed photos tailor-made for use by newspapers and magazines across America. In one of those images, Judy Garland happily reads a copy of L. Frank Baum's book, *The Wizard of Oz*. The photo is a real charmer. Judy is attired and made up as Dorothy, with the now-familiar pinafore and sweet hairstyle. The smile on her face suggests enthusiasm and delight.

Of course, Judy was a professional performer. She'd been on the stage since she was just two years old, and was learning what it meant to be a movie star. She knew how to smile for a camera.

The reality of Judy's role as Dorothy, and the circuitous route to the part that would make her world famous, is more complicated than a sunny smile on a young girl's face. Because *The Wizard of Oz* was going to be an expensive prestige film, shot in three-strip and requiring a wealth of sets, costumes, and special effects, MGM wanted to give itself a guarantee of return on investment.

At the outset of MGM's development of an *Oz* film, the studio's New York–based boss of bosses, Nick Schenck, insisted that Dorothy be played by a bona fide star. Although Judy Garland had been on the lot since September 27, 1935, she was far from the first choice to play Baum's plucky heroine.

Other Faces, Other Voices

Judy had been discovered in 1935, at thirteen, by Jack Robbins, who ran MGM's music-publishing arm, and music arranger Roger Edens. During a vocal audition conducted just days after the sudden death of her father, Frank Gumm, Judy sang "Zing! Went the Strings of My Heart." (Judy inevitably referred to the death of her father as one of the great tragedies of her life, so we can assume that her audition was unusually earnest.)

MGM musical director and would-be producer Arthur Freed was bowled

over by Judy's natural gifts. He talked her up so convincingly that Judy was able to avoid the usual screen-test rigmarole. She was signed in the early fall of 1935 and made her first big impression in a 1936 short subject, *Every Sunday*, which paired her with another teenage singing sensation, Deanna Durbin. *Every Sunday* was Deanna's first appearance before a movie camera. Judy, however, had appeared in short subjects as early as 1929, when she was just seven years old and still little Frances Gumm of the Gumm Sisters. (The first of these shorts was *The Big Revue*, produced by a tiny outfit called Mayfair Pictures.) These were singing appearances, with little or no acting required, so Judy was hardly a movie veteran when she was paired with Durbin.

Every Sunday is an eleven-minute showcase for a pair of sterling singing voices, and a risk-free way for MGM to introduce the newcomers to its leading exhibitors. (Very few members of the general public saw the short when it was new.) What neither Judy nor

Little Frances Gumm was a hardworking performer at age two; here, she's three or four, posing at about the time the Gumm family relocated from Minnesota to Los Angeles.

Deanna knew is that *Every Sunday* was also an audition. Louis B. Mayer realized he didn't need *two* very young, fresh-faced singers on the lot. One of them would have to be cut loose, to make room for the other. Deanna was more slender than Judy, and more "traditionally" pretty. Her soprano was pure and expressive. But Judy's dark eyes and vulnerable quality riveted the exhibitors' attention. And then there was the voice: girlish but already disciplined and unique, with a suggestion of the great emotional power that would come later.

Although MGM studio bosses briefly considered Deanna Durbin for the Dorothy role, Deanna's MGM contract was not renewed. That probably stung Durbin a little, but it was far from disastrous. Deanna was signed by Universal and became that studio's number-one box office attraction of the late 1930s and '40s. If the *Every Sunday* audition had worked out a little differently, it's likely that Durbin would have been cast as Dorothy. MGM tailored scripts to suit the particular talents and appeal of each star. Deanna was charming and sang like an angel. Mervyn LeRoy liked her for the role of Dorothy, and although Universal refused to loan her to MGM, it's no stretch to imagine her as the star of *The Wizard of Oz.*

MGM retained Judy, who was by now earning $200 a week, a step above "beginner" status for a contract player. The studio recognized Judy's talent—and her supposed shortcomings, too. She could sing but, at fourteen, was too mature to be a child star. And because she wasn't as shapely or as overtly glamorous as Lana Turner or Elizabeth Taylor or some other young MGM actresses, Judy wasn't suited for grooming as a traditional leading lady.

That left "kid" and teenage roles, and they came in a succession of pictures in which Judy was cast as somebody's awkward friend or slightly mousy sister. She sang in all of these, in moments usually disconnected from the main plots. (Judy filmed one of her early assignments, 1936's *Pigskin Parade*, while on loan to 20th Century-Fox.)

Then something significant happened. In a 1937 MGM musical called *Broadway Melody of 1938* (in which she danced with Buddy Ebsen before he was cast as the Tin Woodman), Judy looked longingly at a photograph of Clark Gable and sang "Dear Mr. Gable (You Made Me Love You)." Although Judy and Gable worked on the same lot, Judy performed the song as though she were an ordinary teenage girl who has worshipped Gable from afar. The song captures the intensity of teenage emotion with sweetly romantic lyrics that Judy sings with real fervor, suggesting that she's been powerless to resist her feelings for Gable. Audiences noticed, and approved.

Trade critics also realized Judy was special. In its review of *Broadway Melody of 1938, The Hollywood Reporter* said, "Hers is a distinct personality well worth careful promotion. A certain picture star." *Film Weekly* looked at Judy and said, "Obviously a 'find,' of whom more is going to be heard." And thanks to the *Los Angeles Herald-Express*, the general public learned that "[Judy] really walks away with the picture. Here is not only a complete artist, but a personality that takes you by storm."

Could It Be Shirley?

MGM didn't purchase the movie rights to *The Wizard of Oz* until February 1938, but the project had been contemplated throughout 1937, when Judy was singing to Clark Gable. The studio's first inclination was to cast Shirley Temple as Dorothy. Little Shirley, who was just nine in 1937, was a 20th Century-Fox player, and had been America's number-one box office star in 1935, 1936, and 1937. (Clark Gable was number two.) When approached with the idea, MGM's Nick Schenck reasoned that, with Shirley in the lead, *The Wizard of Oz* would be a smash. Hollywood folklore (and Shirley Temple, in her 1988 autobiography) says that Schenck went out on a limb to get the loan of Shirley's services from Fox, offering Gable *and* Jean Harlow in a two-for-one loan-out. According to the story, Fox was agreeable—but then Harlow died of uremic poisoning in the early summer of 1937. The tragedy rocked the Hollywood community, and would naturally have ended the exchange of stars, but Schenck probably never made a serious swap offer to Fox. Anything to that effect that was publicly floated during preproduction was just puffery from the MGM publicity department, or something fabricated by columnists out of thin air.

First Steps to Stardom

Fortunately, Judy had a champion on the MGM lot, musical arranger Roger Edens (who would later arrange the *Oz* vocals and, later still, earn Oscars with his scores for *Annie Get Your Gun, Easter Parade* [a Garland vehicle], and *On the Town*). A member of Arthur Freed's music unit, Edens had written "Dear Mr. Gable" for Judy, and recognized the brilliance of her gifts. He convinced Freed that Judy was perfect for *Oz*. (MGM staff producer Mervyn LeRoy claimed to have been an early Garland supporter, but no evidence of his enthusiasm exists.) Freed, in turn, made his case to Louis B. Mayer, who up to now had regarded Judy as a talented kid who wasn't easy to categorize or cast, and who had no real box-office prospects. Freed persisted. "I knew [Judy] could sing the part of Dorothy like Shirley never could," he recalled. "[I saw her as] an orphan in Kansas who sings jazz."

Mayer's personal assistant, Ida Koverman, also recognized Judy's gifts and advocated on her behalf. Mayer was gradually won over, and he communicated his new enthusiasm to Nick Schenck.

In a January 26, 1938, review, *Variety* celebrated Judy's work in *Everybody Sing*: "The diminutive Judy Garland takes a long leap forward to stardom. She has what it takes." Raves of that sort are noticed, and MGM's qualms about going forward were much diminished. On February 24, 1938, *Variety* noted that MGM's acquisition of film rights to *Oz* was complete and that the key role had been cast. Judy Garland was going to be Dorothy. But by the middle of March, *Variety* wasn't mentioning *anybody* as Dorothy. (It should be noted that, throughout the *Oz* development period at MGM, the public was never made privy to details of casting.)

Nevertheless, MGM felt good about Judy. First, though, more tune-ups that included second billing to Mickey Rooney in *Love Finds Andy Hardy* (1938), one of MGM's very popular "Andy Hardy" family comedies. (Although Judy was a co-star in this, the "glamour" was provided by another MGM starlet, seventeen-year-old Lana Turner.) Although not a leading lady in the grown-up sense, Judy approached the Andy Hardy picture as an opportunity to romance audiences and display her charisma and sheer talent. When the picture was released, MGM sent Judy and Roger Edens on a fifteen-city musical tour, during which Judy greeted the public and sang. She also made some radio appearances, interacting with MGM stars (Wallace Beery was one) and singing. Audiences welcomed her warmly.

Back home in Hollywood, the start date of *Oz* was pushed back to the early fall of 1938. So that Judy would get more film exposure in the meantime, she was handed *Listen, Darling* (1938), a showcase vehicle shot in just sixteen days. Judy played opposite the now-adolescent child star Freddie Bartholomew, and sang one of her signature tunes, "Zing! Went the Strings of My Heart," for the first time. Judy was still filming the final scenes of *Listen, Darling* when she began work on *Oz* in late August 1938. Her activity at that time consisted of posing for makeup and costume test photos. Many of these stills have survived, showing Garland in red and blonde wigs, and heavy makeup that makes Dorothy look like a Manhattan sophisticate rather than a Kansas farm girl. Variations on Dorothy's pinafore also show up in these test shots.

In late September, before a single frame of the film had been shot, Garland went to the MGM recording studios to do the songs that would be used as play-back during filming, and that would be heard on the final soundtrack. The first two songs she recorded (along with Bert Lahr, Ray Bolger, and Buddy Ebsen) were "We're Off to See the Wizard" and "If I Only Had the Nerve."

A director had yet to be assigned to *The Wizard of Oz*, but things had finally fallen into place for Judy Garland. She was becoming well liked across America, and soon, she would start the film that would install her as America's sweetheart.

In a turn that will surprise many people today, not everybody greeted Garland's causing with cheers in 1938. Books were still major parts of American home-entertainment systems (the other components were radio and the phono-graph, and perhaps a family piano), and the Baum books were staples in children's bedrooms. The first novel was particularly well liked, and W. W. Denslow's assertive illustrations were as vivid in people's minds as John Tenniel's drawings for the Lewis Carroll "Alice" books. Denslow's Dorothy was a tiny, squat child who stood about three heads high and looked like a preternaturally clever six-year-old. Although Judy Garland was barely an ingénue, she didn't at all resemble the Dorothy of the novel. Complaints were heard from devotees of the book and, surprisingly, from some of Garland's fans, who felt that their young favorite had been miscast.

No opinion about a subjective matter like this is "wrong," but time has certainly weighed in on the side of Judy Garland. Some thirty years after the shoot, MGM musical director Roger Edens flatly stated, "The discovery of Judy Garland was the biggest thing to happen to the MGM musical." By that, Edens meant not just the numerous MGM musicals starring Judy, but the influence her personality, presence, and way of connecting to an audience via the camera positively affected every musical MGM made for twenty years afterward.

Despite Garland's gifts, MGM was unhappy that the girl was fifteen, going on sixteen. The Dorothy of the *Oz* books was considerably younger (perhaps Shirley Temple's age), so for a while, MGM publicity claimed that Garland was fourteen.

In person, young Judy Garland made vivid impressions as a person and as a performer. Margaret Hamilton, who was struck by what she characterized as Judy's "freshness and vitality," had very fond memories of her co-star, as she told interviewer Gregory Catsos in 1985. Hamilton was particularly struck by Judy's warmth and by the depth of her acting ability. The pair's professional relationship continued immediately after *Oz*, when they worked together in *Babes in Arms*.

For the work that helped maintain MGM's position as Hollywood's greatest and most-envied studio, Judy Garland was paid $500 a week, as part of her guaranteed forty weeks at that sum. Other than what was paid to Terry the Cairn terrier ($125/wk.) and individual Munchkins ($50/wk.), Garland's salary was the lowest of the *Oz* cast.

Grasping for Childhood

On the set, Judy was content to remain solitary between takes, but she became close to "Maggie" Hamilton. Judy wistfully described to the older actress how she had always worked, supporting her family and missing so many of the familiar mile markers of childhood and adolescence—simple play with friends, pets, longtime schoolmates, and dances. Judy had never been allowed to be a child, and now she wasn't allowed to be a teenager, either.

As per California state law, child performers were to have regular, one-hour breaks for schooling scattered throughout the day. MGM maintained a staff of teachers and tutors for that chore, and was invariably eager to point to the MGM "schoolhouse," where young performers were assembled for formal lessons. In 1938, the studio's publicity department concocted a picture story for newspapers' Sunday rotogravure sections; in one absurd photo, Judy and Mickey Rooney stand studiously at a blackboard, studying their French textbooks and writing out their lessons. Very little learning of this sort actually went on at the studio, or at any studio. During the *Oz* shoot, Judy's educational instruction was haphazard, irregular, and on the fly.

Judy struggled to cope with her lost childhood, and although she never acted out, she did develop a self-consciousness that could have derailed her career. She was a perfectionist who never could satisfy herself (even as she delighted millions around the globe). Barely sixteen, but a longtime veteran of the business, she began to second-guess herself. Studio production chief Louis Mayer reckoned that he had gambled bravely when he signed Judy instead of Deanna Durbin. Now, he recognized Judy's enormous talent and box-office appeal, and freely congratulated himself. He still wasn't paying her what she was worth, but he fancied that he had a fond, paternalistic regard for her.

Mayer's horsey, old-fashioned sentimentality was well known around the lot and in town; he once overrode *himself* by giving starlet Ann Rutherford a raise when she told him all she wanted to do was save enough money to buy a house for herself, her mother, and her grandmother. But when serious, long-term expenditures were involved, Mayer was all business. He possessed the grand, vaguely sociopathic self-regard that's not unusual among successful CEOs. He knew his own mind, and he knew what was best for everyone who fell beneath his gaze. Mayer told MGM studio physician Edward B. Jones to help Judy manage her emotional problems.

Jones isn't mentioned in every account of MGM, but he was, in a peculiar way, a key figure at the studio. Sometimes described as Louis Mayer's personal physician, Jones had broader duties. He worked closely with MGM publicity men Howard Dietz and Howard Strickling, and studio vice president Eddie Mannix. The job of these three was to keep an eye on the MGM "family," sniff out embarrassing incidents before they happened, and fix those that did. When Paul Bern, the husband of MGM star Jean Harlow, committed suicide in 1932, it was Strickling and Mannix who "managed" the scene, even before police arrived, and Dr. Jones who claimed that Bern had taken his life because of sexual inadequacy. (That almost certainly is *not* the case.) Jones also helped to conceal the extraction of Clark Gable's teeth and subsequent installation of dentures.

In May 1938, during the shoot of *Love Finds Andy Hardy*, Dr. Jones began to feed Benzedrine to teenage Judy Garland. The amphetamine drug had been developed by Smith, Kline, and French in 1928, and marketed as a decongestant. However, Benzedrine had an unintended side effect: it gave users long-lasting bursts of energy. Because many physicians saw this as an easy way to mask the real reasons for depression and other neuroses, Benzedrine use began to skyrocket around 1935. Illegal trade in the drug grew quickly, and wouldn't dramatically decline until the late 1970s.

The trouble with Benzedrine is that its effects last a little *too* long, which means that if the long-term user wants to go to sleep at the end of the day, that person has to ingest a barbiturate in order to calm down. Barbiturates have numerous legitimate uses, such as an anticonvulsant. But when used to counter the effects of amphetamines, barbiturates encourage a cycle of dependency: bennies to get "up" and barbiturates to come "down," day after day, month after month. Sleep cycles and normal brain activity can be disrupted—and, of course, overdose is always a possibility. Further, the very fact of using the drugs itself becomes a mood depressant. The user may be alternately dull and lucid, convivial and angry. The user also becomes unhappy about being dependent, so the problems that encouraged the use of Benzedrine and barbiturates in the first place are apt to intensify.

Judy was encouraged to imagine that she was fat, and was given other drugs to help her lose weight in lieu of serious dieting. By the time she did her first costume tests for *The Wizard of Oz*, she was taking far too many drugs than were healthy. Although Dr. Jones may not have been aware that what he was feeding Judy was addictive, the fact is that Mayer, Mannix, and Strickling depended on Jones to fix a problem they imagined they saw in their young contract player. Their encouragement, and Jones's casual dispensing philosophy, had started an engine that would eventually misfire and break. (Dr. C. Lewis Gaulden, an MGM physician who dealt with the studio's insurance carriers, was apparently not involved in any of this.)

Although Judy was very young, she'd been involved in show business long enough to understand the value of featured performers. On *Oz*, that performer was she, so her pressures were internal as well as external. The *Oz* shoot had a false start, lasted nearly six months, and was difficult for all. Over the years, tales have floated about MGM's literally criminal treatment of Judy Garland. Some claim that amphetamines were supplied to Judy Garland by her assistant makeup artist or dresser, on executive order. Other studio employees are implicated in other stories. The claims comprise one of the great puzzles of the Garland mythos. As an adult, Judy herself made various assertions to that effect, which she may have embellished or even made up out of whole cloth. On the other hand, the picture business of the studio-system days was ruthless and competitive. It's likely that one level or another of MGM management connived to "calm" Judy's moods and ease her stress.

In Focus: Judy Garland (1922–1969)

Judy Garland has few challengers to the title "greatest entertainer of the 20th century." Of course, many people will cite Sinatra or Elvis, or Callas or the Beatles, Brando or Michael Jackson, but anyone with a special fondness for *The Wizard of Oz* already knows about Judy's remarkably expressive singing and speaking voice, her brilliantly intuitive acting, and the doe-eyed gaze that can touch the stoniest of hearts. Her talent was enormous, off the charts, and people love her not just for her gifts but also for her perseverance. She performed professionally for the first time in 1924, when she was just two years old, and never stopped working. Forty-five years later, on March 25, 1969, she was in Copenhagen for what would be her final concert. She flew to London on June 17. She made her final public appearance on June 18. Four days later, Judy was dead.

It had been a brief lifetime of great success, disappointment, hope, emotional distress, worldwide acclaim, physical ailments, and work. Above all, it had been a life of work.

Frances Ethel Gumm was born in Grand Rapids, Minnesota, on June 10, 1922. Her father, Frank, managed a movie theater; her mother, Ethel, was a housewife with dreams of show-business glory. Baby Frances joined her older sisters, Mary Jane and Virginia, on stage in 1924, as part of the Gumm Sisters. For the next six years, the act performed at increasingly better venues in Minnesota and (after a 1926 move to Los Angeles) on the West Coast. As part of L.A.'s selective Meglin Kiddies troupe, the sisters attracted notice. In June 1929, Mayfield Pictures filmed their act for use in a two-reel short, *The Big Revue*. At the end of the year, the Gumm Sisters did three "Vitaphone Varieties" shorts for Vitaphone/Warner Bros.

The work accelerated in the early 1930s as the sisters began to work San Diego as well as Los Angeles. They did recitals and lodge luncheons; charity benefits and department store fashion shows; farmers' conventions and Kiwanis get-togethers. They played at grade schools and at Hollywood's fabulous Pantages Theater. They did more benefits and more lodge functions. The sisters showed their stuff for the American Legion, a department-store cooking class, and other oddball venues, but also won bookings at Hollywood's Shrine Auditorium, the Paramount Theater, the Fox West Coast in Long Beach, and the Ambassador Hotel's Coconut Grove nightclub.

Little Frances was increasingly singled out for praise by newspaper reviewers in 1932, and she began to appear more frequently as a solo. As "Baby Gumm," Frances performed in a musical revue at L.A.'s Million Dollar Theatre; a reviewer with the *Los Angeles Record* said that ten-year-old Frances was "astounding," and added, "Her singing all but knocks one for a loop, her dancing is snappy and clever. She handles herself on stage like a veteran pro."

By the time Judy shot her last great movie triumph, *A Star Is Born* (1954), she was struggling physically and emotionally. This is a French-release poster.

Solo and as part of the Gumm Sisters, Frances segued into Los Angeles radio, which piqued the interest of booking agents for the RKO vaudeville circuit. The agreement took the Gumm Sisters from their Los Angeles base to theaters as far north as Spokane. The girls did show after show with very few days off between. Frances was enrolled in the Hollywood Professional School in the fall of 1933, but one wonders just when she had time, or energy, to study.

During the summer and fall of 1934, the Gumm Sisters did an eastward tour that took them to Denver, Colorado Springs, and a great vaudeville town, Chicago, where they played the Belmont, the Marbro, the Chez Paree Club—even the Chicago World's Fair. But it was at Chicago's great Oriental Theatre in August 1934 that the popular monologist George Jessel "changed" the girls' name from Gumm to Garland. Barely a week and a half later, the girls were billed at Chicago's Uptown as the Garland Sisters.

A *Variety* reviewer who caught the Garland Sisters during a November 1934 gig at Grauman's Chinese Theater dismissed the act in toto ("As a trio, it means nothing") but was captivated by Frances: "[S]he handles ballads like a veteran. . . . Nothing slow about her on hot stuff, and to top it off, she hoofs. . . . Kid, with or without her sisters, is ready for the East." The reviewer added that, during an earlier date at the Shrine Auditorium, "[Frances] never failed to stop the show."

The Garland Sisters passed a screen test at Universal in January 1935 and were signed for a film that was never made. They continued to play the Southern California vaudeville houses and cut some sides for Decca. During the sisters' June–July 1935 run at Lake Tahoe's Cal-Neva Lodge, Frances changed her first name to Judy, after Hoagy Carmichael's 1934 song "Judy" ("'Cause there's only one in the light of the sun/ That's Judy").

On September 13, 1935, Judy Garland auditioned for Louis Mayer at the MGM studio. A seven-year contract, with options (for the studio to dismiss her) every six months during year one, and one option a year thereafter, brought Judy $100 a week. She was part of the greatest movie studio on earth.

Frank Gumm died in November 1935. Although he'd often been occupied with running his theaters, he believed in Judy's talent, and had been her primary accompanist. Judy had depended on him, and had taken great strength from his love and emotional support. Now, fatherless at thirteen, Judy was particularly vulnerable and insecure. The paternalistic and condescending Louis Mayer enjoyed playing father figure around MGM, but he was no kind of father to anybody on the lot. Mayer would never provide Judy with what she needed.

Judy's mother, Ethel Milne Gumm, had been a child performer who progressed to vaudeville bookings, with Frank, as an adult. Whether because of fate or issues of talent, Ethel never made the big time. As some parents will do, she lived vicariously through her children, and in Judy, she had a child capable of reaching the heavens.

Ethel pushed her most talented daughter hard. In a 1967 television interview, Judy thought back to her mother and admitted, "I was scared of her." Ethel had determined that Judy was going to be a star, and that the journey would be accomplished in steps, throughout the little girl's early childhood and into her teen years and beyond. Ethel was a planner who tried to turn Judy into a performance machine.

When did Judy's unhappiness begin? As a little girl, she had few interactions with other children besides her sisters; she lived and worked in a grown-up world that was frankly cynical and marked by peculiar hours and considerable travel. The vaudeville circuit was a grind of rail cars, second-rate hotels, bad food (often gulped on the run), and a succession of strangers who expected performers to be at their best and put bodies in the seats.

Judy's circumstances became only superficially better after she was signed by MGM. Louis Mayer and some others in the front office were unabashedly critical of Judy's supposed shortcomings, particularly her face and figure. During a 1968 television interview with Dick Cavett, Judy described, with no small bitterness, the studio's attempts to refashion her figure: "I was twelve or thirteen and I was always just given chicken broth with not a noodle in it, 'cause I had baby fat. Everybody can have baby fat, that's not necessarily a criminal offense." Judy loved ice cream cones, but they were strictly forbidden.

The hypocrisy was infuriating; Judy remembered that Louis Mayer and other studio executives would gorge themselves daily in their private dining room. The teenage Judy was admitted to bask in the men's presence during one such feast, and when studio executive Harry Rapf finally took a breath and said, "Mr. Mayer, this is the best piece of apple pie I've ever had in my whole mouth," Judy laughed at him. She was never asked back to the executive dining room.

Judy was discovering that Hollywood was no less callous than vaudeville, and she became the victim of unintended but very real cruelty. The studio had one kind of hope for the teenage Lana Turner, who was already alarmingly sexy, and who had been selected for traditional leading-lady stardom. Although Judy didn't fit the Turner mold, she was nevertheless stuffed into corsets and forced to allow people to fiddle with her teeth and nose. To Mayer and the other MGM lords, Garland was a desirable voice mated to a problematic face and body.

To be sure, most of the popular leading ladies of the day were conventionally beautiful. Lana Turner, who was just coming up, was one of those. A young Columbia player named Rita Hayworth was another. But there was a place for different varieties of beauty. The immense stardom of slender, big-eyed Warner Bros. player Bette Davis proved that. Another young star at the same studio, Ida Lupino, also was unconventionally appealing. 20th Century-Fox was successfully grooming Alice Faye, and Paramount had turned an emphatically sultry German actress, Marlene Dietrich, into a star. Paramount also was rewarded when it developed the gorgeous (but faintly cross-eyed) Miriam Hopkins into a box-office winner. MGM had been willing to take time to develop the waif-like Sylvia Sidney and the resolutely intelligent Myrna Loy into stars. Even MGM's most important female asset, Joan Crawford, was tiny instead of model-elegant, and angular of face rather than girlish.

But Crawford projected force and mature power—qualities that were not yet within Judy Garland's reach as an actress. She was too young and too sweet. She was a pretty child who sang with precocious ability and emotion. The voice excited Judy's vocal coach, MGM music staffer Roger Edens. He helped pull out and shape the genius that happened when the girl opened her mouth and sang.

Judy's professionalism made up for an inability to read music, but because of her years of experience, she memorized melodies and lyrics quickly, and could warble a new song perfectly after just one or two tries.

Although the movie business was confounding, Judy gradually found her path at MGM. She was too unconventional to suit Mayer and some of his toadies, but her gifts were so obvious that Mayer almost had no choice but to keep her on the lot. In the run-up to *The Wizard of Oz*, Judy was looked at for a diverse bunch of projects. One was an Our Gang short, *Our Gang Follies of 1936* (1935; MGM had a late change of mind about this loan-out to studio client Hal Roach). Another was *Born to Dance* (1936), a musical with original songs by Cole Porter (the juvenile role that might have been filled by Judy was eventually eliminated). Other never-were Garland projects include *The Sarah Bernhardt Story* (floated during 1937–38; Judy would have played the young Bernhardt), *The Fanny Brice Story* (1937–38; Judy as the young Fanny), and an untitled sequel to 1936's *Pigskin Parade* (as with *Pigskin*, this would have meant a loan-out to 20th Century-Fox).

Early in 1938, MGM announced *Topsy and Eva*, a film version of the Catherine Cushing musical comedy inspired by Harriet Beecher Stowe's great (and greatly divisive) 1852 novel *Uncle Tom's Cabin*. Judy Garland and Betty Jaynes were announced as Topsy and Eva, respectively. Because neither youngster was widely known, columnist Louella Parsons had to inform her readers on February 27, 1938, "both little Garland and Jaynes are singers." *Topsy and Eva* had been filmed by Feature Productions in 1927; an MGM version was never made, though not for lack of trying: the studio floated the Garland-Topsy idea again during 1943–44, as a follow-up to Judy's role as Magnolia in a proposed MGM remake of *Show Boat* (which was finally filmed, without Judy, in 1951). When the NAACP threatened MGM with an official protest of *Topsy and Eva*, the project was dropped. (Curious fans can see Judy perform a Topsy-like blackface number in MGM's 1938 backstage musical *Everybody Sing*.)

Two suggested Garland projects are particularly intriguing. Late in 1937, independent producer David O. Selznick expressed interest in testing Judy for the part of Carreen O'Hara, the youngest sister of *Gone With the Wind*'s Scarlett O'Hara. Selznick ultimately cast Ann Rutherford.

The Captured Shadow was to have a screenplay by F. Scott Fitzgerald (adapting his own autobiographical 1928 short story), and was evaluated around 1938 as a star vehicle for Judy, Mickey Rooney, and Freddie Bartholomew. Fitzgerald never wrote the script.

Unrealized projects were routine across the industry, and although Judy may have been excited about some of them, she quickly learned not to be crushed when they fell through. And anyway, the studio never allowed her to have any significant off-time. Indeed, Judy's MGM career was always grueling. Even her off-time was supervised by publicity people and other "minders." Early on, she was set up with highly public "dates" with Freddie Bartholomew, Jackie Cooper, and other young actors.

Judy's MGM publicist was Betty Asher, who was prepared for the challenges that might be posed by a very young actress. An early challenge came in the first half of 1939, when Judy fell in love with bandleader/polymath Artie Shaw. Shaw was already a major star, fronting a hugely popular band and astounding millions with his adventurous flair on the clarinet. Late in his long life, he admitted that he was perpetually oversexed, and attracted to young women with great bodies and average brains. When Shaw met Judy, he already had his eye on Betty Grable, as well as the teenage Lana Turner (whom Shaw would later marry). To Shaw's credit, he treated lovestruck Judy like a sister, inviting her to his home to laugh and listen to records. For Judy's seventeenth birthday, Shaw gave her the only copy of a record that he and pal Phil Silvers had recorded and pressed just for her.

The Wizard of Oz attracted huge audiences when it was released in August 1939, and made Judy a bona fide star. That was exciting for everybody. But Judy's mother remarried on November 17, 1939, the anniversary of the death of Judy's father. For the rest of her life, Judy was shocked by the timing of her mother's wedding.

During the first half of the 1940s, Judy starred and co-starred in pictures that played up her girlish enthusiasm: Andy Hardy Meets a Debutante, Little Nellie Kelly, Ziegfeld Girl, Babes on Broadway, Girl Crazy, Meet Me in St. Louis, and others. By mid-decade, Judy was in her early twenties and shifted into more mature and overtly romantic roles. She'd made a lot of money for MGM earlier, but was perhaps the studio's most lucrative asset during 1945–50: The Clock, The Harvey Girls, Ziegfeld Follies, Till the Clouds Roll By, The Pirate, Easter Parade, Words and Music, In the Good Old Summertime, and Summer Stock. Many of these projects overlapped: While completing one, Judy would already be in preproduction, or doing costume tests or rehearsals, for the next. On top of that were contract negotiations, travel and personal appearances, sessions with the studio photographers, numerous radio appearances, studio-managed nights on the town, recording sessions for soundtracks and record release, and her engagement and marriage to composer David Rose.

MGM kept Judy busy because the studio wanted to squeeze as much work as possible from its valuable young player. Judy's rejiggered contract awarded her more money, so Louis Mayer wasn't about to allow her much rest. The studio-sponsored amphetamine use that began during Oz intensified in the two years that followed.

Early in 1942, not long after her marriage to Rose, Judy seemed to reach a crisis. Rehearsals for For Me and My Gal started on February 19 (just a handful of days after Judy returned from a too-brief honeymoon). During the rehearsal phase, February 21 was lost because Judy didn't want to rehearse. Between February 25 and March 31, she was absent eight times, claiming illness.

The cameras finally rolled on For Me and My Gal on April 3. The shoot concluded on July 29. During that span, Judy called in sick on nine days and did not report for work. On two other days, including a June 26 appendicitis attack (which did not require surgery), she reported to the set but was sent home early.

During the rehearsal and shoot of *For Me and My Gal*, Judy was absent twenty days—the equivalent of more than three six-day workweeks. Except for her appendix, she wasn't ill; she was exhausted.

Despite Judy's difficulties, her run of post-*Oz* projects is impressive. She dominates each of them, but she needed help from the carelessly prescribed pharmaceuticals to do her work. She had trouble falling asleep. She struggled to wake up. Her emotional condition was fragile, partly from the drugs and partly because her marriage to director Vincente Minnelli was foundering. Judy was cast in *Annie Get Your Gun* in 1949, and although she rehearsed and did costume tests and began the shoot with co-star Howard Keel, she was in no condition to play Annie Oakley or anyone else. She struggled with the film's director, Busby Berkeley, and couldn't summon the necessary stamina. Judy often came on-set late, or was absent from the studio altogether. Berkeley was replaced by Charles Walters, a director Judy liked, and she gave it another go. However, production of *Annie Get Your Gun* was shut down on May 10, 1949. Judy was replaced by Betty Hutton.

Almost exactly one year later, Judy was called to replace a pregnant June Allyson in *Royal Wedding*. The director, Charles Walters, begged off because of exhaustion and was replaced by a relative neophyte, Stanley Donen. During May and June 1950, Judy appeared on-set as scheduled, but was put off by Donen's insistence that she and co-star Fred Astaire rehearse and rehearse and rehearse, endlessly. Judy was a quick study. She didn't need a great deal of rehearsal, and too much of it tired her physically. According to Garland filmographer John Fricke, in 1960 she remembered her *Royal Wedding* experience:

> I plunged into my work. I learned seven dance routines, a lot of songs, got fitted for costumes, and it happened again. The weight had to come off, so they put me back on Benzedrine and the crash diet. Even my system couldn't stand it anymore; I just couldn't make it.

On September 28, 1950, Judy received a telegram. It was from MGM, and it said that she had been fired.

Judy never worked for MGM again.

Exhaustion never quite let go of Judy after that. She was electrifying in *A Star Is Born* (1954; directed by George Cukor), a Warner Bros. remake of the 1937 original that had starred Janet Gaynor. Uncut, the Garland version is one of the greatest Hollywood pictures of the 1950s. Although Judy is brilliant, even transcendent, her repeated claims of illness, and the lost shooting time that resulted, blew the film's budget and effectively torpedoed Garland's film career. Some voice-over work aside, after 1954 she would work in just three more movies. She supported herself (and perpetuated her fame) with recordings and live concerts.

She did a bit in *Pepe* (1960), Columbia's overblown star vehicle for Mexican comedian Cantinflas, and stunned audiences with the honesty of her portrayal as a simple German woman in United Artists' *Judgment at Nuremberg* (1961), producer-director Stanley Kramer's cutting and pitiless look at one of the lesser war crimes trials in 1948 Germany.

Cartoon fans enjoyed hearing Judy speak and sing, as kitty cat Mewsette, in UPA's feature-length *Gay Purr-ee* (1962). The film's songs were written by Harold Arlen and E. Y. Harburg.

Judy was back at United Artists to co-star with Burt Lancaster in *A Child Is Waiting* (1963), an earnest drama about teachers of developmentally disabled children. Although neither Judy nor Lancaster responded well to the improvisational approach of director John Cassavetes, their performances have a heartfelt immediacy. The film's subject matter didn't warm many audiences, though, and box office was weak.

British director Ronald Neame handled *I Could Go On Singing* (1963), an old-fashioned melodrama that was Judy's final film. In some respects, she played herself: a diva in early middle age with personal problems. The plot was Fanny Hurst stuff: diva re-enters the life of a former lover to see the adolescent son they created. When the kid learns that the diva is his mom, she tearfully leaves his life, and then wows 'em at the Palladium. By all reports from people who were there, Judy was a handful on the set, but she nailed the part, sang powerfully, and impressed co-star Dirk Bogarde and others with moments of brilliance.

By the early 1960s, Judy was deeper still into prescription drugs and patronized pharmacies all over Brentwood and surrounding neighborhoods. CBS-TV's *The Judy Garland Show* lasted just six months in 1963–64.

By this time, Judy had two marriages behind her (to composer David Rose and director Vincente Minnelli). A 1952 marriage to producer-promoter Sid Luft lasted thirteen years, but two later ones, to the obscure actor Mark Herron and to promoter Mickey Deans, were brief and probably ill advised. Still, Judy now had three attractive children and reason to hope for more professional triumphs. She had many more ups than downs with her concert career, most triumphantly a now-legendary 1961 booking at Carnegie Hall.

The *Oz* experience partly defined Garland for the next thirty years of her life. In 1964, following a disastrous and confused concert in Melbourne, a *Time* magazine article uncharitably remarked, "At 41, Judy Garland may have gone over the rainbow for the last time."

On balance, 1964 was a very unhappy year for Judy. Her sister, Mary Jane (Suzy) Gumm, committed suicide almost simultaneously with Judy's nearly successful attempt of May 28, in Hong Kong. When a nurse erroneously announced that Judy was dead (in reality, a valve controlling an oxygen tent had become temporarily dislodged), the news flashed over the radio and across the world. Fortunately, the report was corrected before newspapers had opportunities to print it.

Judy toured for the rest of her life, but another milestone was reached in 1964: her final recording session, which happened on August 5–6, in London.

The emotionally engaged live performances continued, and audiences went wild for the woman described by film historian Doug McClelland as "a tragic wren."

In 1968, when Judy was asked by Dick Cavett to summarize show business, she replied, "I think it's hideous—except the audience."

To the end, Judy loved the strangers that loved her.

Ray Bolger as the Scarecrow

Ray Bolger was originally cast as the Tin Woodman. This is confirmed by a January 31, 1939, memo from Freed to LeRoy; in the same message, Freed suggests Buddy as the Scarecrow—despite some sentimental industry support for sixty-five-year-old Fred Stone to reprise his 1902 stage role as the straw man.

Ebsen was brought on to play the Scarecrow, and Bolger readied himself to become the Tin Woodman. Bolger had read the *Oz* books as a boy, and had seen Fred Stone as the Scarecrow in one of Stone's later tours with the Baum musical. Bolger was a highly skilled improvisational dancer, and was strongly attracted to the Scarecrow's literal brainlessness and apparent lack of bones. In his mind's eye, Bolger imagined giving the character fresh life via an eccentric, loose-limbed style of dance. He made his case to Louis Mayer, who agreed that Bolger and Ebsen should switch roles.

Bolger's gangly physicality encouraged gags that were unique to the movie. For instance, the calamitous yet darkly funny scattering of the Scarecrow's limbs and innards by the winged monkeys is not part of the original Baum novel. Victor Fleming's light touch during the sequence, and exuberant playing by Bolger (and the Tin Woodman's impatient reaction: "That's you all over!"), discovered comic fun in what could have been an interlude of real horror.

Ray Bolger, thirty-four when shooting began, had a narrow, handsome face marked by expressive eyes and mouth. He had a friendly, antic quality that gave the Scarecrow an appealing good humor. Of course, *The Wizard of Oz* was a project about an alternate reality, which meant that many pleasant physiognomies had to be altered. Because of the extensive makeup needed to create Dorothy's friends, Bolger, Ebsen, and Lahr reported to the studio each day at 5:00 a.m. They made their way to the makeup department. Because their mouths would shortly be immobile, or nearly so, they had cups of coffee or Danish, and then they sat. And sat.

Hours beneath heavy makeup and hot lights naturally caused Bolger to perspire. Each day, before too many hours had passed, his makeup would begin to soften and peel from his face. Bolger's makeup man, Norbert Myles, stayed busy with touch-ups intended to keep the Scarecrow looking presentable. The textured chamois that gives the Scarecrow a wonderfully fabric-like face and chin was so firmly affixed during the shoot that Bolger ended up with faint scarring. Bolger didn't realize that until much later. In the meantime, he endured the makeup, using the time in the chair to review his lines or just close his eyes for a while.

Once made up and costumed as the Scarecrow, Bolger *was* the Scarecrow. He knew the role was a showy one that would allow him to create a unique personality. He'd never had a part remotely like it, so the professional opportunities it presented excited him. Bolger was an amiable presence on the set, launching into impromptu dance steps between setups and delighting himself as much as he delighted his co-workers.

Every film star has a stand-in, a person of roughly the same size and complexion who literally stands in place while the cinematographer takes readings with a light meter, and establishes positioning and blocking. On *Oz*, Ray Bolger's stand-in was Stafford Campbell, who later was the regular stand-in for actor Raymond Massey.

In Focus: Ray Bolger (1904–1987)

Raymond Wallace Bulcao was born to middle-class parents in Boston in 1904. He was inspired to pursue a theatrical career after seeing Fred Stone, the Scarecrow of the 1902–03 Broadway *Oz* play, on stage in Boston. Very young when he began to perform, Bolger staged amateur theatricals and won his first professional job at nineteen, with a repertory company. From the beginning, Bolger regarded himself as a comic actor; he once commented that he slipped into dancing sideways during one of his earliest shows, when he blanked on what came next during a comic monologue and covered his lapse by breaking into an impromptu dance. "I've been dancing ever since," he said, "but I'm still a comedian."

Ray Bolger was an agile dancer who had already achieved Broadway stardom by the time Mervyn LeRoy locked him in to play the Scarecrow. On-set, he was an amiable, chatty presence.

Rep was followed by years in vaudeville, and although many dancers that got there *stayed* there, Bolger's unique qualities allowed him to make the leap to Broadway at twenty-seven, in *George White's Scandals* (1931). Other Broadway shows followed. In one of them, *On Your Toes* (1936), Bolger earned special notice with his "Slaughter on Tenth Avenue" dance number.

Bolger made his film debut in 1926 as a supporting player in a minor comedy short called *The Berth Mark*, starring a now-forgotten actress named Peggy Shaw. (*The Berth Mark* is notable, however, as one of the very few live-action shorts directed by Dave Fleischer, a giant of animation who directed more than six hundred cartoons starring Koko the Clown, Betty Boop, Popeye, and Superman between 1919 and 1942. His brother was animation-studio owner Max Fleischer.)

Because of his Broadway success, Bolger signed a one-picture deal with MGM in 1935, at twenty dollars a week for seven weeks. His first MGM assignment was *The Great Ziegfeld* (1936), a fictionalized biography of musical-theater impresario Florenz Ziegfeld. In an all-star cast headed by William Powell (in the title role) and Myrna Loy (as Billie Burke), Bolger played himself, an unusual privilege for a performer who'd never done a feature film before. *The Great Ziegfeld* was released in the spring of 1936, virtually simultaneous with Bolger's new MGM contract, a long-term deal that paid him $3,000 a week.

After *Oz*, Bolger continued in movies as a freelance star. He enjoyed a nice success at RKO in *Four Jills and a Jeep* (1941), returned to MGM for *The Harvey Girls* (1946), and was Doris Day's romantic lead in a Warner musical, *April in Paris* (1952). His feature film appearances diminished after that, though he led the cast of Disney's *Babes in Toyland* in 1961, and toplined a reasonably successful ABC sitcom, *Where's Raymond* (1953–55; as a Broadway star living in suburbia).

Because "Ray Bolger" evokes *The Wizard of Oz* in the minds of millions, it's easy to assume that he was a prolific film actor. Yet he appeared in just twelve movies during his busiest movie-star days, 1936–52. In the main, Bolger was a stage actor, and found his greatest Broadway success (and a Tony) with the cross-dressing musical comedy *Where's Charley?* (1948–50), adapted from the Brandon Thomas play *Charley's Aunt*. The show's highlight was Bolger's star-affirming number "Once in Love with Amy."

In October 1952, Bolger headlined a stage show to help open the Sahara, a brand-new Vegas hotel-casino. Because he hadn't particularly wanted the gig, his wife suggested he ask for a fee so ridiculously high that the casino would never hire him—which is how Ray Bolger traveled to Las Vegas to earn $20,000 a week. Hank Greenspun, a writer for the *Las Vegas Sun*, was swept away by what he saw: "[Bolger] makes you laugh till the tears roll and still there is no slapstick in his comedy. He sings, mimics, is a complete one-man show, but when his feet are moving, that way greatness lies."

Some sources claim that Bolger and Judy Garland later appeared at the Sahara together, which is true and yet misleading: in 1962, Garland headlined "A Date with Judy," a midnight show in the hotel's Conga Room (when the contract was extended, Judy added a 2:30 a.m. show). Bolger's name appeared with Judy's in advertising and on the Sahara marquee, but "An Evening with Ray Bolger," though also staged in the Conga Room, was a separate attraction that went on at 6:00 p.m. (A vintage Sahara ad flyer that transposes the times of the shows is a desirable collectible.)

Bolger remained lean and athletic as the years passed, but unexpected hip failure ended his dancing career in 1984. He retired in 1985, after appearing as himself in various documentaries about MGM or *Oz*.

Throughout his life, Bolger was a dedicated autodidact, a voracious reader with a curiosity about everything. He loved to tell tall tales, but also had a knack for putting life's events into a realistic perspective. He was justifiably pleased with the totality of his career, and knew that the Scarecrow had been a special interlude. Late in his life, Bolger remarked that his work in *The Wizard of Oz* brought him no residuals, "just immortality. I'll settle for that."

Ray Bolger passed away in 1987.

Buddy Ebsen as the Tin Woodman

Buddy Ebsen and *Oz* comprise a "what might have been" tale. At thirty, Ebsen was 6'3", knobby, and seriously underweight. He was an expert, loose-jointed dancer who naturally suggested a scarecrow. He was hired for that role, but when Ray Bolger—already cast as the Tin Woodman—lobbied Louis Mayer for the Scarecrow role, he and Ebsen switched roles. Ebsen was no stranger to MGM. A congenial fit in musicals, he'd freelanced at the studio in 1935 and later signed a short-term contract. When hired for *Oz* in 1938, Ebsen was offered a standard long-term MGM contract (seven years), which he turned down, an act of audacity that puzzled and greatly angered Louis Mayer. Regardless, Ebsen was soon on board to do *Oz*.

Of all the film's principal players, Ebsen came onto the project with the least fuss, debate, and speculation. He and MGM were familiar with each other. Mayer, despite being spurned, appreciated Ebsen's talent, and faintly eccentric looks and manner. If there's any puzzlement here, it's the ease with which everybody agreed that Ebsen should exchange roles with Ray Bolger. The MGM front office was very sanguine about the switch, and Ebsen never reported any disappointment at missing the opportunity to become the Scarecrow. Well, the Tin Woodman promised to be an equally showy part, and as jobs went, it was good one.

As we'll explore in chapter 10, all went well until enough time had passed for Ebsen's body to react to his silvery makeup. The calamity that resulted forced him off the picture, but he was back at MGM by the end of 1938, fully recovered, for a supporting part in a nurses' drama called *Four Girls in White* (1939).

In Focus: Buddy Ebsen (1908–2003)

Dance led Buddy Ebsen into acting, and he got into dance because of his father, a dance teacher. Buddy was born in 1908, and by the time he was in his teens he was skilled at ballet—an art that, although not calculated to win admirers in the school-yard, gave Ebsen the physical and mental discipline he'd use later. Buddy spent the first part of his childhood in southwestern Illinois, and then moved with his family to Florida. He was the perfect age when the Charleston became a dance craze in the 1920s. He danced it avidly and progressed from that into tap. He knew then that he wanted to dance for a living.

In 1928, Buddy moved to New York City, where he was joined a year later by his sister, Vilma. Buddy had been encouraged by work as a chorus boy in a 1928–29 Broadway musical comedy, *Whoopee!*, and was eager to give up soda jerking and make the rounds with his sister, looking for work as a dance duo. (As Adele and Fred Astaire were proving, brother-sister dance acts were popular.) "Vilma and Buddy Ebsen" got into vaudeville and nightclubs, enjoying success by playing off of Buddy's gawkiness and Vilma's good looks. They also found work in the choruses

When he won a role in *The Wizard of Oz*, gangly Buddy Ebsen was a Broadway and vaudeville veteran with three years of movie experience. This portrait (by MGM's Clarence Bull) is from March 1939, just five months after Ebsen's brush with death on the *Oz* set.

of a few Broadway musicals, and after a rave from showbiz columnist Walter Winchell, the Ebsens danced at New York's Palace, the vaudeville circuit's most desirable theater.

For four months during 1932–33, Buddy and Vilma worked as featured performers in another Broadway show, *Flying Colors*, and spent six months in 1934 doing featured turns in *Ziegfeld Follies of 1934*.

Movie production hadn't completely dried up in New York in the '30s, and Vilma and Buddy did a few screen tests for local studios. Some combination of the tests and raves about their stage work earned them a Hollywood screen test with MGM in 1935. Executives liked what they saw and put the Ebsens in their first film, *Broadway Melody of 1936* (1935).

Vilma chose to retire from films after that and appeared as a featured performer in one more Broadway musical, a comedy called *Between the Devil* (1937–38). Buddy pressed on in Hollywood, beginning what would be a sixty-five-year career on film. He worked steadily for the rest of the '30s and into the 1940s at MGM, 20th Century-Fox, and RKO, usually in musicals and comedies (where he danced and provided light comic relief) and in the occasional drama (usually cast as the hero's pal). The illness he contracted on the set of *The Wizard of Oz* during a struggle to play the Tin Woodman put him flat on his back for a while, but it had no long-term effect on his career. In 1939–40, he starred on Broadway in *Yokel Boy*, which had a respectable run of 208 performances.

Ebsen's last picture before leaving for service during World War II was a musical comedy called *Sing Your Worries Away*, toplined by Buddy's *Oz* co-star Bert Lahr. After the war, Ebsen found himself in the position of a lot of second-tier Hollywood personalities: the industry had forgotten about him. In the movies, he'd been making $2,000 a week. When he appeared in a yearlong 1946–47 Broadway revival of *Show Boat*, he earned $750 a week. Minor stage and club appearances brought him $135 a week. Leading Hollywood agent William Morris suggested to Ebsen that he retire.

Buddy tried television in 1949 with a star turn in "Say Good-bye to Larry K," an episode of *The Chevrolet Tele-Theatre*. He struggled along in TV and in occasional features until 1954, when he was cast opposite Fess Parker in the "Davy Crockett" adventures made for TV's *Disneyland* show. Very soon, Ebsen was at the center of a marketing maelstrom that became a cultural phenomenon. Parker played Crockett, but Ebsen's exposure as Davy's pal George Russel was enormous, and he never lacked for work for the rest of his life. He gave a sterling dramatic performance in director Robert Aldrich's savage World War II drama, *Attack* (1956), co-starred with Keith Larsen in TV's *Northwest Passage* during 1957–58, and did high-visibility guest shots on *The Twilight Zone*, *77 Sunset Strip*, and many TV westerns.

By 1961, Ebsen's friendly good looks had grown pleasingly rough-hewn. Executives at CBS-TV liked what he did as a rural type in a prestigious feature film, *Breakfast at Tiffany's* (1961), and convinced him to play transplanted backwoodsman Jed Clampett in *The Beverly Hillbillies*. It became one of the most successful shows in television history, and although much derided at the time, the series was rather smartly satirical—and proved that Ebsen could carry a network show.

The Beverly Hillbillies concluded its run in 1971. The show had made Ebsen wealthy, and he had no financial incentive to work. Nevertheless, he segued easily into another top-rated series, a detective drama called *Barnaby Jones* (1973–80), and was a semi-regular on TV's *Matt Houston* during 1984–85. He took numerous guest-star TV jobs after that, and even did a jokey cameo in a badly conceived 1993 feature, *The Beverly Hillbillies*.

Ebsen retired after 1999.

Buddy complained for decades about suffering unending lung problems caused by the *Wizard of Oz* makeup mishap. That may certainly have been true. On the other hand, when Ebsen died in 2003, he was ninety-five years old.

Bert Lahr as the Cowardly Lion

A February 23, 1938, interoffice memo from Arthur Freed suggests actress Tex Morrissey as the Cowardly Lion. Morrissey, whose given name was Edith Morrissey, was a stage and vaudeville performer who had worked across the USA, and in Cuba, Canada, and Mexico. In 1932, she won national news coverage when she brought her "Hank the Mule" costume novelty act to the Democratic National Convention in Chicago. Her dancing-animal imperson-ation was well received, and she was named the convention's mascot. (Tex Morrissey reprised her "Hank" role at all subsequent Democratic conventions until her death in 1955.) Coincidentally (or not), Hank the Mule is the name of a character created by L. Frank Baum for his 1914 novel, *Tik-Tok of Oz*. Freed probably saw Morrissey in her only film performance, as a specialty dancer in *Double or Nothing*, a 1937 musical comedy starring Bing Crosby.

Hedda Hopper, in her May 3, 1938, column, claimed that LeRoy was consid-ering the MGM lion as the Cowardly Lion. Exactly how that stunt casting might have been pulled off (and received by audiences) was never explained. In any case, a script draft from the previous month suggests that the Lion would be played by a costumed actor.

Bert Lahr may have been considered for the Lion role because of vocal sup-port from E. Y. Harburg. When Lahr received the *Oz* script in the late summer of 1938, he had not heard of the Oz stories. He brought no preconceived ideas to the role; he would have a script, but the core and nuance of his characterization

Bert Lahr's September 9, 1938, contract with MGM stipulated that the actor's salary would begin three days later. Lahr held out for a guarantee of six weeks' work—and ultimately got a lot more.

would begin with a blank slate. Whatever the film's Cowardly Lion became, Bert Lahr was the primary creator—but he had help from an important and often-overlooked collaborator.

Lahr was virtually the only person seriously considered for the Lion, but just to be sure, E. Y. "Yip" Harburg made a point to be a major Lahr booster during the casting process. Yip knew Bert from Broadway, where the actor had appeared in musicals with Harburg's lyrics. Harburg had an inkling of what Lahr could do with the Cowardly Lion, and happily promoted Bert on the MGM lot.

Bert Lahr was by no means handsome in 1938, but he had an open, antic face that was immensely appealing. His professional persona was outsized: expansive, even overpowering. When he was on stage, or on a movie screen, he commanded audience attention. Lahr was a huge talent, but if cast in *Oz*, would he overshadow the other players? Mervyn LeRoy and Arthur Freed didn't think so.

Harburg grasped that Lahr's comic persona combined low humor, sweetness, anxiety, and what Harburg called "comic bravura." Yip later said to John Lahr, "A lyricist is lucky to have a Bert Lahr in his lifetime, who incorporates humor and humanity in his performance."

MGM offered Lahr $2,500 a week with a three-week guarantee. Lahr liked the pay but successfully held out for a six-week guarantee. He signed to play the Cowardly Lion on September 9, 1938. Three days later he went on salary, where he remained until the following March. Lahr got his six weeks and then some.

Harburg couldn't have been happier with the casting. He enjoyed and understood Lahr's gifts so completely that he felt confident as he tweaked some of the Lion's dialogue. Bert Lahr knew Lahr best of all, so he too contributed dialogue—including "Put up your dukes!" and "Unusual weather we're havin', ain't it?"

Lahr had a marvelously distinctive voice and face, as well as a gift for physical comedy. A great deal of his Lion characterization is rooted in what we can see. Some of the pugnacious gestures Lahr devised for the Lion were taken from his 1928–29 Broadway role as a boxer in a musical romance called *Hold Everything*. (When the play was adapted to film in 1930, comic actor Joe E. Brown took the part that had been played by Lahr.) Other visual touches, particularly the Lion's comic takes and the way he carries his body, had been honed by Lahr on the stage, where broad reactions reached folks seated at some distance from the stage.

Lahr took direction easily, not because he felt he needed guidance from a firm hand, but because he knew he could manage his talent, and because he was driven to make each job, every performance, better than the last. A good director came up with good ideas, and when a director's thoughts might help Lahr achieve his goals, he listened.

Lahr was invariably eager for fresh challenges, but the Cowardly Lion disguise tested his patience. The suit alone weighed seventy pounds. It covered him from his neck to the soles of his feet, and was stiflingly hot. While trapped inside of it, he perspired copiously, which led Lahr to describe his too-cozy costume as "a wet mattress." Between setups, he'd shed the costume down to his waist and allow himself to be blow-dried by oversized fans. But the headpiece, which didn't allow his scalp to breathe, could not be easily removed, so Lahr had to put up with it. The facial appliances surrounding his mouth had to be carefully handled, so whenever Lahr was hungry or thirsty, he took soup or water through a straw.

The $2,500 that rolled in every week helped lessen the discomfort of all that heat and makeup. In addition, Lahr knew that the *Oz* script provided him with some unique opportunities. He wasn't going to be able to steal the movie (that was never his intention anyway), but he was going to end up with a lot of dialogue and bits of business that would tickle audiences and get people in the industry talking. The sequence that particularly excited Lahr, "If I Were King of the Forest," turned out to be the actor's finest moment in *The Wizard of Oz*, and one of the most remarkable sequences ever captured on film. The Lion is a fully realized character who brims with infectious good humor as well as a basic absurdity. Besides the Lion's goonish gruffness, Lahr captured the character's internal conflicts and his touching desire to live up to his own fantasies. The Lion is perpetually frightened, but he really does want to please others. The Lion longs to be valued.

On-set, Lahr was a bit of a paradox: a hugely talented man with a kind demeanor but an inclination to be reserved and insecure. Lahr fretted about the quality of his performance, an anxiety that mystified Margaret Hamilton. "There was no reason why he wouldn't or couldn't give a great performance," she said to interviewer Greory Catsos.

In Focus: Bert Lahr (1895–1967)

Bert Lahr was a classic American clown—not strictly in the circus sense, but in the sense of a very physical comic actor who would do anything for a laugh, as long as *he* felt it was going to be funny. Even as Lahr reached a creative and popular peak in the late 1930s, his kind of exaggerated, flamboyant comedy was dying. The real decline set in after World War II, when a more sophisticated public demanded character-driven comedy that was less broad. (Notable exceptions to this postwar "rule" include Jerry Lewis, Milton Berle, and the indefatigable Three Stooges.)

In his introduction to a 1967 book, *The American Musical Theater*, theater critic Brooks Atkinson lamented, "By abandoning buffoons, the musical stage has lost one of its most legitimates assets. They belonged to the musical stage because they, too, were larger than life, and inhabited a fantasy world. They were as legitimate as the music, dancing, and décor."

Lahr successfully defied comedy's evolution. His Hollywood success brought him money and wide fame, but also ignited his fear of being unceremoniously dumped by studio bosses—just when his film income had encouraged him to live more lavishly than before. A very difficult relationship with his mentally incapacitated first wife complicated his personal life and exacerbated his insecurities. He invariably fretted about the next job: Would it pay enough? Would there even be a "next job" at all? Lahr was a glass-half-empty kind of guy. He didn't doubt his talent, but worried that others would react badly to it or, worse, fail to discern it. Bert's son and biographer, John Lahr, described his father as "completely internal," a man who was fully engaged only when performing.

Jack Haley had known Lahr before *Oz* and was a close friend. (Haley was godfather to Bert's son, the noted author John Lahr.) Long after *Oz*, Haley reflected, "Success was Bert's siren, mediocrity his enemy. And for Bert, success meant laughs."

Lahr was born Irving Lahrheim in New York City in 1895. His folks were poor, and Bert's formal education ended when he found work, at fifteen, in the scrappy world of vaudeville. Lahr learned his craft on that circuit. Between 1929 and 1937, he starred in about ten two-reel comedy shorts, variously made by Warner Bros., Educational, and Van Beuren/RKO; in one from 1934, *Henry the Ache*, Bert is a hoot as that king with all the wives.

Lahr got into feature films in 1931, and carried on with movies and television for nearly forty years. He was sufficiently popular and well known to play himself in *Mr. Broadway* (1933), an hour-long nightspot travelogue hosted by *New York Daily News* entertainment columnist Ed Sullivan. (Jack Haley appeared, too.) Bert had colorful supporting roles in features, and was frequently cast in pictures with a show business setting; in *Zaza* (1938), his biggest movie before *The Wizard of Oz*, Lahr played a music-hall performer in France.

Going by numbers alone, however, Lahr's film career was minor; in the thirty years after *Oz*, he appeared in only eight features, often in parts calculated to bring some energy and old-school professionalism to pictures that otherwise wouldn't have any at all. A posthumous release, *The Night They Raided Minsky's* (1968), is rowdy fun, but the one that's most interesting today is *Always Leave Them Laughing* (1949), in which Lahr played a terminally ill stage comic who shares heartfelt career advice with an up-and-comer, played by Milton Berle. Comedy, Lahr tells Berle, has to come from the heart.

Lahr found better opportunities—and dramatic ones, at that—on *The Philco-Goodyear Television Playhouse*, *The United States Steel Hour*, *Omnibus*, and other anthology series of the 1950s. But the theater was always paramount to him. His Broadway experience dated to 1927. Lahr did revues and musical comedies until the mid-1950s, and then set the theater world on its head with his 1956 appearance in Samuel Beckett's remarkable *Waiting for Godot*. The show had a two-week out-of-town tryout in January 1956 at Miami's Coconut Grove Playhouse, where snowbirds who were lured by the star power of Lahr (playing Estragon) and Tom Ewell (Vladimir), and by promotion describing *Waiting for Godot* as "the laugh sensation of two continents," sat mystified and confused. Many walked out. The show opened on Broadway three months later, with E. G. Marshall taking over for Ewell.

Other than Judy Garland, no one in the *Oz* cast had gifts as explosive as Bert Lahr's. His unique voice and manner, and that fabulous rubber face, had made him a star of vaudeville and Broadway—and a man whose personality was almost too "big" to be constrained by the borders of a movie screen. After *Oz*, Lahr did acclaimed work for the remaining thirty years of his life and never lost his enormous popularity.

In brief, *Waiting for Godot* is dominated by two tramps of indeterminate origin and purpose, who stand idly on a country lane (the theater stage decorated by a single, desolate tree) and wait for someone named Godot. In the meanwhile, they exchange comic dialogue, elliptical monologues, and some mordant pondering on What It All Means. Although the two interact with three other characters that happen by, Godot never shows up. At play's end, neither Estragon nor Vladimir, nor the audience, has been illuminated about anything, especially life—except that life itself is almost never truly illuminated.

Waiting for Godot had an acceptable run of two months on Broadway. By June, Lahr was done with it, but his performance established him as one of Broadway's great actors, and pleased and intimidated him for the rest of his life. He had an actor's instincts, not an intellectual's, yet he had been able to connect with the comic elements crafted by Beckett into the purposely opaque material. Lahr turned Estragon into an absurd everyman figure that resonated with tolerant audiences. (In 1956, a recording was made of one performance for release as an LP; that recording can be now be found on the secondary market, and as a two-disc CD and an mp3 audio file.)

Lahr had another Broadway triumph in 1964 with the title role in *Foxy*, a musical-comedy reimagining of Ben Jonson's *Volpone* as a tale of greed among 19th-century miners in the Yukon. When Foxy learns that his friends want to get into his good graces so that they can lay their hands on his gold, he decides to use trickery and disguise to put them in their place. Although *Foxy* ran for just two months, Lahr was awarded a Tony for best lead performance in a musical.

Late in his life, Lahr, like comic legend Buster Keaton, found a new audience via television commercials. In a 1960 or '61 spot for Blatz beer, Lahr is the sole live-action figure amidst cartoon-animated characters. He's captain of an ocean liner that nearly collides with a teeny cargo boat loaded to the gills with Blatz. What a calamity that would have been! In a jiffy, Capt. Lahr is aboard the smaller ship, hoisting a brew and singing— à la the Cowardly Lion—"Blatz is Milwauhahahaha-kee's finest bee-er!"

Lahr's commercials for Lay's potato chips are particularly good-humored. In one from 1967, Lahr is dressed to the nines as Satan, resplendent in a full-body costume topped by a crimson headpiece with dramatic horns. The Lay's tag line, "Nobody can eat just one," is twisted into a taunt by Lahr's devil, whose cardigan-clad victim (also played by Lahr) is indeed enraptured by the single chip he's been offered: "How toothsome!" he exclaims in that inimitable Lahr manner. "I'll have another!" But Satan tells him one is all he's going to get, whereupon the victim hesitates for a moment, and then suddenly snatches the bag from Satan's hand, spilling chips all over but getting what remains for himself. Lahr-Satan rears back and chortles, happy merely to have proved his point.

While commercials signaled a comeback for Buster Keaton, Lahr's spots, and related print ads, were merely added facets of a career that had never gone into remission. Lahr was perennially popular; admirers especially appreciated the great voice. And to just that point, in 1961 a Hanna-Barbera cartoon character named Snagglepuss Lion got under Lahr's skin because voice artist Daws Butler, who did a multitude of Hanna-Barbera characters, played Snagglepuss like Bert Lahr, even turning Lahr's "Heavens to Murgatroyd!" into a Snagglepuss catchphrase. (Lahr had introduced the exclamation in a 1944 movie comedy called *Meet the People*.) In a creative work, impersonation of the sort done by Butler can fall under the rubric of parody.

If anybody was born to play Eve . . . During 1966–67, Lahr became a fixture of magazines and television in a series of very funny ads for Lay's potato chips.

Nevertheless, when the cartoon studio licensed Snagglepuss for use in commercials for Kellogg's Cocoa Krispies cereal, Lahr sued, claiming that viewers would mistakenly believe that he was endorsing the product. The suit was settled out of court with a particularly unusual provision: all subsequent Snagglepuss cereal commercials would carry the tag, "Snagglepuss Voice by DAWS BUTLER."

Lahr died in 1967 of pneumonia complicated by cancer.

On screen, Bert Lahr is a joyously overpowering presence, whose putty face, unique voice, and physical skills combine with his comic instincts to create characters you *have* to look at. You have no choice because Lahr is a pure force of nature. Although Hollywood made no secret that it found Lahr difficult to cast, his genius was highly respected around town, just as it was up and down Broadway. *New York Times* theater critic Brooks Atkinson wrote, "God must have laughed when Bert Lahr was born."

Jack Haley as the Tin Woodman

When *Oz* was being cast in the first quarter of 1938, Jack Haley was a contract player at 20th Century-Fox. When Judy Garland was loaned to that studio to appear in her first feature film, *Pigskin Parade* (1936), Haley appeared in the picture with her. The forty-year-old actor was in demand for movies, and did considerable work in radio, too. On November 4, 1938, 20th Century-Fox agreed to terms loaning Haley to MGM for *The Wizard of Oz*, and on November 8, Haley's casting as the Tin Woodman was confirmed by *The Hollywood Reporter*.

Haley knew that he was stepping into a mildly sticky situation. MGM had explained that Buddy Ebsen had had to leave his role as the Tin Woodman because of "pneumonia." The simultaneous dismissal of *Oz* director Richard Thorpe suggested a production in trouble. Like Margaret Hamilton and some others already in the cast, Haley wondered if the film would be scrapped altogether.

Haley had read Baum's *Oz* books to his son, Jack Haley Jr., so he had more than a passing acquaintance with the world of *Oz* before he was cast in the movie. The actor's ability to project warmth suited the Tin Woodman nicely, but Haley saw nothing particularly remarkable about the part. Like others in the cast, Haley had experience that let him understand how to "sell" a character, so director Victor Fleming went along when Haley suggested that he and Ray Bolger, Bert Lahr, and Frank Morgan adopt what Haley called "storyteller" voices—an occasionally breathy quality that expressed a childlike sense of wonder. The technique was used subtly during the Kansas sequences and became pronounced once the actors were in Oz. Because of the actors' ability to "shade" their emotional pitch, the vocal effect isn't overdone and registers almost subliminally as one more marker telling the audience that Oz is a place unlike any other. The actors understood this perfectly, and Ray Bolger later recalled, "I tried to get a sound in my voice that was complete wonderment, because I [the Scarecrow] was new, so newly made."

Haley's ability to express the Tin Woodman's personality and longings was never in doubt. It was the role's physical challenges that took the actor by surprise. Haley's manner suggests a man of relaxed temperament, and there is truth to that, but the tin and rubber costume that awaited Haley each day filled him with dread. He recalled in his journal, "I shuddered at the thought of climbing into the Tin Woodman's outfit, which I did after a long ritual [each day] with a makeup artist."

Haley got some relief during the regular breaks to change arc-lamp bulbs and to set up shots, and he lived to hear the call of Judy Garland's tutor. State law mandated that child actors receive a set amount of schooling each day, so when the on-set tutor called, "Judy, dear, school!" Haley knew he had another reprieve. The tutoring was done in one-hour segments, so for sixty minutes, anyway, Haley and the others could relax. "I was so tired," Haley said, "I would sleep the whole hour of Judy's lesson." (Haley was able to fall asleep on a slant board that kept his costume in order.) Bert Lahr envied this ability. "That sonofabitch Haley, he can sleep on a meat hook!"

During these protracted breaks, Victor Fleming would kill the arc lamps and slide back the stage doors, to introduce a cooling breeze and allow cast and crew time to step outside.

With an expensive lesson having been learned with Buddy Ebsen, the *Oz* makeup team covered Haley with aluminum paste rather than aluminum dust of the sort that got into Ebsen's lungs and put him in the hospital. But heavy makeup always has a certain risk, and indeed, when some of the aluminum paste got into Haley's eyes, he suffered an infection that took him off the picture for a week. He recuperated at home in a room lit by a red light bulb, his eyes covered with a towel.

Haley was a working actor who had spent years on the road, honing his craft in vaudeville houses grimy and grand. Movies were a special kind of challenge, and Haley was apparently surprised that fans of Oz assumed the shoot was great fun. "Fun?" he said. "Like hell it was fun! It was a lot of hard work. It was no fun at all."

Haley held down another job during the *Oz* shoot. From October 1938 to April 1939, he starred in and co-wrote CBS radio's *The Wonder Show*, a weekly comedy-and-music program, sponsored by Wonder Bread. The program aired live on Friday nights, which meant that Monday through Friday Haley was occupied with rehearsals. He recalled, "That was quite a winter. By the time we did the show Friday night, I was physically exhausted. Emotionally, however, I was very satisfied. I loved doing that radio show."

Haley's interpretation of the Tin Woodman is a disarming marvel of sweetness and sincerity. Haley was a hardboiled ex-vaudevillian, but he believed in the roles he took, and he was confident in his ability to enchant audiences. Margaret Hamilton once noted, with pleasure, that a great deal of Haley's personal charm was evident in his performance. Indeed, of all the star turns in *The Wizard of Oz*, Haley's may be the most underrated.

In Focus: Jack Haley (1897–1979)

Jack Haley had starred or co-starred in more than twenty films before *The Wizard of Oz*. Many of those pictures were featherweight comedies and romances that benefited from Haley's easy charm and bright-eyed good looks. Because he specialized in diffident, well-groomed fops, his casting as the rusty, creaking Tin Woodman was, according to Victor Fleming biographer Michael Sragow, "one giant in-joke."

A second-generation Irish American, John Joseph Haley was born in 1897 in Boston. (Many sources say 1898, some claim 1899, and a few say 1902.) Haley's father, a sea captain, died when Jack was just six months old, and for the rest of his life Haley longed to know and understand his dad.

Jack grew up poor in South Boston, home to thousands of Irish immigrants and their large families. Everybody scrambled constantly for a buck, or a nickel. Haley became enchanted by the stage as a little boy, but before he could pursue it, he roamed the neighborhood, stealing broken cookies to sell from his front stoop and collecting used strawberry boxes; fifteen of them brought him a penny from a neighborhood merchant.

Haley was close to his older brother, Bill. After they became newsboys, they uncorked their fists and successfully defended their corner from other kids that wanted to take over. It was a sweet triumph and a reflection of Haley's scrappy personality.

20th Century-Fox player Jack Haley was a former vaudeville personality and a star of radio and movies before coming to MGM to play the Tin Woodman. Years of performing had honed his nervous, sweetly ineffectual persona. Because he could project a child's sense of wonder, Haley was an especially appealing addition to the *Oz* cast.

While still a kid, Haley worked as a switchboard operator, an office boy, and a theater usher. The stage still fascinated him, and he was thrilled to be able to save enough money to pay a local ex-hoofer to teach him tap dancing.

The kid was too young to be drafted during World War I, but he was plenty big enough to work as an electrician's assistant at the Boston Navy Yard and, later, on Hog Island at the navy yard in Philadelphia. Philly had appealed to Haley because it was close to New York City, the center of show business. Haley bluffed his way into a gig as a song plugger, singing his heart out on stage in order to spark sales of sheet music. Finally, in Hoboken, Haley got himself installed as a background singer in a "girl act" libretto, a minor part of most vaudeville programs, but invaluable training for Haley. The act was called "Soda Fountain Girls," and it eventually played all across New Jersey. Haley was seventeen.

The experience and poise Haley gained with Soda Fountain Girls led him to his first experience in burlesque, *Folly Town*. Haley functioned as a straight man to top banana Frankie Hunter and a confident second banana named Bert Lahr. Haley and Lahr eventually became friends, and remained close for the rest of their lives.

Haley met a pretty vaudevillian named Florence McFadden. The two married in 1921 and were together until Haley's death fifty-eight years later.

After doing a two-man act with comic Charlie Crafts, Haley reached Broadway in 1924 as a cog in a musical revue called *Round the Town*. The show closed after fifteen performances. Jack had considerably better luck with his next Broadway work, *Gay Paree* (1925–26), a musical revue that ran at the prestigious Shubert Theatre for 181 performances. It was a tuneful, well-mounted show headlined by comic Chic Sale and a talented dancer/singer/comic actress from vaudeville, Winnie Lightner.

Haley also was cast in a reworked *Gay Paree* that ran for 192 performances during 1926–27. This time, he was the show's star. Bookers and talent scouts were frankly excited about Jack Haley.

Haley and wife Flo had put together a boy-girl act that they reworked for a road show called *Good News*. Everything in the show played well, particularly in Chicago, and Jack and Flo were invited to Hollywood by Vitaphone (Warner Bros.), where they appeared together, as comic versions of themselves, in a 1928 one-reel short called *Haleyisms*. Flo left the business after this, but Jack was signed by Paramount at the end of 1929, where he starred in a short (*The 20th Amendment*, 1930) and took a supporting role in a feature, *Follow Through* (1930). Then he was back at Vitaphone/Warner, pigeonholed as a one- and two-reel comedy star in fluff the likes of *Came the Yawn* (1932) and *Salt Water Daffy* (1933). Haley played himself in *Mr. Broadway* (1933), an independently produced hour-long Manhattan "travelogue" hosted by Ed Sullivan and featuring plenty of guest stars, including Bert Lahr.

After another stint with Paramount, and flirtations with Hal Roach and Columbia, Haley got his big break in pictures in 1936, when he was signed by 20th Century-Fox. Little Shirley Temple, a Fox property, was then America's biggest movie star, and when Haley was cast in support of her in *Poor Little Rich Girl* (1936), his star began to rise quickly. At Fox between 1936 and 1938, Haley sometimes played himself in all-star revues, but was most familiar in light comedies, as handsome, reticent city fellows who get the girl in spite of themselves. He took the lead, opposite Ann Sothern, in *Danger: Love at Work* (1937); in Fox "A" pictures he had prominent supporting roles, as in *Rebecca of Sunnybrook Farm* (1938; starring Shirley Temple and Randolph Scott) and *Alexander's Ragtime Band* (1938; with Tyrone Power and Alice Faye).

The slightly timid manner Haley brought to the Tin Woodman wasn't much of a departure from what he'd been doing in earlier pictures. Audience reaction was good, of course; it was obvious that Haley was an appealing performer, so he was rewarded with his own radio program—twice: NBC's *Log Cabin Jamboree* of 1937–38 and CBS's *The Wonder Show* (1938–39, and named for its sponsor, Wonder Bread). After each day's shooting on the set of *Oz*, Haley returned home, where he worked with his *Wonder Show* writers from 9:00 to midnight crafting jokes for his live, Friday-night radio broadcast.

The January 20, 1938, episode of *The Wonder Show* included a *Wizard of Oz* sketch with Haley's regular radio foils Lucille Ball and announcer Gale Gordon. (Decades later, Ball and Gordon would work together in TV's *The Lucy Show* and *Here's Lucy*, and enjoy enormous success.)

After *The Wizard of Oz*, Haley filmed at Fox, RKO, Warner, Paramount, and Pine-Thomas, Paramount's prolific B-picture unit that found starring roles for Haley in such trifles as *One Body Too Many* (1944; remembered today only because of co-star Bela Lugosi) and *Scared Stiff* (1945; opposite film noir legend Ann Savage).

Haley worked on Broadway for the remainder of the 1940s and had a big hit in 1948–49 with *Inside U.S.A.*, a musical revue. Except for a cameo in *Norwood* (1970), and another bit in Martin Scorsese's *New York, New York* (1977), Haley's film career ended in 1946. (*Norwood* was directed by Jack Haley Jr., and the female lead of *New York, New York* was the older Haley's daughter-in-law, Liza Minnelli, the daughter of Judy Garland.) Haley had invested well over the years, and he became a generous philanthropist. He didn't have to work, but he indulged himself with occasional guest appearances on episodic TV as late as 1972.

For a long time, the unique sort of stardom Haley achieved because of *Oz* didn't sit well with him. As the years went by, and *Oz* became a television perennial, Haley became impatient with giving autographs. "What a tedious chore," he complained in his journal. He also became fed up with intrusive questions about Judy Garland, and with some people's assumption that he knew all of the actress's deepest secrets—and that he'd spill them whenever asked.

As time passed, Haley better understood the significance of *Oz* and what the Tin Woodman meant to generations of fans. Haley had had a good career, and the Tin Woodman was the obvious highlight. Because Haley had always longed for his father, he came to appreciate that many people accepted the Tin Woodman as a member of their own families.

Jack Haley's journal entry for June 4, 1979, begins, "They are coming to pick me up. I'm headed for intensive care for sure. It's the heart. It seems the 'Heart of the Tin Man' is working overtime, just trying to keep pumping."

The actor died two days later.

Frank Morgan as the Wizard/Prof. Marvel/Gatekeepers

Longtime character actor and MGM contract player Frank Morgan won the title role of *Oz* (and Prof. Marvel) because other actors had turned down the part. Star comic actor W. C. Fields had been nearly everyone's first choice (Yip Harburg agitated strongly for Fields), not least because the churlish Fields persona would mesh perfectly with the notion of the Wizard being a fraud, a humbug. When Fields demanded $150,000 (a sum reported by Louella Parsons in her column of August 4, 1938), negotiations stopped before they'd barely begun. (Another frequently cited Fields salary demand is $5,000 a day.) Fields wanted to be well compensated, but he also may not have liked the ensemble nature of the cast, which would make him but one strong personality among many. Beyond that, the entire project was built around a largely untested young actress. Fields probably didn't regret losing the role at all, even though he must have known that script editor Yip Harburg had written the Wizard's dialogue with Fields in mind. In any case, Fields was committed to do *You Can't Cheat an Honest Man* for Universal, a fact that was noted by a *Hollywood Reporter* story of August 10. The same *Hollywood Reporter* story noted that comic actors Victor Moore and Hugh Herbert were in the running to be the Wizard.

Another able comic, Ed Wynn, passed because he thought the part was too small. He had a point because, in the draft he read, the Wizard appears in just two scenes, and there was no Prof. Marvel at all. According to Mervyn LeRoy's 1974 autobiography, MGM star character player Wallace Beery campaigned for the role after Fields was no longer being considered. Beery, though, was a bit past his box-office prime in 1938, and was never a serious contender.

On August 20, 1938, columnist Sidney Skolsky claimed that Mervyn LeRoy had offered the role to writer and comic monologist Robert Benchley. Little more than a week later, on August 29, Louella Parsons said that Frank Morgan had been cast. But on September 3, *The Hollywood Reporter* said only that Morgan was the leading contender. On September 6, *The Hollywood Reporter* felt compelled to backtrack, saying that character player Charles Winninger had done a screen test. Three days after that report, September 9, 1938, *The Hollywood Reporter* revisited W. C. Fields, saying that the actor and MGM had returned to negotiations. About a week later, "industry reports" (always an amorphous source) said that Fields's salary demands were again a sticking point and that, further, his commitments to Universal were shaping up as roadblocks.

Daily Variety for September 21 brought the news that Frank Morgan had tested for the Wizard role. Finally, on September 22, the same paper reported that MGM had assigned the role to Morgan. Although Morgan was a longtime MGM contract player, he was nobody's choice for the role and had to agitate for a screen test. He had committed the entire script to memory, but took a big chance by having the moxie to ad lib his test. LeRoy and Freed realized that Morgan's suggestion of the Wizard's bombast and pathetic ineptitude was a rare and fine thing.

By mid-November, Morgan did his first costume and makeup tests for the various characters he would play in *The Wizard of Oz*. These tests involved a variety of caps, hairstyles, mustaches, eyebrow treatments, beards and goatees, skullcaps, and hairpieces.

In Focus: Frank Morgan (1890–1949)

Unlike many actors of his generation, Frank Morgan was born into wealth and privilege that were constant companions as he grew up. Francis Philip Wuppermann was born in New York City in 1890. His mother, Josephine Hancox, came from a family that owned a fleet of boats that plied the Hudson River; and Frank's father, George Wuppermann, was a onetime banker who became the sole distributor of Angostura bitters in the United States, Canada, Mexico, and Cuba. As president of Angostura-Wuppermann, George was able to provide handsomely for his wife and eleven children.

Frank was the youngest of the brood. One of his older brothers, Raphael, changed his name to Ralph Morgan when he pursued a stage career. (Ralph Morgan eventually became a familiar character actor in movies.) Francis became Frank Morgan, and another brother, Carlos Wuppermann, changed his name to Carlyle Morgan. Frank was very close to Carlos, and was devastated when the talented writer and poet was killed while serving with army intelligence in Germany in 1919, just after World War I. (One of Carlos's plays, *The Triumph of X*, had a brief Broadway run in 1921.)

Frank wasn't interested in the family business. Instead, he was inspired by Carlos, and Ralph, who had cracked Broadway in 1909, and urged Frank to try his luck. Frank's first Broadway appearance was in *A Woman Killed with Kindness*, which had exactly one performance in 1914. Still, it was a start. Although he broke into films with studios located in New York and New Jersey in 1916 (as Frank Wuppermann, in *The Suspect*), Frank remained focused on his Broadway career. He had a leading role in the 1921 production

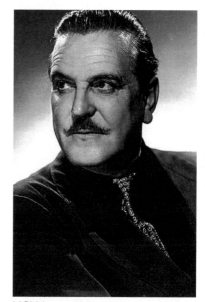

MGM kept numerous top-line character players under contract, but few were as successful or as highly regarded as Frank Morgan. He signed with MGM in 1933 and remained with the studio until his death in 1949. Despite his lofty status on the lot, Morgan had to lobby for the role of the Wizard.

of *The Triumph of X*, won good notices for a 1923–24 drama called *The Lullaby*, and got real acclaim for *The Firebrand*, a 1924–25 costume comedy set in Renaissance Italy. (Frank was in good company: others in the production included Roland Winters, Joseph Schildkraut, and Edward G. Robinson.)

From 1925 to 1932, Frank starred in another dozen Broadway productions, including the 1926–27 hit *Gentlemen Prefer Blondes*. A comic turn as Prof. Topaze in *Topaze* (1930) excited the interest of Hollywood, and Frank signed with MGM in 1933, after freelancing at RKO, Paramount, and elsewhere. Although Morgan made pictures on loan-out to other studios, MGM was to be his professional home until his death.

Social and convivial, Morgan was well liked around town, and added color and wit to his movie assignments. He was nominated for a best actor Oscar for his reprise of his *Firebrand* role as the Duke of Florence in *The Affairs of Cellini* (1934). Morgan did the film while on loan to 20th Century Pictures (20th Century-Fox was formed a year later), and he had even greater professional success opposite Shirley Temple in Fox's *Dimples* (1936). He and eight-year-old Temple made an appealing pair, with Morgan playing Shirley's grandfather, a likable fellow who picks people's pockets while little Shirley diverts the suckers with street theater. The pickpocket is called Prof. Eustace

Appleby, a name that foreshadows the sly deception that characterizes Morgan's performance as Prof. Marvel and the Wizard.

The 1930s and '40s were a golden age for Hollywood character actors. Talented ones worked all the time, and those that were talented *and* unusually popular with audiences, such as Morgan, were assured of "A" picture assignments and co-star billing. Morgan appeared in Jean Harlow's final film, *Saratoga* (1937), in a Nelson Eddy–Eleanor Powell musical called *Rosalie* (1937; Ray Bolger is also in the cast), and in *The Crowd Roars* (1938), a prizefight drama in which Morgan is Robert Taylor's criminally irresponsible, nitwit father. (The part was a nice change of pace for Morgan, in a picture that helped fashion a new image for Taylor, who'd been in enough pretty-boy romantic roles to suit MGM.)

Morgan excelled in five roles in *The Wizard of Oz*, and brought his skill and charm to many superior pictures after that, including *The Shop Around the Corner*, *Broadway Melody of 1940*, *The Mortal Storm*, and *Boom Town* (all 1940); *Tortilla Flat* and *White Cargo* (both 1942); *The Human Comedy* (1943); *Courage of Lassie* (1946); *The Stratton Story* (1949); and *Any Number Can Play* (1949; a rare non-musical produced by Arthur Freed).

Radio demanded some of Morgan's time in the '40s, most famously when he was a regular on *Maxwell House Coffee Time*, a comedy show headlined by Fanny Brice as Baby Snooks.

Morgan owned a yacht and an enormous ranch in Hemet Valley. He was outwardly jovial, but had never recovered from the death of his older brother. Frank was quietly, politely alcoholic, a man who drank steadily rather than heavily. (In a very sad circumstance, his wife and adult son had drinking problems, too.) Without alcohol, his mood could sour. A young woman from MGM's publicity department recalled that Morgan was a little unsteady during his guard-box scene (later deleted) on the *Oz* set, but generally speaking, he was thoroughly professional and prepared throughout his career.

Frank Morgan died quietly of a stroke, at home and in his sleep, in 1949. His last picture, *Key to the City*, was released posthumously in 1950.

Gale Sondergaard as the Wicked Witch of the West

The search to find the ideal actress to play a witch in *The Wizard of Oz*—or multiple actresses to play multiple witches—stands as a good example of how big-budget studio pictures were conceived, evolved, and finally adjusted before a foot of film was exposed.

Early on, the irrepressible Fanny Brice, best known as radio's comically obnoxious Baby Snooks, was considered for the amorphous-sounding role of "a witch." Another actress, long-faced character player Edna May Oliver, was slated to play "another witch." Later, producer Mervyn LeRoy decided that *Oz* would have only two witches with speaking parts: the Wicked Witch of the West and the good witch Glinda. (The third witch, the Wicked Witch of the East, was mainly a pair of slippers and skinny lower legs, and needed no actress at all.)

After an August 20, 1938, interview with Margaret Hamilton, Mervyn LeRoy hired good-looking character actress Gale Sondergaard to play the Wicked Witch of the West. This casting was a direct reflection of the success of Walt Disney's *Snow White and the Seven Dwarfs* (1937). Because that story's evil queen longs to be "the fairest one of all," she has to be physically beautiful, in order that her desire be rooted in reality. After looking at numerous character sketches prepared by his concept artists, Disney

Darkly beautiful Gale Sondergaard (right) was cast as the Wicked Witch of the West, but her unwillingness to shift from "beauty" makeup to a "plain" design encouraged her to leave the project. She's seen here, with Paulette Goddard, in another 1939 release, *The Cat and the Canary*.

approved one done by Joe Grant, of a slim, raven-haired queen with an arrogant and chilly beauty. LeRoy and Freed envisioned the Wicked Witch of *Oz* similarly, playing on the contrast between the witch's good looks and her iniquitous character. Gale Sondergaard was Disney's evil queen come to life.

Gale was fitted for a glamorous, sequined gown and a pointed hat that was elegant instead of vaguely comic. Then Mervyn LeRoy began to have doubts; in the first *Oz* novel, Baum and Denslow's Witch was no beauty. Sondergaard later remarked to *Film Fan Monthly*, "I suppose Mervyn got to remembering that this [the book] was a classic by now, and the children who read it were going to say, 'That isn't the way it was written.' And everybody agreed that you could not do that to *The Wizard of Oz*."

LeRoy's solution was to order Sondergaard done up in "ugly" makeup. Surviving stills of test makeups suggest "drab" rather than ugly, but whatever the case, Sondergaard wasn't having any. She'd built a good career as a sternly beautiful character actress possessed of a grim sort of glamour, and she wasn't going to throw it away on a kids' movie. She announced her intention to quit, and LeRoy didn't stand in her way.

Just twenty-five days after leaving *Oz*, Gale Sondergaard signed with Warner Bros. to play Empress Eugenie in the Paul Muni–Bette Davis vehicle *Juarez* (1939), a biography of the great Mexican leader. She was in another high-profile release in 1939, *The Cat and the Canary*, a semi-comic sendup, with Bob Hope, of John Willard's popular 1922 play.

In Focus: Gale Sondergaard (1899–1985)

By the time she was cast in *The Wizard of Oz*, Gale Sondergaard was a best support-ing actress Oscar winner for her work in *Anthony Adverse* (1936). That film had been directed by Mervyn LeRoy, the producer of *Oz*, so LeRoy was aware of Sondergaard's skill, as well as her penetrating screen presence. As an actress, she was probingly intel-ligent and incisive, almost curt. She was beautiful, too, but darkly sophisticated rather than conventionally pretty.

Edith Holm Sondergaard was born in Minnesota in 1899 to politically progres-sive parents who encouraged her social conscience. She didn't consider acting as a career until her late teens. While at the University of Minnesota during 1918–21, Gale pursued formal studies in dramatics, and gained valuable experience over the summers on the Chautauqua circuit (local or traveling shows dominated by lectures and dramatic presentations designed to provide intellectual uplift). Following stage experience with a traveling Shakespearean troupe, Gale was accepted by New York's prestigious Theatre Guild, where she met Herbert Biberman, a young director who had trained in Moscow. The two married in 1930.

Herbert and Gale received great critical praise for their theater work over the next few years, and by 1934, Biberman was a contract director with Columbia. Gale's film debut, *Anthony Adverse*, was released by Warner Bros. two years later. Audiences were impressed by Sondergaard's dark beauty and the force she brought to the scheming housekeeper, Faith. The Academy Award given to Gale was the first in the new "supporting player" category; the novelty of that, plus Sondergaard's skill after appearing seemingly from nowhere, suggested a film career of great promise.

For the next few years, Sondergaard alternated her film work between villain-esses and sympathetic figures. Although *The Wizard of Oz* didn't pan out for Gale, she earned excellent notices in a lot of prestigious releases from Paramount, Fox, Warner, and MGM: *The Life of Emile Zola* (1937; in a beautifully played sympathetic role as Mme. Dreyfuss), *Juarez* and *The Cat and the Canary* (both 1939), *The Mark of Zorro* and *The Letter* (both 1940). In the last, Sondergaard made an unforgettable impres-sion as the Eurasian beauty who slides a blade into Bette Davis.

In *The Blue Bird* (1940), Sondergaard played Tylette, a "tuxedo cat" transformed by a fairy into a dark, regal beauty wearing a black gown accessorized with white gloves and white bib. Tylette has belonged to a little girl (Shirley Temple), and accom-panies her on a magical voyage to the past and future. Tylette has plans of her own (this *is* Gale Sondergaard, after all), and now longs for luxury. She's resented being a mere housecat; human form is much more to her liking, and she intends to stay that way, even if she must undercut and endanger little Shirley.

After 1940, Sondergaard worked frequently at Universal, one of the industry's "minor majors," where horror and hysterical melodrama were the norm. The actress wasn't entirely pleased by this turn—she felt, for instance, that the foolishly comic *The Black Cat* was "beneath" her (she was right)—but it's for many of these pic-tures that Sondergaard's star still shines brightly today. The most memorable of the bunch are *The Spider Woman* aka *Sherlock Holmes and the Spider Woman* (1944), and a wonderfully over-the-top sequel, *The Spider Woman Strikes Back* (1946). Although these were traditional B-plus features, Sondergaard played the slinky, scheming villainess with the kind of brio associated with the fiendish anti-heroines of Saturday-morning serials.

A solid role as "number-one wife" in an "A" picture, Fox's *Anna and the King of Siam* (1946), put Sondergaard's career on a better track, but everything derailed in 1947, when the opportunistic politicians of the House Un-American Activities Committee (HUAC) began to investigate purported Communist infiltration of the movie industry. Various "friendly witnesses" the likes of Robert Taylor, Adolphe Menjou, and Jack L. Warner cooperated with the committee, and some ratted out friends and co-workers thought to have liberal inclinations.

Gale's husband, writer-director Herbert Biberman, was one of "The Hollywood Ten," a group of principled directors and screenwriters that defied the committee. Biberman refused to testify altogether, which was sufficient to place Sondergaard on an industry blacklist. Biberman and the others of the Ten received prison sentences.

Producer-director Mervyn LeRoy, who had cast Gale in *The Wizard of Oz* nine years earlier, gave her a small role in a prestige drama, *East Side, West Side* (1949). The industry didn't like that, so *East Side, West Side* was the last movie Sondergaard would make for twenty years.

HUAC remained interested in Gale, harassing her into 1951 and expressing mock outrage at her refusal to testify. After the committee finally forced actor Larry Parks to "implicate" Sondergaard in the Communist Party, Gale's film career was taken from her—an ugly irony because she had devoted herself during the 1940s to raising many thousands of dollars at far-flung rallies for war bonds.

Sondergaard put together a one-woman stage show in 1956, and was hauled before HUAC yet again—where she again told the bunch to get lost.

She finally returned to the stage in 1965, and then did TV-movies and guest appearances on episodic television into 1983. She died in 1985, unbowed.

Margaret Hamilton as the Wicked Witch of the West

During the 101 minutes that comprise *The Wizard of Oz*, Margaret Hamilton's Wicked Witch of the West is on screen for just twelve of them. Yet of all the frightening creatures that have paraded across movie screens over the many generations since film began, few, if any, have the pure, primal power to frighten as strongly as Hamilton's Wicked Witch. The role was just another job in the life of a working actress, and she made it legendary.

As we've seen, though, Hamilton wasn't the first choice for the role. In a memo he wrote on January 31, 1938, associate producer Arthur Freed recommended Edna May Oliver for the Wicked Witch. Oliver was a long-faced character actress adept at comedy and drama; before 1939, she had taken prominent supporting parts in comedies, light dramas, and literary adaptations that included *Little Women* (as Aunt March), *Ann Vickers*, *David Copperfield*, *A Tale of Two Cities*, *Romeo and Juliet*, and Paramount's misbegotten 1933 fantasy *Alice*

MARGARET HAMILTON

•

Exclusive Management
Gene Mann-Jess Smith Agency
CR - 1-1135

The twice-yearly *Academy Players Directory* was a useful tool for Hollywood casting agents who might need reminders about the faces and recent credits of available players. The "Characters and Comediennes" section of the 1941 edition included Margaret Hamilton, who sustained a long and very busy career for decades without the security of long-term employment by a single studio.

in Wonderland (as the Red Queen). As a freelance character player, she moved between various studios; her greatest popular success came in the "Hildegarde Withers" mysteries produced by RKO during 1932–35, beginning with *Penguin Pool Murder*. As the incurably snoopy Miss Withers, Oliver was teamed with star character actor James Gleason, cast as the irascible Inspector Piper.

Oliver was a witty actress with stage experience and some fifteen years of movie work behind her. She would have put a unique stamp on the Wicked Witch, but for reasons unknown, Freed's casting notion—like so many that were floated around Hollywood's executive offices—never came to fruition. In a May 20, 1938, memo, Freed notes that the part still has to be cast.

In August, industry trade papers announced Gale Sondergaard as the Wicked Witch.

Margaret Hamilton was familiar with the role, having played the Witch in various stage productions that predated MGM's adaptation. Even while Sondergaard was still in play, Mervyn LeRoy invited Hamilton to read for the part. When LeRoy discarded the notion of a glamorous witch, and Sondergaard didn't care to play an "ugly," Hamilton was again a focus of attention. She was interviewed by MGM casting director Leonard Murphy and was hired on October 10.

Because she was a single mother, Hamilton wanted a two-week guarantee, but her agent asked for six weeks. MGM said it would go to three. In the end, Hamilton's agent was firm on six weeks, and Hamilton was hired. She would work on *The Wizard of Oz* for sixteen weeks—and come close to dying, in the bargain.

In the beginning, though, the Witch was just a good role that Hamilton looked forward to playing. In a 1985 interview with historian Gregory Catsos,

Hamilton said, "It wasn't a very big part, but it was a very good part. The Witch was fun to play because she enjoyed everything she did; it didn't matter whether it was screaming or laughing or threatening Dorothy. . . . The Wicked Witch is the keynote throughout the whole picture. Even though you don't see her all the time, you know she's still there."

Margaret worked on *Oz* for four months, at $1,000 a week, her standard rate at the time. Of course, there were bumps in the road. Hamilton and others in the cast fretted each time another director showed up, worrying that the new man might have his own ideas about casting.

Hamilton had been in pictures for only six years when she did *Oz*, but six years is plenty of time to have seen actors paid off for what remained of their contracts, and sent home. But Hamilton was perfectly cast, and Mervyn LeRoy apparently knew it. He encouraged Hamilton's thoughts about how she might play the character, but the Witch's piercing, menacing laugh was the actress's own creation. She knew that it was vital to the characterization, and she consciously varied the laughter's pitch, so that audiences would remain surprised and engaged.

Because she was a character player in a business that pampered leading ladies, Hamilton was disappointed but hardly surprised when she was given a dreary on-set dressing room that was a black canvas tent with what she described as "a dirty rug" on a portion of the sound-stage floor. This was unintended but very real thoughtlessness on the studio's part. Because Hamilton's professional background differed from those of the other principals, she didn't interact with them very much. The gloomy "dressing room," where Hamilton would have been loath to entertain visitors, was probably an aggravating factor.

In Focus: Margaret Hamilton (1902–1985)

Tour de force, a French term that's been part of English for more than two hundred years, is one of the most abused of all the critical terms tossed around by people that write or talk professionally about movies. Did somebody at a local TV station once call a Tyler Perry "Medea" performance a *tour de force*? Probably. For the real deal, for a true instance of a characterization accomplished with great skill, watch Margaret Hamilton as the Wicked Witch of the West. She's over the top, she's theatrical, and she steals every scene. And that's just what Victor Fleming wanted to happen; Maggie Hamilton delivered a *tour de force*.

The Wicked Witch was born Margaret Brainard Hamilton in Cleveland in 1902. She was attracted to acting while a very young woman, and because she was in theater-rich Cleveland, she had opportunities to do local stage work, notably at the renowned Cleveland Playhouse. Hamilton majored in primary education at Boston's Wheelock College, became a certified kindergarten teacher, and owned a Cleveland nursery school before she was thirty.

Hamilton's obvious talent aside, her severe features marked her as a "type"—a useful actress whose very presence suggests something to audiences. In that, she provided writers with a kind of shorthand: you see Margaret on stage or on the screen and you think, *Uh oh.*

She made her Broadway debut in *Another Language*, a 1932–33 domestic drama that cast her as an unpleasant in-law. The "type" in typecasting had begun! Hamilton repeated her role in her first film, also called *Another Language* (1933), and made another four before a year had passed. By the time she was cast in *The Wizard of Oz*, Hamilton had about twenty-five film appearances behind her.

Hamilton had married in 1931 and divorced in 1938. When she came to *Oz*, she had a three-year-old son and a household to support. Every job was precious, and she never demanded more than $1,000 a week.

Margaret was an industry floater, a character player not attached long-term to any particular studio, but a freelancer ready to go where the jobs were. Before *Oz*, she was in pictures produced by RKO, MGM, Warner Bros., Fox, Republic, and variety of independent producers. Some names of characters she played further suggest what was, for her and the studios, profitable typecasting: Agatha, Lizzie Beadle, Mossy, Maizie, Lucy Gurget, and Beulah Flanders. Post-*Oz*, Hamilton played people named Agatha Badger, Miss Applegate, Clarabelle Evans, Tillie Hutch, Mrs. Klopplebobbler, and Daphne Heap (in *Brewster McCloud*, Robert Altman's *Oz*-inspired fantasy; see the "Fallout from the '60s" sidebar in chapter 19). Besides her work as the Wicked Witch, Hamilton will be familiar to baby boomers as the scowling, hatchet-faced housekeeper in *13 Ghosts* (1960), one of producer William Castle's famously gimmicked horror thrillers.

Hamilton got into television in 1950 and worked steadily there for more than thirty years, in drama anthologies, comedy series, and soap operas. Sitcom fans will recall her as Grandma Frump, Morticia's mother, on *The Addams Family*.

She made her final Broadway appearance in 1969, in a short-run revival of *Our Town*, with Henry Fonda, Ed Begley, and Elizabeth Hartman. Hamilton worked steadily, though, in regional theater, and even returned to the Cleveland Playhouse in 1978 to star in *Night Must Fall*.

Late in her life, Hamilton got into the lucrative world of television commercials as Cora, the homey owner of a general store that stocks no coffee but Maxwell House.

Because she was a jobbing actress, Hamilton never thought in terms of immortality. Many years after *Oz*, she told historian Gregory Catsos, "It never occurred to me that the film would become as big as it is today. Never!"

Billie Burke as Glinda

The first inclination of associate producer Arthur Freed regarding Glinda the Good Witch was to cast singer-comedienne Fanny Brice, an experienced stage performer whose background included burlesque, the *Ziegfeld Follies*, and Broadway. Her torchy performance of the song "My Man" had been wildly popular in 1921 and remained the standard version for many years. Brice brought what would become her signature role, Baby Snooks, to radio on a February 1936 broadcast of *The Ziegfeld Follies of the Air*. Snooks was a loquacious, unintentionally bratty little kid; the character became a permanent part of Brice's repertoire and enjoyed a long run on radio.

Freed recognized Brice's outsized talent and noted that she had worked well with Judy Garland in a 1938 MGM trifle called *Everybody Sing*. However, his notion to cast Brice as Glinda didn't work out—and that was probably a good thing. Brice was a distinctly urban performer who frequently did sketches and songs in Yiddish dialect. She evoked New York's Lower East Side—very much a part of the real world. Her presence in *The Wizard of Oz* might have worked against the film's creation of a place unlike anything audiences had ever seen. Further, Freed and LeRoy would probably have felt obligated to let the big-voiced Brice sing, which would have been manna for Fanny's fans but distracting competition to Garland's vocalizing.

In his character notes, *Oz* screenwriter Noel Langley described Glinda's "high trill of a giggle." Well, that was something Brice could have managed; likewise the quick-witted stage performer Beatrice Lillie, whom Langley suggested for the Glinda role. Lillie was an amusingly sharp-tongued actress-entertainer whose professional experience encompassed vaudeville houses, Broadway theaters, and supper clubs. Canadian by birth but British by upbringing, Lillie utilized song, sketches, and monologues to create a persona that was both sophisticated and knockabout. She became famous for "Mad Dogs and Englishmen" and other comic songs, and she wasn't afraid to take a pratfall, or conclude a performance by lifting her gown and roller-skating off stage.

Although Lillie's vocal facility and mobile face worked best when she could "read" a live audience, she'd had parts in four films when Langley suggested her for Glinda. But like Fanny Brice, Lillie had a big personality that could have taken *Oz* audiences "out" of the story. Mervyn LeRoy wondered whether she'd simply be too funny as the Good Witch. It all became moot when Lillie became tied up with a musical revue in London.

Shortly after a young MGM contract player named Helen Gilbert was cast as Glinda, the inveterate girl-chaser Howard Hughes spirited her away for a fling—with Gilbert's acquiescence, of course. Gilbert was suspended, and the studio, which had been building her as a leading lady, allowed her contract to lapse after 1940. For five months in 1949, Gilbert was married to L.A. mobster Johnny Stompanato. Nine years later, Stompanato was stabbed to death by Cheryl Crane, the daughter of Stompanato's girlfriend, film star Lana Turner. (Besides Stompanato, Gilbert had five other husbands.)

Showbiz columnist Louella Parsons announced on September 12, 1938, that Billie Burke, longtime stage star and film actress, and the widow of famed impresario Florenz Ziegfeld, had been cast as the Good Witch of the South. (The character was from the south in the book; from the north in the film.)

Baum describes Glinda, the Good Witch of the South, as a young beauty with "rich red" hair that "fell in flowing ringlets over her shoulder." Billie Burke was ideally cast as the script's combination of Baum's older Good Witch of the North and the beautiful Glinda. Fifty-three when she shot her scenes, Burke was a mature beauty whose reassuring appearance was complemented by apparent kindness and wisdom.

Burke had vast experience as a stage and film performer, but she wasn't a singer. When Glinda warbles "Come Out, Come Out, Wherever You Are," the voice we hear belongs to uncredited singer Lorraine Bridges, who also provided a Lullaby League vocal *and* played a resident of the Emerald City. Bridges was a capable mimic, too: during 1940–42, she performed uncredited patchwork fixes on vocals by star singers Jeanette MacDonald and Kathryn Grayson.

About a month after Margaret Hamilton's mishap with fire, Burke sprained her ankle while on the set. She had a finely tuned sense of the dramatic, and because her ankle hurt, she wanted special attention. (A limousine came to pick her up at home each morning to spirit her to MGM.) Billie pretended to faint. Very shortly, she was carried to a waiting ambulance.

Because she was Flo Ziegfeld's widow, Billie Burke was show business royalty. She wasn't in the habit of acting as if she wanted everyone else to know that, but she did have a talent for awarding herself the occasional privilege that might upset people on the *Oz* set. One day, after cast and crew had prepared the sequence in which Glinda urges Dorothy to follow the Yellow Brick Road, Victor Fleming was ready to do a take. Where's Billie? Billie had disappeared. Assistant directors Al Shenberg and Wallace Worsley Jr. fanned out with others to find her. They checked the front gate, the commissary, Burke's home, even (according to Margaret Hamilton) "the ladies' room." No Billie.

The search went on. This is what had happened: Besides being picked up by limousine daily, Burke had all-day access to it, and the chauffeur, during the shoot. Burke enjoyed having access to the machine and had simply left on an excursion. When she finally returned, she was approached by Shenberg, who demanded to know where she'd been, and didn't she realize she was upsetting people and costing the production a lot of money? He was very stern. Burke was innocently self-centered—there'd been no malice behind her disappearance—but she was also clever enough to "perform" her way out of an embarrassing situation. Margaret Hamilton told Gregory Catsos that Burke looked at Shenberg and allowed her eyes to overflow with tears before insisting that he was browbeating her. Well, nobody wanted to browbeat Billie Burke, least of all an assistant director. Burke's tears completely disarmed him, and no more was said about her unauthorized absence. When the time came to shoot the scene, Burke was composed and ready to go.

Talent, and particularly her showbiz pedigree, brought Burke a lot of desirable perks. Margaret Hamilton had a dreary, black canvas dressing room, but Burke had a comfortable, proper one done up in pinks and blues, right down to the powder puffs.

In Focus: Billie Burke (1884–1970)

Billie Burke was the daughter of a circus clown. She, too, chose show business, but not her father's sort. A slender, beautiful sylph, she won roles on Broadway, married impresario Florenz Ziegfeld in 1914, and became a major stage star during World War I. Her New York popularity was enormous, and when she was approached by young Hollywood to come west, she spurned the offers, passing up an opportunity to earn wealth above and beyond the finances she shared with her husband.

Mary William Ethelbert Appleton Burke was born in Washington, D.C., in 1884. As a teenager living with her family in London, she became enraptured by the legitimate stage. She began her stage career there, in ingénue parts, in 1902. Burke's first Broadway appearance was 1907's *My Wife*. (A Broadway database cites an 1894 play, Arthur Wing Pinero's *The Amazons*, as Burke's Broadway debut, in the role of Lady Thomasin Belturbet. As Burke was not yet ten years old when the play opened, the credit seems unlikely, particularly since Pinero's stage directions describe Lady Thomasin as "a bright, rosy, rather rough-mannered girl of eighteen.")

Billie Burke took supporting roles in two more Broadway plays during 1908–10, and then won the title role in *Suzanne*, a comedy that managed sixty-four performances during 1910–11. Between 1911 and Flo Ziegfeld's death in 1932, Burke had starring and co-starring roles in another sixteen Broadway comedies and light dramas, One of those was a 1913 revival of Pinero's *The Amazons*, which is the probable source of the confusion about her involvement in the New York production of 1894.

Billie Burke was a stunning beauty of the American stage early in the 20th century and knew equal fame as the wife of tireless theatrical producer Florenz Ziegfeld. After Ziegfeld's death in 1932, Billie thrived as a Broadway producer and as a popular light actress in movies. She was considerably older than the Glinda described by L. Frank Baum, but in retrospect, her casting seems perfect.

Most of Burke's Broadway projects had more-than-respectable runs, but another one by Pinero, *The "Mind the Paint" Girl*, enjoyed a robust 136 performances during 1912–13. W. Somerset Maugham's *Caesar's Wife*, which was produced by Ziegfeld, had eighty-one performances during 1919–20. In all, Flo Ziegfeld produced five of his wife's vehicles, all but one of which ran for between 81 and 103 performances. Two of them, *The Intimate Strangers* (1921–22) and *Rose Briar* (1922–23), were written by the Pulitzer Prize–winning novelist Booth Tarkington.

That ol' devil Fate showed up in 1932 when Flo Ziegfeld died of pneumonia at sixty-five, startling the Broadway community and leaving Billie Burke $500,000 in debt. The couple had owned a $1 million house when a million bucks really meant something, and held many other properties. Like most high-level Broadway producers, Ziegfeld occasionally overextended himself financially, and with his death, Billie was stuck. Toughened by the business, she became a producer and carried on her husband's legacy with the successful *Ziegfeld Follies of 1934*, which mounted 182 performances during the first seven months of 1934. Bobby Connolly, who would later choreograph *The Wizard of Oz*, arranged the show's dances, and future *Oz* lyricist E. Y. Harburg contributed to some of its many songs. Notables (and future notables) in the large cast included Fanny Brice (briefly considered later to play "a witch" in *The Wizard of Oz*); Eve Arden; future Tin Woodman Buddy Ebsen and his sister Vilma; Ina Ray, later a sensational swing-bandleader known as Ina Ray Hutton; teenage June Preisser, who was a bubbly MGM contract player during 1939–41; and the incomparably poised romantic vocalist Jane Froman.

We detail of all this to show that Billie Burke, although trained as an actress, had the wherewithal—and keen powers of observation from her time with Flo—to evaluate talent and succeed as a Broadway producer, one of the most challenging of all show business jobs. During 1936, she had another success, *Ziegfeld Follies of 1936*, which notched 112 performances. Sparkly June Preisser returned, and the great Fanny Brice, who could move easily between comic tunes and torch songs, also came back to do a comic sketch, "Baby Snooks Goes Hollywood," and sing "He Hasn't a Thing Except Me," a comic reversal on her famed torch song, "My Man."

The show got a lot of mileage from eccentric singer and comic actress Cass Daley (later a "novelty" star at Paramount); and from the anarchic stage and movie comic Bobby Clark (dependably amusing with his painted-on eyeglasses), appearing just months after the sudden death of his performance partner, Paul McCullough.

Billie Burke appeared in sixteen movies between 1917 and 1921 before taking a ten-year break to concentrate on her stage work. After Flo's death, Burke spent much more time in Hollywood, with important featured roles during 1932–37 in prestige pictures that included *A Bill of Divorcement*, *Christopher Strong*, *Dinner at Eight*, *Becky Sharp* (the first feature shot in three-strip Technicolor, the process that would distinguish *The Wizard of Oz*), and *Topper* (as the beleaguered Mrs. Topper).

After *Oz*, Billie continued to thrive in movies as an attractive light actress and character comedienne. She made good impressions on screen in *Topper Returns*, *The Man Who Came to Dinner*, and *In This Our Life*, and did a few more turns on Broadway. She didn't appear in *Ziegfeld Follies of 1943* (1943–44), or produce it, either, but licensed the Ziegfeld name and format to producers Lee and J. J. Shubert. The show starred Milton Berle and turned into a smash that racked up 553 performances. (No one claimed the show was sophisticated; in "The Merchant of Venison," a burlesque-style sketch designed around Berle, the comic played a fellow named J. Pierswift Armour.)

As Burke's flighty-sophisticate sort of character went out of style after World War II, she worked at Republic and for various independent producers, and even did a pair of short comedies at Columbia's assembly-line two-reel unit, *Silly Billie* and *Billie Gets Her Man* (both 1948).

MGM's *The Barkleys of Broadway* (1949) and *Father of the Bride* (1950) are obvious late-career high points. Billie's autobiography, *With a Feather on My Nose*, was published in 1949. A second volume, *With Powder on My Nose*, followed in 1959.

Burke got into television in 1950, where she worked for ten years, bringing her long experience and well-established persona to thrillers, dramas, comedies, and even the self-consciously hip *77 Sunset Strip*. A 1952 NBC-TV comedy show, *Doc Corkle*, starred Eddie Mayehoff, Arnold Stang, and Billie, but was canceled after just three episodes had aired.

Billie's last two feature films were major ones, Vincent Sherman's *The Young Philadelphians* (1959) and John Ford's *Sergeant Rutledge* (1960). She retired after that, and died in 1970, at eighty-five.

When Burke reflected on *The Wizard of Oz*, she wrote, "It's a divine part. There's child enough in all of us to be thrilled with the settings and the feeling of this picture. It has terrified me a little to think of living up to the children's idea of what a Good Fairy must be. But I can only hope with all my heart that I won't disappoint them."

Terry as Toto

At the outset of the *Oz* project, Mervyn LeRoy briefly entertained the notion of using an actor in a costume to play Toto. That's possible but unlikely, since audience tolerance for that level of make-believe had been severely diminished by time and the pains of the Depression. Famous actors in animal costumes had bombed in Paramount's *Alice in Wonderland* in 1933—and anyway, there had never been a dearth of talented real dogs in Hollywood. (One of them, in fact, the original Rin Tin Tin, had kept Warner Bros. solvent throughout the 1920s.) LeRoy would have known that finding a suitable real-life dog could be time-consuming, but certainly not impossible.

Although W. W. Denslow's original illustrations of Toto clearly suggest that the little dog is a terrier, MGM spent a long time being befuddled about specifically *which kind* of terrier. Well, although terriers come in many types and sizes, one thing everybody could agree on right away was that Denslow's terrier was a small one. That narrowed things down, but much fretting went on, nevertheless: Is Toto an Australian terrier? (*Do they even have those in Kansas?*) Glen of Imaal terrier? A Cairn? (*Close, but their tails are longer than Toto's.*) Norfolk terrier? Miniature schnauzer? Scottish? (*No, the ears are too long.*) Norwich? A Sealyham terrier? (*I don't know, that one looks awfully short to me.*) A Skye? (*No, no, too hairy!*) Maybe Toto is a West Highland White terrier! (*Yes, perfect, except those are white and Toto is black!*)

Daily Variety reported on September 1, 1938, that MGM was still looking for a "well-educated . . . intelligent" dog to play Toto. Finally, Hollywood animal trainer Carl Spitz showed up at MGM with a female Cairn terrier named Terry. She was one of numerous Cairns that auditioned, but the only one trained by Spitz. Terry had been in pictures since 1934, and had already worked at MGM.

On September 5, Spitz and MGM reached an agreement for Terry to be featured in *The Wizard of Oz*, and to be paid $125 a week.

The film would be Terry's first in color. She was five years old when she was cast. She weighed fifteen pounds, and was invariably attentive to Mr. Spitz. And because she was a doggie, and thus likely to succumb to hints given by her gastro-intestinal tract, Terry was administered an enema before going to work. *Voilà!* No accidents.

Like most trained animals on-set, Terry looked to her master for cues. That was to be expected, of course; the challenge for Victor Fleming, and for King Vidor during the Kansas sequences, was to account for the dog's line of sight and be sure it matched the action of particular scenes. In other words, it couldn't be apparent that the dog was ignoring Judy Garland in order to look off-camera at Spitz. If Terry was required to gaze screen left and then bark happily at Judy, the blocking of two-shots, and in cutaways, had to keep Garland screen left, too. The dog was going to look at Spitz no matter what, so Garland and all other relevant actors had to be inserted between Terry and her trainer.

Terry and Judy Garland got on well, though it's not true that the dog lived with Judy before filming began; that was cooked up by MGM publicity. On-set, Judy joked about Terry's bad breath.

Besides the actual filming, Terry had to be available for countless photo shoots for use in promotion. That was the other aspect of Carl Spitz's skill: Terry had to sit or stand stock-still nearly as often as she had to obey a more active command. The dog followed her cues well, but she was put through her paces rather remorselessly. She often seemed apprehensive to others on the set, and she was particularly spooked by the wind machines.

In Focus: Carl Spitz (1894–1976) and Terry (1933–1945)

Carl Spitz was a German immigrant who left politically unstable and inflation-ravaged Weimar Germany in 1926, when he was thirty-three. After quick stops in New York (where he found work as a firefighter) and Chicago, Spitz was in North Hollywood by 1927, and the owner-operator of Hollywood Dog Training School. Spitz's training regimen was innovative in its use of silent commands—a method that would prove very useful on movie sets.

In an early business handout, Spitz likened dog training to the fundamentals of education learned by a child in elementary school. "Our four-legged pal, the dog, must also undergo elementary schooling," Spitz wrote. "He must be well-trained in the fundamental obedience course before he can be trained to be a hunter, companion to the blind, assistant to the police or a motion picture star. . . . [W]e appeal increasingly to our dog's inherited abilities and instincts, his sense of smell, courage, temperamental soundness, intelligence and alertness."

Spitz owned and trained numerous dogs, and provided canine actors for a few films at the end of the silent era. Unlike some other silent-era actors, dogs had no trouble adjusting to talkies, except that what may have been vocal commands now had to be silent.

Buck, a St. Bernard that appeared opposite Clark Gable in *Call of the Wild*, was a particularly noticeable Spitz success. Buck also worked opposite a snowed-in Stan Laurel in *Swiss Miss* (1938), and helped inspire some of that comedy's biggest laughs. A Spitz Great Dane named Prince was a big part of the generally intimidating atmosphere of *The Most Dangerous Game*, a 1932 thriller based on the famous Richard Connell short story about a hunter whose favorite game animals are human beings.

Carl Spitz's association with Terry began in 1933, when a married couple from Pasadena brought the dog to Spitz for standard house pet training. The pair never paid their bill and never even called for the dog. Spitz liked the dog's intelligence and adopted her. During a nine-year career, Terry appeared in *Ready for Love* (1934; her film debut), *Bright Eyes* (1934; opposite Shirley Temple), and Fritz Lang's *Fury* (1936; as the sweet dog whose needless death stokes the anger of the persecuted character played by Spencer Tracy). Terry worked in Cecil B. DeMille's *The Buccaneer* (1938), *The Women* (1939), *Calling Philo Vance* (1940), Victor Fleming's *Tortilla Flat* (1942), the Jack Benny comedy *George Washington Slept Here* (1942)—nearly twenty in all.

Toto was a female Cairn terrier named Terry. The dog behaved beautifully on-set, avoiding what could have been costly delays. Terry's owner-trainer was Carl Spitz.

In 1942, Terry worked a second time with Margaret Hamilton, in *Twin Beds*, a romantic comedy with Joan Bennett and George Brent, and produced by independent filmmaker Edward Small. Not surprisingly, United Artists (which released the film) saw the publicity possibilities and did a photo shoot in which Hamilton (costumed as a maid) pretends to menace Terry, Witch-style.

In 1940, Spitz took Terry, Prince, Buck, and other dogs on the road to tour the vaudeville circuit. Newspaper adverts placed by the theaters invariably gave top billing to "Toto."

Terry's last film, a minor Universal musical called *Easy to Look At*, was released in 1945, the year of Terry's death.

Spitz's Hollywood Dog Training School and kennel was located at 12350 Riverside Drive. Terry was twelve when she died. Spitz buried her on the kennel grounds. The buildings are long gone, and the land was claimed for the Ventura Freeway in 1958. A faintly macabre outcome, holding that Terry rests somewhere beneath the freeway, is probably true, but that hasn't stopped a wealth of rumors about alternate burial places, including a plot beneath an apartment building that stands on what used to be Spitz's land.

Then there are the taxidermy rumors: Terry was stuffed in 1996 (where on earth was she in the meantime?) and sold at auction for $3,680. In a variant, the stuffed Terry enjoys celebrity status at the Smithsonian.

The best rumor of all contends that Terry is buried all the way across the country, beneath New York's Radio City Music Hall. Good story, but if true it would have meant some heavy, hard-to-hide digging back in '45, because Radio City was built in 1932, long before Terry's death.

Dog owners interested in the Spitz technique will want to know that, around 1960, Spitz and K-9 College Records issued an LP called *Carl Spitz Trains You to Train Your Dog* (K-9 LP-500). The LP occasionally shows up on Web auction sites.

Films never were the dominant part of Spitz's livelihood, but the work gave him valuable exposure and credibility as a trainer. After *Oz*, he and various dogs worked in movies for nearly another forty years. Of Spitz's late-career credits, 1973's *The Daring Dobermans* achieved modest popularity.

The great trainer of dogs died in 1976.

Clara Blandick as Aunt Em

MGM's first choice for the important supporting role as Dorothy's Aunt Em was eighty-year-old freelance player May Robson, a sweet-faced character actress who had been nominated as best actress for her performance as Apple Annie in

This is busy character actress Sarah Padden, on the day she tested (unsuccessfully) for the role of Aunt Em. Padden came to Hollywood from the stage to work in a variety of pictures. After 1940, she became a fixture of lively B-westerns.

Frank Capra's *Lady for a Day* (1933). Robson was born in Australia, and moved to the U.S. in the late 1870s, when she was approaching twenty. She became a playwright and acted on Broadway. The greater portion of her movie work began in 1926, and she remained active, mostly in "A" pictures, until 1942, the year of her death. Robson's failure to be cast as Aunt Em couldn't have hurt her pocketbook: she had featured roles in seven films released in 1939, including *They Made Me a Criminal* (with John Garfield).

A patrician-appearing actress named Janet Beecher was also considered for Aunt Em. Born in 1884, she was twenty-six years younger than Robson. Her Broadway experience stretched from 1903 to about 1930. After that, Beecher stayed busy in Hollywood, with movie work until 1943 and a TV role in 1952. She died in 1955.

On January 31, 1938, Sarah Padden tested for the part. She was fifty-eight at the time, with a resumé that included numerous stops at Universal and Monogram. Casting decisions within the studio system could be very sudden: on February 1, just a day after Padden's test, fifty-nine-year-old Clara Blandick was cast as Aunt Em. Like Robson and Beecher, Blandick had considerable stage experience.

Aunt Em could have been played in many ways, including some that audiences wouldn't have found very sympathetic. Part of the point of the opening Kansas sequence is that Dorothy's aunt and uncle lead gray, perfunctory lives. Daily existence is a struggle. A harsh or bitter Em would have been justifiable dramatically, but wouldn't have given Dorothy a person to long for. The girl misses Aunt Em during every moment of her adventure; audiences had to understand that the love between Dorothy and Em is mutual and strong. Blandick and director King Vidor put together an apt characterization that combined Kansas hardheadedness and gruff tenderness—and an unpretentious morality, too, which we witness when Em tells Miss Gulch that nothing but her faith prevents her from telling the busybody what she thinks of her.

In Focus: Clara Blandick (1880–1962)

Broadway success led character actress Clara Blandick to Hollywood, where she appeared in a handful of features and shorts during 1911–17, returned to the stage, and then resumed her film career in 1929.

Clara took a lead role in an entertaining RKO programmer, *Crime Ring* (1938), as a wealthy woman who helps a reporter expose a gang of phony fortune tellers. In an amusing distinction, she played Mark Twain's Aunt Polly three times, in *Tom Sawyer* (1930), *Huckleberry Finn* (1931), and *Tom Sawyer, Detective* (1938). Blandick is also seen in *The Girl from Missouri* (1934), *Anthony Adverse* (1936), *A Star Is Born* (1937; Janet Gaynor version), *Drums Along the Mohawk* (1939) *The Big Store* (1941), and *Life with Father* (1947). She freelanced throughout her career, taking roles at all the major studios, as well as with Republic and independent producers, too.

Blandick's take on Aunt Em perfectly suits the intentionally ambivalent tone of *Oz*'s Kansas scenes. Emily is a loving aunt who nevertheless has a farm to run. She can be brusque and preoccupied (as when the chick incubator fails), and you get the sense that she's oblivious to Dorothy's growing pains. But in one of the film's most potent reality-based moments, Emily tells off the bullying Miss Gulch: "Almira Gulch, just because you own half the county doesn't mean you have the power to run the rest of

Clara Blandick was comfortable with roles in films of all types. She did costume pictures as well as contemporary drama, and when she dressed up, she was nothing at all like Aunt Em.

us! For twenty-three years I've been dying to tell you what I thought of you, and now, well, being a Christian woman, I can't say it!"

Clara had done movie work continually for more than twenty years when age and arthritis prompted her to retire in 1952. Ten years after that, eighty-one years old, tormented by arthritis that had become mercilessly painful, and on the verge of losing her sight, she committed suicide with sleeping pills and self-asphyxiation. The note Clara left behind is one of Hollywood's most touching mementos. It reads, "I am now about to make the great adventure. I cannot endure this agonizing pain any longer. It is all over my body. Neither can I face the impending blindness. I pray the Lord my soul to take. Amen."

Charley Grapewin as Uncle Henry

Some sources claim that studio decision-makers were unanimous in their feeling that the popular character actor Charley Grapewin should play Uncle Henry. However, an MGM statement issued on February 1, 1938, announced fifty-nine-year-old Harlan Briggs for the role. Although the pugnacious-looking Briggs wasn't nearly as well known as Grapewin (Briggs took numerous uncredited parts throughout his career, 1933–52), he was capable and available. Arthur Freed had wanted Grapewin, but the sixty-nine-year-old actor was considering retirement and demurred. He eventually changed his mind, and Briggs was paid off and released. The studio issued an official announcement of Grapewin's casting on August 12, 1938.

As with Clara Blandick, Grapewin's scenes were confined to one or two sets on a single stage. The setup probably allowed Grapewin to feel immersed in all things Kansas. He expressed Uncle Henry's wry personality with some priceless facial expressions, particularly when Emily lays into Miss Gulch; Henry just scratches the back of his head and allows himself a secret smile. He runs his farm capably, but he's willing to let his wife be the ramrod of the place. Unlike many other of the film's characters (and this may be important), Uncle Henry is secure in who he is.

In Focus: Charley Grapewin (1869–1956)

Charley Grapewin was born just a few years after the Civil War, and like many other screen actors of his generation, he came to films following many years of live performances. Today, Charley Grapewin is fondly recalled not just for Uncle Henry, but also for his heartbreaking performance as the ailing Pa Joad in John Ford's 1940 adaptation of Steinbeck's *The Grapes of Wrath*. Both characters are elderly and rural, and although Pa Joad is more obviously "realistic" than Uncle Henry is (Pa's hopes have become childlike, his health is gone, and he suffers from dementia), Grapewin gave Henry a believably "Kansas" persona.

Charley Grapewin's early show business experience came with the circus. He was very physical and worked as an aerialist and acrobat. Later, he wrote plays and acted in touring stage troupes. He came to Hollywood in 1929 and became a sought-after character actor, adept at playing characters named "Pop" (in numerous films), "Jed," "Dad," "Gramp" (in *The Petrified Forest*, 1936), "Grandpa," "Grandfather," "Uncle Caleb," and "Uncle Frank."

John Ford's *Tobacco Road* (1940; from Erskine Caldwell's "racy" novel) offered Grapewin the opportunity for his liveliest and most weirdly funny performance, as Jeeter Lester, the dimwitted, country-poor dirt farmer whose idea of heaven is a sack of stolen turnips.

In a nice casting turnabout, Grapewin found fresh success during 1940–42, as police inspector Richard Queen in seven independently produced Ellery Queen mysteries distributed by Columbia. (Ellery Queen was played by Ralph Bellamy, and later by William Gargan.) Charley Grapewin remained in demand until his retirement in 1951; he passed away five years later.

In what now seems to have been a terrible lapse, the headline and lead paragraph of Grapewin's February 3, 1956, obituary in the *Los Angeles Times* neglects to mention *The Wizard of Oz*, focusing instead on the actor's roles in *The Grapes of Wrath* and *Tobacco Road*. *Oz* would play on television for the first time later in 1956 and kick off Charley Grapewin's journey to immortality.

Although best known now for playing rural types, Charley Grapewin excelled in a variety of roles in a long career as a stage and film actor. He was considering retirement when he agreed to play Dorothy's Uncle Henry. As things turned out, Grapewin had another dozen years of steady work ahead of him.

Salaries of the Principals, and Weeks Worked

Ray Bolger	$3,000/wk (24 weeks)
Jack Haley	$3,000/wk (22 weeks)
Bert Lahr	$2,500/wk (24 weeks)
Buddy Ebsen	$1,500/wk (2 weeks)
Frank Morgan	$1,500/wk (8 weeks)
Margaret Hamilton	$1,000/wk (16 weeks)
Billie Burke	$767/wk (6 weeks)
Clara Blandick	$750/wk (1 week)
Charley Grapewin	$750/wk (1 week)
Judy Garland	$500/wk (26 weeks; as part of her 40-wk. contractual guarantee)
Terry	$125/wk (26 weeks)
Munchkin players	$50/wk (6 weeks)

Winkies and Monkeys, Who's Who?

Because the end cast credits of *Oz* include the name Pat Walshe, many fans assumed over the years that that actor is the Winkie captain who is astonished by the wicked witch's watery demise, and who says to Dorothy, "You—you killed her!" But Walshe, thirty-nine when *Oz* was released, was a compact 3′8″, and played the leader of the winged monkeys, a role for which he was formally cast on October 4, 1938. Walshe had vaudeville experience dating to his childhood, and was a veteran of Broadway and circuses. (Movies were a minor part of Walshe's career: between 1939 and 1950, he took work in only four films.) As a novelty performer, he had worn animal costumes and other disguises. He could "sell" a character through expressive movement and was an ideal choice

Stage-trained Mitchell Lewis (far right) got into silent films as a leading man and then segued into character roles and bits. MGM liked his size and rugged face, and kept him under contract for many years. He cut an imposing figure as the captain of the Winkie guards.

to play the featured monkey. (Some of the "background" monkeys were played by little people that had also doubled as Munchkins.)

According to imdb.com, Walshe, who died in 1991, was the last surviving credited member of the *Oz* cast.

The Winkie captain was played by general-purpose actor Mitchell Lewis, who was under contract to MGM from 1937 until his death, at seventy-six, in 1956. At 6′2″ and usefully rugged, Lewis was often cast as Arabs, Native Americans, gypsies, and other ethnic "types." His legitimate-stage work dates to 1902, and he first appeared in the movies in 1914, eventually amassing roles in more than two hundred. He was a leading man, for Select and Selznick, for a brief time immediately after World War I, and settled into character roles and bits when he came to MGM, where he was valued for his versatility and rich voice. An apparent lack of ego helped, too: After about 1934, most of Lewis's work was done without screen credit. But it amounted to dependable employment that allowed him to prosper in an industry where the words "job" and "security" were almost never paired in a sentence.

Mitchell Lewis was cast as the Winkie captain in the late summer of 1938.

Fans of movie melodrama will want to know that Lewis is particularly good in a true pre-Code oddity, *Kongo* (1932), as the unscrupulous priest, Hogan.

In Focus: Jimmy the Crow (c. 1937–1954)

In a film career that spanned 1938 to 1954, Jimmy the Crow worked with Betty Grable, Jean Arthur, James Stewart, Bette Davis, James Cagney, Martin & Lewis, and Milton Berle. He appeared in "A" pictures, including *The Wizard of Oz, Moon Over Miami,* and *It's a Wonderful Life,* and in Bs, too, which ranged from *Son of Dracula* to the oddball all-bird romance *Bill and Coo. Oz* came very early in Jimmy's film career. His role, as the crow that brazenly lands on the shoulder of the Scarecrow, is brief but vital to establishing that the Scarecrow can't scare anybody.

Jimmy was owned and trained by a redheaded, onetime cowboy named Curly Twiford (1896–1956), who worked not just with birds but raccoons, a marmoset, and even a rat named Mr. Josephine Beach.

What was Jimmy's favorite role? He never said, but a good guess is that he had two: the Scarecrow's antagonist in *Oz,* and—cast against type, or against *species*—as the raven in *Ellery Queen, Master Detective* (1940). But then again, some sources claim that Jimmy was a raven all along and that he merely happened to excel at playing crows. Is it true? Two caws for yes, one caw for no.

Finding the Munchkins

Show business opportunities for midgets (proportionate dwarfs) existed, but were modest. Aspirants had the best shots at employment with circuses, carnivals, state fairs, and other demanding live venues. The Munchkin troupe eventually included experienced singers, ballet and popular dancers, performers with Broadway and vaudeville experience, and even a circus acrobat.

American movies, naturally enough, seldom clamored for midgets, partly because roles were generally nonexistent, and because any roles that did crop up could promptly be filled by such Hollywood habitués as Harry Earles, Jerry Maren, Billy Curtis, and the very talented Billy Barty. (Of that group, by the way, only Barty—a short-limbed dwarf rather than a proportionate little person of the sort desired by Mervyn LeRoy—did not appear in *The Wizard of Oz*.) Because of this paucity of film work, and because MGM had requested literal busloads of little people, the film would require many that were not normally associated with show business. For the purposes of the Munchkinland sequence, the people's size and proportions were sufficient to recommend them.

In 1938, vaudeville impresario Leo Singer (real name: Leo Singre) was sixty-one years old. A German Jew who sometimes passed himself off as Austria's Baron Leopold Von Singer, he had been active in Europe and South America before settling in the U.S. in 1914. In L. Frank Baum's original novel, Dorothy is greeted by only three Munchkins. Well, MGM was keen to provide more spectacle than that: the studio wanted 125 Munchkins, to be played by midgets. (Over the years, various accounts have claimed that the studio wanted as many as three hundred little people; that number is erroneous.) When *Oz* casting director Bill Grady put out the call for scores of little people, impresario Leo Singer had only eighteen midgets under contract. Undeterred (and more optimistic than he had cause to be), Singer signed a contract with MGM on October 1, 1938. The studio insisted that Singer deliver his troupe on November 11.

Not long before, Singer had provided about forty midgets to the producers of an aggressively peculiar all-midget western, *The Terror of Tiny Town* (1938). (In that film, the midget cast rode Shetland ponies. During his discussions about *Oz*, Singer suggested that Munchkinland showcase a few dwarf animals. His idea was declined.) Finding forty suitable actors for that picture hadn't been easy, and now Singer was looking at the challenge of locating, signing, and delivering three times that many. His challenge was compounded because a British impresario, Fred Roper, was rounding up more than sixty midgets to fill a "Little Miracle Town" attraction for the 1939 New York World's Fair.

Singer located most of his players on the East Coast, which necessitated a New-York-to-L.A. bus run during November 5–10. In order to fulfill the contract date, Singer subcontracted with Dolly and Henry Kramer (proprietors of Henry Kramer's Hollywood Midgets), and Grace and Harvey Williams. A very few midgets were brought in by an impresario who called himself Major Doyle; this handful signed with MGM, not Singer.

The last little person to arrive at MGM was Bill Giblin, who reported for work on November 24, 1938.

Through these impresarios, Singer added about twenty-five people to his troupe. Ultimately, Singer assembled 122 to 124 midgets, though MGM's incomplete records note only 116. Additionally, eight average-sized children (mostly little girls) were hired for background fill. (The children cast as background Munchkins also signed directly with the studio.) At least one of the Munchkins, Johnny Leal, was a midget child. An achondroplasiac dwarf, Elmer St. Aubin, is seen at the head of the marching soldiers. Another, George Ministeri, handles the reins of a horse-drawn carriage.

A requirement of the MGM contract was that Singer carry workman's compensation insurance on his players, including on those who had been located by subcontractors.

Major Doyle, despite having made a few bucks from *Oz*, hated Leo Singer. According to a tale related by John Lahr—and that sounds a little too good to be true—Doyle assembled his little people on a bus that would transport the group from New York to Los Angeles. On the way, Doyle asked that the bus be stopped outside of Singer's apartment, at Sixty-Eighth Street and Central Park West. Doyle asked the doorman to ring Singer and tell him to look out his fifth-floor window. When Singer did so, he was mooned by the major's midgets.

Little people in Singer's employ were encouraged to call him "the Boss" and "Papa Singer." If that sounds to you like condescending paternalism on Singer's part, you're on the right track. Singer probably enjoyed the informal relationships, but he was the undisputed keeper of the pocketbook. He may have been their "Papa," but he wasn't a particularly generous one.

Significantly, no request came from MGM for little people of color. At the time, blacks and Hispanics were scarcely acknowledged in mainstream movies, except in roles as maids, cooks, comic buffoons, or the occasional criminal. Producer Mervyn LeRoy never even entertained the notion. Given the tenor of the day, the presence of "colored" Munchkins would have been assumed to be a sure-fire way to kill the fantasy illusion of Munchkinland, and the ambience of the larger land of Oz. Hollywood, and the USA, still had a lot of growing up to do.

Little People

Nearly all of the Munchkins were portrayed by adult midgets (as distinct from dwarfs). The sort of human dwarfism most familiar to the lay public is achondroplasia, by which the person has an average-sized head (often with a prominent forehead) and chest, with the "long bones" of the arms and legs considerably shorter than the usual. Anomalous hips and inconsistent leg length may impair the gait. Hands are broad, with shortened fingers.

Midgets—who are more properly termed proportionate dwarfs—grow to adulthood with limbs proportionate to the rest of their bodies. Other than overall shortness of stature, midgets present to the layperson no obvious physical deviations from the norm, though the faces of many proportionate dwarfs are rounded and childlike. In strictly nonmedical shorthand, a midget is a miniature adult. Proportionate dwarfism is not a factor in longevity, or lack of it. People with the condition experience normal life spans.

Sincerely, The Doll Family
Tiny—Harry—Daisy—Grace

Lollipop Guild player Harry Earles (top) and his sisters (who also appear in *Oz*) were born in Germany and enjoyed long careers on America's circus and vaudeville circuits. Although Harry's real name was Kurt Schneider, he called himself Harry Doll when working in live venues. As Harry Earles, he made a powerful impression as the sympathetic star of *Freaks* (1932).

The term "midget" is now considered a pejorative. It came into common usage in the mid-19th century, derived from the word *midge* (a sand fly). The term entered conversation via popular literature and, especially, circus promoter P. T. Barnum, who featured a proportionate "midget" dwarf called General Tom Thumb (Charles Stratton) from 1843 to 1878. Tom enjoyed enormous popularity around the world, enchanting the public with his frankly doll-like appearance. (Tom became even more popular in 1863, after his well-publicized marriage to a proportionate dwarf named Lavinia Warren.) Tom Thumb reached his full height of 2'11" in 1862, when he was twenty-four years old.

Leo Singer worked primarily with midgets, calling his enterprise, alternately, the Singer Midgets and Singer's Midgets. Achondroplasiac dwarfs are relatively common today in movies and television (one, Peter Dinklage, is a bona fide star and sex symbol), but those toiling in show business in the '30s were seldom seen outside of carnivals and circuses. The public was most intrigued by proportionate dwarfs—hence the wealth of work in golden-age Hollywood for midgets.

"Pimping and whoring"

Once arrived in Los Angeles, the Munchkin players were quartered in two hotels, the wedge-shaped Culver, on Culver Boulevard; and the Adams, on Washington Boulevard. The greater number were lodged at the Culver. (The Adams was condemned in 1987 and razed a year later, but the Culver endures. In 1997, the Culver hosted a Munchkin reunion.)

Rehearsals began about a week after the November 11 arrival date. Singer was paid $100 a week per player; each player received $50 a week.

Most of the players were slated for "background" duty—standing, reacting, waving, and with a bit of dancing.

Charley Becker played the mayor. An erroneous story circulated by the Associated Press in 1984 reported the mayor's death. The deceased actor, though, wasn't Becker but a gentleman named Prince Denis. For years, Denis claimed to have played the mayor of Oz. Apparently, his actual role, as a sergeant-at-arms, didn't strike him as sufficiently prestigious.

A Munchkin woman, Hazel Derthick, was tall at 4′4″ and was still busy twenty years later as the stand-in for child actor Jerry Mathers, the star of TV's *Leave It to Beaver.*

Harry Monty did double-duty as a Munchkin and as a winged monkey. He later became a busy stunt double and played a variety of peculiar creatures on television's *H.R. Pufnstuf* and *Lost in Space.*

The average Munchkin weighed about fifty-five pounds. Heights varied, but most of the players were well below four feet. Besides Derthick, some of the taller players were Alta Stevens, who stood 4′5″, and Tommy Cottonaro, who was 4′6″. Many of the taller actors, twenty-five in all, were cast as the smartly marching soldiers.

Nearly all of the Munchkins were played by adult little people, but a handful hired to provide background were children of average size. Of that group, the names of three are known: Betty Ann Cain, Raynelle Lasky, and Priscilla Montgomery. Cain, under the name Betty Bruno, later became a TV news reporter in Oakland. While on-set, the children were tutored by a teacher named Mrs. Carter.

One midget player, ten-year-old Margie Raia, was asked to leave the lot because she was underage. MGM had found the average-sized children hired to play background Munchkins, and made separate contracts with their parents and guardians. Leo Singer, though, had been expected to provide adult players.

Margie's older brother, Matthew Raia, remained to play a Munchkinland city father. The Raias were Italian immigrants who played the carnival sideshow circuit, often for Cetlin & Wilson. A vintage photograph that includes Margie appears on the sleeve of the 1972 Rolling Stones LP *Exile on Main Street.*)

Another player, Elsie Schultz, left during filming because of injuries suffered in an auto accident.

"Little Billy" Rhodes, who co-starred as bad guy Bat Haines in *The Terror of Tiny Town* (1938), is the Munchkinland barrister. Rhodes was very busy in shorts and features throughout the 1930s. His film work fell off dramatically after 1945, but he remained active until 1966. Today, he's well known to comedy fans for a featured role, as a belligerent bellboy, with the Three Stooges in *You Nazty Spy!* (1940).

Many of the Munchkin players came from vaudeville, circuses, and carnivals, but some were showbiz neophytes. Ruth Duccini was just a teenager when she traveled from Minnesota to play a Munchkin villager. Before arriving at MGM, Ruth had never seen another little person. She was both startled and reassured by her revelation. Duccini left show business a few years after *Oz* and worked as a riveter during World War II. She said, "I could get in all the small places the bigger people couldn't get to."

English was not the first language of numerous Munchkins, many of whom had origins in France, Hungary, Czechoslovakia, Germany, Italy, and Russia. (In a turnabout, the very Germanic Meinhardt "The Coroner" Raabe was born not in Europe but in Wisconsin. He was, in fact, a twenty-three-year-old graduate of the University of Wisconsin—all $4'0''$ of him.)

Jack Haley recalled the Munchkin players in his memoirs: "Some of dem sang mit de Cherman agzent. They couldn't speak English and when they sang together it was the damndest conglomeration of noise you ever heard."

Day to day, assistants lifted some of the smallest Munchkin players on and off the toilet. According to a story told years later by Bert Lahr, one diminutive gentleman fell into the bowl. Columnist Hedda Hopper embellished the story, erroneously identifying the victim as midget actor Billy Curtis and claiming that singer-actor Nelson Eddy "saved him from drowning." In another column, Hopper reported that Curtis tried to "date up Judy Garland, but she prefers Jackie Cooper"—a clever way to do a favor for a juvenile actor whose star had faded.

At best, crew reaction to the Munchkin players was condescending. "Little dolls," "little toys," and "cute little things" were common judgments.

On off days, the Munchkins behaved as tourists would, hitting nightspots, taking day trips in the region, and visiting local landmarks. The filmmaking community was tightly knit and didn't react kindly to the little people, who were regarded as bizarre outsiders. The semi-literate Hedda Hopper stoked the fire (and probably began the "Munchkin menace" nonsense) in a piece published late in 1938. Working from puffery handed to her by MGM and, probably, her own imagination, she wrote, "On the *Wizard of Oz* set, they've added 50 school children to the 150 midgets, being sure the kids were the same size [as the little people]. Makes it mighty difficult for Miss Macdonald and her staff of school teachers, because the minute a scene is finished, they grab the kids for their lessons, and nine times out of 10, what they find on their laps is a midget." (As we've seen, only eight children played Munchkins, and the total number of little people amounted to fewer than 125.)

Later, still sucking at the MGM publicity teat, Hopper claimed that a studio receptionist who was puzzled by disembodied voices looked over her desk at "three midgets," and was horrified.

Much later, after *The Wizard of Oz* had grown into folklore and Judy Garland became a living legend, the star became an accomplished *raconteur*—never mind that not all of her stories were strictly true. She delivered one of her most infamous reminiscences in 1967, on *A Funny Thing Happened on the Way to Hollywood*, an NBC television special hosted by Jack Paar. Nearly thirty years after the *Oz* shoot, and for the edification of Paar and the audience watching at home, Garland pretended to have been horrified by the rambunctious Munchkins, who, she claimed, were collected each morning "in butterfly nets." Garland seems unusually garrulous and self-conscious during these remarks, smiling and laughing rather fiercely, and punctuating her words with sweeping gestures and vigorous movement of her head and upper body. She seems not only false but also desperate, as if the entire future course of her career depended on handing Jack Paar a juicy story. In the end, Garland did the Munchkins, and herself, a disservice.

A self-contained movie studio was a small place with an eagerness for gossip, and a tendency to make good stories better, and even to fabricate a story when there was really no story at all. This is the sort of insular culture that helped encourage Garland and LeRoy, years after the fact, to wax about marauding midgets.

John Lahr repeated the "pimping and whoring" part of the story in *Notes on a Cowardly Lion*, his 1969 biography of his father. In Mervyn LeRoy's ghosted 1974 memoir, *Take One*, the *Oz* producer talked about Munchkin "orgies," and historian Roland Flamini's 1975 history of the making of *Gone With the Wind* claimed that a laborious shoot of "Ding! Dong! The Witch Is Dead" had to be halted when somebody realized that the Munchkins were lustily singing "the bitch is dead." (Can this tale be supported following a moment's rational thought?)

A 1975 book about the Freed unit picked up the unwholesome theme, saying, "This unholy assemblage of pimps, hookers, and gamblers infested the Metro lot and all of the community." If these words were intended to demonize the little people and cast them as grotesque "others," the writers succeeded.

The fabrications were elaborated on by *Under the Rainbow*, a wretchedly unfunny 1981 comedy about a fellow hired by MGM to keep tabs on the randy Munchkins, only to run afoul of German spies. In just the most obvious of the film's many deviations from the truth, most of the movie's little people are achondroplasiac dwarfs rather than the proper proportionate dwarfs.

Babylon Heights, a 2006 play by British novelist Irvine Welsh (*Trainspotting*) and screenwriter Dean Cavanagh, revived the well-worn trope of Hollywood as a den of unavoidable sin, where the Munchkins were free to indulge their baser instincts. Striving to force dramatic emotion and thus suggest that all of us are little people at the mercy of large, unkind forces, the play limits itself to four characters, three men and a woman, who "swear, steal, fight, drink, and smoke opium" (quoting AP writer Jill Lawless, in her August 2006 review of the Dublin production). Inexplicably, the mixed-gender group has been quartered in a single hotel room, where tempers, regrets, and desires quickly boil over.

In interviews, Welsh demurred, saying that the play celebrates the strength and "self-reliance" of the marooned little people, but he gave implicit encouragement to journalists eager to resurrect the hoary, latter-day tales of Munchkin orgies and hostility. If *Babylon Heights* has a clever stroke, it's that the four little people are played by average-sized actors on oversized hotel and restaurant sets.

Munchkin "mischief" during *Oz* was about the same as one might expect from any troupe of grown-ups housed and working in close quarters. The little people were small, but they were grown-ups, with every virtue and vice of adulthood. Some of the players were couples with marital baggage. The troupe experienced some jealousies and some spats. Margaret Williams (later Margaret Pellegrini, and just fifteen years old when she did *Oz*) witnessed one midget husband pull a knife on his midget wife. (The incident is obliquely referred to in a December 30, 1938, interoffice MGM memo written by *Oz* production manager Keith Weeks.) Some little people at the Culver and the Adams got noisy inside their rooms, and were warned by management. Well, big people sometimes get noisy too. The difference is that not every big person is assumed to be a troublemaker.

The Munchkin and the Glamazon

Munchkin player Billy Curtis was a handsome man with an insatiable eye for the ladies, whether small, average, or even king-sized. In a January 1938 ceremony at Miami Beach, the 3′2″ Curtis married a 6′4″ bouncer/showgirl/stripper named Lois De Fee. (Columnist Walter Winchell dubbed De Fee "the Eiffel Eyeful.") According to the February 27 edition of the *Milwaukee Sentinel*, Curtis left beautiful, 3′4″ Olive Brasno in order to be with De Fee. Olive and Lois allegedly hurled insults at one another; as a *Sentinel* cartoonist imagined it, the exchange went like this:

> Olive: "You're a midget snatcher."
> Lois: "Can I he'p it if I love him?"
> Olive: "He was my man—and you done me wrong!"
> Lois: "Maybe, but I'VE GOT HIM!"

Meanwhile, Billy disappeared from the honeymoon suite and didn't return. Did he plan to pick up again with Olive? Or was the whole thing (as the unnamed *Sentinel* writer speculated) a publicity stunt? The article described this tangle of relationships as a "strange, by no means equilateral triangle," and then contradicted its own suspicions, quoting De Fee as saying that she "falls like nobody's business for little bitsy men, collapsing all in a heap." Further, one of De Fee's previous husbands (Billy Curtis was number three or number seven, accounts vary) was a jockey "whose head didn't come up to [De Fee's] shoulders." And Billy, although not with his bride, "pointed out, just before he went into hiding, [that] he is supporting her, and to back up that statement he exhibited two receipts for money orders he had sent her."

When the marriage was annulled a day or two after the ceremony, De Fee stopped playing coy. "It was just a stunt to get in the papers," she said. "We didn't—I mean, we were married at three o'clock in the afternoon in Miami, and the half pint took a plane for New York at seven o'clock in the evening, and we didn't—that is—oh, hell! We didn't."

Billy claimed to have sued for divorce, complaining to *Time* magazine, "She treated me like a doll."

Billy Curtis enjoyed a long and successful career. Other Munchkin players, though, were less versatile than he, and less committed to pursuing film work. As the Munchkinland shoot approached its end during the December 1938 holiday season, Judy Garland presented the little people with an enormous box of chocolates—a gift that was sweet in more ways than one, but hardly the gesture of one professional to a group of peers. Dorothy enjoyed the company of the Munchkin players, but everyone's relative position in the studio hierarchy was very clear to her.

Principal shooting on the Munchkinland set wrapped on December 30. After the first of the year, about twenty midget players worked, for two days, mainly on one scene: when the Munchkins excitedly chase after and wave goodbye to the departing Glinda.

A few of the Munchkins found immediate work at MGM and stayed on. Billy Curtis and others were cast as pygmies in director Richard Thorpe's *Tarzan Finds a Son!* (1939), the installment that introduced Johnny Sheffield as Boy. Jerry Maren was cast in an MGM Our Gang short, *Tiny Troubles* (1939), as Light-Fingered Lester, a criminal who joins Alfalfa's household when Alfalfa trades his annoying baby brother for another "child."

For many of the Munchkin players, *Oz* meant a lifetime of fame. Not all cared to exploit their participation, but those who did, and who enjoyed meeting fans, frequently appeared on the TV talk show circuit and at film conventions. With the advent of home video, some of the players appeared in "bonus" features. Munchkin players became familiar "talking heads" in *Oz* documentaries.

Miami residents reacted with amusement to the January 1938 wedding of diminutive Munchkin player Billy Curtis and 6′4″ showgirl Lois De Fee. Curtis was a known lady-killer, but this publicity-inspired union lasted barely forty-eight hours.

Movie Midgets Before *Oz*

The human fascination with physically anomalous people is ancient. Sometimes, people who did not look as others did were venerated as mystics and seers. Others, because of disease, quirks of birth, or local superstition, were shunned or driven from their communities or even killed. Photography, motion pictures, the circus, and a simultaneous burst of global exploration in the early 1900s exposed Westerners to unusual-looking people from earth's hottest and coldest climes, and everyplace in between. Documentarians Robert Flaherty and Merian C. Cooper startled movie audiences with epic narratives of Inuits and Bakhtiari Iranian nomads. For a while in the 1920s and '30s, public interest in so-called "Ubangi" women, with great discs inserted into their lips, and Padaung (Burmese) women with shoulders pushed downward by successively placed metal rings (giving the illusion of a very long neck), was practically a fad. Much fuss was also made about unusually tall Masai and other Africans, and "pygmies" from Africa, Papua New Guinea, South America, and elsewhere. The explorer-cartoonist Robert Ripley built an oddball empire founded largely on "strange" people. All of that, as well as postcards, *National Geographic* magazine (established in 1888), radio, and newsreels nursed public fascination with what many called "human oddities."

Little people of European origin attracted particular attention. Of course, midgets had appeared in Hollywood films prior to *The Wizard of Oz*. German-born Harry Earles (see "In Focus: The Men of the Lollipop Guild," this chapter) enjoyed a good film career in the 1920s and '30s, most famously in *Freaks* (1932).

A proportionate dwarf brother-sister vaudeville act, George and Olive Brasno, had been featured in a pair of Hal Roach's Our Gang shorts, *Shrimps for a Day* (1934) and *Arbor Day* (1936). In 20th Century-Fox's *The Mighty Barnum* (1934), George and Olive played real-life stars Tom Thumb and Lavinia Warren. Olive Brasno's husband, Gus Wayne, accepted work as a Munchkin, but Olive had to decline because of road obligations. (Ray Bolger had worked with midgets in vaudeville. Reminiscing about *Oz*, he recalled "a delicious-looking little woman named Olive." Some fans speculate that Bolger was referring to Olive Brasno. Although Brasno wasn't cast in *Oz*, it's possible that she visited her husband during the shoot.)

Tiny Lawrence and Clarence "Major Mite" Howerton played scowling, larcenous adults disguised as babies in another Our Gang comedy, *Free Eats* (1932). For additional laughs, their dialogue was dubbed by deep-voiced actors, and Howerton chewed a cigar. (Howerton was later cast in *Oz*, pulling double-duty as a Munchkin trumpeter and one of the sleepy-eyed "hatchlings.")

Before *Oz*, the most ambitious Hollywood use of proportionate dwarfs was producer Jed Buell's *The Terror of Tiny Town* (1938), a poverty-stricken novelty western with no novelty other than that the entire cast is comprised of midgets. Various of the players, including hero Billy Curtis, leading lady Yvonne Moray, and femme fatale Nita Krebs, appear in *Oz*. (Curtis went on to have a fruitful, nearly fifty-year career in films and television. He enjoyed some highlights, but the best was a heavily dramatic, co-starring role in Clint Eastwood's mystical 1973 western *High Plains Drifter*.)

And then there's actor Mickey Rooney (1920–2014), a longtime friend of Judy Garland, who enjoyed his first taste of stardom as a boy during 1927–34, when he headlined more than sixty "Mickey McGuire" comedy shorts for producer Larry Darmour. Because Rooney was tiny and precociously talented, some moviegoers were convinced that Mickey McGuire was a midget. Perhaps viewers got that impression because in his film debut, a pre-McGuire comic short called *Not to Be Trusted* (1926), young Mickey Rooney played . . . a midget.

In Focus: The Men of the Lollipop Guild

As arrayed on screen from left to right, the men of the Lollipop Guild are Jackie Gerlich, Jerry Maren, and Harry Earles. Although their voices were provided by Ken Darby and others, the actors make a wonderfully pugnacious impression, strutting to Dorothy with shoulder-rolling swagger and congratulating themselves after their greeting.

Jakob "Jackie" Gerlich (1917–60) was born in Vienna to Abraham Fuks and Regina Gerlich. He arrived in the United States in March 1936, with the sponsorship of impresario Leo Singer. Census records reveal that Jackie lived in Singer's home in Oakland, California, at about the time of *The Wizard of Oz*. Regina Gerlich, who came to the U.S. sometime between 1936 and 1940, lived in Los Angeles.

Jackie relocated to Tampa after *Oz* and performed with Florida-based Ringling Bros. and Barnum & Bailey circus during 1946–55. His Ringling personnel card describes him as a "clown-midget." Jackie's starting salary was fifteen dollars a week, but by 1955, he was earning sixty. A 1955 RB/B&B circus program identifies Jackie as being part of Clown Alley: "Merchants of Mirth, they'll trade you a bruise for a chuckle or a laceration for a belly-laugh."

Beginning in 1956, Jackie clowned for the Polack Bros. circus (sometimes known as the "Shriner Circus"), assisting popular clown Lou Jacobs in Jacobs's "Lunimobile" act.

Although Viennese by birth, Jackie held Polish citizenship. He never married.

Gerlich was a resident of Sarasota, Florida, when he died there on December 27, 1960.

Modest intrigue may surround Jackie. His brother, David Fox (who died in 2011), claimed that Jackie was born in 1925 as Leo Gerlich. Because Leo's parents wanted him to accept work with Leo Singer, they provided Singer with the birth records of an older brother, Jakob. According to this account, David and the true Jakob arrived in the United States in 1939, three years after Leo. David and Jakob changed their last name from Fuks to Fox; Leo, meanwhile, continued to pass as Jakob/Jackie.

Neither Leo's Ringling Bros. personnel card nor his death certificate note a Social Security number (the death certificate reads "UNKNOWN"), which lends some credence to David Fox's claim about fraudulent birth records.

Leo/Jackie's death was attributed to natural causes, but David insisted that his brother died after being given a doctored drink (a Mickey Finn) in a Sarasota bar.

At this writing, Lollipop Guild member **Jerry Maren** (b. 1920) is the last surviving Munchkin player. Because of his longevity, amiability, and long experience as a trained actor, Maren became one of the most successful and best-known Munchkin actors. He was born Gerald Marenghi in Roxbury, Massachusetts, near Boston, and began to train as a dancer before he was five years old. He became a handsome young man and worked as a comic dancer on the Massachusetts vaudeville circuit.

Maren settled in Hollywood in the 1930s and made his film debut in the famed "all-midget" western *The Terror of Tiny Town* (1938). He maintained an active movie career until 2010, working in pictures as diverse as *Superman and the Mole Men* (1951) and *Hello, Dolly!* (1968). Not unexpectedly, Maren was frequently cast for comic effect, as when he took the role of ventriloquist Edgar Bergen's dummy Charlie McCarthy (in "walking" long shots) in *Here We Go Again* (1942). He was Little Professor Atom in *At the Circus* (1939), a young ape in *Planet of the Apes* (1968), and a slick heist man in *Little Cigars* (1973). In *The Dreamer of Oz*, a 1990 TV-movie about L. Frank Baum, Maren was Mr. Munchkin. And, inevitably, he played a Munchkin in *Under the Rainbow* (1981).

There was plenty of work in television after 1950: *The Beverly Hillbillies*, *The Wild Wild West*, *Bewitched*, *Here's Lucy*, *Get Smart*, *The Odd Couple*, *The Gong Show*, *Seinfeld*, and many others. Jerry was a costumed regular on the Sid and Marty Krofft kiddie show *Lidsville*.

In between film and TV roles, Maren did radio and television spots as Buster Brown for Buster Brown shoes; traveled with the Wienermobile as Little Oscar for Oscar Meyer; and played Mayor McCheese in commercials for McDonald's.

Maren was a public face of *Oz* at innumerable conventions, awards ceremonies, and anniversary celebrations. On September 18, 2013, two days before the Hollywood IMAX premiere of *The Wizard of Oz 3D*, ninety-three-year-old Jerry Maren inscribed his signature, and left his handprints and footprints, in the forecourt of the renovated and newly named TCL IMAX Chinese Theatre. (A collective "Munchkins" star had been laid at the Hollywood Walk of Fame in 2007.)

Maren dramatically slowed the pace of his public appearances after his wife's death in 2010, but continued to make himself available to interviewers.

Over the years, Jerry gave honest accounts of *The Wizard of Oz*, neither inflating his own participation nor diminishing anybody else's. He became invaluable to film historians and was much beloved by local-TV news programmers that needed a sure-fire two-minute filler.

Maren's autobiography, *Short and Sweet*, was published in 2008.

And now, a change of pace. There is a moment in *The Unholy Three* (1925) in which a nattily dressed midget who is being taunted by a small boy rears back from his perch on a tabletop and savagely kicks the child flush in the face. Director Tod Browning intended the scene to shock, and he succeeded. Nearly ninety years later, this unexpected violence can extract gasps from audiences. The midget actor was Lollipop man **Harry Earles** (1902–85). Although he appeared in barely a dozen shorts and features between 1925 and 1939, his movie work is of special interest to historians.

Born in Germany as Kurt Schneider, Earles had eight siblings. Five were of average size, and the other three—Frieda, Hilda, and Elly—were proportionate dwarfs. In 1913, an American promoter named Burt Earles caught Kurt and Frieda's "Hans and Gretel" dance act. With Earles working as their manager, Kurt and Frieda (later named Gracie) settled in America and became featured dancers at Coney Island's Dreamland Circus sideshow. By 1920, Kurt and Frieda were performing as Harry and Grace Doll.

Siblings Hilda (Daisy) and Elly (Tiny) came to the States in 1925, and all four Dolls made good livings on the vaudeville stage and with the Ringling Brothers and Barnum & Bailey circus (where Harry's closest friend was Jack Earle, the sideshow's giant).

Harry and Daisy adopted the surname Earles for their screen work. Harry's first film, *The Unholy Three*, cast him as Tweedledee, one-third of a criminal group whose other members are a murderous strongman (Victor McLaglen) and a ventriloquist (Lon Chaney) who masquerades as an old lady. The plot machinations encompass Tweedledee in a baby carriage, rich people that buy talking parrots, and safes that beg to be cracked. *The Unholy Three* is unique, and alternately funny, absurd, and shocking.

Harry followed up with the expected turns as comic midgets in features and in shorts starring Our Gang and Laurel and Hardy. In 1930, he reprised his Tweedledee role in a talkie remake of *The Unholy Three*. This one was directed by Jack Conway rather than Tod Browning, and although less atmospheric than the original, it allowed Earles to use his German-accented English to bring a fresh dimension to the diminutive criminal. Most notably, the remake gave Chaney, who died later in 1930, his only role in a talking picture.

Not long after, Tod Browning and MGM story executive Irving Thalberg became excited about "Spurs," a short story by Tod Robbins about the hothouse atmosphere of a traveling circus. Browning directed the adaptation, to memorable effect, as *Freaks* (1932). Although frequently recalled as a horror film, *Freaks* is mostly about surrogate-family loyalty, which asserts itself when wealthy and lovestruck Hans (Earles) is slowly poisoned by his wife, Cleopatra (Olga Baclanova), an average-sized trapeze artist in league (and in bed) with the show's strongman, Hercules (Henry Victor). Hans ignores warnings from Frieda (Daisy Earles) and his other sideshow companions. After he's rescued by the other "freaks," Cleopatra and Hercules wish they'd never been born.

Harry Earles is sweet and touching as Hans. He's tiny but clearly a grown man; when he finally discovers what Cleopatra is up to, his tiny features scrunch into a storm cloud of fury. Earle's performance is both sympathetic and intimidating, and has real force.

Freaks was an MGM production, and the studio regretted it almost immediately. The story's revenge angle has a frankly grotesque resolution, and Browning's decision to use genuine sideshow oddities in his cast unsettled critics and audiences. Before *Freaks* had a real opportunity to show what it could do at the box office, MGM pulled it from distribution and subsequently handed the prints to small-time distributors for states-rights playdates as *Nature's Mistakes* and other titles.

Earles never again had a role as good. His next full-length movie, *The Wizard of Oz*, was his final screen work. (Sisters Daisy, Gracie, and Tiny are in *Oz*, too, as Munchkin villagers.) Harry Earles and the rest of the Dolls remained active in vaudeville and the circus, working for the Cristiani Brothers show before retiring to Florida around 1960.

In Focus: The Women of the Lullaby League

The petite ballerinas that greet Dorothy in Munchkinland were (from left to right on screen) Nita Krebs, Olga Nardone, and Yvonne Moray (Bistany). So charming are they that they've become the subjects of eagerly collected figurines, music boxes, and other latter-day *Wizard of Oz* merchandising.

Actress-dancer **Anna "Nita" Krebs** (1905–91) was born in Czechoslovakia to average-sized parents. The country was hit hard by World War I, and Nita's father, a shoemaker, bartered shoes for food. Nita studied ballet and sang in children's choruses before traveling to Prague, where she saw other little people for the first time.

Nita came to the United States around 1916 and later signed with promoter Leo Singer. She established herself on the Pantages vaudeville circuit as a glamorous specialty dancer, often doing modified ballet. In September 1934, she showed up in a widely published Wide World photograph, posing in a brief costume with the similarly attired 5′9″ Helene Hampton. Wide World's caption announces that Nita and Helene are among the contestants in the "American Beauty" pageant.

Nita made her film debut in *They Gave Him a Gun* (1937), an MGM vehicle for Spencer Tracy. After that, she co-starred as the dance hall seductress in producer Jed Buell's oddball "all-midget western," *The Terror of Tiny Town* (1938).

Nita was thirty-three and again associated with Singer when she worked on *Oz*. Just 3′8″, she was pretty and perfectly proportioned. Relative to her size, she was long-legged, so the ballerina role was ideal for her. She reappears a few minutes later as a Munchkin lady in green who exhorts Dorothy to "Follow the Yellow Brick Road!"

During the shoot, Nita and some other Munchkin players spent a free day exploring Forest Lawn cemetery, Glendale; at least one photo exists of Nita and three others standing before one of the famously ornate Forest Lawn monuments.

After *Oz*, Krebs returned to vaudeville as part of Nate Eagle's Hollywood Midgets, in an act called Tenee, Tiny, and Toni (Mary Burbach, Krebs, and Marie Wood). In 1946, Nita and two other Munchkin veterans, Billy Curtis and Jerry Maren, had bits in MGM's *Three Wise Fools*.

Nita built a home in Sarasota, Florida, in 1949, and retired there in 1960. She remained active as a hostess to tourists at the town's Circus Hall of Fame. In 1990, she was profiled by *St. Petersburg Times* columnist Rick Bragg in an article called "Little Women Look Back on a Lost World." It's a melancholy piece that notes how few little people remained in Sarasota, the former winter home of Ringling Brothers and Barnum & Bailey, and where many performers once spent the winter months.

Olga Nardone (1921–2010) was, like Nita Krebs, a vaudeville veteran with ballet experience. She was variously billed as Princess Olga and Little Olga, and sometimes worked as part of a dance duo with an average-sized male.

The Wizard of Oz is apparently Olga's only film. Very tiny at 3′4″, she was not only part of the Lullaby League but one of the first Munchkin villagers to greet Dorothy, as well as one of the just-hatched "Sleepyheads" (because Olga was one of the few who could fit into the prop nest).

Various MGM contract players visited (or were sent to) the Munchkinland set, where they were photographed for publicity purposes. One visitor was Myrna Loy, who was snapped as she greeted Olga.

Although very pleased later in life that she overcame her initial reluctance to audition for *Oz*, Nardone avoided public appearances in her later years and seldom consented to interviews. She passed away at home in Massachusetts in 2010, having outlived very nearly the entire *Oz* cast.

During the *Oz* shoot, publicity flaks at MGM dubbed **Yvonne Moray** (b. 1917; date of death is unknown) "the miniature Garbo." Greta Garbo was an MGM contract player, and one story, possibly apocryphal, holds that the great star went to the Munchkinland stage for a look at Yvonne. She got one and then left, apparently unimpressed.

Moray was indeed very pretty, but her film career was slight, with appearances in *Oz*, *The Terror of Tiny Town* (as the heroine), and a 1937 Vitaphone short called *Movie Mania*.

Show business occupied Moray for many years after *Oz*. Publicity described her as a "tiny, sugary comedienne" nicknamed Miss Dyna-Mite. Throughout the 1940s and '50s, Yvonne toured theaters and clubs in Los Angeles, Miami, and elsewhere, sometimes struggling to manage a full-sized stand-up bass and sometimes working as a foil to Jack E. Leonard and other comics.

In the spring of 1962, Yvonne headlined at Toledo, Ohio's Town House Motel. Newspaper ad copy promoted her as the "Smallest Girl Vocalist" and "RCA Recording Artist."

Yvonne did her fourth and final movie at about that time, *Confessions of an Opium Eater* (1962), a thriller with Vincent Price. Moray played Child, a tiny adult Chinese locked in a cage in San Francisco's Chinatown and left to starve. She explains to the astonished Price, "When wife dead, husband can marry again. They no kill us, just no give us food. If they kill, then our ghost would haunt always."

Yvonne had traveled a long way from Munchkinland.

Munchkin Masquerader

As MGM's *The Wizard of Oz* grew into something legendary, the occasional little person falsely claimed to have been a Munchkin. A 1989 AP story, for instance, reported that an Iowa native, 4'6" Dale Paullin, had played one of the Lollipop Guild. Paullin informed the reporter that he'd been recently hired to help promote a home video release of the "uncut" *Oz*. Trouble was, Paullin hadn't been a Lollipop kid, and isn't in *Oz* at all. Nevertheless, AP bought Paullin's story. But *Oz* historian Stephen Cox didn't bite, and neither did numerous surviving Munchkins that joined Cox within days of the story's publication to pronounce Mr. Paullin a fraud.

Many years later, in 2010, the by-now eighty-six-year-old Paullin was at it again. During an interview with Waterloo, Iowa, television station KWWL at Waterloo's Home Instead Senior Care, Paullin repeated his claim that he'd been a Lollipop Guild Munchkin. Then in 2013, Des Moines TV station WHO sent a crew to see Paullin at his residence, Villa del Sol Senior Center in Marshalltown. Paullin reiterated that he'd been a Munchkin and reminisced about chatting on-set with Judy Garland, but added that he had recently learned his footage had been cut from the final-release version of *The Wizard of Oz*. He wanted, he said, to make that clear.

During the 2013 interview, Paullin appears happy and active, using his feet to scoot himself along the hallways in his wheelchair and holding court in the nursing home dining room. Then, as confabulators will do, he gave himself away. He said he got his role after a friend had shown him a trade ad in 1938: Warner Bros. needed five hundred little people to play Munchkins. So young Dale hustled over to Warner and was cast. *Five hundred little people. At Warner Bros.* Well, that was two strikes, and who, really, had to hear a third?

Why did Paullin suddenly qualify his *Oz* claim by saying his part had been cut? By 2013, only two Munchkins were known to survive, and Paullin—according to every standard reference—was not one of them. With virtually no other Munchkins to provide figurative cover, Paullin tidied up his tale by invoking the cutting-room floor.

Paullin's further claim in the same 2013 interview, of having been a member of Henry Kramer's Hollywood Midgets in the late 1930s and '40s, cannot be confirmed—which isn't to say that Kramer never employed him; only that contemporaneous photos of the Kramer troupe that are available for examination do not include Paullin.

What is known is that Paullin starred in a perceptive and fascinating 1950 B-movie called *It's a Small World.* Just twenty-six at the time, Paullin (credited under a stage name, Paul Dale) is completely winning as an adult midget who struggles to find a place—and romance—in a big persons' world. The picture was sensitively directed by William Castle, who made his name a decade later as producer-director of *House on Haunted Hill* (1959), *The Tingler* (1959), *Thirteen Ghosts* (1960), and the best of the *Psycho* knockoffs, *Homicidal* (1961). *It's a Small World* was originally released by Eagle-Lion and became part of the Warner Bros. Archive Collection in 2010. The picture is the indisputable oddity of Castle's career and a splendid showcase for Paullin. That alone ought to be enough past glory for anybody.

Over the Rainbow and Beyond

The Score and Songs

The Wizard of Oz was awarded two Oscars: best song and best original score. The latter was shaped and supervised by Herbert W. Stothart, a skilled composer of programmatic music. The Oz score was his responsibility—that is, he was expected to deliver one—but he had some talented collaborators whose contributions have become a little obscured with time.

Stothart had two more 1939 film credits other than *The Wizard of Oz*, *Broadway Serenade* and *Balalaika. Broadway Serenade* was particularly demanding, requiring that Stothart function as composer and arranger of a music-heavy musical. Stothart's workload mandated that less highly regarded studio talents be assigned to provide helping hands on *Oz*. However, let's be clear that "less highly regarded" is no insult, but simply an acknowledgment of the highly stratified nature of studio-system rank. Stothart was higher in the pecking order than the men that assisted him on *Oz*, because the studio said he was.

Anonymous contributions to the *Oz* score were made by George Bassman (the cyclone sequence, the Haunted Forest, the Emerald City, and Dorothy's initial meetings with the Scarecrow, the Tin Woodman, and the Cowardly Lion), Robert Stringer (the poppy field), George Stoll (portions of the Munchkinland sequence, plus the Haunted Forest and the Emerald City) Murray Cutter (the muted brass and woodblocks of the Tin Woodman underscore), Ken Darby, and Paul Marquardt. The work of these gentlemen was in the nature of secondary compositions, arrangements, and orchestrations. "Secondary," though, isn't the same as "unimportant." Although the cyclone sequences lasts just ninety seconds on screen, George Bassman struggled with the sequence's underscore for three weeks and wasn't satisfied until his sixth version. Bassman scored the sequence for ninety instruments, including thirty violins. Naturally, an unusually large orchestra demanded complex scoring and arrangements. Bassman's ninety seconds of cyclone music filled about sixty score sheets. (For big-budget pictures at MGM, a fifty-piece orchestra was the norm, but *Oz*, on average, was a bit more modest, as Stothart scored a great deal of the music for fewer than forty instruments.)

In some instances, Stothart and others tackled the same sequence; he collaborated with Stoll and Bassman, for instance, on the score for Dorothy's first meeting with the Scarecrow and our heroine's later adventures in the Haunted Forest.

Stothart was a pragmatist as well as an artist: when Dorothy and her friends attempt to escape from the Witch's castle, the composer reused a cue from his 1938 score for *Marie Antoinette*.

Effective scores have repeated motifs designed to link sequences and remind listeners of particular characterizations. A good example is Stothart's ominous, seven-note "Witch's Theme" (do-do do-do do-do dooo), which is heard eleven times.

Because the background score of *The Wizard of Oz* helps create and reiterate the film's emotional coloring, viewers who are swept away by the story may hardly notice what Stothart and his collaborators created. With its echoes of Mendelssohn, Mussorgsky, and Schumann, the score is variously subtle and programmatic, reflective and insistent, soothing and jarring. Occasional snatches of popular songs are fun for people who catch them. It is a brilliant piece of work that will floor any music lover who listens carefully to it. (The score sounded particularly impressive during the October 2013 IMAX screenings of *Oz*.)

Roger Edens had overall responsibility for the film's vocal arrangements, but much of the day-to-day work was done by Ken Darby. Darby was particularly adept at audio manipulation during recording and playback. He created the deep voices of the Winkies by recording the vocals of baritone and bass singers at faster than normal speed. During normal-speed playback, Darby said, the voices "dropped a perfect fourth lower." (Darby himself provided the singing voice of the Munchkin mayor.)

In 1939, film credits weren't nearly as detailed and exhaustive as they are today. On *Oz*, Stothart was credited with "Musical Adaptation," while George Stoll is noted as "Associate Conductor." "Orchestral and Vocal Arrangements" were attributed to Bassman, Cutter, Darby, and Marquardt. None of this was especially illuminating to audiences then (or now), but it was sufficient to satisfy the studio's internal rules for on-screen acknowledgment.

During preproduction and postproduction recording sessions, Stothart and George Stoll alternated as conductors. Stoll (who often called himself Georgie Stoll) had been a violin prodigy who later played the instrument in vaudeville jazz bands in the 1920s and was named studio music director in 1937.

When Judy Garland and Mickey Rooney toured big-city theaters in support of *Oz* in 1939, the traveling orchestra was conducted by Stoll. (He later won an Oscar of his own, for his work on *Anchors Aweigh* [1945].)

In Focus: Herbert W. Stothart (1885–1949)

Like Max Steiner at Warner Bros., Milwaukee-born Herbert W. Stothart was identified with a single studio; in his case, MGM. Because Stothart died in 1949, before the final collapse of the studio system, he worked *only* at MGM, never having to freelance late in his career. Stothart was with the studio for twenty years, 1929–49. The only Stothart film work not done for MGM was the composer's first credit, a co-scoring job (with Vladimir Lurovski) on an important 1927 Soviet feature directed by Vsevolod Pudovkin and Mikhail Doller, *Konets Sankt-Peterburga* (*The End of St. Petersburg*).

Among Hollywood composers, Stothart is especially intriguing because his initial university training wasn't in music at all, but in history. He began to compose while at the University of Wisconsin and found his first successes with ambitious amateur stage productions. One of those was professionally staged in Chicago and was sufficient to propel Stothart into musical jobs in vaudeville and the legitimate stage. While still in his twenties, Stothart was hired by stage composer Rudolf Friml and lyricist Oscar Hammerstein II to be the traveling musical director of *High Jinks*. Throughout most of the 1920s, Stothart learned the nuts and bolts of composing by assisting Vincent Youmans and other established composers. Stothart wrote some original pieces in the early 1920s and gradually increased his output. His high-profile contributions to *Rose-Marie* (with Friml) and *Song of the Flame* (with George Gershwin) brought Stothart the weight he needed for an invitation by MGM to come west.

Stothart became MGM's leading composer for varied reasons. He was a competent manager, which was vital in the collaborative environment of movies. He was a splendid, emotionally charged melodist, and he felt comfortable providing musical ideas for a variety of genres and periods. He also had a grasp of the realities of the Hollywood film business: whenever asked to compose a bit of new melody to be incorporated with existing stock music (in other words, patchwork composition), Stothart fell to the task. He subsumed a bit of ego in order to please producers and the front office, and meet whatever small challenge the assignment demanded.

Stothart favored 19th- and 20th-century Romantic composers, particularly Chopin (whose brilliant use of melody appealed to him) and Mussorgsky (whose dark bombast thrilled Stothart); echoes of their work can occasionally be heard in Stothart's film scores. Stothart also was fond of Tchaikovsky, whose preoccupation with musical melancholia informed Stothart's work.

Another Romantic, Robert Schumann, particularly appealed to Stothart because of Schumann's emotional range: turbulent in one piece and sweetly contemplative in another.

Before *The Wizard of Oz*, Stothart wrote and supervised significant scores for *Rasputin and the Empress* (1932), *Viva Villa!* (1934), *Treasure Island* (1934), *David Copperfield* (1935), *Mutiny on the Bounty* (1935), *San Francisco* (1936), and *Marie Antoinette* (1938).

In February 1939, Stothart unwittingly made himself a pawn in David O. Selznick's push for composer Max Steiner to complete the score of *Gone With the Wind*. Selznick felt that Steiner was being pokey, so he secretly commissioned Franz Waxman to get to work on a *GWTW* score, too. Selznick reasoned that if Steiner were unable to deliver, Waxman's score would save the day. Stothart didn't know about Waxman's involvement, but he was aware of Steiner's deadline, and lobbied

Selznick for the *GWTW* assignment. Selznick was noncommittal, but Stothart, whom *GWTW* historian Roland Flamini described as "not exactly the soul of discretion," loudly announced that he had been commissioned to bring his talents to *GWTW*. That was sufficient to spur Steiner, who sped up his output and delivered one of cinema's most memorable scores.

Post-1939, Stothart wrote effective scores for *Ziegfeld Girl* (1941), *National Velvet* (1944), *The Picture of Dorian Gray* (1945), *The Yearling* (1946), and *The Three Musketeers* (1948).

Since Stothart's death, his music and songs have been adapted for use in some sixty feature films and TV shows, more than half of those instances coming after 1990. In recent years, his work has been heard in a diverse bunch of films and TV series that includes *Queer as Folk*; *Sky Captain and the World of Tomorrow*; *Girl, Interrupted*; and *Wreck-It Ralph*.

Freed and Harburg: A Partnership for the Ages

Associate Producer Arthur Freed's experience as a successful theater and movie lyricist encouraged Mervyn LeRoy to cede some of his producer's power to Freed with regard to the songs and the songwriters. Freed recognized music's potential uses in film and was open to fresh ideas, not just melodically and lyrically, but in the way songs might be used to delineate character and propel a story. In such matters of narrative, Freed's indulgence allowed lyricist E. Y. "Yip" Harburg to become a major force behind *The Wizard of Oz*.

Naturally enough, Freed had a special interest in who might write the lyrics for the *Oz* songs. Yip Harburg had successfully partnered with songwriter Jay Gorney on Broadway revues in the very early 1930s, and later made a name in Hollywood, working with numerous melodists (see "In Focus: E. Y. 'Yip' Harburg," this chapter). Like a lot of other industry people, Arthur Freed had been impressed by Gorney and Harburg's "Brother, Can You Spare a Dime," a showstopper of a tune from a 1932 revue called *Americana*. Harburg's lyrics were heart wrenching.

Harburg responded positively when Freed felt him out about becoming involved with *The Wizard of Oz*. Harburg hadn't been offered a contract yet, but he began to think about songwriters who might be congenial fits for him, and for *Oz*. He'd already worked with a top songwriter, Harold Arlen. Harburg and Freed were well aware of Arlen's gift for melody, but there were other melodists in town, and Harburg wasn't entirely sure that the *Oz* melodies had to come from Arlen. After additional thought, Harburg remembered how well he and Arlen had fed off each other during their first collaboration, a successful 1934 Broadway revue called *Life Begins at 8:40*. During that job, they worked together almost instinctively—suggesting, adding, and building.

Freed liked Arlen's work and could envision a successful collaboration with Harburg. Still, Freed mulled over other teams, including Al Dubin and Nacio Herb Brown; and Jerome Kern and Ira Gershwin/Dorothy Fields. Kern, though, was recovering from a heart attack and was unable to take on a major assignment. Then there were Mack Gordon and Harry Revel, who had done three songs for *Love Finds Andy Hardy* while on loan from 20th Century-Fox. A March 17, 1938, studio press release announced that that team had been hired for *The Wizard of Oz*, but the announcement was premature and erroneous.

The April 18, 1938, edition of *Daily Variety* tabbed Dubin and Brown, on loan from Warner Bros., as the *Oz* songwriters. This made sense because Brown, a lyricist, had been Arthur Freed's songwriting partner. However, Dubin and Brown did no work on *Oz*.

Most of the major songwriters in town wanted the job. In the end, Freed went with Arlen and Harburg because he trusted Harburg's judgment about Arlen, and because Freed had enjoyed the light whimsy of one of the pair's songs, "In the Shade of the New Apple Tree," from a successful 1937–38 anti-war stage musical, *Hooray for What!* The Arlen-Harburg team was signed on May 3,

E. Y. "Yip" Harburg wrote beautiful lyrics to Arlen's melodies and contributed mightily to the *Oz* script, too.

1938, with a fourteen-week guarantee at $25,000, with one-third of that amount an advance on songwriting royalties.

Arlen and Harburg got to work on May 9, 1938, working from a solo screenplay draft by Noel Langley. (Ryerson and Woolf wouldn't be hired to do rewrites until June.)

Although Hollywood treated screenwriters with indifference or outright contempt, songwriters fared a little better, probably because the nature of their work eliminated the need for addle-brained executives to have to *read* anything. The bosses could just listen and then pronounce aye or nay. As in any business, real power in Hollywood was awarded to executives, schmoozers, salesmen, and dealmakers. "Creatives" were regarded as 1) necessary evils and 2) chattel. During the studio-system era, songwriters had little power. They performed work for hire. If a song was liked by the front office, it became studio property.

Well versed in Hollywood's frequent ill treatment of the people that did the heavy creative lifting, Harburg nevertheless focused on the assignment, and pushed for an "integrated score." Instead of the story simply stopping dead so that somebody could do a song, or a musical dance number, Harburg favored tunes and lyrics that related to the story directly, and not merely in matters of tone or setting. Harburg believed it was important that songs elaborate on plot and character points that had already been established, and that the songs actively move the story forward. The Broadway production of Kern and Hammerstein's *Show Boat* had been executed in this way, and there had been some film musicals, too (such as *Love Me Tonight* and *High, Wide, and Handsome*), that followed that template.

The melodist, Arlen, worked out chords and progressions at the piano. When Arlen had a melody, he played it for Harburg over and over. Harburg absorbed the notes, and soon, as Harburg once explained, he "could hear words."

The pair decided to tackle the lighter tunes first—the ones referred to by Arlen as "lemon-drop songs." Into this group, he and Harburg included what they called "Ding! Dong! The Witch Is Dead" and "We're Off to See the Wizard." The first song they completed, though, was the lightest of the light, "The Jitterbug," which was finished in May.

Early June brought "If I Only Had a Brain" ("a Heart"/"the Nerve"). The melody came from "I'm Hanging On to You," a song that had been dropped from the team's 1937 show *Hooray for What!* The opening bars recall the melody of Harburg's 1930 Broadway tune "C'mon Get Happy," and then segue into a very strong, four-note motif, with an extended hold on the third note.

At 101 minutes, *The Wizard of Oz* is of standard length for an "A" picture of the period. The studio had feared that if the film ran longer, it would cause children in the audience (and MGM expected a lot of children) to grow restless. Unusually long pictures meant fewer showings per day, which cut into box-office receipts. With overall running time in mind, some of the Arlen-Harburg songs, or specific performances of them, were discarded. Dorothy's reprise of "Over the Rainbow" was cut; likewise, a post-melting reprise of "Ding! Dong! The Witch Is Dead" (which incorporated "We're Off to See the Wizard"). A reprise of "The Merry Old Land of Oz" was axed, and the now-legendary "Jitterbug" sequence was eliminated altogether.

Arlen and Harburg did some work on something called "Horse of a Different Color" before abandoning it. The first Emerald City sequence already had plenty of music, and another tune just wasn't needed. A protracted version of "Lions and Tigers and Bears" never developed very far; likewise, a full-song version of "We're Out of the Woods."

Harburg deftly inserted lyrics. By late June, the complex Munchkinland song-and-dialogue sequence had been written. As per Arthur Freed, Yip Harburg enjoyed considerable freedom here, writing not just song lyrics but a great deal of the dialogue that surrounded and connected the tunes. These songs, not all of which made the film's final cut, helped delineate character and push the narrative forward: "Come Out, Come Out, Wherever You Are," "It Really Was No Miracle," and "Ding! Dong! The Witch Is Dead," plus the "We Welcome You to Munchkinland" sentiment warbled by the Lullaby League, the Lollipop Guild, and the Mother Goose League.

"We're Off to See the Wizard" (which includes a "Follow the Yellow Brick Road" refrain written by Freed) was to be reprised during the poppy field sequence. Instead, Arlen, Harburg, and Herbert Stothart wrote a new song, a brief choral piece called "Optimistic Voices." By telling Dorothy and her friends that they are "out of the dark," the Voices mark a clear transition to the next phase of the narrative. (If the interlude has a problem, it's that the precisely harmonized, syncopated female vocals now sound dated.)

Swatting "The Jitterbug"

Entire sequences cut from movies are sometimes unintentionally referenced in dialogue or visuals that remain in the final cut. In the case of the discarded "Jitterbug" number from The Wizard of Oz, the clue comes in the Witch's castle, when she instructs her winged monkeys to capture Dorothy and Toto, and waylay Dorothy's friends. As the monkeys begin to fly off, the Witch says to Nikko, the monkeys' captain, "They'll give you no trouble, I promise you that. I've sent a little insect on ahead to take the fight out of them." Many people have seen Oz dozens of times without registering that line.

As shot by Victor Fleming, Dorothy and the others grow wary as they move deeper into the Haunted Forest. They call for Glinda, who provides the group with an oversized insect spray gun, an enormous monkey wrench, and a butter-fly net (these burlesque-style props must have tickled Bert Lahr). The principals begin to sing when they hear a peculiar buzzing sound, and in a moment the pesky, pink-and-blue bug (which was to have been cartoon animation) appears. (While writing "The Jitterbug," Harburg found inspiration for the song's frantic pace in the aggressive bees of Baum's novel.) The song's tempo increases, the weapons are forgotten, and the characters' dancing becomes increasingly energetic. Lahr is particularly animated. Even nearby trees bend and sway to the rhythm, clapping their branchy "arms" and "hands."

The dance combines a linked-arm roundelay and more traditional jitterbug styles; in an especially amusing bit, Dorothy dances with the Scarecrow, while the Lion and the Tin Woodman pair off to do the same.

A version of the tune specially recorded for release on record runs about 3:30; the early portion of this recording includes the principals' vocals, but then moves into an up-tempo instrumental lasting from 2:05 to 3:28. In the discarded film footage, the characters speak to each other throughout the dance, and even engage various talking trees in conversation. Internet sources claim that the trees pass Toto back and forth, but in the only surviving footage of the sequence—silent, color home-movie footage of a dress rehearsal shot by composer Harold Arlen—there is no evidence of that. (The public saw Arlen's amateur footage for the first time on an October 1983 broadcast of *Ripley's*

The on-set still photographer captured this image of Dorothy and her friends as they await the arrival of the Jitterbug, the pesky menace sent by the Wicked Witch. The lively song-and-dance sequence was shot but later discarded.

Believe It or Not. Since 1989, the snippet has been a staple "extra" of *Wizard of Oz* home-video releases.)

The sequence ran about six minutes as filmed and ate up five weeks during its rehearsal and shoot. It cost between $80,000 and $100,000, but wasn't well received at an early preview (probably San Bernardino or Pomona). Audience taste, then, helped lessen the financial sting.

There is an enduring rumor about "The Jitterbug" and Bert Lahr, and it goes like this: The song was cut because the sequence allowed Lahr to dominate Judy Garland and steal the whole interlude. Nothing in the Arlen home movie suggests that Lahr would have had an opportunity to do that, and if Victor Fleming had seen such a thing coming, he would have spoken with Lahr and adjusted the sequence.

The "Jitterbug" sequence is lively and imparts a sense of fun, but it stops the story's forward momentum cold, and unwisely lightens the tone of what should be a grim situation.

Further, with its syncopated swing tempo, the song is obviously a product of the late 1930s. (According to *Merriam Webster's Collegiate Dictionary*, the word "jitterbug" dates to 1938.) Yip Harburg recalled later that there was some fear that the number might date the film, but that sounds like hindsight. The real issue may simply have been that the number was a mere diversion that wasn't integral to the plot. If the song sequence had been retained in the final cut, it would have been the only *Wizard of Oz* element we'd hesitate to call "timeless."

"Over the Rainbow"

Freed grasped the potential difficulty faced by his songwriters, and was particularly preoccupied with the challenge of a narrative song to set up the transition from Kansas to Oz. He depended on Arlen and Harburg to develop a suitable tune. But the songwriters had doubts of their own. They knew that this would be the picture's central ballad, and was vital not just to the establishment of a central theme, but also to the movie's commercial prospects.

The song that became "Over the Rainbow" was the last one tackled by the songwriting team. Arlen was on a drive with his wife along Sunset, and asked her to pull into the parking lot of Schwab's drug store. A melody had come to him, a melody with the sort of "long, broad line" he'd been trying to conjure. He wrote it out and immediately felt good. He later recalled, "It was as if the Lord said, 'Well, here it is, now stop worrying about it!'"

When Arlen played the melody for his collaborator the next day, he did so with a lot of flourishes. Harburg felt the melody was too "big" for a youngster. But when Arlen played it for famed lyricist Ira Gershwin, he played more simply. Gershwin loved the melody and insisted that it be part of the film. Although he had no official role with the *Oz* project, Ira Gershwin carried enough professional weight to sway Arlen and Harburg's opinions.

The "Over the Rainbow" melody was nearly done, but the tune lacked a bridge. With Harburg giving encouragement, Arlen began to whistle in the manner he whistled for his dog, Pan. Very shortly, he had the melodic line that Harburg later augmented with the words, "Someday I'll wish upon a star."

As the lyricist, Harburg had to express various aspects of Dorothy's character and longings, *and* provide a philosophical and emotional bridge connecting Kansas to Oz. That challenge to Harburg's ability was made greater because the lyrics had to avoid adult longings and adult reasoning. Dorothy isn't a sophisticated character from one of the Arlen-Harburg Broadway musicals, but an untutored girl with a girl's dreams.

After Yip Harburg had a good handle on the lyrics, he wanted to call the song "Over the Rainbow Is Where I Want to Be." The shorter final title came about, in part, because Harburg got hung up on Dorothy's eagerness to escape "someday." Harburg played with the first two notes of Arlen's melody: "I'll go-o-o . . ." and "Some-daay" were two lyric ideas that Harburg came up with and then decided he didn't care for. It was when he stopped thinking about Dorothy's interest in *when* and concentrated alternatively on *where* that he came up with "Some-where. . ."

With the notion of a *place* in hand, Harburg had a plan when he wrote the Aunt Em–Dorothy dialogue exchange that leads into the song. Aunt Em impatiently urges Dorothy to "find yourself a place where you won't get into any trouble!" Dorothy wonders aloud, "Some place where there's no trouble. Do you think there is such a place, Toto?" A moment later, the music bed for "Over the Rainbow" comes up, and Dorothy sings.

During a talk he gave many years later, Harburg remarked, "You always have trouble writing a ballad. Of course, I was writing for a situation of a little girl who was desperate, had never seen anything beyond an arid Kansas where there was no color in her life. It was all brown and sepia, and at a moment when she was troubled in a childish way, she wanted to escape, in a song of escape—where could she go? The only colorful thing that she's ever seen in her life was the rainbow."

The Baum novel makes no mention of rainbows. Instead, the book describes "bright sunshine" that floods Dorothy's room after the house has landed in Oz.

The song's lyrics had a resonance in 1939 that may elude contemporary fans. When Harburg was tasked to find words for Arlen's melody, America was still gripped by the Depression. Enormous rural areas had withered beneath the failed economy and unprecedented drought. Harburg began to think about the drabness of Kansas and the plain, exhausted faces of the people that lived there. He also was compelled to reconsider his early life in New York's slums, where he perpetually longed for light that would allow him to fly away and escape, as on a rainbow . . .

Melodically and lyrically, "Over the Rainbow" was a titanic, yet beautifully simple, achievement. Judy Garland and Roger Edens loved it immediately, but various MGM executives still had to be convinced. The music division's executive producer, Sam Katz, told Louis Mayer, "This score ["Rainbow"] is above the heads of children." Jack Robbins, chief of MGM's music publishing, grumped, "Why, it's like a child's piano exercise. Nobody will sing it! Who'll buy the sheet music?"

Further, some on the lot were disposed to take exception to Arlen and Harburg's working methods. Unlike some other MGM songwriters, neither Arlen nor Harburg was a nine-to-five kind of guy. The two often worked together at night, and frequently in the home of one or the other. Fortunately, Freed's

The soaring melody and sensitive lyrics of Arlen and Harburg's "Over the Rainbow" established a great deal about Dorothy and set the tone for her adventure. The song functions not simply as a piece of music but as an integral part of the story. Some MGM executives claimed to dislike "Over the Rainbow" and nearly succeeded in permanently banishing it.

musical background encouraged him to squash objections to the team's schedule. He knew that musical inspiration often struck at unconventional hours and places. When asked about "Over the Rainbow" years later, prolific songwriter Harry Warren confirmed that Freed grasped the occasionally non-linear creative process.

Louis Mayer was fine with Arlen and Harburg's way of working, but the steady drumbeat of executive objections to "Rainbow" began to wear on him and he wavered. After listening to the song during the movie's first preview, Mayer said "Over the Rainbow" should go. Suddenly, Mayer had even more supporters than before, including numerous MGM producers eager to assure Mayer that he was right. However, their support was grounded in ignorance (Harry Warren once complained that producers "ordered a song like they were ordering a steak dinner") and grounded in studio politics and the taint of self-interest, too. Some producers that had been on the lot long before Mervyn LeRoy regarded him as an interloper—not least because LeRoy was smart and talented, and thus a threat to them. Fueled by jealousy and insecurity, and bent on undercutting LeRoy, the anti-"Rainbow" faction clamored to Mayer that the notion of an MGM leading lady singing "in a barnyard" was, at the least, unseemly. Some said that the idea was completely outrageous.

Arthur Freed was adamant in his defense of the song. He told Mayer, "The song stays, or I go. It's as simple as that." Although a freshly minted executive, Freed had gifts that were plain for Mayer to see. "Over the Rainbow" was reinstated.

Judy did the soundtrack recording of "Over the Rainbow" on October 7, 1938, a full five months before she and director King Vidor would shoot the accompanying scene.

On October 11, Judy got together with Ray Bolger, Bert Lahr, and Buddy Ebsen (the first actor cast as the Tin Woodman) to record the soundtrack version of "We're Off to See the Wizard." In the completed film, whenever Dorothy sings the song with her three friends, or when the friends sing it as a trio, you are listening to the voice of Buddy Ebsen. Buddy's replacement, Jack Haley, recorded "We're Off to See the Wizard" just once, when the Tin Woodman sings it with Dorothy and the Scarecrow.

"We're Off to See the Wizard" and "Over the Rainbow" were particularly popular in Australia, which is located so far from Europe and America that it's "somewhere over the rainbow." Further, the familiar "Aussie" nickname was pronounced "Ozzie," and Australians began to refer to their nation as Oz. (The designation was eventually picked up by Hollywood trade publications, and to this day, movie news from Australia comes from "Oz.") During World War II, "We're Off to See the Wizard" was frequently sung by Australian troops as they marched into battle.

Judy's Oz Recording Sessions

Soundtrack recording sessions are an invisible but vital part of the progress of a movie musical. They can be time-consuming, and often overlap with singers' scheduled times to be on-set before the cameras.

This log of Judy Garland's recording-studio activity gives a suggestion of just one of the many *Oz*-related demands that were placed on her.

September 20, 1938

"We're Off to See the Wizard" (duo with Ray Bolger)
"We're Off to See the Wizard" (trio, with Bolger and Buddy Ebsen)
"We're Off to See the Wizard" (quartet, with Bolger, Ebsen, and Lahr)

October 6, 1938

"The Jitterbug" (with Buddy Ebsen)

October 7, 1938

"Over the Rainbow"

October 11, 1938

"We're Off to See the Wizard" version 1 (alternate lyrics)
"We're Off to See the Wizard" version 2 (alternate lyrics)
"We're Off to See the Wizard" version 3 (alternate lyrics)
"If I Were King of the Forest"

October 16, 1938

"The Wind Began to Twitch"

October 17, 1938

"Over the Rainbow" (reprise; cut from film)

October 30, 1938

"The Merry Old Land of Oz"

December 22, 1938

"Follow the Yellow Brick Road"/"We're Off to See the Wizard"
"The Jitterbug" (with Jack Haley replacing Ebsen; revised opening)

December 28, 1938

"The Merry Old Land of Oz"
"The Merry Old Land of Oz" (alternate take)

January 3, 1939

"The Merry Old Land of Oz" (alternate take)

February 28, 1939

"If I Only Had a Brain"

Songs as Story

Fleming told Harold Arlen that Dorothy should depart Munchkinland with a song. With that directive, Arlen and Harburg created "Follow the Yellow Brick Road."

"Over the Rainbow" and "Follow the Yellow Brick Road" do not cause the film's action—or story—to stop in its tracks. To the contrary, Arlen and Harburg designed songs that were vital to the story and necessary to its forward momentum. Their songs were integral parts of the narrative. Before *The Wizard of Oz*, most Hollywood musicals had treated songs as "showpiece" numbers, by which the singer (perhaps accompanied by other singers) exited the plot to perform numbers that had been designed not for story purposes, but to dazzle audiences and ensure heavy sales of sheet music. *Oz* changed all of that (though "Over the Rainbow" became a sheet-music favorite).

Contributing screenwriter Noel Langley was confident in Arlen and Harburg's abilities. He knew that they had been asked to expand the screenplay. These were not just songs; these were *story*. Langley wrote later, "The basic laws of genuine fantasy are far more rigid than the laws that govern an ordinary screenplay, and *The Wizard of Oz* gained its indestructibility by adhering to these laws. As Harburg and Arlen accepted this assignment, I had no fears. Less experienced men might well have tried to reduce the movie to a 'whimsy' level. Any kind of patronizing condescension in tone, *even unintentional*, is fatal to a project of this nature. Fantasy must appeal to the adults in all children, and the child in all adults."

Langley had already written books designed for children, but now he wanted a layered sort of whimsy that would engage adults as well as children. He was coming very close to achieving that with the characterizations suggested by his early drafts, and he knew the songs must do the same. Yip Harburg's way with lyrics was dazzling—sophisticated yet universal; thoughtful yet rooted in honest emotion. He gave audiences a lot to enjoy: the Scarecrow's "riddle" and "individdle," and the Lion's "elephant" and "cellophant." Kids loved the anarchic sound of the made-up words; adults were taken with the rhymes' ingenious charm.

Yip Harburg used carefully chosen lyrics to tell rich stories, and establish characterizations, within the confines of songs. He was in every sense a writer, and in fact contributed to the *Oz* script proper after Victor Fleming was brought aboard, but before Fleming hired screenwriter and script doctor John Lee Mahin. Harburg contributed whole passages of dialogue and wrote virtually all of the "awards" sequence, one of the film's funniest and most touching. Dorothy's friends get what they think they need (brains, a heart, courage), when, of course, they had those qualities all along. (Example: In the Witch's castle, it is the supposedly foolish Scarecrow who eyes the rope leading to the heavy chandelier and swings the Tin Woodman's axe sharply into it.)

The undercurrent of the awards sequence is subtly clever, implying issues of perception—not simply one's own perceptions, and the perceptions of others, but the ways in which perception can be manipulated, for trickery (the technical fakery that creates the blazing Wizard head) and for kindness (the redundant awards). Our reactions to the presumed reality of the world and ourselves, Harburg was telling us, are frequently misapprehended. In a moment that was cut from the final film, the Wizard has handed out the awards, and then amazes the group by pulling a chicken from thin air. The Wizard explains, "The chicken was always there. All I did was make you see it."

What Oz Owes to *Show Boat*

Many industry insiders assumed that MGM's *Wizard of Oz* would utilize the songs from the 1902–03 stage musical. But LeRoy and Freed realized that those tunes could not be easily integrated into their vision of the narrative. And as we've seen, they wanted a new sort of "narrative" song. The 1939 *Oz* made brilliant use of that tack, but it wasn't the first film to do so. The big breakthrough had been made on stage by *Show Boat*, the smash 1927 Broadway musical with songs by Jerome Kern and Oscar Hammerstein II. This stirring, very emotional story of forty years on a Mississippi River showboat concerned itself with a love story that turns tragic because of racial attitudes, particularly what used to be called "miscegenation." That in itself is sufficient to mark *Show Boat* as a theater revelation, but on top of that were more than twenty highly melodic and emotional songs *that helped to tell the story*. Some, like "Can't Help Lovin' Dat Man," "Ol' Man River," and "Make Believe," have become much-loved standards. Others, such as "Cap'n Andy's Ballyhoo," "You Are Love," and "Bill" (originally written by Kern and P. G. Wodehouse in 1917, for *Oh, Lady! Lady!*) are alternately lively and heart-rending.

A part-talkie 1929 film adaptation from Universal told the story from Edna Ferber's source novel, but took almost nothing from the Broadway adaptation. Universal tried again—this time adapting Kern and Hammerstein—in 1936, with a *Show Boat* that thrilled movie audiences and was one of Universal's greatest popular and "prestige" successes of the 1930s.

MGM looked at the film's success with not a little envy—and some surprise, as well, because Universal was (along with Columbia and RKO) one of the "minor majors." It wasn't in the same league as MGM, but it had trumped the bigger studio with a fresh, new sort of musical that was adored by audiences. *Show Boat* helped to greenlight the narrative song style of *The Wizard of Oz*.

Side note: Rights to the Universal version were purchased by MGM in the 1940s because Louis Mayer planned a remake to star Jeanette MacDonald and Nelson Eddy. In order to build anticipation, and to encourage the public to "forget" the earlier film, MGM kept the Universal version out of circulation. Although the MacDonald-Eddy version of *Show Boat* never happened, MGM continued to keep the Universal adaptation buried, and then finally produced its own in 1951. This was a splashy Technicolor experience with pleasing texture, a wooden leading man (Howard Keel), and a lot of heart, particularly from Ava Gardner as the tragic Julie. This *Show Boat* was a box-office hit—one of the last engineered at MGM by Mayer, who had lost touch with the postwar audience expectations and was forced out of his job in the spring of 1951.

In Focus: Harold Arlen (1905–1986)

Harold Arlen was a writer of sophisticated melodies that, in form and length, defined songwriting conventions of the day. Yet he was an obvious cut above many of his contemporaries. Listeners often could not tell where Arlen's melodic lines were going. His musicality simply couldn't be anticipated. A listener would expect a bridge, for instance, but the bridge might be postponed. You might wait for a melodic phrase to be repeated *here*, only to be pleasantly surprised when it did not, and a new musical idea was introduced instead. (George Gershwin, remarking on Arlen's "Stormy Weather," was struck by this aspect of Arlen's work.)

During the post–World War I era, Tin Pan Alley encouraged an inoffensive predictability in popular music, but Arlen saw himself as better than that. In his inventiveness, and the intellectualism that informed his personal life as well as his work, he was more akin to a classical composer than a movie-studio employee who labored for a salary. Arlen invariably gave more than what was expected.

As a young man in show business during the 1920s, Harold Arlen was pulled and motivated by his two greatest talents: singing and songwriting. Because he wanted to be the best at whatever he did, Arlen knew he had to concentrate on just one of his vocations. Although Arlen was a singer of professional caliber, with aspirations to become a jazz vocalist, songwriting won out. His true course became clear to him in 1930 when he wrote a sprightly melody that Ted Koehler filled with words and called "C'mon, Get Happy." (Ruth Etting popularized the tune in a Broadway musical called *The Nine-Fifteen Revue*.) From that time, and for the next thirty years, Arlen penned the melodies of hit after hit. He was one of the greatest American songwriters of the 20th century.

His ear as both singer and songwriter arose mainly from two influences: Jewish liturgical singing and (a bit later in his life) black American musical tradition. As Hyman Arluck, the young Arlen sang with his Buffalo, New York, synagogue choir, absorbing the structural and emotional imperatives of melodic phrases and changes. The jazzed urgency of secular music interested Arlen most of all, never mind that his father was a cantor. (Music historian Ken Bloom has pointed out that in the matters of culture and personal ambition, Arlen was very much like Jakie Rabinowitz, the young, culture-conflicted protagonist of 1927's breakthrough talkie *The Jazz Singer*.)

While barely in his teens, Arlen took jobs as a pianist in movie theaters and with various Buffalo-based vaudeville acts. By fifteen, he headed a musical group called the Snappy Trio and shortly formed the Southbound Shufflers, a five-man band that played Buffalo-area venues and on Lake Erie ferries and other day-trip vessels. A later group, the Buffalodians, was particularly successful and brought Arlen into contact with a rangy young dancer named Ray Bolger, who would become one of Arlen's best friends.

After touring with the Buffalodians, Arlen settled in New York City, where he sang, arranged, and played piano for the Arnold Johnson dance band. Although Arlen wrote his first song, "My Gal, My Pal" (with lyricist Hyman Cheiffetz), in 1924, and composed a solo piano piece with Dick George, *Minor Gaff* (*Blues Fantasy*), in 1926, he remained most committed to performing. When he left Arnold Johnson, Arlen took to vaudeville as a solo act, and in 1929, he collaborated with lyricist Lou Davis to write "The Album of My Dreams," which became his first hit song. The same year, Arlen won a featured role in a Vincent Youmans musical called *The Great Day*. When the show's piano accompanist fell ill during rehearsals, Arlen was asked to fill in. When he grew tired of repeating the pickup phrase that cued the dancers, he began to vamp and noodle around on the keyboard, coming up with a musical phrase that became the core of his first major hit song, "C'mon, Get Happy."

This success helped Arlen realize that his future was as a writer rather than a performer. During the first half of the 1930s, Arlen and Koehler wrote material for New York's famed Cotton Club, where the performers were black and the patrons were white. Like some other major music clubs, the Cotton Club mounted elaborate, original revues, and one of those, 1931's *Rhythmania*, produced the Arlen-Koehler hits "I Love a Parade," "Between the Devil and the Deep Blue Sea," and a brazen drug tune, "Kickin' the Gong Around" (which saw its greatest popularity via bandleader/vocalist Cab Calloway). For a 1932 Cotton Club show, *Cotton Club Parades*, Arlen and Koehler came up with "I've Got the World on a String." (If you're getting the idea that Ted Koehler is a major figure of 20th-century music, you're on the right track.)

For the 1933 *Cotton Club Parades*, the Arlen-Koehler team produced "Stormy Weather," which became an enormous hit when recorded by Ethel Waters. (It later became the signature tune of singer Lena Horne.)

Although Arlen and Koehler continued to work for the Cotton Club until 1934 (two years before the place closed its doors), both men juggled side projects. In 1932, Arlen collaborated for the first time with a lyricist named E. Y. "Yip" Harburg (see "In Focus: E. Y. 'Yip' Harburg"), on an unmemorable tune, "Satan's Li'l Lamb," for a busted revue called *Americana*. But the pair (along with co-lyricist Billy Rose) had much better success later in 1932, when they wrote "If You Believe in Me" for a Broadway show called *The Great Magoo*. When the tune was retitled "It's Only a Paper Moon" for use in a movie called *Take a Chance* (1933), it became a hit.

The *Take a Chance* assignment was Arlen's first work in Hollywood, and he settled there in 1935. He had met a teenage showgirl and Powers model named Anya Taranda in 1932, fell in love, and married her in 1937.

Prior to *The Wizard of Oz*, Arlen worked with various lyricists on the hits "Fun to Be Fooled" (with Ira Gershwin); "Ill Wind" (Koehler); and "I Love to Sing-a" (Harburg). The last was written for a 1936 Warner Bros.–First National feature called *The Singing Kid*. The catchy tune was instantly popular, and Jack Warner, via the Warner cartoon unit headed by Leon Schlesinger, promoted it further (and goosed its sheet-music sales) in a 1936 Merrie Melodies cartoon called—what else?—*I Love to Singa* (sans hyphen). The cartoon was reissued to theaters in 1944 and has since played endlessly on TV and home video, making "I Love to Sing-a" one of the most familiar and best-liked Arlen-Harburg compositions.

The humorous "Lydia, the Tattooed Lady" (famously sung by Groucho Marx) was written with Harburg in 1939 and was followed by many songs that have since become standards: "Blues in the Night" (with Johnny Mercer), "That Old Black Magic" (Mercer), "One for My Baby (and One More for the Road)" (Mercer), "Ac-cent-tchu-ate the Positive" (Mercer), "Come Rain or Come Shine" (Mercer), "The Man That Got Away" (Ira Gershwin, for the Judy Garland film *A Star Is Born*), and "I Could Go On Singing" (Harburg).

Arlen never left the stage entirely; *Jamaica*, a 1957 Broadway musical designed around Lena Horne and with songs co-written by Yip Harburg, was a smash that ran for more than five hundred performances. A modern classical piece, *Blues Opera Suite*, was performed at Carnegie Hall by Andre Kostelanetz and the New York Philharmonic in 1957.

A son, Samuel, was born in 1958. Twelve years later, Arlen's wife Anya died from a brain disorder. After Anya's death, Arlen became increasingly remote and appeared to have lost interest in his work. Harold Arlen died in 1986.

At birth, Arlen was one of a set of male twins. Because his brother lived only a few days, it's tempting to suggest that Arlen entered creative partnerships with lyricists as a way to "complete" himself. Whether he ever gave a thought to this is unknown, but what we can say for sure is that Harold Arlen had a prodigious talent, suited for the blues, jazz, and ballads, too, like "Over the Rainbow."

In Focus: E. Y. "Yip" Harburg (1896–1981)

Yip Harburg was born Isidore Hochberg in New York City. ("Yip" was from "Yipsel," which may or may not have been Harburg's middle name.) He grew up on the city's Lower East Side and fit the familiar mold of many songwriters of his era: Jewish, street smart, and a person of considerable native intelligence. Ira Gershwin was a friend and City College classmate, but Harburg needed time to get into his true calling. In the early 1920s, he worked in the institutional-meat business, and later sold appliances. When the 1929 stock market crash derailed his business career, Harburg told himself that he was going to be a lyricist.

That same year, Ira Gershwin helped Harburg get together with songwriter Jay Gorney to write tunes for *Earl Carroll's Sketch Book*. The show enjoyed a very healthy run of 392 performances during 1929–30 and gave plenty of people the opportunity to enjoy the amusing stuff by Gorney and Harburg, which included "Legs, Legs, Legs," "Kinda Cute," and "Papa Likes a Hot Papoose."

Yip Harburg became an immediate fixture on Broadway, writing lyrics for, among others, *Garrick Gaieties* (1930; with Vernon Duke), *Earl Carroll's Vanities* (1930–31; with Duke and Gorney), *Shoot the Works* (1931; with Gorney), and *Ballyhoo of 1932* (1932; with Lewis E. Gensler).

A 1932 revue, *Americana*, was highlighted by "Brother, Can You Spare a Dime," a gem of a Depression-era ballad with melancholy melody by Jay Gorney and downbeat lyrics by Harburg. He told interviewer Max Wilk, "I didn't make a maudlin lyric of a guy begging. I made it into a commentary. It was about the fellow who works, the fellow who builds, who makes railroads and houses—and he's left empty-handed."

Harburg was a fierce progressive, with a mistrust of institutions, deep concern for working people, and (after World War I) an intense dislike of swaddled men who sent younger men off to die in foolish wars. Harburg's feelings, at least as expressed in his lyrics, were suited to the times, and he and Gorney were offered contracts by Paramount Pictures.

Another tune from *Americana*, "Satan's Li'l Lamb," brought Harburg and Arlen together professionally for the first time. ("Satan's Li'l Lamb" had a second lyricist, Johnny Mercer.) Later in 1932, Harburg and Arlen collaborated again, on "If You Believe in Me," a tune for Ben Hecht and Gene Fowler's *The Great Magoo*. (There was a second lyricist on this song, too: Billy Rose.) *Magoo* ran just eleven performances, but produced a Billy Rose–E. Y. Harburg song that would become timeless, "If You Believe in Me"—but only after it was retitled "It's Only a Paper Moon."

Walk a Little Faster, a 1932 Broadway team-up with melodist Vernon Duke, produced one for the Great American Songbook, "April in Paris."

Life Begins at 8:40, a long-running 1934–35 show starring Ray Bolger and Bert Lahr, brought Harburg and Arlen together again. Arlen subtly experimented with beats and rhythms in the show's songs, and earned a great deal of attention. The songs' lyrics were no less audacious, as Harburg and co-lyricist Ira Gershwin used "Beautifying the City (Life Begins at City Hall)" to poke fun at New York's Mayor LaGuardia and First Lady Eleanor Roosevelt (who was in the audience on opening night and thoroughly enjoyed herself). Another tune, "Quartet Erotica," cast Bolger as Boccaccio and Lahr as Balzac, for a bright but unmistakably sarcastic comment on sex, ribald literature, and censorship.

Two other songs from the show, "Fun to Be Fooled" and "You're a Builder Upper," also scored.

Hollywood was lucrative but even more messily collaborative than Broadway. Still, film musicals were very much in vogue during the early sound era, and work was plentiful. Yip Harburg was only one of many who jumped in. He worked on pictures made at Paramount, Warner Bros., Universal, and elsewhere, with numerous collaborators—frequently Arlen: *The Sap from Syracuse* (1930; with Vernon Duke), *Lady Killer* (1933; with Joseph Meyer), *Metropolitan* (1935; with Arlen), *Manhattan Moon* (1935; with Karl Hajos), *Stage Struck* (1936; with Arlen), *The Singing Kid* (1936; with Arlen; this vehicle for a fading Al Jolson includes the sprightly "I Want to Sing a Mammy Song," which purposely suggests that "mammy" tunes are out of date). There were many others.

The Wizard of Oz marked one of the first times that a very broad public was exposed to a wealth of brilliant Harburg lyrics. "Over the Rainbow" was well amortized over the years; Yip Harburg lived long enough to hear the song performed by many artists in dozens of features, shorts, and TV episodes.

Songs for the 1940–41 stage production of *Cabin in the Sky* were written by Vernon Duke and John La Touche; Harburg and Arlen were assigned to add three more to the 1943 MGM adaptation: "Life Is Full of Consequence" (performed by Lena Horne and Eddie "Rochester" Anderson), "Li'l Black Sheep" (performed by Ethel Waters), and the quite lovely "Happiness Is a Thing Called Joe" (performed by Waters).

Harburg collaborated on many other original songs for films throughout the 1940s, and he and songwriter Burton Lane enjoyed a monster of a Broadway hit with *Finian's Rainbow* (1947–48): 725 performances. The production (for which Harburg co-wrote the libretto) had a strong streak of liberal humanism, and biting satire, as well, including a racist white senator who becomes a black man. The show became a Broadway perennial and was revived in 1955, 1960, and 2009. (A watery film version appeared in 1968.)

By the time *The Wizard of Oz* came to television in 1956, Harburg was already in trouble with the House Un-American Activities Committee's lamebrained investigation of supposed Communist influence in the film industry. Yip's work on a 1944 picture, *Song of Russia*, had come back to haunt him. During World War II, the Roosevelt administration approached different studios about doing films with pro-Soviet sentiments. The Russians were America's chief ally in the awful battle against the Nazis, and Washington felt a need for some unsubtle propaganda. MGM went along with the request, but the caveat from Washington was that the public must never know that the requests were made. The enforced secrecy ensured that when HUAC began snooping in the late 1940s, *Song of Russia*, *Mission to Moscow* (Warner Bros.), and other wartime polemics were impossible to defend to the committee's satisfaction. Harburg's liberal mindset was no secret around town, and the tune he and Jerome

Kern had written for *Song of Russia*, "And Russia Is Her Name," struck the HUAC wolves as altogether too chummy.

Harburg fell onto the Hollywood blacklist. Although songs he had written years before continued to be re-recorded for new use, original movie assignments dried up. Although Arthur Freed's politics were right wing, he was upset by the bad treatment Harburg was suffering and agitated to get movie work for Yip, but none was offered.

Broadway sustained Yip during this period, notably *Jamaica* (1957–59; with Arlen), a smash that put together 555 performances. (An anti–witch hunt musical Yip did with Sammy Fain in 1951, *Flahooley*, died after forty performances.)

Harburg's first original film work in a decade was with Arlen, on a cartoon-animated feature called *Gay Purr-ee* (1962); Judy Garland provided the voice (and singing) for heroine Mewsette. Arlen and Harburg collaborated on Garland's final film, *I Could Go On Singing* (1963)—and that was the end of Harburg's movie career.

The final Broadway original with which Harburg was involved was *Darling of the Day* (1968; with Jules Styne), a sharp-edge musical about a young widow's romantic relationship with a reclusive, older painter.

As a reaction to the April 1968 assassination of Martin Luther King Jr., Harburg and Arlen collaborated to write "Silent Spring."

A late collection of poems was titled *Rhymes for the Irreverent*.

Yip Harburg was inducted into the Songwriters Hall of Fame in 1972. For the next decade, he occupied himself with songwriting and verse. On March 5, 1981, days before he was to accept the Hall's Johnny Mercer Award, Harburg died in Los Angeles traffic, from a car accident or a fatal heart attack; sources differ.

Curiosity about people, and affection and dismay, as well, drove Harburg's life and art. He was an entertainer who was determined to challenge, and even provoke. Years after becoming successful, Harburg said, "Words make you think a thought. Music makes you feel a feeling. A song makes you feel a thought."

In Focus: Ken Darby (1909–1992)

Ken Darby had experience as a vocalist before working in the film industry as a studio composer, arranger, and vocal coach. He was a Nebraska boy who grew up in Santa Monica, where he played trumpet and piano, and studied composition, counterpoint, and harmony. While still a teenager, he provided live organ accompaniment to silent movies. He also developed as a singer and was a founding member of the King's Men vocal group in 1929. The group found frequent radio gigs and became well known for an upbeat style and close harmonies.

Between 1933 and 1950, Darby appeared on screen many times, usually as one of the King's Men, and sometimes as a solo. He also provided off-screen vocals.

Darby was later a songwriter at Disney for a period during the 1940s, most successfully for a pair of 1946 releases, *Make Mine Music* and *Song of the South*. A bit later, he was at 20th Century-Fox, where he collaborated with famed film composer Alfred Newman and did orchestral and vocal arrangements for scores of Fox releases.

During 1940–69, Darby brought his commercial writer-composer's touch to dozens of songs. Few of them are memorable, but they're somehow evocative, sentimental, heart tugging, or what people used to describe as "snappy and peppy." Darby was a professional, and like many professionals in the creative arts, he had a sure sense of what was desired by his bosses and the public. The songs he wrote for Fox star Marilyn Monroe, for example—including "River of No Return" and "I'm Gonna File My Claim"—are deft, calculated, and rote.

But Darby had more talent than he was usually allowed to show, and it peeked out sometimes, as it did with his vocal and musical arrangements for *Oz*, the melody of "I Wish I Could Shimmy Like My Sister Kate" (for Fox's *Wabash Avenue*; 1950), an amusingly lusty, self-spoofing score for Fritz Lang's sexually charged 1953 western, *Rancho Notorious*. Darby also wrote that film's songs, including two for co-star Marlene Dietrich that evoked the actress's smoldering Weimar allure, "Get Away, Young Man" and "Gypsy Davey."

During the late period of his Fox career, Darby was Elvis Presley's vocal coach and wrote the lyrics for one of Elvis's best early ballads, "Love Me Tender." (The melody came from "Aura Lee," a Civil War ballad.) Although song-publishing agreements mandated that Darby not be credited as the song's writer (Elvis and Darby's wife, Vera Matson, were awarded that distinction), the Ken Darby Trio (drums, bass, guitar, and background vocals) backed Elvis at the "Love Me Tender" recording session.

Generally, Darby's most prestigious assignments involved vocal supervision and orchestral arrangements rather than songwriting. Some of his better credits are *Down to the Sea in Ships* (1949), *With a Song in My Heart* (1952), *The Girl Can't Help It* (1956), *The King and I* (1956; Academy Award, with Alfred Newman), *South Pacific* (1958; Oscar nomination), *Porgy and Bess* (1959; Academy Award, with Andre Previn), *Flower Drum Song* (1961; Oscar nomination), *How the West Was Won* (1962; Oscar nomination), *Camelot* (1967; Academy Award, with Newman), and a charming novelty, *The Whale Who Wanted to Sing at the Met* (1946), a two-reel Disney cartoon that gave Darby opportunities to do specialty arrangements of Wagner, Donizetti, and Rossini.

Let the Munchkins Sing!

All of the Munchkins' singing had been recorded at slower-than-normal speeds, over eight sessions, to give a "chipmunk" effect during normal playback. (Several of the sessions included Judy Garland and Lorraine Bridges, who sang for Billie Burke.) In order to ensure proper timing as well as a high-pitched tone, vocal arranger Ken Darby (who had been brought on to the project by Herbert Stothart) devised complicated mathematical formulae timed to film speed of ninety feet a minute (as opposed to the standard sixty feet per minute), for the desired tempo, tones, semitones, octaves, and major thirds. Darby said, "[W]e found we needed a machine that would play back our click track [a musical track overlaid with audible, pre-set metronomic clicks] and piano key at sixty feet per minute and slow the vocal performance of the singer proportionally." The machine mentioned by Darby was built by supervising sound recorder

Douglas Shearer. A reverse procedure (slower to faster) was used to create the baritone vocals of the Winkies.

The vocals were backed with a forty-five-piece orchestra playing Stothart's score, arranged and orchestrated by Murray Cutler.

Because few of the Munchkin actors were singers, their solos and group vocals were juiced by studio professionals. (A handful of Munchkin players did perform their own vocals.) The Debutantes, for instance, who had an association with MGM dating back to 1934, sang for the Lullaby League; radio listeners would already have heard the Debutantes singing with the Ted Fio Rito orchestra.

The King's Men (John Dodson, Bill Linn, Rad Robinson, all of whom had had prior association with Ken Darby) vocalized for the Lollipop Guild. These professional singers were equally comfortable with soundtracks, records, stage work, and live radio.

Darby overdubbed the Munchkinland mayor, actor Charley Becker. Choral voices heard beneath the Munchkinland sequence were recorded by the St. Joseph Choir of St. Joseph's Church in Los Angeles. The choir was recruited by the church's musical director, Roger Wagner, who had joined the MGM chorus in 1937. He later formed the Roger Wagner Chorale and the Los Angeles Master Chorale, both of which enjoyed considerable success live and on record.

The choral voices that sing "Optimistic Voices" when Dorothy and her friends are "out of the woods" and in sight of the Emerald City belonged to the Rhythmettes, a female trio that gained some notice in the early 1930s on Los Angeles radio station KMTR and, by 1933, as part of Al Pearce's *Happy-Go-Lucky Hour*, which originated from L.A. radio station KHJ, for the NBC Red network. The aforementioned Debutantes also assisted with "Optimistic Voices."

As with many largely anonymous musical groups of the day, the Rhythmettes saw personnel changes throughout the '30s. Two members, Dorothy Compton and Mary Moder, had provided the voices for two of Walt Disney's *Three Little Pigs* in 1933. The name of the third Rhythmette is unclear, and a 1937 story in the *Oakland Tribune* muddies things further by identifying the Rhythmettes as "Doris, Dell and Kay of radio fame."

A later group called the Rhythmettes, which sang across Indiana and in Chicago in the late 1940s, is not related to the *Oz* group. Likewise, the Rhythmettes vocal groups that recorded for RCA Victor, Brunswick, and Alvic (a small Kentucky label) during 1955–60 have no connection to *Oz*.

7

Conferrin' with the Flowers

The Screenplay

L ike other studios of Hollywood's golden age, MGM had a system of production and an overarching philosophy. Those things helped ensure efficiency and consistency. When the stars aligned—as they often did at the big studios—*quality* also resulted. MGM's goal of superior family entertainment mandated that every project be done promptly, but with proper review. The studio often hired writers from the world of novels or other disciplines to write scripts, with everyone understanding that staff writers and even other outsiders were apt to take a hack at the thing after it was written.

The script of *The Wizard of Oz* strikes many as perfect, and it may be. MGM's system worked. As we'll see, one brilliant writer laid a foundation and a frame. Then two others, who were somewhat less brilliant but nevertheless pretty clever, changed the foundation a little, tore down some of the frame, and constructed their own. This continued for quite a while, finally involving many more writers than could comfortably fit into a limousine. Or into two limousines.

As producer Mervyn LeRoy and other MGM executives looked at various script drafts, story conferences held during the greater part of 1938 entertained an array of plot points, narrative concepts, and characterizations. In an early set of notes kept by LeRoy's assistant, William Cannon, the Scarecrow is described as a real man dressed in straw by the Ozites, because they consider him thick-headed. A similar tack was floated for the Tin Woodman, a real man whose tin suit is a punishment meted out because of his heartless bullying.

Cannon himself suggested that the Wizard be made infallible. Through all of this, Mervyn LeRoy insisted that the story be fantasy. No real people forced to wear costumes; no godlike Wizard. As LeRoy saw it, the film would rise or fall on the strength of its sense of whimsy.

Baum's Prince and Princess were dropped, though a role for the Princess was considered as late as January 1938. If the character had remained, she would likely have been played by seventeen-year-old MGM contract player Betty Jaynes. Despite pleasing looks and a precocious operatic voice, Jaynes's film career was minor and brief. Jaynes is most familiar to film fans as Molly Moran in *Babes in Arms* (1939), in which she was seventh-billed behind, among others,

Mickey Rooney and Judy Garland (with whom she sings a duet). If Jaynes had been cast in *The Wizard of Oz*, plans were for the Princess to engage Dorothy in a vocal sing-off: opera vs. jazz.

Tenor Kenny Baker, who had become popular as Jack Benny's radio foil, was penciled in to play the Prince, if the character had made the cut. If he had, he and the Princess would have sung to each other after being imprisoned by the Wicked Witch.

The Many Inventions of Noel Langley

Between March and June 1938, twenty-six-year-old Noel Langley, a playwright, script doctor, and neophyte screenwriter with just a handful of Hollywood credits, completed a forty-three page *Wizard of Oz* treatment, followed by four *Oz* screenplays. He returned to the project for various polishes and rewrites that kept him busy, off and on, until Halloween 1938. Not just an imaginative thinker, Langley was a blazingly fast writer capable of turning out a complete, polished screenplay in less than a workweek (or, that is, in fewer than six days).

Langley was an invaluable contributor to the movie, not least because he suggested a critical narrative point: Dorothy's adventure in Oz is a dream. That's a direct contradiction of Baum, whose Oz is a very real place. On the other hand, Langley's early drafts retained Baum's China Country and its fragile inhabitants. Matching Baum, Langley allowed Toto to pull back the curtain on the Wizard (though in the book, the dog merely tips over a screen).

Completely independent of Baum, Langley created Miss Gulch and a pair of farmhands, Hunk and Hickory, and even provided the hands with detailed backstories (that were eliminated from later drafts). As for Aunt Em, Langley's first inclination was to make her vaguely unsympathetic to Dorothy's concern for Toto; it's Em, in fact, who tells Dorothy that the dog must go because he bit one of Dorothy's classmates. A later Langley draft eliminated Toto's nip of the classmate and expressed Aunt Em's sympathy for Dorothy via her vocal unhappiness with Miss Gulch.

Four witches populate Baum's novel, and Langley, who was aware of the dangers inherent in dividing audience attention with unnecessary characters, reduced the four to just two. Langley also grasped the dramatic necessity of establishing early on that the Wicked Witch was going to be a real menace to Dorothy; hence their early meeting in Munchkinland. In the novel, Dorothy is aware of the Witch but doesn't actually encounter her until after leaving Munchkinland.

Dorothy's sweetly amusing first encounter with Glinda was filmed almost exactly as Langley originally wrote it.

Critically, the young screenwriter devised one of the film's most well-liked inventions: that Dorothy's friends, and even Miss Gulch, have counterparts in Oz. (This, along with Langley's whimsical and intentionally absurd images that pass Dorothy's window when the house is aloft, is a clear hint that the adventure we are about to experience is a dream.) Langley further suggested that Hickory and Hunk sing to Dorothy about Oz and then reprise the number in the poppy field.

Langley's first inclination had been to get rid of the poppy-field interlude altogether, partly because he couldn't imagine how—as in the book—Dorothy and her friends could be rescued from their on-screen stupors by legions of mice. (When the idea was resurrected for the 1974 Broadway run of *The Wiz*, the mice were actors in costume.) Langley took his later "snowfall" resolution from Baum's 1902 stage play.

Much—though not all—of the Lion's comically pugnacious dialogue came from Langley, who suggested that the Lion be tested by a "monster." In various drafts that followed, the Lion's adversary was a dragon, a gorilla, and another lion.

A Langley draft describes how the Witch's winged monkeys brazenly kidnap Dorothy from the hot air balloon, thus eliminating any narrative need for Dorothy's tortuous journey to find the Witch.

According to Langley, the Horse of a Different Color is a *talking* horse that acts as a guide when the Scarecrow, Tin Woodman, Cowardly Lion, and the Wizard traipse through China Country in search of Dorothy. That might have worked out agreeably, but Langley, like Herman Mankiewicz before him, began inventing characters that didn't appear in Baum's book. Not content to create Hunk and Hickory (Zeke would be imagined later), Langley came up a female hand, Lizzie Smithers, who would have a counterpart in Oz, as the Wizard's assistant. During the Kansas sequences, Lizzie would be romantically attached to Hunk (the Scarecrow).

Once begun with this sort of thing, Langley apparently couldn't stop himself from inventing other Kansans with doppelgangers in Oz: *Walter*, Miss Gulch's son (in Oz, he's *Bulbo*, the son of the Wicked Witch); *another son to the Witch*, designed as a counterpart to Uncle Henry (!); *Sylvia*, Miss Gulch's niece (*Princess Sylvia*); *Kenny*, Sylvia's boyfriend (*Prince Florizel/Prince Kebelin/Prince Kenelm*; different drafts suggest different names). And if it bothers you, whether Langley explained how Miss Gulch came by a son is unknown.

The prince runs afoul of the Wicked Witch and is turned into the Cowardly Lion. Then, in a stroke that would have made audiences jump from their seats (and probably not in a good way), the Lion *kills* the Wicked Witch.

Finally, although Baum describes Dorothy's slippers as silver, Langley indicated them as ruby red, an acknowledgment of the anticipated use of Technicolor. But Langley had little interest in the slippers' magical powers, and did little to develop that critical part of the story.

Freed Wants Changes

Very shortly, Langley and other writers who were working simultaneously but separately had become overly invested in eccentric characters, and peculiar features and customs of the Land of Oz. Some treatments took the film's title too closely to heart and suggested that the Wizard's adventures were more important than Dorothy's. Arthur Freed knew that if he allowed all of this to continue, he'd end up with a one-note novelty film. So, in an April 25, 1938, memo, Freed instructed the writers to invest the narrative with emotional meaning. The memo mentioned the "urgent necessity of getting a real emotional and dramatic quality through the Oz sequences. I would like to see Dorothy in some spot in Oz with her companions, utterly crestfallen and lost with a complete feeling of despair. . . . [W]e should go into this phase of the story very fully so that when the picture is over, besides our laughs and our novelty, we have had a real assault upon our hearts." Langley and others absorbed the memo and were able to increase the story's sense of menace, and develop and maintain Dorothy's deep longing for home, friends, and family.

Not surprisingly, Freed found Mankiewicz's idea of an office-bound Wicked Witch insufficiently menacing. In keeping with the sentiments of his memo, Freed wanted Dorothy's antagonist to be deeply formidable. It was because of this directive that the Wicked Witch grew, in dramatic terms and in the impact of her environment. The fabulously sinister castle we know from the finished film is light years removed from Mank's conception of an office, and all to the good. In all, Freed wanted Dorothy's saga to have much more weight and consequence than what he'd seen so far.

Freed doubted the dramatic value of Sylvia and Kenny, and asked whether the dragon (or whatever the Lion's nemesis turned out to be) was necessary.

Freed also wanted the songs to advance the plot and underline the film's themes, work that would fall later to songwriter Harold Arlen and, especially, lyricist E. Y. "Yip" Harburg.

Gags by Brecher and Changes by Langley

In early March 1938, LeRoy brought in twenty-four-year-old screenwriter Irving Brecher to look over scripted byplay between the Scarecrow, the Tin Woodman, and the Cowardly Lion; punch up the gags; and add new ones. By 1938, Brecher had written just one picture, *New Faces of 1937*, a comedy revue starring Milton Berle and radio comic Joe Penner. LeRoy had encountered Brecher during production of *Fools for Scandal* (1938), a romantic comedy that LeRoy had directed; Brecher was on that picture as one of numerous writers that contributed "additional dialogue."

Through no fault of his own, Brecher's tenure on *Oz* was brief, and ended when he was needed to write the screenplay for another MGM–Mervyn LeRoy picture, the Marx Brothers' *At the Circus* (1939).

Brecher went on to have a successful career that included directing episodic television, creating the radio and TV iterations of *The Life of Riley*, and writing scripts for *Go West* (1940; the Marx Brothers) *Shadow of the Thin Man* (1941), *Meet Me in St. Louis* (1944), and *Bye Bye Birdie* (1963), his last. Brecher died in 2008.

His posthumous 2009 autobiography (written with Hank Rosenfeld) takes its title from an honorarium bestowed upon him by Groucho Marx: *The Wicked Wit of the West.*

Meanwhile, Noel Langley continued to write. He turned in his fourth script on June 4, 1938. This one was the first to include *two* trips to the Emerald City— one to find the Wizard and a second to deliver the broomstick. Dorothy's dream of flying home to Kansas via balloon is destroyed not just by the Wizard's ineptitude, but also by balloon-busting woodpeckers. (Dorothy's last-second search for Toto, and the balloon's premature ascent, would appear in later scripts.)

New characters Sylvia, Kenny, and Lizzie had been exiled to the ether, but for the time being, Walter/Bulbo remained. Prof. Marvel was given a pet lion. Most crucially, Langley was faithful to Baum in the manner of the Witch's demise: Dorothy kills her with water. (In the book, Dorothy doesn't act in order to save the Scarecrow, but empties the bucket onto the Witch in an impulsive fit of pique, after being tripped by an invisible iron bar and losing one of the slippers.)

Langley completed a first-draft screenplay sometime in May 1938 and did revised versions into the summer.

In Focus: Noel Langley (1911–1980)

Although not exactly a prodigy, Noel Langley was scripting British movies as early as 1935; wrote a clever backstage novel, *There's a Porpoise Close Behind Us*, in 1936; and published a very popular children's book, *The Tale of the Land of Green Ginger*, a year later. It was *Green Ginger* that caught the attention of MGM. The studio invited Langley to Hollywood to take a crack at a script for *The Wizard of Oz*.

Born in South Africa, Langley began his movie career in Britain in 1935, scripting or co-scripting four films before he came to America for *Oz*. He impressed studios in Hollywood and Britain with his rich imagination, and divided his time between continents for many years. Langley was a facile, intelligent screenwriter who offered the added lure of versatility: *They Made Me a Fugitive* (1947) is crackling Brit noir; *Trio* (1950), *A Christmas Carol* (1951), and *The Pickwick Papers* (1952) are adaptations from literature; and *Ivanhoe* (1952) and *Knights of the Round Table* (1953) are sturdy, self-important historical epics.

Simultaneous with all of that was Langley's work as a novelist. *The Inconstant Moon* (1949) is a retelling of Dante's love for Beatrice, with the twist being that this Dante is young and callow. Other Langley books for grown-ups include *Hocus Pocus* (1941), a comic take on Hollywood; *Cage Me a Peacock* (1948), a risqué novel of ancient Rome that casts Lucrece as the central character; and *Nymph in Clover* (1948), in which Langley recast the Lysistrata tale as a comic how-to for married couples.

And there were numerous stage plays, as well, two of which reached Broadway: *Farm of Three Echoes* (1939–40; starring Ethel Barrymore) and *Edward, My Son* (1948–49; co-written with actor Robert Morley).

In the 1940s and '50s, Langley settled into a lucrative groove as a short-story writer for the *Saturday Evening Post*, *Good Housekeeping*, and other "slicks"; seven of those tales are collected in a 1950 book, *Tales of Mystery and Revenge*.

As sometimes happens to successful writers, Langley saw his aura dim as the 1950s went on, and during the latter part of his life he wrote the screenplays for *The Search for Bridey Murphy* (1956), based on an unintentionally fraudulent non-fiction best seller about reincarnation; and *Snow White Meets the Three Stooges* (1961), which commits the unpardonable sin of being decorous and boring.

For a 1958 episode of TV's *Shirley Temple's Storybook*, Langley adapted *Rip Van Winkle*.

One of Langley's last books was *Edgar Cayce on Reincarnation*, a 1968 trifle about the late, self-promoting 20th-century mystic, scribbled by Langley "under the editorship of Hugh Lynn Cayce."

Like many screenwriters, Langley had a strong appreciation of his own gifts, and like most of them, he disliked rewrites of his work done by others. He saw *The Wizard of Oz* for the first time at a matinee screening in 1939. He felt the picture had no inner life, and claimed privately to have been so appalled that he cried. Because he had been a very young man in 1938–39, Langley lived long enough to witness the first four theatrical re-releases and, more critically, the remarkable elevation of the film's stature that began when MGM sold the movie to television in the 1950s. By the early 1960s, when Langley was barely into his fifties and *Oz* was universally beloved, the writer could hardly claim to "loathe" (his word) the phenomenon he had helped create. For the remainder of his life, he professed great fondness for the film. He probably meant it.

Although Langley worked on a screenplay based on Baum's second Oz novel, *The Marvelous Land of Oz*, he may never have completed it.

Screenplay, with Woolf and Ryerson

Langley's final script was examined by LeRoy, Freed, and others. They felt it needed work. Production executives always say that, but this time they were right. During the first week of June 1938, LeRoy gave the okay for the studio to bring in two additional, and very experienced, screenwriters, Edgar Allan Woolf and Florence Ryerson, who were hired on June 3. Although not a self-created team, Woolf and Ryerson worked together on *Oz* for nearly all of June and into July. Freed encouraged them to revise and delete, making clear, however, that his chief interest was in the story's emotional center.

Because the film's casting process was heavily informed by the particular talents and personas of each actor (for instance, Bert Lahr's uncouth gruffness), LeRoy and Freed considered it useful that Woolf had once written vaudeville sketches for Frank Morgan. In this, Woolf was expected to function as Irving Brecher had with Dorothy's friends, punching up the Wizard's dialogue with comedy. But Woolf contributed considerably more. He and Ryerson thought hard about Dorothy and decided she needed a more intense emotional core if she were to connect with audiences. To that end, Woolf and Ryerson heightened Dorothy's sentimental attachment to Kansas and the people she'd left there, involved her more directly in the story (in other words, she would be more than just a plot pivot), and increased the level of danger she faced. In a bit of a paradox, the pair regarded the *Oz* project as a children's movie and insisted that no character die during the course of the story—not even the Wicked Witch. And now, paradox on paradox: Ryerson and Woolf didn't object to the Witch being melted, as if that Baum-created fate were something less than fatal and hideous. To the contrary, they suggested that the moment be given a more suspenseful buildup, and thus a greater dramatic payoff. But, they cautioned, Dorothy must be faithful to Baum and dispatch the Witch accidentally.

Woolf and Ryerson addressed Langley's disinterest in the ruby slippers by heightening the shoes' power, the Witch's desire for them, and Dorothy's determination not to give them up. The writers understood that Dorothy's attachment to the slippers had to be linked to the girl's overwhelming desire to go home. Without that, the ruby slippers were just an unusual pair of shoes. When mated with the notion of "home," however, the slippers achieved a unique and touching resonance.

Ryerson and Woolf struck a far more fanciful note when they created a Rainbow Bridge that connects Kansas to Oz. Dorothy and Toto are able to climb the bridge and travel all the way to Munchkinland. (This idea was dropped after LeRoy wondered about the special-effects challenge, and when Louis Mayer decided that however it was to be accomplished, it would cost too much.)

Ryerson and Woolf came up with Prof. Marvel (remember, the only Kansans in Baum's novel are Dorothy, Toto, Aunt Em, and Uncle Henry), and rewrote the Emerald City sequence so that, among other things, the Wizard is seen in multiple roles as a gatekeeper and other minor functionaries (which allowed Woolf to write comic bits for Frank Morgan). One dubious idea, casting the Wizard as an Emerald City bootblack—in blackface, no less—was proposed and then abandoned.

Ryerson and Woolf liked the Horse of a Different Color, but shifted the animal from the Emerald City sequence to Munchkinland. In a major departure from the Baum text, the writers eliminated the death-by-house plot point involving the Wicked Witch of the East.

Woolf and Ryerson's second script, dated July 5, 1938, discarded the Witch's son, Bulbo, and the character's Kansas counterpart, Walter. The Witch's plan to make war on the Emerald City was dropped, and a startling scene in which she feeds a Winkie to her aged, caged lion also got the heave-ho.

By the time MGM's *Oz* got rolling, dwarf actors like Angelo Rossitto and Billy Barty had made modest screen careers in bits as gnomes, precocious babies, and, well, dwarfs. Traditional witchcraft tales maintained that witches were served by "familiars"—semi-magical toadies that carried out the witches' bidding. Working from that bit of folklore, Ryerson and Woolf created a dwarf to assist the Wicked Witch, a role that was eventually manipulated to create

Nikko, the leader of the winged monkeys. ("Nikko," by the way, is the Japanese city that boasts the original "three wise monkeys" sculpture: "Hear no evil, speak no evil, see no evil.")

For their *Oz* climax, Ryerson and Woolf envisioned complex mayhem during which the Wizard is unmasked, and he, Dorothy, and the others are attacked by the furious residents of the Emerald City. The writers retained Noel Langley's balloon-busting woodpecker, but in this draft, the balloon bursts into flames, necessitating a quick rescue by Glinda and the Munchkinland Fire Department. The Scarecrow, Tin Woodman, and Cowardly Lion have active roles in saving the day and realize that they've always had the qualities they've longed for. (The first Baum book features *two* good witches, the unnamed "little old woman" [the Good Witch of the North] who greets Dorothy in Munchkinland; and Glinda, the Good Witch of the South. The MGM movie combines the two into Glinda, the Good Witch of the North.)

At the urging of Freed and LeRoy, Ryerson and Woolf added the "There's no place like home" homily that concludes the film. For all the upset and controversy this teeny bit of homey wisdom has engendered over the years, a person could be forgiven for assuming that MGM pulled the notion out of thin air, in brazen defiance of L. Frank Baum's intentions. But no: the idea is grounded in Baum—if noticeably more sentimental in MGM's hands. Here is Baum:

> "My darling child!" [Aunt Em] cried, folding the little girl in her arms and covering her face with kisses; "where in the world did you come from?"
>
> "From the Land of Oz," said Dorothy, gravely. "And here is Toto, too. And oh, Aunt Em! I'm so glad to be at home again!"

The Ryerson-Woolf elaboration of Baum's thought could be termed treacly (in the hands of an actress less assured that Garland, it could have been awful), but Freed and LeRoy knew that it would appeal to Louis Mayer, who adored uncomplicated sentimentality. When this draft was returned to Noel Langley, he was told to keep his hands off the final lines of dialogue.

Finally, *Oz* lyricist Yip Harburg had emphasized to Freed that the dialogue leading into and out of musical sequences was just as important as the songs' lyrics. Freed felt that Harburg was right about that and assigned him to work with Ryerson and Woolf to ensure that the tone and meaning of those critical dialogue passages jibed with the emotional tones and narrative intentions of the songs. Harburg assumed these duties when he already was writing the film's songs with Harold Arlen. The pair mounted a big push from May through August 1938, and completed most of the tunes.

In Focus: Woolf and Ryerson

Every film historian who writes about *The Wizard of Oz* gives considerable, and deserved, attention to co-scripter Noel Langley, but the movie would have been very different if not for the two MGM staffers brought on board for revisions, Edgar Allan Woolf (1881–1943) and Florence Ryerson (1892–1965).

Edgar Allan Woolf was writing for the movies as early as 1914, but he had professional credits going back even earlier. In June 1906, a sprightly Woolf musical revue, *Mam'zelle Champagne*, was playing at the rooftop garden of the original Madison Square Garden when the venue's architect, Stanford White, was accosted there and shot to death by millionaire Harry K. Thaw. White had become known in fashionable circles as the lover of one of the great beauties of the day, twenty-two-year-old model and occasional stage performer Evelyn Nesbit. Trouble was, Nesbit was Thaw's wife, and Thaw had a history of mental illness. At the moment Stanford White was killed, the show's cast was singing "I Could Love a Million Girls," and Evelyn was seated next to her lover. The foofaraw that followed became known as the Trial of the Century. (Following a hung jury in his first trial, White was later found not guilty because of insanity.)

None of this would have much real bearing on Edgar Allan Woolf (or on this book) except that Woolf eventually put aside the whimsy that characterized *Mam'zelle Champagne* to focus on screenplays that were propelled by murder, wealth, greed, revenge, and the grotesque: *A Black Hand* (1914), *Gang War* (1928), *The Man Who Laughs Last* (1929; short), *Freaks* (1932; additional dialogue), *The Mask of Fu Manchu* (1932), *Flesh* (1932), *Murder in the Private Car* (1934), *The Casino Murder Case* (1935), *Mad Love* (1935; uncredited), *Mad Holiday* (1936; a shipboard thriller co-scripted by Florence Ryerson), *Moonlight Murder* (1936; a murder tale with musical elements). The reason for the sharp turn in Woolf's career is easy enough to surmise: Although an incidental player in the Trial of the Century, he came away with some notoriety. When he was signed by MGM in 1931, with three crime pictures already behind him, he was kept on that track, at least for much of the time.

Why, then, was Woolf assigned to a rewrite of *The Wizard of Oz*? Well, he was a known quantity at MGM, and his background in musical theater was a big selling point (that is, he understood how to integrate story and music). In addition, Woolf had done screenplays for the comedies *Hit of the Show* (1928) and MGM's *A Tailor Made Man* (1931), and two MGM musicals, *Broadway to Hollywood* (1933) and *Everybody Sing* (1938; co-written with Florence Ryerson, and starring Allan Jones and Judy Garland). Equally promising was that Woolf had revealed a zany sensibility with his original story for MGM's *Hollywood Party* (1934), a music-and-comedy oddity with eight directors and extended cameos by Laurel and Hardy, Jimmy Durante, Lupe Velez, and many lesser lights that had come to Hollywood by way of vaudeville and the musical stage. (*Hollywood Party* is still popular with film buffs today.) Given Woolf's experience with Judy Garland, and the challenging mix of genres, tones, and situations suggested by Noel Langley's *Oz* drafts, Woolf's assignment to the project seems, in retrospect, almost obvious.

Like Edgar Allan Woolf, Florence Ryerson had screenwriting experience from before 1920, and really got going in the '20s and '30s, when she freelanced around town, at Universal, MGM, Paramount, and lowly Educational. She had an important early credit as screenwriter of a popular early talkie from Paramount, *The Canary*

Murder Case (1929; starring William Powell as Philo Vance, with Jean Arthur and Louise Brooks). The same year, Ryerson scripted a high-profile Paramount musical, *Pointed Heels* (starring William Powell and Helen "boop-boop-a-doop" Kane). Shortly after, Ryerson got into heavier stuff: *The Return of Dr. Fu Manchu* (1930), *The Drums of Jeopardy* (1931; a revenge thriller from low-rent Tiffany Productions), *The Reckless Hour* (1931; an unwed motherhood melodrama starring Dorothy Mackaill), *The Crime of the Century* (1933; a psychological murder mystery), and *A Wicked Woman* (1934; a domestic-violence melodrama).

Ryerson became an MGM staff writer in 1936. Although she and Woolf were now at the same studio, both had been pursuing separate careers; that the two added dialogue to an MGM romantic drama called *Have a Heart* (1934) hasn't much significance (each almost certainly worked independent of the other), except that they were on the same lot and had established a link, however tenuous.

Ryerson and Woolf worked separately on *This Side of Heaven* (1934; a family drama involving a false accusation of embezzlement), but this time they may have ultimately collaborated. Both are credited with the screenplay. A year later, the pair shared screenplay credit for *The Casino Murder Case*, and in 1936 they cooked up their first verifiable collaboration, *Tough Guy* (1936), for which they shared original story and screenplay credit. MGM came to regard Ryerson and Woolf as a congenial team. The two collaborated again on *Mad Holiday*, *Moonlight Murder*, *Everybody Sing*, *The Ice Follies of 1939* (1939), and *The Kid from Texas* (1939). Then came *The Wizard of Oz*. As if sensing that *Oz* would be their most noteworthy credit, the pair took out a full-page ad in *Daily Variety* when the picture was released. The text was as self-aggrandizing as such industry ads always are, but included this pleasing sentiment: "Every moment we worked on the 'Wizard' with Mervyn LeRoy was a moment of joy."

Following *Oz*, Woolf and Ryerson did an uncredited treatment for Garland's *Babes in Arms* (1939; Noel Langley was a script doctor on this one). *Babes*, though, was the last Woolf-Ryerson collaboration, and Woolf's final staff work for MGM, though he returned in 1945 to do uncredited tweaking (along with more than thirty other writers!) of the script for *Ziegfeld Follies* (1945). The last was Woolf's final big-screen work—little wonder, for it was released two years after his death.

Florence Ryerson's career also wound down after *Oz*, though not quite as precipitously as Woolf's. She left MGM after *Henry Goes to Arizona* (1939; a light thriller starring Frank Morgan), and had just three more big-screen credits (one screenplay, two stories) between 1939 and 1946. After a handful of television credits between 1948 and 1956, Ryerson retired.

Writers Coming out of the Woodwork

During the spring and summer of 1938, while Langley, Ryerson, and Woolf were engaged in their various labors, LeRoy and Freed engaged still more writers: Herbert Fields, Samuel Hoffenstein, and Jack Mintz. Precisely what Fields contributed during his April 19–April 22 stint is unknown. Hoffenstein, who was engaged from May 3 to June 3, wrote a two-page outline of the Kansas sequence that involved Walter and "Dr. Miffle," two characters that never reached the shooting stage. Jack Mintz contributed some jokes. None of that amounts to a great deal, but there was nothing capricious or ill advised in the hiring of these gentlemen. They'd all been around the block in Hollywood and had long lists of solid credits.

Fields's entrée into the business had come in the late 1920s, via his credentials as a playwright. One of those plays, *Present Arms*, became Irene Dunne's first film, *Leathernecking* (1930). Fields was comfortable with musicals and did original stories and screenplays for pictures with songs by Rodgers and Hart, Cole Porter, and Harold Arlen and Ted Koehler. Fields's grasp of how to incorporate songs into narrative, plus his skill with dialogue, suggests that he contributed ideas based on Freed's "song as story" philosophy.

Samuel Hoffenstein had come to Hollywood in 1931 after success as a newspaper reporter, columnist, and short-story writer. He hit pay dirt right away, earning an Oscar nomination for his adaptation and screenplay for the Rouben Mamoulian–Fredric March version of *Dr. Jekyll and Mr. Hyde* (1931). Hoffenstein later did ghost work for Ernst Lubitsch's excellent *Design for Living* (1933), and won screenplay or co-writer credits for *Wharf Angel* (1934; a grotty oil-and-water romance starring Victor McLaglen and Dorothy Dell) and *Desire* (1936; a pleasing crime romance directed by Frank Borzage and designed to showcase Marlene Dietrich). After *Oz*, Hoffenstein was a script doctor on the Spencer Tracy version of *Dr. Jekyll and Mr. Hyde* (1941), and continued to do credited work on other high-profile movies: *Flesh and Fantasy* (1943), *Phantom of the Opera* (1943; with Claude Rains), and *Laura* (1944; a noir gem that is one of the most significant Hollywood films of the '40s). When Hoffenstein died in 1947, he was just fifty-six years old. His final credit, *Give My Regards to Broadway* (1948), was released posthumously.

Jack Mintz, who worked on *Oz* from August 3 to September 2, left a few pages of notes containing fresh gags. He's more obscure than some of the other *Oz* writers, and more intriguing, too. He was a film actor as early as 1915 and filled a variety of behind-the-scenes roles from the 1920s to the 1960s: dialogue director, assistant director, joke writer, and script doctor. A late-career association with producer Hal Wallis found Mintz at work as an assistant producer and dialogue coach on comedies starring Martin and Lewis and the solo Jerry Lewis, and on Elvis Presley pictures. Mintz retired in 1963 and died twenty years later.

Yip Harburg, Script Doctor

Noel Langley's imagination was highly valued by LeRoy and Freed, so, unlike Herman Mankiewicz and others, Langley hadn't been paid off and encouraged to go on his way when his work ostensibly ended. Instead, at the end of July he was given Ryerson and Woolf's final draft and told to have another go.

Langley looked over the changes and was very unhappy. He described Ryerson and Woolf's script as "so cutesy and oozy that I could have vomited." As

Langley saw things, Ryerson and Woolf had misinterpreted Freed's demand for emotional weight as a plea for adorableness (never mind that there's nothing very adorable about the Emerald City convulsed in a murderous riot). Langley came perilously close to confronting Mayer and LeRoy to insult them but reconsidered, and simply announced that he wanted his name removed from the script.

Freed believed that Langley was too valuable to be allowed to divorce himself from the script, but the associate producer also felt that this latest draft was too heavy with dialogue; he wanted a more visual experience and more "music" expressed in dialogue, too. With Mervyn LeRoy's approval, Freed engaged *Oz* lyricist E. Y. "Yip" Harburg to be the script editor, the person responsible for consistency of tone and focus. Harburg and his partner, melodist Harold Arlen, had already written most of the movie's songs. (See chapter 6). Now it was up to Harburg to shape and integrate the best from the Langley solo drafts, and from the Langley-Woolf-Ryerson draft. Although Harburg said, years later, "*The Wizard of Oz* was just for children," he took his assignment seriously, intent on smoothing the narrative and heightening its emotional impression.

Harburg's arrangement with Freed and LeRoy was highly unusual, but because the executives had already bought into Harburg's notion of songs-as-narrative, they felt confident that he could effectively shape the story. The involvement of Freed was critical at this juncture. Like Harburg, he was a music man who grasped the narrative potential of songs, and ways in which dialogue and music might profitably be mated. The rhyming dialogue that greets Dorothy in Munchkinland, for instance, was written by Harburg.

Because he was a lyricist with a well-developed story sense, Harburg's interest in songs went far beyond sonics. He said, "The function of a song is to simplify everything, to take the clutter out of too much plot and too many characters, to telescope everything into one emotional idea." Harburg went on: "You have to throw out the unnecessary. *And lots of things not in the script have to be invented* [in new dialogue] *to make the songs work*" (emphasis added).

Armed with a mandate from Freed, Harburg felt free to indicate that he preferred Langley's work to what Woolf and Ryerson had done. He retained Langley's brilliant notion that people in Dorothy's Kansas life have counterparts in Oz—though with fewer players than Langley had envisioned. Under Harburg's counsel, and in keeping with Freed's desire for a more pictorial experience, some set pieces that had been explicated in dialogue—notably Dorothy's arrival in Munchkinland and the group's arrival in the Emerald City—now were related almost entirely in song and dance. Both sequences—as pointed out by Harburg biographers Harold Meyerson and Ernie Harburg—are rudely cut short by the Witch, so that the audience is startled, character is delineated, and the narrative is forced forward. And it was Harburg who conceived of an awards ceremony acknowledging the best qualities of the Scarecrow, Tin Woodman, and Cowardly Lion.

Harburg felt that the early part of the Munchkinland sequence, in particular, needed work. Rather perfunctory "Gee, where am I?" dialogue was replaced by Harburg with charming, rhymed dialogue exchanges involving Dorothy, Glinda, and the Munchkins; it's a stylized, carefully syncopated way of speaking that is effective as narrative and in purely audio terms. The Harburg dialogue "sets up" the particular rhythms of the songs. Everything is of a piece.

Naturally enough, Noel Langley was in favor of Harburg's fondness for his script and began yet another revision. He was particularly motivated because Woolf and Ryerson had scuttled a great deal of his dialogue—which Langley promptly reinstated. He worked quickly, and a draft of the Langley-Woolf-Ryerson script was typed and circulated to studio executives on July 28. After front-office review, Langley was officially brought back onto the project on July 30. He polished the dialogue he had restored and dumped Woolf and Ryerson's Rainbow Bridge. He was told by Freed, however, to leave Prof. Marvel alone.

The Langley Draft, August 2, 1938

A ninety-six-page screenplay draft, credited to Noel Langley, is dated August 2, 1938. This draft is based on Langley's own earlier work and the work of Ryerson and Woolf. Further, it incorporates early contributions by Yip Harburg. The cover is repeatedly stamped "DO NOT MAKE CHANGES." (That directive would be ignored.) This version retains the vital instruction that had come from writer Herman Mankiewicz six months before: shoot the Kansas sequences in monochrome.

Langley described the tornado sequence in detail and retained Ryerson and Woolf's notion of a Rainbow Bridge that Dorothy climbs all the way to Oz.

Many of Yip Harburg's lyrics are incorporated into this draft script, although neither "Over the Rainbow" (which wouldn't be written until the following month) nor "We're Off to See the Wizard" is in place. "If I Only Had a Brain" is in this draft, though the Scarecrow-Dorothy dialogue is very different from the exchanges shot later by Victor Fleming.

When Dorothy and the Scarecrow depart together for Oz, Langley's script indicates a tune called "The Marching Song." Later, when Dorothy, the Scarecrow, and the Tin Woodman link arms and head for Oz, all three say "To Oz!" and then skip off to another mention of "The Marching Song." Dialogue that segues into songs was written by Harburg.

When the friends (by now joined by the Cowardly Lion) arrive at the Emerald City, the script reverts to an outline format, as if Langley had been unsure as to precisely what Freed and LeRoy wanted there or were willing to attempt in terms of sets and special effects.

Glinda, who arrives in Munchkinland in a bubble, is called "the North Witch" in this script and is described as a matronly older woman. (Baum's Good Witch of the North is a "little old woman" who is otherwise unnamed.

"Glinda" is Baum's name for the "beautiful and young" Good Witch of the South. Langley's Glinda takes elements from both Baum witches.)

The Rainbow Bridge appears again when Dorothy and her friends use it to leave the Witch's castle (which is surrounded by a crocodile moat) and start on their return to the Emerald City.

Revised Draft and Shooting Script, October 7, 1938

Still another revised screenplay was circulated on October 7. This one is credited to Langley, Ryerson, and Woolf. Yip Harburg has no credit on this draft, but, as before, he made crucial suggestions regarding thematic and tonal continuity, and dialogue "setups" for songs.

The October draft runs 112 pages. Assuming the "rule" that one page of script equals one minute of screen time, we have the makings of a movie considerably longer than the 101-minute cut we know. This draft, or a modest revision, would be the one that Richard Thorpe worked from when he began his shoot on October 13.

"Worked from" raises an important distinction. Although Thorpe had a revised screenplay on October 7, he didn't have what he really needed: a shooting script. A screenplay and a shooting script are different animals. A screenplay is the story the movie will tell, suggested by the writer(s) via dialogue and indications of setting, but with few or no suggestions for camera placement, camera movement, blocking, or anything else that's the bailiwick of the director and cinematographer. Typically, those two work together to break down the mechanics of each scene and fashion the screenplay into a tool that describes what the director needs to know in order to instruct his or her cast and crew how to accomplish what needs to be done. For instance, a shooting script notes that the camera will dolly in here; that single-source lighting will be used there; and that the camera crane will be lowered here, to reveal actors A, C, and B, in that order. Those and similar decisions are the director's and are informed by suggestions from the director of photography and other technical crew.

Thorpe and cinematographer Harold Rosson began to fashion their shooting script in September 1938 and continued to alter technical ideas, as well as dialogue and other screenplay elements, on-set in October. Thorpe began his shoot on October 13, 1938. He occupied himself with Dorothy's meeting with the Scarecrow and with scenes inside the Witch's castle. As we'll see, Thorpe lasted just two weeks before producer Mervyn LeRoy replaced him. The Thorpe footage was scrapped.

Naturally, most of Thorpe's shooting script got the heave-ho, and the screenplay continued to evolve. Those changes were probably for the better, because the October draft incorporated some peculiar elements. Prof. Marvel no longer has a pet lion or a dwarf assistant. Instead, he has a timid assistant named Goliath (a precursor to Bert Lahr's Zeke, who had yet to be created). The "Jitterbug" sequence, with lyrics, is here, as it would be in all later drafts.

At this juncture in the picture's development, the Wicked Witch of the West is a creature of sinister glamour, in the Gale Sondergaard mold, and is named (hang on) Gulcheria.

One script note that accompanies the opening Kansas sequence specifies that a "Negro baby in a bathtub" will breeze past Dorothy's window when the house is aloft in the middle of the twister. There was a built-in racial gag in there that audiences of the day would have understood; for years, novelty postcards with illustrations of black infants and children in bathtubs, and the words "How Ink Is Made," could be found in neighborhood groceries and five-and-tens across the South and lower Midwest. The gag was no less stupid and foolish then than it is now, but it would have raised plenty of smiles among racist white audiences. The flying baby bit was never filmed, probably not because of concerns about racial insult, but because 1) the sudden appearance of a black baby lifted from the farmlands of Kansas might strike white audiences as anomalous, and 2) a black face, even a baby's, would inject a level of realism that wasn't desired. (Granted, the Wicked Witch that we meet later has green skin, the Tin Woodman is silver, the Lion is brown and furry, and so forth—but the characters' underlying Caucasian backgrounds were clear—and comforting—to audiences.)

Worsley's Booklet

A production-breakdown booklet annotated by script clerk Wallace Worsley Jr. came to auction in the spring of 2010. (Worsley also functioned as one of the picture's two uncredited assistant directors; Al Shenberg was the other.) Worsley's eighty-eight-page booklet jiggers the shooting script into an efficient, day-by-day plan for on-set activity, with schedules for actors and other personnel, props, mechanical effects, and other things that would be needed for each day of the shoot. One of Worsley's production charts notes that lots of bees would be required on-set on a specific day because, according to the shooting script, the Wicked Witch was going to make good on her threat to turn the Tin Woodman into a beehive.

Mank

In February 1939, LeRoy assigned *Oz* script chores to Herman Mankiewicz, a onetime Chicago newspaperman and Hollywood veteran with more than a dozen years of credits dating back to the late-silent era. Prior to the *Oz* assignment, Mank had worked at RKO, Paramount, and elsewhere. He had fallen prey to alcohol and gambling, but MGM regarded him highly because of his brilliant script (with Frances Marion) for the studio's *Dinner at Eight* (1933), and as a script doctor at other studios (*Love Among the Millionaires*, 1930; and *The Lost Squadron*, 1932). Two years after the release of *The Wizard of Oz*, Mank's name

Herman Mankiewicz (left) is most famous for collaborating with Orson Welles on the script for *Citizen Kane*. Mank worked on *The Wizard of Oz* for just a month but contributed a vital idea: shoot the Kansas sequences in monochrome and save the Technicolor for the Oz part of the story. In this 1943 photo, Mankiewicz leaves court with attorney Norman Tyre after arraignment on a drunk-driving charge.

would be the talk of the town because of his co-writer credit (with Orson Welles) on *Citizen Kane* (1941), a screenplay that won the Academy Award.

Mankiewicz had no particular experience with fantasy—which was good, because he knew that the fantasy elements of *Oz* would have to be grounded in a recognizable reality in order to be accepted by audiences. He was particularly interested in Dorothy's Kansas origins. Here, he felt, was the real-world anchor that the rest of the picture could be tethered to. L. Frank Baum had not written a protracted Kansas sequence to open his novel, but what he did write was starkly eloquent. Here is a sample from Baum:

> When Dorothy stood in the doorway and looked around, she could see nothing but the great gray prairie on every side. Not a tree nor a house

broke the broad sweep of flat country that reached the edge of the sky in all directions. The sun had baked the plowed land into a gray mass, with little cracks running through it. Even the grass was not green, for the sun had burned the tops of the long blades until they were the same gray color to be seen everywhere. Once the house had been painted, but the sun blistered the paint and the rains washed it away, and now the house was as dull and gray as everything else.

This concise prose anticipates such later writers as John Steinbeck, Erskine Caldwell, and James Agee. Mankiewicz, himself a writer with a gift for the terse, well-placed word, was impressed with Baum's simple, declarative realism, and was inspired to turn in a seventeen-page outline for "the Kansas sequence." LeRoy liked it and encouraged Mankiewicz to flesh it out. In about a week, Mank turned over a fifty-six-page script for the Kansas sequences, with instructions that the footage be shot in black and white. This is a very important innovation that, as we've seen, may have been inspired by animator Ted Eshbaugh's 1933 cartoon short *The Wizard of Oz*. (Years later, LeRoy awarded himself credit for the monochrome idea.)

Although Mank generally stayed close to the Baum book, he did invent some fresh characters, including an out-of-left-field wealthy mother and daughter that visit the Gale farm.

His work on Kansas complete, Mankiewicz remained on the *Oz* payroll for another two weeks, concentrating on particulars of the cyclone and Dorothy's arrival in Oz. Mank created two more characters out of whole cloth, the Princess and the Grand Duke, and brought an intriguing twist to the Wicked Witch, whom he delineated as a peculiar sort of bureaucrat who keeps an office! The words on her office door read, "Cruelties, Tortures and all kinds of Devilments."

As written by Mankiewicz, Dorothy is so puzzled by the goings-on in Oz that she asks, "Does everybody in this country dance when he's happy?"

Mankiewicz was relieved of his *Oz* duties sometime in March 1938. Although he receives no on-screen credit, his contribution can hardly be overestimated.

Herman Mankiewicz was just fifty-five years old when he died in 1953, but not before he wrote other major movies: *The Pride of the Yankees* (1942), *The Enchanted Cottage* (1945), *The Spanish Main* (1945), and *A Woman's Secret* (1949).

Dorothy and the Hero's Journey

As set down by L. Frank Baum and, more pertinently, by MGM, *The Wizard of Oz* is the story of a journey and the creation of a hero. Dorothy is called to adventure by a monstrous cyclone that sweeps her to Oz, a place that, to her, is very strange. She's greeted there by Glinda, who becomes Dorothy's guide and mentor.

After leaving Munchkinland, Dorothy meets new friends and an intimidating new enemy, too. Dorothy's fear gives her pause, but she resolves to complete her journey because she has a goal: to return home. Because that return apparently hinges on Dorothy's acquisition of the Witch's broomstick, Dorothy's journey assumes the stature of a quest.

Various obstacles continue to test Dorothy's mettle, but with help from her allies, she continues forward, emerging not simply alive but triumphant, and in possession of the broomstick. But Dorothy's quest isn't over.

The beginning of her journey back to her ordinary life gets off to an unpromising start (the Wizard really is hopeless), but Dorothy's hopes are realized moments after articulating for Glinda the wisdom she's acquired.

Back home in Kansas, Dorothy's people don't believe her tale. Nevertheless, Dorothy has returned from her journey with an elixir of knowledge. Her kindly nature, and new self-awareness, will motivate her to share that knowledge with everyone she encounters.

Readers familiar with the 20th-century American thinker Joseph Campbell will already have recognized in the paragraphs above some of the phrases and descriptors Campbell utilized to understand the shape and sequence of what he called "the hero's journey"—a shape and substance that's shared by the great preponderance of fictional adventure. Campbell admired Carl Jung, the creator of analytical psychology; like Jung, Campbell became preoccupied with archetypes ("the mentor" is one) common to all storytelling cultures, and how those archetypes are expressed and become like myths—and the ways that myths become a *lingua franca* that spans continents and the centuries.

People's shared understanding ("grasp" might be a more precise word) of quest adventures isn't quite genetic, but it is firmly implanted in us by every tradition of storytelling, from tales told around the fire after the hunt, read in a book, or enjoyed on a movie screen. In Campbell's logical, goal-oriented progression of events, we find comfort and satisfaction. In the bargain, we learn about our own limitations and capabilities.

In all of this, L. Frank Baum's imagined world and MGM's expression of that world share a heroic tradition with works as diverse, and yet essentially alike, as *Beowulf* and *Lord of the Rings*; *The Odyssey* and *Gulliver's Travels*; *Moby Dick* and *Heart of Darkness*; *The Hunger Games* and *The Four Feathers*; and *Star Wars* and *Watership Down*.

The narrative underpinnings of *The Wizard of Oz* are ancient, and although Dorothy is from Kansas, she's also from everywhere, and from every time. She's the heroine celebrated by storytellers since the beginning of recorded history. Dorothy is epic.

8

A Horse of a Different Color

Production Design

M GM production design was supervised by Cedric Gibbons, who was assisted by supervising art director Elmer Sheeley, Wade Rubottom, and lead scenic artist George Gibson. Associate art director William A. Horning worked particularly closely with Gibbons. The vast physical resources of MGM promised that there would be no shortage of building materials or workers; very nearly anything that Gibbons and Horning might come up with could be made real.

General Design

Baum's book provided Gibbons and Horning with very little usable reference. Original *Oz* illustrator W. W. Denslow had created strong images for the story's principal characters but few detail of places. (Baum and Denslow had rightly concluded that the book's readers would relate most strongly to the tale's characters. Places could be described primarily through prose, but readers would long for—and eagerly accept—visualizations of Dorothy and the others.)

Denslow chose to depict the Emerald City two ways: from afar (the metropolis assumes a vaguely Moorish silhouette) and in close-up details, such as an ornate gate (in these, the city seems medieval). Gibbons wasn't satisfied with Denslow's paucity of detail. Working at a time when a future-oriented kind of modernism dominated many areas of design, Gibbons wanted to make a particular visual statement with the Emerald City. Hence, the city's towering, densely packed spires and towers. Gibbons took some of his inspiration from a German sketch that predated World War I. Another likely influence, also German, was film director Fritz Lang's vision of the great, complex towers that comprise *Metropolis* (1927).

From a distance, the exterior skins of the great buildings appear smooth and featureless. Many of the tower tops are rounded, which reflects the shift to streamlined architecture and industrial design (the famed Zephyr train is a good example) that had taken firm hold of the design world by 1938. (A great

This test shot of the living room at the Gale farmhouse reveals the nature of set construction. Note the thinness of the flats (walls), and the rigging above. Most or all of the furniture and other items were standard stuff in MGM's prop department.

deal of streamlined, modernist design was created for the 1939 New York World's Fair.)

Relatively low, translucent domes situated at the approach to the city suggest what urban designers call "mixed use," by which areas of commerce and residence are combined.

And in a nod to a design conceit that had been popular a century before Gibbons got to work on *Oz*, some Emerald City details, such as narrow, horizontal windows and ornately carved exterior door frames, recall Orientalist art of the 19th century. Napoleon's up-and-down military fortunes in Egypt during 1798–99 sparked the imagination of explorers and artists who journeyed into what we now know as the Middle East (Iraq, Persia, Palestine, Lebanon, and Arabia), as well as Turkey and North Africa. Specialist and lay interest in the region grew rapidly, and the Orientalist movement was a sort of worldwide fad throughout the 1800s. The Middle East was romanticized and eroticized, and cast as a place of perpetual mystery and intrigue. (Because of latter-day pop-culture interpretations of the Middle East, Western misapprehensions about the region were perpetuated and encouraged, so that by 1955, moviegoers could experience the sublime absurdity of grinning, Oklahoma-born actor Dale Robertson as *Son of Sinbad*.)

Orientalist art and design depended heavily on color to impart exoticism. In the Emerald City, even horses were exotic and proved to be more challenging

These test photos of the Yellow Brick Road reveal obvious differences between the visions of director Richard Thorpe and replacement director Victor Fleming. In the Thorpe conception (top), the road has no curbs and is paved with ovoid bricks. Fleming asked for curbs and bricks that were precisely rectangular. In the Fleming photo, sheeting (below) protects the bricks from the weight of the cameras and other equipment. Both shots show the upper limits of the painted backdrop.

than may have been assumed. Trial and error determined the proper dye levels needed to create the "horse of a different color." Some early trials failed because the colors ran, or were too dense. Others just looked unappetizing; Gibbons remarked, "[I]f you paint a gray horse green, the color won't turn out too pleasing."

When the ASPCA rep finally said "No more dye," Gibbons's team created a new formula that was Jell-O-based. The concoction gave a good visual effect, but the horses (there were two of them, Arabians named Ike and Mike) wanted to lick it off because it tasted good.

Art Direction

Many of the film's most important design concepts, such as Munchkinland, were closely collaborative efforts begun with loose sketches prepared by William Horning and followed by sketches and drawings by Malcolm Brown and the lead sketch artist, Jack Martin Smith. Smith was a very important figure at this stage of the production, as he supervised art department staffers who created progressively more polished and detailed drawings rendered at a quarter-inch to the foot. Cedric Gibbons involved himself throughout the process, supervising meetings and contributing his own sketches and drawings.

Smith also prepared detailed notes on materials; in the case of the Munchkinland set, the notes indicated a great deal of plaster and decorative paint.

Horning did the initial designs of the Witch's hourglass and other purpose-built props. His rough sketches were refined by Smith and the sketch crew.

Finished drawings were sent to the construction department, which was housed in a massive space with a glass-panel roof and a main floor stretching more than one hundred feet. The department was staffed by 500 carpenters, 150 laborers, 50 plasterers, 20 scenic artists, and 15 plumbers. Studio-era construction crews are typically unsung, but it is their craft that brings reality to movies made before computer-generated effects. The complex environments built by MGM's construction crew were architecturally and materially sound, and although the construction encompassed only what would be visible to the camera, the structures were nevertheless solid and real. Gerald F. Rocket was the construction coordinator on *The Wizard of Oz*.

Construction of the Munchkinland set began on Stage 27 on December 5, 1938, when director Victor Fleming was shooting on other stages. The work was supervised by Edwin B. Willis. With its painted backdrops, the completed set towered dozens of feet above the stage floor and covered more than two acres. The buildings and other elements were built to one-quarter normal size. Dozens of painters applied scores of colors.

Many years after *Oz*, Jack Haley remembered that when a teenage Munchkin player saw the Munchkinland set for the first time, she was overwhelmed by its beauty and began to cry.

Another test shot from the Thorpe shoot. At the request of replacement director Victor Fleming, designers subtly reworked the crystal globe and other props seen here. The latticework of shadows prepared for Thorpe would remain, though the ceiling piece was never visible on screen.

A technician holds the slate identifying the prop gadgetry used by the Wizard to create the fearsome "Wizard head." The hanging microphone is a lovely relic of 1930s industrial design.

When a particular set or object simply couldn't be built, the item was created in paint. The Witch's castle is a marvel of malevolent-looking architecture, but only portions of it could be constructed. Candelario Rivas's matte painting of the ramparts of the Witch's castle was optically combined with the castle tower, which was a miniature. The final effect is a stunner. A simpler matte effect, the rays of sunshine that beam down on Munchkinland after Dorothy's arrival, is another audience-pleaser.

The film's matte work fell under the aegis of special-effects supervisor A. Arnold "Buddy" Gillespie and was supervised by Warren Newcombe, a special-effects Oscar nominee for *Mrs. Miniver* (1942), and a winner for *Thirty Seconds Over Tokyo* (1944) and *Green Dolphin Street* (1947). Each of those was an MGM production. Newcombe's professional career began in New York City, where he was a successful commercial artist and portrait painter. He segued into films by producing and directing an experimental, one-reel fantasy short called *The Enchanted City* (1922; one critic praised its "remarkable romantic grandeur"). After working briefly with D. W. Griffith at the famed director's Mamaroneck, New York, studio, Newcombe moved to Hollywood in the mid-1920s. He was shortly hired by MGM, where he remained for some thirty-five years. In the 1930s, matte paintings were typically painted on glass that would later be positioned before the camera in front of a set (sometimes full-sized, other times a miniature). The matte painting and the real-world element were shot simultaneously for an illusion of depth and reality. Some mattes indicated foreground elements; others, painted in subdued tones, suggested a landscape or other element of the background. Matte paintings also could be captured on film and then mated with a separately filmed element, such as actors or a stop-motion puppet (à la *King Kong*), in an optical printer.

Warren Newcombe had his own ideas about how to do matte paintings. He abandoned glass for large sheets of black cardboard, four feet wide, onto which he applied crayon pastels. The distant view of the Emerald City's gleaming spires was one of those four-feet-wide matte paintings. Because the high-quality work coming out of Newcombe's department suggested that pastels gave better color values and softer edges than oil paint, the "Newcombe method" became one of MGM's closely guarded, proprietary secrets.

Some paintings were not mattes in the usual sense but painted backdrops, sometimes with forced perspective (like the expanse that stretches ahead of Dorothy as she prepares to leave Munchkinland) and carefully contrived color "fade" that gave the illusion of distance between object and observer. Besides the real-world degradation of color with distance, horizon lines also had to be carefully worked out. Without proper care, a painter or painters would lose track of the supposed horizon, and the backdrop would be untrue to its own visual logic and have to be scrapped. In a finished work, a backdrop with a mismanaged horizon might appear to float, or sit too low relative to the actors.

The cornfield backdrop behind Ray Bolger and Judy Garland on Stage 26 was painted on an expanse of muslin that measured 400 × 35 feet. As for other

This test photo for the "Jitterbug" sequence reveals tree designs that were exclusive to this discarded number. Note the vertical slit at the back of the tree on the left, to allow a technician's egress, and hidden manipulation of branches left limbs. Two pieces of equipment are also visible: an arc lamp and a bell horn used in music playback.

Among the props assembled for Richard Thorpe's shoot in the Witch's castle were two items designed and made especially for the film: a silver chalice with a lizard top and a jeweled box with a snake-and-eagle lid. A Wide World story described designer H. B. Crouch as an "ingenious Welsh jeweler."

Oz backdrops, the cornfield paint was mixed with glue, which acted as a binding agent. The painting was the work of about a dozen painters who worked from color sketches by Jack Martin Smith. The painters stood on a scaffold that was twenty feet long, applying color according to a predetermined palette indicated on the muslin by a grid. The painting of backdrops was supervised by scenic-art department chief George Gibson, who came to MGM in 1934 after being laid off by Fox.

In order to allow for necessary perspectives and sight lines, alignment, and to avoid shadows inadvertently cast on the muslin, backdrops were set up beyond the back edge of the sets, leaving a gap of twelve feet. Cast members had to remain mindful of the space.

When all scenes involving a particular backdrop had been shot and vetted in dailies, the muslin was painted over and reused.

In Focus: Cedric Gibbons (1893–1960)

The striking and impressively varied production designs put forth in *The Wizard of Oz* and other MGM movies of the golden age came from the production-design department of Cedric Gibbons. He supervised the look of more than a thousand movies, designed the Oscar statuette (with sculptor George Stanley), and designed and built a fabulous art deco home for himself and his movie-star wife, Dolores Del Rio. Gibbons was moved by beauty, and that, along with his marvelous gifts, helped make him one of the finest production designers the industry has ever produced.

Austin Cedric Gibbons was an Irish kid born in Dublin and brought up in Brooklyn. As a teenager, he attended Art Students of New York school and worked for his father, an architect. He shortly segued into advertising. Gibbons became interested in the movies during World War I; after three years of work for Edison Studios, he came to the Sam Goldwyn company in 1918 as an art director. Goldwyn was based in New Jersey in those days, but when the company merged with the Loew's/Mayer/Metro partnership that created MGM in 1924, Gibbons remained with the new entity and followed it west.

Gibbons had refined sensibilities, as well as a sharp understanding of the realities of moviemaking. To say that he was motivated by business and balance sheets would be an overstatement, but he knew that numbers mattered. He invariably pushed himself and his department to produce quality work on time and on budget. And during his peak in the late 1920s and '30s, he pushed for the *new*.

The sleek and *moderne* art deco movement was flourishing in Paris in the mid-1920s. When Gibbons visited there, his artistic vision was altered. His work on an early Joan Crawford vehicle, *Our Dancing Daughters* (1928), excited audiences, and when Gibbons followed up with similarly deco designs for *Our Modern Maidens* (1929) and *Our Blushing Brides* (1930), "Hollywood deco" became a sensation in the studios of home-interior designers on both coasts.

Gibbons enjoyed suggesting on-screen wealth and sophistication with designs that shattered the musty, old conceptions of the rich (dark mahogany, and so forth) by

Cedric Gibbons had a keen interest in art deco, which is evident in this shot of the cast at the Emerald City.

placing characters in strikingly modern environments dominated by circles, curves, and arches (as in *Grand Hotel*, 1932), and by bringing eye-popping tonal values to black-and-white film stock (as with the "white room" design for *Dinner at Eight*, 1933).

Among film designers, Gibbons was an early proponent of indirect lighting, which softened the contours of furniture and faces, and suffused everything with a sophisticated glow. His lighting schemes soon began to appear in the houses and apartments of the rich and well-off. At the same time, his aesthetics were enthusiastically received by "regular" moviegoers who had been battered by the Depression and wanted to enjoy elegant, unostentatious beauty.

With over a thousand screen credits (as per his contract), Gibbons obviously didn't function as principal designer on every project. He supervised dozens of art directors, designers, sketch artists, illustrators, draftsmen, and architects, and remained aware of the progress and "look" of every project. His sensibilities had helped propel MGM to the top, and he ensured that every design was tasteful and practical—that is, it would photograph properly. Gibbons was firm with his staff but quick to defend them—as a group and as individuals—from what he felt was unwarranted or ignorant criticism.

In the vein of studio costume designer Gilbert Adrian, Gibbons was a dandy—an elegant study in Continental grays and black, complete with kid gloves and a felt Homburg hat. He drove a Duesenberg and may have been the best-accessorized man in town after marrying Del Rio in 1930.

Gibbons entertained a wish to get into the Directors Guild, which would explain his co-directing credit (with Jack Conway) on *Tarzan and His Mate* (1934), which was mostly directed by Conway.

Gibbons remained with MGM until his retirement in 1956. He moved with the times, adjusting his aesthetic to suit musicals (notably, *Singin' in the Rain* and *An American in Paris*), comedies, westerns, thrillers, war films, and all manner of traditional dramas. During his career, Gibbons was Oscar-nominated thirty-nine times (including for *The Wizard of Oz*, and often for multiple films in a single year) and had eleven wins for projects as varied as *The Merry Widow* (1934), *The Yearling* (1946), and *Julius Caesar* (1953).

And the Art Deco house Gibbons built for Del Rio? It's still pristine and a favorite of architectural magazines and Web sites.

9

Only Bad Witches Are Ugly

Character Design and Costumes

Wizard of Oz makeup was supervised by Jack Dawn, who designed key characters. He supervised more than forty adept makeup artists and lab technicians, a full three dozen of whom were staff added expressly for the *Oz* project. Nighttime labor was the norm.

Rather than use greasepaint (which gives a false, theatrical look) or masks (which are impressive in long shots but immobile and lifeless in close-ups), Dawn created prosthetic appliances: foam rubber pieces molded from the contours of plaster-of-paris life masks (or partial masks) taken of key cast members. Dawn wanted each actor's face and personality to be apparent despite the makeup. In the most dramatic cases—Bolger, Haley, Lahr, and Hamilton—he was stunningly successful. Dawn was undoubtedly aware of the immobile masks created by Wally Westmore and Newt Jones for Paramount's *Alice in Wonderland* (1933); he knew he could accomplish something more artful, and he was right. When the *New York Post* reviewed *The Wizard of Oz* in August 1939, the writer made special note of the "miraculous makeup." A trade publication, *Picture Reports*, was even more effusive: "Those character makeups by Jack Dawn are alone worth the price of admission."

Rubber pieces and latex appliances were freely utilized, for such things as the Tin Woodman's hat, nose, and chinstrap; the Witch's nose and chin; the Lion's face above his lower lip; and the Scarecrow's burlap face and neck.

Costumer Adrian (professionally, he dispensed with his first name, Gilbert) and cinematographer Hal Rosson did Technicolor tests of costumes during the second half of 1938, between late summer and early winter. Both men had to remain mindful of the Technicolor camera's tendency to read certain brown tones as green and its inability to recognize pure white. On screen, snowy white would be practically invisible, so if Rosson and Adrian wanted to show that tone, they had to "cheat" by doctoring whites with a pale blue rinse. For general use during the shoot, Rosson devised a "relative color value list" that was consulted during prep of makeups, sets, costumes, matte paintings, painted backdrops, props—everything.

MGM's chief of makeup, Jack Dawn. Imaginative and tireless, he was an industry pioneer in molded prosthetics.

Eccentricities of color recognition aside, Technicolor was a dream challenge for Adrian, whose designs would be realized by a studio wardrobe department of more than 180 people. Among that number were milliners, pattern cutters, seamstresses, beaders, and dyers. Cleaning and pressing of most costumes was done overnight, off-site. However, particularly visible costumes, as well as those with ornate or delicate accessories, were cleaned on the lot, by hand.

Throughout much of Adrian's involvement with *The Wizard of Oz*, the designer grew unhappy with Technicolor color director Henri Jaffa, a Technicolor employee who was on-set. He and Adrian disagreed about the color of the film's costumes and which colors would and would not photograph accurately. Although Adrian was an important figure in the MGM hierarchy, he was subservient to studio manager Eddie Mannix, who ruled in Jaffa's favor after art director Cedric Gibbons interceded on Jaffa's behalf.

Dorothy

The central character of the *Oz* novel and film is, of course, Dorothy Gale. In order to succeed on film, Dorothy had to be not just charismatic, but appealing and likeable. Much of that appeal would come from her appearance.

Considerable time was devoted to the sort of makeup and costume Judy Garland would wear. Dorothy's hair was a particular challenge, probably because variations of hairstyle and color are almost endless, even when the mandate is as seemingly simple as "Kansas girl." Wigs in various degrees of dark blonde were tested; likewise a brace of auburn ones. Some had narrow pigtails, but most had softer, modified pigtails that swept gently onto Dorothy's upper chest, as in W. W. Denslow's original illustrations.

A costume and makeup test for Judy Garland's Dorothy, probably from the late summer of 1938. Things changed dramatically following the October dismissal of director Richard Thorpe: costumer Adrian came up with far simpler pinafore designs; and hair stylist Sydney Guilaroff and makeup chief Jack Dawn discarded the "glamour" feel of Dorothy's appearance.

One of Dawn's many facial-makeup experiments was dominated by heavily rouged cheeks, glossy lips, and pronounced eye shadow. It frankly made for a peculiar-seeming Dorothy, because the overall effect was at odds with itself. The bound breasts, simple dress, and plain shoes suggested a little girl, but the blonde wig and glamour makeup evoked a grown woman (or, maybe, a child-woman, which has an unwholesome air all its own). The blonde hair was particularly distracting, partly for its shade and partly because it drew attention from Judy's striking, enormous eyes. Beyond that, this Dorothy didn't at all suggest the innocence of a Kansas farm girl—and yet the look was approved by LeRoy and Freed.

Costume tests with Judy Garland began in August 1938. Adrian executed numerous designs for Dorothy's gingham checked pinafore, with variations to sleeves, collars, patterns, bodices, and other elements—all of which were coordinated with a variety of test wigs prepared by Sydney Guilaroff. The white portion of the famed gingham dress was blue and pink, rather than blue and white; under the arc lights and on Technicolor stock, white photographed too "hot." With a slight pink tone to the dress and blouse, the film stock registered the color as white. Careful allowance had to be made for the ruby slippers' tendency to reflect light from the arc lamps.

Adrian made the dress with a twenty-seven-inch waist, which exposes Louis Mayer's notion that Judy Garland was overweight as ridiculous. Still, Judy wasn't the childlike, flat-chested Dorothy imagined by original Oz illustrator W. W. Denslow. She was a young woman who had to suffer the discomfort and indignity of a binding brassiere that would make her figure appear as childlike as possible. Already preoccupied with what she imagined as her sub-par physical appearance, Judy wasn't happy at the prospect of millions of people seeing her with the figure of a ten-year-old.

These test images are from Halloween 1938, when the *Wizard of Oz* troupe had already been idle for a week. Judy's makeup was now more in line with what we know, and her hair and pinafore were shading closer to their final versions.

The slippers were fitted to Garland and then transformed by the costume department. The shoes (there were multiple pairs) were covered with fine netting, onto which closely spaced sequins were sewn, one by one.

The Scarecrow

Many years after *The Wizard of Oz*, more than one horror film turned scarecrows into engines of terror. As scripted for *Oz*, though, the Scarecrow was kind and loving, and although his makeup had to suggest a living scarecrow, the overall effect could not be allowed to veer into the grotesque. The Scarecrow had to be as unthreatening as he was real. In that regard, long-faced and handsome Ray Bolger was ideally cast.

Bolger, like Lahr and Haley, reported to makeup each morning at 5:30, so that Dawn's people could get in thirty minutes of work before the Munchkin players arrived at 6:00.

In August 1938, a plaster cast was made of Bolger's face and neck. Elsewhere in the shop, clear acetate that had been placed over a life-sized 8″× 10″ Bolger

This October 31, 1938, costume and makeup test image shows subtle alterations to Ray Bolger's face, and a re-think of his pants, too.

portrait allowed Dawn and his staff to noodle possible Scarecrow designs in grease pencil. Shortly, the acetate (one sheet after another) gave the sculptors a useful surface from which appliances could be modeled.

As summer became fall, a very thin latex mask that had been fashioned from the plaster cast became the basis for further refinement. The burlap texture of the Scarecrow's face was tricky and required a lot of starts and stops. When Dawn and his staff achieved an acceptable texture, the burlap pattern was etched onto a thin layer of clay overlaid on the latex mask. The "burlap" was cast in latex, and when all was in order, the Scarecrow's head gave the impression of a bag loosely tied around the neck, as per W. W. Denslow's 1900 illustrations. (Dawn referred to the slightly flared, loose-seeming bottom part as "wings.")

The finished mask was attached to Bolger's face with spirit gum and other adhesives, a process that required about an hour. At night, another hour was needed to remove the mask. Not surprisingly, it was impossible to peel off the mask from Bolger's face without tearing the latex, so the facial mold was used over and over throughout the shoot, as fresh latex was cast nightly, for use the next day. (Dawn's "wings" were more sturdy because they didn't adhere directly to Bolger's face, so the "bag" portion of the makeup didn't have to be replaced every day; during most weeks, three or four were used. In all, some one hundred Scarecrow masks were cast during the shoot.

Bolger was patient, but after some weeks of the makeup going on and off and on again, the skin of the actor's face acquired a faint, but discernable, burlap pattern. The marks didn't fade until weeks after production had wrapped.

As with many other aspects of the film, some trial and error was involved as the Scarecrow's "look" was settled. In some tests, liberal amounts of straw stuck from beneath the Scarecrow's "collar" (the open bottom of the burlap bag). Different amounts of straw also appeared from beneath the soft cap and from elbows and sleeves.

Simultaneous with all of this were many variations of eye treatments, including one with thin black circles drawn all around the eye orbits, which made Bolger look like Our Gang's Pete the Pup. Eyebrows also came in for a lot of grave scrutiny. There seemed to be early agreement that they should be composed of straw, but should they be diagonal slashes (which gave an unintended angry look) or soft arches? Mouth shape, and the shape and color toning of the nose, were also labored over. A mouth that went with the circled eyes had a clearly intentional circus-clown look, with lips that were extended horizontally in red.

There also were many treatments of the Scarecrow's frown lines and other "character lines." He had to look weathered and rustic, but he couldn't seem aged or intimidating.

Scarecrow had a soft cap almost from the outset, and changes to it as the rest of the makeup progressed were minor. One version of the original Scarecrow costume later found a home at the Smithsonian Institution.

Development of Ray Bolger's Scarecrow costume went routinely and changed only modestly from early conceptions to final design. Evolutionary changes to Bolger's facial makeup were more pointed. Early sketches of the Scarecrow's head and face makeup from late summer 1938 led Jack Dawn to create very light initial makeups, with Bolger's features barely obscured. In other words, anyone could plainly see that the actor was Ray Bolger. This less-is-more approach was influenced by the fundamental mistake committed by Paramount with 1933's *Alice in Wonderland*, in which the faces, and even entire bodies, of many stars and popular actors were completely obscured beneath masks, and molded costumes and headpieces. Audiences hadn't cared for that at all.

The Tin Woodman I

Lanky dancer Buddy Ebsen, originally cast as the Scarecrow, took the Tin Woodman role following encouragement from Ray Bolger. The first attempt at a Tin Woodman costume was formed from sheet aluminum. The pieces were rigid, and the overall effect was physically inexpressive and hindered Ebsen's movement. Designs that followed (some of which incorporated stiff paper) had smoother, progressively less-dramatic shoulder, elbow, and knee joints. A skirt-like piece that hung from the lower edge of the torso piece, like a knight's tasset, was tested and then abandoned.

A subsequent idea for the Woodman's main body utilized metallic cloth painted silver and sewn over buckram, which allowed Ebsen to move more freely.

Early tests put Ebsen in storybook facial makeup dominated by darkly circled eyes and deep character lines running from the sides of the nose to the edges of the Tin Man's horizontally stretched mouth. In principle, Jack Dawn's wide, very rigid, rubber chinstrap design followed W. W. Denslow's original artwork, which depicted the Tin Woodman's mouth as dominated by a high-hinged

Tin Woodman Buddy Ebsen, attired here in a design proposal for the Winkie uniforms, joined the rest of the cast in poses showing makeup and costume concepts. Ebsen's facial treatment, with the unwisely immobilizing chinstrap, was still in place when the actor shot his scenes.

lower jaw that defined the lower lip and stretched across the width of his face. But the chin piece also gave the Tin Woodman an unintended pugnacious look, and anyway, so much of Ebsen's lower face was covered that he was on the verge of no longer being Buddy Ebsen (*Alice in Wonderland* all over again). Nevertheless, the conception was still in place when Richard Thorpe began shooting.

The visible parts of Ebsen's face were layered in blued white makeup dusted with fine aluminum. The nose was rigid rubber.

Illness forced Ebsen off the project.

The Tin Woodman II

Following Ebsen's departure, the role was recast with Jack Haley. Although the strap remained as part of the Haley makeup, its contours were softened so that the piece had a less dramatic "hinged" aspect. The center part of the chin piece was glued to Haley's skin to allow natural-appearing movement of the mouth and jaw.

The flesh of Haley's face and neck was covered in a neutral base, with silver-toned aluminum paste blended over it. But the paste didn't match the tone of the costume, so Dawn repeated a trick he'd done with Ebsen, adding bluing that allowed Haley's face to photograph properly. Dawn also darkened Haley's lips, so that the actor's teeth wouldn't be "lost" in the expanse of silver around his mouth. Each of the Tin Woodman's facial rivets was applied by hand, with positioning carefully noted and recorded so that each day's shoot was consistent with the others.

Haley's costume was, like Ebsen's, buckram and leather painted silver. Because Ebsen was a dancer, bendable joints had been important. That wasn't quite so necessary with Haley, so his costume was relatively rigid. At a glance, it differed from Ebsen's mainly in detail involving the funnel cap, elbow joints, the lower portion of the main chest piece, and the shoes. Although the final costume weighed forty pounds and effectively suggested the stiffness of a man made of tin, it allowed Haley considerably more movement in the arms than the earliest conceptions. But once Haley had been welded inside the costume, he was in it for the entire day. At day's end, the welder had to return, to free Haley.

During tests, cinematographer Harold Rosson became aware of the costume's tendency to reflect light and devised plans to combat it.

The Tin Woodman costume did not survive long beyond the shoot. It was dismantled and the pieces separated.

The Cowardly Lion

Of all the actors who toiled beneath the hot lights needed to provide illumination for the Technicolor film stock, Bert Lahr suffered the most. Yes, Haley's heavy, stiff Tin Woodman costume meant that he had to relax on a slant board between takes, but he wasn't required to carry fifty pounds of sewn lion skin shaped with thick, sweat-inducing padding. Indeed, Lahr perspired copiously inside the costume and had to shed it down to his ankles between setups, so that he could be dried with forced air. Real lions on the veldt had it easier.

Jack Dawn's design of the Lion's head and face, which required that Lahr's features be almost completely covered, is a miracle of cleverness: the Lion is clearly a lion, but none of Lahr's sparkle or personality was lost. His head and face were layered in rubber prosthetics molded and cast to fit his features perfectly. Built-in tensioners pulled up the Lion's nose to give what Lahr called a comically "retroussé effect." The lower-cheek and upper-lip pieces were contoured to suggest the slightly puffed cheeks of a cat. The inner edges of the appliances descended vertically on each side of Lahr's mouth, before sweeping back into comically heavy jowls. The Lion's "hair" and "beard" were made of fur. Lahr's eyes and portions of his cheeks were the only facial elements left largely untouched.

Because of the complexity of the appliances, Lahr wasn't allowed to eat solid food because chewing would have had a disastrous effect; liquids only.

Dawn and his Lion team came up with many variations on a central element: the Lion's mane. Early concepts suggest the pompadour of a pampered lap dog. Gradually, the mane was refined, until the fur swept straight back from the Lion's forehead and fell grandly on both sides of his face and onto his chest. (The design allowed great comedy during the Lion's first visit to the Emerald City, when solicitous hairdressers curl his lower mane into delightful ringlets.)

The heavy whiskers were individually inserted into Lahr's lower-cheek pieces. Lahr's tail was manipulated by fishing line handled by technician Harry Edwards (or possibly property master Jackie Ackerman, accounts differ), who was stationed on catwalks situated above camera range.

Two Lion costumes were made, and both survive (see chapter 19).

Dawn himself worked on Bert Lahr, who regarded the whole process with considerable apprehension, not just because of the potential discomfort but because, like any comic actor whose fortune was his face, he worried that his features would be obscured.

The genius of Jack Dawn's makeup design for Bert Lahr is that the sculpted prosthetics did not obscure Lahr's marvelously expressive face. The actor's eyes are essentially untouched, and the upper-lip piece mates perfectly with Lahr's real lower lip and chin, allowing complete expressiveness.

As the Lion's face evolved, various design ideas played with the size and shape of the ears, the crest of the mane, and the color of the nose (it was initially black).

While in costume and makeup during the shoot, Bolger, Haley, and Lahr ate each day in a reserved bungalow located close to a sound stage. In what sounds like urban legend, some sources claim that the actors ate separately because other MGM employees who ate in the general commissary had been put off by the men's stylized makeup. But MGM was a movie factory where the unusual was commonplace. To imagine that filmmaking professionals would be discouraged from eating because of the make-believe appearances of other players is absurd. More likely is that Dorothy's friends ate separately so that they didn't have to move far for their breaks, and so that their costumes wouldn't be damaged. And the bungalow was hardly a gulag; indeed, it had three dressing rooms and a common lounge.

The "exiled from the commissary" tale makes more sense vis-à-vis the Munchkins—not because of their appearance, but because of their status on the MGM lot (low) and their numbers (great). And they did indeed eat as a group, in a special area created for them at the studio and at restaurants on nearby Motor Avenue. (The commissary rumor was floated about *Oz* probably because of an earlier MGM picture, *Freaks* [1932], which cast people with real-life physical and intellectual anomalies. These players did eat in a private area, partly out of deference to them, but primarily because of the presumed insalubrious effect they would have on commissary diners.)

During lunch and other lengthy breaks, Bolger and Lahr occupied themselves with spirited games of gin.

The Wicked Witch of the West: False Start

Gale Sondergaard's stern, unconventional beauty was to be the visual linchpin of the Wicked Witch of the West. Adrian created a dark, sequined gown, and Jack Dawn's people created "beauty" concepts that were applied and photographed beginning on September 22, 1938. These had dramatically arched eyebrows; dark, false lashes; and liberal use of dark lipstick, with a carefully drawn upper lip.

For Gale Sondergaard, cast as the Wicked Witch of the West, early costume designs (created when the Witch was still envisioned as an evil glamour girl) were highlighted by a face-hugging cowl headpiece. The effect was regal and stylish, as well as sinister. Her hat and gown were black fabric, festooned with dark sequins.

As had been envisioned, Sondergaard did indeed evoke the wicked queen of *Snow White*—which itself had found inspiration in *She* (1935), a "lost civilization" thriller with Helen Gahagan Douglas in the title role, as "She who must be obeyed." Douglas's costume is ornate and cowled, and anticipates not just the queen of *Snow White* but the early Sondergaard glamour conceptions.

Producer Mervyn LeRoy looked at the test photos of the intimidatingly beautiful Witch. He remained enthused about Sondergaard, but began to wonder if the Witch should be ugly instead of glamorous. Sondergaard sat down in the makeup chair again on October 3, this time to become more conventionally witchlike. The result wasn't ugly—just

This early, and discarded, Wicked Witch makeup for Margaret Hamilton allowed her hair to fall around her face and retained the natural contours of the actress's chin. Both of those details were later changed.

very plain, even drab, with no apparent eye makeup or lipstick and a prosthetic piece that enlarged the tip of the actress's nose. When Sondergaard saw the tests, she decided she didn't want to be captured on screen that way. "Drab" just wouldn't enhance her cultivated grim glamour. She wished to be relieved of the assignment, and when word reached LeRoy, he approved Sondergaard's exit.

The Wicked Witch of the West: A Keeper

The sharp-featured character actress Margaret Hamilton wasn't tall (in fact, she was tiny, barely more than five feet tall), but she had an angular frame that could suggest an imposing kind of menace. Her prior film work suggested to her how to emote physically. She knew that gestures and general body language would be important parts of the characterization, but if her facial makeup weren't right, the Wicked Witch wouldn't "work."

Jack Dawn's makeup department busily fiddled with Hamilton's makeup before arriving at a design that pleased everyone. Various treatments of nose and chin came and went. Different shades of green were tried, too, and after each test the makeup would have to be wiped off, which finally irritated Hamilton's skin so badly that the actress had to see a doctor.

Hamilton's green makeup was copper-based and toxic. For that reason, she couldn't eat solid food, but had to take water, soup, and beverages through a straw. The makeup eventually embedded itself in Hamilton's pores, leaving a green tinge that lasted for weeks, causing friends and even strangers to wonder if Hamilton were well.

Hamilton's morning makeup sessions began at 6:45 a.m. and required two hours. Makeup was applied slowly and carefully, beginning with a layer of cold cream that was the medium for the green paint. The rubber nose and chin pieces, and the Witch's famed wart, were attached with adhesive. (The chin piece Hamilton wore during the Richard Thorpe shoot was very subtle. It would become more pronounced after Thorpe's departure.) False nails made of celluloid were carefully laid and attached to Hamilton's fingertips. Although Jack Young, an assistant to Jack Dawn, was Hamilton's personal makeup man, Dawn supervised each morning's application of the base and indicated where highlights and other tonal shifts should be.

When Richard Thorpe began his aborted shoot, Hamilton wore a black wig with long tresses that fell on either side of her face. The style didn't exactly make the Witch appear girlish, but it did have a softening effect. When the shot resumed under Victor Fleming, the Witch's tresses remained tucked beneath her hat, the better to accent the harsh planes created by Dawn's makeup design.

The Wizard

Frank Morgan was cast in five roles: the Wizard, Prof. Marvel, a gatekeeper, a hansom driver, and a soldier. His costume tests, which began in mid-November

Carefully molded prosthetics made from a cast of Frank Morgan's face gave the Wizard benign (yet amusingly ineffectual) apple cheeks and round-tipped nose. In this publicity still, Dorothy speaks truth to power.

1938, were a whirligig of variations on coats, collars, buttons, hats, ties, ascots, epaulets, belts, watch chains, and other accessories.

In tests for his role as the Wizard, Morgan was fitted with a prosthetic nose and rounded cheeks. His gatekeeper makeups involved false mustaches, headpieces, and wigs. The wigs were particularly varied: some were ornate in their swirls and spit curls.

An early, rejected Wizard makeup for Frank Morgan looked very much like Prof. Marvel, but with a bald head. LeRoy felt that the makeup was insufficiently distinct and urged Dawn and his staff to try again.

Prof. Marvel's Coat

Because Prof. Marvel is a bit of a charlatan who lives in a wagon and subsists on hot dogs, Adrian knew that a fellow in such circumstances couldn't be expensively garbed. His wardrobe should be emphatic, but a little threadbare. With that mandate in hand, Adrian's staff combed the MGM costume department, looking for off-the-rack items that would be suitable for the professor. When a properly old-fashioned coat was located, it was pulled from Wardrobe and readied for actor Frank Morgan. Then somebody noticed a sewn label inside the coat. The label said "L. FRANK BAUM."

The tale eventually made its way into MGM publicity, and over the years, it came to be widely doubted. The coincidence of it seemed contrived and absurd. But during the *Wizard of Oz* shoot, the original studio tailor and Baum's widow, Maud, confirmed the coat's authenticity. Frank Morgan was delighted to have an article of clothing that had been worn by the father of *Oz*.

Glinda

Alone among the characters of *The Wizard of Oz*, the good witch Glinda required an emphatically gorgeous costume and overt "beauty" makeup. Billie Burke's fulsome gown had been worn by Jeanette MacDonald in MGM's *San Francisco* (1936). For use by Glinda, Adrian augmented his own design with a pronounced silvery collar. Although Burke was accustomed to stage and film roles that put her into gorgeous costumes, she looked at Glinda's fabulous gown and joked, "I look like a refugee from German opera."

Burke was a natural redhead, but her hair was neither sufficiently long nor colorful to take full advantage of Technicolor. The red wig she wore was tinted to suit her natural coloring.

The Munchkins

Adrian examined the *Oz* script and realized that he would be designing costumes for more than a hundred Munchkins and three hundred residents of the Emerald City. He'd be very busy, and so would MGM's seamstresses. Except for Prof. Marvel's coat and some farm attire seen in the Kansas sequences, every costume you see in *The Wizard of Oz* was designed and manufactured on the MGM lot expressly for *Oz*. Even frequent viewers of the film aren't aware of each and every piece. A wardrobe department checklist from one day in July 1938, for instance, notes that costumes had been readied for "20 men shopkeepers" and "8 girls to throw flowers."

Every Munchkin costume had to be designed and purpose-built. Each one was an individual creation; off-the-rack was naturally impossible. Working with Munchkin wardrobe mistress Sheila O'Brien, costume designer Gilbert Adrian employed a huge variety of fabrics. Insofar as *Oz* was concerned, comfort was relatively low on the costumer's list of prerequisites. Because the preponderance of costume designs went to the Munchkins, Adrian wanted fabrics that would accept novel colors and could hold the shapes of oversized collars, tails, and other accoutrements. Many Munchkin outfits were of reinforced felt, which held its shape—and caused the wearers to overheat beneath the hot Technicolor arc lamps.

Costume designer Adrian worked from one of his own creations, a gown worn by Jeanette MacDonald in *San Francisco*, to create Billie Burke's "Glinda" gown. Adrian fit it to Burke, of course, and lengthened the sleeves, raised the neckline, and added more tulle to the puffy sleeves. The underskirt hoop of the Glinda version is very pronounced.

The small stature of the Munchkin players encouraged costume designs that played off of that with oversized hats and belts, enormously padded shoulders, and blousy trousers. Diminutive statures were further emphasized with big collars, slightly overlong sleeves, vests, hard-to-miss shoes with curling toes (those toe pieces were unexpectedly hard to construct), and coats with tails and oversized buttons. (Many years later, Munchkin player Ruth Robinson Duccini recalled the "heavy costumes" and "long hours.") Large, gaudy plaids brought an even more whimsical air, as did tassels, watch chains, and gaudy leggings. (Of the particularly ornate costumes, only a Lollipop Guild outfit and the Cowardly Lion's lion skin survive intact today.)

Comically sized and shaped hats, some with nodding flowers and other wonky details, forced audience attention to the players' small faces and helped highlight Jack Dawn's cheerful (yet vaguely unsettling) character makeups, which involved prosthetic nose and chin pieces, bald caps, and carefully shaped wigs.

Green is the predominant color in the Emerald City—green everywhere! Some of the necessary green fabric was purchased off-lot, but most of it was dyed by the costume department, where dye-room personnel (supervised by Vera Mordaunt) sometimes worked thirteen- to sixteen-hour days.

Munchkinland, of course, demanded vividly colored sets and costumes. Although much of Adrian's film work, and many of his later label designs, made dramatic use of black-and-white fabrics, color values were invariably important to Adrian. For *The Wizard of Oz*, and Munchkinland in particular, he needed to be sure that his tones were in synch with the colors and patterns established by the production designers. Cinematographer Hal Rosson, too, had to be accommodated, via filmed tests for color register, possible reflection from the arcs, and other issues visible on film but unseen by the naked eye.

The daily assembly line that was the Munchkin makeup process began at 5:30 a.m., when the makeup artists assigned to Munchkin duty arrived. The diminutive players showed up at 6:00 a.m. and were fully transformed by 8:30 a.m. Munchkin costumes were challenging, and the facial makeup and hair treatments were no less complex. Munchkin makeup was accomplished at discrete stations, with one artist handling noses, another dealing with bald caps and hair, and so forth. Years later, Jack Dawn recalled the Munchkins during a conversation with John Lahr. "There was a great deal to learn about working with them. They were adults, not children, and sometimes we forgot. They did not want us to touch them or lift them up into the makeup chairs. They climbed into the seats by themselves."

Some of the Munchkin players, such as Harry Earles, were show business veterans. Others, like thirty-three-year-old Hazel Resmondo, were getting their first taste of the industry. The makeup process was a grind, and, like everybody else, the Munchkins suffered beneath the hot arc lamps (temperatures on the stage could hit 100 degrees). The Munchkins' days were full ones that usually ended at 8:00 p.m.

The Winged Monkeys

The actors cast as the Wicked Witch's winged monkeys wore furred, full-body suits

layered with short, open tunics. The monkeys' wings had various shapes that were exaggerated versions of the wings of eagles, pelicans, and bats. The smallest wing designs were given limited movement by battery packs hidden on the actors' persons. The monkeys were sent aloft on wires attached at the top to a catwalk track and hooked to hidden harnesses worn by the actors. Whenever a wire broke, the setup had to be reshot, which caused the monkeys to demand extra pay. They got it.

The tri-tone wings hadn't yet been abandoned when this flying-posture test photo was snapped.

Because the monkeys' wings had to move as well as present an intriguing appearance, Jack Dawn and his crew experimented with many sizes and shapes. Dawn ultimately abandoned the tri-tone treatment worn here by Sid Dawson. On screen, the wires that elevated the monkeys are nearly invisible; the wire in this photo may have been present to test the attachment point affixed to the flying harness. The hands and feet in this study are partially finished preliminary designs.

Actors cast as "background" monkeys wore relatively simple molded rubber masks. Because the mask worn by actor Pat Walshe (who was cast as the chief monkey, Nikko) had to withstand the challenges posed by close-ups, the appliance was made of multiple pieces, with underpinnings molded to Walshe's features and applied as prosthetics. The appliances protruded from Walshe's face, allowing a broad, flattened nose and sinus area—two critical parts of monkey facial anatomy.

The monkeys viewed in long shot against the dark blue sky were miniatures, of course, constructed from hard rubber at lengths of about eight to nine inches, depending upon the required scale. (Sources disagree as to whether the miniature rubber monks were solid or hollow.) Each miniature figure was supported by four wires. As with the "real" monkeys, a reshoot was done whenever a miniature popped a wire.

Smaller wings highlight this test image of makeup and costuming. Although hands and feet are close to their final forms, the natural opening of the tunic was ultimately wider, and the decorative "X" pieces sat higher on the chest.

A miniature Dorothy, with stiffly kicking legs, was constructed similarly.

The Winkies

Towering, furred hats and heavy, ornate greatcoats (total weight: about fifty pounds) characterized the Winkies, the chanting soldiers that guard the Witch's castle. Various eyebrow and mouth variants were tried. Some combinations were more menacing than others, and the final version was a reasonable compromise that made the Winkies appear fearsome but not monstrous. The elongated prosthetic nosepieces were relatively late additions.

Because numerous Winkies were to be in medium close-ups at the film's climax, the makeup of actor Mitchell Lewis (cast as the captain of the Winkie guard) was no more ornate than that of the other Winkie players who are visible in the scene.

Men of Emerald City

These costumes were designed to be ornate, but in proportion with the actors. In other words, the costumes complemented the actor's faces and frames, rather than exaggerating one quality or another.

Women of Emerald City

Jack Dawn's character makeups brought out the doll-like facial qualities of the pretty actresses and extras hired to play the Emerald City's female citizens. The costumes were complex layers of robes, shawls, and snoods (mesh hair wraps).

A close-up of Helen Seamon, who plays the rosy-cheeked Emerald City beauty who can't hang on to her restless Siamese cat, gives a particularly good view of Ozite makeup and costuming. Other beauty makeups, which can't be seen as clearly because of camera distance, were created for actress Lois January and the other young women cast as Emerald City beauticians.

In Focus: Helen Seamon (1919–2001) and Lois January (1913–2006)

During the final Emerald City sequence in *The Wizard of Oz*, many viewers are enchanted by a beautiful woman in green who holds a Siamese cat. She's young and achingly pretty, with heavy makeup (including wildly rouged cheeks) that gives her a doll-like appearance. The character is an anonymous citizen of Oz and is important only because her cat catches the attention of Toto—a moment that culminates in the Wizard going aloft in his balloon without Dorothy.

For many years, that actress was erroneously identified as Lois January, a dancer and B-western star. January never claimed to be the cat lady, a part that was played by Helen Seamon, an Arkansas girl who studied dance in Los Angeles and fell into pictures. (One Web source correctly notes that Seamon played the cat lady—and then claims that she was "one of the diminutive actors" hired to play Munchkins!)

Between 1935 and 1943, Seamon put together twelve uncredited film appearances. She's certainly striking in *Oz*, but had an opportunity to show off her dance moves in a kinetic specialty jitterbug number in *Broadway Serenade* (1939). During 1948–57, Seamon appeared in four Broadway productions, including *The Waltz of the Toreadors*, which had a healthy run of 132 performances in 1957. In her only off-Broadway appearance, Helen co-starred in a 1957 revival of Sartre's existentially bleak *No Exit*. Critical reactions to her performance as the narcissistic Estelle ranged from neutral to enthusiastic. Helen found work in television in 1951, and again in 1955.

A few years after her death, locals in Pine Bluff, Arkansas, claimed that a theater in which she performed as a child was haunted—but not by Helen.

As for Lois January, she *is* in the Emerald City sequence, playing the redheaded beautician (in white cap) who assures Dorothy, "We can make a dimpled smile/Out of a frown." Except for *Oz*, not a lot about Lois January is uniquely interesting. She was a pretty starlet in a town that overflowed with them, and although she found more success than most, she remained obscure. In that, she's emblematic of the unending tide of prom queens, stenographers, and small-town beauties that longed to make it in Hollywood. January's story is a reasonably familiar one, so she gives a face to

Actress-dancer Lois January, who played an Emerald City beautician in *The Wizard of Oz*, was the featured "Star of Stage and Screen" in a 1942 magazine campaign for Chesterfield cigarettes.

the struggles of thousands. She also reminds us that success isn't always the same thing as fame.

Unlikely though it seems, "Lois January" was her real name. She was a Texas girl who was prodded into show business by her mother, whom Lois described as "pushy." When Lois was in middle school, the family relocated to Los Angeles. She studied dance and joined the prestigious Denishawn troupe led by Ruth St. Denis and Ted Shawn. Not yet twenty, she was poised and good-looking, and found work as an actress in L.A. stage productions. She was noticed in one of them and was spirited to the Columbia two-reel unit, where she did her first film work, co-starring with Broadway actor Jack Osterman and Mary Shea in *Umpa* (1933). The short was part of the "Musical Novelty" series that includes *Woman Haters* (1934), the Columbia debut of the Three Stooges. Like *Woman Haters*, *Umpa* is propelled by music, with dialogue recited in rhyme. (The short's catchy central melody was lifted a year later for *Woman Haters*, but given fresh lyrics.) Osterman falls for Shea and can't stop saying "Umpa!" That's the joke, and the short struggles to sustain it for sixteen minutes.

Lois January played a nurse, attired strangely but fetchingly in a satin uniform. Lois dances briefly with second-billed Gloria Shea, sings a bit, and leads a tap-dancing chorus line. When she looks at Osterman and blurts, "His umpa's coming out!" she explicates nearly the entire plot.

Lois did another five shorts for Columbia and had uncredited bits in features. Her best break (or possibly her worst) came in 1935, when she was cast as the leading lady opposite ex-football star Reb Russell in an independently produced B-western called *Arizona Bad Man*. For the next two years, Lois co-starred in nearly a dozen Saturday-morning oaters, the best of which (like 1937's *The Red Rope*) were from Republic, where she played opposite cowboy star Bob Steele. But when players fell into B-westerns, their larger career aspirations could usually be considered dead.

January went on to do the bit part in *The Wizard of Oz* and assisted Bobby Connolly with the film's choreography. As Lois's film career petered out, she relocated with her husband to New York. She did nightclub work and appeared in a pair of Broadway musicals, *Yokel Boy* (1938–39; starring Buddy Ebsen), and *High Kickers* (1941–42).

In 1942, she achieved her greatest fame as WABC radio's *Reveille Sweetheart*, spinning records for stateside GIs, singing a bit, joking, and keeping everybody's wartime morale up. Because WABC (now WCBS) was the CBS flagship, its programming received considerable attention in New York and the surrounding region. (In 1942, network radio programs were not usually rebroadcast via transcription, though exceptions were made for shows that might be enjoyed by servicemen. For that reason, it's possible that *Reveille Sweetheart* was transcribed onto so-called V-discs and made available for national and even overseas broadcast.) Lois became well known and was tapped by Liggett & Myers Tobacco to do a national print ad for Chesterfield cigarettes.

Lois worked very sporadically in movies after the war (you can catch her in 1962's *Don't Knock the Twist*) and focused most of her energies on television, where she worked for thirty years. She had real roles (no more bits) on shows as diverse as *My Three Sons*, *Marcus Welby, M.D.* (seven appearances during 1972–76), *Lola* (Lola Falana's variety show), and *Kolchak: The Night Stalker*. Lois retired after "Double Agent," a 1987 installment of *Walt Disney's Wonderful World of Color*.

Lois January never became a name, but she persevered. Late in her life, she discovered that her B-western work was fondly remembered. She attended western-movie conventions, met happy fans, and probably reflected that things hadn't worked out so badly after all.

In Focus: Jack Dawn (1892–1961)

Faces fascinated John (Jack) Dawn, and as a boy in Kentucky he was driven create them out of sandstone. He had already shown some skill as a painter, and one of his first professional jobs was as a sign painter in New York City. He headed west to get into the picture business in 1907, experimenting with makeup and teaching himself how to ride horses and drive cars and trucks. With those skills, he found work as an extra at Mack Sennett's Keystone Studios and elsewhere. War broke out in Europe in 1914, and because the U.S. wasn't yet involved, Dawn went to Canada to enlist. He was back in Los Angeles in 1919, doing bits that were more prominent than before, sometimes wearing makeups of his own design. As his skills became more sophisticated, Dawn created makeup for Fox Studios, 20th Century Pictures, and finally MGM. By 1935, he was on salary at the big studio and remained at MGM until his retirement in 1951.

A dedicated, very large makeup annex was built at MGM in 1938, and Dawn was named makeup director a year later. From the outset, he realized that if the studio's multitude of productions were to be adequately served, he would need to find and hire many apprentice makeup artists. The best would become experts in various disciplines: beards and wigs, ethnic designs, body makeup, dental appliances, beauty work, age makeup, and so on. Day to day in the studio, Dawn supervised at least thirty artists and technicians, keeping everybody on task and servicing multiple productions simultaneously.

Historian Jonathan Shirshekan quotes a 1983 interview in which Dawn's onetime MGM assistant William Tuttle described his boss's search for recruits: "He got some of the people from the [studio's] messenger service and the mail room, and had them over there [for hiring]. And they're the ones who are in the makeup business today, they became so interested in it." Tuttle added, "[A]ll of the [makeup] techniques that were involved . . . have never really been duplicated. And there's really nothing new that's come along since then. The entire field of makeup was encompassed in that picture." (Tuttle himself went on to be MGM's director of makeup.)

Although makeup technique has become very sophisticated since Tuttle made his comments in 1983, what Dawn and his people achieved on *Oz* in 1938–39 remains completely remarkable. Not simply a brilliant designer blessed with a sense of whimsy, Dawn was also an imaginative technician. He was an early proponent of facial prosthetics, which he crafted from a vinyl-and-resin mix he called Vinylite. He held the patent on the stuff and used it to brilliant effect on *The Good Earth* (1937), transforming actors of European heritage into Chinese.

The Good Earth required makeups that established personality and allowed the actors a full range of facial expression. Further, the designs had to play to the particular strengths of each actor. (He'd face the same challenges on *Oz*.) A makeup artist the caliber of Dawn is a master illusionist, and the illusion of *The Good Earth* is that the characters designed by Dawn were born that way.

Jack did particularly vivid work on two other 1937 releases, *Lost Horizon* (Sam Jaffe's old-age makeup) and *Conquest* (transforming Charles Boyer into Napoleon). He had already made German-born star Luise Rainer appear Asian for *The Good Earth*, and when he got his hands on her for *The Great Waltz* (1938), he turned her into an eighty-year old. Dawn also created a fine age makeup for Robert Donat in *Goodbye, Mr. Chips* (1939).

In a novel reversal, Dawn was asked to make real-life vaudevillians twenty years younger for *Babes in Arms* (1939). Makeup historians Al Taylor and Sue Roy report that when Dawn asked sixty-three-year-old Irene Franklin if he'd captured her younger self, she answered, "Almost. One thing that is missing is a certain optimistic expression in the eyes."

For a sentimental 1939 drama called *Joe and Ethel Turp Call on the President*, Dawn brought twenty-two-year-old supporting player Marsha Hunt into early middle age. For co-star Walter Brennan, who was forty, Dawn shaved off fifteen years, gradually brought the actor back to forty, and then aged him even further. At one point in the film, Hunt and Brennan appear to be the same age.

While Jack carried on at MGM during World War II, he developed his own company, Jack Dawn Inc.; and donated his time to the San Diego naval hospital, where he created noses, cheeks, and other appliances for disfigured soldiers who longed to appear normal to their families and strangers. One of Dawn's assistants on the project was a young lieutenant named Gordon Bau, who later became director of makeup at RKO and Warner Bros.

Jack Dawn retired in 1951, after nearly forty years in the business. He died in 1961, twenty years before the Motion Picture Association of America introduced an Academy Award category for makeup. That's a shame, but for three generations, makeup artists and fans have spoken his name with a kind of awe.

Jack's brother, Lyle Dawn, did makeup before his premature death in 1944. Jack's sons, Bob and Wes Dawn, became very successful movie makeup artists, and Bob's son, Jeff Dawn, followed suit. A great-grandson, Patrick Dawn, works in the business as a grip and production assistant.

Jack Dawn's Partners in Wonder

Jack Dawn supervised a crew of nearly thirty on *Oz*, almost all of whom pursued careers into the 1950s. Most worked throughout the '60s, and some were active into the 1970s and '80s. Reference sources list "credits" for these people, but not every job earned the makeup artist an on-screen acknowledgment. Many who were salaried members of a studio makeup department, for instance, seldom received screen credit. For many of these artists, low-budget, independent pictures provided the best opportunity to see their names on the screen.

Some who worked with Dawn on *Oz* remained at MGM for many years. Others freelanced. Some careers were sporadic; others seem to have had no down time at all. The careers of an intriguing few are marked by equal numbers of schlock and prestige projects.

Here are *partial* filmographies for those makeup artists that had the longest, most varied, or otherwise notable careers. Some were assistants; others were assigned to maintain the makeup of a particular cast member or work with a particular element of makeup technology. All of them learned at the side of Jack Dawn.

Del Armstrong (1915–2003)

The Wizard of Oz was Armstrong's first film work. He established a career of considerable longevity and variety.

- *Behind Locked Doors* (1948)
- *Detective Story* (1951)
- *A Star Is Born* (1954; another association with Judy Garland)
- *Anatomy of a Murder* (1959; "black-eye" makeup for Lee Remick)
- *Gargoyles* (1972, TV; amusing "creature" makeups for this well-liked TV-movie)
- *The Day of the Locust* (1975; sometimes-grotesque period makeups in this Hollywood story set in the 1930s)
- *Jaws* (1975)
- *Caveman* (1981)
- *Honey, I Shrunk the Kids* (1989)
- *Teenage Mutant Ninja Turtles II: The Secret of the Ooze* (1991)

Max Factor Jr. (1904–1996)

He was born Frank Factor and eventually controlled and expanded the makeup empire founded by his father. Factor's film resumé is slight, but his company provided cosmetics to movie studios for many years. He was wig supervisor on *Oz*.

- *Abe Lincoln in Illinois* (1940)
- *Joan of Arc* (1948; effectively unglamorous makeup for Ingrid Bergman)

Sydney Guilaroff (1907–1997)

If you wanted the best "hair man" in Hollywood, you got in touch with Sydney Guilaroff. During a long association with MGM, he demonstrated an unmatched facility with hair and hair design. Active from 1937 to 1989, Guilaroff worked on more than four hundred films. On-set for *Oz*, he looked after Judy Garland's hair and hair extensions.

- *Gone With the Wind* (1939; designs for Vivien Leigh)
- *The Pirate* (1948)
- *Little Women* (1949; 19th-century hairstyles for June Allyson and others in a large female cast)
- *Show Boat* (1951)
- *Forbidden Planet* (1956; hair designs for Anne Francis)
- *7 Faces of Dr. Lao* (1964)
- *Who's Afraid of Virginia Woolf?* (1966; the marvelously scary hairstyle sported by Elizabeth Taylor)
- *The Graduate* (1967)
- *They Shoot Horses, Don't They?* (1969; a wide range of striking designs for this drama set in the 1930s)
- *New York, New York* (1977; '40s-style hairstyles for Liza Minnelli and Robert De Niro)
- *The Legend of Lylah Clare* (1968; a provocative mix of present-day and 1930s styles)
- *Speedway* (1968; one of numerous times Sydney attended to the coif of Elvis Presley)
- *Sweet Charity* (1969; amusing styles for Shirley MacLaine and others playing taxi dancers)

Jack Kevan (1912–1997)

Film buffs are familiar with Kevan's imaginative "monster" designs of the 1950s, most of which were done for Universal-International. His *Oz* job was his first in the picture business.

- *Abbott and Costello Meet Frankenstein* (1948)
- *Ma and Pa Kettle* (1949)
- *It Came from Outer Space* (1953; "Xenomorph" designs)
- *Creature from the Black Lagoon* (1954; Millicent Patrick and Kevan were the creative forces behind a crew ostensibly led by Bud Westmore. The Creature is one of the greatest full-body designs ever achieved.)
- *Monster on the Campus* (1958)
- *The Monster of Piedras Blancas* (1959; Kevan produced this surprisingly gruesome independent thriller and did full-body design for the savage-looking title creature)

Emile LaVigne (1913–1990)

LaVigne was an amiable man who recalled his B-picture and "A" picture designs with equal pride and pleasure. He was particularly imaginative when he had virtually no money to work with. Steve McQueen and Lee Marvin took a liking to him and hired him many times. On *Oz*, he attended to Jack Haley.

- *Fort Apache* (1948)
- *Abbott and Costello Meet Frankenstein* (1948)
- *Land of the Pharaohs* (1955; LaVigne faced the frankly impossible task of turning British stars Jack Hawkins and Joan Collins into Egyptians)
- *Dig That Uranium* (1955; just one of LaVigne's numerous associations with the Bowery Boys)
- *Invasion of the Body Snatchers* (1956)
- *World Without End* (1956; gnarly cave-mutant designs for this time-travel thriller from Allied Artists)
- *Queen of Outer Space* (1958; beauty makeup for a full crew of lovelies, including Zsa Zsa Gabor, who does *not* play the title character. That actress was Laurie Mitchell, whom LaVigne made hideous on a makeup budget that wouldn't have paid for one of the Cowardly Lion's whiskers.)
- *The Atomic Submarine* (1959; the infamous space-cyclops-that's-just-goop-on-somebody's-forearm was created by other hands. LaVigne invented some effective burn makeups.)
- *The Magnificent Seven* (1960; LaVigne's first with Steve McQueen)
- *The Hypnotic Eye* (1960; a low-budget roughie with alarming makeups showing burns, damaged eyes, and scarring)
- *West Side Story* (1961)
- *The Great Escape* (1963)
- *Bullitt* (1968)
- *The Reivers* (1969)
- *Le Mans* (1971)
- *Prime Cut* (1972; LaVigne's first with Lee Marvin)
- *The Iceman Cometh* (1973)
- *The Klansman* (1974)
- *The Towering Inferno* (1974; more McQueen, plus a lot of startling burn effects)

Norbert Myles (1887–1966)

Myles had a particular facility for "exotic" characters. Already a ten-year movie veteran by the time he worked on *Oz*, he looked after Ray Bolger's makeup.

- *Dr. Jekyll and Mr. Hyde* (1931; assisted Wally Westmore with the repellent Hyde makeup)

- *The Bitter Tea of General Yen* (1933; Danish actor Nils Asther becomes "Chinese")
- *The Good Earth* (1937; more Asian impersonations)
- *The Thief of Bagdad* (1940; fine work on Rex Ingram's Djinn)
- *Duel in the Sun* (1946; Jennifer Jones is transformed into a dusky, hot-blooded "half-breed")
- *Hamlet* (1948; subtle and imaginative designs for Laurence Olivier and others)
- *Tarzan's Savage Fury* (1952)

Gustaf (Gus) Norin (1905–1988)

Norin had a gift for unglamorous, "documentary"-style makeups that suggested everyday people in difficult situations. He was assigned to prosthetics work for *Oz*.

- *The Grapes of Wrath* (1940)
- *Body and Soul* (1947; rugged prizefight makeups)
- *Force of Evil* (1948)
- *Champion* (1949; brutal prizefight designs)
- *Cyrano de Bergerac* (1950; Norin designed Jose Ferrer's marvelous nose)
- *Bride of the Gorilla* (1951; transitional makeups for Raymond Burr, who becomes a gorilla)
- *High Noon* (1952)
- "Five Minutes to Doom" (1953; and nearly eighty other episodes of *The Adventures of Superman*. Consistently effective work on lean budgets.)
- *Tarzan and the She-Devil* (1953)
- *The Mad Magician* (1954; a nice variety of character makeups and disguises)
- *20,000 Leagues Under the Sea* (1954)
- *Around the World in Eighty Days* (1956)
- *Witness for the Prosecution* (1957)
- *Duel at Diablo* (1966; torture makeups and other bloody designs)
- *Willard* (1971)
- *History of the World: Part I* (1981)

Web Overlander (1902–1975)

Overlander's beauty and character designs impressed John Wayne, who hired the artist numerous times. On *Oz*, he helped attend to Judy Garland's facial makeup.

- *The Blue Dahlia* (1946)
- *The Feathered Serpent* (1948)
- *Bomba the Jungle Boy* (1949)
- *The Quiet Man* (1952; Overlander's first with John Wayne)

- *The High and the Mighty* (1954)
- *The Conqueror* (1956; Overlander made a valiant stab at turning John Wayne into Genghis Khan)
- *The Barbarian and the Geisha* (1958; unlike some other makeup artists assigned to projects set in the Far East, Overlander worked with genuine Asians in this one)
- *The Alamo* (1960)
- *The Sons of Katie Elder* (1965)

Robert J. Schiffer (1916–2005)

Schiffer worked on more than two hundred films and was equally at home with beauty makeups and grotesqueries. He was the first person to create makeups for three-strip Technicolor.

- *Horse Feathers* (1932; Groucho Marx and Thelma Todd—from the ridiculous to the sublime)
- *Becky Sharp* (1935; first feature film in three-strip Technicolor)
- *The Devil-Doll* (1936; clever and amusing "old lady" makeup for Lionel Barrymore)
- *The Good Earth* (1937)
- *The Hunchback of Notre Dame* (1939; the makeup worn by Charles Laughton in the title role is startling but invites great sympathy)
- *Gilda* (1946; Rita Hayworth, at the apex of her beauty and glamour)
- *The Lady from Shanghai* (1947; beauty makeup that complements Rita Hayworth's newly blonde hair)
- *The Killer That Stalked New York* (1950; sweatily convincing "illness" makeup for Evelyn Keyes, playing a woman suffering from smallpox)
- *The 5000 Fingers of Dr. T* (1953; faintly nightmarish whimsy from Dr. Seuss)
- *Kiss Me Deadly* (1955; a variety of injury and wound makeups, plus many actresses in glamour roles)
- *Gigi* (1958)
- *Judgment at Nuremberg* (1961; age makeup for Burt Lancaster and "plain" designs for Judy Garland)
- *Birdman of Alcatraz* (1962; character and age makeup for Burt Lancaster)
- *What Ever Happened to Baby Jane?* (1962; pure grotesque, ranging from Bette Davis's over-use of cosmetics to Joan Crawford's miserable descent into starvation)
- *Cleopatra* (1963)
- *My Fair Lady* (1964)
- *Bedknobs and Broomsticks* (1971)
- *The Shaggy D.A.* (1976)
- *TRON* (1982; cutting-edge futurism)
- *Splash* (1984)

Charles H. Schram (1911–2008)

Schram attended to Bert Lahr's makeup needs on the *Oz* set. Later in his career, Schram created a number of unusually distinctive period and character makeups.

- *Around the World in Eighty Days* (1956)
- *Carnal Knowledge* (1971)
- *Papillon* (1973)
- *The Godfather: Part II* (1974)
- *Mommie Dearest* (1981)

Howard Smit (1911–2009)

Smit was a versatile designer who did beauty, ethnic, and specialty prosthetic makeups. He worked twice for Alfred Hitchcock.

- *She* (1935)
- *Gunga Din* (1939)
- *Code of the Silver Sage* (1950; and many other B-westerns of the 1940s and '50s)
- *The Birds* (1963)
- *Marnie* (1964)
- *Planet of the Apes* (1968)
- "Bad Man on Campus" (1968; and nearly one hundred other episodes of *Mod Squad*)

William Tuttle (1912–2007)

Tuttle, like Jack Dawn, is one of the towering figures of Hollywood makeup history. He succeeded Dawn as director of makeup at MGM, where he oversaw hundreds of films and created many distinctive designs.

- *Mark of the Vampire* (1935; "spook" makeup for Bela Lugosi and Carroll Borland)
- *Show Boat* (1951; period character and glamour designs)
- *Singin' in the Rain* (1952; lovely makeups evoking the 1920s and '20s Hollywood)
- *Julius Caesar* (1953)
- *Blackboard Jungle* (1955; restrained glamour makeup for Anne Francis, plus various injury makeups)
- *Forbidden Planet* (1956)
- *Jailhouse Rock* (1957)
- *Cat on a Hot Tin Roof* (1958)
- *The Time Machine* (1960; the sloe-eyed, animalistic Morlocks)
- *Mutiny on the Bounty* (1962)

- "Nightmare at 20,000 Feet" (1963; the creature on the airplane wing; *The Twilight Zone*)
- "The Masks" (1964; the awful family whose faces come to reflect their failings; *The Twilight Zone*)
- *Young Frankenstein* (1974; fresh approaches to venerable characters)
- *The Fury* (1978; complex special-effects makeups)

Jack H. Young (1910–1992)

Young was a talented all-around makeup artist whose career spanned six decades. He is especially remembered by fans of science fiction from the 1950s. On the *Oz* set, Young looked after Margaret Hamilton's makeup.

- *The Cyclops* (1957; intentionally overstated "melted face" design of the title character)
- *War of the Colossal Beast* (1958; an uncannily clever makeup suggesting a missing eye and half-exposed cheek and jaw)
- *Skullduggery* (1970)
- *Ben* (1972)
- *Fat City* (1972; effective boxing-match makeups)
- *Apocalypse Now* (1979)
- *The Brood* (1979; eccentric horror designs)
- *Salem's Lot* (1979; TV; effectively repellent vampire designs reminiscent of *Nosferatu*)

In Focus: Adrian (1903–1959)

It makes perfect sense that Hollywood's most gifted costume designer, Gilbert Adrian, had been part of the prestigious MGM family for ten years when development work began on *The Wizard of Oz*. Hardworking and endowed with a chic sensibility, Adrian famously "dressed the stars."

Born Adolph Greenberg in Naugatuck, Connecticut, Adrian was with MGM from 1928 to 1941, responsible for dressing the studio's most glamorous and valuable leading ladies. One key to Adrian's great success was his versatility. He was equally comfortable doing fabulous gowns for Garbo as with designing Judy Garland's simple gingham dress—a believable Kansas outfit created by a man who had been formally fashion-educated in New York and Paris, and found his first success on Broadway in the early 1920s. Adrian was a cosmopolitan who had a bedrock understanding of how costume can illuminate screen characters of every sort. He dressed Dorothy so beautifully because he understood her.

Adrian was equally comfortable with period stories (*Marie Antoinette*) and modern-day pieces (*The Women*). He became famed for particular screen designs: dashing costumes for Rudolph Valentino; an insouciant slouch hat worn by Garbo; padded shoulders that accented Joan Crawford's powerful upper body; ornate gowns that perfectly complemented the thrilling voice of Jeanette MacDonald.

A 1932 film, *Letty Lynton*, featured the "Letty Lynton dress," a white organza gown dominated by dramatically layered ruche at the shoulders and designed for Joan Crawford. The dress caused such a stir among American women that it was copied by Macy's, where half a million examples, at twenty dollars apiece, went out the door.

In *The Women* (1939), the nature of the costuming indicated character, such as Joan Crawford's sensual flirt, who wore outfits that displayed a lot of shoulder and bare midriff. (Yes, Adrian seems to have had a particular affinity for Crawford. Although tiny, she wore good clothes beautifully.)

Adrian was dedicated to fashion in film and felt that it could—and should—be a legitimate influence on Parisian design. In 1942, just a year after leaving MGM, he had his own design house and his own label. His egalitarian spirit moved him to create not just couture but ready-to-wear clothing, too.

He was a dandy in his personal life and made himself a walking exemplar of sophisticated fashion. Beauty preoccupied him, and he was married to one of the screen's loveliest actresses, Janet Gaynor, for twenty years, until his death.

Classiq fashion blogger Ada describes Adrian's creations as "an intangible mix of fanciful and taste, dramatic and grace, whimsical and elegance." Adrian lived for glamour, but also indulged his love of simple, elegant practicality. Many of his MGM designs were suitable for everyday wear, and thus appealed to female moviegoers that looked for a similar approach from label designers.

Most major designers employ platoons of sketch artist. Adrian did not. He preferred to sketch his ideas himself, and could in fact complete a useful concept sketch in pencil or pen and ink in about five minutes—a bit longer if he enhanced the drawing with watercolors, as he often did.

Adrian enjoys scant coverage in published histories of couture, probably because he dared to design for "everyday" women, and not simply for fashion models and the very few women that could afford pricey original designs.

Adrian's responsibility to his design house mandated that he slow his film work during the 1940s. Because there was no Academy Award category for costuming until 1949, Adrian (who did just one movie after that year) never had an opportunity to bring home Oscar.

People Come and Go So Quickly Here

The Struggle to Find a Director

D uring a 1969 interview with film historian Kevin Brownlow, silent-era actress Louise Brooks rhetorically asked, "Isn't Victor Fleming an inspired director of the beauty of childhood?"

Brooks was quite right in her assessment, of course, but her opinion was widely shared only *after Oz* had been screened and publicly applauded. Although a versatile filmmaker who functioned equally well with drama, adult comedy, and adventure, Fleming had no experience with children's material, and no personal interest in it, either. A powerful (and profit-making) presence on the MGM lot, Fleming could have risked the ire of Louis Mayer and declined *Oz*. During the studio-system days, moneymaking directors occasionally requested a pass on particular projects, and most of them got away with it—partly because, moneymaking or not, directors were considered by front offices to be inter-changeable. *Well, X doesn't want to do it so we'll assign Y. Y's track record is just as good as X's, and he can aim a camera just as well as X, too, right?* To studio moguls, talent was valuable but replicable. Frank Capra, a contemporaneous director who aspired to creative independence, described staff directors as "organization men, as anonymous as vice presidents of General Motors."

Major-studio staff directors made very good livings, but even the finest of them were just parts of a larger machine. Naturally, Victor Fleming wasn't the only top-notch director on the MGM lot. To the contrary, the studio had plenty of superior craftsmen: George Cukor, Clarence Brown, Jack Conway, Robert Z. Leonard, Woody Van Dyke. Each of these men had distinct ways of working, but each also toed MGM's stylistic and attitudinal line: "Do it Right, Do it Big, Give it Class." MGM exemplified old Hollywood's dedication to a "house style." Directors were not expected (or invited) to put their personal stamp on projects. Their mandate was to deliver films that would look and play like other pictures from that studio. MGM product had gloss. Warner and Columbia had grit. Films from 20th Century-Fox had sparkle. RKO excelled at somber mood. Universal pictures had a splash of the gaudy. Paramount was dedicated to polish. Every studio sold a particular, identifiable style. As West Coast production chief, Louis Mayer was expected to enforce MGM's "big and class" mandate.

Mervyn LeRoy, freshly arrived at MGM from Warner Bros. in February 1938 and assigned by Mayer to produce *The Wizard of Oz*, wanted to direct the film, as well. LeRoy's qualifications as a "box-office" director were clear enough, but Mayer had the objectivity necessary to tell LeRoy that producing *and* directing would be just too much work and responsibility. The studio would find a staff director to assume on-set responsibility for *Oz*.

Norman Taurog

In the spring of 1938, LeRoy resigned himself that he would not direct *Oz*. He assigned the project to MGM staff director Norman Taurog, who had won the best director Oscar for his work on Paramount's *Skippy* (1931), a Jackie Cooper weepie involving an endangered dog and city plans to dispossess a poor neighborhood. An important 1938 Universal project directed by Taurog, *Mad About Music*, was a smash-hit showcase for sixteen-year-old Deanna Durbin. At Selznick International, Taurog's *The Adventures of Tom Sawyer* (1938) did solid box office. After joining MGM later in '38, Taurog impressed LeRoy and the MGM front office with rushes from *Boys Town*, another picture with strong focus on youngsters. (The final retakes and inserts for *Boys Town* wrapped in early August 1938; the picture would be a major hit when released later in the year.)

Taurog's appointment to *Oz* was announced in the July 16, 1938, edition of *The Hollywood Reporter*. The paper reiterated this on August 12. LeRoy was sure that Taurog had the background and on-set efficiency needed to guide Judy Garland in a prestige production. By industry standards, Taurog was a perfectly acceptable choice to helm *Oz*—a far more likely one, in fact, than the eventual credited director, unsentimental and virile Victor Fleming.

LeRoy was ready to announce Taurog's hiring in May, but the front office asked that nothing be said until Taurog neared completion of *Boys Town*. *The Hollywood Reporter*, like every other trade paper in town, was immensely curious about the identity of the director selected to helm MGM's risky fantasy project, but had to wait for its scoop.

Taurog got to work at the end of the month, inspecting sets, costumes, and makeup, and shooting test footage. But at the beginning of August, after just three days of work, MGM pulled Taurog from *Oz*, in order that he could begin preproduction for another major picture, *The Adventures of Huckleberry Finn*. The shoot of that film was scheduled to begin in November, which meant that Taurog would have no more time for *The Wizard of Oz*. Taurog had already done *Huckleberry Finn* for Paramount in 1931, so he was a natural choice for the remake. As far as the studio was concerned, Taurog was a good choice for *Oz* but a better one for its version of *Huckleberry Finn*. When MGM staff director Richard Thorpe was dismissed from *The Wizard of Oz* in late November (see below), Taurog was removed from *The Adventures of Huckleberry Finn* and replaced by Thorpe, who completed the project and got sole screen credit. Only in the highly structured and systemized environment of Hollywood's golden age was this kind of revolving-door filmmaking possible. It may have been chaos, but it was *controlled* chaos.

Over the years, sources have erroneously claimed that the MGM front office pulled Taurog from *Oz* in order to put him to work on *Boys Town* (which Taurog was already wrapping up at the time of the *Oz* announcement); or *The Adventures of Tom Sawyer* (a Selznick picture that had been released on February 11, 1938).

In later years, Taurog claimed to have no memory of ever having been approached about *Oz*—and then came August 2013. That was when PBA Galleries, a San Francisco auction house, offered a treasure trove of twenty-seven candid, 3¾" × 4¾" photographs from the Norman Taurog estate (the director passed away in 1981), snapped at various times during the prep and shoot of *The Wizard of Oz*. The original prints had been tipped into the inside cover of a small photo album.

Seven of the images were printed in sepia, the rest in black and white. Of the nine sample images provided on the PBA Web site, one clearly shows Victor Fleming on the Munchkinland set, supervising a dolly shot. Others capture MGM costumers at work on the fabrication and assembly of the Tin Woodman costume.

The most revelatory photo was snapped in Munchkinland months before Fleming went to work on that set. Makeup artist Charlie Schram kneels to touch up the face powder of Lollipop Guild player Harry Earles. Two people stand behind Schram, observing. One is Bobbie Koshay, Judy Garland's stand-in. The other is Norman Taurog.

PBA's pre-auction estimate for the Taurog *Oz* photos was $3,000–$5,000; the actual sale price was $36,000. The identity of the buyer (who bid by phone) was not revealed.

In Focus: Norman Taurog (1899–1981)

Short, stout Norman Taurog is recalled today mainly for having directed more Elvis Presley movies than anybody else (nine) and for getting child actor Jackie Cooper to cry on cue by telling him that a studio guard had just shot the kid's dog. The latter incident happened during the filming of *Skippy* (1931), when Cooper was just nine years old. That's a hell of a thing to be remembered for, and the ironies are that Taurog was little Jackie's uncle as well as his director, and had himself started in the business as a child actor, before 1910. Taurog abandoned acting when he outgrew his cute phase and moved behind the camera in 1920, working for the next eleven years as director of nearly a hundred minor comedy shorts featuring Joe Rock, Johnny Arthur, Clark & McCullough (who became reasonably popular later, in the early 1930s), and Larry Semon (director-star of the 1925 *Wizard of Oz* feature). The Taurog shorts were variously produced by Fox Film, Goodwill, Jack White's Mermaid, and Vitagraph.

Taurog directed his first feature in 1928, and *Skippy* came along three years later. The picture was a tremendous hit for Paramount and brought Taurog the Academy

Norman Taurog, still the youngest person to win the best director Academy Award, was MGM's first choice to handle *The Wizard of Oz*. Taurog was an experienced storyteller who had worked well with juvenile actors. The nature of his approach to *Oz* is an enticing "what if?"

Award for best director. Just thirty-two at the time, Taurog remains the youngest person to take home the directing Oscar.

Taurog's success with *Skippy* suggested to the industry—perhaps rightly, perhaps wrongly—that Taurog had the magic touch with kids. Some of the pictures he directed later were built around such child actors as Jackie Searle, Jackie Coogan, Junior Durkin, Tommy Kelly, Jackie Moran, and Marcia Mae Jones. A bit later, Taurog became adept at light comedy; *We're Not Dressing*, a 1934 vehicle for Bing Crosby and Carole Lombard, is typical.

At Universal, Taurog directed one of young Deanna Durbin's early hits, *Mad About Music* (1938), and signed with MGM the same year. Taurog directed the smash hit *Boys Town* (1938), getting a sterling performance from eighteen-year-old Mickey Rooney, helping Spencer Tracy to a best actor Oscar, and earning a best director nomination for himself. All of this encouraged Mervyn LeRoy to bring Taurog onto *The Wizard of Oz*. Through no fault of his own, Taurog's very brief tenure on that project consisted of little more than test footage. He remained on staff at MGM, directing class-A musicals, romances, and the occasional drama (the best of those is *The Beginning or the End*, 1947, a timely piece about the development of the atomic bomb).

Although Taurog never formally directed Judy Garland in *The Wizard of Oz*, the two did work together afterward: *Little Nellie Kelly* (1940), *Presenting Lily Mars* (1943), *Girl Crazy* (1943), and *Words and Music* (1948).

In the 1950s, Taurog directed six Martin and Lewis comedies, including one of the team's funniest, *You're Never Too Young* (1955). Taurog's association with Elvis began with *G.I. Blues*, which was released in 1960, immediately after Elvis's real-life Army service. The period is recalled as the beginning of the push by Elvis's manager, Tom Parker, to neuter his explosive star and make him bland, cheerful, and unthreatening. Taurog obliged by doing little more than point the camera during the subsequent shoots of *Blue Hawaii*, *Girls! Girls! Girls!*, *Tickle Me*, the dire *Double Trouble*, and others. And somewhere in there, Taurog made time to direct a Vincent Price–Frankie Avalon farce, *Dr. Goldfoot and the Bikini Machine* (1965), for American International Pictures.

Taurog retired after 1968. He did some university lectures but was slowed by diabetes that eventually cost him his sight. Norman Taurog passed away in 1981, at eighty-two.

Richard Thorpe Gets to Work

With Taurog out of the picture, LeRoy assigned *Oz* to another experienced studio staffer, Richard Thorpe. Although MGM's decision to go with Thorpe was made some time in the forepart of August, *The Hollywood Reporter* didn't break the news until its September 1, 1938, edition; Thorpe's assignment was confirmed by MGM on September 7, a day after dance director Bobby Connolly had begun rehearsals with Judy Garland, Ray Bolger, and Buddy Ebsen.

The Wizard of Oz was originally scheduled as a four-month shoot. The studio had wanted the *Oz* shoot to begin in September 1938 (the 15th, the 20th, and the 23rd were hopefully announced by the studio as start dates). As those dates came and went, Garland and other principals stayed busy with color tests and prerecordings of musical numbers. (Those prerecordings began on September 30, with a full orchestra supervised by Herbert Stothart.)

A *Daily Variety* report from October 7, 1938, said that Thorpe, production manager Joe Cooke, and assistant director Al Shenberg would leave the next day to scout Southern California locations that might double for Kansas. *The Hollywood Reporter* embellished this claim (which almost certainly originated in the imagination of someone in MGM publicity) on October 8, saying that the story's Kansas scenes would be shot in Kansas.

Filming finally began on October 13. Thorpe started with Dorothy's first encounter with the Scarecrow and the "If I Only Had a Brain" number, but on October 15, he moved on to the imprisonment and rescue sequence inside the Witch's castle. He began in the tower room and then filmed on larger areas of the castle set. As scripted, Judy was to do a reprise of "Over the Rainbow" while held captive. When Thorpe filmed the number on Monday, October 17, Garland sang live, on set, accompanied only by Roger Edens's piano. Although some sources say that Judy overdubbed her vocal the following May, the whole point of Judy singing the number live was that she'd find it impossible later to voice-match her halting, highly emotional rendition. (The surviving audio is heartbreaking; Dorothy's fear and despair are palpable.) The reprise was cut because it slowed narrative momentum, and only increased the film's running time. Whether the abject emotionalism of the performance had a bearing is unknown. The on-set audio, as well as Judy's (less emotional) soundtrack recording, survive and have been included on various DVD and CD packages since 1993.

At Thorpe's request, writer Sid Silvers was brought on board to help with on-set script revisions. Silvers was an on-again, off-again film actor who segued into writing in 1930. He was primarily an "original story" man who co-wrote the occasional complete screenplay, did rewrites of scripts written by others, and punched up dialogue. Prior to *The Wizard of Oz*, Silvers's greatest success was as co-screenwriter for a good MGM musical, *Broadway Melody of 1936* (1935).

Scenes inside the castle continued. Thorpe's professionalism kept on-set activity moving. Dorothy's confrontations with the Witch seemed to play effectively, and if Thorpe had any doubts about Judy Garland's precociously glamorous appearance, he kept them to himself. Thorpe's Dorothy has cascading dark blonde tresses (the blonde wig was created by *Oz* hair stylist Beth Langston, under the oversight of wig supervisor Max Factor Jr. and wig designer Fred Frederick). The café-society makeup was created by Web Overlander and supervised by Jack Dawn. In this early footage, Dorothy wears a pinafore and slippers that are different from what we have come to know; the change was just one of many suggested later by George Cukor, who acted as a consultant following Richard Thorpe's departure from the project.

No 35mm studio footage of the blonde Dorothy exists. If it did, it surely would have shown up as an extra on more than one of the film's home-video releases. However, black-and-white silent footage (probably 16mm) taken outside on the MGM lot during the time of the Thorpe shoot reveals Judy Garland in the blonde wig. Because Garland acknowledges the camera by turning around to curtsy, it's possible that the footage was part of newsreel coverage of the film's shoot, or a general tour of the MGM lot.

The pressure of an important starring role gnawed at Judy, who was in great emotional distress as the *Oz* shoot commenced. She had long doubted her own attractiveness, and now she was entangling herself in tragic, unwarranted self-criticism. She hated her neck, she hated her legs, she hated her body, she hated her face. On the MGM lot, she was surrounded by gorgeous starlets. Some were talented, others were not. A few would succeed, but most would fail. Nevertheless, their beauty was all that was apparent to Judy. Oblivious to her own unique beauty and other gifts, she fretted herself into complete misery. (In 1939, after she had established a friendship with bandleader Artie Shaw, Judy compared herself unfavorably to one of Shaw's vocalists, Billie Holiday.)

Richard Thorpe was a good technician but not "an actor's director"—and certainly not the best person to guide an insecure, very young leading lady. From the outset of his shoot, Thorpe was more interested in the story's physical environment. The massive central stairway that dominated the castle interior intrigued Thorpe, who brought in a camera boom that utilized compressed air to reach as high as eighty feet. The director had a grasp of the climax's pictorial possibilities, and he wanted cinematographer Harold Rosson to help him to exploit them. (Thorpe and Rosson had worked together once before, on 1937's *Double Wedding*.) The October 22, 1938, edition of *Daily Variety* remarked on a dolly tracking shot that "followed [the principals] diagonally at a distance of 150 feet for the take, said to be the longest boom shot ever made in color."

Buddy Ebsen rested between setups on a slant board, and Bert Lahr quickly discovered the horrors of being encased in lion skin for hours at a stretch. When he was hungry or thirsty, he took nourishment through a straw.

Hedda Hopper visited the set. Shortly after, she commented in her *Los Angeles Times* column, "Never expected to live long enough to see a zipper on a lion." That was a deliberately snarky comment meant to imply that something about the *Oz* project was shoddy and substandard. Thorpe naturally shot so that no secrets of anybody's costume would be revealed. Hopper knew that but felt compelled to pretend otherwise in order to make a weak joke at the film's expense.

Aluminum Poisoning in Oz

The most important ingredient of Buddy Ebsen's silvered Tin Woodman makeup was aluminum dust, on a layer of clown-white. Of all the minerals in earth's crust, aluminum is the most common. Normal exposure is harmless, but when excessive amounts are breathed or ingested, aluminum becomes a toxic agent. Very prolonged exposure can decrease the body's number of red blood cells, and thus the amount of oxygen circulating through the body. Seizures, bone pain, and confusion are familiar symptoms of aluminum poisoning. In some cases, victims have difficulty with speech or experience muscle weakness.

Ebsen was stricken on-set, on Friday, October 21, 1938, nine days after the start of Oz's principal photography, and after many days of makeup tests that preceded filming. The lanky actor was suddenly gripped by profound shortness of breath, which he described as a "panicky feeling I hadn't breathed at all." He was rushed to a hospital and placed beneath an oxygen tent. A few days later, severe muscle cramps caused his arms to curl toward his chest, and in just minutes, his legs seized and involuntarily bent at the knees. When Ebsen felt the cramping move into his chest, he was certain he was about to die.

What had happened? Aluminum overdose is particularly harmful to the lungs, which become no longer able to provide the victim with full breaths. That's the complication that manifested itself on the Oz set. The involuntary muscle movement that followed is another familiar complication, caused by a compromised nervous system.

Ebsen remained in the hospital for two weeks and needed another month to recuperate. In the meantime, Mervyn LeRoy hired Jack Haley to play the Tin Woodman. Because Ebsen seemed to have vanished at the same time as dismissed director Richard Thorpe, many in the Oz cast and crew assumed that Buddy, like Thorpe, had been fired. That may now strike some of us as unnecessarily paranoid, but the people that worried weren't on the wrong track. Studio-era Hollywood was very hierarchical—quick to assign blame and designed to protect those at the top. Doo-doo rolled downhill like an umber avalanche, stopping to bury a person of reasonable importance and then continuing on, growing larger, sweeping aside lesser lights that may not have been guilty of anything at all. Circumstance, and the director's particular vision of Oz, had conspired against Thorpe, and he was out. Buddy Ebsen, through no fault of his own, was also lost to the ages. In countless similar cases, the avalanche would have continued to roll beyond Buddy, growing fat with the careers of actors, cinematographers, and others. In the end, MGM bore no ill will against Thorpe, and the only actor gone MIA was Ebsen. Garland was never in danger, of course, but the other principals might have been. The remainder of the cast was retained, and there were no changes in cinematographer, set designer, or any other tech job.

Ebsen's singing voice remains, however. You will hear him in two performances of "We're Off to See the Wizard," the first time with Garland, Bolger, and Haley; and later, with Garland, Bolger, Haley, and Lahr.

Despite the illness that forced him from *Oz*, Ebsen had featured roles in two films released in 1939: *Four Girls in White*, an agreeable nurses-meet-doctors drama; and *The Kid from Texas*, in which uncouth cowboys appall the upper crust when they take up polo. Both pictures were produced by MGM.

Because of Ebsen's illness, the enormous dressed *Oz* stages weren't getting full use, which was money down the drain. That didn't improve the disposition of anybody, including Mervyn LeRoy, who looked at daily rushes and felt that Thorpe wasn't achieving the magical quality the film needed. LeRoy went to Louis Mayer to explain the problem and to ask once again to direct the picture himself. Mayer once more said no.

LeRoy fired Thorpe on the day Ebsen was stricken, October 24. The studio announced Thorpe's departure a day later, claiming the director was "seriously ill."

In the 1970s, during an interview with historian Doug McClelland, Thorpe said, "I don't believe any of the footage remains made during the few days I was on the picture." That's disappointing to *Oz* fans and film historians, but pieces of other films long thought to have been lost have a habit of turning up unexpectedly, decades later, and in unexpected places. (Twenty-five minutes of footage from Fritz Lang's 1927 German masterpiece *Metropolis* were discovered in 2008, in a long-restricted, semi-private film archive in Argentina.) We may yet see portions, or even most, of what Richard Thorpe shot on the *Oz* sets in the autumn of 1938.

In Focus: Richard Thorpe (1896–1991)

Over the many years of the studio system, Hollywood saw plenty of directors like Richard Thorpe. These were filmmakers who began with B-pictures, where they learned how to frame a shot and tell a story with reasonable competence. They worked quickly and with professional craft, inspiring no one among the cast and crew but getting the pictures done on schedule, or earlier. From an industry standpoint, this kind of filmmaker was as valuable as gold. The business has always been about product, and these directors cranked out a lot of it. Most of them, like Phil Rosen (*Phantom of Chinatown*), George Blair (*The Ghost Goes Wild*), Lee "Roll 'em" Sholem (*Jungle Man-Eaters*), and William "One-Shot" Beaudine (*Broadway Big Shot*), bounced from studio to studio and among independent producers, picking up great numbers of minor assignments. Many eventually made their way to episodic television, where their careers were greatly prolonged. A very few had the luck and political instincts to become installed as staff directors at a major studio. Those who managed the transition worked with better budgets and bigger stars than most of their similarly talented contemporaries.

Richard Thorpe was one of those.

He began his professional career as an actor and entertainer in vaudeville and the legitimate stage. Between 1921 and 1924, he worked as an actor in a handful of B-movies and directed his first, *Rough Ridin'*, in 1924, when he was twenty-eight. Throughout the remainder of the silent era, and into the early 1930s, he directed dozens of budget westerns, many featuring cowboy star Buddy Roosevelt, for Chesterfield, Tiffany, and other Poverty Row production companies.

In 1935, Thorpe came on staff at MGM, where he remained for the next twenty-nine years and some seventy movies. He became a brisk, able filmmaker who was confident with increasingly large budgets and important stars. The suspenseful and well-crafted *Night Must Fall* (1937) is one of Thorpe's pre-*Oz* highlights. Others are *Tarzan Escapes* (1936), *Double Wedding* (Powell & Loy; 1937), and *The Crowd Roars* (Robert Taylor; 1938).

Thorpe's *Oz* assignment was a testament to his professionalism, but he and the material weren't a congenial fit. It's important to note that as far as Louis B. Mayer and the rest of the industry were concerned, Thorpe's heave-ho from *The Wizard of Oz* was not a slap at the director's competence, or a suggestion that he couldn't stand—commercially—with any of his contemporaries. *Oz* just wasn't his cup of tea. Well, that was all right. Thorpe had already proved himself. No harm was done to his career.

After 1939, in fact, the projects that came Thorpe's way grew increasingly more prestigious: *Tarzan's New York Adventure* (1942), *White Cargo* (with Hedy Lamarr as Tondelayo; 1942), *Cry "Havoc"* (Margaret Sullavan; 1943), *Ivanhoe* (Robert Taylor, Elizabeth Taylor; 1952), *Knights of the Round Table* (Robert Taylor, Ava Gardner; 1953), and *Jailhouse Rock* (Elvis Presley; 1957). A bit later, perhaps because of the presumed "kid appeal" of *Jailhouse Rock*, Thorpe undertook a series of young-romance comedies featuring Steve McQueen, Jim Hutton, Paula Prentiss, Connie Francis, and other new stars: *The Honeymoon Machine* (1961), *The Horizontal Lieutenant* (1962), *Follow the Boys* (1963), and another with Elvis, *Fun in Acapulco* (1963).

After leaving MGM, Thorpe continued in the "youth" vein with a Bobby Darin–Sandra Dee vehicle, *That Funny Feeling* (1965). These

Although infrequently mentioned in studies of American directors, Richard Thorpe was a competent professional who knew how to put pictures in the can on time and on budget. He was a valuable staff director at MGM, and although his sensibility didn't mesh with *Oz*, the studio never held it against him. To the contrary, Thorpe prospered at MGM for many years to come.

Nikko receives his instructions. Victor Fleming shot this scene with the camera inside the Witch's castle, looking toward the window and at the sky outside. This publicity still taken during the Thorpe shoot shows the reverse angle, with the camera looking in at the castle from the outside.

romances are innocuous and forgettable; what's significant is that Thorpe, in his late sixties, still made profitable movies.

MGM star Esther Williams, who worked with Thorpe four times, described him in her autobiography as a "dyspeptic" sourpuss whose preoccupation with the buck caused him to bully actors who didn't live up to his time-clock standards. Thorpe was particularly annoyed by inexperienced players, and by any cast member that came on the set in a cheerful mood. When Thorpe and Williams were suffering through their third film together, he confided to her, "I hate actors."

Very little about Thorpe's two-week tenure on *The Wizard of Oz* was apparently ever recorded. In later years, cast members had virtually nothing to say about him. Although a former actor himself, Thorpe apparently pretended to be oblivious to the challenges of that job. Even if he was cordial to young Judy Garland, he could not have been very encouraging to her.

But competence should be rewarded. Richard Thorpe was a team player who made a lot of money for the industry. In 1960, he was given a star on the Hollywood Walk of Fame. Thorpe was ninety-five when he died in 1991.

In Focus: Harold Rosson (1895–1988)

In the history of Hollywood filmmaking, few directors of photography have been as esteemed as Harold "Hal" Rosson. A native of New York state, he got into movies in 1908, as an actor and extra, when American movie production was still centered in or near New York City. For Rosson, this meant the Vitagraph Studios located in the Flatbush section of Brooklyn. At the Mark Dintenfass studio around 1910, Rosson began to explore cinematography, and by the end of 1914, he was in California, working as an assistant to Metro Pictures cinematographer Arthur Cadwell.

Following service in World War I, Rosson was back on the East Coast. Star actress Marion Davies had her own production company, and she was impressed with Rosson's work on one of her vehicles, *The Dark Star* (1919). It was through that association that Rosson became a director of photography, initially working on pictures starring Jack Pickford, the less-famous brother of film star Mary Pickford.

Before Rosson joined MGM in 1930, he shot many films for one of early cinema's great (and most efficient) craftsmen, Allan Dwan (who worked from 1911 to 1961 and is probably best known to latter-day audiences as the director of 1948's *Sands of Iwo Jima*). From Dwan and others in those early days, Rosson learned the value of preparation and quickness.

Rosson's professional introduction to Victor Fleming came in 1922 (*Dark Secrets*), and they went on to collaborate on seven more projects, including *Red Dust* (1932), *Bombshell* (1933), *Treasure Island* (1934), *The Wizard of Oz* (1939), and *Gone With the Wind* (1939).

Red Dust and *Bombshell* starred MGM's greatest female asset, the fabulous Jean Harlow. Rosson shot Harlow five times in all (the others were *Red-Headed Woman*, *Hold Your Man*, and *The Girl from Missouri*); his photography highlighted Harlow's platinum hair, yet also gave her an accessible, "real" appearance that endeared her to audiences. Rosson and Harlow were married in 1935, and divorced two years later.

Red Dust, with its oppressively sweaty South American setting, allowed Rosson to utilize his gift for carefully lit cinematography that suggests the sensual qualities of a place. *Red Dust* and *Kongo* (1932) suggest oppressive humidity, the particular lighting and great expanses of the sea are captured in *Treasure Island* and *Captains Courageous* (1936), and a rough-hewn rawness defines *Boom Town* (1940) and *Honky Tonk* (1941).

Rosson was a star cinematographer at the best studio, so he worked with skilled directors on a lot of very good projects: *Madam Satan* (1930; Cecil B. DeMille), *Tarzan the Ape Man* (1932; Woody Van Dyke), *Hell Below* (1932; Jack Conway), *The Ghost Goes West* (1935; René Clair), *Meet Me in St. Louis* (1944; Vincente Minnelli), *Thirty Seconds Over Tokyo* (1944; Mervyn LeRoy).

As movies became grittier after World War II, Rosson developed a naturalistic "you are there" look; John Huston's *The Asphalt Jungle* (1950) was Rosson's greatest

Harold Rosson was one of the best cinematographers in Hollywood, and handled the monochrome and color sequences of *Oz* with equal skill. This 1936 photo shows him with society matron Yvonne Crellin, whom he later married.

achievement of that sort. But he could shoot musicals, too, and with delightful and chromatically brilliant use of color: *Singin' in the Rain* (1952), *Dangerous When Wet* (1953; starring sleek and slippery Esther Williams), and the unforgettable "Born in a Trunk" number from Judy Garland's last great film, *A Star Is Born* (1954). (Rosson's first experience with color, for a 1936 loan-out project for Selznick called *The Garden of Allah*, took him completely by surprise, He had had no idea he was to shoot in color. He had serious doubts about his ability to pull it off—but he did, and won an Academy Award in the bargain.)

Louis B. Mayer took considerable pride in the polished look of the MGM product. Mayer once said to Rosson, "If it's an MGM film, it has to look like an MGM film." This was the mandate Rosson needed. During a superb career, he drove the studio to the visual excellence that distinguished it for decades.

These Things Must Be Done Delicately

Cukor Offers Advice

Not surprisingly, no one in the industry believed that Richard Thorpe was ill. Hollywood was (and remains) a small company town where news traveled quickly. Thorpe's dismissal excited some local interest because of the financial risks MGM had already assumed with this prestigious adaptation of a well-liked children's book. The studio was aware that the circumstances of Thorpe's dismissal might be embellished to the point that the entire *Oz* project might seem to be in jeopardy. Stories might swirl that Judy Garland was somehow inadequate, or that the budget was already out of control. Perhaps, rumors might insist, *The Wizard of Oz* was unfilmable.

Executives from every studio claimed not to be concerned with the Hollywood rumor mill, but that's only partially true. The particular nature of specific rumors probably didn't concern them (almost anything could be rectified with a publicity counterattack); what bothered those in power was that something had happened to *cause* the rumor. Executive authority in the movie business was as much about perception as about real power. Nobody wanted to be identified as the leader who allowed a project to stumble. Fortunately, a quick remedy to help *Oz* was available right on the MGM lot.

MGM staffer George Cukor, a particularly accomplished and urbane director, was brought onto the *Oz* project on October 25, 1938, just a day after the dismissal of Richard Thorpe. Cukor's appointment was made public on October 26. Although *The Hollywood Reporter* claimed that Cukor would reshoot some of Thorpe's scenes before beginning on fresh material, Mervyn LeRoy made clear to the *Oz* unit that Cukor's role would not be as a "shooting" director but as a temporary consultant. David O. Selznick's independent production of *Gone With the Wind* was scheduled to start shooting in January 1939, and Cukor had been penciled in as that project's director since 1936. He performed his tasks for *The Wizard of Oz* simultaneously with preproduction work on *GWTW*.

George Cukor was justly famed for his taste and appreciation of subtlety and nuance. (Because of those gifts, he was incidentally able to calm scripter Noel Langley, who had been upset with rewrites of his work. Cukor assured the writer that many of the added ideas were uncinematic and would eventually go by the wayside.) Cukor was not known as a fantasy director—none of the staff directors at MGM had that distinction—but he grasped the written and visual possibilities of characterization.

Because he was a practical filmmaker involved in the creation of sophisticated entertainment, Cukor had no qualms about his own opinion of the *Oz* project. He disliked it. He disliked the Oz books, too, feeling that Baum's universe wasn't simply childlike but childish. (Years later, Cukor sniffed, "I was brought up on grander things. I was brought up on Tennyson.") But although Cukor valued his own opinion, he wasn't going to let it diminish his professionalism. As he saw things, *The Wizard of Oz* was in trouble—and he could address the problems successfully.

Mainly, Cukor was struck by the inappropriateness of Dorothy's appearance; given Dorothy's Kansas-farm girl backstory, the heavy makeup (which he termed "doll-like") and blonde hair were absurd and would have to go. On October 26, Cukor began supervising film and photo tests of revised hair and makeup treatments. He tried and then discarded various wigs, as well as Judy Garland's own hair, with natural braids. On October 31, Cukor felt he was getting closer, when he got pleasing results with subdued makeup and Judy's own hair, augmented with a fall.

Cukor's impression from the Thorpe rushes was that Judy had been encouraged to give a mannered performance suggesting that the actress (and Dorothy) was very conscious of the tale's fairytale aspects. Cukor told LeRoy that Judy had to project a natural quality because Judy/Dorothy had to function as the "reality" that made the other characters, and the plot, acceptably believable. As Cukor saw things, Dorothy should be *in* Oz but not *of* Oz. When he met with Judy Garland, he asked the young actress to remember that Dorothy was "just a little girl from Kansas." That, he felt, was the essence of whatever charm others found in the books and in the MGM script. Dorothy was loved because she was an innocent.

While occupied with Dorothy, Cukor also turned his attention to other characters, bringing the Witch's hair off her shoulders and asking that Hamilton's nose and chin pieces be given greater emphasis. He also asked that the Scarecrow have a more human appearance.

An October 31 interoffice memo from publicity chief Howard Strickling to studio advertising director Howard Dietz revealed that Victor Fleming would take over *Oz*. The industry trade papers announced Fleming's appointment on November 1, 1938.

George Cukor's last day as consultant to *Oz* was November 3, when Cukor and hair technician Sydney Guilaroff agreed that Dorothy looked best with dark, almost auburn hair parted in the middle, for a "schoolgirl" appearance. When Mervyn LeRoy signed off on the design, Cukor's work on *Oz* was done, and he was free to devote all of his time to *Gone With the Wind*.

In Focus: George Cukor (1899–1983)

Hollywood made itself a specialist in brightly comic, brightly arch comedy-dramas in the 1930s, and one reason so many of those films turned out so, well, brightly, is that they were informed by the taste and bitchy intelligence of George Cukor. Granted, it's not extravagantly easy to go awry when you're working from screenplays by Anita Loos, Donald Ogden Stewart, Ruth Gordon and Garson Kanin, Howard Estabrook, Frances Marion, Moss Hart, and Herman Mankiewicz. Without Cukor, though, a clutch of the best-liked and best-regarded American films from the early 1930s to the mid-1950s wouldn't have the elastically funny body language that delineated character, or the quick flick of a gaze that was more cutting than two pages of "you stink" dialogue. For many years, Cukor has been described as "a woman's director," which does him a disservice and probably ought to be taken as an insult to women. Cukor was interested in the foibles of everybody, and if many of his pictures involve the quirks of women, it's because when Cukor was at his height, Hollywood studios okayed a lot of great parts for a lot of wonderful actresses.

Cukor was born in New York City and began his career as a Broadway performer in 1919. He was better suited to be a director and gained notice his second time out, for his tasteful but emotionally sharp handling of *The Great Gatsby* (adapted by Owen Davis). The production helped to confirm the stage stardom of James Rennie (as Gatsby), and saw a very nice run of 112 performances. Between 1927 and 1929, Cukor directed another half dozen Broadway plays and then went to Hollywood, initially as a writer. He was dialogue director on a couple of early talkies that include a classic,

Director George Cukor came onto *Oz* as a consultant shortly before Halloween 1938. Although he had no fondness for the material, and was preoccupied with pre-production of *Gone With the Wind*, he attended to *Oz* smartly, insisting that Dorothy's glamorous appearance be toned down. Cukor also established that "straight" playing was essential if audiences were to identify with the characters and accept the story's fantasy elements.

All Quiet on the Western Front. That was 1930, and after a few assignments as a co-director, Cukor made his solo debut with *Tarnished Lady* (1931). The star was Tallulah Bankhead, who had had plenty of Broadway experience but was yet to achieve her full theatrical stardom. Nevertheless, Paramount knew it had a live wire and gave her top billing in *Tarnished Lady*. She could be a handful, but Cukor negotiated her moods. He was a closeted gay; Bankhead was a bisexual sensualist; perhaps they reached some sort of congenial understanding.

During the next twenty years, Cukor put together an enviable resumé, highlighted by ensemble pictures (*Dinner at Eight*, *Little Women*), satire (*What Price Hollywood?*, *Ninotchka*), some sterling adaptations of established classics (*Romeo and Juliet*, *David Copperfield*, *Camille*), and sophisticated urban comedies (*The Philadelphia Story*, *Adam's Rib*, *Born Yesterday*, *Pat and Mike*, *It Should Happen to You*).

Cukor handled heavy suspense dramas, like *Gaslight* and *A Double Life*, imaginatively and with a lot of bite, and also shone as a director of musicals, notably the greatest version of *A Star Is Born* (1954; starring Judy Garland and James Mason), and one of his late triumphs, *Les Girls* (1957).

He worked almost exclusively for MGM from 1933 to 1950 and subsequently found success and quality material at Columbia and 20th Century-Fox. Although the accelerated breakup of the studio system in the late '50s did nothing to diminish his gifts (in other words, he didn't need the prime material and other "protection" offered by MGM or any other single studio), it did lead Cukor—like many other very fine directors—into a landscape of shifting audience demographics, executive indecision, and some glossy but empty projects that were frankly beneath him; *Heller in Pink Tights* (1959), *Let's Make Love* (1960), and an overblown but meek "sexposé," *The Chapman Report* (1962), spring quickly to mind.

However, being an éminence grise conferred certain advantages, such as Cukor's opportunity to direct a wildly anticipated musical, *My Fair Lady* (1964). He did it to a T, of course, but it was his last important project. Cukor retired after *Rich and Famous* (1981).

During his professional prime, George Cukor suffered only one real reversal: being fired from *Gone With the Wind*. That David Selznick didn't like what he saw in rushes, or what he may have heard from Clark Gable (who may have said nothing at all about Cukor), bothered the director, but not so seriously that his natural enthusiasm for work didn't allow him to recover quickly. His availability to act as an adviser to *The Wizard of Oz* was a lucky stroke, and he probably saved the movie from going down a woefully inappropriate path.

King of the Forest

Victor Fleming Steps In

MGM's greatest male star of 1938–39, Clark Gable, was the kind of fellow other men wanted to spend time with. He was jocular and unreflective, very much at home with motorcycling, hunting, and other outdoor pursuits. MGM staff director Victor Fleming was made of the same stuff and was frequently a part of Gable's outings. Fleming and Gable had worked together in the past, notably on the very satisfying *Red Dust* (1932). Fleming pumped up Gable's virility quotient on that one and coaxed a funny, raunchy performance from fast-rising leading lady Jean Harlow. Given his resumé, it's no surprise that Fleming was nobody's first choice for *Oz*.

Fleming had been unusually busy immediately before *The Wizard of Oz*. When he was assigned to the *Oz* restart, the forty-nine-year-old director was, well, pooped. A physically strong and active man, Fleming was nevertheless

John Lee Mahin (left) was one of Hollywood's most capable script doctors and made important revisions to *The Wizard of Oz*. A publicity photographer snapped this shot of Mahin, Jean Harlow, and Victor Fleming on the set of *Bombshell* (1933). Mahin and Fleming had a mutual respect and worked together many times.

bowing beneath the accumulated weight of four projects in quick succession during 1937–38 and pre-production for MGM's adaptation of Marjorie Kinnan Rawlings's *The Yearling*. (When the novel was finally filmed in 1946, it was directed by another MGM staffer, Clarence Brown.)

But Fleming was proud of his stamina, and he was a company man, too. He said that *Oz* sounded okay and that he'd take it on. In all, Fleming would devote three and a half months to *The Wizard of Oz*, earning $3,000 a week. He grasped the challenges posed by this very ambitious project but was undeterred, once remarking, "Don't get excited. Obstacles make a better picture."

Fleming was a confident professional, but he knew he couldn't hurdle all the obstacles by himself. He wanted to put his own imprint of *Oz*, so he hired screenwriter John Lee Mahin for rewrites. Fleming and Mahin had enjoyed amiable working relationships on *Red Dust*, *Treasure Island*, and others, and Mahin had written sharp, smart stuff for *The Beast of the City* and *Scarface* (both 1932), *China Seas* (1935), *Captains Courageous* (1937), and many others. Fleming had great respect for Mahin's talent and kept the writer on the set throughout his portion of the *Oz* shoot. (Later, Fleming brought Mahin to Selznick International to assist on *Gone With the Wind* following the dismissal of George Cukor. As he had on *Oz*, Mahin provided Fleming with on-set rewrites.)

Mahin looked at the *Oz* script and began his adjustments at the beginning, rewriting the opening so that conflict and anxiety are immediately established. In Mahin's rewrite, Dorothy is introduced as she hurries home to complain about Miss Gulch's treatment of Toto. Where there had been two farmhands, there now were three: Mahin created Zeke (Bert Lahr) to round out the parallelism of the Kansas/Oz sequences and to provide Dorothy with yet another sympathetic farmhand to talk with. Because Fleming and Mahin felt it was critical that Dorothy experience the story's initial conflict essentially alone, Mahin added the bit of business about Aunt Em and Uncle Henry's preoccupation with the sickly chicks and the incubator. Dorothy almost *demands* their attention, but her aunt and uncle are too busy to give it. By establishing that Dorothy must rely largely on herself, Mahin not only goosed the opening sequence and developed Dorothy's character, but also set up Dorothy's need to live by her wits once in the Land of Oz.

Mahin provided Fleming with fresh dialogue almost daily. Fleming would look at what Mahin had done and add changes of his own. This collaboration allowed Fleming to shape the story, and manage characters, as he wished.

Mahin was adept at gags as well as with structure and characterization. After sensing an opportunity for a funny quip when the Scarecrow, Tin Woodman, and Cowardly Lion overpower the Winkies and prepare to enter the Witch's castle, Mahin consulted with Jack Haley, who provided him with a venerable vaudeville gag that culminates in the Lion's wonderful "Talk me out of it!"

Although Mahin was kept busy throughout Fleming's time on *Oz*, the writer refused on-screen credit.

Where Richard Thorpe had wanted to highlight Toto and explore him as a character, Fleming and Mahin saw the wisdom of using the dog simply as a device to propel the plot. The story was, after all, about Dorothy, not Toto.

Fleming and Mahin felt that the Langley, Woolf, and Ryerson script had too many instances of innocuous, uninteresting lightness: Dorothy on a pony, Dorothy engaging a real scarecrow in a one-sided conversation, and so on. All of that was scrapped. If Dorothy's dreary Kansas existence was to be made clear, and if the danger she faced in Oz was to have impact, viewers mustn't be distracted by fluff.

On the *Oz* set, Fleming wasn't an unsmiling taskmaster, but he conducted himself like a professional, and he expected the people he worked with to do likewise. He understood the nuts-and-bolts *process* of moviemaking as well as any of his contemporaries, and he valued talented collaborators. If you demonstrated to Fleming that you were part of the MGM family for a reason, everything was fine. That was a bit of relief to cinematographer Harold Rosson, who knew from experience that when a director is released from a film, the director of photography often goes too, as a sort of symbolic housecleaning. When Richard Thorpe was dismissed from *Oz*, Rosson prepared himself for another assignment and was pleased, and a bit surprised, to be retained. He worked throughout the project, with Victor Fleming and King Vidor as well as Thorpe.

A typical Fleming day on the set began at 8:00 a.m. and lasted until 5:00 or 6:00 p.m. Six of MGM's twenty-nine sound stages were continually on call, giving Fleming the flexibility needed to move efficiently from one sequence to another, as schedules, unforeseen delays, and other factors manifested themselves. By design, of course, the sound stages allowed Fleming complete control over lighting, wind effects, sound—everything that could easily be compromised during filming on genuine exteriors. Throughout the shoot, crews moved between Stages 14, 15, 25, 26, 27, and the newest, 29. Carpenters and scenic artists were constantly, endlessly busy, erecting sets on one stage, tearing them down on another, and then putting up fresh ones.

Fleming had been told by the Technicolor people that the colors had a tendency to blur on screen if the camera remained static. Harold Rosson agreed, saying that camera tests had resulted in "just a mass of nothing." In order to avoid the unwanted blending, Fleming had the camera mounted on a Chapman boom and kept it in almost constant motion. This technique, which is particularly noticeable in the Munchkinland sequences, gave the film a subtle visual urgency, as well as a way to avoid the hazards pointed out by the folks at Technicolor.

Al Shenberg was assigned as assistant director, to fulfill the usual requirements of that job: preparer and coordinator of daily call sheets; awareness of the production schedule; wrangling cast members and doing other logistics; answering questions from the crew; and looking after the safety of the cast and all others on the set.

Fleming worked on *The Wizard of Oz* from November 4, 1938 (his first day of shooting was November 11), through February 17, 1939, and then did a few retakes and inserts in March. Mervyn LeRoy left Fleming alone and didn't distract him with too many visits to the set. As a director himself, LeRoy knew that intrusive executives were resented and ultimately counterproductive. And anyway, Fleming was smart, focused, and efficient. He didn't have to be guided.

On Fleming's first day, he took the troupe to Stage 26, where he supervised a reshoot of Dorothy's first meeting with the Scarecrow, a scene that Thorpe had shot on October 13. Because Jimmy, the crow on Bolger's shoulder, misbehaved (he flew into the riggings and stayed there), not much was accomplished that first day. (See "In Focus: Jimmy the Crow," chapter 5.)

By the second week of November, Fleming had finished with the talking apple trees and completed Dorothy and the Scarecrow's first encounter with the Tin Woodman. Because of a blocking error involving the apple trees, Judy Garland was momentarily framed full-figure, allowing inadvertent exposure of the comfortable brown shoes she wore during setups in which the ruby slippers wouldn't be visible.

Because Dorothy's early moments with the Scarecrow were cobbled together from footage Fleming shot on different days, Dorothy's pigtails are different lengths from shot to shot. Another error could not be allowed to stand:

Victor Fleming disliked the "morning stars" on the Witch's chandelier and had the whole thing redesigned.

Haley's Tin Woodman costume, like Ebsen's, was shiny—but shouldn't be, because the Woodman was supposed to have been standing in the elements for ages. He should be rusty, not shiny. This dawned on Fleming after three days of filming with Haley and the others, and half a week's work had to be dumped. By November 15, Haley was posing for test shots of the "rust" makeup. When Fleming resumed shooting, the Tin Woodman's metal body was artfully adorned with subtle streaks and spots of rust.

The abandoned Haley footage featured an old-style long-necked, bottom-squeeze oil can; in the replacement footage, Dorothy uses a modern, more compact can, with a pistol grip. The reason for the change is unknown, though a guess is that the modern style allowed oil to flow more easily and made the possibility of botched takes less likely. (Chocolate syrup was used instead of oil because it photographed better than the real thing.)

Besides correcting mistakes, Fleming altered aspects of the production design. He examined the production sketches of the Kansas farm and said the place should appear more poverty stricken, and even vaguely threatening. The change was intended to heighten the drama of the opening sequence and provide a more startling contrast to the rich color of Oz, and to that place's happy aspects. (Of course, it was King Vidor, not Fleming, who directed the Kansas sequences.)

As test shots were made of various sets, Victor Fleming (background, left) examined the tangle of Winkies beneath the Witch's chandelier.

When Fleming cast an eye on the Yellow Brick Road that had been prepared for Richard Thorpe, with modestly oval stones and no curbs, he ordered it changed to a curbed road with rectangular stones. Early Technicolor tests of the road had printed as green instead of yellow, so an appropriate yellow paint was mixed by MGM scenic artist Randall Duell. (Duell was a Hollywood art director by 1944 and made important contributions to *The Postman Always Rings Twice, The Asphalt Jungle, Singin' in the Rain, Blackboard Jungle, Silk Stockings, Party Girl,* and many other prestigious pictures. Duell later designed theme parks and had his first great success with Six Flags Over Texas, which opened in 1961.)

Fleming dramatically accelerated the pace of the shoot during November–December 1938. (Cast and crew were given only two days off for Christmas—and Christmas that year fell on a Sunday, a day the company wouldn't have been working anyway!) The Munchkinland shoot promised to be unusually challenging because of sets, props, costumes, special effects, lengthy interludes of song, and a lot of actors that weren't especially familiar with film work.

As Fleming moved from set to set, he realized that Richard Thorpe had imposed many of his own ideas onto the interior design of the Witch's castle. Some big ones, like the Witch's chandelier and other oversized props, didn't appeal to Fleming at all and were scrapped. He fiddled with various smaller elements, too, including the Witch's crystal globe, which was increased in size.

Director Victor Fleming takes a moment on the Munchkinland set (probably during December 1938) to counsel Munchkin player Jack Glicken. The two actors to the right are Charley Becker (as the mayor) and "Little Billy" Rhodes (as the barrister).

(The crystal ball used by Prof. Marvel during the King Vidor shoot was a handsome prop that had been used in an earlier MGM film starring Boris Karloff, *The Mask of Fu Manchu* [1932].)

November 19, 1938, brought Garland, Bolger, and Haley together for the "We're Off to See the Wizard" number. As the camera rolled, Jack Haley lip-synched to the audio track, which included the voice of Buddy Ebsen. Fleming and choreographer Bobby Connolly staged this and the other Technicolor musical numbers by asking the players to match their singing and other movement to the recorded tracks that had been laid down weeks and months before. (As noted elsewhere in this book, Buddy Ebsen's voice is heard on nearly all of the "We're Off to See the Wizard" sequences.)

On November 25, as Fleming was completing Dorothy's first encounter with the Cowardly Lion, Judy Garland was awarded her first dressing room, a yellow trailer decorated inside with Degas reproductions. In the blatantly hierarchical setup of studio life, a private dressing room was enormously symbolic. The yellow trailer was tangible evidence of Garland's ascension from "featured player" to "star." That the teenage Judy was given the dressing room long before the public would see *The Wizard of Oz* was a clear affirmation of Louis Mayer's faith in her earning potential. Now she was one of the anointed.

The "honey bee" sequence from the March 15, 1939, script was shot but ultimately discarded. Here, the Tin Woodman laments having accidentally killed one of the little insects.

This was an occasionally happy time for Judy. Not just a star, she also was a young actress having a ball with Bert Lahr, whose performance caused her to break up with laughter. Fleming treated Judy Garland gently, not simply because he realized she'd respond best to that approach, but because he genuinely liked her. Fleming called her Judalein, an endearment that, years later, was given to the son of Judy's sister, Jimmie.

Because of her age, and because Fleming was one of the few people in her life that wasn't pressuring her, Judy developed a teenager's romantic attachment to Fleming. At the end of the shoot, Fleming gave her a motorbike. She reciprocated by giving him a cocker spaniel. Fleming's daughters loved the dog and named it Judy.

Except for a break on December 1 to shoot Dorothy's water-toss and the melting of the Witch, November 28 through December 3 were devoted to the poppy field. As an "exterior" shot indoors, on Stage 29, the carpet of flowers was augmented with matte paintings and false perspective. But if the sequence was going to be convincing, the "real" part of the set had to be of considerable size. One way to achieve that was to bring in *forty thousand* artificial flowers, which were set in place by twenty men over the course of a week. In order to achieve low shots that would accentuate the field's vast size, effects manager A. Arnold "Buddy" Gillespie designed and built a unique underslung dolly that positioned the camera mere inches above the stage floor.

Dorothy and her friends are rescued from the poppies by, of course, Glinda, who sends snow. (Sticklers complain that Glinda's intervention is a *deus ex machina*; and, further, that Glinda could intervene at many other critical moments but doesn't. A similar objection to contrivance is lodged against the bucket of water that destroys the Wicked Witch.) Even today, special-effects technicians have their hands full with fake snow. Over the years, the fluffy stuff had been impersonated (to greater and lesser success) by painted corn flakes, soap flakes, cellulose, instant potato flakes, foamite (fire extinguisher material), paper, starch, and other materials. For the snowfall that covers the poppy field, Gillespie okayed chrysotile asbestos fibers—which looked terrific on screen but are (as is now well known) carcinogenic.

For four or five days after December 3, Fleming returned his attention to the Witch's castle. Some of these setups, particularly as the climax approaches, are complex and filled with principal cast and actors who played the Winkies. Dog-actor Terry was underfoot in close quarters during these sequences, and during a rehearsal sometime in that first week of December, a Winkie accidentally stepped on Terry's paw, sending her home until the middle of the month with a sprain. In the meantime, trainer Carl Spitz found another Cairn terrier to fill in.

The greater part of December 1938, the 9th through the 30th, was devoted to the Munchkinland sequences (although principal cast members were periodically taken away to do other things, as on December 10, when Fleming shot additional scenes inside the Witch's castle; and December 22, when Garland did the soundtrack recording of "Follow the Yellow Brick Road").

Given the challenges of set design and construction, cast members with widely varying levels of experience, the ever-present considerations mandated by Technicolor, and ambitious special effects and camera movement, nobody thought that the Munchkinland sequence was going to be a breeze. Sure enough, it proved to be very complex and laborious. Assistant director Al Shenberg was kept busy with assembling the Munchkin players for sequences involving all of them. Then he had to shift gears to deliver featured Munchkin players, such as the mayor and coroner, to their designated places.

Harold Rosson shot on Technicolor's latest film stock, which had been in use for less than a year and was considerably faster than the previous standard. He (and the omnipresent Technicolor Corporation advisers) worked out color schemes with Fleming, who was pleased to have Rosson aboard—even though Rosson's brother, Arthur, had been the first husband of Fleming's wife. (If everyone in Hollywood had refused to work with people who had had sexual and/or romantic relationships with people in their orbits, nobody would ever have worked with anybody.) Rosson worked unusually long hours on *Oz*, 7:00 a.m. to midnight, because once cast and crew went home, he had to set lights for the first of the following day's shots and calculate what he'd need for subsequent setups.

The Technicolor cameras were huge (*Oz* required that MGM rent nine of them) and not easy to come by. Technicolor Corp. had fewer cameras than were needed to satisfy industry demand, so the units had to be reserved far in advance. Shooting of *The Wizard of Oz* frequently took place at night, when the cameras were available.

Enormous amounts of light had to flood the Munchkinland stage in order to take full advantage of what Technicolor offered. More than 100 thirty-six-inch arc lamps, and the time and expertise needed to rig them, added to the budget. The lamps were powered by two generators located in a corner of the Munchkinland stage; the light they produced was enough to illuminate five hundred average-size houses. Because the lights were brutally hot, the set was periodically visited by a city fire inspector. The visits ate up valuable time. Further, the positions of the large and unwieldy lamps had to be altered with each significant alteration to point of view. That took time, too, so Fleming was able to manage only a handful of Munchkinland setups each day.

Active stages were physically opened every one to two hours for cool air and ventilation. Filming was naturally suspended during such interludes, as it was suspended every thirty minutes, when the carbon elements of the arc lights had to be changed. The lamps had to be literally ignited, so fresh carbon was a must.

Fleming got through the Munchkinland rehearsals as efficiently as he could, mindful that everybody was sweltering. (Nothing at all would have been gained by shutting down the arcs during rehearsals, because once turned off, the lamps needed considerable time to get going again.)

Lighting costs for *Gone With the Wind* (supervised by cinematographers Ernest Haller and the uncredited Lee Garmes) came in at more than $130,000, a sobering sum that *Oz*, with a lighting tab of $226,307, handily topped by nearly $100,000.

If *The Wizard of Oz* had been shot in black and white, lighting costs would have been about $140,000 less. In 1938, black-and-white film stock used "cold" incandescent lights and required hot arc lamps only for crisp delineation of shadows. Technicolor stock had to be used with hot arcs all the time. (By 1950, color stock across the industry no longer required arc lamps, and cinematographers were free to use incandescents.)

At the wrap of each satisfactory scene, a crewmember holding a 6′ × 9′ color-correction card called a "Lilly" stepped into frame. The Lilly told the processing lab that the cinematographer had lit correctly, front and sides, for optimum color values. Adjustments could be made by color timers during processing, but because of time, expense, and the possibility of human error, everybody worked to ensure that the only color adjustments needed in the lab would be minor.

The Majesty and Melodrama of Technicolor

Because relatively few American households had color television before the late 1960s, millions of *Oz* fans were astonished the first time they saw the movie in color. They were swept away by Herbert and Natalie Kalmus's Technicolor film process, which, in 1938, utilized bulky, proprietary cameras running three separate film magazines on top: one for red, one for green, and one for blue. (This "three-strip" process was an improvement on Technicolor's earlier, two-strip technology, which mainly gave shades of red and green; see the 1933 Warner Bros. horror classic *Mystery of the Wax Museum*.)

The earliest Technicolor process printed two negative records onto two positive films; after processing, everything was cemented back to back to make a final print. In the late 1920s, the Kalmuses altered and improved their technology, so that two-strip prints were finalized by transferring dye images from a matrix film, with an image in relief, onto stock coated with absorbent gel. The improved process was called imbibition printing and became the basis of the later three-strip setup.

During filming in three-strip, the three reels of film were exposed simultaneously. When combined in the lab during processing, the dyes yielded a deep, saturated color palette that, frankly, was *better* than the colors of real life.

The Technicolor Motion Picture Corporation had been founded in 1915 by MIT physics grad Herbert T. Kalmus; his artistically trained and technically minded wife, Natalie; and two partners. Young people who had been married only since 1902, the Kalmuses created the innovation that defined color Hollywood cinematography during the 1930s and '40s, and that put Natalie Kalmus's name in the credits of every picture shot in Technicolor, often as "Technicolor Color Director" or "Color Supervisor."

If you wanted Technicolor, you got Natalie, too. Her presence was no token acknowledgment made by studios. The Technicolor Corp. owned every

Technicolor camera. The cameras were in great demand, and studios had to reserve them months in advance. The camera rental fee was ninety dollars a week. Any necessary repairs were paid for by the studio. Cross-scheduling became problematic when a single studio was shooting more than one Technicolor film at a time.

When the camera arrived, so did a Technicolor employee who operated the camera, as well as Natalie, a color director, a color consultant, and various assistants, who were on-set to ensure that lighting, costuming, and set decoration would take optimum advantage of Technicolor and reflect well on the process.

Scheduling and specific assignments of Technicolor camera operators weren't standardized and could become baroque. The company insisted that, along with each of its cameras, a so-called first cameraman had to be brought on at $250 a week; *plus* a second cameraman (called a color technician) at $125 a week; *or* an assistant cameraman at $62.50 a week. For *Oz*, MGM paid the salaries of a Technicolor first cameraman, a second cameraman, and an assistant cameraman. This was surely no surprise to Technicolor Corporation, which knew that MGM would go whole hog on this very important project. MGM staffer Harold Rosson was lead cinematographer, with very real responsibilities, but like everyone else, he had to put up with the meddlesome Technicolor people. (Rosson didn't arrive in *Oz* as a color naïf; to the contrary, he had already shot a picture in Technicolor, without screen credit: Selznick International's *The Garden of Allah* [1936].)

In the late 1930s, the salaries of the Technicolor people were paid by the studios, and easily topped $100,000 per picture.

Every color decision was reviewed by Natalie Kalmus and her subordinates. This mandatory hiring of consultants was part of what the Kalmuses called the Technicolor Advisory Service. The arrangement not only protected the corporation's patented technology but fattened profits.

Because neither the camera operators nor Natalie were employees of any studio, bad feelings and even resentment were inevitable, partly because Natalie was an intrusive and overbearing colormaster who once had the temerity to tell top cinematographer James Wong Howe that he would no longer be allowed to shoot in Technicolor! (Mrs. Kalmus had objected to Howe's lighting of *The Adventures of Tom Sawyer* [1938].) Natalie was naturally preoccupied with technical matters and insisted that color be used not just for visual excitement, but to reflect themes, too. Her interest in the intellectual use of Technicolor, although not unreasonable, was a clear intrusion into territory commanded by directors, cinematographers, set designers, costumers, and many other professionals.

While on the set of *Gone With the Wind*, Natalie annoyed producer David O. Selznick, who wrote in a memo, "The Technicolor experts have been up to their old tricks of putting all sorts of obstacles in the way of real beauty."

While at Warner Bros. for the shoot of *The Adventures of Robin Hood* (1938), Natalie continually pestered star cinematographers Tony Gaudio and Sol Polito, as well as veteran director Michael Curtiz, declaring that, as lit, the movie would be hypercolorful and unrealistic. The exasperated Curtiz, fumbling to respond in his broken English, said, "But that is what we are wanting!"

In a turnabout that, to all at MGM, must have been both unexpected and welcome, Natalie Kalmus visited the *Oz* set very few times. During the shoot, the most-frequently-seen Technicolor employee was Natalie's assistant, color director Henri Jaffa. Except for the damnably hot arc lights that brought temperatures up to 100 degrees, the on-set use of Technicolor brought with it no special problems. Jaffa's only gripe was that his weekly salary of about $125 amounted to only a fraction of what Natalie received.

Fred Detmers was the Technicolor cameraman assigned to *The Wizard of Oz*. Some thirty-five years after the shoot, Detmers explained Technicolor film and camera technology to film historian Aljean Harmetz:

> We had to design something that would work. In 1938, there was no film that would record color. The negatives were black-and-white negatives and you filtered the light. You used a colored gelatin between the object and the film, which would cause one strip of film to record the green aspect, one the blue aspect, and one the red aspect. There were two mechanisms, two movements in the camera Technicolor designed. One mechanism had one film in it. The other had two pieces of film face to face with the emulsion sides together. Between those two apertures was a prism block, a glass prism which had a mirror between two blocks. It was a cube with a diagonal cemented interface that had a mirror in it that reflected part of the light to the aperture that had two films in it.

An intriguing sidelight of the Technicolor story is that Herbert and Natalie Kalmus had divorced in 1921 but told no one, and continued to live together. The divorce settlement guaranteed Natalie screen credit on every Technicolor movie. She, Herbert, and the corporation prospered for nearly the next thirty years, but in 1948, when Natalie discovered that her ex was about to remarry, she went to court to retain what she felt was her rightful share of Technicolor. In the settlement, Natalie retained her company stock and was awarded a yearly income of about $20,000, a healthy sum at the time.

Natalie wanted more money, however, and launched one unsuccessful legal assault after another. By the mid-1950s, she was exasperating judges just as she had once tried the patience of directors and cinematographers. She finally gave up on the courts. Natalie still had shares in Technicolor Corp., but was prevented from taking part in the company's operations. She turned her attention to the design of wallpaper, furniture, and even a line of "Natalie Kalmus Television" sets.

Herbert T. Kalmus died in 1963, at eighty-one. Natalie Kalmus followed in 1965, at eighty-six.

Because of the salaries of added personnel, lighting costs, and other expenses incurred by studios that used Technicolor, the technology was restricted almost exclusively to big-budget projects. Beginning in the late 1940s, though, filmmakers had some alternatives. Eastman Kodak's Eastmancolor (and that system's follow-on, DeLuxe color) produced startlingly vivid hues at less cost. Anscocolor (derived from Germany's Agfacolor) was mildly popular; so was an unsophisticated but inexpensive process called Cinecolor, (which began in the early 1930s, when its backers bought out Howard Hughes's Multicolor). The '40s also brought "monopak" cameras, which, conveniently, used just a single strip of color film rather than Technicolor's three. (Technicolor came up with its own monopak unit, but the processed film was grainy.)

Technicolor's patents expired in 1950, and although a color process called Technicolor continued to exist, it was less visually impressive than before, and the name gradually came to mean a processing system rather than a unique film stock. The first American movie shot in three-strip Technicolor was Pioneer Pictures/RKO's *Becky Sharp* (1935). The last was *Foxfire* (1955), a modern-day western produced by Universal-International.

Ironically, the "look" of vintage three-strip Technicolor now can be duplicated digitally, as was done with selected segments of Martin Scorsese's 2004 biography of Howard Hughes, *The Aviator*.

Although digital moviemaking threatens to make 35mm film obsolete, Technicolor, now owned by a French conglomerate, carries on, occupying itself with digital manipulation.

Crafting Illusions On-Set

The forced perspective of the Munchkinland set demanded that Fleming and Rosson line up their shots carefully and maintain a consistent point of view during master shots. Without that consistency, the forced perspective could have been given away.

The entrance and exit of the Wicked Witch of the West involved precise timing of smoke and mechanical effects (more on this later), and Glinda's comings and goings would be composited in the optical printer.

When the cameras rolled, the Munchkin players spoke and sang in their everyday voices. Contrary to what had become usual during the shoots of musicals, they did not "mouth" the words to a pre-recorded audio track. Instead, Munchkin dialogue and vocalizing were specially recorded after the shoot, with professional singers and other voice artists carefully synching their voices to the film images. The reversal was called for because to expect scores of moving people to synch their singing to an audio track was unrealistic and unreasonable.

One of the most pleasing Munchkinland shots, the awakening of the "Sleepyheads," required special attention. This was an elevated tracking shot, with the camera boom in motion to capture the Sleepyheads and the other Munchkin goings-on below. The little people cast as the Sleepyheads had to listen for a verbal cue so that they'd emerge from their eggs just as the camera was poised to pass.

Through all of these challenges, Fleming remained professional and pleasant with the Munchkin players; he knew that many of them were neither actors nor dancers, so although he carried on with his characteristic efficiency, he didn't expect the moon from players unable to deliver it. He knew who the strongest players were and focused on them, awarding them featured bits and dialogue. Other Munchkins may not have been great performers, but they were hardly less valuable to Fleming, who brilliantly utilized them as onlookers that gave depth and liveliness to the sequence.

Considerable credit also goes to dance director Bobby Connolly, who was assisted by assistant dance directors Arthur "Cowboy" Appel and Dona Massin, and by bit player Lois January (an experienced dancer). Like Fleming, Connolly was eager to work with the strongest of the Munchkin players, cultivating players that could be "leaders" during the dance sequences. Others had to simply follow those leaders and execute the steps.

Because Munchkinland and other *Oz* sound stages were enormous, some sequences were shot simultaneously with six or more cameras, so that whole segments wouldn't have to be restaged to accommodate the industry standard, which was one camera. Multiple cameras were naturally more expensive than one, but gave better coverage (always appreciated by film editors) and decreased shooting time.

Judy Garland treated the Munchkin players as her sweet nature would have encouraged her to treat anybody of "lower" status around the studio. She regarded them as professionals and freely chatted between setups. During the shoot, she never made an issue of her star status, but it was inevitable that it was Judy who granted audiences to the Munchkins, and not the way around.

"She's on fire!"

Margaret Hamilton had worked with Victor Fleming before, on a Janet Gaynor–Henry Fonda romance called *The Farmer Takes a Wife* (Fox, 1935). Despite that modest familiarity with her director, Hamilton was apprehensive about a fire stunt during the climax in the Witch's castle, when she had to lower her broomstick to a torch and then touch the flames to Ray Bolger's arm. ("Want to play ball, Scarecrow?") Victor Fleming instructed Hamilton to look as if she enjoyed her sadistic mischief, but the stunt required five or six takes, which only increased Hamilton's apprehension. But it was another stunt involving fire that made December 23, 1938, Hamilton's most memorable day on the *Oz* set. In order to squeeze maximum drama from the Witch, the script suggested that her arrivals and exits be accompanied by smoke and flame—two visually exciting elements. During the Witch's unexpected arrival in Munchkinland, the effect was achieved by positioning Hamilton's double, Betty Danko, beneath the stage floor, where she stood on a platform that was catapulted to floor level by a hydraulic ram. It was important that Danko's upward movement be choreographed with the smoke and fire very carefully. If one or the other were triggered too soon or too late, or out of sequence, the illusion would be ruined. Before any of that could be accomplished, dance director Bobby Connolly, who had been running the Munchkin players through their paces, accidentally stepped through the thin, well-disguised yellow-painted aluminum that would be pulled aside the instant the catapult was engaged. Connolly fell into the hole and directly onto Betty Danko's shoulders. Danko was able to complete the stunt, but temporarily lost full movement of her arms and had to make visits to a chiropractor.

In order to execute the Witch's dramatic exit, the whole process had to be repeated, only in reverse. Danko tested the downward movement of the hydraulic elevator. The test was done slowly, and Danko's only complaint was that the opening in the floor was narrow, and one's shoulders might easily be caught on the way down. Because an abrupt cutaway from Margaret Hamilton (in close-up) to Danko (in long shot) would diminish the effect and probably give the whole game away, Hamilton had to do the stunt herself.

The action was choreographed so that Hamilton had to take steps backward and stop precisely on the bit of aluminum flooring above the elevator. The timing was tricky, and Hamilton's floor-length costume had the potential to cause a stumble. As an aid to her placement, Hamilton was instructed to key her sight on an object attached to the camera. When the object was directly in front of her, she would know she had reached the predetermined spot.

Victor Fleming was pleased because the first take went perfectly: the smoke and fire came up on cue, and the platform smoothly and rapidly lowered Hamilton below the stage (where she was steadied by two grips). But Fleming, like many directors in comparable circumstances, asked for "insurance" takes. After a break for lunch, Hamilton repositioned herself on the platform—and then things began to go wrong. During take two, the smoke appeared too soon. During the next, the smoke and flames appeared too late, and take number four was ruined because no flame came up to accompany the smoke. Fleming grew impatient, shouting that he wanted the shot done—now.

Hamilton and the technicians made ready for take five. After Margaret stepped back onto the platform, the rigged smoke and flames came up too soon; heat licked against her face and hand.

When Hamilton reached the subfloor, she was unaware of having been burned. She was pleased with what she thought had been a successful take, but the grips who awaited her down below were aghast. Hamilton, who still wasn't aware that she'd been burned, wondered why the men were fussing over her.

Assistant makeup artist Jack H. Young was one of those who came to Hamilton's aid. He, the grips, and others put out the fire on the hat and broom, and on Hamilton's skirt. Then they hustled the actress to a first-aid area at the back of the stage. There, it became obvious that Hamilton's face and right hand had been seriously burned. The flesh was burned away from the right wrist to the fingertips, and burns covered Hamilton's nose, chin, and right side of her face. Worse, her green makeup had a toxic copper oxide base and impregnated

Hamilton's skin via the burned areas. Margaret was beginning to feel pain now and really suffered moments later, when the makeup—which had to come off—was removed by makeup man Jack Young with alcohol. Young had to *rub* the swap across the burned flesh. Now the pain was breathtaking.

Hamilton was a single mother. She needed her salary, and her first fear was that she'd be replaced. The studio—partly from concern and partly from fear of a lawsuit—later assured her that her role was safe. Hamilton wouldn't have sued anyway. She had been in the business long enough to know that "troublemakers" were blackballed. If she wanted her career to continue, she'd have to bear the pain and wait to heal.

At the hospital, Margaret was covered with salve and bandaged. She was away from the *Oz* set for six weeks (when someone from the studio called before then to inquire when she might return to work, Hamilton's physician gave the caller holy hell). When Margaret returned, her face had healed well enough to accept makeup, but nerves in her hand remained exposed. For the rest of the shoot, she wore green gloves. Early on February 10, 1939, her first day back on the set, Victor Fleming expressed curiosity about her hand—so he roughly grabbed it for a closer inspection. The pain was unbearable, and Hamilton nearly lost consciousness. Fleming apologized and then assured Hamilton that that long-ago first take was "great." In other words, everything that had happened after that first take was unnecessary.

The next day, February 11, was scheduled for the close-up that opens the skywriting sequence, Hamilton looked at the Witch's broomstick, which had been fitted with a concealed pipe designed to bellow black smoke. The broom was topped with a saddle-like seat hidden beneath the folds of the Witch's cloak. Once Hamilton sat herself in it, the entire rig would be raised by four wires ten to fifteen feet above the stage floor. Hamilton took a second look. Then she refused to get onto the broomstick.

In Hamilton's dressing room, production manager Keith Weeks insisted that the gag was safe and promised that if Hamilton didn't get right on that saddle, he'd tattle to Louis Mayer. Hamilton, who noted that her costume was now fireproof, refused to budge. Weeks summoned Fleming and effects director Buddy Gillespie. Neither could persuade Hamilton. They could fire her right then, she said, but she wasn't getting anywhere near smoke or flames again.

In the end, Margaret agreed to sit on the broom, at floor level, for close-ups only, *after* the smoke pipe had been detached and taken away. When Fleming decided he wanted more coverage (and the smoke), Hamilton's stand-in, Betty Danko, agreed to ride the smoking pipe—even after the device was moved from the rear of the broomstick to a dangerous spot beneath the saddle. (The change was necessary because Fleming wanted the Witch's cloak to flap in the wind.) Hamilton warned Danko not to do it, but Betty, who earned only eleven dollars a day as Hamilton's stand-in, was persuaded by the thirty-five dollars the stunt would pay.

Danko was lifted above the stage floor. She controlled the smoke with a hidden hand button. Gillespie shot two perfect takes before Fleming wandered over to ask for a third. Fleming called action—and Danko was promptly blown sideways off the saddle when the smoke pipe exploded. She saved herself from falling by instinctively looping one leg around the rig, but the explosion left the leg with a wound that was two inches deep. The Wicked Witch was going to spend another eleven days in the hospital.

Although Gillespie had supervised two good-looking takes, Fleming remained unsatisfied. The stunt was completed to Fleming's satisfaction—without explosives—by stunt double Eileen Goodwin.

As is readily apparent, the long shots of the witch flying in the sky high above Emerald City utilized a miniature witch and broom. As filmed, the broom's smoke spells out SURRENDER DOROTHY OR DIE! LeRoy and others felt that was too descriptive, so the sequence was cut to show just the SURRENDER DOROTHY that has become folklore. (The effects shot of the Witch's skywriting was done in May 1939, three months after Victor Fleming's departure and four months after Garland and others in the cast had filmed their reaction shots.)

The prop hourglass thrown to the floor by the Witch as a prelude to the story's climactic chase had been drilled with holes by the mechanical-effects staff and attached to a sloping wire. This ensured that Margaret Hamilton's toss would be controlled and that the hourglass would strike the floor exactly where it should.

The climactic melting of the Wicked Witch is one of the movie's best-known and most startling scenes. (It's cleverly presaged in the opening Kansas sequence, when Miss Gulch travels with an umbrella.) The melting gag was achieved after fastening Hamilton's costume to the stage floor surrounding a descending hydraulic platform. As dry ice inside the Witch's cloak gave off dramatic, smoke-like vapor, Hamilton was slowly lowered beneath the level of the floor. By the time the Witch was completely out of sight, only her smoking hat and cloak remained. The moment's real power, though, comes from Hamilton, who brought fury, regret, and even a little pathos to the Witch's death.

Hamilton and other principals later recalled Victor Fleming as a generally pleasant, very competent director, who came to the set very well prepared and expected cast and crew to do likewise. Wasted time and anything else that seemed unprofessional raised Fleming's ire. He insisted on efficiency, but he also took the time to work with the actors—and gave on-the-spot praise when something was done especially well.

Challenges in Emerald City

By the beginning of 1939, Stage 26 had been dressed as the Haunted Forest, with artificial trees and undergrowth, forced perspective, and a painted cyclorama suggesting a changing sky. The Haunted Forest has some cute touches, such as the hooting owls and the "I'd Turn Back If I Were You" sign. "Lions and Tigers and Bears" is a wonderful lead-in to the climax of the sequence: the winged monkeys' attack on Dorothy and her friends, and Dorothy's aerial abduction. (Bobbie Koshay doubled Judy Garland when Dorothy is grabbed and carried aloft.) Fleming had begun tests of the monkeys' takeoffs, flight, and touchdowns during the previous October and December. The elaborate sequence was shot during the first three weeks of January.

Some problems must have been anticipated. Wires that suddenly broke sent monkeys crashing to the stage floor, and some of the players struggled to remain in their wire-rig harnesses. One problem took the production by surprise: the monkeys' demand for an altered pay structure. As originally set up, the players that would fly were to be paid by the day. But when retake after retake suggested that the shoot of the sequence might go on for a while, the winged monkeys asked for—and got—pay based on the numbers of takeoffs and landings, rather than on a flat daily fee.

One group of monkeys, the miniature ones seen in the expansive long shot of Dorothy and Toto far away in the sky above the Haunted Forest, made no salary demands. The grips that manipulated wires and pulleys to animate the miniatures (as well as the full-size monkeys) were sanguine because their union contracts guaranteed extra pay for extra work.

Fleming and the troupe began shooting the Emerald City sequences on January 14, 1939, with 300 to 350 costumed extras. MGM publicity claimed that the Emerald City set covered twenty-eight hundred square feet. That's not an unreasonable size, and it's easy to believe, especially given how many extras were able to assemble there.

Directing an enormous number of people demands a gift for crowd control and clear communication between director and assistant director. A lazy director might have been satisfied to function as a traffic cop, doing little camera movement and simply relying on the great masses of people to give the sequence life. Fleming, of course, wasn't built that way, so the Emerald City crowd sequence not only has the inherent interest created by all those people and costumes, but smart, graceful use of crane shots and dollys. Fleming's direction is active and controlled.

The beautician sequences were straightforward medium shots that were made complicated by the need for cast members to lip-synch to the prerecorded music track. Much of the footage involving the principals and the beauticians is a subtle dance, carefully choreographed to fill confined spaces. That very lack of room had to be accounted for by Fleming and choreographer Bobby Connolly.

The restuffing of the Scarecrow was carefully rehearsed to ensure the desired energy and rhythm; likewise, the buff-up of the Tin Woodman, a mechanical effect involving a large, moving prop that had to function smoothly *and* get a laugh.

The latter portion of January, and much of February, was devoted to scenes inside the Wizard's palace. These weren't overly complicated for the actors, at least physically: there were lines to deliver, some walking, and a great deal of standing when Dorothy and her friends address the Wizard. Frank Morgan wanted to play the Wizard expansively, with comically broad line readings and reactions, as if he were on stage. Fleming wanted Morgan and the Wizard to be lively without being overbearing. The director had to ask Morgan to tone down his performance. Fleming had come to depend on Bert Lahr for larger-than-life humor; Morgan wasn't needed to fill that function.

Once ground rules had been established by Fleming, Frank Morgan's scenes after his unmasking as a humbug were simple enough. But the palace sequence hinged nearly as critically on special effects as on the cast. Matte paintings, miniatures, and pyrotechnics were involved; likewise sound effects. (Remember the Wizard's terrifying voice?) None of that had any bearing on the cast *except that they had to react to an environment that wasn't there.* This accounted for a great deal of the acting challenge on the palace set.

When Dorothy and her friends enter the palace and nervously tread on the long, long corridor inside, precious little other than the floor was there. The towering arched walls were matte paintings that were mated with the live-action footage long after Garland and the others had done their scenes. There was no bellow from the Wizard's head (although Fleming or someone else probably threw Garland and the others the Wizard's dialogue, as cues). There was no Wizard's head. No flame, no smoke. When Dorothy, the Scarecrow, the Tin Woodman, and the Cowardly Lion stepped forward for their brief, terrifying audiences with the phantasmagorical Wizard, they weren't gazing upon the awful face that's visible to us. Judy and the others were looking past the camera, past Victor Fleming, cinematographer Harold Rosson and Rosson's cameraman, past the script girl and the sound recordists and various grips and other crew, past snaking cables and arc lamps, looking at—nothing, other than an empty section of the sound stage.

The trickery of this sequence, and of so many others, isn't just what we see on the screen. The real trickery often is whatever the actors must do in order to convince themselves—and thus convince us—that their environment is total, overpowering, and real.

In the second week of February 1939, Judy Garland fell ill. She was absent from the set for a few days, so Fleming shot around her. That was no calamity, but as February wore on, MGM's front office became concerned about the length of the shoot, as if the executives had forgotten that the search for a director had had all the cool competence of a back-alley craps game. Norman Taurog had helped with conceptual matters, George Cukor had been an enormously helpful consulting director, and Richard Thorpe helped LeRoy and other executives realize what they didn't want. The job had finally been given to Victor Fleming, who conducted himself with confident professionalism. Largely because of the musical chairs, proposed release dates had come and gone; one press release, in fact, had promised a March 1939 release!

If March strikes you as a "nothing" time to release a major film, you're right—from a present-day perspective. In 1939, however, movies in all genres and at all levels of ambition and execution rotated into and out of theaters endlessly. The "summer movie" phenomenon was some thirty-five years in the future (*Jaws* is usually fingered as the culprit that ushered in that go-for-broke marketing philosophy). Even *Gone With the Wind* wasn't an "event movie" quite as we understand that term today. Although *GWTW* had separate New York and Los Angeles premieres in late December 1939, the picture didn't open wide until January 17, 1940—well after the holiday break, and when people had been back at work and school for two weeks. Some movies, such as MGM's *A Christmas Carol* (December 16, 1938), practically demanded timed releases. Then again, a bit of holiday fluff that arrived later, Warner Bros.' *Christmas in Connecticut*, was released in August 1945. That sort of disregard for release dates confirms Hollywood's understanding of the world in the 1930s and '40s: people went to the movies all the time, two and three times a week, year round. A picture could be released—and find an audience—at any time. The eventual August 1939 opening of *The Wizard of Oz*—that is, a summertime release—was more serendipity than the result of calculated planning by studio accountants and marketing staff.

Still, when MGM promised a March 1939 release of *The Wizard of Oz*, the studio shot, and wasted, part of its publicity ammunition. The early tingle of audience anticipation that had been built up for March had been squandered. The publicity department would have to reignite public interest.

Revised Shooting Script, March 15, 1939

When Victor Fleming went to work on *Oz*, he began with those portions of the script that were ready to be shot. Because the screenplay still inspired debate among LeRoy and other executives, Langley and the other writers continued their work. Four months after Fleming had begun the shoot, a script dated March 15, 1939, and credited to "Noel Langley, Florence Ryerson and Edgar Allan Woolf," was circulated. This script was the basis for the remainder of a Fleming-Rosson shooting script, as well as for a subsequent cutting continuity, which indicated fades and edit points, as well as how to handle the dialogue, including certain words or phrases that should be heard from off-screen (o.s.).

The March 1939 draft is considerably closer to the film we know, but it does retain some elements that were later eliminated, including Hickory's enthusiastic description of his latest invention (Hickory was played by Jack Haley). Dorothy is in the barnyard, struggling to tell her aunt and the farm-hands about her trouble with Miss Gulch. After Hunk (Ray Bolger) reminds Dorothy that "Your head ain't made of straw, you know," Dorothy enters the barn, where Hickory has been tinkering with a machine. Oil suddenly spurts onto Hickory's face.

HICKORY

Oh! Oh, it feels like my joints are rusted.

Listen, Dorothy, don't let Hunk kid you about Miss Gulch.

She's just a poor sour-faced old maid that—she ain't got
no heart left. You know, you should have a little more heart
yourself, and have pity on her.

DOROTHY
Well, gee, I try and have a heart.

HICKORY
Now look, here's something that really has a heart.
This is the best invention I ever invented.

DOROTHY
This?

HICKORY
Sure. It's to break up winds, so we don't have no more dust
storms. Can you imagine what it'll mean to this section of
the country? I'll show you. It works perfectly now.
Here's the principle. You see that fan—that sends up air
currents into the sky.
[Something goes wrong with the machine.]
These air currents—oh, stop it!

The sequence resumes with Zeke (Bert Lahr) prodding pigs into the pen.

Because the Kansas sequences were shot last, it's unlikely that King Vidor ever filmed the exchange quoted above. The clunky, stilted dialogue suggests an effort to link Hickory's invention to the real-life Dust Bowl calamity, and to force a connection between Hickory and the Tin Woodman, and the wind machine and the cyclone. All of it is pointless and superfluous.

One intriguing note is that this March 15 script includes stage directions for Dorothy as she moves around the barnyard, singing "Over the Rainbow" (walking slowly, leaning against the haystack, and so forth). Vidor said years later that he had wanted to avoid a static number of the sort that slowed so many film musicals. Because he began work on the *Oz* set on February 19, it's likely that these stage directions were inspired by his wishes.

A bit later in the March 15 script, Dorothy returns home after consulting with Prof. Marvel. The winds are picking up, and the farmhands are rounding up animals. Uncle Henry calls for Hunk to set the horses free, but Hunk is preoccupied with his invention. When Uncle Henry tells him to knock it off, Hunk mutters that Henry will be sorry.

In this draft, some of the Wicked Witch's dialogue is even more threatening than what ended up in the final cut. When the Witch bursts into Munchkinland, she confronts Dorothy and says, "I'm here for vengeance!" As we'll see, that menacing tone returns later in the story.

The March 15 Langley script continues: Dorothy and the Scarecrow have a run-in with the apple trees, meet the Tin Woodman, and are cowed by an abrupt visit from the Wicked Witch. She hurls a fireball at the Scarecrow and threatens to turn the Tin Woodman into a beehive. When she departs, the Tin Woodman's courage begins to return. He scoffs at the Witch's threat, and then notices that a bee has landed on Dorothy's arm. He plucks it off. When Dorothy asks him if *he's* been stung, he begins to cry: a bee has bent its stinger against his tin and died. The Tin Woodman laments, "I killed that poor little honey bee! It's only a man without a heart that could do a thing like that. Poor little bee."

Dorothy dries the Tin Woodman's tears and assures him that it's "just an old drone bee, and it would have died anyway."

This is a peculiar sequence, preoccupied with death and a hint of mercy killing. The interlude is obviously intended to suggest that the Tin Woodman does indeed have a heart, but we don't need to be beaten over the head to get the idea. And Langley's cleverness with dialogue seems to have deserted him here.

At the Emerald City, the friends are spruced up by tinsmiths, beauticians, and other workers. After the Witch's ominous skywriting, the friends are told that they can't see the Wizard after all. One guard emphasizes the point and then excuses himself: "Pardon me. We've gotta change the guards." With that, the guard steps into what Langley calls a "revolving sentry house." Once inside, the guard turns his false mustache upside down, and then emerges—supposedly a whole new person. This absurdly funny bit of business was filmed but ultimately cut. That's a loss but not a great one. The cut is significant because it leads to a continuity gaffe: the guard's mustache is initially right-side up and then it's upside-down. But as filmed, it wasn't a gaffe at all. The oversight happened during editing, when editor Blanche Sewell had to allow the slip because the "second guard" has pertinent dialogue.

In the Haunted Forest on their way to the Witch's castle, the Lion carries an enormous butterfly net and an oversize spray gun that he calls "my Witch Remover."

The Scarecrow grabs the spray gun and tosses it aside. Then it vanishes, and a second later, the butterfly net is invisibly pulled from the Lion's paws. The Lion confesses, "I do believe in spooks!" The Witch observes the scene in her crystal and instructs Nikko, the leader of the winged monkeys, to fetch Dorothy and Toto. She adds that she's dispatched "a little insect" to soften up Dorothy and her friends.

You don't have to be unusually astute to wonder about the insect that we hear no more about. The words refer, of course to the Jitterbug, a creature designed to occupy Dorothy and the others until the winged monkeys arrive.

In the Haunted Forest, Dorothy and the others are spooked by an odd sound and then dance away from the "rascal" bug; even the trees are compelled to twist and dance. Dorothy and her friends sing about the bug's "terrible horrible buzz." Thus preoccupied, they can't react in time when the winged monkeys arrive. (For more about "The Jitterbug," see chapter 6.)

Still more situations and dialogue prepared for the Wicked Witch were modified or deleted. In the script's March 15 draft, when the Witch gets Dorothy inside the castle and reaches for the ruby slippers, her hand merely "trembles" as she reaches for them. In the finished film, of course, she's given a righteous electrical shock, courtesy of some sterling visual and audio effects.

The Witch reacts with "Those slippers will never come off, as long as you're alive!"

DOROTHY
What are you going to do?

WITCH
What do you think I'm going to do?

The horrid, matter-of-fact nature of the Witch's response gives a clear indication of why the line was cut.

Meanwhile, Toto has alerted Dorothy's friends, and as they make their way to her, Dorothy sobs through a few of the lyrics of "Over the Rainbow." This reprise was cut from the finished film.

Other unused bits of business in the March script are minor, such as idle, pointless chitchat between the Scarecrow, Tin Woodman, and Lion after the three have fought the Winkie scouts and taken their uniforms; and some slapstick just before the Tin Woodman uses his axe to chop through the door that imprisons Dorothy. (The Lion won't stop shouting, "Open the door! Open the door!" and all three are bumping into each other. If the interlude had been preserved, it would have derailed the sequence's fine, frantic pace.)

The Witch and the Winkies trap Dorothy and her friends in the castle's main hall. The Witch rhetorically asks, "Can you imagine what I'm going to do to you?" That scary line, too, was cut.

Then the water is tossed, and the Winkies are elated that Dorothy has melted the Witch. The captain confesses his relief that the Witch will no longer be around to hit them with her broom.

If you find it difficult to imagine the hard-bitten Winkies being upset because the Witch swats their bottoms, you're not alone. The Winkie captain's remark is ridiculously mild and sucks the fright of the past five minutes right out of the room. The comment didn't survive the final revision. A reprise of "Ding! Dong! The Wicked Witch Is Dead," sung by Dorothy, her friends, and even the Winkies, was also eliminated.

In the next sequence, in the Emerald City, Dorothy, friends, and Ozites (the script calls them "Oz people") continue the tune, with some fresh, colorful lyrics about the Witch being with the goblins, "below, below, below"—that is, in Hell.

Glinda eventually arrives to reveal the special power of the ruby slippers. Dorothy taps her heels, and she's immersed in a montage of sound and images that recap her adventure and even some of her life in Kansas. She imagines the Munchkins, the Wicked Witch, and the Wizard revealed behind his curtain. She sees Glinda leading the Munchkins in a dance, the Tin Woodman's axe biting into the locked door, Hickory's wind machine. There's one of Uncle Henry's horses and some chickens, and Aunt Em offering the baked crullers. Finally, Dorothy's head returns to the pillow in her bedroom. In the movie's final cut, all but the pillow shot is gone.

This March script has Langley's variation on Ryerson and Woolf's "no place like home" ending, which had been mandated by LeRoy and other executives. Although Hickory's wind machine is indicated as part of the montage, a moment in which Hickory asks Dorothy to wait for him while he's at agricultural college is absent from the bedroom sequence.

The Writers of Oz

For handy reference, here are the screenwriters and others who contributed to various script drafts of MGM's The Wizard of Oz during 1938–39.

William H. Cannon, February 1938; unused four-page treatment (Cannon was an assistant to Mervyn LeRoy)

Herman Mankiewicz, February–March 1938; suggests Kansas B&W, Oz color

Noel Langley, March–June 1938, July–October 31, 1938

Irving Brecher, March 1938

Robert Pirosh, March 1938, in collaboration with Brecher

George Seaton, March 1938, in collaboration with Brecher

Ogden Nash, March–April 1938; unused four-page treatment

Arthur Freed, April 1938–June 1939; concept contributor who insisted that Dorothy's adventure allow the girl to help others and seek the love she longs for

Herbert Fields, late April 1938, assisting Noel Langley

Samuel Hoffenstein, May–June 1938; unused two-page outline

Florence Ryerson, June 3–July 1938; rewrites of Langley draft

Edgar Allan Woolf, June 3–July 1938; rewrites of Langley draft

E. Y. "Yip" Harburg, July–October 1938; spring 1939 (likely); fresh dialogue and script editing

Jack Mintz, August–September 1938; jokes

Richard Thorpe, October 1938; unknown revisions and shooting script

Sid Silvers, October 17–22, 1938; on-set revisions for Richard Thorpe

George Cukor, October–November 1938; revised character concepts

Victor Fleming, November 1938–February 1939; unknown revisions and shooting script

John Lee Mahin, November 1938–February 1939; script doctor working on-set with Victor Fleming

Jack Haley, 1938–39; some dialogue

Bert Lahr, 1938–39; some dialogue

King Vidor, February–March 1939; unknown revisions and shooting script (Kansas sequences only)

In Focus: Victor Fleming (1889–1949)

MGM contract director Victor Fleming was a rugged, largely self-educated "man's man" who hunted, drove hot rods, and rode motorcycles. He preferred the company of men and was seldom effusive. Fleming would not seem to have been a natural choice to direct *The Wizard of Oz* but for three things: his intense professionalism and his two young daughters, whom he doted on and loved dearly.

Fleming was born in Pasadena and was doing stunt work in movies by 1910. Like *Oz* cinematographer Harold Rosson, Fleming benefited from an early association with director Allan Dwan, and another with D. W. Griffith. The young man's taste for adventure was thwarted during World War I, when Lt. Fleming remained stateside as a cinematographer with the Signal Corps. (He finally got to Europe *after* the war, as a photographer accompanying President Wilson in 1918.)

Fleming directed his first feature, *When the Clouds Roll By*, in 1919. The picture starred Douglas Fairbanks, another determinedly male man. (The two later collaborated on a documentary, *Around the World with Douglas Fairbanks* [1931].)

After a decade with Paramount, Fleming became an MGM staff director in 1932. One of his first pictures for the studio, *Red Dust* (1932), is a salty, steamy tropical romance starring two of the studio's biggest assets, Clark Gable and Jean Harlow. Fleming became a close friend of Gable, who was cultivating an outdoorsy image to offset his on-screen romantic appeal.

Fleming worked comfortably in numerous genres. He brought a modern, masculine touch to films set in the present day and capably handled westerns, thrillers, musicals, and period pictures. Among Fleming's credits are *Captains Courageous, Treasure Island, The Great Waltz* (co-director), *The Virginian, Gone With the Wind*, and *Dr. Jekyll and Mr. Hyde* (the Spencer Tracy version). Poor material didn't faze Fleming, either: he managed to wring some verve from a dire adaptation of an even more dire play, *Abie's Irish Rose*, a huge Broadway hit that found alleged humor in Jewish and Irish stereotypes.

Besides his wife, Lucile, the people most central to the domestic side of Fleming's private life were his young niece, Yvonne, and his two young daughters, Victoria (usually called Missy) and Sally. He was particularly close to his daughters and doted on them in a manner that might have surprised Hollywood associates who knew him only as a rugged individualist. He was, frankly, lovingly preoccupied with his girls and thought of them continually as he worked on *Oz*.

Fleming had come on to that project when it was struggling to find a workable director; in one of the more remarkable and historically noteworthy feats in Hollywood history, Fleming subsequently assumed control of another troubled production, *Gone With the Wind* and directed both pictures back to back. (In fact, he edited *Oz* at night after working all day on *GWTW*.) For this feat alone, and for the quality he brought to both movies, Fleming should be celebrated as one of Hollywood's greatest filmmakers, but most film historians have regarded him only as a polished craftsman. (That dismissal began to be redressed in 2008, with the publication of Michael Sragow's thorough and perceptive biography, *Victor Fleming: An American Movie Master*.)

A Guy Named Joe (1943) is a touching romance imbued with a sense of loss, and was a big hit. Fleming's final MGM picture, *Adventure* (1945), was a commercial success and a profound critical bust that badly damaged the career of Clark Gable. Fleming was thinking about retirement even before making the film, but plenty of money convinced him to stay around the studio for one more assignment.

A few years later, free of MGM and working on the "Victor Fleming Production" of *Joan of Arc* (1948), Fleming fell deeply, obsessively in love with the film's married star, Ingrid Bergman. He'd had affairs before, but they'd been flings. This was profound. Fleming was betraying his wife and abandoning his home, and setting himself up to be racked with guilt—but Bergman mesmerized him. The film was an ambitious period epic about one of the most famed women in history. Because money was tight, the shoot was done on cramped stages at the Hal Roach studio. Bergman knew the project was crucially important to her career (not least because she, Fleming, and producer Walter Wanger had co-financed it), and so off screen she matched Fleming tryst for tryst . . . for a while. As the shoot wound down, Bergman suddenly cooled, and Fleming was devastated. He began to reconcile with his wife, but died of a heart attack in January 1949, less than two months after the release of *Joan of Arc*. Fleming was fifty-nine.

Buzz

Although Bobby Connolly had been on board as the picture's choreographer since August 1938, Mervyn LeRoy had had another idea as early as May, when he wanted famed choreographer Busby "Buzz" Berkeley to direct the film's musical sequences. Berkeley was a onetime stage actor who had turned himself into a sought-after Broadway musical-dance director in the 1920s. He came to Hollywood in 1930 and made indelible impressions at Warner Bros. with stupendously choreographed numbers involving dozens, frequently scores, of dancers moving in astonishing lockstep and counterpoint on eye-poppingly elaborate sets. (The "narrative" portion of an early Berkeley triumph, *Gold Diggers of 1933*, had been directed by LeRoy, and Buzz's other Warner projects from before 1935 were helmed by Ray Enright, Lloyd Bacon, and other capable journeymen. Beginning with *Gold Diggers of 1935*, though, Berkeley was made responsible for his pictures in their entireties.)

Although Berkeley came from the theater, he grasped film's visual principles and then expanded them, employing a restive, gliding camera and often shooting down on his dancers as their moving bodies created kaleidoscopic geometric patterns or the illusion of flower blossoms. (This sort of invention was, indeed, pure cinema because, as presented in the films' narratives, the numbers were performed for live-theater audiences, who could never have appreciated the overhead artistry!)

In Warner pictures like *42nd Street*, *Footlight Parade*, and *Dames*, Berkeley dazzled audiences with precise, excitingly photographed numbers—that stopped each film's storyline cold. This was in direct opposition to Arthur Freed's vision for *The Wizard of Oz*, of course, and could have precipitated a clash of wills. Regardless, LeRoy remained enamored of his hiring idea.

In May 1938, Berkeley was still under contract at Warner, so if LeRoy wanted him, somebody was going to have to pay for him. In the meantime, LeRoy brought choreographer Bobby Connolly, with whom LeRoy had worked at Warner, onto *Oz*. Connolly began dance rehearsals with the cast in September. Four months later, in January 1939, Berkeley declined to sign a one-year, "no raise" contract extension offered by Jack Warner (despite the recent box-office success of a straight drama directed by Berkeley, *They Made Me a Criminal*). Berkeley paid Warner Bros. $10,000 to cover what remained of his existing contract and then signed a one-picture deal with MGM.

Berkeley's association with *The Wizard of Oz* wasn't without some complications. His presence presented a possible conflict with Bobby Connolly, and the cornfield sequence, which was to be the first thing Berkeley tackled, had already been shot by Victor Fleming the previous November. Further, Berkeley's contract brought him to MGM only for a musical called *Broadway Serenade*. Nothing in his agreement with MGM connected Berkeley to *Oz*. Regardless, LeRoy brought Buzz onto the *Oz* set to choreograph and direct a lengthy dance-and-music revision/addendum featuring the Scarecrow. As devised by Berkeley, the Scarecrow laments to Dorothy that the crows aren't afraid of him. With that, he launches himself into a protracted bit of business involving the birds, who scatter from the cornstalks as the Scarecrow crashes and blunders through the field. Toto nudges a pumpkin that's rolled onto the Yellow Brick Road, and in a moment, the pumpkin sends the Scarecrow end over end and into such violent contortions that he ricochets from side to side along the split-rail fence that lines the road, finally breaking right through the wood. The wirework utilized to send the Scarecrow leaping into and out of the cornfield is childishly exaggerated. Worse, obvious reverse-motion makes a burlesque of the Scarecrow's flailing. Bolger's physical efforts are heroic, but, as shot and printed, the sequence seems designed for three-year-olds. At about four minutes, it feels more like a tedious ten. None of this business adds a thing to the narrative or characterizations, and it was wisely cut.

No record exists that Berkeley was involved in any other *Oz* musical number.

Berkeley biographer Jeffrey Spivak reports that Victor Fleming looked at the Berkeley footage and sent Buzz a note: "I've just run the Scarecrow number. It's simply great. You should have directed the whole picture."

Or maybe not.

The Berkeley sequence survives and has been included with various special-edition *Wizard of Oz* home-video releases.

Throughout January 1939, as MGM negotiated the tricky terrain created by the presence of Busby Berkeley, Victor Fleming and the cast busied themselves with the "Jitterbug" sequence; scenes with Frank Morgan in Oz, including Emerald City interiors; and the Wizard's hot-air balloon. More Emerald City sequences, including Lahr's brilliant "If I Were King of the Forest," occupied cast and crew from late January until the middle of February.

Jack Haley said that Judy was "born to brilliance"—which is the sort of compliment not often handed out by battle-scarred vaudevillians. On-set, Judy was a startlingly quick study, whose already prodigious gifts flowed from her easily and naturally. Whatever doubts she had about her appearance did not hurt her work. She had been in the business for most of her life and had no need to doubt her talent. To a cast and crew of show-business veterans, she was a revelation.

Cast members were captivated by the sweetness and enthusiasm of the young star. Margaret Hamilton recalled for *Filmfax* magazine that when Judy stepped onto the set, "the lights got brighter."

Three Dirty Hams?

Judy Garland had been a performer nearly all her life. Still, when the cameras rolled on *Oz*, she was only sixteen—a kid who would be amenable to direction. Haley, Bolger, and Lahr were different. They weren't exactly cynical, but they were grown men who'd struggled to the top on the daunting stairway of vaudeville. They were willing to take direction, but because each had honed a specific personality and performance style, they weren't going to be pushed into doing anything that didn't feel right to them. Bert Lahr told his son John, "Vic Fleming had never experienced guys like us. Some legitimate [theater] directors can't imagine anybody thinking about something else when he yells 'Shoot'—just going in and playing. [On *Oz*,] we'd kid around up to the last minute and go on. You could see [Fleming] got mad and red-faced. Some actors try and get into the mood. They'll put themselves into the character. I never did that. I'm not that—let's say—dedicated."

Of course, Bert Lahr was being a little disingenuous here. He was enormously invested in every performance he ever undertook, and if the Cowardly Lion struck Lahr at the time as just another job, he nevertheless brought his best game to the set every day. The vaudeville work ethic—which might more properly be termed a *sweat* ethic—informed Lahr, Haley, and Bolger's approaches to their roles. Before the cameras rolled on *Oz* sequences involving all three, they'd chorus "Smith's premium ham!"—a private exhortation akin to "Go get 'em!" When the guys mentioned the ham, they were in the zone.

Among the things implied by the word "professional" is a respect for other performers. For years after *Oz*, Judy Garland and others told stories about how Haley, Bolger, and Lahr intentionally stole scenes from her, literally crowding her behind them or out of the frame altogether. No one would blame the actors if they resented these tall tales, but Haley, writing years later in his journal, took the high road and responded to the charges of scene-stealing by simply telling it as it was: "How could that be? When we go off to see the Wizard we're locked arm in arm, and every shot is a long shot. [Some were medium shots, but the establishing shots were filmed, as Haley says, from a distance.] How can you push someone out of the picture with a long shot?"

In her 1967 television interview with Jack Paar, Garland garnished the story by claiming that when Fleming saw what the ex-vaudevillians were doing to his star, he shouted, "Hold it! You three dirty hams, let that little girl in there!" (A particularly inane Internet claim says that the trio of ex-vaudevillians *resented* Judy Garland.)

All of this is not to say that mischief didn't go on. Haley and Lahr were especially close, with a friendship going back to 1922 or 1923, when Lahr took the inexperienced Haley under his wing after Haley joined a summer burlesque troupe in New York City. On the *Oz* set, the two amused themselves between takes by setting up Ray Bolger, whose desire to be the center of attention encouraged him to brag. Whatever subject or event Haley and Lahr cared to discuss— difficult vaudeville engagements, street fights, sports—Bolger came back with a "personal" story about it. "If you dwell on it [in conversation]," Haley wrote, "Bolger will tell you he's done that." Haley remembered a conversation that he and Lahr steered to boxing. "Then you wait," Haley said. "And here's the line. You know this line is coming; you could lay book on it. Bolger says, 'I was a boxer once.' 'You were?' 'Yeah, I wasn't very good but I had a few fights.' And then he'd tell you an incident about one of his 'bouts.'"

Dailies revealed that Judy Garland could more than hold her own with Bolger and the others. The studio was encouraged to think more highly of her. As evidence of Judy Garland's new star status, February brought the young actress an assistant, a worldly, good-looking blonde named Betty Asher. Although the twenty-two-year-old Asher reported to MGM publicity chief Howard Strickling, and was carried on the books as a publicist, her duties around the lot were more personal; Garland biographer Gerald Clarke describes her as "a hand-holder and a fixer, someone who did whatever it took to keep her client happy and productive." As with other "clients," Asher insinuated herself into Judy's good graces, feigning girlish friendship while reporting Judy's every move to Strickling. As the years passed, Judy became emotionally dependent on Asher, unaware that hurtful lies fed to her by Asher helped destroy her 1943 romance with married actor Tyrone Power. (Asher played another, peripheral part in Judy's life when she interceded with Lana Turner to save that star's marriage to Artie Shaw, the musician who had once captured Judy's fancy.)

The Tin Woodman Was a Quarterback

As Dorothy's friends scale the cliffs surrounding the Witch's castle, the Tin Woodman clutches the Lion's tail and pulls on it with his full weight. Costume designer Adrian added an "anchor" made of shoe leather that reinforced the lion's appendage and helped Jack Haley hang on. (Viewers can easily glimpse the leather piece's boxy shape.

In other sequences, the tail was manipulated from above with fishing line.) During medium shots of the climbing sequence, Haley was doubled by 185-pound USC quarterback Ambrose Schindler. Schindler remembered that, in a discarded take, "I pulled the tail right off" and "fell like a hunk of lumber." Before the stunt was attempted again, Schindler was fitted for a much lighter Woodman costume that would put less stress on the "stunt tail."

Some sources claim Schindler also played a Winkie, but neither Schindler nor his son mentioned that in a 2011 interview.

Ambrose Schindler led the 1939 USC team to the 1940 Rose Bowl, where he scored the first touchdown himself—the first score made against opponent Tennessee in sixteen games— and passed for a second. The Trojans won the game, 14–0. Because the NFL paid very low wages in 1940, Schindler decided to become a high school coach, but before that, he made uncredited appearances in a pair of comedies released by 20th Century-Fox in 1940, *Sailor's Lady* and *Yesterday's Heroes*.

Later in life, Schindler drove a Jaguar with a license plate reading X USC QB.

Because *The Wizard of Oz* was an expensive novelty musical built around a gifted and very young studio player, people on the MGM lot were naturally curious about what was going on in all those sound stages. Greta Garbo, Walter Pidgeon, Norma Shearer, Spencer Tracy, Eleanor Powell, Victor McLaglen, and Myrna Loy were among the MGM contract stars that visited the set. Our Gang's Alfalfa (Carl Switzer) showed up one day (MGM assumed production of the popular short-subject series from Hal Roach in the late spring of 1938). Wallace Beery brought his daughter with him, and Joan Crawford showed up with her niece. (Crawford did not adopt Christina, the first of her five adopted children, until 1940.) Mickey Rooney, Judy's always-dependable friend, dropped by the set to give encouragement.

When little Warner LeRoy visited the set, he ran headlong into a painted backdrop on the Yellow Brick Road. Four-year-old Victoria Fleming took a gander at the talking apple trees and got scared.

Later, when the MGM front office began to worry about the picture's expense, and its presumably limited audience, the sets were closed to visitors and most of the press to remove time-consuming distractions and to preserve some of the mystery of what was being filmed.

Cast and crew were aware, at least in general terms, of the production's troubles. Concerns about budget and other things were just more burdens loaded onto the film's young star. Despite emotional stress, physical discomfort, and long hours, Judy was buoyed during the first four months of 1939 by construction of her first house, at 1231 Stone Canyon Road in Bel Air, near Sunset Boulevard. The handsome, dormered colonial had four bedrooms and a wide, covered front porch. A pair of large bay windows looked out on the large backyard, which was handsomely bisected by a flagstone walkway. Judy intended the house for herself and her mother.

On February 13, 1939, independent producer David O. Selznick and director George Cukor announced Cukor's departure from *Gone With the Wind*. When the announcement came, Cukor had worked on the Civil War epic for a mere three weeks. He had never cared for the script, and the picture's male lead, Clark Gable, may not have cared for Cukor. Selznick realized that nothing was to be gained by retaining a director who wasn't in synch with all aspects of the project. Every day without a director meant that actors, standing sets, costumes, and myriad other elements were doing nothing to amortize their cost. A new director was needed, and right away. Selznick approached King Vidor, a major talent and MGM staff director who had risen from comic shorts made before 1920 to sweeping, emotionally gripping dramas.

But Vidor didn't like the script any more than Cukor did and declined.

Selznick met with Louis Mayer and then approached Victor Fleming. Fleming had worked long hours on *Oz* during three and a half months of six-day weeks. He felt as droopy as one of Frank Morgan's false mustaches, but agreed to take over *GWTW* because of his personal relationship with Gable. MGM informed the trade press of Fleming's decision on February 14, 1939, adding that what remained of *The Wizard of Oz* would be directed by King Vidor.

Still, Fleming was set on completing the Technicolor portion of *Oz* and had to tell Selznick that he wouldn't be able to meet the producer's February 20 start date. His last day on the *Oz* set was February 17, 1939, when he shot the Emerald City awards sequence with the Wizard and Dorothy and her three friends. His replacement, King Vidor, came to the set that day. Vidor recalled, "Victor Fleming was a good friend, and he took me around to all the sets that had been built and went through the whole thing. He left that night and I took over." Late in the day, Fleming enjoyed a farewell party.

Fleming had directed the color portion of *Oz* with efficiency, imagination, and extraordinary confidence. Mayer was comfortable with Fleming's shift to *GWTW*, a picture that MGM would bring to theaters via its distribution arm, giving the studio a considerable financial interest.

Tired but invariably professional, Victor Fleming accepted the *GWTW* assignment with equanimity—but he also decided that he wasn't done with *Oz*, not by a long shot. He had invested a lot of himself in the film and hadn't forgotten that he wanted to please his little girls. Under the studio system, very few staff directors were allowed to supervise the edit of their projects. The system dictated that a director shot a movie, and when he was done, it was edited by other hands, while the director was already involved with his next project. Fleming, however, had clout. He was an assertive presence who had earned the respect of not just his peers but of Louis Mayer. So it was that after February 17, Fleming divided his time between *GWTW* (directing) and *Oz* (cutting). Either of those tasks would have given an ordinary mortal plenty to do, but Fleming was determined.

Before leaving *Oz*, Fleming oversaw the effects in the twister sequence and shot the awards sequence (brains, heart, courage) in the Emerald City.

Fleming biographer Michael Sragow praises the firmness and aggressive professionalism that informed Fleming's career. The director expressed those virtues via enormous technical ability, a gift for organization of script and on-set activity, and his seldom-discussed touch with actresses, comedy, and music. Freed, Langley, and Harburg are some of the other behind-the-scenes geniuses of *Oz*, but it was Fleming who gave the film much of its joy and—even more critical—its air of reality. Although Dorothy's Oz is fanciful, it also seems *possible*. Victor Fleming did that.

Oz and Judy's State of Mind

Dorothy Gale was an indelible role that Garland played with enthusiasm and grace. To millions, Judy and Dorothy were inseparable. Completely without Garland's approval, Dorothy came to define the actress for much of the rest of her life. She already was a veteran performer when she did *Oz* and had been immersed in the competitive, often cynical reality of show business. She played Dorothy with capped teeth (MGM's idea) and a binder that flattened her breasts. She wore girlish pigtails at a time when she was already a young woman with longings that Dorothy would not have imagined. During the *Oz* shoot, it's likely that the studio was already feeding amphetamines to their teenage star. (One source suggests a wardrobe worker as Judy's studio-appointed supplier, though there's been no evidence to suggest that Victor Fleming ever knew of this.)

The studio's continual "readjustment" of her body and emotions was a trial. She knew that the studio regarded her as an asset and that many other people worked when *she* worked. She felt the weight of that responsibility. The studio did nothing to relieve her of that. She'd been busy with other films, including various Andy Hardy pictures, which were modestly budgeted and shot quickly. After *Oz*, she realized that all her subsequent projects would rise or fall on her shoulders. She was involved in touring and other personal appearances, and spent a lot of time singing in recording studios.

At seventeen, Judy developed an unrequited romantic love for musician Artie Shaw, who loved her like a sister. Although Shaw was unfailingly generous and kind to her, Judy misinterpreted his brotherly attitude as rejection, and as just more proof that her figure and everything else the studio complained about were indeed sub-par.

On top of that, there was Ethel, Judy's mother, and other family members, all of whom demanded, with varying degrees of vociferousness, that she provide for them.

This was no childhood. This was work, doubt, and pressure.

Years after *Oz*, Judy reflected on the way Dorothy Gale informed the rest of her career: "I played that part so many times, acting so darn happy!"

Of course, Judy wasn't happy at all.

Lions and Tigers and Bears—Together?

As Dorothy and her companions enter the Haunted Forest, they worry aloud about wild animals, finally settling into the much-loved litany of "Lions and tigers and bears, oh my!" Many things are possible in the fantasyland of Oz, but in the real world, lions, tigers, and the sorts of bear familiar to Dorothy occupy different continents and do not co-exist. (Winged monkeys aren't easy to find in the real world, either, but that's another story.) At Noah's Ark, however, a nonprofit animal sanctuary and rehabilitation center in Locust Grove, Georgia, an African lion, a Bengal tiger, and a North American black bear not only live together, but also share the same enclosure, where they play and tumble as friends.

In 2001, when they were still cubs, the animals were rescued from a neglectful drug dealer and later taken in by Noah's Ark owners Jamie and Charles Hedgecoth. When the cubs were separated, none of them thrived, so the Hedgecoths tried to forget what they knew about "apex" predators and reunited the three youngsters. At this writing, Leo the lion, Shere Khan the tiger, and Baloo the black bear are contented, playful companions.

13

Up Like Thunder

Special Effects and Sound

According to MGM's organizational chart, A. Arnold "Buddy" Gillespie's special effects unit was part of the larger art department and answered to Cedric Gibbons. Although Gibbons never allowed himself to be kept in the dark about what the effects crew was up to, he respected Gillespie's technical proficiency and gift for project management. Gillespie wasn't exactly a free agent, but he did enjoy a great deal of freedom. He was mindful of budget and able to hold down costs. But whenever he had a reasonable idea, he tried it.

Gillespie's effects supervisor was Edwin Bloomfield. Marcel Delgado (who had contributed mightily to *King Kong* in 1933) handled miniatures. J. McMillan Johnson was senior effects technician, and effects were rigged by Don Trumbull (the father of later special-effects whiz Douglas Trumbull). The effects assistant was A. D. Flowers.

Because *The Wizard of Oz* was a fantasy with a wholly artificial environment, the special effects had to be sensational *and* bring a measure of physical realism. If audiences didn't buy the effects work, much of the story's magic would be lost. Gillespie and his crew utilized many materials and techniques to bring special life to *Oz*. The belligerent apple trees were constructed of sculpted rubber, in the eighty-person MGM sculpture department headed by Henry Greutert, who would ultimately be a thirty-year MGM employee. Besides the apple trees, Greutert's staff did particularly fine work on the Haunted Forest, including those famously peculiar owls and decorative details of the Witch's castle. (Later in his career, Greutert created seating molds in the fashion of ancient Pompeii for the gardens of the Getty Villa at Pacific Palisades and created the faux Mount Rushmore that's central to *North by Northwest* [1959].) Each apple tree was slit up the back, allowing easy egress for the men who made the trees move. Actor Abe Dinovitch gave voice to the tree that snatches the apple from Dorothy's hand and scolds her. Dinovitch was a husky type and a small-part actor often cast as sailors, cab drivers, and laborers.

The apple trees were a mechanical special effect: they were created in real time, on-set, as the cameras rolled. Another such effect, the charming toot of

The surly apple trees were sculpted latex. The technicians that manipulated the trees from inside did not provide the memorable voices; actors recorded those later, in post-production.

steam that issues from the Tin Woodman's cap, was achieved with a hidden compressed-air unit that sent forth a tiny geyser of talcum powder.

When Dorothy and the Scarecrow begin to oil the Tin Woodman, they neglect to do his feet, which stay rooted to the ground and allow him to lean precipitously one way, then the other. This effect, which always brings smiles, was achieved on-set with metal runners set into the stage floor and designed to accommodate Haley's shoes.

An on-set effect that may have been considered and later abandoned is suggested by the sawhorse that's visible during the introduction of the Tin Woodman. In the first *Oz* book by Baum, a sawhorse comes to life. On the other hand, perhaps Victor Fleming simply felt that a Tin Woodman would naturally have a sawhorse.

A particularly dramatic mechanical effect on is display when the panicked Lion (stunt player George Bruggeman, filling in for Bert Lahr) dashes down the Wizard's corridor and launches himself through a window to escape. The "glass" was a breakaway unit made of a hot mixture of resin and mercury that had been poured into the window frame and allowed to cool. The material held its shape, splintered nicely, and gave every impression of glass. Sound effects added in post-production helped the illusion.

"It's a twister! It's a twister!"

An effects-heavy adventure film called *Twister* was released in 1996. By that date, filmmaking was well into the digital age, and the movie's effects crew had the ability to use computer-generated imagery to create the story's numerous tornadoes. The effects are impressive (excellent sound work helps a lot), but occasional reviewers were reminded of the *Oz* twister—and decided that it was considerably more frightening than anything that had come from the computer. The *Oz* storm, which is used to propel the narrative and suggest the very brisk pace of events to follow, is terrifying and completely believable, but it didn't get that way without struggle.

Buddy Gillespie and his crew did cyclone-effects tests on MGM's Stage 14, during three discrete periods. In August 1938, the crew tested what Gillespie called a "water vortex," which proved difficult to control and even harder to maintain in a proper shape. The unit also experimented with an $8,000 rubber cone that turned out to be far too stiff to simulate the liveliness of a real twister. In November, Gillespie did his first tests with a cloth tube. He returned in late January 1939 to do further tests of what he referred to as a "small" cloth tube and to make photographic adjustments to the miniature buildings and farmscape designed and built for use in long shots. It should be noted that "miniature" doesn't mean something that Buddy Gillespie could pop into his pocket. To the contrary, the farm buildings, trees, fencing, and other elements were built three-quarters of an inch to the foot, meaning that the Gale farmhouse stood about three feet high. Two sets of buildings were used during the tests.

The January work also included tests of the sky and dust, and of the dark, menacing clouds, some of which were back-projected film footage; others were made of cotton attached to moving glass that was positioned to mate seamlessly with the other sky elements. The glass panels served another purpose: they masked the gantry and other equipment.

Just a single day in August 1938 had been devoted to cyclone tests, and a single day in November. Gillespie needed more time: four days in January 1939 and ten in February. By then, the "small" cloth tube had grown to a thirty-five-foot piece of muslin laced with reinforcing wire—a sort of stocking—attached at its top to a $5,000 gantry crane designed by Gillespie. The crane was purpose-built by Consolidated Steel, a Los Angeles firm that made streetcars, iron and brass castings for various sorts of machinery, pumping plants, water mains, HVAC systems, and freight and passenger elevators. The effects gantry was hung from the stage's roof trusses. The muslin was rotated at the top by an electric motor that was designed to tip when necessary, to give the twister some "English." The tube was moved around the stage floor by a motor winch attached to a miniature "car" hidden on tracks at the stocking's base, and

Buddy Gillespie's crew used muslin, Fuller's earth, miniatures, back projection, and other sleight of hand to create the terrifying Kansas twister.

operated by crewmembers beneath the set. Additional visual interest was provided by air jets that kicked up Fuller's earth as the cyclone battered the ground. This "dust" (as Gillespie referred to it) wasn't easily managed, and the effects crew devoted two days to achieve the kickup effect Gillespie wanted. Fuller's earth that was carefully dribbled into the open top of the muslin softened the twister's contours.

The rest of the miniature setup was whipped by two wind machines and six fans; a similar technique was used later, when Judy Garland and the other actors dashed around the full-size farm sets. (Total electrical cost for the lights, wind machines, and other power implements used during the tests was about $3,600.) In the final composite, back projection places the cast in convincing proximity to the storm.

Gillespie's cameraman was Max Fabian, a DP who had devoted himself to special visual effects after 1930. (He had a hand in two other MGM releases known for sensational special effects, *San Francisco* [1936] and *Forbidden Planet* [1956].) Fabian used 35mm, 40mm, and 50mm lenses for the twister tests, shooting at forty-eight frames per second, or two times normal speed. When projected, the twister footage would assume the majestic slow motion that's so effective in the film's final cut.

The brief upward shot, from Dorothy's point of view, of the twister's interior used more rotating, reinforced muslin, which was painted with subtle stripes and photographed with a madly whirling camera.

The January–February tests were shot during mornings and afternoons; no test work was done during the night. A typical day's work involved Gillespie and Fabian, plus an effects foreman, ten to eighteen mechanics, and a handful of grips and helpers.

Set construction independent of its later operation was an approximately $10,500 expense. Total operating cost was about $12,400. All of that, plus other expenses, brought the cost of Gillespie's twister tests to $27,000. (The $5,000 special mount for the gantry is not part of that figure.)

The whimsical parade of flying people that passes Dorothy's window was done later with back projection and superimposed images. The superimposition was purposely executed as simply as possible, so that the objects are transparent and seem to move on a plane quite divorced from the twister. This, along with the earlier scene of the window frame striking Dorothy's head, is the best early clue we have that what we will see is the girl's dream.

Seventy-five years after audiences first witnessed it, the twister effect remains a marvel of the art. It's been indelibly etched in the minds of millions. Today, computer-generated images can easily create more visual thunder than what Gillespie could manage, but who, really, remembers any of the tornados in *Twister* (1996)? The *Oz* cyclone has personality.

The storm was far too effective to be used by MGM only once. It appears in *Cabin in the Sky* (1943) and may be in other films, as well.

In Focus: A. Arnold "Buddy" Gillespie (1899–1978)

In 1936, Buddy Gillespie was asked to knock the hell out of a great city and, while he was at it, kill hundreds of people. In his role as head of special visual effects at MGM, he and his crew did all of that for *San Francisco*, a period romance that re-creates the earthquake that leveled the city in 1906. Seven cameras captured the devastation: floors ripple, ceilings sag. Walls bend and collapse. A crammed theater balcony comes loose from the wall and droops on one side, bending into an inverted V before crashing to the floor below. A towering domed building crumbles in stages, like a sand castle. Enormous exterior brick walls tear loose and crash to the street. The dust is everywhere, and it's blinding. People who haven't time to react are crushed beneath a rain of debris. Streetlamps are levered from the streets. Water mains burst and explode. A piano that's propelled through a second-story window squashes a man on the street below. Immense statuary topples. People are running—running everywhere.

It's the damnedest two minutes you'll ever see.

Remember that Gillespie achieved all of this ages before computer-generated images, working with mechanical effects that encompassed miniatures, full-size breakaways, tricked-up sets, and real people amidst real objects.

Albert Arnold Gillespie was born in El Paso, Texas, in the waning days of the 19th century. While a very young man, he lived in Oklahoma City, and then saw France during World War I. He attended Columbia University and the Art Students League, sold cars in California, worked as a draftsman for Cecil B. DeMille's art director, and became an assistant art director at Paramount in 1922.

Gillespie (known to friends and associates as Buddy) was associated with MGM from 1925 until 1962, becoming head of the special effects department in 1936. Although subordinate to chief production designer Cedric Gibbons, Gillespie never-theless ruled an effects shop staffed by about forty people. Together, they created what was needed for more than six hundred movies: miniatures and matte paintings; explosions and tidal waves; a plague of locusts and an atomic explosion (before a single photograph of a mushroom cloud had been released to the public). The crew did opticals and animation; car crashes and floods; great battle fleets and a flying saucer; whipping windstorms and a comet that crashes against the moon. The assign-ments were astonishingly varied, and every one was executed from the department's own precisely scaled drawings and blueprints. Gillespie was as much a practical scien-tist and engineer as he was a moviemaker.

As an art director, Gillespie worked on *Ben-Hur* (1926), *London After Midnight* (1927), *The Crowd* (1928), and *Mutiny on the Bounty* (1935). Later, as head of effects, he did *The Good Earth* (1937), *Test Pilot* (1938), *Thirty Seconds Over Tokyo* (1944), *Quo Vadis* (1951), *Forbidden Planet* (1956), *North by Northwest* (1959), *Ben-Hur* (1959), *Cimarron* (1960), and *Mutiny on the Bounty* (1962). He was a thirteen-time Oscar nominee and a four-time winner.

Because of the generosity of the Gillespie family, the Margaret Herrick Library of the Academy of Motion Picture Arts and Sciences holds 4½ linear feet of 8″ x 10″ effects stills and frame blowups, with Gillespie's notes about dates, technique, budget, and personnel.

When Buddy was interviewed in retirement by *Film Comment*, he reflected, "The whole physical end of movies . . . was so interesting because whether the picture was modern, whether it was in the future, whether it was a dream world like *The Wizard of Oz* or in outer space like *Forbidden Planet*, it was an illusion made real."

Surrender Dorothy

From January 23, 1939, to May 1, Gillespie and his crew busied themselves with (among other things) the smoky, skywritten message to Dorothy that the Wicked Witch expels from her broomstick from high above the Emerald City. The script described the message as SURRENDER DOROTHY OR DIE—WWW. In all, Gillespie needed nineteen days to design and execute the skywriting satisfactorily: two days in January, two in February, six in March, eight in April, and one in May. (By April, Gillespie had the advantage of a newly assembled rough cut of the film that ran about two hours, or some twenty minutes longer than the eventual general-release version.) Crew size varied according to the complexity of the day's work, but a typical day involved Gillespie, a foreman, four mechanics, and a grip. The number of crewmembers doubled on days when electricians were needed. And, of course, there was a cameraman, Max Fabian. Work was done during mornings and afternoons.

The obvious challenge Gillespie faced was how to create and maintain the shapes of letters. An airplane was out of the question because the aircraft would have to be optically obscured later in post-production. And anyway, the Witch's message was a long one; even a practiced skywriter would struggle to complete the message before the early letters dissipated. That suggested that the effect would have to be done in miniature. Skywriting was possible in normal air only because of the letters' great size. To get a similar effect in miniature was impossible.

Gillespie realized that liquid, rather than air, was the suitable medium. Plain water wouldn't do (it was too thin to hold letter shapes, and too transparent to give the letters a background that would make them readable). Water with whitewash, or a similar white agent, was a likely solution.

As tests began in January, Gillespie's first challenge was what he called "drift": the letters' natural tendency to dissipate and lose their shapes, with some of them drifting upward and others drifting down. By experimenting with the viscosity of the liquid, Gillespie was able to correct the drift on the first day of February. Additional corrections, and many takes and retakes, followed. March 29 brought a satisfactory take of the letters SUR. The complete message was achieved March 30 and refined during retakes a day later. But on April 1, "DOROTHY" had to be redone and reshot.

Much of the April activity involved the miniature Witch and broom, which were optically mated later to a miniature castle battlement. The figure was about one-and-a-half inches long. Max Fabian used a 50mm lens to film the letters at sixty-four frames a second, so that the action would be slowed when projected at the normal rate of twenty-four fps.

Gillespie summarized the key aspects of the process in his cost- and schedule-breakdown sheet:

> For Witch Skywriting a $6' \times 6' \times 4''$ tank with glass bottom was framed $12'$ above the stage floor with camera shooting up and thru glass into $2''$ of white translucent water. The smoke which formed the letters was a black liquid released under slight pressure thru a stylus made with a hypodermic needle upon which a small black profile of witch was fastened. This was moved by operators from above[,] forming the letters required. Wind drift was made by causing slight drift of water across tank. Black and white shots were printed into color sky.

Gillespie noted on his sheet that his original cost estimate had not taken into account the number of separate cuts that would be required to create the message; he had originally hoped it could be accomplished as a single shot. Prep, materials, construction and rigging, electrical, film stock, and personnel brought the cost of the skywriting effect to more than $6,500.

Because producer Mervyn LeRoy and others wondered later about the appropriateness of the "OR DIE" portion of the message, those words, and the Witch's initials, were cut. In the years since, "Surrender Dorothy" has become part of the American lexicon.

Gillespie also was asked to devise an unusual main title. LeRoy hoped that something novel could be done with the words "The Wizard of Oz." Gillespie again used white liquid, this time in a clear glass ball. The title was painted onto the top surface of the ball and looked like this:

The
Wizard
of
OZ

The ball was dropped from what Gillespie's reports referred to as the "runway" of Stage 14 onto a section of floor covered in black cloth. The ball

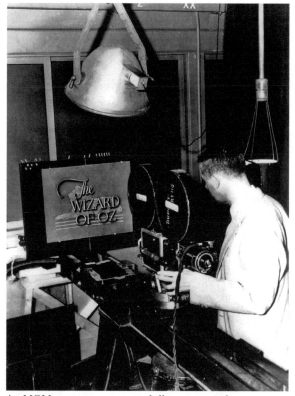

An MGM cameraman uses a dolly mount to shoot a never-used *Oz* title card.

shattered. When the film was printed in reverse, the title appeared to coalesce from a splash and travel toward the camera eye. The title halted at the point at which the ball had been dropped.

This title design required considerable time and ingenuity, but the effect was nevertheless discarded. Subsequently, nearly three dozen variations were tried and debated: some in Technicolor, others in black and white, and with a wealth of fonts and word placement. In the end, of course, the chosen design had elegant black and white letters, in quotes, optically overlaid on black and white clouds, and all dyed sepia:

"The
WIZARD
of OZ"

Sound Recording

Sound came under the supervision of Douglas Shearer, an imaginative and very experienced technician whose entrée into Hollywood had been facilitated by his sister, top MGM star Norma Shearer. His early movie experience was as a camera assistant, and although he and his crews won a dozen Oscars for sound recording during his nearly thirty-year career (encompassing nearly a thousand films), he returned to camera-related technology in the 1950s, working with Panavision to create Ultra Panavision, a distortion-free widescreen system that MGM dubbed MGM Camera 65. Shearer's background allowed him to consider ways in which sound recording and sound design might be best integrated with a film's images.

Years before *Oz*, Shearer had broken precedent by suggesting that the singers in musicals synch their voices to pre-recorded tracks played on-set. That became standard industry practice and was used on *Oz* (which explains, for instance, why Buddy Ebsen's voice, and not Jack Haley's, is occasionally heard during "We're Off to See the Wizard" moments: the vocals had been recorded before the cameras rolled). As we've seen, the Munchkins' songs were the exception to the lip-synch method.

One of Shearer's staff, Michael Steinore, was the supervising sound editor. He and his crew were particularly mindful of audio levels during the edit of song sequences and took care to ensure that the vocalizing had presence appropriate to the settings. In short, Steinore had to retain the best elements of these studio recordings while simultaneously reducing the audio artificiality that studio recording inevitably brings.

Special sound effects encompassed an enormous range of sounds, including footsteps, background dialogue, barks, the rustle of the Scarecrow's hay, the hollow thump of the Tin Woodman's chest, and on and on. Even the most sophisticated microphones of the day (or of today, either) are not acute enough to pick up every ancillary sound at appropriate levels, tones, and durations. Frequently, a sound effect that may be indicated during filming (such as the *toot* from the Tin Woodman's cap during his solo dance) doesn't exist at all until audio technicians work with the footage weeks later.

Additionally, multiple camera setups are frequently used in single scenes. Each time the camera is relocated, the mics must be moved as well. An unaugmented soundtrack would reflect that, with varying levels of volume and clarity. For consistency, this must be addressed after principal photography is complete.

Then there is the issue of make-believe. Something that appears to be metal on screen may be made of rubber that can't provide the desired sound. The appropriate sound effect must be created later. Post-production sound effects recording is the art of bringing audio realism to make-believe.

Doug Shearer addressed the challenge of the sound of the twister by bringing Italian-born sound engineer O. O. Ceccarini onto the project. (Ceccarini's first name was Olindo.) Ceccarini had worked at MGM once before, as a sound technician on *The Broadway Melody* (1929). In 1930, working on behalf of MGM, Ceccarini devised what the U.S. Patent Office called an "optical system for photographic purposes," by which the horizontal and vertical components of a projected image appear simultaneously in a single plane. Images are also, as described in the patent application, "definite, clear and brilliant." In December 1933, the patent office recognized Ceccarini as the inventor and assigned the patent to MGM. Before that, in 1932, Ceccarini won a patent for a "damped light valve" that accurately modulated recorded sound to film. He also had a hand in technology that allowed multiple audio tracks to be combined, so that a particular scene in a film could have, for instance, main dialogue, background dialogue, ambient noise, and background music (the underscore).

In a press release, MGM described Ceccarini as a mathematician who devised more than two hundred pages of "delicate mathematical calculations" that indicated the proper volume, pitch, and frequency of the funnel cloud.

Other sound effects were considerably simpler. The sounds of the sweetly twittering birds that help welcome Dorothy to Munchkinland, for instance, were fashioned from manipulated birdcalls recorded on Catalina Island, located twenty-two miles south-southwest of Los Angeles.

Let Pinto and Billy Say It

About eighty uncredited actors did overdub work for various Munchkin vocals. Two of the most notable are Pinto Colvig and Billy Bletcher.

Pinto Colvig (1892–1967) was one of the finest and busiest of all Disney voice actors. His first vocations, though, were the circus, the clarinet, and newspaper cartooning. He got into the movies in 1925 with occasional live-action roles, but nearly always as a voice actor in cartoons. He was an animator with the Walter

Lantz/Universal animation unit in the very early 1930s, but shortly began a long association with Disney. Although best known, even to casual cartoon fans, as the original voice of Goofy in dozens of cartoon shorts, Colvig provided Disney with voices for an immense array of human beings and anthropomorphic animals. He was Grumpy and Sleepy in *Snow White and the Seven Dwarfs* (1937), the Aracuan Bird in *The Three Caballeros* (1944), the Flamingo in *Alice in Wonderland* (1951), and Ichabod Crane in *The Adventures of Ichabod and Mr. Toad* (1949). Colvig reprised Goofy in the features *The Reluctant Dragon* (1941), *Saludos Amigos* (1942), and *Fun and Fancy Free* (1947; compilation). The voice of an often-revived Mickey Mouse spin-off, the conniving Mortimer Mouse, was originated by Colvig.

Disney was just one of Colvig's clients; he did voice work for most of the major cartoon units in Hollywood, including Warner Bros., MGM, Fleischer Studios (where Pinto voiced Gabby in *Gulliver's Travels*, 1939), and Walter Lantz.

In *The Wizard of Oz*, Colvig provided voices for various Munchkins, including one of the Lollipop Guild.

His final work was as Goofy in *Donald Duck Goes West* (1965).

For **Billy Bletcher** (1894–1979), early success in silent comedies came because of his masculine face and physique, which were mated to a total height of 5′1″ or 5′2″. He broke into movies with Vitagraph in 1914, working as an actor in comedy shorts. Later jobs took him to Fox Film, Vim, and other producers. Bletcher was usually a supporting player but had leads in a short-lived series of comedy shorts produced by Christie Film Company around 1920. Appearances in feature films became more common for him after World War I, but the greater part of his work for forty years was in one- and two-reelers, including voice-over work for live-action dogs in MGM's very peculiar "Dogville" shorts of the early 1930s. In *The Wizard of Oz*, he did voice-over for the mayor of Munchkinland and for one member of the Lollipop Guild.

Billy had a rich, baritone speaking voice. He hooked up with Hal Roach around 1930, where he did voice-over work as police dispatchers and radio announcers, and appeared on camera, too, most notably with Our Gang in *The First Round-Up* (1934). Wally, Spanky, and the other kids plan to go camping. They're a little scared of the dark, but Wally's father (whom we see only as a head in a window) reassures the kids and tells his wife that camping is great. "Oh, I went through all of that when *I* was a boy," he says, "and look what it's done for me!" With that, he steps into the doorway, looking hearty but very, very short.

Billy had long associations with Disney and the Warner Bros. animation unit, compiling hundreds of cartoon-voice credits over three decades. He also found uncredited voice work at Republic and other producers of B-westerns, whenever an authoritative or menacing voice was called for.

Television took hold after 1950, and Billy returned to real-life performances on *The Millionaire*, *The Real McCoys*, *Get Smart*, and many other shows. His last work was as Pappy Yokum in a 1971 TV version of *Li'l Abner*.

What's a Humbug?

Moments after Toto unmasks the Wizard, Dorothy and her shocked friends denounce him as a humbug, a word that's clearly meant to be a devastating reproach, but that has lost nearly all of its bite with the passing decades. According to Merriam-Webster, "humbug" dates to 1751; in noun form, it means "a willfully false, deceptive, or insincere person." Well, that's not a good thing to be, but it's not a charge guaranteed to put a hardboiled recipient on the floor, either. So why does Dorothy's "humbug" label carry such weight?

Eighteenth-century accounts of the word suggest an origin in student slang, which may take us into the realm of so-called vogue words like today's "proactive" and "synergy." Appropriate to the passions of youth, early uses of "humbug" suggested hypocrisy as well as deceit. In other words, the humbug follows a course quite different from—perhaps even the opposite of—the course he loudly espouses.

By the 19th century, "humbug" had acquired a vaguely comic or farcical tone, thanks mainly to Ebenezer Scrooge's "Bah, humbug!" pronouncement about the holidays in Dickens's *A Christmas Carol*. Circus showman Phineas T. Barnum also had a hand in this. His supposed "moral instruction" of the public played out (according to circus historian Noel Daniel) via exhibitions of medical oddities, sideshow freaks, "Ubangi savages," and other bald appeals to voyeurism. Although Barnum held a sincere dislike for purposeful deceit, he nevertheless dubbed himself "the great humbug."

During 1957–58, *Mad* magazine creator Harvey Kurtzman published and edited *Humbug*, an illustrated humor magazine that skewered misleading advertising, formulaic moviemaking, Cold War opportunists, white man's burden, and other sorts of humbuggery. And in 1958, country singer Lefty Frizzell sang "You're Humbuggin' Me," an angry reprimand to a faithless lover.

"Humbug" may have gone out of style, but humbuggery, alas, has not.

14

A House with a Picket Fence

King Vidor Brings It Home

The single most famous sequence of *The Wizard of Oz* was not shot by the man who receives on-screen credit as the film's director. Although Fleming shot every moment that takes place in the Land of Oz, the film's timeless musical moment, Garland's rendition of "Over the Rainbow," is part of the Kansas sequences—all of which were directed, without credit, by King Vidor. (Contrary to what he claimed after Fleming's death, Vidor did not shoot any iteration of "We're Off to See the Wizard.") John Lee Mahin wrote considerable portions of the Kansas segments, under the guidance of Victor Fleming, but the entirety of these heavily stylized "home" scenes was directed by Vidor, who stepped onto the set, ready to shoot, on February 19, 1939.

Except for reshoots of some color scenes, "Kansas" accounted for the last elements of *The Wizard of Oz* to be filmed. From the start of preproduction, these sequences were scheduled to be addressed last; the timing had nothing to do with Fleming's departure, or Vidor's arrival.

Vidor was a self-assured filmmaker who believed in editing in the camera, which is a polite way to say that he dedicated himself to giving editors relatively few choices at the cutting stage. He knew exactly what he *wanted* to shoot. Because Vidor habitually worked out what he wished to see on the screen even before shooting began, he saw no point in shooting, say, a close-up or a pan shot that he didn't want in the film in the first place. (Vidor gave producer Sam Goldwyn a few headaches by pursuing this on-set philosophy two years earlier, during the shoot of *Stella Dallas* [1937].) No evidence has emerged to suggest that *Oz* producer Mervyn LeRoy objected to Vidor's in-camera editing, or that Vidor's methods offended the people who cut *The Wizard of Oz*, Victor Fleming and Blanche Sewell.

Vidor began with Dorothy's interactions with the farmhands, Hickory (Haley), Zeke (Lahr), and Hunk (Bolger), straightforward scenes that got a little tricky and required rehearsals for proper choreography and timing, when Dorothy falls into the pigpen.

One of the last on-set duties handled by Victor Fleming was to supervise the cyclone special effects—not the bedroom-interior process shots in which people and objects fly past Dorothy's window, but the moving, raging cyclone itself. Because the cyclone wasn't real, the only people who felt threatened by it were on the special-effects crew. Delay, or an ineffective simulation, was unacceptable. In a minor bit of irony, Judy Garland was unusually fearful of natural disasters. A childhood experience with a modest L.A. quake scared her, and thereafter she was unnerved at the thought of earthquakes, thunderstorms, and tornados.

The Kansas sequences weren't scripted to have the obvious theatricality or expense of the rest of the film, but they did present special challenges for Vidor and his technicians. Like the rest of the movie, the Kansas scenes were shot on sound stages—a tricky proposition when nearly every Kansas shot is an "exterior," and when the "reality" of Kansas must be established in order to create a powerful contrast to the fanciful land of Oz. The decision to shoot Kansas on black-and-white film stock was brilliant. Narratively, the monochrome suggests the bleakness that stifles Dorothy and prompts her to dream of another, better place. Visually, the black and white eliminates the need to light sound-stage "exteriors" for color, which is literally impossible if your aim is realism. A true exterior has only one source of light: the sun. A stage exterior utilizes many sources: a strong arc to simulate sunlight and numerous less emphatic lights for fill. (Think back to color TV shows of the 1960s and '70s that relied on sound-stage exteriors; *Bonanza* is a good example. When characters ambled down daylit, oddly pastel-colored streets, they threw multiple shadows—an impossibility in life unless you're beneath street lamps or at a night baseball game.) Color Kansas "exteriors" would have had the multiple-light-source problem, plus the undamped brilliance of three-strip Technicolor. Colors in life are relatively subdued; in Technicolor, colors were heightened. Kansas in color would have been an aesthetic disaster.

Audiences of 1939 had become accustomed to black-and-white images of American farmland shot by photojournalists and WPA photographers. Newspapers and magazines printed photos in monochrome more frequently than in color. Even *LIFE* magazine, *the* general-information source of the day, used color pages sparingly. Newsreels, too, were shot in black and white. The reality of Kansas, as it existed in the minds of moviegoers, was monochrome. The further decision to dye the black-and-white film stock in sepia wasn't just to suggest nostalgia, as it does today, but to evoke the dingy tones of earth and weathered buildings. Cinematographer Harold Rosson is rightfully lauded for the lighting he devised for the film's color sequences, but isn't praised as often for his work on the Kansas sequences. What he achieved is gorgeous and moving.

Sepia Tone

The gentle brown tone that suffuses the Kansas sequences of *The Wizard of Oz* is sepia, and was a purposeful attempt to impart the presumed virtuousness, and occasional hardships, of what used to be called "homely values": family and friends, work and rest, satisfaction and reflection. As the world teetered on the brink of war during 1938–39, many Americans looked back with longing to what seemed to be simpler, better times. To them, sepia suggested nostalgia and security.

Sepia tone, which was common to still photography until about 1920, comes from chemical toner, functioning as a dye, that's added during the processing of raw film. Although long out of fashion when utilized in *The Wizard of Oz*, sepia continued to carry emotional weight. (Today, it's a cute gimmick, utilized, for instance, in Old West dress-up portraits and other novelty photography.)

Color toning dates from motion pictures' earliest days. A useful 1917 book by Colin Bennett, *The Guide to Kinematography*, discusses how to bathe raw black-and-white film stock in chemical dyes to achieve appropriate color effects for candlelight, fire, bright sunlight, and moonlight. Early in 20th-century moviemaking, color toning of scenes and whole sequences was common.

The framing device of *The Wizard of Oz*—that is, the Kansas sequences—was shot on black-and-white film stock and dyed sepia in the lab during the processing of the raw stock.

Although some online sources devoted to *Oz* refer to "Sepiatone" film, such stock has never existed.

Distinct from toning is *tinting*, a sophisticated color method involving precisely selected and apportioned chemicals that create color effects in the silver-based black-and-white film stock. These effects are more subtle than those possible with simple toning. For instance, various ratios of vanadium show as a range of greens, copper brings ranges of red to brown, and sulfide (one sulfur atom attached to two carbon atoms) creates sepia.

For specialty color effects, such as the blue of the ocean below the red-orange of a setting sun, tinting and toning were employed in combination.

In *The Wizard of Oz*, the startling transition from sepia to Technicolor occurs after the farmhouse has landed in Oz and Dorothy opens the door to reveal the riot of color that is Munchkinland. Although preceded by a tracking close-up of Judy Garland (who moves out of frame before a cut), the act of opening the door was done by Judy's stand-in, Bobbie Koshay, who is seen only from the back. Rather than cut elaborate stencils to hand-color Dorothy and the doorframe in sepia, frame by frame, King Vidor shot the sequence in Technicolor, on a sepia-painted set, with Koshay clad in a black-and-ochre gingham dress and a sepia wig. (Rather deep shadows help to sell the illusion.) Although arguably the most startling visual effect in *The Wizard of Oz*, the transition to color is also one of the simplest—a mechanical (on-set) effect rather than an optical one.

When the film was put into general theatrical re-release in 1949, MGM saved processing costs by striking prints with the Kansas sequences printed in black and white instead of the original sepia. If audiences complained in 1949, or during the 1955 re-release, MGM did nothing to address the alteration. Nothing changed in 1956, either, when MGM struck a deal with CBS for national TV broadcasts of the movie. (Very few American homes had color television in

1956. MGM undoubtedly reasoned that nothing was to be gained by bothering with the sepia, when even the Technicolor footage would be seen by relatively few viewers.) Indeed, audiences didn't see the original sepia sequences again until fresh prints were struck for home video release commemorating the film's fiftieth anniversary, in 1989.

In an atypical lapse, the splendid MGM-*Oz* historian Aljean Harmetz dismissed Vidor's Kansas as "painfully literal." That's not only incorrect but misses the point of what Vidor aimed to achieve. Despite the careworn Gale farmhouse and barns, despite the rough attire of the farmhands and the dowdy outfits worn by Aunt Em and Miss Gulch, and despite that "dirt" color mentioned above, Vidor's Kansas is highly stylized and miles removed from "literal," painful or otherwise. We are immersed in an *impression* of late-Depression Kansas. The low, cloud-smudged skies aren't strictly "real" but evoke reality via their painterly stylization. When Dorothy and Toto walk alone along the dirt road, Dorothy's voice has greater presence than it would in the true outdoors of the Plains, and we wouldn't hear the mutter of insects as clearly. Vidor and Rosson created an impressively consistent visual tone—and thus a consistent emotional one, as well. The farmhouse interiors are no less austere than the landscape outside. Dorothy isn't miserable, but her life isn't a picnic, either. Merely by looking, we understand. Reality can't always be counted on to provide this kind of tonal consistency, but a film director's smart manipulation can make it happen.

Vidor's Kansas is full of surprises. Dorothy's sudden topple into the pigpen is a clever combination of humor and fright that leads to effective characterization of farmhand Zeke (Lahr). On the set, Judy Garland's first attempt to negotiate the fence surrounding the pigs went fine, except that she agitated the mother pig by landing amidst the piglets. Assistant director Al Shenberg quickly snatched Judy from harm's way.

"Over the Rainbow" is one of the movie's many highlights. Vidor recalled being on *Oz* for about two and a half weeks and was especially gratified for the opportunity to work with Garland on the song. Some thirty years after the fact, Vidor told film historian Richard Schickel, "[My time on *Oz*] included 'Somewhere Over the Rainbow' [*sic*]. It's run all the time, and whenever I hear it, I get a tremendous kick out of knowing that I directed that scene. I always wanted to do a musical film [and he had: *Hallelujah*, in 1929; Vidor undoubtedly meant he'd wanted to do a musical with state-of-the-art sound and recording technology]. I wanted to keep the movement going, just as we had in silent pictures."

In Focus: King Vidor (1894–1982)

When film historians wish to make some point or other by discussing directors who are "American primitives," they almost invariably cite Sam Fuller, the ex-newspaperman and World War II combat dogface who wrote and directed *Pickup on South Street* (1953), *The Naked Kiss* (1964), and many other uncomfortably honest,

King Vidor was the sixth and final director involved with *The Wizard of Oz*. He brought his interest in high emotion, and his consummate visual sense, to the film's Kansas sequences.

sensationalist tales hinged on the darker emotions of people. Sometimes the historians talk about western specialist Budd Boetticher in a similar way; like Fuller, he prospered in B-pictures, and if you like the "American primitive" label, Boetticher fits it. But almost nobody discusses King Vidor in those terms. (The very astute historian David Thomson is a rare one who does.)

Vidor's immensely successful career bridged the silent and sound eras, and has great artistic significance. He was a top studio director from the 1920s into the '50s and worked exclusively in "A" pictures; how "primitive" could he possibly have been? Well, the satisfying, emotionally violent surprise of King Vidor is that, for all the gloss he brought to his pictures, he had a tabloid writer's preoccupation with the id, exposed. Vidor wasn't necessarily the ideal director to handle the Kansas sequences of *The Wizard of Oz*, but he was uniquely equipped for the job and did it superbly.

King Wallis Vidor was born in Texas, where he grew intrigued by moving images and became a kid projectionist and newsreel cameraman. He was in Hollywood by about 1915, picking up work as an extra, assistant director, and prop man, before variously writing, co-writing, and directing nearly twenty-three comedy shorts during 1917–18, for Universal, Nestor Studios, Victor, and Boy City Film.

Vidor moved into features with *The Turn in the Road* (1919) for Famous Players-Lasky and was directing John Gilbert and other big stars before 1925. From very early in his career, Vidor was preoccupied with the tempo and rhythm of screen images, and in fact choreographed the marching scenes of one of his early triumphs, the unvarnished World War I drama *The Big Parade* (1925), to a bass drum. Another Vidor classic, a communal-farming drama called *Our Daily Bread* (1934), has a key scene in which a long line of men labors to dig a ditch—action that Vidor choreographed with a metronome at his side.

Vidor was devoted to honest portrayals of human lives and motivations, and was aware of the German Expressionist film movement. Although he never was overtly Germanic in his work, he nevertheless cultivated a talent for skewed visual perspectives and boldly mobile camerawork. *The Crowd* (1928), a bittersweet story of the repetitive and seemingly drab lives of office workers, captures the hustle of the city, and even brings considerable pictorial interest to sequences in plain rooms and offices. *Hallelujah* (1929), a black-cast talkie musical that Vidor directed before the availability of sound equipment capable of doing justice to the songs, is rescued by its players, and Vidor's restless imagery.

Vidor was adept at comedy and even light satire, as he demonstrated in *Show People* (1928) and two others with the delightful Marion Davies, but he marshaled his most powerful instincts for heightened melodramas. *The Champ* (1931), a tearjerking story set in the world of professional boxing, is entirely about emotion stripped bare; the fast-paced fight sequences are merely setup for the loving and aggressively tragic relationship between the aging fighter and his young son. In *Stella Dallas* (1937), Vidor and Barbara Stanwyck explored some hugely unhappy aspects of motherhood. A later Vidor gem, the thrillingly pictorial *Duel in the Sun* (1946), is propelled by a love triangle—made up in part by Jennifer Jones, absurd but fabulous as a fiery "half-breed." The tangle of emotions ignites the screen, creating what may be the first big-budget "camp" western.

The notion of camp wouldn't arrive on the cultural scene for another twenty years, and anyway, Vidor would never have viewed his work that way. He was serious about the tone of his movies, and it was no accident that the stars of *Duel in the Sun* carry their emotions not just on their sleeves, but practically painted on their faces. If Vidor hadn't believed in the honesty of his method, he would never have gone even further in *The Fountainhead* (1949), in which Gary Cooper is a rough-hewn architect who prefers to violently destroy one of his buildings rather than allow it to be compromised by the interference of a committee of no-talents. The script was done by Ayn Rand, adapting her didactic and fascinating novel; as screenplays go, it's truly awful, with pages of hectoring monologues and self-righteous preening—Rand's tedious, failed attempt to give her inherently unpleasant Objectivist philosophy some physical life. The entire enterprise was rescued by Vidor, who incorporated architectural designs into a soaring visual sensibility. Moreover, he developed the novel's flat central romance between the earthy architect and a sexually repressed rich beauty (Patricia Neal) with real brio: in this world, small emotions do not exist, and mere glances speak volumes.

It's no accident, then, that the Kansas sequences of *Oz* are a-tingle with fundamental emotion. A staid director might have staged the scenes with a competent realism and little more. Vidor gave them poignancy and a respectful understanding of Dorothy's longings.

Vidor retired from studio pictures after *Solomon and Sheba* (1959), but worked with film students on 16mm projects, including a 1964 short about metaphysics. His last film, *The Metaphor*, is a documentary short about the painter Andrew Wyeth. It was released in 1980, by which time Vidor had been a filmmaker for some sixty-five years.

He remained interested in commercial movies to the end of his life, pleased with their unprecedented frankness. In 1982, he earned some warm notices for a supporting role in James Toback's *Love and Money*.

Vidor believed in the importance of people's emotional lives. When he said to historian Richard Schickel, "I don't believe in a bad world," he was confirming that life itself is a joy.

Judy and "Over the Rainbow"

If Judy Garland ever grew tired of "Over the Rainbow," the public never knew. She was taken with it the day composers Arlen and Harburg first sang it for her, with simple piano accompaniment. Some twenty years later, Garland said, "I was terribly impressed by Mr. Arlen's great genius and very much in awe of him. . . . 'Over the Rainbow' has become a part of my life. It is so symbolic of everybody's dream and wish that I'm sure that's why people sometimes get tears in their eyes when they hear it. I have sung it dozens of times and it's still the song that is closest to my heart. It is very gratifying to have a song that is more or less known as my song, or my theme song, and to have had it written by the fantastic Harold Arlen."

Judy recorded her signature song for the first time on October 7, 1938, for the *Wizard of Oz* soundtrack. When she and King Vidor shot the barnyard scene five months later, she lip-synched to the October 7 recording. When Judy sang for servicemen during World War II, the troops invariably demanded "Over the Rainbow." Many years after that, singer Mel Tormé suggested to Judy that they parody "Over the Rainbow" in an upcoming television special. Judy said absolutely not. She told Tormé, "It's kind of sacred."

Judy signed with Decca Records on June 5, 1939, and was at the Decca studio on July 28 to record "Over the Rainbow" and "The Jitterbug," the dance tune cut from the movie.

Decca has flogged this early recording of "Rainbow" for decades, on the Decca, EMI, Brunswick, Polydor, PolyGram, and JSP labels. In 1939, the single parked itself on the charts for twelve weeks, topping out at number five on the Hit Parade.

In April 1940, a session Judy did at Decca included a tune called "(Can This Be) The End of the Rainbow"—an obvious nod to the original "Rainbow" tune. A 1944 V-Disc recording of "Over the Rainbow" paired Judy with the Tommy Dorsey Orchestra; the record's B-side was "I May Be Wrong (But I Think You're Wonderful)."

A 45 rpm Decca release from 1952 paired "Over the Rainbow" with "(Dear Mr. Gable) You Made Me Love You."

A 1955 recording of "Rainbow," on Capitol (Judy's recording "home" after her time at Decca) was the B-side of a 1956 single, "Maybe I'll Come Back." During Judy's lifetime, the song was featured on numerous 45 rpm releases.

Various Garland versions of "Over the Rainbow" are included on these albums and LPs released during the singer's lifetime: *The Wizard of Oz* (Decca, 1940; Decca re-recordings with Victor Young Orchestra) • *The Wizard of Oz* (Decca, 1947; reissue of *The Wizard of Oz*) • *Judy at the Palace: Judy Garland Singing Songs She Made Famous* (Decca, 1951; although Judy performed at New York's Palace Theatre in 1951, this is *not* a live album, but a compilation of previously recorded Judy/Decca tunes) • *The Wizard of Oz* (Decca, 1955; reissue of 1940 Decca release, to tie in with 1955 re-release of the movie) • *Judy*

A timeless interlude in movie history: Arlen and Harburg's "Over the Rainbow," sung by
Judy Garland and directed by King Vidor.

Garland: Greatest Performances (Decca/Brunswick, 1955; compilation) • *Miss
Show Business* (Capitol, 1955) • *The Wizard of Oz/Pinocchio* (Decca, 1956; reissue of Decca's *The Wizard of Oz*) • *The Wizard of Oz* (MGM, 1956; the first true
soundtrack release, with songs and dialogue; issued to coincide with the film's
TV premiere) • *Great Moments of the Movies* (EMI Records, UK release only;
compilation; various artists; songs from soundtracks of various MGM musicals,
1939–54) • *Garland at The Grove* (Capitol, 1959; recorded live at L.A's Cocoanut
Grove in 1958; "Over the Rainbow" is part of the LP's opening medley, and is
later sung in its entirety) • *Judy at Carnegie Hall* (Capitol, 1961; recorded live,
1961; "Rainbow" is part of the opening medley and is later sung in its entirety)
• *The Judy Garland Story Vol. 2: The Hollywood Years* (1962, MGM; compilation)
• *Magnificent Moments from MGM Movies* (MGM, 1962; compilation; various
artists; songs from soundtracks of various MGM musicals, 1939–58) • *The
Wizard of Oz Starring Judy Garland* (MGM, 1962; reissue of 1956 soundtrack LP,
with gatefold packaging) • *My Greatest Songs* (Brunswick [Germany], c. 1963;
compilation) • *The Best of Judy Garland* (Decca, 1963; compilation; reissued
under the same title by MCA in 1973) • *The Very Best of Motion Picture Musicals*
(MGM, 1963; reissue of *Magnificent Moments from MGM Movies*) • *The Very Best
of Judy Garland* (MGM, 1964; compilation) • *Lo major de Judy Garland* (MCA/
Decca. c. 1965; Argentina release; compilation) • *Judy Garland and Liza Minnelli,*

"Live" at the London Palladium (Capitol, 1965; recorded 1964; "Rainbow" is part of the opening medley and is later sung in its entirety, solo, by Judy) • *Judy Garland in Song* (Metro Records, 1966; compilation) • *Judy Garland at Home at the Palace* (ABC Records, 1967; recorded live at the Palace Theatre, NYC, 1967; "Rainbow" is heard in the opening and closing medleys only) • *24 Karat Gold from the Sound Stage* (MGM, 1968; compilation; various artists; songs from various MGM musicals and non-musicals, 1939–67) • *Judy. London. 1969.* (Juno, 1969; selected from live performances at London's Talk of the Town club during a four-week period in 1968–69).

Since Judy Garland's death, various Garland recordings of "Over the Rainbow" have been included in an enormous catalog of compilations from Decca (and its follow-on labels), Capitol, and numerous licensees.

As a side note, artists other than Judy had success with "Over the Rainbow" during the first blush of the tune's popularity. A 1939 cover by Glenn Miller and Orchestra, with vocal by Ray Eberle, was released as a ten-inch single by Bluebird. Miller's version was the number-one record in America for seven weeks. The Bob Crosby and Larry Clinton orchestras also found success with the song, reaching number two and number ten, respectively, on the singles chart.

Judy Garland sang "Over the Rainbow" on television just three times; the last was on *The Mike Douglas Show* from August 9, 1968.

What's a Cruller?

Early in the first Kansas sequence of *The Wizard of Oz*, Aunt Em mildly berates her farmhands for general foolishness and then offers them a snack. "Have some crullers," she commands, thrusting a piled plate in the workers' direction. Hunk (Ray Bolger) is particularly enthusiastic. Naturally enough, King Vidor didn't shoot an insert close-up of the crullers because he had no need to. In this scene, the food is simply a device—a way to alter the rhythm of the narrative, add a bit of dialogue and visual interest, and suggest the simple, homespun quality of Kansas farm life.

Well, that's great, but what's a cruller?

Simply, it's a doughy fried treat. The Krispy Kreme cruller, for instance, is round and has a hole in the middle, like a traditional doughnut (in keeping with the shape of other Krispy Kreme products), but the dough is heavily ridged and corkscrewed, as if the whole concoction had been twisted before frying. To this writer's eye, the contours of the KK cruller suggest the thick, heavy treads of an earthmover tire. And indeed, urbandictionary.com defines "cruller" as a "tractor-tire-shaped donut."

Deeper investigation reveals that the traditional American cruller, unlike the round Krispy Kreme type, is a twisted oblong of dough. We glimpse that sort of shape on Aunt Em's plate. The word *cruller* is an Americanization of various forms of the Dutch *krulle* (circa 1800), which, as *krullen*, means "to curl." A more precise etymology, also from the Dutch, is *krulle-koken*, a rolled cake.

The dough is made from water, butter, sugar, salt, flour, and eggs—all of which would have been available in Aunt Em's kitchen. Modern recipes suggest that the shaped dough be fried in vegetable oil, but it's a virtual certainty that Aunt Em fried hers in artery-clogging lard.

Although frosted glazes are popular on modern crullers, Aunt Em eschewed that fancy-Dan sort of thing, so her crullers had less sugar than today's examples. But whatever the finer recipe points, a cruller has virtually no food value. It's mostly sugar, fat, cholesterol, sodium, and carbs—all good stuff for fellows that work outdoors and need quick infusions of energy. So Em wasn't being particularly kind when she brought out those crullers; she was giving her shiftless farmhands a carbohydrate power shot so that they'd work harder and longer.

And just maybe have enough energy to fight a twister.

Principal photography of *The Wizard of Oz* wrapped on March 16, 1939, when Victor Fleming was already directing *Gone With the Wind*. On that day, Vidor shot a few moments with Margaret Hamilton as Miss Gulch, with Frank Morgan as Prof. Marvel, Judy Garland's "Over the Rainbow," and assorted retakes. Including pre-production, MGM's *The Wizard of Oz* had already been an active project for thirteen months. Pickups, inserts, and reshoots would be shot, off and on, for a few months more. Victor Fleming and MGM staff editor Blanche Sewell worked to assemble a rough cut even as recording of various songs and portions of the score continued. Editing, sound effects, and many other technical duties would be largely completed in just three months, in time for the first sneak preview in June. Work would continue after that, until the picture's official release in August.

To commemorate the end of the shoot, Ray Bolger gave Judy a handsome edition of *The Raven*, by her favorite poet, Edgar Allan Poe. Days after finishing, Judy Garland left Hollywood for a five-week personal appearance tour. Very shortly after that, on April 30, she was in rehearsals for her next picture, *Babes in Arms*, and reported to the set on May 12, for the start of shooting.

Margaret Hamilton and Billie Burke, both of whom had moved on to other projects, were called back for pickup shots in early May 1939. Other retakes were done sporadically until the end of June.

On June 30, 1939, Judy had to leave the *Babes in Arms* set to do one final bit of work on *Oz* consisting of retakes, including scenes with Ray Bolger, directed by King Vidor. Prior to that, in early May, Billie Burke was called back for pickups, possibly reaction shots.

During April through July, varying numbers of musicians and background vocalists participated in ten recording sessions supervised by Herbert Stothart and George Stoll.

April 12–13 were devoted to the final Munchkin voice tracks. These were done by the St. Joseph Choir and directed by Roger Wagner. Simultaneously, Herbert Stothart's ambitious underscore continued to be recorded. As an imaginative, subliminal joke, Stothart inserted snippets and cues from well-known melodies into his music (much in the manner of Warner Bros. cartoon composer Carl Stalling). In the Kansas sequences, bits of Robert Schumann's sprightly "Happy Farmer" (from the composer's 1848 *Album für die Jugend*) can be heard in the Kansas sequences; and melodies from a 19th-century William Gooch–Harry Birch song, "Reuben and Rachel," are used beneath the cyclone. Dorothy and the Scarecrow's misadventure with the apple trees inspired Stothart to incorporate some of "In the Shade of the Old Apple Tree," a sweetly lovelorn 1905 tune by Egbert Van Alstyne and Harry Williams. Toto's escape from the Witch's castle is enlivened by a few bars of Felix Mendelssohn's Scherzo in E Minor, a solo piano piece from 1829. A bit later, portions of Modest Mussorgsky's imperious and foreboding *Night on Bald Mountain* (which Walt Disney would use to great effect a year later in *Fantasia*) underline Dorothy's rescue.

The Edit

An editor works with film footage to give it the shape, rhythm, emphasis, and dramatic qualities desired by the director. In Hollywood's classic era, few directors had the juice that would allow them to edit their pictures, but Victor Fleming did. Even as he was directing *Gone With the Wind* in March 1939, he was also at work with MGM editor Blanche Sewell at night, cutting *The Wizard of Oz*. Principal photography was already in hand, and the final effects footage was ready for Fleming and Sewell around April 1. The two of them, and Sewell's supervisor, Margaret Booth, worked toward Fleming's first goal, a two-hour rough cut.

Sewell, Booth, and Fleming weren't merciless in their treatment of the *Oz* footage, but Fleming, in particular, was determined to make the picture as lean as possible. The initial rough cut topped two hours at a time when most important studio films were between 90 and 100 minutes. (Imagine, then, the audacity of David O. Selznick, whose *Gone With the Wind* clocked in at 222 minutes—plus overture and intermission.)

Fleming asked for some significant cuts:

- An extended version of "If I Only Had a Brain," with an especially hyperactive Ray Bolger.
- The Emerald City celebration for Dorothy and her friends, to "Ding! Dong! The Witch Is Dead." Some of this footage appears in one of the *Oz* trailers, and music from the sequence was preserved on a Decca children's audio release.
- Dorothy's mournful reprise of "Over the Rainbow," when she's held captive in the Witch's castle.
- The entire "Jitterbug" sequence, including the song, and Dorothy trying to deal with grabby "Jitter Trees" (the Jitterbug itself was cartoon animation).
- The so-called "renovation sequence," when Dorothy and her friends return to the Emerald City with the Witch's broomstick.

General reaction to *Oz* among studio executives was enthusiastic, and many of them predicted a long life for the film. Margaret Hamilton, a working actress who had seen numberless movies come and go, thought that was an absurd notion. She was particularly concerned that the "Jitterbug" sequence would date the movie, because the tune played off of a then-popular dance craze that would go out of fashion sooner rather than later. Various studio executives agreed with that, but Victor Fleming, whose instincts were usually top-notch, liked the sequence and wanted to keep it. In the end, associate producer Arthur Freed agreed with the executive staff, and "The Jitterbug" was dumped. Silent, color 16mm footage shot on-set by Harold Arlen is the only visual record of "The Jitterbug" that remains. (This footage has been widely seen in documentaries and as a DVD "extra.") However, the original-soundtrack version of the tune, which Judy recorded at MGM on October 6, 1938, before the *Oz* shoot began, has survived, as well as various record- and LP-only "Jitterbug" recordings Garland made later. Because the Jitterbug was to be an animated cartoon, he's not visible in Arlen's footage, but the agitated jumping around of Dorothy and her friends suggests that the bug was designed to be a major pest.

Another cut that Fleming did not ask for was Dorothy's barnyard rendition of "Over the Rainbow." For years afterward, Yip Harburg claimed that the order to kill the sequence had indeed come from Fleming, and with such vehemence on Fleming's part that producer Mervyn LeRoy was cowed into going along. What really happened is that various MGM executives, feeling compelled to justify their salaries by throwing out their opinions, said that the song slowed the story and killed the film's pace. Louis Mayer heard this assessment often enough to finally agree. Not unexpectedly, King Vidor and Arlen & Harburg were dismayed. Fleming, too, was convinced that to cut the song would be a dreadful mistake. In the end, pressure brought to bear by LeRoy and Freed convinced Mayer to reinstate the sequence.

Oz was at last whittled to 101 minutes. In that form, it has about 650 edits; a typical present-day movie of similar length has 2,000 or more. That says something about diminished attention spans (the more cuts, the more lively a film seems to be), but says more about Fleming and Sewell's judgment. Fleming had dealt with *Oz* day after day, for months, but despite his closeness to the material, he wasn't afraid to cut. And Sewell had good instincts: by 1939 she'd already cut about forty pictures, including a seminal prison drama, *The Big House* (1930), and one of Fleming's best movies, *Red Dust* (1932). She had an aggressive storytelling sense that was just as favorable to performances and characterizations as to purely visual elements. (Sewell worked at MGM until the end of her life; when she died in 1949, she was just fifty years old.)

15

The Miracle Wonderland Carnival Company

The MGM Publicity Machine

MGM's publicity department was located on the studio's Lot 1. The department promoted new and upcoming releases by working with newspapers, magazines, radio, and other media; and by arranging product tie-ins calculated to benefit MGM and boost sales of, say, Lucky Strike cigarettes. The department was particularly interested in cultivating relationships with anybody who could help the studio sell its product, or anybody who had access to a person that could do that. Schmoozing, flattery, swaps, payoffs, threats, and other cajolery were directed to newspaper reporters and columnists, magazine editors and prominent feature writers, authors, radio executives, advertising account execs, chambers of commerce, the Rotary, politicians, district attorneys, judges, notables in popular fields other than show business, a hero Eagle Scout—anyone who might bring something to the table.

The department also did damage control, working to protect the studio's reputation by shielding wayward stars from bad press and even prison. Drunkenness, car wrecks, accidental homicide, adultery, out-of-wedlock children, bothersome ex-spouses and lovers, police records, wife-beating, and bad trouble with siblings and other family members could be expertly covered up. Any hints of same-sex romance or interracial relations brought the hammer down.

MGM publicity intruded into stars' personal lives in other ways, too, arranging "romantic" dates to public places and even suggesting—or suggesting against—marriage. Having children was almost never a good idea, and MGM publicity staffers helped married stars understand that. Don't drink too much, find a better class of friends, and for god's sake lose some weight.

Contract players were tutored in how to comport themselves during interviews, especially with powerful figures like gossip columnist Walter Winchell and Hollywood gossips Hedda Hopper and the Gorgon-like Louella Parsons.

Howard Strickling directed MGM publicity, and another powerful executive, Howard Dietz, was responsible for advertising. As you might imagine, they had their hands full with many things, but above all, they were clever salesmen. For *Oz*, as with any other release, Strickling and Dietz made sure that people across America knew the film was coming. They blanketed the nation, paying particular attention to major urban areas, where more and bigger theaters were located. Publicity went to where the people were, so although the hardies in Montana had an inkling of *The Wizard of Oz*, folks in New York and Los Angeles and Cleveland and other big cities knew a lot more.

"Selling" a movie was simpler in 1939 than today and more challenging, too. Studio publicity wasn't easy, but it was reasonably straightforward. Trailers were cut together and sent out to captive audiences in MGM-owned theaters and indie houses. The department cooked up bogus "news items" and behind-the-scenes stuff for insertion into newsreels. For other exposure, Strickling and Dietz concentrated on print media and radio. Their department placed trade ads in *Boxoffice* and similar trade publications, hoping to excite the interest of exhibitors. Because most households took a morning and an evening newspaper in those days, and bought or subscribed to many magazines, the studio churned out print ads and encouraged feature stories. Stories that ran in some of the movie-fan magazines were actually written by publicity people and bylined with the names of stars or others who had had nothing to do with the piece. And because stars' lives were protected and proscribed, marquee players could be safely sent on the road to do personal-appearance tours, big-city stage shows, charity drives—many things.

On the other hand, because there was no commercial TV or cable, no Internet or streaming, no Twitter or Facebook, there were only modest opportunities to create what we now call buzz. Magazine stories and newspaper items were essentially passive. Radio was good, and it was heard coast to coast, but it wasn't visual, so the excitement quotient was limited. Personal appearances stimulated the public, but only in areas relatively close to the venues. Because of all of that,

Howard Dietz was a successful songwriter as well as the chief of advertising at MGM. Among the studio's executives, Dietz was one of the four most powerful.

Strickling and Dietz had to time their campaigns carefully and choose their forums well. Every movie was unique, so no two campaigns were precisely alike.

In contrast to the aggressive buildup given *Gone With the Wind* (a book that fueled fan excitement for a film adaptation the moment it was published in 1936), MGM's promotion of *The Wizard of Oz* was managed very closely. Dribs of information and publicity were released while the picture was being shot, and then a great deal as the release date(s) approached, and for a period thereafter. Information fed to *The Hollywood Reporter* and other trade press might be picked up by astute hometown dailies, and that would have been acceptable—even

As the release date neared, MGM's publicity department issued intriguing still photos. This good-looking example (probably shot by studio photographer Clarence Bull) spells D-A-N-G-E-R.

desirable—because the information was scant and gave away very little about the film's content.

Oz promotion was handled jointly by the studio's Hollywood and New York publicity offices. Strickling and Dietz supervised both offices and became aggravated when anticipated release dates came and went as the shoot dragged on. A planned Christmas 1938 release was never realistic. Easter 1939 was more reasonable, except that as things developed, principal photography didn't wrap until March 16, 1939. (Easter Sunday fell on April 9 in 1939, and pickup shots for *Oz* were underway until the end of June.)

When Easter 1939 had still seemed realistic, publicity arranged for *The Wizard of Oz* to have a prominent presence in the January 1, 1939, Tournament of Roses Parade in Pasadena. Judy Garland's stand-in, Bobbie Koshay, rode an elaborate float (co-sponsored by Culver City and MGM) with Charley Becker, Karl Slover, and two more Munchkin players; Stafford Campbell (Ray Bolger's stand-in) as the Scarecrow; Harry Master (Jack Haley's stand-in) as the Tin Woodman; and Pat Moran (Bert Lahr's stand-in) as the Cowardly Lion. The event was guaranteed to score newspaper, magazine, and newsreel coverage— what a shame that the movie wouldn't go into wide release for nearly another eight months.

MGM released teaser stories about a "Munchkinland" exhibit planned for the 1939 New York World's Fair. Because the fair was scheduled to open in April, the timing seems to have been fixed to an Easter release. Strickling and Dietz had been encouraged to do the exhibit because of something similar, Stanley R. Graham and Nate Eagle's "Midget Village" at the 1933 Century of Progress International Exposition of Chicago aka the Chicago World's Fair. The "village" was good-natured, exploitative novelty entertainment designed for Depression-weary Americans that might be diverted by a midget barbershop, a midget wedding, a midget hula dance, even midgets playing craps—until the game was broken up by midget cops.

Built as a self-contained town where the performers actually resided, Midget Village was so popular that it was quadrupled in size and renamed Midget City for the Chicago fair's 1934 season. In "City" guise, the exhibit had a mayor, a city council, a church, and other everyday institutions. The program book noted that, "Every detail of midget life is faithfully carried out for the entertainment of the visitor."

Promoters Graham and Eagle re-created their Midget City at the 1935 California Pacific International Exposition, in San Diego. This attraction, much closer to Hollywood than Chicago, further intrigued MGM.

Whether MGM honestly wanted to mount a 1939 New York Munchkinland exhibit is unknown. If the studio were serious, it was aced out by Morris Gest, a theatrical producer who brought his Little Miracle Town to the '39 World's Fair. The official Little Miracle Town program book touted "the world's greatest midget artistes." All had been assembled, under subcontract to Gest, by British impresario Fred Roper, who was well known in the UK and on the Continent for his "Wonder Midgets."

Although less elaborate than the Graham and Eagle attraction, the Gest-Roper Little Miracle Town nevertheless featured more than sixty of Roper's international cast of midgets (predominantly German). They played their parts in a midget-sized castle (with a midget guard of honor), a midget "Honeymoon House" (with midget newlyweds), stables (with miniature horses), midget ping-pong exhibitions, a midget stage show, and many other attractions. The program book claimed that the "British midgets" dressed each day for tea.

When MGM conceived the Rose Parade float and the World's Fair notion, *The Wizard of Oz* was to be limited to major theaters in big cities, with advance-ticket admission set at "road-show" prices. The picture would be screened only twice a day. A typical adult theater admission in 1939 was twenty-five cents (about $3.95 in inflation-adjusted dollars); a child got in for ten or fifteen cents. Under the road-show plan, adult admission to *The Wizard of Oz* would be set at a dollar, and even children wouldn't be admitted for less than fifty cents.

Road-show saturation was usually achieved after about six months. At that juncture, *Oz* would open in second-tier metropolitan theaters. The advance-ticket model would be abandoned and admission prices cut by half. When that pricing ran its course, the film would open wide at small-town and neighborhood theaters, with admissions set at "popular prices."

The road-show idea was abandoned, partly because a big MGM release from 1938, *Marie Antoinette*, hadn't done well at all with the setup.

When general release was finally achieved on August 25, 1939, *The Wizard of Oz* played on four hundred screens (a very wide rollout for the time) at regular prices. Strickling and Dietz arranged for splashy newspaper and newsreel coverage of the August 15 Hollywood premiere, and pushed follow-on newspaper articles and Sunday-supplement rotogravure features. Comic-strip sections about *Oz* also appeared in Sunday papers around the country.

What's Playing? Other Movie Choices During August–September 1939

During this especially robust time in the life of the studio system, movies cycled in and out of theaters (particularly smaller "nabe" houses) at least twice a week. The major studios functioned like assembly lines, and that there was *not* a glut of product was due mainly to careful control of exhibition by MGM and the other vertically integrated studios. Although *The Wizard of Oz* was guaranteed lengthy playdates at large, first-run houses owned by MGM's parent company, it certainly wasn't the only movie searching for an audience in the late summer of 1939. Film historian Mike Cline has compiled a list of movies that opened at various theaters in Rowan County, North Carolina, during a span of eighty years. His information about titles and playdates at the Capitol, Victory, State, and Spencer theaters for August and September 1939 is usefully representative of the competitive environment *Oz* found itself in by the time the picture had made its way to small theaters.

During August and September, only one theater in the county, the Capitol, had *The Wizard of Oz*, which opened there on Thursday, August 31. But suppose Dad or Sis was disinclined to go to *Oz*. Well, at the nearby Victory, a Wallace Beery vehicle, *Sergeant Madden*, also opened on the 31st. The same day brought *Fisherman's Wharf*, with Henry Armetta and child star Bobby Breen, to the State; while the Spencer ran two pictures on August 30–31, *Boy Slaves* and a Bing Crosby musical comedy, *East Side of Heaven*.

Oz continued at the Capitol for September 1–2. (The theater was closed on Sunday the 3rd, and when it opened again on the 4th, the new feature was *When Tomorrow Comes*, with Charles Boyer and Irene Dunne.) Meanwhile, a Charles Starrett western, *Riders of Black River*, did the September 1–2 frame at the Victory; it was accompanied by installments from two serials, *Buck Rogers* and *Daredevils of the Red Circle*.

September 1–2 at the State brought Conn Pictures's *Swing It, Professor*, a minor 1937 musical comedy on a belated second run (probably on a per-screen basis rather than as a general re-release), plus a chapter of *The Oregon Trail*, with Johnny Mack Brown. Over at the Spencer during September 1–2, Errol Flynn and Bette Davis starred in *The Sisters* (1938), doubling with a new Gene Autry western, *Blue Montana Skies*.

Later, on November 20–21, the Victory had its turn with *The Wizard of Oz*; and the Spencer showed it during December 4–5. Competing pictures in the county during these dates: *The Adventures of Sherlock Holmes*; Greta Garbo in *Ninotchka*; Claude Rains and John Garfield in *Daughters Courageous*, paired with Tom Neal in *They All Come Out*; Joe E. Brown in *$1000 a Touchdown*; Nelson Eddy and Jeanette MacDonald in *Rose Marie* (1936); and bandleader Kay Kyser in *That's Right—You're Wrong*.

Besides renting from MGM and the aforementioned Conn Pictures, the Rowan County theaters booked pictures from RKO, Warner Bros., Paramount, Columbia, Republic, Sol Lesser/RKO, and Universal during the local runs of *The Wizard of Oz*. So not only was *Oz* looking at competition from films in a wide variety of genres at the neighborhood level, but from nearly every studio in Hollywood. Flagship theaters in big cities could produce flashy box-office numbers, but a great deal of a given picture's revenue came from the hinterlands, where the movie played for a day here, two or three days there, quietly earning, and pleasing audiences that no studio dared ignore.

In Print

The specific nature of each piece of *Oz* print publicity was carefully matched to the publication in which it would appear. Material provided to *Photoplay* and other fan magazines naturally emphasized the stars and their private lives, and a bit of behind-the-scene information, too. The major general-interest

Read **WIZARD OF OZ — $3,000,000 SCREEN HIT!**

SCREEN Romances

AUGUST
25¢
NOW
10¢

EVERY STORY A MOVIE HIT

THE OLD MAID · *Starring* BETTE DAVIS, MIRIAM HOPKINS *and* GEORGE BRENT
CONFESSIONS OF A NAZI SPY — *With* AN ALL-STAR CAST
GOOD GIRLS GO TO PARIS — *Starring* JOAN BLONDELL *and* MELVYN DOUGLAS

The August 1939 issue of *Screen Romances* featured a five-page narrative synopsis of *Oz*, illustrated with sepia-toned stills. The cover art is the work of fan-magazine stalwart F. Earl Christy.

magazines were *LIFE, Look, The Saturday Evening Post, Liberty,* and *Cosmopolitan.* (The July 17, 1939, issue of *LIFE* magazine carried a two-page color spread advertising the movie.) Publicity and advertisements sent to those publications was broad in nature and likely to tie in to the interests of both men and women.

Good Housekeeping, McCall's, Family Circle, and *Harper's Bazaar* were among the major women's magazines. It was assumed that those readers would be interested in stories about Judy Garland and the film's songs and score. Advertisements for products that tied into *Oz* were common across the board, but were especially domestic, and frequently meal-oriented (Jell-O, for instance), in the women's magazines.

Trade columnists usually got to the truth of what was going on inside all those elaborately dressed sound stages, but those that catered to the public happily accepted MGM publicity handouts with updated *Oz* "news." Many of these anecdotes were embellished reality; others were apocryphal—a publicist's fancy. In her December 19, 1938, column for the Hearst newspaper chain, Louella Parsons claimed that MGM star Greta Garbo appeared on the *Oz* set one day to "give the pint-sized Yvonne [Moray] the once-over." According to Parsons, Garbo had heard that the tiny Moray was her double, in miniature. Walter Winchell, Louella Parsons, Ed Sullivan, and writers of other syndicated columns were assiduously fed items.

Stories manufactured by the studio were passed to movie-fan magazines, which had enormous influence in those days before *Entertainment Weekly*, TMZ, and the 24-hour celebrity news cycle. By establishing symbiotic relationships with the studios, movie magazines were able to keep fans informed about upcoming movies and the lives of the stars. In return for positive coverage of stars (often with a wholesomely domestic slant) and the occasional front cover, fan mags were supplied with photographs (including carefully negotiated "exclusives"), studio-approved news, and stars willing to sit for interviews. All of that, plus studio-managed "making of" stories and similar *Wizard of Oz* promotion disguised as editorial content, were published in *Movie Mirror, Screen Guide, Movie Story, Photoplay, Motion Picture*, and other popular titles.

Much of the material devised by Strickling and his subcontractors was frankly erroneous. One handout claimed the film had "a cast of 9200" and "3210 costumes," when the actual numbers were about 600 and fewer than a thousand, respectively. Another publicity piece claimed that the "hundreds of midgets who play the Munchkins were gathered from 42 cities in 29 states." Well, most came from the East Coast, and the story made no mention at all of the European origins of many Munchkins.

Besides magazines and gossip columns, *Oz* was promoted in a pair of syndicated newspaper-cartoon panels: Wiley Padan's square-shaped *It's True!* (which, coincidentally enough, focused exclusively on MGM) and *Seein' Stars*, a handsome horizontal panel by radio personality/sports cartoonist Feg (Frederic) Murray. (*Seein' Stars* wasn't exclusively beholden to any one studio and covered them all, even lowly Republic.) These panels offered tidbits of *Oz* trivia timed to coincide with the picture's release. Murray's October 29, 1939, panel, for instance, includes a small portrait of Frank Morgan and a claim that the Wizard once purchased an oil well when he was kidded about being an actor and not a businessman. The well, according to Murray, turned into "a gusher." (Yes, people really were supposed to be fascinated with this kind of stuff.)

Other cartoonists, either on staff at MGM or contractors hired by Strickling's publicity department, were called upon to work in the Padan and Murray styles (which frankly resembled Robert Ripley's) on panel-strip magazine advertisements.

Because a great proportion of Americans kept pianos for home entertainment, sheet music was a booming publishing specialty. MGM saw to it that various issues of *Oz* sheet music and lyrics were available.

Very little pre-release promotional material pictured the Wicked Witch of the West, even incidentally. MGM felt that Margaret Hamilton's frightening scowl would deter parents from taking their children to see the movie. A notable exception was a shot of the long-haired Witch (from the Richard Thorpe shoot) that was published in the September 1939 issue of *Screen Guide*. Print promos and advertising emphasized the ensemble cast, with countless photo variations with Garland, Bolger, Haley, and Lahr. Somewhat fewer images added Frank Morgan to the mix, Judy was pictured alone in product tie-in ads, and the MGM still photographer took many portraits of her as Dorothy. But she was most often pictured with her co-stars.

Billboards were another form of print advertising that was employed to sell *Oz*. These hard-to-miss signs stood near roadways or were erected on the sides of tall buildings. They were attention grabbers that reached thousands of people in New York, Los Angeles, Chicago, and other big cities.

Kodachrome

In order to make the *Oz* color experience complete, many of the publicity photos taken on-set and in posed settings were shot in Kodachrome, Eastman Kodak's revolutionary color film. It had been developed as movie film in the mid-1920s, eventually added a still-photo application, and became commercially available in 1935. In promotional material, Eastman Kodak noted Kodachrome's thinness, despite five layers of color emulsion. The most obvious appeal of Kodachrome was the brilliance of the colors it captured, particularly in the eye-catching red range. Like three-strip Technicolor, Kodachrome provided images more vivid than life. *National Geographic* magazine gave the film to its photographers almost immediately and said later that Kodachrome "changed the way we document the world."

During America's involvement in World War II, Kodachrome photos brought startling reality to home-front and battle images. That sort of uber-verisimilitude was paradoxically ideal to sell the fantasy elements of *The Wizard of Oz*. People who saw the publicity photos in magazines and Sunday supplements were set up to unconsciously accept the reality of MGM's fantasy musical.

Kodak's alternative to Kodachrome, Ektachrome, was introduced in the early 1940s. It gave good color and could be processed in home labs by amateurs—something that wasn't possible to do with Kodachrome. Ektachrome also was faster than Kodachrome, which meant it functioned well in low light. Unfortunately, Ektachrome prints aren't durable and have a tendency to fade and warp over time. Kodachrome prints, on the other hand, including those shot for *Oz* publicity, retain their brilliance. Eastman Kodak discontinued production of Kodachrome film in 2009, by which time only one lab was certified to process the film in the United States.

Promoting Oz on the Radio

Radio spots, and guest appearances by *Oz* stars on regularly scheduled radio shows, brought news of the movie into America's living rooms. Radio was still the dominant form of home entertainment, and exposure on the airwaves was priceless to anyone with something to sell.

When Howard Strickling and his staff got to work, one highlight of June 1939 was a radio reading of the first Baum book, performed by Fred Stone, who had played the Scarecrow in the 1903 Broadway production of *The Wizard of Oz*.

Days on the *Oz* set were long, and frequent nighttime radio appearances made them even longer for Judy. The day's shoot complete, the young star hurried to the appropriate CBS or NBC studio for rehearsals and did final broadcasts live. Just as today's film stars appear on television chat shows to talk up their latest releases, Judy was sent out to do *Oz* cross-promotion on the radio. She sang and did sketches on these programs, appearing on some of the shows more than once. For example, as a "regular," she did fifteen episodes (and rehearsals) of *The Pepsodent Show*, with Bob Hope, in 1939.

Sometimes, Judy was the show's featured guest. In other instances, she was one of numerous celebrities that took the mic. During the 1938–39 *Oz* shoot, Judy's radio co-stars included Joan Crawford, Jack Benny, Robert Taylor, and Mickey Rooney; Cary Grant, Myrna Loy, and Maureen O'Sullivan; plus some of her companions from *Oz*: Bert Lahr, Ray Bolger, Frank Morgan, and Billie Burke.

None of Judy's 1938 radio work was *Oz*-specific, though the film was mentioned in the chitchat that preceded songs and sketches. The publicity push increased in 1939, with appearances by Judy that coincided with the *Oz* shoot and guest shots that came during the spring and summer, after the shoot had been completed. Two of Judy's 1939 radio broadcasts revolved around *Oz*: the June 29 airing of *Good News of 1939* ("Behind the Scenes at the Making of *The Wizard of Oz*") and the September 10 episode of *Maxwell House Coffee Time* (when the movie had been in theaters a bit longer than two weeks).

Ray Bolger and Bert Lahr joined Judy as guests on the *Good News* broadcast; Yip Harburg was on-mic, too, as well as an unidentified actor who impersonated *Oz* producer Mervyn LeRoy. Frank Morgan and Fanny Brice (who was at one time considered for a role in *Oz* as a witch) were *Good News* regulars. Popular film actor Robert Young acted as host and had the opportunity to introduce veteran Scarecrow actor Fred Stone to Bolger.

In a sketch, Morgan learns that he's been cast as the Wizard. Brice did her weekly Baby Snooks sketch with her *Good News* partner, actor Hanley Stafford (as Snooks's perpetually irritated father). Snooks—innocently obtuse, as always—is curious about *The Wizard of Oz*, and Daddy struggles to explain it to her.

Bert Lahr was the focus of a sketch in which he pretended to rehearse. In another sketch, Bobby Connolly "rehearsed" the Munchkin players.

Portions of the film's Munchkinland sequence were re-created. Judy and others engaged in a re-creation of studio-approved on-set chatter, with actor Robert Young, who was the show's emcee, taking the Jack Haley/Tin Woodman part. Backed by the Meredith Willson orchestra and chorus, Judy sang "Over the Rainbow" and Lahr performed "If I Were King of the Forest." (Willson later found fame as the creator of a Broadway smash, *The Music Man*.)

This June 29 installment of *Good News of 1939* was Judy's first radio performance of "Over the Rainbow." This is when millions of Americans heard the song for the first time. Not long after this broadcast, the song went to number one on the national Hit Parade that tracked record sales and jukebox plays. (The broadcast was issued on CD by Jass Records in 1991, under the title *Behind the Scenes at the Making of The Wizard of Oz*.)

So powerful was MGM and its parent, Loew's Inc., that it produced and distributed its own radio program, *Leo Is on the Air*. The program adapted screenplays to suit its fifteen-minute running time, with an announcer setting up various scenes that were represented by soundtrack dialogue clips. Songs and other soundtrack music were prominently featured. (A similar but far more ambitious radio show, CBS's *Lux Radio Theatre,* ran for an hour and did condensed reenactments of popular movies, usually with at least one or two members of the original casts reprising their roles.)

MGM provided *Leo* to radio stations in the form of sixteen-inch audio discs. Each disc was labeled "For Sustaining Program Only. Not to be played on a sponsored program other than a program sponsored by a theater in which Metro-Goldwyn-Mayer pictures appear. Please destroy after use." (A sustained radio show had no sponsor, and was paid for by the network.) Because some stations ignored the request to destroy, some of the *Oz* broadcast discs have survived. The audio runs 12:53 and has been available since 1991 as part of various *Wizard of Oz* home-video sets and on bootleg CDs and mp3 files. Completists value the Leo broadcast because it includes an alternate take of Judy Garland's "Over the Rainbow" vocal.

A newspaper sports cartoonist named Robert Ripley wrote and drew his first *Believe It or Not* panel in 1918. That first cartoon was sports oriented, but when Ripley broadened his view, *Believe It or Not* became a wildly popular newspaper feature. At its peak in the late 1930s, the panel was syndicated to more than three hundred papers around the globe; Ripley historian Jack French estimates a weekly readership of eighty million. Following success on the lecture and personal appearance circuits, and simultaneous with the beginning of a 1930–31 run of *Believe It or Not* movie shorts for Warner Vitaphone, Ripley was offered his own NBC radio show in 1930. Airing mainly on NBC's Blue network, *Believe It or Not* was broadcast from 1930–32 and 1934–38. The program moved to CBS radio early in 1939. Although a stiff and minimally trained speaker, Ripley brought enthusiasm and charm to his duties as host to dramatized tales of freaks and oddities. But there was less of that than during the NBC years. CBS insisted on interludes of music and other traditional entertainment, so a typical broadcast might include a singer or a comic. Topicality was also important, so the September 22, 1939, radio broadcast of *Believe It or Not,* which promoted the upcoming *Oz* movie, was no shocker. It was a clear plug, and audiences didn't mind. Besides chatter about the movie, the show had a special guest, Maud Baum, widow of *Oz* creator L. Frank Baum.

During the broadcast, Maud Baum revealed that Frank's mother, Cynthia Stanton Baum, encouraged Frank to write and that without her, "there might never have been *The Wizard of Oz.*"

Besides the programs mentioned above, Judy made appearances on the following radio shows during the *Oz* shoot, post-production, and exhibition: *America Calling, Gulf Screen Guild Theater, Council of Stars, Good News of 1938, Tune Up Time, The Fred Waring Show, Mobilization for Human Needs, National Redemption Movement Program, Leo Is on the Air, Premiere of Marie Antoinette,* and *The Rinso Program.*

Oz at the Movies

Newsreel coverage of *The Wizard of Oz* unspooled at every Loew's theater in the country, and at many others, as well. Although spurious as news items, the vignettes were agreeable light-feature stuff that took viewers onto the MGM lot and behind the scenes; a few words from this star or that were dropped in to excite more interest. During the 1930s, MGM distributed News of the Day (formerly Hearst-Metrotone News), which gave its theaters a newsreel voice.

Generally, though, newsreel units gave most of their attention to hard news, bringing a vivid eyewitness feel to stories that audiences had already heard about on the radio or read about in the newspapers. Newsreel units had film crews on staff, and a small army of stringers, that roamed the world in search of dramatic footage. Still, there was usually room for fluff. Units affiliated with studios other than MGM, such as Fox Movietone News, Universal Newsreel, Pathé News (which was distributed by RKO), and Paramount News, were naturally not in the habit of promoting rivals' product. The leading independent newsreel outfit, The March of Time, was willing to devote thirty seconds or a minute to any studio's new-movie promotion disguised as news.

Tie-ins

Today we take for granted that movies targeting young audiences will have product tie-ins. In 1939, the practice was new and very novel. Universal had done some publishing cross-promotion of its horror films earlier in the '30s, but when MGM decided to license tie-ins to *The Wizard of Oz*, the studio took its cue from Disney, which had placed a wealth of *Snow White* products on shelves in 1937.

A 1939 magazine ad cross-promoted the movie and the New York World's Fair with the words, 'The Wizard of Oz' is a World's Fair in itself. A World's Fair in Technicolor."

Toys were a natural marketing hookup. Manufacturers issued dolls, bisque figurines, masks (in paper, gauze, and linen), and *Oz*-illustrated drinking glasses. Parents could also treat their children to *Oz* costumes, soap figurines, jewelry, card games, and board games. And in a marketing scheme calculated to make parents happy because the kids might actually keep their rooms clean, Bissell issued the "Wizard" sweeper, a kid-sized push-push with a base of pressed steel and wood sides, with rubber wheels. The base was red and stamped in yellow with simple *Wizard of Oz* cartoon caricatures. The wood handle measured twenty-eight inches.

Exhibitors were encouraged to stir up *Oz* fever in anticipation of the picture's scheduled opening on their screens. Local theaters sponsored coloring contests, costume parties, even mind readers.

Oz-related publishing for kids took off, bringing to market watercolor books, kiddie adaptations of the first Baum novel, picture books, valentines, and stationery. Bobbs-Merrill, the longtime publisher of the Baum novels, reissued the first book as a special movie edition (commonly called the Photoplay Edition), with photo-illustrated endpapers. A banner beneath the title (above a colorful jacket painting done in the style of original *Oz* artist W. W. Denslow) reads, "THE ONLY EDITION CONTAINING THE COMPLETE ORIGINAL TEXT ON WHICH THE FAMOUS METRO-GOLDWYN-MAYER MOVIE IS BASED."

Movie tie-in editions were published in Great Britain, and editions printed in languages other than English were distributed in Spain, Mexico, Portugal, Brazil, Denmark, and Sweden.

Along the way, *The Wizard of Oz* was promoted by tie-ins to some unlikely products. One multiple-column color advert included *Oz* trivia, pictures of the principals, and a plug for pectin, which the ad said was essential to effective jelly making. Via word balloon, Judy/Dorothy advised, "*ANYBODY* CAN BE A WIZARD AT JELLY-MAKING!"

Recordings that had been pressed for distribution to record stores and radio stations were strictly embargoed. The Brunswick label, however, jumped the gun when it issued the Larry Clinton band doing "Over the Rainbow" and "The Jitterbug" in April 1939. The record was quickly withdrawn after Brunswick was sobered up by MGM's promise of litigation if it were not.

A Nod from Mervyn

On a page from the August 21, 1939, *Hollywood Reporter*, Mervyn LeRoy promoted *Oz* to the trade and to exhibitors, and implicitly acknowledged himself, by thanking "all the Wizards who made *The Wizard of Oz* possible." As promotion, the ad wasn't bad; in industry terms, it was a nice gesture because it gave the names of many people, attached to numerous MGM departments, who had gone unnamed in the film's credits.

Wizard of Oz "Sell" Lines

In order to promote *The Wizard of Oz*, MGM publicists unlocked the adjectives box and came up with breathless sell copy for posters, industry trade ads, and magazine adverts—all intended to excite exhibitors and lure audiences to theaters.

In that late-Depression period of real-life disappointments, MGM was careful to avoid revealing that *The Wizard of Oz* was a fantasy. *Snow White*'s success aside, movie audiences had little tolerance for the fantastic, so the publicity copy emphasized the film's color, spectacle, presumed stage origins, and music.

Here are some of the most vivid *Oz* printed sell lines (similar language was part of the film's trailers), with original use of capital letters and punctuation:

- Metro-Goldwyn-Mayer's WONDER SHOW OF SHOWS!
- It's METRO-GOLDWYN-MAYER'S TECHNICOLOR TRIUMPH!
- Gaiety! Glory! Glamour!
- MAGNIFICENT IN ITS BRILLIANT TECHNICOLOR SPLENDOR!
- BIGGEST SENSATION Since "SNOW WHITE"!
- THE MIGHTY MIRACLE SHOW THAT IS THE TALK OF AMERICA!
- . . . Movieland's triumph of 1939.
- AMAZING SIGHTS TO SEE!
- SCREEN'S MOST SPECTACULAR MUSICAL!
- Every moment different, thrilling! . . . a new experience at the movies!
- GREATEST MAGIC FILM EVER TO BE MADE!

Some of MGM's publicity flacks were at their best in long-form copy:

- A musical wonder show so spectacular that it cost as much as *ten* average good pictures!
- THOUSANDS OF LIVING ACTORS IN A SENSATION UNMATCHED SINCE THE WONDERS OF FAMED "SNOW WHITE"!
- 80,000,000 American readers in 38 years have been delighted by this wonder story. Now it comes to thrilling life . . . The story of a girl from Kansas who finds fantastic, strange adventures in a wonderful land east of nowhere at the end of the Rainbow's trail!
- Every moment *different, thrilling* . . . a new experience at the movies!
- Two exciting years in preparation! Thrilling with a multi-star cast . . . amazing settings . . . eye-filling dances . . . alluring girls . . . all elaborately combined in the richest, most daring entertainment the screen has ever known!
- From the hit musical play that ran on Broadway for 4 solid years and toured all America for 7 record-breaking years thereafter!
- Leo's hot-weather parade of hits is the talk of the industry! . . . ISN'T IT WONDERFUL! . . . And what company but M-G-M would give you a multi-million-dollar show in August like this Technicolor sensation! 'THE WIZARD OF OZ' . . . THE FRIENDLY COMPANY all year around!
- 9237 persons in the actual cast! 68 incredibly beautiful sets! Augmented orchestra of 120 pieces! Chorus of 300 rousing voices!—It's the BIGGEST SHOW you ever saw!
- A BOOK FAMOUS IN FICTION . . . A PLAY CELEBRATED ON THE AMERICAN STAGE . . . A PICTURE THAT IS TRULY A TRIUMPH!

And the *coup de grace*: a huge billboard outside the MGM gates that read:

- "THE GREATEST PICTURE IN THE HISTORY OF ENTERTAINMENT in Glorious Technicolor."

16

Come Out, Come Out, Wherever You Are

The Public Journeys to Oz

The Sneak Previews and "World Premieres"

The first sneak preview of *The Wizard of Oz*—all 121 minutes of it—was held at San Bernardino's California Theatre in mid-June (probably the 15th) 1939. The unannounced screening went well, but mid-level MGM executives complained to Louis Mayer that "Over the Rainbow" slowed the Kansas sequences and should be cut. (One source claims that the first sneak was at a theater in Santa Barbara and that the song was excised following that screening. Another source notes San Luis Obispo as the location of a sneak preview.) Mayer followed his underlings' advice and ordered the song cut. Arthur Freed, Harold Arlen, and Yip Harburg were furious. The "Jitterbug" number also got the axe after the San Berdoo screening (too long and the wrong narrative tone, executives felt), as was the unnecessarily protracted slapstick dance of the Scarecrow that had been staged and directed by Busby Berkeley.

Another June 1939 sneak, on the sixteenth in Pomona, went well, though (according to Friends of the Pomona Fox president John Clifford in 2010) audiences were uncomfortable with the heightened emotion of the "Over the Rainbow" reprise in the Witch's castle. That number was cut, leaving no trace at all of what would become the movie's signature song.

Not too long after the San Bernardino and Pomona screenings, Dorothy's barnyard rendition of "Over the Rainbow" was reinstated, partly because Louis Mayer usually warmed to on-screen expressions of sentimentality, and because he happened to be receptive the day LeRoy and Freed begged him to reinstate the tune.

At some point after the San Bernardino and Pomona screenings, editor Blanche Sewell and director Victor Fleming tightened the film further. A lengthy montage bridging Dorothy's return home from Oz was cut. Some apple tree dialogue was eliminated, as well as some of the climactic castle chase. Hickory's description of his cyclone-preventer, and all other references to the gadget, was removed. To speed things up, and in deference to parents of very young children, some of the Wicked Witch's lines were cut, notably the sinister rhetorical question she directs to Dorothy: "Can you *imagine* what I'm going to do to you?" And a splashy celebration in Emerald City that began after the grateful Winkie hands the broomstick to Dorothy was discarded, too.

At least one source claims that the first *Oz* sneak preview took place on July 18, at L.A.'s Westwood Village Theatre. The date is reasonable enough, but the location is highly unlikely. In order to avoid the presence of industry insiders from the Hollywood trade papers or executives from other studios, sneak previews were unannounced (they usually unspooled after the evening's main feature) and took place in areas geographically removed from Hollywood. Hence, San Bernardino and Pomona.

Audience reaction to the sneak previews encouraged additional work by Sewell and Victor Fleming, who shaped the 121-minute cut into a tighter, leaner 101 minutes. The picture would remain at that length. Next step: the world premiere.

By late July, the MGM lab was processing enough film for five hundred prints of *The Wizard of Oz*. On August 7, the film was copyrighted by MGM.

A "premiere" is distinct from a preview. By definition, a premiere can happen only once. Nevertheless, *The Wizard of Oz* had more than one "premiere" showing. Because MGM remained eager to have a sense of audience response from regions that would not be covered by major papers (thus, no plot surprises given away and no negative reviews going coast to coast), one of the first

Grauman's Chinese Theatre hosted the gala Hollywood premiere of *The Wizard of Oz* on August 15, 1939. Billie Burke was among the cast members that attended. Jerry Maren (second from left) did not play the mayor in the movie, but filled in for the unavailable Charley Becker.

The Rialto Theater in East Rochester, New York, screened *Oz* for two days in August 1939.

advertised public showings of *The Wizard of Oz* took place at Kenosha, Wisconsin's Gateway Theater (now the Rhode Center for the Arts) on the evening of August 11, 1939. The same evening, *Oz* unspooled at the Cape Cinema in Dennis, Massachusetts, on Cape Cod.

A day later, August 12, the film opened an advertised five-day engagement at the Strand Theatre in Oconomowoc, Wisconsin. It also played on that date at the Venetian Theatre, in Racine, Wisconsin. Time and the inevitable blurring of facts have led to Oconomowoc being regarded—and regarding itself—as the *Oz* "world premiere" site.

The Hollywood premiere for industry insiders was mounted at 8:30 p.m. on Tuesday, August 15, 1939, at Grauman's Chinese Theatre, prominently located on Hollywood Boulevard. The theater's forecourt was dominated by a faux cornfield.

Although Judy Garland was already in New York City for the August 17 Loew's Capitol opening and her live show there, the Grauman's event was attended by other cast members, Victor Fleming, and Mervyn LeRoy. Maud Gage Baum, widow of L. Frank Baum, attended, along with L. Frank Baum's granddaughter, Frances Ozma Baum. Fred Stone, who had played the Scarecrow in the 1903 Broadway *Wizard of Oz*, also was an honored guest.

Typical of any high-profile Hollywood premiere of the time, the *Oz* gala was attended by a gaggle of stars. Eddie Cantor, a great fan of the Oz stories, was on hand. Others were Wallace Beery, Ann Rutherford, Bonita Granville, Harold Lloyd, and Orson Welles (less than a year after his *Mercury Theatre* "War of the Worlds" radio broadcast scared the pants off America).

Most of the Munchkin players had left Hollywood months before, but a few who remained were recruited to appear in costume at Grauman's: Nona Cooper, Tommy Cottonaro, Billy Curtis, Jerry Maren (as the mayor, filling in for Charley

Becker), and Victor Wetter. Most of the opening-night Munchkins remained for the duration of the Grauman run.

The cost of reserved-seat admission to this gala event at one of the finest movie theaters in Los Angeles was two dollars, plus twenty cents for tax. (An admission ticket from the premiere—center left section, row 28, seat 1—sold at auction for $6,083 in the spring of 2013.) Those at the Grauman premiere received the requisite souvenir program. Fans could do star spotting from the relative comfort of five thousand specially erected sidewalk bleacher seats. The bleachers filled quickly, and the surrounding area was clogged by another three thousand fans that stood.

An after-screening party was held at the Trocadero nightclub, on Sunset Boulevard.

Days after the Grauman's event, Maud Gage Baum wrote to Mervyn LeRoy to express her pleasure with the faithful translation of her husband's "kindly philosophy."

The Wizard of Oz opened at New York City's Loew's Capitol Theatre on August 17, to long lines (people were attracted by a live Judy Garland–Mickey Rooney stage show) and fabulous word of mouth.

Claims of an August 17 screening in Spirit Lake, Iowa, with many journalists in attendance, cannot be confirmed.

Evangelist Aimee Semple McPherson, who had enjoyed an enormous cult-like following in the 1920s, was in serious professional decline by 1939, but still filled the five thousand seats in her cavernous Los Angeles place of worship, Angelus Temple. (The Temple had been designed, at Sister Aimee's insistence, to mimic the décor and sight lines of a movie theater.) McPherson had found inspiration in popular storytelling for years. Earlier in the 1930s, she had mounted a series of elaborate fairy-tale productions cum sermons, including "Little Miss Muffet," in which the spider was the Devil, who descended on a thread to tempt Little Miss. On August 20, 1939, Sister Aimee worked with her scenic designers and lighting technicians to spin the tale of the Second Coming of Christ, in the context of "Over the Rainbow."

In a 2012 rumination on Sister Aimee, blogger Kayti Sweetland Rasmussen revealed that her grandmother had been a McPherson follower who eventually became disillusioned, realizing that "Aimee was merely another false Wizard of Oz, hiding behind a shiny curtain."

Coincidentally, Judy Garland had a lifelong interest in Sister Aimee; in 1967, she mentioned to "Broadway Ballyhoo" columnist Radie Harris that she hoped to produce a McPherson biopic.

The Wizard of Oz had its national rollout on August 25. Various promotional activities continued. Four costumed Munchkins toured Philadelphia (these were probably not original-cast members), and publicity caravans covered the east and Midwest in and near Chicago, Indianapolis, St. Louis, Kansas City, Minneapolis, Atlantic City, and Long Island.

General Release, and Judy and Mickey on Tour

A key part of MGM's heavy publicity push for *Oz* was the pairing of Judy Garland and Mickey Rooney for live appearances at key big-city theaters in New York City and elsewhere in the northeast from August 6 to August 30. In support of that were newspaper and magazine ads that emphasized the cast, the songs, and the Technicolor. Judy and Mickey pushed themselves hard to maintain their energy during the tour (which also promoted *Babes in Arms*). They were appearing at major theaters with large audiences that expected to be entertained.

Following a four-show engagement at Washington, D.C.'s 3,234-seat Loew's Capitol Theatre that drew huge crowds, Judy and Mickey were at New York's Loew's Capitol on August 17. This was the flagship of the many MGM theaters, with 5,230 seats situated in a stunning rococo interior. The Depression had made stage shows economically infeasible at the Capitol after 1935, but an exception was made for the Garland-Rooney engagement. (The New York Capitol reinstated stage shows in 1944, a wartime boom year.) Instead of four shows daily, Judy and Mickey did five on weekdays (bracketed by seven screenings of *The Wizard of Oz*) and a staggering seven shows (with nine screenings) on weekends.

The pair typically worked past 7:00 p.m. Because Judy was a minor, local authorities levied workplace fines against Loew's and the theater manager. MGM unwittingly contributed to the enactment of the penalties not simply by insisting that Judy work late, but by claiming in publicity material that she was fifteen years old. In fact, Judy turned seventeen before the release of *The Wizard of Oz*. She found MGM's interest in keeping her a child aggravating on general principle, and it hurt her in specific terms, as well, since the studio's shenanigans came when Judy was romantically

The Judy Garland–Mickey Rooney stage show that toured in support of *The Wizard of Oz* came to the Loew's Capitol in New York City in August 1939.

attracted to bandleader Artie Shaw and was hoping (in vain) that he would regard her as something other than a pal.

Mickey Rooney traveled with a drum kit, which he played exuberantly if not expertly. In its August 23, 1939, edition, *Variety* commented, "He's far from being a topflight skin-beater," but added that the sheer novelty was "swell" and was much appreciated by "the jive hounds." The

During their NYC stage tour, Mickey and Judy met fans and enjoyed celebratory luncheons.

paper described Judy as "a cute, clean-cut girl with a smash singing voice and style." The importance of that praise was significant. Although Judy was a show-business veteran with years of film credits, she was nevertheless doing a sort of "coming-out party" with *The Wizard of Oz* and the live tour. Her activity of summer 1939 was her step into broad, mainstream exposure. *Variety* was the movie business's bible, and people noticed when the reviewer acknowledged Judy's star quality. In one stroke, her star was dramatically elevated within the industry. And it didn't hurt that people lined up around the block to see *The Wizard of Oz* at Loew's Capitol.

On August 30, Judy and Mickey were at Madison Square Garden for the *New York Daily News*'s Harvest Moon Ball (an amateur dance contest founded in 1932), where they performed in front of a packed house of twenty thousand. Ray Bolger, Jack Haley, and Bert Lahr were on hand and were joined by the Jimmy Dorsey Orchestra. Other big stars appeared in discrete sets: 20th Century-Fox singing star Alice Faye; Fox skater-actress Sonja Henie; and Warner Bros. leading men John Garfield and George Raft.

After the Madison Square Garden performance, Rooney returned to Hollywood to begin work on *Judge Hardy and Son*. For the remainder of the Capitol engagement (which ended on September 6), Judy was joined by Lahr and Bolger. The three did sketches, danced, and sang, including "The Jitterbug."

New York and New Jersey were dotted with seventy Loew's theaters, which would be visited by Judy, Bolger, Haley, and Lahr. As Judy made the rounds, she was greeted at each venue by a local boy and girl that had been selected by each theater to be ambassadors. In addition, about 150 kids were hired from across the region, to fan out and drum up interest for *Oz* and the live show.

Young fans all along the circuit were well behaved, though there were inevitably enough of them that they had to be confined behind police barricades at each theater. Overflow filled nearby restaurants, soda fountains, candy stores, five-and-tens, and burger stands. For her crowd-pleasing effort, Judy was awarded a "voluntary bonus" of $10,000 by MGM.

The seventeen-year-old star found the theater tour exhilarating but exhausting. When she wasn't on stage, she was occupied with prearranged radio and newspaper interviews, radio guest appearances, luncheons, and supper parties (including one put together by teenage socialite Brenda Frazier). The activity put Judy in a goldfish bowl that only seemed more confining when she was made to do personal appearances before groups of influential locals.

At the World's Fair

August 27, 1939, found Mickey and Judy at the New York World's Fair, the nation's most popular and best-publicized live event of the year. They appeared on television (which was still semi-experimental and beamed to only a few hundred receivers in all of New York), were filmed by newsreel crews, and schmoozed with Mayor LaGuardia. The stars returned, more or less unannounced, later the same day, to enjoy the fair during special late-day hours.

OZIFIED !

This hastily prepared advertisement celebrating healthy box-office returns appeared in the September 2, 1939, edition of *Motion Picture Herald*. The "OZ" in "OZIFIED!" (a humorous take on "ossified") was printed in red.

Box-Office Results

Although most trade and public adverts suggested that *Oz* was a "big" film that could only have come from MGM, the public may never have quite gotten the "event" nature of the release. In retrospect, a slower rollout across the country, perhaps as a road-show attraction with higher prices and reserved seats, might have encouraged more buzz.

Two-thirds of audience members that saw *Oz* on its initial run were children. That was good news for theater owners concerned with margins at their concession stands, but not so good for MGM. Why? Because kids' prices were significantly lower than adult admissions. Depending on the theater and time of day, a child's admission fee could be as low as ten cents, in a day when adult prices averaged about forty cents for standard engagements. (Limited-release "road-show" pictures inevitably cost more to see.)

Oz did very strong business in cities, but relative box-office was weaker in small towns.

Because of delays caused, in significant part, by the film's sheer scope and technical ambition, Oz exceeded its budget by about 65 percent. The final cost to MGM—including production, prints, and marketing—was $3.7 million. Although The Wizard of Oz was number seven among 1939's top ten movie releases, its $3,017,000 first-run take, though splendid for the day, wasn't enough to recoup its cost and put the film into the black. Oz went on the books with a $750,000 loss and wouldn't show a profit until its very successful 1949 re-release. (Some sources cite the loss at $1 million or slightly more.)

It's possible that the picture would have broken even or even posted a wee profit on first release if it could have been routinely held over by prestige theaters in big cities. But, as we've seen, 1939 was a movie year of astonishingly high quality. A lot of other high-quality product,

Gaiety! Glory! Glamour!

THE WIZARD OF OZ

with
**JUDY GARLAND
FRANK MORGAN
RAY BOLGER
BERT LAHR
JACK HALEY**

BILLIE BURKE
MARGARET HAMILTON
CHARLEY GRAPEWIN
and THE MUNCHKINS

A VICTOR FLEMING *Production*
SCREEN PLAY BY NOEL LANGLEY, FLORENCE RYERSON AND EDGAR ALLAN WOOLF FROM THE BOOK BY L. FRANK BAUM
Directed by   *Produced by*
VICTOR FLEMING · MERVYN LEROY

It's
**METRO-GOLDWYN-MAYER'S
TECHNICOLOR TRIUMPH!**

Charmingly modernist caricatures are highlights of this 1939 poster.

much of it from MGM, was waiting for release in Loew's theaters during the last quarter of 1939, so after reasonable runs, Oz had to make way for other attractions.

Another consideration is that film fantasy wasn't the sure-fire audience-pleaser in 1939 that it is today. MGM had known it was exploring a risky genre, but as we've seen, the success of Disney's Snow White was a strong motivator to proceed. The first-run gross generated by The Wizard of Oz was probably at the outer limits of what the studio could have reasonably expected. America's middle-aged adults had come of age during World War I. Young adults had been battered by the Depression. On top of that, Europe and Asia were gearing up for another world war, one that would probably involve the United States. Grown-ups were preoccupied with grown-up things. Fantasy was for kids.

Early in 1940, *Variety* suggested that *Oz* would have been profitable if it, like Disney's *Snow White*, had been an animated cartoon. (A recurring tale that MGM considered doing *Oz* as a cartoon feature is almost certainly erroneous. As things turned out, *Variety*'s assertion was off the mark, because Disney's second animated feature, *Pinocchio*, underperformed following its February 1940 premiere.) Although time-consuming, animation was nevertheless far less expensive than unusually complex, design-heavy live-action. *Snow White* confirmed that a feature-length cartoon could succeed without star names attached to the voice work. (After all, the industry asked, who was Adriana Caselotti?) No stars meant no star salaries. Yet monies paid to the stars of *The Wizard of Oz* had relatively little impact on that film's overall budget. Judy Garland was a newcomer that MGM felt justified in underpaying, and the other principals were freelance or on-loan light leads and character players who worked for considerably less than major stars. The two best-paid members of the *Oz* troupe, Ray Bolger and Jack Haley, each earned $3,000 a week. The lowest salaries were penurious: Judy Garland ($500/wk), Terry ($125/wk), and the Munchkins ($50 each/wk). MGM spent lavishly on sets and other visual elements, but effectively controlled the expense of on-screen talent.

MGM was naturally disappointed with the film's failure even to earn back its cost. The tally was especially stinging because some other prestigious MGM releases of 1938/39, including *Broadway Serenade*, *The Great Waltz*, and *Marie Antoinette*, had also lost money.

Contrarily, the relatively low-budget Rooney-Garland musical *Babes in Arms* cleaned up, grossing $3.3 million (foreign receipts included), for a profit of $2.8 million. The combined monies from *Oz* and *Babes in Arms* were sufficient to propel Judy onto Hollywood's top ten box-office list for 1939; Bette Davis was the only other woman. (A Warner Bros. star, Davis had four films in release in 1939: *The Private Lives of Elizabeth and Essex*, *The Old Maid*, *Juarez*, and the wildly popular *Dark Victory*.)

Bad Business in Europe

Oz grossed nearly a million dollars abroad on first release—a nice sum that would have been greater if events in Germany hadn't cast a pall over MGM's foreign business. Although Germany was an important market for Hollywood films, local, anti-American violence directed again American film exchanges in Germany began shortly after Hitler's 1933 ascension to power. Most of these attacks, such as Nazi thugs' 1934 assault on the Warner Bros. Berlin exchange, were more anti-Semitic than anti-American (the Warner rep, for instance, was Jewish). Warner closed its German exchange after that insult, and other studios grew wary of Germany. Wariness, however, didn't mean a halt to business. De facto Hollywood censor Joe Breen involved himself in the industry's money side as well as with scenes or plots he deemed unacceptable for public consumption. During the first days of 1936, he asked Louis Mayer to tone down the anti-Nazi sentiment in the screenplay for *Three Comrades*. Cravenly, Mayer and MGM obeyed, to forestall objections from Nazi Berlin that might have jeopardized MGM's profits in Germany.

Later in 1936, Louis Mayer hoped to undercut Nazi domination of Austria's film industry with MGM-backed film production in Vienna, but the idea never got off the ground. (Austria was ostensibly free until "annexed" by Hitler in March 1938.) Paramount's German exchange posted a modest loss in 1936, by which time only that studio, 20th Century-Fox, and MGM still distributed films in Germany.

In December 1938, Nazi Austria's puppet government seized some MGM film prints, and although they were returned after Arthur Loew protested to the Gestapo (via the U.S. embassy in Vienna), it was clear that MGM's business relationship with Germany-Austria was dying on its feet.

Loew, Nick Schenck, and Mayer knew full well that Hitler was persecuting German, Czech, and Austrian Jews, but maintained a cynical and irrational hope that business might still proceed. In June 1939, the studio warned contract star Myrna Loy to knock it off with her criticisms of Hitler; Greta Garbo and Hedy Lamarr were similarly cautioned.

Everything collapsed after Germany invaded Poland in September 1939. MGM and the rest of Hollywood finally grasped that, for the foreseeable future, there would be no American product on German screens, or elsewhere on the Continent. The start of World War II is obviously far more momentous than MGM's balance sheet, but the fact remains that political events deprived *The Wizard of Oz* of much-needed foreign revenue.

Oz and the Death of *War Eagles*

War Eagles is one of the most tantalizing of Hollywood's "what if?" stories. The brainchild of *King Kong* producer Merian C. Cooper, this epic fantasy-adventure about Norse warriors who harness and pilot giant eagles to defend New York City against a European invader was greenlighted by MGM in the early autumn of 1938. Studio chief Louis B. Mayer had no head for fantasy, but he could see clearly what Cooper and *Kong* had done for RKO's balance sheet in 1933. Many drafts of a *War Eagles* script were written before one was completed by Cyril Hume during 1938–39. The greater part of the story is set on an isolated South American plateau, where American pilot Slim Johansen discovers the enormous eagles and their riders, and assists in air and ground battles against dinosaurs. In the climactic New York sequence, war eagles by the dozens clash with waves of enemy fighter-bombers and a gigantic dirigible with a pulse weapon that grounds all American aircraft. (Popular media of the day frequently reported that Germany was at work on a "death ray," so the invaders' weapon was timely as well as exciting.) Atop White Eagle, a gigantic bird that no Norseman had thought could ever be tamed and brought to harness, Slim marshals his aviator's skill in an epic battle that concludes atop the Statue of Liberty.

Because *Oz* was not a moneymaker in first release, and because foreign makets were drying up, MGM chief Louis Mayer decided to shelve *War Eagles*, a lavish fantasy proposed by the team responsible for *King Kong* (1933). This pre-production illustration was done by Duncan Gleason.

If any Hollywood producer could have carried this off, it was Cooper, whose business acumen was complemented by a brilliant story sense and a flair for promotion. Special-effects wizard Willis O'Brien had brought Kong to life with stop-motion animation and was hired to do the same with the massive eagles. With the right cast, *War Eagles* could have been a fantasy adventure for the ages.

However, the failure of *The Wizard of Oz* to recoup its costs during its first release allowed Louis Mayer to pretend to be suddenly mortified by the potential expense of Cooper's film. This concern was a bit of a sham, but Mayer had a more legitimate worry: that pre-war (but already aggressive) Germany would take offense at the unidentified but intriguingly ruthless invaders and refuse German playdates to *War Eagles*. If that happened, the rest of Europe might do the same, and in the end, *all* of MGM's future product might be refused bookings in Europe. To the great disappointment of Cooper, O'Brien, and the rest of the team, *War Eagles* was abruptly canceled during pre-production, leaving nothing but a script, many concept sketches, and a few minutes of test footage. MGM's one-two punch of *Oz* and *War Eagles* was not to be.

Oz Reviews, 1939, or: What Ever Happened to Victor Fleming?

What follow are excerpts from trade publications, newspapers, and consumer magazines on the 1939 release of *The Wizard of Oz*. You'll see that *The Hollywood Reporter* and other trade publications focused on the film's studio and producer, and on box-office potential. Daily papers, such as the *Los Angeles Herald Express*, and mainstream magazines, such as *McCall's*, were particularly concerned with story, fantasy elements, visual appeal, and character values. Critical reaction to Judy Garland was very favorable, but the real raves were directed to Bert Lahr. His performance is still a revelation today, and it's to the credit of contemporaneous reviewers that they were enthusiastically impressed.

Reviewers seem split as to the success of the film's alternate reality. Some critics felt that the brightly colored literalness of Munchkinland, Oz, and the Emerald City paradoxically undercut the fantasy. Others were enchanted. Contrarily, a few critics that missed the point complained that the Kansas sequences were excessively earthbound.

Makeup supervisor Jack Dawn was frequently singled out for praise. If anything about the 1939 reviews is apt to surprise today's audiences, it's that the Arlen-Harburg songs were received with only mild approval and, in some reviews, with indifference or worse.

Relatively few of the reviews from 1939 mention director Victor Fleming, which is instructive today, when professional reviews are frequently *dominated* by acknowledgment of directors and critical evaluation of the directors' creative contributions. Numerous critics regard the director as the most important force behind a movie.

The notion that the director is the "author" of a film was proposed in France around 1955. This so-called *auteur* theory subsequently gained credence in Europe because of idiosyncratic directors like Jean-Luc Godard, Michelangelo Antonioni, Federico Fellini, and François Truffaut, but didn't pull a lot of weight in America until the 1968 publication of *The American Cinema: Directors and Directions 1929–1968*, by Brooklyn-born critic and essayist Andrew Sarris. Now an essential, if often debated, part of every film scholar's library, Sarris's book supposes that talented directors (and even not-so-talented ones) have unique, personal visions that drive narratives, themes, and stylistics, and are consistent and recognizable, film after film.

What the Directors Guild of America (DGA) calls a possessory credit ("Joe Director's *Adventures in Movieland*" or "A Film by Jane Director") was never encouraged by studios during the studio-system era, but was allowed (and probably made good business sense) if the director was known to the general public and famed for movies of special excellence or popular appeal. As early as 1915, director D. W. Griffith awarded himself a possessory credit for *Birth of a Nation*. Later, during the studio era, George Stevens, Alfred Hitchcock, Frank Capra, King Vidor, and a few others successfully negotiated possessory credits.

When the studio system began to fall apart after 1950 and other directors clamored for possessory credit, the Writers Guild of America (WGA) took exception, claiming that if any individual is the "author" of a film, that person is the screenwriter. That's not unreasonable, except that Hollywood films often have multiple writers that may work in partnerships, or alone, or sometimes as discrete teams that might have been hired by different executives at widely separated stages of the projects' development. Individual screenwriters often have no interaction with other writers who contribute. Writers may not even be aware of each other's existence until late in the script stage. Then there are rewrite specialists and script doctors, who are brought on after a screenplay is completed, to rearrange scenes, add new ones, or punch up dialogue.

A 1967 attempt by the WGA to allow possessory director credits only after WGA review was successfully squelched by the DGA, an act that effectively awarded directors authorship of movies. Just so that the issue might be clarified, a 2000 DGA ruling said that the union would not restrict *any* director's ability to negotiate a possessory credit. Naturally, directors want that sort of on-screen credit, which has led to absurdities such as this one from 2007: "A Susan Hippen Film *Sorority Sister Slaughter*."

Meanwhile, critical appreciation of Victor Fleming remains as unforgivably scant as it was in 1939 (though Fleming's biographer, Michael Sragow, took a giant stride toward remedying that with his very fine 2008 book *Victor Fleming: An American Movie Master*).

Naturally, none of this is to say that *Oz* should have opened with "A Victor Fleming Film" or "A Film by Victor Fleming." He was one of six directors that contributed, and he worked with a brilliant cast and dozens of technicians to bring life to the ideas of a small platoon of writers. *The Wizard of Oz*, like all films, was a collaborative effort. Still, the absence, in 1939, of critical acknowledgment of Fleming is modestly startling, particularly since he had already proved himself a reliable and competent hit-maker.

Trade Publications

"A completely charming and wholly delightful film in a direction rarely attempted. Production boundaries have given way to new approaches in sets, costuming and conception which make Oz a beautiful thing to behold in gorgeous Technicolor." —*Boxoffice*

"*Oz* is likely to perform some record-breaking feats of box office magic. Favorable word-of-mouth on the unique and highly entertaining features of the film should spread rapidly. It's a pushover for the children and family biz. Nothing comparable has come out of Hollywood in the past few years." —"Flin," *Daily Variety*

"Oz should find a ready-made audience practically everywhere. It is engrossing and amusing. Class houses will get the best returns. Parents will bring their children. It will fail to attract the young adults and action fans." —*Film Bulletin*

"Handsomely mounted fairy story should click solidly at the box office. Leo the Lion is privileged to herald this one with his deepest roar—the one that comes from way down—for seldom if indeed ever has the screen been so successful in its approach to fantasy and extravaganza through the medium of flesh and blood. [A] corking achievement, all the way through." —*The Film Daily*

"Oz will, beyond question, be accorded recognition as a milestone in motion picture history. It scintillates with artistry, yet it possesses such an abundance of qualities which predict broad audience success that there can be no question of its being headed for spectacular playing time and grosses. The picture will undoubtedly reflect great credit on the industry at large. [The film is] brilliantly inventive, arrestingly beautiful and dramatically compelling to the eye, the ear, and the emotions. LeRoy has captured a spirit of earthy drama of a strong moral flavor and combined this with outright fantasy and striking effect. . . . The production is remarkable in every department." —*The Hollywood Reporter*

"To me, the outstanding feature of the production is the astonishingly clever performance of Judy Garland, holding the picture together, being always its motivating feature, and so natural is she, so perfectly cast, one scarcely becomes conscious of her contribution to the whole. Praise is due this accomplished child: her performance strengthens my conviction that in a few years she will be recognized as one of the screen's foremost emotional actresses." —*The Hollywood Spectator*

"Oz is of the essence of screen entertainment that lives for a long time. It probably will prove to be a popular revival at appropriate seasons. It has been given lavish treatment and impeccable direction [and it is] a box office attraction of major importance. Weakness is apparent in the whimsy itself. Dating from the year 1900, it may or may not appeal to sophisticated adults in the year 1939. Valiant attempts have been made to inject a modern note and, while in itself it clicks tremendously, in the surroundings it appears quite out of place. . . . Lahr turns in the No. 1 performance. The makeup job calls for a special award." —Alfred Finestone, *Motion Picture Daily*

"Dust off the adjectives and prepare for extended runs. . . . Direction, scripting, musical ingredients, playing are on a scale of the highest. Add those elements and then multiply for the Technicolor job—so entrancing and engrossing as to make it tough on the next black-and-white picture you view after *Oz*. . . . The picture marks a great break in the screen career of Garland. Technicolor and

Judy mate perfectly, and the youngster's real talent takes sympathetically to the role. . . . Stothart's score is a gem, musical numbers by Arlen and Harburg sparkle. . . . Skillful Bobby Connolly handled the dance numbers on the same clear-cut, while highly imaginative, plane that distinguishes the entire production." —*Movie Digest*

"It is truly a magnificent spectacle, a towering achievement in the technical magic of motion pictures. . . . The picture will still be playing to delight a coming generation. . . . The music is really delightful. Too much credit cannot be given to Victor Fleming. He brooks no apologies in presenting a fable and keeps events steadily marching forward without pause. . . . Garland deserves stardom for her performance. She is everything admirers of the character could want her to be, and her role is unusually long and exacting. Bolger, Lahr, and Haley are perfection itself." —*Picture Reports*

"A great adventure . . . a charming, exciting, and beautiful picture." —Clark Wales, *Screen and Radio Weekly*

Newspapers and Other Mainstream News Outlets

"*Oz* was unveiled to the public Tuesday night [at Grauman's], bringing 'ohs' and 'ahs' from the colony's upper crust and an almost unheard-of outburst of raves from usually blasé critics. The best picture that Metro has turned out in many a day." —*Associated Press*

"There is a warming fantasy in its conception, lovely color in its execution, and there should be an Academy Award, even if a special award has to be created, for Bert Lahr." —John Gibbons, *Boston Transcript*

"It is gorgeous, fantastic, radiant with Technicolor. It teems with midgets. It is alive with trick photography, is jeweled with hummable tunes, and features a Kansas tornado that makes you want to live anywhere but in Kansas. . . . Judy Garland was a perfect choice for Dorothy. She portrays, without a false move, an honest-to-goodness little girl, genuinely flabbergasted curious, terrified, game, lonely, ecstatic, as the case may call for—and you're just going to love her." —Mae Tinée [pseudonym], *Chicago Daily Tribune*

"Two splendid hours of melody and magic. The technical trickery is perhaps even more impressive than the story itself. Witches and hobgoblins have been reproduced with realism which may be too terrifying for the very youngest." —*Christian Science Monitor*

"One of the most expensive (and also one of the most beautiful) examples of film fantasy ever to grace the American screen. . . . The social angle of the picture is comparatively nil. But as pure entertainment (at the same time regretting that MGM neglected this opportunity to satirize dictators), we heartily recommend Oz." —Howard Rushmore, *The Daily Worker*. Note: *The Daily Worker* was a newspaper published in New York City by the Communist Party USA.

"Disney's best cartoon technique could never duplicate the rubber-legged movement of Ray Bolger. . . . Haley also is as effective as an artist might have drawn. While Disney might have sketched the Lion, he couldn't possibly get Lahr on his pencil point. Lahr's impersonation is among the acting triumphs and one of the singing high spots of the year. . . . The well-fed Miss Garland is surprisingly effective as Dorothy, bringing a wide-eyed naivety to the role and nothing of a dreaded simper, coo, and yodel. She plays seriously, earnestly, and without disturbing mannerisms." —John Rosenfield, *Dallas Morning Star*

"Judy Garland is rosy-cheeked, starry-eyed, and more alluring than a glamour girl." —*Hollywood Citizen-News*

"Three generations will see their gayest dreams come true in Oz. . . . Don't miss this movie. You may want to see it every day this week." —Jack Moffat, *Kansas City Star*

"The whole production is careful and affectionate but, unless you are one of the 'young in heart' to whom the film is dedicated, you may find Oz a little on the tedious side. The character most in tune with its theme is the Cowardly Lion. Lahr is uproariously timid, in a wonderfully effective makeup. Garland is sweet and sensitive, with an exceptionally good voice, and it is to her special credit that at the last she manages to touch the heart even in her unpredictable predicament. Hamilton is a triumph of villainy." —*Los Angeles Evening News*

"*Oz* completely fascinated the sophisticated audience of first-nighters [at Grauman's]. Enthusiasm over the amazing achievement of MGM was heard on all sides. . . . This is little Judy Garland's great triumph and the best thing she has ever done. I thought at first she would be far too robust and energetic for Dorothy, but Judy grows on you and before the end of the picture, you find yourself enthusiastic over her conception of the Baum heroine. You'll love Lahr, who is such a sissy that he has a permanent wave. Bolger is excellent, Haley is splendid, [and] the inimitable Frank Morgan gives his own original interpretation to the Wizard." —Louella Parsons, *Los Angeles Examiner*

"The real triumph of the picture is the fantastic land of Oz. The eye is assailed with surprises, each more beautiful or more impressive in its camera magic than the last. The photography is gorgeous, the art direction is superb, and the special effects are a source of constant wonder. If there is any jarring note, it is in the early reels where there is a tendency to go musical comedy. . . . None

will deny that *Oz* is one of the greatest novelties ever offered on the screen."
—Harrison Carroll, *Los Angeles Herald-Express*

"First and foremost a technician's triumph, *Oz* offers a constant series of surprises in fascinating sights. . . . a lush and lovable production, told with laughter, song and pathos, acted with zest. Lahr has a field day . . . it is the hit performance of a hit picture. The best picture of the year . . . the perfect piece of entertainment." —Harry Mines, *Los Angeles Illustrated Daily News*

"A new experience and a new thrill dawned last night. . . . *Oz* is living up fully and more than fully to the expectations of those who appraised it scarcely a week ago at preview. The film is one of those marvels of moviedom which come all too seldom—a pioneering step and an artistic realization at once. The story [is] joyous, inspired make-believe. And the audience undoubtedly actually 'rooted' for Dorothy and her companions, for applause punctuated the way." —Edwin Schallert, *Los Angeles Times*

"[I]f sheer fantasy is likely to trouble you, no doubt you will not be able to share in the delight the great majority of us are going to find. . . . We'll just be sorry for you and pray for your spiritual rejuvenation." —Merle Potter, *Minneapolis Tribune*

"[A] delightful fantasy. . . . Garland is perfectly cast as Dorothy. She is as clever a little actress as she is a singer, and her special style of vocalizing is ideally adapted to the music of the picture." —Kate Cameron, *New York Daily News*

"[*The Wizard of Oz* is] a vastly entertaining and delightful offering. . . . Many of the scenes are the sort to stick in one's memory for a long time. . . . [T]he production itself is always handsome and intriguing and that the principal characters are impersonated with feeling, humor, and charm. . . . *Oz* [is] more of a Hollywood than a Baum conception, but it has the capacity to hold your interest throughout. Thank the performers for much of this. . . . Thanks to its pictorial splendor and engaging portrayals, *Oz* is first-rate entertainment, but I would not call it a great piece of screen fantasy." —Howard Barnes, *New York Herald*

"A spectacular show . . . an outstanding achievement. It's Mr. Lahr who romps off with the acting honors, and a good deal of the credit for the proceedings goes to Jack Dawn. Outstanding, too, is the musical score." —*New York Journal American*

"[*Oz*] lacks that spontaneity which is the spirit of all great fantasy. It is surprisingly short on comedy . . . the makeup men are the real stars of the film. The songs are rather dull. Oz has a pleasant quality, the sense of re-reading a childhood favorite. But its elaborateness smothers much of its charm." —Eileen Creelman, *New York Sun*

"A delightful piece of wonder-working which had the youngsters' eyes shining and brought a quietly amused gleam to the wiser ones of the oldsters. . . . It is all so well-intentioned, so genial, and so gay that any reviewer who would look down his nose at the funmaking should be spanked and sent off, supperless, to bed. . . . Judy Garland's Dorothy is a pert and fresh-faced miss with the wonder-lit eyes of a believer in fairy tales, but the Baum fantasy is at its best when the Scarecrow, the Woodman, and the Lion are on the move. . . . Mr. Lahr's lion is fion." —Frank Nugent, *The New York Times*

"Through trial and error, and month on month of toil and sweat, Oz finally emerged, and the results are a near-miracle for the movie industry." —Kaspar Monahan, *Pittsburgh Press*

"I am one of those nuts that still reread occasionally children's stories and still like 'em, and so I toss bouquets at MGM for Oz, because it is the first one that ever came to one hundred percent specification for me. Five gets you ten it will run close to Snow White in receipts." —Claude LaBelle, *San Francisco News*

Magazines

"Splendorous Technicolor, fantastic settings, makeups, staging, swell tunes and lyrics add a new vividness to the Baum story. The brightest spots are the meetings between Dorothy and her new friends. The cleverest are Bolger, whose gay dancing and song are delightful, and Lahr, whose impersonations of timidity and toughness are a masterpiece of travesty. Billie Burke's saccharine Good Witch hardly compensates for Margaret Hamilton's evil Bad Witch. A six-year-old sitting next to me loved the whole proceedings; he bit off all his nails, but was gleeful most of the time." —Philip T. Hartung, *Commonweal*

"Pinning elusive fantasy down to literal camera shots is one of the ultra-precarious jobs. Disaster is just around the first close-up. That this expensive, streamlined version of Baum's fantasy is entertaining, sometimes quite lovely, and frequently amusing is, in itself, a triumph. There are innumerable amazing camera tricks and . . . lavish hues, perhaps in too garish color. Music enlivens every foot of the film, and there are some mildly tinkling tunes. You will find Judy Garland a pleasant and wholesome Dorothy. Of the rest, I liked best Bert Lahr [whose] Lion is a richly amusing character, right after Androcles' own heart. [four-star rating]" —*Liberty*

"It was fairly courageous on the part of MGM to try to put Baum's story on film. But 'put' is hardly the word. 'Hurled' is more accurate. Oz has the most awe-inspiring sets ever put on the screen and the most colorful and successful Technicolor work I have seen to date. But the picture seems tiresome, for the

most part, simply because you do not believe you are in Never-Never Land."
—Pare Lorentz, *McCall's*

"'The Wizard of Oz' was intended to hit the same audience as 'Snow White' and won't fail for lack of trying. It has dwarfs, music, Technicolor, freak characters and Judy Garland. It can't be expected to have a sense of humor as well—and as for the light touch of fantasy, it weighs like a pound of fruitcake soaking wet." —Otis Ferguson, *The New Republic*

"[Baum's] whimsy has been broadened by antics after the musical comedy manner and the interpolation of patter songs in Stothart's excellent score. Magnificent sets and costumes, vivid Technicolor, and every resource of trick photography bolster the competent cast that strikes a happy medium between humor and make-believe. The more fanatic Ozophiles may dispute MGM's remodeling of the story, but the average moviegoer—adult or adolescent—will find it novel and richly satisfying to the eye." —*Newsweek*

"I sat cringing before MGM's . . . Oz, which displays no trace of imagination, good taste, or ingenuity. . . . I say it's a stinkaroo. The vulgarity . . . all through the film is difficult to analyze. Part of it was the raw, eye-straining Technicolor, applied with a complete lack of restraint. . . . Bert Lahr is funny but out of place. If Bert Lahr belongs in the Land of Oz, so does Mae West. . . . I don't like the Singer Midgets under any circumstances, but I found them especially bothersome in Technicolor." —Russell Maloney, *The New Yorker*

"As long as *Oz* sticks to whimsy and magic, it floats in the same rare atmosphere of enchantment that distinguished *Snow White*. When it descends to earth, it collapses like a scarecrow in a cloudburst. No children's tale is MGM's *Oz*. Lavish in sets, adult in humor, it is a Broadway spectacle translated into make-believe. Most of its entertainment comes from the polished work (aided by Jack Dawn's expert make-up) of seasoned troupers Lahr, Bolger, and Haley. . . . Its Singer Midgets . . . go through their paces with the bored sophisticated air of slightly evil children." —*Time*

The Wizard of Oz Is Released Abroad

The film's September 14, 1939, Canadian release was the first outside of the USA. (Some sources say Canada first saw *Oz* on August 21.) The film premiered in Brazil, Argentina, and the Philippines in November. (A broader Philippines run began early in 1953.)

The film was released in the United Kingdom in November. British censors, always prickly about violent or frightening content, demanded that children be accompanied into theaters by adults. Some Brit reviewers, including Graham Greene, publicly lamented that decision. (Historically, British film censors were far more concerned with violence and scare issues than with sex, an indisputably European mindset.)

A clutch of important foreign releases took place throughout 1940 in Mexico, Estonia, Hungary, Denmark (where the Cowardly Lion was called Lion Afraid Trousers [Scaredy-Pants]), Sweden, Ireland, and Australia (where the film became a big hit with Aussie troops on their way to war). The last foreign release before America entered World War II was in Portugal in December 1940. There were just two wartime foreign releases after 1940: Finland in November 1943 and Spain in March 1945.

The Wizard of Oz opened in France in June 1946, eleven months after the end of the war in Europe. Other foreign rollouts continued to the end of 1947: Belgium and the Netherlands (1946) and Hong Kong in 1947. The only Axis nation to see the movie during the '40s was Italy (1947). The other Axis members didn't see *Oz* until years later: Austria in 1950; Germany (by now West Germany) in 1951; and Japan at the close of 1954. (The other big Japanese fantasy release from that year was *Gojira* aka *Godzilla*.) India, an Allied nation, finally saw *Oz* in 1952. Other postwar release venues, for which dates cannot be pinned down, are Czechoslovakia, Turkey, and Persia (present-day Iran).

The Soviet Union, never scrupulous about observance of copyright law, published a pirated version of the first Baum book in 1939, but never saw the MGM movie in its first run. During later years, as the Kremlin loosened travel restrictions and home video (official and pirated) proliferated, Soviets became familiar with MGM's version of Dorothy and her friends.

Oz was well received in all foreign markets and was especially popular with audiences in Great Britain and Australia.

Le Magicien d'Oz finally opened in France in 1946.

Italy had been an Axis nation during World War II, so theaters there had to wait until 1947 to show *Il Mago di Oz*.

Foreign releases were frequently preceded by publication of translated versions of the Baum novel. Languages included Spanish, Portuguese, Danish, Italian, Swedish, Tagalog (for the Philippines), Romanian, Hungarian, French, and German (for distribution in Switzerland). Some of the foreign editions preserved the original Denslow illustrations, but many more mated the translated Baum text with images from the movie. Some of the books re-created the entire film in text and stills, with the most visual examples done panel-style, like comic books.

That Magnificent Movie Year, 1939

A favorite game of film buffs begins with the question, "What was the best-ever year for American movies?" Nineteen thirty-nine long ago became the standard, and widely accepted, answer. While some other years can make legitimate claims to the prize (look at what was released, for instance, in 1950 and 1967), it's difficult to mount strong arguments against 1939. For all the excellence of *Oz*, and its status at or very near the top of all 1939 releases, it was just one of a staggering number of the year's enduringly admired releases.

In alphabetical order, here are some of them:

- *The Adventures of Huckleberry Finn* (MGM)
- *At the Circus* (MGM)
- *Beau Geste* (Paramount)
- *Confessions of a Nazi Spy* (Warner Bros.)
- *Dark Victory* (Warner Bros.)
- *Destry Rides Again* (Universal)
- *Dodge City* (Warner Bros.)
- *Drums Along the Mohawk* (20th Century-Fox)
- *Each Dawn I Die* (Warner Bros.)
- *Golden Boy* (Columbia)
- *Gone With the Wind* (Selznick International Pictures/MGM)
- *Goodbye, Mr. Chips* (MGM)
- *Gunga Din* (RKO)
- *The Hound of the Baskervilles* (20th Century-Fox)
- *The Hunchback of Notre Dame* (RKO)
- *Intermezzo* (Selznick International Pictures/United Artists)
- *Jesse James* (20th Century-Fox)
- *Juarez* (Warner Bros.)
- *The Little Princess* (20th Century-Fox)
- *Love Affair* (Paramount)
- *The Man in the Iron Mask* (Edward Small Productions/United Artists)
- *Mr. Smith Goes to Washington* (Columbia)
- *Ninotchka* (MGM)
- *Of Mice and Men* (Hal Roach Productions/United Artists)

- *The Oklahoma Kid* (Warner Bros.)
- *The Old Maid* (Warner Bros.)
- *Only Angels Have Wings* (Columbia)
- *The Private Lives of Elizabeth and Essex* (Warner Bros.)
- *The Roaring Twenties* (Warner Bros.)
- *Son of Frankenstein* (Universal)
- *Stagecoach* (Walter Wanger Productions/United Artists)
- *Stanley and Livingstone* (20th Century-Fox)
- *The Story of Vernon and Irene Castle* (RKO)
- *They Made Me a Criminal* (Warner Bros.)
- *Union Pacific* (Paramount)
- *The Women* (MGM)
- *Wuthering Heights* (The Samuel Goldwyn Co./United Artists)
- *You Can't Cheat an Honest Man* (Universal)
- *Young Mr. Lincoln* (20th Century-Fox)

Audiences could choose from among all of these, plus well-done series pictures featuring Andy Hardy, Maisie, Charlie Chan, Mr. Moto, the Dead End Kids, the Saint, and Tarzan; *and* these top-flight serials: *Buck Rogers, Daredevils of the Red Circle, Dick Tracy's G-Men, The Lone Ranger Rides Again*, and *Zorro's Fighting Legion.*

A few important things are apparent from the list. First, it's dominated by major Hollywood studios, particularly Warner Bros. and 20th Century-Fox. (The other "majors," MGM and Paramount, are uncharacteristically underrepresented.) Second, it's clear that the "mini-majors" (RKO, Universal, and Columbia) were capable of excellence, a quality that wasn't beyond the reach of independent producers, either, as evidenced by the likes of David O. Selznick and Walter Wanger.

Third, the year's best releases were aimed at adults (at a time when the industry assumed that most moviegoing decisions were made by Mom).

The most intriguing takeaway from the list is that *The Wizard of Oz* is 1939's only important fantasy release. (*Son of Frankenstein* is more properly termed a horror movie, and the *Buck Rogers* serial is science fiction.) Contrarily, movie-year 2013 brought moviegoers nearly thirty fantasy releases that included *Thor: The Dark World, Jack the Giant Slayer, The Hobbit: The Desolation of Smaug*, and *Oz the Great and Powerful*. In addition, computer-animated fantasy was represented by more than half a dozen titles, including *Frozen, Despicable Me 2*, and *Monsters University*.

Overall, fantasy continued to be an important film genre in 2013 and performed extraordinarily well at the box office, dominating the list of top ten grossers and attracting adults as well as younger audiences.

The lively genre that had been marginal on the eve of World War II had become mainstream.

Academy Awards for 1939

The Academy of Motion Picture Arts and Sciences recognized *The Wizard of Oz* with six Oscar nominations: best picture, best visual effects, best art direction, best original score, best original song, and best cinematography, color. There was no *Oz* nomination for Victor Fleming (who won for *Gone With the Wind*), nor for Bert Lahr, which seems a particularly glaring oversight, especially considering the rapturous critical reaction to his performance.

Work that came to screens in 1939 was honored at the twelfth annual Academy Awards ceremony, at Hollywood's Ambassador Hotel on February 29, 1940. For the first time, the host was Bob Hope (who would perform that duty seventeen more times, off and on, until 1978). And for the final time, the names of winners were released to the press before the ceremony.

Although Judy Garland wasn't nominated as best actress, she nevertheless went home with Oscar, via a special "juvenile award." Later in her career, Judy garnered two more Oscar nominations, for her brilliant and emotionally complex performance in *A Star Is Born* (1954; best actress) and a wrenching cameo in *Judgment at Nuremberg* (1961; best supporting actress). She did not win in either instance.

In a toughly competitive Oscar year, *Oz* took home two statuettes, for Harold Stothart's score and Arlen and Harburg's song "Over the Rainbow."

No cast member was Oscar-nominated for work in *The Wizard of Oz*, but early in 1940 Judy Garland was honored with a special "juvenile" Academy Award. The presentation was made by her good friend Mickey Rooney.

No Academy category for best costume design existed until 1949; hence the seeming snub of Gilbert Adrian's brilliant *Oz* costumes. A generation later, the 1979 Oscar telecast (honoring releases of 1978) was produced by Jack Haley Jr. A highlight came when the costume award was presented by Jack Haley Sr. and Ray Bolger. (The winner was Anthony Powell, for *Death on the Nile*.)

The Academy Award for makeup wasn't established until 1981 (although *Oz* assistant makeup man William Tuttle took home an "Honorary Academy Award for Makeup" in 1964, for his work on *The Seven Faces of Dr. Lao*).

Here are the 1939 Academy categories in which *The Wizard of Oz* was nominated. For comparison purposes, a very brief synopsis is included for each competing film.

Winners are indicated by **boldface**.

Best Picture

Dark Victory. Socialite Bette Davis contracts a fatal brain tumor.

Gone With the Wind. Southern belle Scarlett O'Hara (Vivien Leigh) taps her inner strength to survive and find love during the most challenging days of the Civil War.

Goodbye, Mr. Chips. Chilly schoolteacher Robert Donat is softened by love and becomes a favorite of his students.

Love Affair. Charles Boyer and Irene Dunne develop a shipboard romance.

Mr. Smith Goes to Washington. Idealistic young Jimmy Stewart is elected to Congress and learns that politics is a bare-knuckle business.

Ninotchka. Glamorous Russian agent Greta Garbo unexpectedly finds love in Paris.

Of Mice and Men. Two drifters (Burgess Meredith and Lon Chaney Jr.) struggle to survive in Depression-plagued California.

Stagecoach. When stagecoach passengers are attacked by Indians, they work with outlaw John Wayne to meet the threat.

The Wizard of Oz. Young Kansas girl finds wonder and danger in the fabulous Land of Oz.

Wuthering Heights. Class prejudice sabotages the romance of Heathcliff and Cathy (Laurence Olivier and Merle Oberon).

Best Cinematography, Color

Drums Along the Mohawk, Ray Rennahan and Bert Glennon. In upstate New York, farmer Henry Fonda and wife Claudette Colbert are drawn into the violence of the Revolutionary War.

The Four Feathers, Georges Périnal and Osmond Borradaile. After resigning his commission and being wrongly accused of cowardice, a British officer (John Clements) undertakes a masquerade and a hazardous journey in order to redeem himself.

Gone With the Wind, Ernest Haller and Ray Rennahan.

The Mikado, William V. Skall and Bernard Knowles. From the fanciful Gilbert and Sullivan operetta, Japanese lovers Nanki-Poo (Kenny Baker) and Yum-Yum (Jean Colin) play cat and mouse with the royal executioner.

The Private Lives of Elizabeth and Essex, Sol Polito and W. Howard Greene.

The Wizard of Oz, Hal Rosson.

Best Art Direction

Beau Geste, Hans Dreier and Robert Odell. Three brothers in the French Foreign Legion battle Arabs and their own sadistic commander.

Captain Fury, Charles D. Hall. An escaped Irish convict (Brian Aherne) leads a rebellion against a cruel landowner.

First Love, Jack Otterson and Martin Obzina. A beautiful orphan (Deanna Durbin) goes to live with her uncle and finds a beau.

Gone With the Wind, Lyle Wheeler.

Love Affair, Van Nest Polglase and Alfred Herman.

Man of Conquest, John Victor Mackay. Lavish and exciting tale of Texas empire-builder Sam Huston (Richard Dix).

Mr. Smith Goes to Washington, Lionel Banks.

The Private Lives of Elizabeth and Essex, Anton Grot. Queen Elizabeth I (Bette Davis) loves the Earl of Essex (Errol Flynn), but worries that his popularity might undercut her position as monarch.

The Rains Came, William S. Darling and George Dudley. In Ranchipur, Indian physician Tyrone Power carries on a dalliance with bored Myrna Loy until natural disasters rearrange everyone's priorities.

Stagecoach, Alexander Toluboff.

The Wizard of Oz, Cedric Gibbons and William A. Horning.

Wuthering Heights, James Basevi.

Best Song

"Faithful Forever," Ralph Rainger and Leo Robin, *Gulliver's Travels*. Elaborate cartoon-animated version of the Jonathan Swift satire.

"I Poured My Heart into a Song," Irving Berlin, *Second Fiddle*. Although a studio publicity man (Tyrone Power) falls for a new, young star (Sonja Henie), he cooks up a phony romance between the girl and another actor.

"Over the Rainbow," Harold Arlen and E. Y. Harburg. *The Wizard of Oz*.

"Wishing (Will Make It So)," Buddy de Sylva, *Love Affair*.

Best Original Score

Dark Victory, Max Steiner.

Eternally Yours, Werner Janssen. Loretta Young impulsively marries a philandering magician (David Niven) and lives to regret it.

Golden Boy, Victor Young. Cynical Barbara Stanwyck convinces a promising young violinist (William Holden) to pursue his dream of boxing, but then has second thoughts.

Gone With the Wind, Max Steiner.

Gulliver's Travels, Victor Young.

The Man in the Iron Mask, Lud Gluskin and Lucien Moraweck. The Three Musketeers rescue Philippe (Louis Hayward), who has been unjustly imprisoned by his brother, King Louis XIV (Hayward).

Man of Conquest, Victor Young.

Nurse Edith Cavell, Anthony Collins. A British nurse (Anna Neagle) in German-occupied Belgium during World War I helps establish an escape line for captured Allied soldiers.

Of Mice and Men, Aaron Copland.
The Rains Came, Alfred Newman.
The Wizard of Oz, Herbert Stothart.
Wuthering Heights, Alfred Newman.

Best Visual Effects

Gone With the Wind, Jack Cosgrove, Fred Albin, and Arthur Johns.
Only Angels Have Wings, Roy Davidson and Edwin C. Hahn. The fatalistic Geoff
   (Cary Grant) leads a close-knit group of air mail pilots in South America;
   the group is disrupted by the arrival of a showgirl (Jean Arthur) and a new
   pilot (Richard Barthelmess) with a bad past.
The Private Lives of Elizabeth and Essex, Byron Haskin and Nathan Levinson.
The Rains Came, E. H. Hansen and Fred Sersen.
Topper Takes a Trip, Roy Seawright. When a friendly ghost (Constance Bennett)
   inadvertently upsets the marriage of Cosmo Topper (Roland Young), Cosmo
   takes his wife (Billie Burke) on a trip to France.
Union Pacific, Farciot Edouart, Gordon Jennings, and Loren Ryder. Railroad
   troubleshooter Joel McCrea tries to keep construction of the Union Pacific
   on schedule while battling an old friend (Robert Preston) and falling in love
   with the local postmistress (Barbara Stanwyck).
The Wizard of Oz, A. Arnold "Buddy" Gillespie and Douglas Shearer.

Dorothy, the Crime of the Century, and America's Love of Childhood

Audiences went to see *The Wizard of Oz* expecting to be entertained, and they
were. On that very basic and important level, the film was a triumph. What a
gift to the world!

The movie has enjoyed enduring popularity partly because it's equally
satisfying for children and adults. The film's spectacle is obvious, and all of it
unfolds in the service of a thrilling quest adventure with intriguing, sympathetic
characters. That sort of achievement brings pleasure to everyone. The adult
portion of today's audiences, though, can focus (if it wishes) on ideas reflected
in the film that help us to a clearer understanding of the world of America in
1938–39. The most apparent example is the drab nature of the Gale farm, which
is an intentional reflection of the Depression and the Dust Bowl that parched
crops across the plains states and wiped out thousands of family farms. The
Depression was tamed by the New Deal and eliminated by the employment
brought to America by World War II, and rain eventually came again to the
Great Plains, but when *The Wizard of Oz* was released, audiences understood the
reality that was hinted at by Dorothy's Kansas.

The film alludes to other ideas and issues that grew in popularity during
the 1920s and '30s: sleep, dreams, and psychoanalysis; adult education and

self-improvement; dangerous women (the Ruth Snyder murder case was still fresh in people's minds in 1939); and "humbug" leaders (such as President Harding and self-serving evangelist Aimee Semple McPherson). There was the Technocracy movement (as reflected by the Wizard's supposed governance via technological trickery), brutal warfare in Asia (the Witch's army of Winkies and winged monkeys), the lengthening shadow of war in Europe (the Witch's threats against Dorothy), and the love of family and other homely virtues that mattered greatly in an America that was still conservative and provincial. The movie may be at its most piquant, though, in its continual allusions to the vulnerability of children.

"Childhood" wasn't invented until the rise of an educated middle class in Britain and America during the second half of the 19th century. Industrialization and commercial agriculture freed great numbers of people from laborious piecework and the fields, and although many children of the underclass continued to work in punishing conditions, more than ever before were allowed to be children, as we understand the concept today. They were encouraged to read and play. They ate well and wore clothing that was designed just for them. (No more cut-down adult clothes.) Because middle-class parents now had the luxury of valuing their offspring as something other than field hands and laborers, childhood ceased to be an unavoidable and inconvenient way station on the path to useful adulthood. Instead, it was an end in itself but transient, and even more precious because of that. New attitudes of educators, social workers, health-care professionals, philanthropic organizations, and women's clubs promoted the well-being of children and the concomitant happy glow of proud parents. Childhood became idealized and sentimentalized. Children were loved (and often displayed) as tangible evidence of couples' status and success. Publishers, clothing companies, toymakers, piano manufacturers, pharmaceutical concerns, catalogue companies, and many other businesses created children's products for middle-class buyers. By the time L. Frank Baum wrote his first Oz book in 1900, childhood was on its way to becoming an institution.

Although the American Depression staggered that conceit, the middle class didn't disappear. Even when American unemployment reached 25 percent in 1933, three-quarters of workers were still employed, and many in that number were middle class. The idealization of children continued.

In MGM's Oz, Dorothy endures hardship (life on the farm) and wonder (the beauties of Oz). But she wants desperately to return home. The road back is difficult and dangerous, and it's plain that Dorothy is frighteningly vulnerable. That vulnerability had special resonance for audiences of 1939 because one of the biggest and most sensational news stories of the century was at that time only seven years in the past: the 1932 kidnap-murder of the infant son of Anne and Charles Lindbergh. A fearless and visionary aviator, Charles had flown alone across the Atlantic in 1927 and became, literally, the most famous person in the world. For the remainder of the 1920s, his celebrity eclipsed that of all other public figures. He leveraged the adoration he received to fashion himself into an aggressive advocate for commercial and military aviation, involve himself in international relations (he admired Adolf Hitler), and answer requests for his thoughts on many subjects, including some (such as the crackpot eugenics movement) for which he was unqualified to offer opinions. But because he was "Lindy," America and Europe listened.

Twenty-month-old Charles Lindbergh Jr. was taken from his second-floor nursery at the Lindberghs' New Jersey estate sometime during the evening of March 1, 1932. A series of thirteen ransom notes delivered to the Lindberghs and an intermediary between March 1 and April 2 variously demanded payments of $50,000 or $70,000. Fifty thousand dollars was finally delivered on April 2 to an elusive man known as "John." John told the intermediary that the boy was alive and could be found on the *Nellie*, a small boat anchored at Martha's Vineyard, Massachusetts.

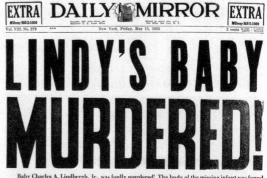

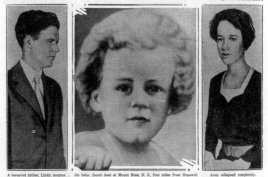

The kidnap-murder of Charles Lindbergh Jr. shocked and preoccupied all America, and suggested that *everybody's* children might be at risk at any time. For grown-ups who saw *Oz* in 1939, the crime made young Dorothy Gale's on-screen peril doubly frightening.

Charles Lindbergh Jr. was not on or anywhere near the boat.

The baby's body was finally found, partially buried, in a wooded area some four miles from the Lindbergh home, on May 12, 1932. A German immigrant named Bruno Richard Hauptmann was eventually arrested and convicted of the crime. He was executed on April 3, 1936, but that was small solace to the Lindberghs and not much of a salve to the rest of America's parents, either.

The world's greatest hero had suffered a stunning loss. It seemed impossible, but it had happened. Mothers and fathers across America absorbed the obvious lesson: if it can happen to Lindy, it can happen to us.

The preciousness of children, already a national preoccupation, became an obsession. Although America could summon only modest sympathy for the Chinese children already being slaughtered by the Japanese in Manchuria, the well-being of American kids became an issue of national importance.

When movie audiences witnessed Dorothy's abduction in *The Wizard of Oz* and stared at that rapidly emptying hourglass, they inevitably thought of the Lindbergh baby and worried for their own children. In this regard, The *Wizard of Oz* was one of the most timely and affecting movies of Hollywood's golden age.

The 1949 Re-release

MGM re-released *The Wizard of Oz* on June 1, 1949, coincidentally, just days after the studio suspended Judy Garland for unexcused absences from the shoot of *Annie Get Your Gun*. (The production was troubled from the outset. Judy returned but continued to struggle, and was finally dismissed from the project in September 1949. She was replaced by Betty Hutton.) Prior to the re-release of *Oz*, moviegoers were teased by one of the color trailers from 1939, with a new printed tag: "MGM A MASTERPIECE REPRINT Brought back in response to more requests than for any other picture" (capitalization style in original; "Masterpiece Reprint" was MGM's elevated term for "re-release").

In a poorly considered cost-saving measure, lab work for the '49 reissue printed the Kansas sequences in black and white rather than the original sepia. MGM's box-office projections for the re-release were modest (which may explain the "so what?" decision to print in black and white). The studio marketing department just wasn't thinking very clearly, but was rewarded, nonetheless, with an enormous $1.5 million gross (the equivalent of $14.7 million in 2013 dollars)—a sum sufficient to put *The Wizard of Oz* into profit for the first time.

This great success also was a testament to the gifts of Judy Garland and the level of popularity she had achieved since 1939.

Promotional materials for the '49 reissue featured post-*Oz* photo portraits of Judy Garland that had been snapped during the production of *Meet Me in St. Louis* (1944).

Time magazine, a prominent opinion maker since the 1930s, raved about *Oz* in May 1949: "The whimsical gaiety, the lighthearted song and dance, the

Oz finally went into the black when MGM re-released the film to theaters in June 1949. The "1939" Judy dominated the dress-up banner beneath the marquee of the Loew's Orpheum in Boston (shown), while the side posters showed a more contemporary image.

lavish Hollywood sets and costumes are as fresh and beguiling today as they were ten years ago when the picture was first released. Oldsters over ten who have seen it once will want to see it again. Youngsters not old enough to be frightened out of their wits by the Wicked Witch . . . will have the thrill of some first-rate make-believe."

The first re-release coincided with the 1949 publication of the fortieth authorized *Oz* book, Jack Snow's *The Shaggy Man of Oz*.

The 1955 Re-release

When Judy Garland received a 1954 best actress Oscar nomination for brilliant work in a Warner Bros. release, *A Star Is Born*, MGM felt the time was perfect for another big-screen re-release. But the industry had changed dramatically since the previous re-release of 1949. MGM executives stopped to think for a while. How could they get maximum profit from a second reissue?

Because television was providing free entertainment (the only work required of the viewer was an ability to sit through commercials), the Hollywood studios fought back with technical innovation and spectacle. 20th Century-Fox's most important 1954 release, *The Robe*, is a costume epic about the Roman military unit that oversaw the crucifixion of Jesus. Fox front-loaded *The Robe* with stars, including Richard Burton, Jean Simmons, and Victor Mature, but gambled that the real attraction for audiences was going to be the studio's new, proprietary shooting and projection system called CinemaScope. Prior to *The Robe*, Hollywood films had been projected in an industry-standard 1.37:1 aspect ratio, by which the image was about one-third wider than it was tall. (Silent-era movies had been 1.33:1.) At a glance, the projected 1.37:1 image appeared to be square.

CinemaScope upended all of that, shooting with special Bausch and Lomb lenses that anamorphically "squeezed" the image laterally, to a 2:1 ratio. (The word "anamorphic" is a 1954 invention of 20th Century-Fox; the proper term, which Fox found unwieldy, is *anamorphotic*.) During exhibition at properly equipped theaters, projectors with unique lenses eliminated the squeeze and threw a very wide 2.55:1 image onto new, rectangular screens designed to accommodate it. Because of the opportunity for lavish visuals, and a sense of being enfolded by the image, CinemaScope was a smash. So valuable was the process's name, in fact, that when Fox applied the technology to its B-films, opening credits referred to the widescreen process as "Regalscope."

Similar tech innovations quickly followed, chiefly VistaVision (from Paramount) and Panavision (a proprietary camera system that could be rented by any studio). After taking these developments into consideration, the brainiacs at MGM decided that the 1955 re-release of *Oz* should be in widescreen in big-city theaters—never mind that the film had been shot in the 1.37:1 ratio. Regardless, a simulation of widescreen was easily created by simply masking the image to create a horizontal, 1.85:1 expanse that, quite unhelpfully, deleted the top and bottom of every frame. The false widescreen (which MGM called Metroscope) was an aesthetic disaster. In 1938–39, with markedly horizontal screens still fifteen years in the future, Victor Fleming and the other *Oz* directors had no reason to make allowance for image areas that would be lost to top-and-bottom masking.

MGM pre-release hype for 1955 said, "Let's go 'OVER THE RAINBOW' with Judy in her greatest hit!" (The song that had nearly been cut in 1939 had become, by 1955, a major selling point!) The re-release posters for 1955 were dominated by photo portraits of Judy that dated from somewhere during the previous ten years. *The Wizard of Oz* opened across the country on June 17, 1955, and went on to gross $931,000, the equivalent of $8.1 million in 2013 dollars.

As in 1949, though, not everyone at MGM was thinking with a clear head. Some of the playdate situations of 1955 were not completely desirable—in smaller urban theaters, *Oz* was often paired with vastly inferior second features, and it was parked at too many second-run houses, where admissions were lower than at first-run hardtops. The $931,000 was welcome at the studio, but the sum could have been considerably greater if more care had been taken with distribution.

Despite the solid 1955 box office for *Oz*, MGM later had second thoughts about the phony widescreen setup. The 1.85:1 *Oz* never aired on television, nor has it been issued in any home-video format. Others in the industry, though, weren't shy about widescreen created on the cheap. A false widescreen process similar to the sort that bollixed up *Oz* in '55 had begun to be used by other studios, with reasonable effectiveness, at about the same time. The most common was called Superscope. With that process, movies that had been shot with standard equipment at 1.37:1 were fiddled with in the lab, via optical printer, so that the tops and bottoms of the frames were masked to produce a 2:1 ratio. When directors knew ahead of time that their projects were going to be screened in Superscope, they compensated by framing shots with unnecessary visual information, top and bottom. When the frames were cropped in the lab, nothing vital was eliminated. Superscope was originally used by RKO, during that studio's final few years. It also was picked up by smaller outfits, including American Releasing Corporation (later American International Pictures) and Allied Artists.

The 1970 and 1971 Re-releases

In both of these years, *The Wizard of Oz* returned to theaters as part of a daytime attraction that MGM called the Children's Matinee. As suggested above, these (and all subsequent theatrical and TV showings) preserved the movie's original 1.37:1 aspect ratio. (In a rather unpleasant irony, Judy's fans were surprised and hurt in 1967 when the actress revealed on Chicago's *The Irv Kupcinet Show* that MGM had refused to *sell* her a 16mm print of *Oz* for her private use—during a period of profitable TV showings and theatrical re-releases.)

The 1970 trailer begins with a Children's Matinee logo and then offers a breathless, male voice-over: "Imagine, you're over the rainbow, in a *fantastic* land of tiny people *half* your size!" Consistent with the presumed children-only audience, the real names of cast members are not given.

The other MGM films in the Children's Matinee package were *Lassie Come Home* (1943), *The Yearling* (1946), and *Kim* (1950).

The 1998 Re-release

Broadcast mogul Ted Turner acquired the classic-era MGM film library in 1986. Under his directive, *Oz* was restored, remastered, and remixed for distribution to theaters by Warner Bros. Unfortunately, this was another spurious widescreen release. Further, a very slight misalignment of the original three-strip Technicolor produced a slightly degraded image.

In conjunction with MGM's "Children's Matinee" re-release of 1970, Margaret Hamilton, Ray Bolger, and Jack Haley did a quick reprise of their iconic roles.

Early plans to reinstate the full "Scarecrow dance" sequence that had been directed by Busby Berkeley were abandoned.

Gross receipts for this re-release were $11.3 million.

The 1999 Re-release

This was the 1998 restoration, released only in Australia, to commemorate the film's 60th anniversary.

The 2002 Re-release

This was a limited theatrical run, in the original 1.37:1 ratio.

The 2009 Re-release

The Wizard of Oz was shown in select American theaters on two nights only: September 23 and November 17. Total gross was $910,000.

The 2012 Re-release

On June 30, an original 1939 print of *The Wizard of Oz* was shown at the Saban Theatre in Beverly Hills.

The 2013 Re-release

Other than the faux-widescreen reissue, this one stirred mild controversy among purists because it was released in 3-D. Of course, *The Wizard of Oz* had not been shot with 3-D exhibition in mind. Some fans were outraged, but many more were curious, and excited, about this new development.

"Dimensional" movies hit big in 1952, when Arch Oboler's jungle programmer *Bwana Devil* was shot and screened in 3-D. "A lion in your lap!" the ads promised. "A lover in your arms!" Other 3-D movies quickly followed, notably *House of Wax* (1953) and *It Came from Outer Space* (1953). Very shortly, even comic books were in 3-D, with "free" glasses. The fad burned itself out after three or four years, with some studios, independent producers, and exhibitors taking such baths that the term "3-D" became poison.

The technology, improved by now, returned in the early 1980s, mainly in horror films (notably in 1982's *Friday the 13th 3-D*, in which human viscera, and not lions, were in your lap). Some of these thrillers did big box office, but, as before, the technology had no legs and was quickly gone again. Worse, the technology had been stained by its link to gruesome horror.

But time forgives a lot. By the millennium, movie audiences were younger than ever before, far less sophisticated than they assumed, and thus ripe for 3-D technology that had become startlingly effective. The cardboard glasses with a red lens and a green one were long gone, and with them the headache-inducing fuzziness and distortions of earlier years. 3-D glasses now were sturdy plastic with clear, subtly toned lenses. 3-D screen images were sharp and bright. Many films that went on to become huge hits were shot and exhibited in 3-D (*Gravity* [2013] may be the most sterling recent example); others that had been shot "flat" were transformed into 3-D with technology that hadn't been available even ten years earlier. Sometimes the decision to do this was made to goose a new film that had been shot flat and still awaited release, such as *World War Z* (2013). In other instances, profitable 3-D versions were made from past blockbusters that had been shot and exhibited flat in their first releases, like *Titanic* (1996). Studios saw that fresh commercial success was possible with conversion to 3-D, particularly when played off as "event" engagements on enormous IMAX screens, at premium admission prices.

Pre-release hype for the IMAX *Oz* was frankly tantalizing, though one IMAX executive delivered a howler when he claimed that "it's a movie that very few people alive have seen in a movie theater." The 3-D conversion was executed by Prime Focus World, which worked from the original Technicolor camera negative, which had been restored and remastered in the original 1.37:1 aspect ratio. The 3-D conversion was accomplished over fourteen months. Prime Focus World producers identified scenes that introduce and establish key characters and settings—what they called "hero shots"—and used them as the touchstones for the entire conversion.

The dimensional effect is startling but subtle; nothing is aggressively shoved into the viewers' laps. Prime Focus did say, though, that the 3-D was brought up a notch for certain images, notably close-ups on the Wicked Witch's face. On screen, her pointed nose and chin are particularly unnerving. Dimensionality was manipulated so that the Munchkins appear particularly small in relation to their environment. One Prime Focus producer, Justin Jones, was especially pleased with the new detail and impact of the Lion's curls after his mane has been given a permanent by Emerald City beauticians.

In all, some 1,500 Prime Focus employees and contract workers had a hand in the conversion.

The Wizard of Oz 3D was an IMAX exclusive that opened in 318 IMAX theaters on September 20, 2013, for an advertised one-week engagement that Warner Bros. was ready to extend if business was sufficiently brisk. High-profile IMAX venues in the United States include Chicago's Navy Pier, Atlantic City's The Quarter at Tropicana, and Manhattan's Loew's Lincoln Square. The biggest, though, is Hollywood's TCL IMAX Chinese Theatre, formerly Grauman's Chinese Theatre. Grauman's had been in financial trouble since the 1990s and had had more than its share of technical troubles, too—such as speakers that blew in the middle of screenings. Talk of converting the space into a nightclub shocked longtime theater buffs. It was finally decided that the Chinese would carry on as an IMAX venue that could also show non-IMAX movies. The theater closed for retrofitting at the beginning of May 2013 and underwent conversion construction until mid-September. The theater reopened on September 20, with *The Wizard of Oz 3D* as its first attraction. With 986 seats, the TCL Chinese has the greatest capacity of all IMAX venues.

Immediately after the Grauman's IMAX release, Internet chatter suggested that the brilliantly pristine print and 3-D effects were very well liked by fans; many viewers reported the excitement of seeing visual details that they'd never seen before. Details of makeup, such as the Scarecrow's burlap-textured face and neck, and the precisely fitted Munchkin bald caps that were dressed with wigs, could now be fully appreciated. Michael Phillips, film critic for the *Chicago Tribune*, was moved because he could see a hint of Judy Garland's girlish freckles beneath her foundation makeup. Other viewers noticed details of fabric and set decoration; even the individual grains in the Witch's hourglass were clearly visible. (Because sand resisted attempts to dye it, the hourglass's individual grains are uncooked strawberry Jell-O. Some sources make the unlikely assertion that the grains were pulverized red sequins.)

The 3-D enhanced the film rather than distracted from it. The depth effects gave Kansas and Oz much greater spatial reality than before; even the gorgeous matte paintings (such as the hills that stretch behind the Scarecrow's cornfield) were divided into discrete planes. Viewers didn't feel like participants (the 3-D technicians never intended that anyway), but like intimate observers.

In the *New York Post*, reviewer Lou Lumenick said, "It looks fantastic, sounds great, and the 3-D effects (reportedly labored over for 16 months by a thousand technicians) are both subtle and respectfully applied. . . . If I could convene a séance, I'd guess that this presentation of 'The Wizard of Oz' would get a big thumbs up in the sky from Victor Fleming [and the entire cast and crew]."

Claudia Puig of *USA Today* wrote, "The blend of old-fashioned, classic storytelling with cutting-edge technology is undeniably enthralling." Puig praised the clarity of the digitally restored print, and was particularly delighted to be able to see heretofore-obscured details of makeup and the word "OZ" emblazoned on the green T-shirts worn by workers in the Emerald City.

In a bit of a gaffe, Puig wondered why the Kansas sequences ("memorably in black and white," she wrote) were "tinted to sepia." Apparently unaware that those scenes were in sepiatone in original-release prints from 1939, and in nearly all prints struck since then, Puig assumed that the switch to sepia had been engineered for the IMAX release. She found the reasoning for this "unclear."

In *Newsday*, Rafer Guzman sounded pleased to report that "[h]igh-resolution technology means the Technicolor palette really pops, but without losing the dreamy, soft-grain feel of old-fashioned celluloid." He questioned the value of the 3-D, but concluded that the overall technical upgrades to the visuals and the audio "make this restored version of the 1939 classic worth the hefty [IMAX] ticket price—up to $19."

The nationwide 3-D IMAX re-release of September 2013 was a thrill for *Oz* fans. What had been scheduled as a one-week engagement stretched to four.

Virtually every reviewer was unanimous that the film

had lost none of its magic over the many years and that it has earned its place as an enduring classic.

Because it's a cultural icon, *The Wizard of Oz* didn't escape the critical notice of Peter K. Rosenthal, film critic for *The Onion*, the satiric newspaper and Web site that is "America's Finest News Source." (That's what *The Onion* says, and why should we argue?) In a video review posted on theonion.com, Rosenthal combined an obvious admiration for the film with a straight-faced lunacy that led to this: "The beloved family movie has aged tremendously well, due to its brilliant and still resonant central thesis: that all women become lost and helpless when isolated from the firm guidance of an adequate male suitor or guardian."

During its first weekend, *Oz 3D* launched itself to number nine on the national box office top ten by taking in $3.1 million at the box office, a remarkable achievement for a seventy-four-year-old film playing on just 318 screens (important releases typically open on 2,500 to 3,000 screens). The $3.1 million easily tops the opening-weekend take of two other IMAX-only re-releases from earlier in 2013: *Raiders of the Lost Ark* ($1.6 million) and *Top Gun* ($1.9 million).

After a national IMAX run of four weeks, *The Wizard of Oz 3D* had grossed $5.6 million. The movie's domestic lifetime gross, not adjusted for inflation, stands at $22.2 million.

17

A Real, Truly Live Place

Oz in Live Performance After 1939

Since 1939, more professional, semi-professional, and amateur productions of *The Wizard of Oz* than can be counted have been staged. Adaptations of Baum, the MGM film, and combinations of the two have been put on by legitimate theaters, auditoriums, circus tents, and ice rinks. Aspiring young actors have done stage versions in pre-schools, grade schools, junior highs, high schools, and colleges. *Oz* shows have been hosted by county fairs, theme parks, theaters in the round, dinner theaters, and chamber ensembles, barbershop quartets, children's theater troupes, and even medical schools.

Various stage versions have been presented around the world, from Russia to Peru.

No *Oz* completist could have had a hope of keeping up with them all—or would even want to.

Here are a few of the more notable or unusual performances.

The Wizard of Oz (1942)

The St. Louis Municipal Opera commissioned this adaptation, with book by Frank Gabrielson (borrowing heavily from the first Baum novel and the 1939 film) and familiar Arlen and Harburg tunes. This is an unusually good adaptation that's been revived by the Municipal Opera and other companies around the country.

The Wizard of Oz (1950)

The Suzari Marionettes were featured in this New York production.

The Wizard of Oz (1951)

A puppet production featuring the Reed Marionettes.

The Wizard of Oz (1959)

A women's group production staged at Brooklyn College.

The Wizard of Oz (1960–61)

This was the touring Ice Capades show for 1960–61 and marked the occasion of the extravaganza's twenty-first anniversary. Between July 1960 and May 1961, the troupe made more than 245 playdates in twenty-four major and mid-sized cities across America and southern Canada. (An alternate tour that visited thirty-five U.S. and Canadian cities during August 1960 to April 1961 put on the twentieth anniversary Ice Capades show.) "The Wizard of Oz," with eighteen-year-old skater Lynn Patsy Finnegan as Dorothy and 150 ice dancers in support, was a highlight of the twenty-first anniversary show. The thirteen-minute segment was narrated by prominent radio actress Betty Lou Gerson, who had played Glinda in the 1950 *Lux Radio Theatre* presentation of *Oz* starring Judy Garland. (Gerson was the voice of Cruella De Vil in the 1961 Disney animated feature *One Hundred and One Dalmatians*.) Other highlights of the show were a Rodgers and Hammerstein tribute, Rimsky-Korsakov's *Scheherazade*, and "Ballet Militaire."

The Wizard of Oz on Ice (1960)

This United Kingdom production utilized the MGM film score.

The touring Ice Capades show for 1960–61 included a *Wizard of Oz* extravaganza.

The Wizard of Oz (1960)

Dorothy's adventures were staged by the Ringling Brothers and Barnum & Bailey Circus.

The Yellow Knight of Oz (1963)

Oz with a science-fiction twist, staged by the Willow Grove (NJ) Park Playhouse.

Snow White Meets the Wizard of Oz (1963)

Willow Grove (NJ) Park Playhouse.

The Wizard of Oz (1964)

A live presentation staged at the Tupperware convention and awards ceremony, Northern Illinois University. Throughout the 1960s, other Tupperware dealer conventions screened a 16mm motivational film, *The Wizard of Ours*.

The Wizard of Oz (1966)

In September, Baum's *The Wizard of Oz* was staged in Chicago by Ralph Kipniss's Royal European Marionette Theater. The cast was comprised of fifty-five detailed, oversized puppets.

The Emerald City of Oz (1971)

Gayle Cotterell's play opened on June 28 at Salt Lake City's Memorial Theatre for a monthlong run.

Trolmanden fra Oz (1973)

Copenhagen's Det Lille Theater staged *Trolmanden fra Oz*, a play based on the Classics Illustrated Junior comic book adaptation of 1957. The show opened on September 20.

The Marvelous Land of Oz (1974)

Writer Martin Williams's *The Marvelous Land of Oz* was staged at the Smithsonian Institution Puppet Theater.

The Wiz (1975)

The celebrated black-cast musical version of *The Wizard of Oz* staged tryouts in Baltimore before opening at New York's Majestic Theatre on January 5, 1975, enjoying a robust run of 1,672 performances. (The show shifted to the Broadway Theatre about halfway through the run.) Stephanie Mills, playing Dorothy, wowed audiences with her perky presence and big voice. Others in the cast were Hinton Battle as the Scarecrow, Tiger Haynes as the Tin Man, Ted Ross as the Cowardly Lion, Mabel King as Evillene (the Wicked Witch), Dee Dee Bridgewater as Glinda, and André De Shields as the Wiz. A future Broadway star, Phylicia Rashād, played a Munchkin.

Music and lyrics were by Charlie Smalls; the libretto was written by William F. Brown. Geoffrey Holder—a longtime actor-director-dancer—directed.

Audiences enjoyed the score and songs; two tunes, "Ease on Down the Road" and "Everybody Rejoice (Brand New Day)," were especially popular.

The Wiz scored big at the 1975 Tony ceremony, winning for best musical, original score, direction of a musical, choreography (George Faison), and costume design (Holder). Tonys also went to cast members Ross and Bridgewater. In addition, *The Wiz* took home four 1975 Drama Desk Awards.

Mills and Holder returned for a 1984 Broadway revival that ran just thirteen performances. Over the years, the show has had greater latter-day legit success in Chicago and Los Angeles, and in cities abroad. A 2004 Broadway revival was planned but ultimately abandoned.

In 1978, Motown and Universal collaborated to adapt the play to film. The movie version of *The Wiz* starred Diana Ross as Dorothy; to some people, the casting of the thin-voiced Ross was a detriment that couldn't be overcome. Ted Ross and Mabel King reprised their stage roles. Other principal cast members were Michael Jackson as the Scarecrow, Nipsey Russell as the Tin Man, Lena Horne as Glinda, and Richard Pryor as the Wiz.

The stage version maintained the fantasy settings set down by Baum and perpetuated by MGM. For the film adaptation, though, director Sidney Lumet and screenwriter Joel Schumacher chose to open the story in Harlem and transport Dorothy (now a schoolteacher rather than a Kansas girl) to a fantasyland version of New York.

Despite the powerhouse cast and the advantages of familiar source material, *The Wiz* was a critical and commercial disappointment that enchanted almost nobody. On a $24 million budget, it managed a gross of just $13 million.

The Wizard of Oz (1979)

Staged at South Kingstown, Rhode Island's Theatre-by-the-Sea, featuring Fred Barton as the Wicked Witch of the West (see below).

Miss Gulch Lives! (1983)

This one-man musical revue about the storied life of Almira Gulch was written and performed by Fred Barton, at Palsson's Supper Club in New York City. Songs: "Born on a Bike," "Pour Me a Man"—and "I'm a Bitch," which, according to Miss Gulch, was rudely cut from the MGM version of *Oz*. Following Margaret Hamilton's death, the show's name was changed to *Miss Gulch Returns!*

The Wizard of Oz (1983)

This stage play was produced in Tokyo and sponsored by Seiby department store. Chika Takami played Dorothy.

ODDysey in Oz (1983)

This stage play by Virginia Koste premiered in Ypsilanti, Michigan's Quirk Theater.

Royal Shakespeare Company's The Wizard of Oz (1987)

This production was adapted from the 1939 film by John Kane and closely follows that film's script. The Arlen-Harburg songs were retained. Dorothy was played by Imelda Staunton (who more recently has appeared as Prof. Umbridge in various Harry Potter adventures).

Holiday in Oz (1988)

Staged by the famed Pasadena Playhouse for Christmas audiences, this lively musical incorporated Robin Hood, Friar Tuck, and Mr. and Mrs. Santa Claus. The Playhouse brought the show back during subsequent holiday seasons. Written and directed by co-star Steve Cassling.

Radio City Music Hall's The Wizard of Oz (1989)

Created to tie in with the fiftieth anniversary of the MGM release, this elaborate show used prerecorded music and dialogue. It flopped in New York, and a planned seventy-city tour was canceled.

Was (1994)

Chicago's Victory Gardens Theater staged this Albert Williams play based on Geoff Ryman's 1992 novel of the same name. On the surface, the premise seems nothing but bluntly exploitative: Kansas orphan Dorothy Gael [*sic*] is exiled to the slow death of Kansas, where she so upsets her Aunt Em that Em kills Toto; and finds herself the victim in an ongoing sexual affair engineered by her Uncle Henry. A kindly schoolteacher, Mr. Baum, tries to help, but over time, Dorothy goes mad. At this juncture, the story expands beyond the merely shocking to become a metaphysical and heartfelt rumination on the power of art and the importance of fantasy. After Dorothy is discovered following fifty years of confinement in an asylum, she sees *The Wizard of Oz* on television and loudly proclaims that the filmmakers got it all wrong.

In a related parallel story, Dorothy's past is investigated by an AIDS sufferer named Jonathan. He's a former horror-movie star who struggles to resist a child-based obsession with MGM's *Oz*. Jonathan's psychiatrist, Bill, had been an orderly at the mental hospital where Dorothy spent the greater part of her life. Separately and together, these characters probe and dig at the relationship of fantasy to reality, and art to truth.

Twister! A Musical Catastrophe for the Millennium's End (1994)

One Flew Over the Cuckoo's Nest author Ken Kesey wrote this *Oz*-inspired psychedelic piece that incorporates (take a breath) Norse legend, Toto's accidental castration (by a flying violin), AIDS, computer viruses, the Cold War, climate catastrophe, Frankenstein's monster, right-wing militias, and the consequences of Dorothy's careless sexual behavior. When the play was presented at city's New Fillmore in May 1994, the lead players were Kesey and his Merry Pranksters—all of whom had created anarchic conceptual art happenings in the 1960s.

The Wizard of Oz on Ice (1995)

Another adaptation for a cast of skaters, presented by Kenneth Feld. The costumes designed for Dorothy, the Wizard, and the Winkies were inspired by the MGM movie. The Jitterbug makes an appearance in this show.

The Wizard of Oz in Concert: Dreams Come True (1995)

Star-studded musical reinterpretation of Noel Langley's MGM script was staged live at New York's Avery Fisher Hall, Lincoln Center for the Performing Arts, in October 1995, as a hybrid play-concert, and filmed for later broadcast on the TNT cable network. Television actor Darrell Larson wrote, produced, and co-directed (with Louis J. Horvitz), retaining the Herbert Stothart score and Harburg-Arlen songs (with some new, additional lyrics). MGM's discarded "The Jitterbug" was revived, and among nearly a dozen new tunes were the Wicked Witch's "Cyclone" and "Poppies." The show provided an impressive showcase for Jewel Kilcher, a new, young singer-actress who called herself Jewel. She was Dorothy in a strong cast that included Jackson Browne as the Scarecrow, Roger Daltrey (doing a bit of Stan Laurel) as the Tin Woodman, Broadway's Nathan

Lane as the Cowardly Lion, stage star Joel Grey as the Wizard, and Debra Winger as the Wicked Witch of the West. Others in the cast: Natalie Cole (Glinda), Lucie Arnaz (Aunt Em), Ronnie Spector (Winkie captain), James Waller (Toto), the Boys Choir of Harlem (Munchkins), and Alfre Woodard (host). On-stage musical support came from Phoebe Snow and Ry Cooder.

The Wizard of Oz (1997)

Shortly after the wrap-up of her long-running sitcom, comic actress Roseanne Barr played the Wicked Witch of the West in this opulent, MGM-based production that opened May 7 for a scheduled forty-eight performances at Madison Square Garden. Fifteen-year-old Jessica Grove was Dorothy. Others in the 1997 cast: Lara Teeter as the Scarecrow, Michael Gruber as the Tin Woodman, Ken Page as the Cowardly Lion (he had played another version of the Lion in the original Broadway production of *The Wiz*), and Gerry Vichi as the Wizard/ Prof. Marvel. When the show embarked on a national tour in 1998, Vichi was replaced by Mickey Rooney, a real-life friend of Judy Garland. Michael Gruber was replaced by Dirk Lombard, and Barr left the production as well, opening the door for Eartha Kitt as a memorably sexy—and singing—Wicked Witch. Kitt became the actor most closely identified with the 1998 tour. (When Kitt fell ill for a time in 1999, JoAnne Worley took the role.) The show toured until late in 1999.

Munchkin Holiday (2002)

Rob Papineau presented the Pippin Puppets in this whimsical production staged at the Theatre Guild in Livonia-Redford, Michigan.

Sing-a-Long Wizard of Oz (2002)

A screening of the 1939 film presented as an audience-participation musical, Chicago Ford Theater.

Oz: A Twisted Musical (2003)

Another purposely provocative spin on the familiar tale, this ambitious high-school production by Bill Francoeur (music and lyrics) and Tim Kelly (book) posits Dorothy as a street-smart grunge teenager and the Wicked Witch as a devotee of S&M. The musical was staged at Producer's Club II in Manhattan, following an award-winning 2002 run at the Jay Todd Theater, Hudson County (NJ) Schools of Technology. (Paper Mill Playhouse Rising Star Award, best overall musical in New Jersey.) Kyla Garcia appeared as Dorothy.

Wicked: The Untold Story of the Witches of Oz (2003)

Wicked began as an extraordinarily popular 1995 novel by Gregory Maguire, an academic who reimagined Baum's *The Wizard of Oz* as the journey to adulthood undertaken by Elphaba, the mysteriously green-skinned, razor-toothed girl of Oz who is destined to become the Wicked Witch of the West. Dorothy doesn't appear until late in the story, to drop her house on Elphaba's sister and prompt Elphaba to seek justice. That won't be simple because of Elphaba's deeply troubled soul and the crimes of the evil Wizard.

Part coming-of-age tale, part contrarian fable, and part exploration of identity and private dreams, *Wicked* wowed readers, despite a final hundred pages that are flat and feel superfluous. The book presents other challenges: Maguire's conception of Oz wants to be gloriously rich, but feels rushed and arbitrary. Even diligent readers are apt to be put off by the novel's clumsy plotting, contrived "surprises," and too many threads that lead nowhere. Still, the novel is blindingly imaginative and has a peculiar majesty—of intention if not of execution—and can be bracingly vivid. Certainly, the story has the central hook, the melodrama, and the vulgar energy needed to engage Broadway audiences. (Maguire elaborated on his conception of Oz in three later novels: *Son of a Witch* [2005], *A Lion Among Men* [2008], and *Out of Oz* [2011].)

Although Maguire had already sold book rights to Universal for a live-action movie adaptation (which remains likely), the studio saw the property's theatrical potential. An agreement was reached whereby Marc Platt (a Universal executive), David Stone, and Universal acted as co-producers. (Stone had Broadway and off-Broadway producer's credits going back to 1994, including *The Diary of Anne Frank* and *The Vagina Monologues*.)

The adaptation, by Stephen Schwartz (music and lyrics) and Winnie Holzman (book), is smartly streamlined. A great deal of extraneous stuff is gone, and many of the novel's gaps in plot are successfully addressed in song.

Wicked, which focuses on the melodrama attending the lives of the witches of Oz, has been a stage sensation around the world.

Used by permission of Playbill

After tryouts in San Francisco, *Wicked* opened at New York's Gershwin Theatre on October 30, 2003, directed by Joe Mantello and choreographed by Wayne Cilento.

Powerhouse singer-actress Idina Menzel, as Elphaba, headed the original cast, which also included Kristin Chenoweth as Glinda and Joel Grey as the Wizard. Audiences have been captured by the play's physical spectacle and soaring songs; "Defying Gravity" and "As Long as You're Mine" are particular crowd-pleasers. But the spectacle embodied in oversized, animated sets and props is as distancing as it is impressive and can overwhelm scenes and characters.

Wicked earned Tony awards for best actress (Menzel), costume design (Susan Hilferty), and scenic design (Eugene Lee). The original-cast CD won a Grammy in 2005.

At this writing, *Wicked* continues to play to sold-out houses at the Gershwin, passing four thousand performances and on its way to the top ten of longest-running shows in Broadway history.

A big-city U.S. tour was undertaken in 2005. The musical came to London's West End in 2006 and has since been staged around the world.

Entertainment Weekly magazine, a dependable booster of accessible middle-brow culture, has called *Wicked* "the best musical of the decade."

Was (2004)

This *Was* was a musical version of the Geoff Ryman novel of the same name, staged by Dayton, Ohio's Human Race Theatre Company.

End of the Rainbow (2005)

End of the Rainbow, a musical drama by Peter Quilter, was first presented in Sydney, Australia, in 2005 before opening on London's West End in 2010 and on Broadway in 2012, where it enjoyed a respectable run of 160 performances. The play is biographical and is set in London's Ritz Hotel during December 1968, as Judy struggles with emotional challenges while working with fiancé (later husband) Mickey Deans and her pianist in rehearsals for an upcoming engagement at London's Talk of the Town Club. Much of the play's piquancy comes from the awareness of Quilter, and audiences, that Judy's Talk of the Town dates would be smashing successes—and that Judy would be dead six months later.

The play features about a dozen songs (the number varies), all from the Judy Garland catalogue. "Over the Rainbow," Garland's signature tune, is the only one that originated in *The Wizard of Oz*. Other songs include "The Man That Got Away," "Zing! Went the Strings of My Heart," "The Trolley Song," and "I Could Go On Singing." In 2011, a cast recording of the London production, with belter Tracie Bennett as Judy, was issued on CD. A similar disc, with Bennett and the cast of the Broadway production, was released in 2012.

At this writing, *End of the Rainbow* carries on as an international success.

Unauthorized Magic in Oz (2005)

This Edward Einhorn puppet presentation was staged in Brooklyn at St. Ann's Warehouse Theatre.

Babylon Heights (2006)

This Munchkin-focused drama that explores various sorts of morale-depleting discrimination in Hollywood and the larger world had its world premiere at San Francisco's Exit Theatre on June 14. The play was written by Irvine Welsh, author of *Trainspotting* and other novels.

The Wizard of Oz (2011)

Following previews, Andrew Lloyd Webber's *The Wizard of Oz* opened in London's West End, at the London Palladium, on March 1. An intriguing mix of the Herbert Stothart score, new score elements, and new songs, the show also used numerous Arlen-Harburg tunes and took many plot elements, and dialogue, from the 1939 movie. In one of the new songs, a Webber–Tim Rice composition called "Red Shoes Blues," the Wicked Witch fancies herself a femme fatale. Danielle Hope played Dorothy, with understudy Sophie Evans doing the role each Tuesday. Michael Crawford played the Wizard. After cast changes and more than 550 performances, the show closed in September and then embarked on a world tour. At this writing, the tour is scheduled to continue into the early summer of 2014. As with another latter-day, *Oz*-inspired stage hit, *Wicked*, audiences were pleased by the show's spectacle, technical ambition, and set design. Danielle Hope was widely praised, but most critics felt that the new songs paled next to the Arlen-Harburg numbers and that the show's visual splendor prevented audiences from becoming fully engaged with the story.

Illinois- and Wisconsin-based Spotlight Youth Theater is a nonprofit children's theater arts program. During the 2013–14 season, the group mounted *The Wizard of Oz* and nearly thirty other shows.

"In Color and Black and White"

MGM's Oz on TV

MGM had ridden *The Wizard of Oz* into profitability in 1949, during the film's first theatrical re-release. Additional profit came from the second re-release in 1955. Even with those successes, *Oz* had a limited hold on the American imagination. As far as the industry was concerned, *Oz* was merely another movie that had been unable to turn a profit on its initial release. Audiences had responded well to the theatrical re-releases, but the public wasn't exactly clamoring for *Oz*. Film historian John McElwee has noted that, at the time, "*Snow White and the Seven Dwarfs* . . . was a bona fide cultural phenomenon and *Oz* was not."

Television, the film industry's presumed mortal enemy, changed all of that. Not only has the TV career of *The Wizard of Oz* generated enough gravy to float a navy, it provided the platform—and huge audiences—sufficient to elevate *Oz* to *essential* status in the culture. MGM's hunger for additional return on its original investment, plus a little bit of studio foresight, transformed *Oz* into America's best-loved movie.

MGM's first deal for television airings of *The Wizard of Oz* was made with CBS in July 1956, with Robert Weitman, the network's vice president of program development, negotiating on behalf of the network. The contract agreement, which was signed on August 2, 1956, allowed for four showings at a per-broadcast cost to CBS of $225,000. An option clause established another seven broadcasts at $150,000 apiece.

Studios other than MGM (and even some executives within MGM), as well as theater owners, objected to the TV sale. By 1956, exhibitors had invested heavily in CinemaScope screens and projection, stereophonic sound, and other upgrades designed to meet the threat posed by television. They resented the sale of enormous film libraries to television and were particularly worried that *Oz* might be followed to the home screen by other high-profile pictures. Exhibitors wondered how they could continue to compete.

The Wizard of Oz made its television debut on CBS on Saturday, November 3, 1956, in the rather late 9:00 p.m. to 11:00 p.m. time slot, EST. This initial airing was the farewell telecast of *Ford Star Jubilee*, an anthology program that the network had already canceled. Fifty-three percent of all American televisions that were on during the nine o'clock and ten o'clock hours were tuned to the movie. That astonishing figure accounted for 45 million people in nearly 13 million households and topped competing-network offerings with comics George Gobel, Sid Caesar, and cornball music meister Lawrence Welk. Only a televised campaign speech by Vice President Richard Nixon, aired opposite *Oz* during the film's last half-hour, gave the movie any real ratings competition. (The '56 presidential election fell on November 6, just three days after the *Oz* broadcast.)

The broadcast's smash ratings couldn't have pleased theater exhibitors, whose worst fears seemed to have been confirmed by a study done shortly afterward by entertainment analysts with Sidlinger & Company, who found that the Saturday-night *Oz* telecast caused a $2 million loss in nationwide theater revenue—a 7.7 percent decline in attendance. (In 2013 dollars, that $2 million deficit is equal to $17.2 million.)

Because of Ford's sponsorship, the MGM soundtrack album (the first true *Wizard of Oz* soundtrack LP; see chapter 14) was available at Ford dealerships. The 1956 telecast carried twelve minutes of Ford Motor Company commercials for the new '57 line—"action-test a new kind of Ford . . . the most elegant Ford ever," with a "long, low silhouette."

Judy Garland had been set to host the inaugural telecast, from backstage at New York's Palace Theatre, but changed her mind because of logistical problems and an attack of anxiety. Regardless, Judy watched some of the film on a Palace TV set. One can only imagine the myriad thoughts that raced through her mind. Nineteen thirty-nine probably seemed worlds away.

The 1956 broadcast was "in color and black and white" and was hosted by Bert Lahr; Garland's daughter, ten-year-old Liza Minnelli; and a twelve-year-old L. Frank Baum expert named Justin G. Schiller, who loaned CBS his first edition of *The Wonderful Wizard of Oz*. As Lahr read portions of the book aloud, he seated Minnelli and Schiller on his knees. (Schiller founded the International Wizard of Oz Club in 1957 and went on to become a successful and highly respected New York City dealer in antiquarian children's books.)

The film was not broadcast during 1957–58, but CBS resumed its involvement, by now with an intention to broadcast annually, in 1959, with an airing on Friday, October 16. Popular film and CBS-TV comic Red Skelton hosted, with help from his twelve-year-old daughter, Valentina. This time, *The Wizard of Oz* aired from 6:00 p.m. to 8:00 p.m, EST. After a broadcast layoff of two years, the *Oz* numbers for 1959 were bigger than in '56.

Before the 1960 broadcast, the 1956 contract was altered to the benefit of both parties, so that CBS was given broadcast rights for 1960–64, with MGM receiving $200,000 annually. (A subsequent contract continued the MGM-CBS relationship beyond 1964.) Partly because color television was rather exotic at the beginning of the 1960s, CBS elected to broadcast the entirety of *Oz* in black and white in 1961 and 1962.

Although color TV didn't begin to make real inroads into American homes until about 1965, it's likely that *The Wizard of Oz* would have been broadcast in color during those early years if the television rights had been held by NBC, which pioneered color-TV broadcasting, and which was owned by TV-manufacturer RCA, an aggressive proponent of color sets. But until 1989, the Kansas sequences in TV prints provided by MGM were in black and white, and not the original sepia.

The annual CBS airings became much-anticipated events, hosted by personalities with links to the network. For instance, Richard Boone, the 1960 host (with son Peter), was then starring in the CBS western *Have Gun, Will Travel*. (If the thought of craggy, faintly menacing Richard Boone hosting *The Wizard of Oz* strikes you as a little peculiar, you're not alone.) CBS star Dick Van Dyke hosted in 1961 and 1962. There was no broadcast of *Oz* in 1963, but in 1964, Danny Kaye, star of CBS's *The Danny Kaye Show*, began a particularly amiable four-year stint as host, 1964–67.

Throughout the greater part of its stewardship, CBS elected not to show the original MGM end credits; instead, the screen faded after Dorothy's final line and faded in on the CBS logo.

After a ten-year association with CBS, *Oz* peaked in the ratings in 1966, when it was the number-one show during the week it aired.

The Wizard of Oz finally came to NBC in 1968 and played on that network through 1975. By that period, *Oz* was frankly more valuable than ever before, and because inflation had gotten a grip on the American economy, the annual broadcast fee demanded by MGM was $800,000, too rich for CBS but agreeable to NBC.

Comic actor Danny Kaye hosted CBS-TV showings of *Oz* from 1964 to 1967.

Because hosts ate up valuable airtime that could be sold for commercials, NBC did away with the concept, with one exception, which was prompted by Judy Garland's death in June 1969. The first television showing of *Oz* after that tragic event, on Sunday, March 15, 1970, included a prerecorded tribute to Judy hosted by film star Gregory Peck and directed by the movie's producer, Mervyn LeRoy. (This was LeRoy's first and only foray into TV.) Not surprisingly, this broadcast of *Oz* attracted the largest audience to date: sixty-four million viewers. The broadcast had a single sponsor,

Singer, a perpetuation of a one-sponsor setup that had been the case since the first telecast in 1956.

Because of the $800,000 per-broadcast fee, NBC was determined to wring every cent from its two-hour broadcasts of the 101-minute film. To that end, the network sold commercial time to multiple advertisers (as it was by now doing on its regularly scheduled shows) and cut about a minute of footage from Dorothy's arrival in Munchkinland. The cuts ran deeper after CBS reacquired TV rights in 1976, parting with $4 million for five broadcasts (1976–80). That was a significant amount of money, even for one of television's titans, so CBS took its scissors to *Oz* in order to sell still more commercial time. The network butcher that cut the film was especially tough on the opening Kansas sequence, eliminating some gorgeous and important narrative moments: Dorothy and Toto's lonesome walk along the empty dirt road and much of the buildup to the twister. The minute that NBC had cut from Munchkinland was not restored, and snips were made to pictorial moments in the poppy field and during the trek of Dorothy's friends to the Witch's castle. Even the charming title dedication that opens the film—". . . and to the young in heart we dedicate this picture"—was discarded. *Oz* historian John Fricke calls the hacking "indiscriminate" and adds that the cuts "tore up the background score in several places."

The Wizard of Oz aired on British television for the first time on December 25, 1975. Whether the British broadcast version reflected the American TV cuts is unknown.

A special (if accidental) insult was levied against Chicago viewers in 1978, when a computer at the local CBS outlet threw a clot and replaced the film's final moments with forty-two seconds of commercials.

CBS renewed with MGM in 1981, agreeing to pay $1 million for each telecast through 1985. For years, fans of TV's *Star Trek* had complained that episodes in syndication were time-compressed (speeded up) without being cut, allowing local stations even more commercial revenue. That indignity happened to *Oz* in 1985, on the Friday, March 1, CBS broadcast. Although traditional editing is time compression of a sort—you don't have to witness every step a character takes while making her way downstairs and finally into her car to "get" her from apartment to car—the broadcast compression we're interested in here is something relatively subtle. If the networks had wanted to be ham-handed about it by the 1980s, they would have continued to cut portions of scenes from *The Wizard of Oz*, or even whole sequences. Naturally, viewers strongly familiar with the film would have noticed and objected. Sponsors, as well as the network, would have been blamed. Contrarily, time compression for broadcast is simply an acceleration of playback. If, over the course of a 100-minute movie, time compression squeezes thirty seconds off the original running time, the network has created thirty seconds of additional ad revenue. Most *Oz* TV viewers never noticed the compression, but when the technology is applied to source footage that's shorter than feature length (say, the fifty-two minutes of an original *Star Trek* episode), or if the broadcaster gets carried away while time compressing a

When CBS broadcast *Oz* in 1985, the film was time-compressed so the network could sell one or two additional commercial spots.

feature, audio may be distorted, most noticeably as speeded-up dialogue. A common visual symptom of poorly done time compression is a perceptible choppiness of pans and dolly shots. (Present-day time compression is digital and thus even more devious: the computer can be programmed with algorithms that eliminate "redundant" frames or that remove content on a regularly timed basis.)

The CBS decision for the 1985 broadcast was surely applauded by people in the network's ad-sales department, but because the *Oz* visuals and audio were altered, the technology amounted to an assault on an American treasure.

By the mid-1980s, the videocassette revolution (which allowed viewers to watch *anything* on their sets) began to hurt the ratings of the annual CBS broadcast of *Oz*. Airings during the first thirty years of the film's TV career averaged 26.4 in the ratings, meaning that more than a quarter of American homes with TV were tuned to the movie. But in February 1986, *The Wizard of Oz* had its weakest showing to date, managing a Saturday-night rating of 18.4, when CBS had hoped for a considerably better showing. (By way of contrast, the top-rated broadcast from February 10–16, 1986, was an episode of *The Cosby Show*, which garnered a 35.2.)

In 1987, CBS extended its agreement with MGM (and broadcast mogul Ted Turner, who by now owned much of the MGM film library) yet again. Ratings were robust through the 1980s, except in 1988, when CBS inexplicably ran *Oz* on a Wednesday night rather than on Sunday.

The Wizard of Oz was released to videocassette in 1980 and lost its once-a-year appeal. But it was no less popular than before, and by the late '90s it had been aired by numerous eager networks, including Ted Turner's TBS and TNT. Like CBS and NBC, those networks ran commercials, but *Oz* prints that ran there were restored to full length and were allowed to occupy a time slot longer than the traditional two hours.

After the millennium, *Oz* was moved to Turner Classic Movies (TCM), the most congenial TV home the movie has ever had. TCM is commercial-free, and resident host Robert Osborne is unfailingly knowledgeable and enthusiastic. Special weekend daytime broadcasts have been hosted by actors John Lithgow, Bill Hader, and others.

TCM broadcasts *The Wizard of Oz* multiple times in a single year, running the best available prints (lately in HD) and giving viewers the best possible small-screen *Oz* experience.

Many film actors avoid watching themselves on screen. Nevertheless, it's a bit of an irony that Judy Garland may have watched a complete telecast of *The Wizard of Oz* only once, on Sunday, January 9, 1966. She recalled for a newspaper reporter soon after that she'd spent too much time during previous viewings reassuring her children that the Munchkins were harmless. She even had doubts about the whole film. "I think it's too scary for kids," she said.

Shirley Temple Finally Gets to Oz

Serious discussion of Shirley Temple playing Dorothy was short-lived at MGM in 1938, and the young actress stayed busy with other projects. Not too long after, she became a pretty teen star who never connected with audiences as she once had. Temple's opportunity to visit Oz came decades later (and more than ten years after the end of her film career), on *Shirley Temple's Storybook*, an anthology show that aired on NBC-TV during 1960–61. Thirty-two years old and lovely, Temple acted as host and occasional star of adaptations of *The Little Mermaid*, *Babes in Toyland*, *The House of the Seven Gables*, and other venerable tales. "The Land of Oz" was broadcast on September 18, 1960, with Shirley as Princess Ozma. Others in the cast were Agnes Moorehead as Mombi the Witch, Jonathan Winters as Lord Nikidik, Ben Blue as the Scarecrow, Sterling Holloway as Jack Pumpkinhead, Gil Lamb as the Tin Woodman, and Arthur Treacher as Graves, Nikidik's butler. Indefatigable voice artist Mel Blanc played the Sawhorse.

Although a budget-conscious production, the experience is appealing, not least because Temple had made an honest commitment to bring quality material to children.

"The Land of Oz" is available on DVD as part of a double feature, with the *Storybook* adaptation of "The Reluctant Dragon."

Oz on Home Video

One of the great horrors facing children of the 1950s and '60s was the fear of missing the annual television broadcast of *The Wizard of Oz*. Worse than a pop quiz, worse than a Dutch rub, worse even than a Halloween costume made by your mother, a year without *Oz* was unendurable. Any unusual circumstance could spell doom. You could be stuck in traffic with your parents, bored out of your skull at your cousin's wedding reception, lost in Carlsbad Caverns—why, *anything* could happen.

The Wizard of Oz finally came home when MGM released the film on VHS and Beta tape in 1980. Fans fired up their forty-pound videocassette machines and thanked God that they'd lived long enough to see this miraculous technology, and to experience *Oz* at home, whenever they wished. This was bliss.

Still, MGM didn't have a good grasp of the property's commercial value. A 1985 videotape release was marketed by MGM/UA under its "Viddy-Oh! For Kids" label, as if the studio's marketing department had reasoned that since everyone who would ever want *The Wizard of Oz* had bought it back in 1980, nothing was left but to fob it off on little kids. In a happy turn, *Oz* was marketed much more appropriately in 1989, when a 50th anniversary VHS set, with a book and other extras, was issued. Ever since then, home-video releases have given fans continually improved quality and an increasing number of extras.

Oz came to the high-quality laser disc format in 1982, on the MGM/UA label. In 1989, the movie's 50th anniversary brought a pair of new laser disc releases; the one from MGM/UA was reconstructed from a Technicolor print with the Kansas scenes in sepiatone. (For many years, MGM's television prints diminished Kansas to plain black and white.) Bonus materials included the excised Busby Berkeley/Ray Bolger Scarecrow dance; "Jitterbug" audio and the Harold Arlen home-movie footage of that sequence; and Buddy Ebsen's version of "If I Only Had a Heart." There also were original trailers, a glimpse of Judy Garland accepting her special Oscar, and a coupon redeemable for a 32-page "making of" booklet.

The 1989 Criterion laser disc was licensed from MGM/UA and Janus Films.

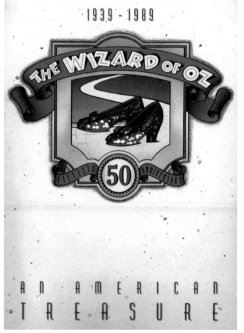

A pair of high-quality laserdisc releases for the 50th anniversary restored sepia tone to the Kansas sequences.

This was a deluxe, two-disc release with many extras: the Arlen home movies; the Buddy Ebsen song audio; an *Oz* radio broadcast; a feature about the 1903 stage play; an excerpt from Larry Semon's 1925 *Wizard of Oz* film; an interview with Munchkin player Jerry Maren; a promotional short; and views of posters and other promotional paper. The 1955 re-release trailer is also included, though the sleeve mistakenly identifies it as being from 1956. Commentary was provided by film historian Ronald Haver.

Before laser disc technology went the way of the passenger pigeon, *The Wizard of Oz* was released in that format in 1991, 1993, 1995, and 1996. The '93 release, *The Ultimate Oz*, was particularly appealing. It was a three-disc set featuring the restored film, a "making of" documentary, five glossy film stills, a $24'' \times 36''$ poster, an oversized brochure (*Your Guide to the Ultimate Oz*), and a replica of the March 15, 1939, shooting script. This release was processed in THX sound.

The first *Oz* DVD arrived in 1997 and featured the restored 1993 print of the *Ultimate Oz* laser disc. Although VHS was fading badly by this time, a videocassette version was available.

An enormous upgrade was made for the 1999 DVD/VHS release, as the print was the gorgeously restored 60th anniversary theatrical re-release. The 1999 set included everything that had been in *The Ultimate Oz* and added lobby card reproductions and striking new green packaging.

Another upgrade arrived in 2005, with a two-disc DVD set highlighted by a new "Ultra Resolution" digital master that was the best print yet. *Oz* historian John Fricke did the commentary track. Other features: two documentaries about the film and a featurette about its restoration, outtakes, a stills gallery, the making of the twister, the Arlen footage, profiles of the supporting cast, and a storybook read by Angela Lansbury. Plus vintage featurettes and a wealth of archival comments from original cast and family members, as well as behind-the-scenes personnel. Finally, six hours of audio-only material brought back original radio shows, recording sessions, and promotional material.

In the same year, 2005, Warner issued a *three-disc* DVD set containing everything from the 2005 two-disc issue, plus extensive coverage of L. Frank Baum and information about *Oz* films that preceded the 1939 version (the complete 1925 feature, restored and with a new score by Robert Israel, is included). The set also had replicas of MGM's in-house newspaper and material from the 1939 Grauman's Chinese premiere, reproductions of original MGM Kodachrome stills, and the 1939 *Photoplay* study guide.

The first Blu-ray release of *Oz*, from September 2009, was marketed as *The Wizard of Oz 70th Anniversary Ultimate Collector's Edition*. The movie was remastered for this four-disc release, achieving unprecedented clarity and brilliance. The soundtrack was enhanced with Dolby TrueHD audio. Nearly four hours of bonus material were new to this release, including documentaries about Victor Fleming, the Munchkin players, and *The Dreamer of Oz*, a 1990 TV-movie with John Ritter as L. Frank Baum. The set offered two of Baum's Selig films, *The Magic Cloak of Oz* and *The Patchwork Girl of Oz* (both 1914); a fifty-two-page book; and a collectible *Wizard of Oz* 70th anniversary watch.

Celebration of the movie's 75th anniversary, and promotion of the 2013 IMAX 3-D theatrical release, kicked off in October 2013 with another box set, *The Wizard of Oz 75th Anniversary Collector's Edition*. This numbered, five-disc issue had Blu-ray and Blu-ray 3D discs, and discrete DVD and HD UltraViolet discs. Disc number five was devoted to an extensive selection of extras.

Besides the variously formatted *Wizard of Oz* discs, the 75th anniversary box featured every extra from earlier special releases and added a new "making of" documentary; a journal, a ruby slippers sparkle globe, an oversized map of Oz, a three-piece "awards" enamel pin set (brains, heart, courage), and a forty-eight-page hardcover book. A 4 GB Wicked Witch of the East flash drive was an Amazon.com exclusive available in sets purchased from that Internet retailer.

The 75th-anniversary *Wizard of Oz* was also available on stand-alone DVD, stand-alone Blu-ray, and as a three-disc set containing Blu-ray, Blu-ray 3D, and HD UltraViolet.

Merry Old Land of Rumors

Decades of TV exposure imprinted *Oz* in viewers' minds and encouraged the steady growth of rumors about the film. Much of the appeal of rumors comes from the usually erroneous supposition that they're rooted in secrecy, and that they're secret because of a conspiracy. *Somebody doesn't want us to know the truth! But we won't be denied! Truth to power!*—and so on and so forth. Rumors typically swirl around people or things that are known to great numbers of people. Shared knowledge—of, say, *The Wizard of Oz*—encourages rumors and allows them to endure over years, even over generations. Of course, some rumors are true.

Rumor-mongering can be a lot of fun, but that doesn't mean it's a particularly intelligent pursuit. Explanations that reveal the truth behind false rumors are usually very simple, and because they're simple, they're no fun. Therefore, the rumors persist.

Here are some rumors that have developed around MGM's *The Wizard of Oz.*

The rumor: MGM wanted Shirley Temple to have the role of Dorothy. **The facts:** The idea was kicked around the studio during the earliest phase of the *Oz* project. Ten-year-old Shirley was a box-office champ of the 1930s. She wasn't cast as Dorothy because 1) her star had faded a bit by 1938; 2) she was under contract to 20th Century-Fox, and no deal for her services could be worked out; and 3) Louis B. Mayer and other MGM executives realized that Temple didn't have a prayer of fulfilling the role's musical requirements.

The rumor: "Over the Rainbow," now one of the world's most popular songs, nearly didn't make the final cut. **The facts:** Very true. See chapter 6.

The rumor: Producer Mervyn LeRoy approved the casting of Otto, a dachshund owned by Margaret Hamilton, to play Dorothy's four-legged companion. Judy Garland filmed the "Over the Rainbow" sequence with Otto, but the pooch was shortly replaced because of growing anti-German sentiment in America. The dog part was recast with a Norwich terrier that would be called "Toto," an anagram of Otto's name. **The facts:** Oh, where to begin? The rumor implies that "Over the Rainbow" was shot very early in the *Oz* production process, giving the studio time to reconsider and make the change. To the contrary, the sequence was one of the *last* things to be shot, by which time all casting would have been long settled. The claim that the name "Toto" was created from "Otto" is incredibly naïve and uninformed, ignoring that L. Frank Baum had created Toto's name nearly forty years earlier. And Terry (who played Toto) was a Cairn, not a Norwich. Additionally, no matter what sort of dog the studio wanted, the animal would never have been the house pet of a cast member, but a dog belonging to a professional trainer. A clever Photoshop image (the only one that ever accompanies the dachshund claim) depicts the wiener-like Otto perched on a farm implement while Dorothy sings. One of these rumor sites, a handsome WordPress blog devoted to dachshunds, adds that "nearly a decade later," "in the sunset of his short life," Otto co-starred in *Hogan's Heroes*, as Col. Klink's canine companion. "Nearly a decade later" suggests 1947 or 1948, but *Hogan's Heroes* didn't go into production until 1965, by which time Otto would have been, at minimum, twenty-seven years old and thus, well, *dead.*

The rumor: An unidentified Munchkin who hanged himself (or, possibly, herself) on the forest set is visible in the background when the Wicked Witch confronts Dorothy and her friends at the Tin Woodman's cottage. A variant rumor revolves around a heartbroken, suicidal grip. **The facts:** Of all the *Wizard of Oz* rumors, this is the most persistent and widespread. But it doesn't jibe with reality: the sequence was shot before any Munchkin players were on the set, so that kills the rumor's most common version. As for the grips, all of them—happy, suicidal, and in-between—were accounted for when shooting wrapped. The figure glimpsed amidst the trees is a Sarus Crane, one of numerous animals rented from the Los Angeles County Zoo (the place needed money at the time) and brought onto the set for "color." But the "hanging Munchkin" rumor hasn't gone to its grave easily; one Internet blogger, for instance, soberly wrote, "[W]hether there is any truth behind it or not is based entirely on opinion," as if truth is completely subjective. One theorist declared, "i [*sic*] know for sure some hanged themsevles [*sic*] on set because you can see someone clearly swing back and forth then it stops." Another poster offered this comment: "i just saw the scene of the hanging munchkin, i totally never want to watch the wizard of oz again. it used to be my favorite movie. what do you think? couldn't they have edited that part out or something instead of lying saying it was a stork or a bird. i mean come on we are not dumb."

Although one blogger admitted having seen the bird shake out its feathers, the same writer was compelled to add, "But that is actually to the left of the hanging person dude." The "hanging Munchkin" assertions go on in this brand of certitude, endlessly. Many bloggers claim that the hanging Munchkin is clearly visible in the first VHS release of the movie and is absent from subsequent releases. According to this line of thought, the dead body was "edited out" and "replaced by a bird" on later DVD releases.

The creator of a hoax YouTube video posted in 2012 used motion-track software to mask out the crane and cleverly insert what could be mistaken for a hanging little person. Naturally, enough, a lot of people have been taken in by this trickery.

The rumor: A crane rented from the Los Angeles Zoo chased after Ray Bolger to peck the Scarecrow's straw. **The facts:** Although Sarus Cranes are omnivorous and sometimes aggressive, the rumor cannot be confirmed or denied.

The rumor: A suicidal Lollipop Guild Munchkin hanged himself on the forest set. **The facts:** This is an obvious variation of the rumor described above. Besides that, no Munchkins had yet been on-set when the sequence was filmed, the post-*Oz* lives of the three Lollipop actors are well documented, and no other people were cast in any of the three roles.

The rumor: An *Oz* producer hanged himself on the forest set because the movie was over budget. **The facts:** *Oz* did go over budget, but post-filming, all producers were accounted for.

The rumor: The director's daughter hanged herself on the forest set because she was passed over for the role of Dorothy. **The facts**: Assuming that the rumor refers to a daughter of *Victor Fleming*, credibility is strained because when the film was cast in 1938, Fleming's daughters were aged three and one. *King Vidor* had three daughters; one is still living, one of the others passed away in 2003, and another in 2012. *Richard Thorpe* had a son but no daughters. *George Cukor* had no children. *Norman Taurog* had a daughter, who was six in 1938. (A second daughter, adopted by Taurog, was born many years later.) *Busby Berkeley* was, like Cukor, childless.

The rumor: A Munchkin who hanged herself is visible in a crowd of Munchkins during the "We thank you very sweetly" sequence. **The facts:** What may appear to be a noose around the neck of the barely glimpsed background player is a decorative collar or bow. Keep in mind, too, that this rumor depends on the assumption that MGM was in the habit of printing takes with suicides that had been witnessed on-set by scores of people.

The rumor: The Munchkins (the Singer Midgets) came from Europe, and many of them used the jobs as good reasons to flee Hitler's Germany. **The facts:** Some in the Singer troupe were indeed originally from Europe, and some, like Harry Earles, were born in Germany. However, the Munchkins were gathered in America, mostly on the East Coast. If any were "imported" from Europe, no record survives. And anyway, by 1938, virtually *no one* was getting out of Germany.

The rumor: The little people cast as the Munchkins ran riot in their hotel, tearing the place to pieces, drinking like fish, brawling, and having sex like rabbits. **The facts:** This is another particularly sturdy rumor; like the common cold, it's always around. The Munchkins were lodged in two hotels and behaved just like anybody else. Some were loud; most were not. Large-scale mayhem never happened. The rumor can be traced to Judy Garland, who became too imaginative because she wanted to tell a good story during a 1967 television interview. A miserable 1981 movie comedy, *Under the Rainbow*, perpetuated the rumor, and in an unpleasant way, too.

The rumor: All the Munchkins were children. **The facts:** Admittedly, this is a very anemic rumor, but it does float around, existing in direct opposition to the hotel-Munchkins rumor noted earlier. As we've seen in chapter 5, all but a dozen Munchkins were played by adults.

The rumor: Six-year-old Elizabeth Taylor played a Munchkin. **The facts:** Although Liz Taylor was an MGM contract player, she didn't become one until 1942. Further, she lived in England until 1939, when she was seven, and didn't do a screen test until 1941.

The rumor: Terry, who played Toto, was paid more than the Munchkins. **The facts:** Terry was paid $125 a week; each Munchkin earned $50. On the face of it, this may seem wildly unjust, but keep in mind that Toto was a featured player involved in many difficult scenes. Individual Munchkins, though important to the film's texture and story, were parts of an ensemble.

The rumor: Wicked Witch of the West Margaret Hamilton nearly died one day on the set. **The facts:** Hamilton could indeed have died, from burns sustained during a misfired special-effects gag. See chapter 12 for details.

The rumor: Margaret Hamilton sued MGM after being burned on-set. **The facts:** Although Hamilton considered suing, she realized that to do so would effectively blackball her in Hollywood. She took no legal action, but was very clear that she'd never work with fire again.

The rumor: Margaret Hamilton's green makeup was poisonous and almost killed her. **The facts:** The makeup's green hue was achieved with a copper-oxide base. Copper is indeed poisonous, but Hamilton (who took her liquid meals through a straw) was never in danger of ingesting any. However, her skin had a faint green tinge for weeks after shooting had wrapped. (Hamilton may also have acquired a green tinge to her hair. She never mentioned this, but it is one result of prolonged copper-to-skin contact.)

The rumor: The sparks that fly from the ruby slippers when the Wicked Witch tries to remove them from Dorothy's feet were created with lemon juice. Some versions of the story claim apple juice. **The facts:** Although Buddy Gillespie's original special-effects notes report that an early attempt was made to capture the spark effect by "using high tension juice shot at speed," Gillespie almost certainly was referring to electricity: "juice."

The rumor: The guy that played the Tin Woodman almost died. **The facts:** This is true, as we've seen in chapter 10. The guy was Buddy Ebsen, whose potentially fatal reaction to aluminum dust in his facial makeup caused him to be replaced by Jack Haley.

The rumor: When the Winkies march into the Witch's castle, they chant, "Oh we love the OLD one." Or: "All we own, we OWE her." Or perhaps: "Oh we loathe the OLD one." **The facts:** The *Wizard of Oz* continuity script dated March 15, 1939, indicates no lyrics for the chant. In the finished film, the Winkies simply repeat martial-sounding nonsense syllables: "Oh wee oh! Ee OH ah!"—and so on.

The rumor: Lyrics from Pink Floyd's *Dark Side of the Moon* LP synch up perfectly with scenes from *The Wizard of Oz*. **The facts:** This contention boils down to subjective reaction. If you believe it's true, well, no one is going to dissuade you, but Pink Floyd isn't on the same page.

The rumor: By pure chance, Prof. Marvel (Frank Morgan) wore a coat that once belonged to original *Wizard of Oz* author L. Frank Baum. **The facts:** Although wildly unlikely, this rumor is true. Director Victor Fleming wanted the professor to appear a little ragged; during costume tests, he asked the wardrobe department to search for a coat that was nicely designed but well worn. (At this time, Fleming assumed that he would direct the Kansas sequences, which were ultimately done by King Vidor.) Wardrobe purchased a rack of old coats from a local used-clothing store. Fleming liked one of them, a Prince Albert coat with a velvet collar. When Frank Morgan later looked into a pocket, he saw a name, L. Frank Baum, sewn inside. Baum's widow, Maud, and Baum's tailor confirmed the coat's provenance. After the shoot, the coat was given to Maud Baum.

The rumor: When L. Frank Baum was trying to come up with a name for his fantasyland, he glanced at a file cabinet drawer that was marked O–Z. **The facts:** This is an appealing story, but its truthfulness can't be confirmed. The claim isn't particularly improbable, except that a more typical division of file contents is S–Z. Then again, if Baum had relatively few items in his file, O–Z would have served him just fine.

The rumor: MGM may never have made *The Wizard of Oz* if not for Walt Disney's animated-cartoon feature *Snow White and the Seven Dwarfs*. **The facts:** Studios were leery of fantasy in 1939. Paramount's generously budgeted, star-studded *Alice in Wonderland*, a 1933 adaptation of Lewis Carroll, was a box-office bomb, but *Snow White* (1937) was a tremendous hit. Its success, and the popular appeal of its female protagonist, encouraged MGM to risk the expense of *Oz*.

The rumor: In the film's original ending, Dorothy looks beneath her bed and finds the ruby slippers, suggesting that her adventure hasn't been a dream. **The facts:** No such ending was ever scripted or shot, and there is nothing similar in the Baum novel (which presents Dorothy's journey as having been real). Regardless, many bloggers and other Internet habitués insist they remember seeing the alternate ending during television broadcasts.

The rumor: MGM was prepared to follow *The Wizard of Oz* with a sequel. **The facts:** Although sequelitis is epidemic in present-day Hollywood, the practice was relatively rare during the industry's golden age. Instead, *remakes* (such as versions of *The Maltese Falcon* from 1931, 1936 [as *Satan Met a Lady*], and 1941) were far more common. MGM, for instance, successfully remade one of its silent thrillers, *London After Midnight* (1927), as *Mark of the Vampire* (1935). Remakes were appealing because they were re-dos of proven hits, and because they could be disguised, if desired, with fresh settings and plot tweaks. Remakes could even be perpetrated by one studio against another, as in 1939, when Warner Bros. purloined MGM's 1934 smash *Manhattan Melodrama*, remaking it as *Angels with Dirty Faces*; and when Columbia did a brazen raid on Universal's *Dracula* (1931; with Bela Lugosi) to make *The Return of the Vampire* (1944; also starring Lugosi).

Alternatively, series pictures, such as MGM's Andy Hardy and Tarzan franchises, don't qualify as sequels, even though cast members returned time after time. Each entry in a series was essentially a stand-alone story rather than a concerted continuation of an earlier movie.

Sequels involved some risk, mainly because one that wasn't well received by audiences could dim the appeal of the original idea and poison the well for a later re-release or remake. In rare instances, a sequel would be as good as or even better than the original; Universal's *Frankenstein* (1931) and *Bride of Frankenstein* (1935) testify to that. More often, though, a typical sequel failed to match the quality of the first film, sometimes because a studio refused to allow the original creative team enough time and money to execute the project properly, and sometimes because, in the rush to push a sequel into theaters, the studio would assign the follow-up to a fast-working but quality-challenged B-unit. When RKO produced a sequel to its magnificent 1933 epic *King Kong*, the studio cut corners—which was disappointingly obvious to everyone who went to see *Son of Kong* later in 1933.

MGM made no immediate sequel to *The Wizard of Oz* for a variety of reasons. Although the picture attracted enthusiastic audiences and a healthy gross, it couldn't recoup its costs in 1939, let alone show a profit. Studio executives and their accountants were invariably put off by that sort of outcome. International politics, and the foreseeable loss of lucrative European markets, also militated against an *Oz* sequel. Further, a sequel would demand that a significant part of the original cast be reunited, which wouldn't be a simple thing because not everybody was under contract to MGM, and because actors' schedules are inevitably in conflict. As we've discussed, movie fantasy didn't have nearly the audience appeal in 1939 it enjoys today. Louis Mayer liked idealized, homespun stories with solid American virtues. By nature, he was disinclined to place MGM's human capital and other valuable resources in the service of another big-budget fantasy (it would *have* to be big budget because, after all, this was MGM). Mayer wouldn't have seen any sense in doing another major movie that would draw crowds of kids that got into theaters at kids' admission prices.

Ironically, the biggest obstacle blocking a sequel to *The Wizard of Oz* was the picture's brilliant young star. By the time a sequel could be mounted, Judy Garland would be at least a year older, maybe two. Her already-womanly figure would have become even more apparent, and subtle changes to her face and bearing would further hobble her characterization of the simple farm girl, Dorothy. Then there was Mayer's vision for the course of Judy's career. He knew that Judy was most valuable in proven genres. She was going to be a light actress and a musical star. MGM could mount a handsome musical for a fraction of the cost of *The Wizard of Oz* and show a profit. Indeed, the six Garland films released by MGM after *Oz* were sprightly, pleasing, and essentially unimaginative comedies and songfests: *Strike Up the Band*, *Andy Hardy Meets a Debutante*, *Little Nellie Kelly*, *Ziegfeld Girl* (this one is more adult than the others), *Life Begins for Andy Hardy*, and *Babes on Broadway*.

The rumor: Dozens of winged monkeys on loan from the Los Angeles Zoo escaped the set one day and flew into downtown Culver City, where they looted stores, abducted citizens, and took liberties with bananas. **The facts:** Okay, I made this one up. See how easy it is?

Our Fascination with Boo-Boos

Movie Web sites large and small, smart and silly, devote a lot of bytes to "find the boo-boo"—errors in continuity; camera crews reflected in windows and other physical mistakes; obviously post-synced dialogue; anachronisms; inconsistent points of dialogue, and numberless other things. The game is fun in a "so what?" kind of way, but there's something a little arrogant about it, too, as movie fans feel superior because they've caught Victor Fleming or Orson Welles or whoever directs the *Jackass* movies in a mistake.

Of course, the boo-boo hunters know that they have the advantage of DVDs and DVRs with PAUSE, ZOOM, and other specialized controls. They're aware that they're eyeballing the movies in ways that no original audience ever was able to. Mistakes that are very apparent when scenes are played and examined repeatedly on a home screen were never apparent to theater audiences, or to people who know the film from old television broadcasts. When characters and plots are engaging, our minds don't become wired to anticipate goofs that have no bearing on character or plot. We don't notice them because they don't matter.

Movies are shot piecemeal, and individual scenes are commonly assembled from bits of footage shot days or even weeks apart. Mistakes happen. The continuity supervisor (a position that was once called "script girl") works very hard to ensure that dialogue and visual elements (costumes, hair, props, shadows, and so on, infinitely) match from cut to cut, scene to scene. Occasionally, though, the supervisor may not notice (even with photographic reference) that, for instance, the star's jacket, which was buttoned with two buttons during yesterday's shoot, is now closed with only one button. Unattended "hot sets" that will be used again later, and that must not be touched in the meantime, may be inadvertently altered in small ways. A necktie may have a noticeable wrinkle in close-ups and no wrinkle in two-shots. A cigarette held between the fingers might be two inches long in one setup and then three inches in a cutaway. An unwanted edge of shadow from a person or object on the set may be visible on a wall. The camera crew might be momentarily reflected in a store window or on the bodyside of an automobile. And then there's that all-time favorite, the shadow of a boom mike that moves on the wall above the actors. Often, film editors have no choice but to cut in problematic footage because that's the *only* footage.

Even mighty MGM, the paragon of Hollywood moviemaking before World War II, was fallible. In *The Women*, another MGM picture from 1939, Joan Crawford removes her coat, and in the next cut, the coat is back on again. As Robert Young climbs a mountain in MGM's *Idiot's Delight* (1939), his shadow falls on a painted backdrop of faraway peaks. In the studio's *Another Thin Man* (1939), the suspenders worn by actor Harry Bellaver mysteriously disappear. And as Greta Garbo tells a joke in one of MGM's greatest successes, *Ninotchka* (1939), objects on the desk in front of her move around from cut to cut.

The Wizard of Oz has no more and no fewer errors than any other major film of its time. But for the record, and because lists of any sort are fun to compile and difficult to resist, here are some boo-boos from *The Wizard of Oz*, which you'll see if you're looking for them:

- Dorothy is rescued after toppling into the pigpen and emerges without a single spot of dirt.
- Moments before Dorothy sings "Over the Rainbow," a broken fence post behind her is intact in a subsequent shot.
- When Aunt Em tells Uncle Henry she can't find Dorothy (as the twister approaches), the dialogue doesn't match the movement of her mouth.
- During the storm, stage lights are reflected in one of Dorothy's bedroom windows.
- The moving shadow of a camera boom is visible on the nest of hatching Munchkins.
- The tallest Lullaby League representative (actress Nita Krebs) shows up minutes later as a lady in green who helps cheer Dorothy's departure for the Emerald City.
- An unseen Munchkin screams in fright an instant *before* the Wicked Witch materializes in Munchkinland.
- When the Wicked Witch of the West approaches Dorothy's downed house, rear-projection cinematography makes it obvious that actress Margaret Hamilton was looking at a rear-projection screen or a still photo; the grain of the film stock behind the Witch is very coarse. **Note:** Although not a true flub, this brief shot is the film's most obvious technical lapse. The best guess as to the reason for it is that Victor Fleming decided after the Munchkin set had been struck that a transition shot was needed to establish a visual link between the house and the Witch of the West.
- A shrub near the curled feet of the Wicked Witch of the East vanishes after the Wicked Witch of the West has examined her deceased sister.
- The edge of a trap door is visible at the Wicked Witch's feet as she departs Munchkinland.
- When Dorothy skips along the Yellow Brick Road on her way out of Munchkinland, the floor-level seam of the painted flat (depicting the distant hills) is plainly visible.
- The pole that supports the Scarecrow in the cornfield rises to different heights above the Scarecrow's head.
- The length of Dorothy's pigtails fluctuates during her first scene with the Scarecrow. **Note:** Judy Garland's hair extensions were still being fiddled with after Victor Fleming came on board to direct. The studio gambled, correctly, that audiences wouldn't notice.
- Pumpkins that line the Yellow Brick Road appear and disappear as Dorothy approaches the Scarecrow.
- During Dorothy's first meeting with the Scarecrow, various sections of fence are intact and then broken. **Note:** In Busby Berkeley's deleted sequence of

the Scarecrow's dance, the Scarecrow flings himself into the fencing, breaking sections of it.

- Long shots of the apple orchard reveal brown, tired-looking soil. In closer shots, the ground is covered with healthy grass.
- As Dorothy reacts when startled by the angry apple tree, a hand (probably belonging to trainer Carl Spitz) summons Toto forward.
- As the Scarecrow is knocked down by apples hurled by the surly trees, Dorothy wears plain shoes rather than the ruby slippers. In the next cut, the ruby slippers are back.
- Although the Tin Woodman explains that he rusted "right in the middle of a chop," his frozen pose is static. **Note:** The Tin Woodman was speaking figuratively.
- When the Tin Woodman staggers away from Dorothy and the Scarecrow shortly after meeting them, his oil can falls from Dorothy's basket. In the next cut, the can is back where it belongs.
- When the Tin Woodman removes his hat in order to smother a flame near the Scarecrow, Jack Haley's silvered hair is visible. **Note:** If the Tin Woodman has a tin mouth and a tin nose, he can surely have tin hair.
- As the Tin Woodman complains about the Witch's threat to turn him into a beehive, Toto is being held by Dorothy. In a close shot on Dorothy an instant later, Toto is gone. **Note:** This continuity error arose when the Tin Woodman's prolonged reaction to a dead bee was later cut.
- The three-shot of Dorothy, the Scarecrow, and the Tin Woodman that's seen immediately after the Tin Woodman's dismissal of the Witch's beehive threat was printed flopped, so that the positions of the Tin Woodman and the Scarecrow matched the previous cut. **Note:** Haley and Bolger had changed position during the deleted "dead bee" interlude, forcing this optical adjustment.
- At the beginning of the "Lions and Tigers and Bears" number, Judy says "Oh, my!" but her mouth doesn't move.
- Dorothy can barely keep from laughing when she meets the Cowardly Lion and appears to bring Toto up to her face in order to hide her smile. **Note:** One tale, which has been related by numerous sources, maintains that Fleming slapped Garland across the face to stop a giggle fit. Given Garland's professionalism, and Fleming's real fondness for his young star, the story smacks of the apocryphal.
- When the Tin Woodman struggles to regain his feet after being elevated and then dropped in the Haunted Forest, a bit of underclothing is visible beneath his chest piece.
- Dorothy stumbles slightly as she skips from the poppy field. **Note:** Another "mistake" that didn't warrant a retake.
- The mustache of the Emerald City gatekeeper changes shape from one shot to another. **Note:** A deleted scene, in which the gatekeeper steps aside to remove his false mustache and then repositions it, was cut.

- During the "King of the Forest" number, the Tin Woodman smashes a flowerpot and sets it on the Lion's head as a crown. When the crown falls off later, it bounces rather than shatters. **Note:** Some props are safest when they're made of rubber.
- During some full-figure views of the Cowardly Lion during the "King of the Forest" sequence, the wire that manipulates his tail is faintly visible. **Note:** It's visible to us as we look at remastered prints on hi-def flat-screen TVs; pre-war movie-screen resolution, even when the screen is twenty feet high, wasn't sufficiently sharp to reveal the wire.
- A handkerchief in Dorothy's hand during "King of the Forest" vanishes and then reappears.
- The Lion sings, "What makes the Sphinx the Seventh Wonder?"—even though the Sphinx is not one of those famed artifacts of antiquity. **Note:** "Sphinx" is inherently funnier (and scans more effectively) than "Great Pyramid of Giza."
- Dorothy trips slightly as she holds the Lion's "cape" during "King of the Forest." **Note:** This was an acceptable fluff, which Victor Fleming apparently did not reshoot.
- When the Emerald City gatekeeper is moved by Dorothy's unhappiness, he begins to shed a waterfall of tears, which seems to originate in his eyebrows and forehead. **Note:** Surely not a mistake of any sort, but a purposeful bit of burlesque. If Victor Fleming and the special-effects crew had wanted tears to come from the gatekeeper's eyes, that's what would have happened.
- As the group approaches the Haunted Forest, the Tin Woodman carries a large wrench, which mysteriously disappears. **Note:** This error was inadvertently created when the "Jitterbug" sequence was cut.
- The Witch prepares her winged monkeys to abduct Dorothy, noting aloud that she's sent "a little insect" on ahead to "take the fight out of them" But nothing more is seen or heard about the insect. **Note:** The line of dialogue was a setup for the excised "Jitterbug" sequence.
- Winged monkeys are in the air even before the Wicked Witch finishes giving Nikko her kidnap instructions. **Note:** A smart subordinate always anticipates his commander.
- The winged monkeys snatch the Tin Woodman's axe from his hand, but a moment later, he's holding it again.
- As Dorothy runs from the winged monkeys, her hands are empty; and then, in a closer shot, she's carrying a basket.
- During Dorothy's abduction in the Haunted Forest, a winged monkey swoops down and scoops up Toto; a moment later, a winged monkey swoops down and scoops up Toto. **Note:** Victor Fleming followed industry practice by shooting stunts multiple times. During the edit, Blanche Sewell inadvertently retained an alternate take of Toto's liftoff.
- The red sand in the Witch's hourglass passes into the lower portion very quickly in close-ups, but the overall level seems to have changed very little

whenever it's revisited by the camera. **Note:** Moviemakers frequently manipulate time for dramatic effect.

- When the Tin Woodman pulls on the Lion's tail in order to scale a cliff-side, the boxy outline of a reinforcing piece is plainly visible at the Lion's hindquarters.
- After Dorothy's friends subdue the Winkie scouts, the Tin Woodman carries a Winkie spear; but inside the castle, he has his axe again. **Note:** You could hide a Buick beneath one of those Winkie greatcoats. The Tin Woodman had his axe all the time.
- Inside the Witch's castle, various candles are lit, then unlit, and then lit again.
- As the Wicked Witch enters the small room where she will perish, she lifts her skirt in order not to trip. The flesh of her lower legs is flesh-colored instead of green.
- When Toto reveals the Wizard's fakery, the curtain is pulled back not by Toto's teeth, but by a wire attached to the dog's collar.
- When Dorothy scoops up Toto after the Wizard has been revealed, she removes the string from around the dog's neck.
- After receiving a diploma from the Wizard, the Scarecrow rapidly recites the Pythagorean Theorem—incorrectly. **Note:** Ray Bolger's inaccurate burst of dialogue was either a mistake by whomever wrote the line or (more likely) a comic acknowledgment that the Scarecrow has been smart all along—just not about everything.
- As the Cowardly Lion proudly shows off his medal, the award disappears from his hand (to rest against his chest) and then reappears in his hand.
- The Wizard's balloon leaves without Dorothy because the Tin Woodman has undone the anchor rope. **Note:** Three possibilities here. 1) Victor Fleming asked actor Jack Haley to undo the rope so that the scene's action could proceed. 2) The Tin Woodman wants the Wizard to leave without Dorothy. 3) The Tin Woodman undoes the rope because he plans to hold it secure himself.
- In the film's final scene, Dorothy says, "There's no place like home"—but lip readers can see that she actually says, "There's no place like Cleveland." **Note:** Okay, just kidding about this one.
- Toto was played by Terry, but the end credits note that the part was played by Toto. **Note:** How much clout could a small dog named Terry possibly have?

Other mistakes and lapses in continuity are minor and almost endless: a dirty floor that becomes a clean floor; minor props that change position; instances of extras (background players) that change position from one shot to another; errant, unintended shadows of cameras or booms; clumsily handled post-synched dialogue; and misplaced sound effects. Because of the immense popularity of *The Wizard of Oz*, the film has been endlessly examined. If you're a persistent sleuth, you've already discovered well over three hundred boo-boos.

Congratulations! Your OCD certificate is in the mail.

My Little Party's Just Beginning

Selling Oz, and Reinventing It, Too

T o the engineers of any commercial entertainment endeavor, the "sell" is always more important than content or product integrity. Few popular creations remain stand-alone experiences; somewhere, someone is always planning ancillary merchandise. Familiar real people (living and dead), fictional characters, exploitable brands (like *Garfield, The Hunger Games,* "Marvel Comics," "LeBron James"), sports franchises, and too many other things to easily list are exploited with a staggering array of licensed products: calendars and video games; jigsaw puzzles and bath towels; coffee mugs and Halloween costumes; throw pillows and plush toys; posters and food items. If the product has a surface area sufficiently large to display an image, a name, or a logo, it's ripe for merchandising.

Today, licensed-merchandise gurus function in an artificial world of surveys, rigmarole intended to justify the presumed experts' fat salaries and retainers. The savvy merchandiser—that is, the man or woman that doesn't want to appear stale or out of touch—is continually on the alert for "emerging retail trends." Brilliant indeed is the licensing expert that can predict *now* that in five years people will demand, say, Iron Man anchovy paste. Any blockhead can license a hot property to a toy company; smart indeed is the guru who *creates* a merchandising trend. (As far as I know, there are no plans for Iron Man anchovy paste. However, if I ever see that product on a supermarket shelf, someone is going to get a phone call.)

During Hollywood's golden age, only two studios, Disney and Republic, created product designed primarily for children. Republic survived for many years on slick, action-packed serials and B-westerns, and didn't begin to make "quality" pictures until well into the '40s. Republic was a small studio that existed on thin margins and maintained a relatively small staff. Cash flow was vital, so after 1940, Republic routinely sold book, comic book, and toy licenses based on its western stars (Gene Autry and Roy Rogers were the most popular) and "hillbilly" comedienne Judy Canova.

Disney was larger, more prosperous, and, frankly, far more visionary. Alone among important Hollywood studios of the 1930s and '40s, Disney vigorously pursued merchandising. Licenses were awarded to makers of toys, coloring books, watercolor sets, games, puzzles, and anything else with built-in kid appeal. What began in the late 1920s with Mickey Mouse rapidly expanded to encompass each successive character success: Minnie Mouse, Donald Duck, Pluto, Goofy, and others.

Each of those characters made a mark in cartoon shorts, but when Walt Disney moved forward with his daring plan for a feature-length animated cartoon and released *Snow White and the Seven Dwarfs* in 1937, his studio was transformed, and so was the licensing business. Unlike Mickey and the other Disney characters, Snow White didn't develop merchandising appeal over a course of years. She arrived like a comet and was instantly popular. An avalanche of licensed products followed. For 1939, Disney successfully licensed its latest animated feature, *Pinocchio*.

Although MGM had been interested in *Snow White* mainly in box-office terms, few at the studio overlooked what Disney had accomplished with licensed products. (Yet another 1939 feature-cartoon release, Max Fleischer-Paramount's *Gulliver's Travels*, inspired dozens of licensing deals.) MGM made sleek, superficially sophisticated movies for grown-ups, but *Oz* was a children's picture that presented an opportunity for profits linked to things other than traffic in and out of theaters.

A complete catalogue of *Oz*-related merchandise, 1939 to the present, is beyond the scope of this book. A full accounting would require years of research, and if the subject were to be treated properly, the book would be an oversized, hundred-dollar coffee-table book. Until that book arrives, here is acknowledgment of just a fraction of products that have had the *Wizard of Oz* imprimatur.

- Sheet music
- "Dorothy" pinafores (for the serious Dorothy collector)
- Halloween costumes and masks
- Collector dolls, including a gingham-miniskirted Barbie/Dorothy (2010) and a traditional Dorothy modeled on Judy Garland (2013)
- Beanbag dolls
- Plush dolls
- "Dancing" bendable dolls and other "play" dolls
- Gumball machines
- Phone cases
- Mr. Potato Head set
- Teapots
- Pencil holders and pencil sharpeners
- Canvas wall art
- Character figures in vinyl, wood, ceramic, china, porcelain, pewter, and other materials
- Musical figurines
- Pinball games

- Cookie jars
- Jewelry, ranging from kid-priced to seriously expensive
- Posters and lenticular posters
- Jigsaw puzzles
- Jack-in-the-boxes
- Hand puppets, finger puppets, and marionettes
- Night lights
- Trading cards
- Decorative lamps, including a Wicked Witch of the East leg lamp
- T-shirts, caps, flip-flops, and other casual apparel
- Countless book adaptations, some with MGM characters mated to the original Baum text; others adapting the movie
- Collector plates
- Personal checks and checkbook covers
- Valentine's and other greeting cards
- Bookmarks
- Salt and pepper shakers
- Coin banks
- Decorative aprons
- Snow globes and water globes
- Stationery and postcards
- Limited-edition prints and lithographs
- Decorative boxes
- Mounted, collectible 35mm film frames
- Mouse pads
- Statues, busts, and maquettes
- Wall clocks, mantel clocks, and alarm clocks
- Video games
- Bumper stickers
- Music boxes
- Watches
- Pet costumes
- Christmas lights and other ornaments; a 2000 Hallmark ornament of the terrifying green head of the Wizard is particularly dramatic
- Doorstops (frequently, the legs and feet of the Wicked Witch of the East)
- Backpacks, purses, and tote bags
- Broadway shows
- Pillows and throws
- Comic book adaptations
- Key chains and luggage tags
- "Exclusives" from the Franklin Mint and other high-end collector sources
- Wastebaskets
- Infant apparel
- Standees

- Pinback buttons, magnets, and tin signs
- Photo frames
- Bobbleheads
- Lunch boxes
- Pen and pencil sets
- Snack foods
- Land of Oz amusement park (see discussion later in this chapter)
- Fast-food tie-ins
- Board games, including an Oz-centric Monopoly game
- Colorforms
- Coffee mugs, travel mugs, cups, and tumblers
- Coasters
- Tea lights and votive holders
- Paint-by-number kits
- Ornate, multi-piece play sets
- Journals and datebooks
- Calendars

Oz Merchandising Today

Although MGM effectively capitalized on licensing opportunities created by *Oz*, the studio didn't generally venture into that arena; nor did most other studios. But today, licensed, movie-related products are omnipresent and unavoidable. What accounts for this change? The obvious answer is that the youth culture that began to manifest itself after World War II has since become *kid culture*. A considerable proportion of product merchandising and marketing is aimed at very young, undiscriminating consumers—as well as at adults that have been enchanted by kid stuff. (It's not just ten-year-olds that buy Iron Man tchotchkes.)

The less-apparent explanation for the growth of licensed movie product is that today's movie studios aren't studios in the 1939 sense of the word. The MGM of Nick Schenck and Louis B. Mayer dedicated itself to film production, theater ownership, and distribution. Secondarily, a music division ensured ownership of songs heard in the studio's films. Like other Hollywood studios of the era, MGM was primarily about making movies. Today, the major studios are enormously diversified. Some, like Columbia, are parts of multinational conglomerates.

As the years passed, MGM remained independent, partly because of its creation of a successful TV division. But beginning in the mid-1960s, MGM suffered a succession of individual and corporate owners that, unlike Louis Mayer, had no real interest in movies. Studio leadership changed with alarming frequency. If not for the James Bond films and a few other profitable franchises, MGM would be financially adrift. (Indeed, the studio went through Chapter 11 bankruptcy during December 2010.)

Despite internal and external upsets of the past thirty years, MGM followed the acquisitive business model of the late 20th century, buying interests in other film libraries and investing in television production, cable television, theatrical distribution, home video, TV syndication, movie downloads, video on demand, and, most famously, the hotel and resort business. With each successive acquisition, MGM gained marketing and licensing expertise.

The stunning irony vis-à-vis *The Wizard of Oz* is that since the late 1990s, the 1939 film has been controlled by Warner Bros., a subsidiary of Time Warner. In 2012–13, Warner allotted $25 million for its 75th anniversary IMAX promotion of the MGM classic and earned millions from numberless licensing deals. And like other entities heavily involved in licensing, Warner is very protective of its property. In 2011, for instance, the studio went to court to halt the sale of Kansas wines called Ruby Slippers, The Lion's Courage, Broomstick, Flying Monkey, and the clunkily named Dorothy of Kansas and Toto.

Unauthorized and Pirated Merchandise

Unauthorized *Wizard of Oz* products, occasionally homemade but usually the products of small, clandestine factories in America and nations around the world can be found at flea markets, parking-lot "art" marts, transient "pop-up" holiday and closeout stores, and other déclassé venues. Cheap, knockoff ceramics made in Mexico are particularly common. Abroad, public interest generated by the movie's 75th anniversary has been reflected in goods hawked by stall and sidewalk vendors in Mexico (Tijuana is particularly rife with such stuff), South Asia, Africa, and Eastern Europe. Even Warner Bros. (the present copyright holder) hasn't the capability to chase down and prosecute every offender, so the mischief continues.

Video pirates focused on *Oz* as soon as the film had legitimate videotape release in 1980. The movie had various-label laserdisc releases from 1982 to 1996. The first *Wizard of Oz* DVD went on sale in 1997. Trade in pirated copies of *Oz* is particularly brisk in China and other parts of Asia; a 2013 news item reported that many of the pirated *Wizard of Oz* DVDs originate in Australia.

Not Your Grandma's Oz

In 1976, softcore porn producer Bill Osco announced that Kristen de Bell would star in *Dirty Dorothy*, a bare version of *The Wizard of Oz*. Osco had had unexpected success two years before with *Flesh Gordon* (1974), a fitfully amusing parody of the Flash Gordon serials of the 1930s and '40s. With that triumph under his belt, Osco apparently felt ready for even loftier challenges. Unfortunately for him, and fortunately for the rest of us, *Dirty Dorothy* was never produced. Instead, Osco's release for 1976 was *Alice in Wonderland: An X-Rated Musical Fantasy*. (Greater achievements were to come: in 1995 Mr. Osco thrilled the world with *Art of Nude Bowling*.)

Screen standards loosened considerably after Bill Osco's 1970s heyday, and video technology promised to turn any mope into a moviemaker. Makers of skin films felt encouraged to become ever bolder. A 1988 ruling by the U.S. Supreme Court (*Hustler Magazine, Inc. v. Falwell*) held that parody is protected speech if the parody displays no intentional malice toward its inspiration. That decision helps explain the existence of *Not the Wizard of Oz XXX* (2013), a direct-to-video musical parody from a Los Angeles production company called X-Play. Crushingly overlong at ninety-seven minutes, the sepia-and-color spoof features a bevy of awful actresses headlined by twenty-three-year-old Maddy O'Reilly, who plays Dorothy. The petite O'Reilly (who appeared in seventy-two pornographic films from her 2011 debut to 2013) is seductively pretty, with eyes so cold that her gaze could freeze alcohol. She looks curvy in a gingham mini and curvy without it, too, which is frequently.

X-Play's ad campaign trumpeted the film's "seven sex scenes and five songs." One of those songs, "I Wonder What Is Happening," is the Cowardly Lion's unexpectedly tuneful and amusing lament about his confused sexual identity. James Bartholet is the Lion, and he sings with verve and real gusto, and seems not to belong in this movie. Then again, maybe he does, since his previous screen credits include *Not M*A*S*H XXX* (as Klinger), *Beverly Hillbillies XXX* (as Mr. Drysdale), and *Not the Three Stooges XXX* (as Curly).

We could list a few of Miss O'Reilly's other credits, too, but we'd better not.

The 1970 MGM Auction, and Aftermath

By the late 1960s, the once-splendid MGM back lot in Culver City was used more often for television episodes than for motion pictures. MGM's increasing reliance on big-budget spectaculars during the 1950s and '60s had produced too many flops. Salaried studio staff had been winnowed away since about 1950, and MGM's immense physical plant, and holdings of props and costumes, had become too expensive to maintain. Movie studios were being absorbed into larger corporate entities that maintained film studios merely as part of a port-folio of investments. Hollywood was no longer about the creation, distribution, and exhibition of movies. It was about movies as a kind of loss leader—highly visible holdings to be leveraged via cross marketing that might ultimately be more lucrative than the movies themselves. Soundtrack albums, hit songs, toys, beach towels, TV spin-offs, and myriad other products might provide more income than the film. Louis B. Mayer was gone; movies weren't entertainment and business and a philosophy anymore—they were just business.

In the spring of 1970, the public was invited to tour the back lot—not strictly in the tourist sense, but as an appetizer for a studio-sponsored memorabilia auction that would clear sound stages and other depositories of "junk" that was of no interest to MGM's new owner, investor Kirk Kerkorian, and his pick for studio president, James Aubrey. Kerkorian had purchased MGM in 1969 not to make movies, but to leverage its assets in order to build the MGM Grand Hotel in Las Vegas. Aubrey immediately fired about half the studio staff.

People who walked the lot saw European, New York, and other replica streets that had become shabby and overgrown. The ground was littered with trash and occasional decorative pieces that had come loose from neglected façades.

On Lot 2, the steeple from Andy Hardy's neighborhood still stood. Nearby was a locomotive seen in *The Harvey Girls* and *Annie Get Your Gun*. You couldn't have the steeple, but the locomotive was going to be for sale.

The pre-auction festivities began on May 2, 1970, with a black-tie charity dinner. The following day, Sunday, May 3, was the first of what auctioneer David Weisz expected would be three weeks of bidding and buying. (As things developed, the auction stretched over seventeen days.) Weisz owned International Fastener Research Corporation, which bought unsold stock and other assets, as well as entire businesses, to sell at auction. MGM accepted $1.5 million from Weisz for outright ownership of between 300,000 and 350,000 items from the studio's props and wardrobe departments—enough stuff to fill seven of the MGM sound stages. Weisz planned to part with only a tenth—about 30,000 pieces. Weisz, who died in 1981 at age seventy, didn't do many things small. During his career, he bought and sold 468 fully stocked clothing stores of the bankrupt Robert Hall chain; and the assets of Glasgow's Wolf Shipyards, where the *Queen Mary* was built.

Joining the MGM locomotive on the block were replica ships and carriages; musical instruments; vintage automobiles; crossbows, revolvers, and myriad other weapons; circus props and wind machines; special-effects miniatures; clocks, statuary, paintings, vases, crystal, and furniture, including many desirable antique pieces. And of course, there were the clothes and costumes.

Weisz published five discrete catalogs, ranging from 48 to 232 pages, that itemized every piece. May 3 was Weisz's "Star Wardrobe" day. He had rented MGM's Stage 27, where more than five thousand people showed up to ogle and bid on some of the auction's most desirable pieces. (One obvious irony of all this is that Stage 27 was where the Munchkinland sequence had been shot, some thirty years before.)

Weisz had hired 137 people to help him stage the sale. He could only guess that the first day would be successful, but he was an old hand at this sort of thing. He knew how to encourage bidders; how to clean house. In total, more than six thousand people had paid $100 apiece for the privilege of sitting in a chair, on a day of their choosing, to watch, listen, and, maybe, to buy. (People who bought nothing got their hundred bucks back, a nice gesture in a cold business.) Weisz got to work.

Rock Hudson, Debbie Reynolds (an aggressive bidder), Shirley Jones, and some other celebrities were present. The other participants were antique dealers and speculators, the curious, and collectors whose budgets ranged from a little to a lot. An outfit worn by Lana Turner in *The Bad and the Beautiful* sold for $225.

Marilyn Monroe's clingy pants suit from *The Asphalt Jungle* put a gleam in some eyes. But *Oz*. What about *The Wizard of Oz?*

An almost priceless piece of film history, Bert Lahr's Lion costume (Lot 950A), went for $2,400 to Dr. Julius Marini, a West Covina general practitioner (many accounts erroneously describe him as a chiropractor). Today, anybody would jump at the chance to pay so little, but in 1970, $2,400 was a great deal of money for a fur suit.

The greater part of public and media attention went to one frankly remarkable lot: Dorothy's ruby slippers (size 4½). It was widely assumed at the time that the slippers were the only legitimate pair, an assumption later proved erroneous. At any rate, the slippers had been discovered in a wardrobe-department bin, wrapped in a towel. Culver City wanted very much to own the slippers, in order to keep them close to the place where Judy Garland wore them. Mayor Martin Lotz politely requested that no one outbid Culver City, which could offer only $7,500 raised from pledges and other contributions. Alas, Culver City was not destined to retain the slippers, which aroused enthusiastic bidding. Two other bidders were Debbie Reynolds (then collecting items for a proposed Hollywood museum) and Harry Robbins, president of Carolina Caribbean Corporation, owner of the Land of Oz theme park. When the bidding paused at $15,000, David Weisz tried to get to $20,000, to no avail. He asked for $17,500. Nothing. So, just forty-seven seconds after bidding began, an attorney representing Dick Carroll, a Beverly Hills haberdasher, locked in the winning bid of $15,000.

Of numerous *Oz* items that came up for auction at MGM in 1970, Dorothy's ruby slippers excited the most interest. Many assumed that only one pair still existed, which was certainly *not* the case.

No surviving members of the *Oz* cast had wanted the slippers.

Carolina Caribbean's slipper budget was $11,000, so they fell short, but the company did put in winning bids for one of Dorothy's gingham dresses ($1,000), the Wizard's suit ($650), the Wicked Witch's hat ($450), and the Witch's dress ($350).

Not long before her death in 1985, Margaret Hamilton acknowledged to interviewer Gregory Catsos that MGM offered her the opportunity to buy the Witch's hat before the auction began. She declined, feeling that the hat and other items on the block belonged in a museum, and that the whole auction was "foolish." And even if she did buy the hat, she would have had no idea what to do with it.

MGM movies released in 1970 lost $8.3 million. In a none-too-amusing irony, the seventeen-day Weisz auction brought in $9.8 million, validating the auctioneer's instincts and pulling the curtain on the magic that had been MGM.

The auction inadvertently revealed that, for the moment, anyway, Hollywood's past was grossly undervalued, and the present wasn't looking so good, either. By 1970, MGM's Las Vegas hotel and casino was more profitable than the movie arm. Following the auction, great piles of sketches, blueprints, and other memorabilia were shipped there, to be used as decorations or sold in the hotel's gift shop.

As the years passed and a succession of owners took charge of what had been MGM, the remainder of the carefully designed back lot streets and faux buildings were razed. The land was sold and subdivided for condominiums, a shopping center, and other commercial use. Although a hugely disappointing development, one might reasonably assume that that kind of activity was inevitable. Los Angeles was still growing, and real estate had become too valuable to be allowed to sit idle. Rising land values were killing off drive-in theaters around the country; now the same thing was happening to a place that once made the movies. (Famously, and most unfortunately, much of the 20th Century-Fox back lot also went the way of condos at about this time.)

The real sin of what happened at MGM in 1970, and for decades afterward, is that almost no care was given to the contents of archives, files, storage rooms, and film libraries. Between 1970 and 1975, reams of original correspondence of Louis B. Mayer were tossed. Sometime in the mid-1970s, the studio hired cleanup specialists to get rid of the rest of the junk and clutter—like the matte painting of the Emerald City. (Fortunately, someone with the hauling company rescued the painting that MGM didn't care about. It sold, at private auction around 1990, for $44,000.)

Early in 1987, priceless—and gorgeous—blueprints for thousands of MGM sets were accidentally thrown away. They had been stored in enormous bins, and because blueprints for sets used in TV shows lay on top of the files, someone assumed that the whole lot of it was worthless (a development suggesting that TV blueprints have no value, which is certainly not the case). The accident happened because nobody at MGM cared, and because employees were still discombobulated by Ted Turner's recent sale of the lot to Lorimar. Warnings and pleas from the Academy of Motion Picture Arts and Sciences had been ignored.

Fortunately, Lorimar chairman Merv Adelson appreciated film history and took steps to see that items still warehoused were preserved and that things that had gone missing (like a pair of imposing, carved-wood MGM lions) were located and preserved. But no one ever expected Adelson to be at MGM forever. New owners continued to come and go, which meant that studio enthusiasm about preserving MGM's past waxed and waned.

By 1990, commercial trade in original movie memorabilia had become robust. Because private collectors grasped the unique importance of such items, the wholesale dumping of treasures stopped. It stopped cold. Original items now fetched prices well into six figures. The enormous, general-interest auction houses Christie's and Sotheby's got involved, as well as smaller houses that chose to focus almost exclusively on movie-related items. (Museums and archives also recognized the value of the memorabilia, but typically hadn't a prayer of matching the funds available to wealthy individuals or speculators with pooled resources.) People had been reasonably impressed back in 1970 when the haberdasher parted with $15,000 for a pair of ruby slippers. In 1988, another pair, just as genuine as the first, was auctioned by Christie's for $165,000.

Although cash is chilly, a sum like that nevertheless suggests that, at last, the physical remains of MGM's *The Wizard of Oz* were beginning to be properly regarded.

A Tail of Two Costumes

Two Cowardly Lion costumes have survived, a fact that's almost never been noted during many years of news stories about Lion-costume sales, auctions, restorations, more auctions, and attempts at sales. You'll see that the story is a little tangled; some dates and purchase prices don't jibe.

Lion Costume #1 (a completely arbitrary designation selected for lack of a better one) was created in 1938–39 by MGM's wardrobe department, for actor Bert Lahr. This costume was one item in a 300,000- to 350,000-piece collection of MGM materials that went to auction in 1970.

On the first auction day, May 3, 1970, Costume #1 was purchased for $2,400 by a West Covina physician. This owner engaged a taxidermist to restore the costume, and then put it into cold storage.

In 1985, Los Angeles sculptor Bill Mack purchased Costume #1 and later pursued a complete restoration. Following refurbishment, Costume #1 stood upright on a human-shaped frame, the fists raised in the familiar "Put 'em up!" pose. Because Costume #1 lacked a headpiece when found, Mack executed an extraordinarily handsome sculpture of Bert Lahr in the Lion makeup.

The costume and headpiece are mounted on a flexible steel armature; the completed figure stands on a simulated portion of the Yellow Brick Road, bordered on two sides by artificial poppies. The entire piece rests on a two-tier wooden base.

Working on Mack's behalf, the Profiles in History auction house conducted live eBay bidding in December 2006. The pre-auction estimate was $400,000–$600,000; in the event, Costume #1 sold for $826,000. (Some sources cite this auction as having taken place in 2011 or 2012, with a purchase price of $700,000.)

A Brief Paws

Having dealt with **Costume #1**, we can move on to **Lion Costume #2**. It too was created in 1938–39 by MGM's wardrobe department, for actor Bert Lahr. The costume vanished after the shoot but was discovered in 1973 on what remained of the MGM lot, during final cleanup of studio warehouses. Because of years of neglect, Costume #2 was dirty and partly decayed. Regardless, a worker stuffed it into a garbage bag and took it home.

Here's Bert Lahr in full Cowardly Lion regalia. Visual cues suggest that of the two (or possibly more) Lion costumes made, this is the primary one.

In 1991 (or 1996, accounts vary), Costume #2 was discovered—somewhere—by a junk dealer and subsequently purchased by TV and movie memorabilia collector James Comisar. (In the "1996" version of the story, Costume #2 is rescued at the curb by an antiques dealer, who contacts Comisar.)

In 1996, Comisar undertook a careful restoration of Costume #2, in conjunction with textile experts at the Los Angeles County Art Museum. By matching the costume's distinctive fur patterns with *Wizard of Oz* stills and freeze frames, Comisar and the experts determined that Costume #2 was the one worn by Bert Lahr during some of the movie's key sequences, including "If I Only Had the Nerve" and "If I Were King of the Forest." Because the headpiece of Costume #2 was missing, artists hired by Comisar re-created the Lion's face after taking a facial mold from Bert Lahr's older son, Herbert. The paws were reconstructed, and a new wig and mane were fashioned from human hair. The $22,000 restoration was completed in 1998.

Costume #2 was mounted for display in a standing position in front of a canvas painting of the Emerald City. The paws of Costume #2 are held at the Lion's waist, with arms slightly bent.

Comisar's primary interest was vintage television. In order to help finance a TV museum, Comisar worked with Profiles in History to put Costume #2 up for auction. The event was held at the Paley Center for Media, in Beverly Hills, on December 15–16, 2011. Profiles in History estimated Costume #2's auction value at $3 million. Costume #2 did not sell at this auction. Potential buyers, who would have been aware of the under-$1 million auction price for Costume #1, may have been put off by the much higher estimate for Costume #2.

In March 2013, Comisar announced that he was going to try again, but this time with a straight sale, no auction. Comisar's 2013 asking price for Costume #2 wasn't made public. At this writing (February 2014) Lion Costume #2 is still looking for a buyer.

As collector pieces, each of the two Lion costumes has virtues. Costume #1, with the delightful "Put 'em up!" pose, is gorgeous as a costume *and* as a display piece. The elaborate base is very handsome, and because Bill Mack is a widely collected sculptor, his sculpt of the Lion's face brings added dimensions of beauty, exclusivity, and dollar value.

Although the presentation of Costume #2 (hands at waist) isn't as flamboyant as that of Costume #1, #2 has been identified as the primary Lion costume. You can observe and identify it on screen—and that's a thrill that may be priceless.

Oz in the Comics

The Wizard of Oz has engaged the interest of collectors and investors, and it has inspired simpler pleasure, too: it's conquered the world of comics. Comic strips were fashioned into important parts of American newspapers in the 19th century, when big cities had multiple dailies and circulation wars were common. The simple, graphic appeal of daily and Sunday comic strips was a reliable way to bring in and retain readers.

Oz came to newspaper comics pages in 1904, just four years after L. Frank Baum's first Oz novel. *Queer Visitors from the Marvelous Land of Oz* ran as a syndicated Sunday strip from September 4, 1904 to February 26, 1905. The strip was written by Baum and illustrated by New York–based Walt McDougall, a ballsy editorial cartoonist of thirty years' experience. McDougall was famed for his willingness to go after corrupt politicians and other scoundrels, but he also created his own children's stories. Although he and Baum gave every appearance of collaborating well, McDougall became publicly critical of Baum after the strip concluded.

Original *Oz* illustrator W. W. Denslow wrote and drew fourteen Sunday installments of *Scarecrow and the Tin-Man*, which chronicled the friends' adventures in Mexico and the Caribbean. Intriguingly, the strip's period of publication—December 10, 1904, to February 18, 1905—overlapped considerably with Baum and McDougall's *Oz* strip.

The year 1904 also brought *Adventures Across America*, a strip that was a thinly disguised promotional piece for Baum's 1904 Oz novel *The Marvelous Land of Oz*. Book and strip were illustrated by John R. Neill.

In 1932, Detroit-based C. C. Winningham Inc. syndicated *The Wonderland of Oz*. The strip was written and drawn by Walt Spouse, who combined material from five *Oz* books (including the introduction of Jack Pumpkinhead) into a single continuity. A Spanish-language version was prepared for distribution across Mexico.

Although *The Wonderland of Oz* ran just sixteen months as a Monday through Friday feature, the strip was twice reprinted in comic book form, in Dell's *The Funnies* in 1938 and Hawley Publications's *Hi Spot Comics* in 1940.

Spouse's detailed drawings are both realistic and fanciful, with considerable appeal to modern-day readers. During 2006–2007, handsome trade-paperback "graphic novel" editions of Spouse's *Wonderland* were published by Hungry Tiger Press, as *The Emerald City of Oz*, *The Land of Oz*, and *Ozma of Oz*.

As readership of newspaper strips began to decline in the 1950s, comics writers and artists devoted more of their energy to comic books. Gilberton Publishing's Classics Illustrated line was created in 1942 to adapt great literature to comic books. A series for younger readers, Classics Illustrated Junior, was launched in 1953. Baum's *The Wizard of Oz* was adapted as a Junior title in 1957, with crisp art by penciler Mike Sekowsky and inker Joe Giella. (Just a few years later, the two were at DC, doing beautiful work on *Justice League of America, Adam Strange*, and other superhero series.) Although adapting Baum, the Classics Junior *Oz* found visual inspiration in the books and in the 1939 movie; Dorothy and the Tin Woodman are particularly reminiscent of the Garland and Haley characters.

Dell was a paperback-book powerhouse that also thrived with comic books. ("Dell Comics Are Good Comics.") Most of the latter were licensed products adapting TV westerns, animated cartoons, and kid-friendly movies. A handsome 1956 adaptation, titled *The Wizard of Oz*, was published as part of the Dell Junior Treasury series. The comic included many Baum characters that are not part of the 1939 film, but some character designs and settings (particularly the Yellow Brick Road and the poppy field) showed a clear MGM influence.

A 1962 Dell adaptation of TV animator Rankin-Bass's *Tales of the Wizard of Oz* carried on R-B's space-age-modern cartoon style that burdened most characters with enormous, squash-like heads and teeny tiny feet.

By the mid-1960s, West Coast car and bike culture had spread across the country, with widespread interest in hot rods, super-cycles, custom cars, low riders, and muscle cars. Magazine publishers jumped in with traditional car and motorcycle titles, and with gearhead magazines dominated by edgy, black-and-white one-panel gags and complete comic book stories. *CARtoons, Drag Cartoons*, and *Hot Rod Cartoons* entertained car buffs, while *CYCLEtoons* catered to bikers.

What has this to do with *The Wizard of Oz*? The highlight of the June 1973 issue of *CYCLEtoons* is "Hogg in Oz," writer-cartoonist Bill Stout's amusing ten-page "cycle fairy tale" dropping muscular biker Hogg into a mash-up of Baum, MGM, and fable, carefully drawn in the style of fantasy comics of the 1950s.

A highlight of *Oz*'s association with comics arrived in 1975, as a licensed retelling of the MGM film that was the first co-publishing venture of Marvel and DC Comics. Resplendent with heavy board covers and a mighty $12'' \times 18''$ trim size, the comic was executed by Marvel staffers and freelancers. Top Marvel writer-editor Roy Thomas adapted the original Langley-Ryerson-Woolf film script into seventy-two pages penciled by Marvel's most brilliant draftsman and storyteller, John Buscema, famed for his work on *Fantastic Four*, *The Silver Surfer*, and *The Avengers*. His work was inked by Tony DeZuniga. The comic's front and back covers were drawn by *Spider-Man* artist John Romita. Cover price was $1.50.

Nearly all key dialogue from the film was retained, and although settings and character designs were clearly MGM, Buscema's interpretation, though faithful, was more dynamic, with aggressive "camera setups" and staging. In a clever stroke, the Kansas sequences were colored in muted shades of blue and gray.

One- to three-page ancillary features at the back of the book were variously written by Thomas and Don Glut, and illustrated by Romita, Buscema, Marie Severin, and Ed Hannigan.

A 1986 DC Comics publication, *The Oz-Wonderland War*, is a cheeky, frequently imaginative collision of Baum and Lewis Carroll, featuring DC's anthropomorphic "funny animal" superhero group, the Zoo Crew. The adventure was written by E. Nelson Bridwell and illustrated by Carol Lay.

During 1991–92, comics writer Alan Moore, best known as the author of the nihilistic *Watchmen* superhero series, created grown-up versions of Dorothy, Carroll's Alice, and *Peter Pan*'s Wendy for a proposed epic called *Lost Girls*. The young women meet at a hotel in 1913, where they reveal their troubled pasts and explore their private and shared desires. Typical of Moore, the script is purposely provocative (Dorothy is what used to be called "promiscuous"), gratuitously offensive (depictions of child sex rightly scared off many retailers), and occasionally jejune (the Mad Hatter, for instance, is a hermaphrodite). The richly colored, explicitly sexual illustrations (done in the handsome style of vintage bookplates) are by Melinda Gebbie. Moore has an intellectual interest in the divide between fantasy and reality, and although *Lost Girls* has a go at that already well-explored line of thought, the comic inevitably falls into the "sexual awakening" category—and is likely to be best enjoyed by people who haven't had one yet. Early portions of *Lost Girls* were published in *Taboo* magazine, and a much-expanded version was issued in 2006 as a three-volume hardcover set; a single-volume hardcover followed in 2009.

On a lighter note, Marvel's *What If?* . . . #100 (1997) includes "There's No Place Like That Place Where You Sleep and Keep Your Stuff," which placed the company's marquee superhero team, the Fantastic Four, in Oz. Sue Storm (the Invisible Girl) is the Dorothy character. Devoted superhero fans are most likely to "get" this mildly amusing tale, which was written by Robert Piotrowski and drawn by Rurik Tyler (pencils) and Harry Candelario (inks).

Fallout from the '60s: *Oz* and *Brewster McCloud*

Screenwriter Doran William Cannon and director Robert Altman referenced MGM's *Wizard of Oz* in their odd and touching 1970 film *Brewster McCloud*. Although shot in and around Houston (notably, inside the Astrodome), and invoking such things as serial killings, a policeman's car chase of a murder suspect, and dreadful loneliness, *Brewster McCloud* is essentially a fantasy. The hook is that the young title character (played by Bud Cort) is struggling to construct immense, artificial wings, so that he can fly—that is, so that he can escape a very chilly world that has no tolerance for dreamers. His daily life, in a windowless air raid shelter beneath the Astrodome, is bearable only because it is there that he labors over his wings.

In the end, Brewster does take flight, but not for very long. His dreams—and his personal failings—have been too consequential to allow him the freedom he's yearned for.

Besides the partial resemblance to the wistful theme of *The Wizard of Oz*, *Brewster McCloud* invokes the MGM classic in other important ways. Although the face of actress Margaret Hamilton is never seen, her Wicked Witch voice gives a suggestion of the nature of the character she plays. After she becomes a victim of the serial killer, we *still* don't see her face, just her legs and the ruby slippers on her feet.

Various characters assume functions akin to that of Dorothy's friends. A fallen angel (Sally Kellerman, with scarred shoulders) guides Brewster through his misadventures, and a slightly spacey Astrodome tour guide (Shelly Duvall, in her first film) supports Brewster's ambitions, to a point. The third woman in Brewster's life is a gingham-frocked beauty named Hope (Jennifer Salt). At film's end, when Altman parades his cast as costumed circus performers (à la one key sequence in Fellini's *8½*), Hope wears a Dorothy dress and cradles a Cairn terrier.

Other characters and sequences in *Brewster McCloud* evoke, or spoof, Fellini's *La Dolce Vita*, the Wright brothers, Steve McQueen and *Bullitt*, the legend of Icarus, and the biblical fall from grace.

So what does this determinedly loopy, unsubtly symbolic coming-of-age fable mean? Well, maybe a lot, or maybe very little. As a reflection of the disappointing aftertaste of the 1960s, the movie is an edgy social document. As entertainment, it's dependent upon the tolerance and generosity of its audience. Some viewers are put off by the film's fantastical elements and endless allusions; others take delight in its attack on conformity and celebration of aspirational dreams.

The "No place like home" Controversy

When MGM made *The Wizard of Oz* during 1938–39, the homely virtues that underscore the film's actions and the motivations of its characters—home, love, responsibility, modesty—were at the forefront of American thought (and were *idées fixes* of studio chief Louis Mayer, too). Despite the brief national adventure abroad during the final year of World War I, late-Depression America was unsophisticated and parochial. Alternate ways of life existing beyond America's borders were beneath notice; the strange ways of "foreigners" bored braver Americans and frightened the timid ones. Tolerance for anything other than the white Anglo-Saxon ideal was modest at best.

Statistically speaking, almost no adult Americans of 1940 had been to college; by the time they were thirty-five years old, Americans born in 1905 had attained, on average, just 9.2 years of education.

Franklin Roosevelt was in the White House, but during the tenure of his predecessor, Herbert Hoover, America was firmly, even self-righteously, isolationist. The prompts to adventurism abroad made by Teddy Roosevelt at the beginning of the century had been forgotten. When Hoover's term was sputtering to a close in 1932–33, the United States had a military that barely ranked in the world's top twenty in terms of men and materiel. America wasn't a superpower; the nation wasn't even particularly influential on the world stage. This is borne out by British prime minister Neville Chamberlain's capacity to tell FDR to take his unasked-for advice about foment in Europe and, in essence, get lost, when Chamberlain confidently prepared to meet Adolf Hitler at Munich in 1938. Indeed, Britain was *the* superpower, ruling not just the waves but unimaginably vast areas of the world. Britain mattered; the United States was an overgrown upstart. (Of course, Roosevelt was dead right in his warning to Chamberlain before Munich, but that's another story.)

The remarkable thing is that Americans weren't concerned by the nation's lowly status. Let the Brits spend their treasure abroad. We'll stay home, thank you, and mind our own business. We have plenty of domestic trouble to occupy our time. National unemployment had peaked at a staggering 25 percent in 1932–33. The idea of capitalism had been in serious peril. Communism wasn't just a chic notion that had engaged East Coast intellectuals; it was beginning to seem reasonable to millions of Americans that had lost jobs, farms, homes, and hope. Labor unrest was met with institutionalized violence and even out-and-out murder. Ten thousand banks failed between 1929 and 1933, and many states closed their borders to destitute "outsiders" that might be looking for ways to feed themselves. (MGM actively encouraged this sort of police-state mentality in 1934 by creating a faked "newsreel" of hobos and Bolsheviks headed for California to overwhelm the state's public resources; as intended, the ploy put an end to author-progressive Upton Sinclair's credible bid to become California's governor.) The nation's roads and rail lines were clogged by hundreds of thousands of men—including teenagers and men in their twenties—who had given up all hope in the farms and cities, and who had nothing but an urge to keep moving. At great risk, and often in disguise, desperate young women traveled with these men. The social fabric was unraveling, and as Franklin Roosevelt campaigned for the presidency in 1932, he rightly feared that the United States was on the verge of armed rebellion.

After taking office in March 1933, Roosevelt ruled via a compliant Congress and executive order. Unemployment had dropped to about 10 percent by the middle of 1937, but a severe and unexpected recession during 1937–38 shot the figure to 20 percent by the early summer of 1938. Americans were frightened all over again.

Into this atmosphere came MGM's *Oz*, tremulous in its heart-rending emphasis on home lost and home regained. Given the establishment-oriented perspective of MGM, we might today interpret "there's no place like home" as the filmmakers' unconscious plea: *Yes, the nation is in trouble, we see that just as clearly as you do, but things will be better because we're Americans and the American way is the best way.* It's a plea made by people desperate to believe that they're being justifiably optimistic and not just foolishly hopeful.

The real weight of "home" in the context of MGM's *Oz* draws from the national unease, but is more focused and personal. In the film, the word links closely to a particular, fictional person, as well as to all young people, particularly girls and women, who will come after. Over the three generations since the movie's initial release, Dorothy's great relief at being back in her own bed is perceived not as a joyful rebuke to timidity, and not even as a triumph of focus and ingenuity, but as a surrender to the suffocating expectations of a society that limited women's horizons and encouraged them to diminish their dreams. Many present-day detractors who are troubled by Dorothy's "There's no place like home" are mortified by the less-often-quoted, "[I]f I ever go looking for my heart's desire again, I won't look any further than my own back yard, because if it isn't there, I never really lost it to begin with." (In Baum, Dorothy says only, "I'm so glad to be at home again!")

On the face of it, the film's central sentiment about home isn't very encouraging. We can easily imagine an older Dorothy, sallow and a little stooped, living on the same farm or one so similar that any differences are irrelevant. That kind of Dorothy is easy for us to foresee because the human imagination is by nature catastrophic. When we assume the worst, we keep vigilant and we stay alive. When we assume the worst for others, we're trying to be empathetic.

But Dorothy is a smart kid. She's a stolid and straightforward little toughie in the Baum book and a person of great intellectual and emotional gifts in the film. Because the movie makes clear that Dorothy's exotic adventure is her dream, *the Dorothy that we see in Oz is precisely the same Dorothy as the one in Kansas.* Kansas-Dorothy created all of it. Every challenge and every solution, every friendship and moment of selflessness, every instance of cleverness and guts, every awareness of evil and perfidy—it all comes from Dorothy. Kansas-Dorothy is precisely as she appears during her adventure in Oz. Who, really, is unable to like and admire this young woman? Who cannot be hopeful for her future?

When Dorothy says "back yard," she means the limits that define her—and we've already seen that her metaphorical yard is enormous. Big metaphoric yard = big personal destiny.

We will do ourselves a favor by keeping in mind that Dorothy does *not* say "There's no place like Kansas" or "There's no place like this farm." She says "home," and what is home, after all, but a subjectively discerned place that is part reality, part memory, and part desire? Home is our personal world that gives us security and purpose, and a sense of belonging to someplace. Home is wood and plaster and shingles, and it also is an idea that we construct and nourish in our minds. It's very much about our definitions of ourselves.

Dorothy's home of the mind has enabled her to express her own virtues as qualities expressed by the characters she imagines. Her Oz friends are uniquely brilliant because Dorothy is brilliant. (In this vein, it's *Dorothy*, and not the Scarecrow, that chops the rope supporting the Witch's chandelier.) The girl is filled to bursting with bravery and imagination, love and intelligence. She will persevere and grow. Via her dream, she's realized (and allowed us to see) that she can manage complicated relationships and life-threatening situations. She's conjured up dangers in Oz, but she's also devised ways around them, and even a way to return herself to where she wishes to be. If she can manage all of that in Oz, then she surely can figure out a way to get the heck out of Kansas—or at least carry herself to a fresh start in the bustle of Kansas City.

"There's no place like home" isn't a fence. It's an open door to freedom.

Dorothy Has a Hairy Chest: Looking for the Lesson of *Zardoz*

John Boorman's *Zardoz* (1974) is a science-fiction/fantasy epic that borrows one idea from L. Frank Baum and embeds it in a humorless parable about religion and power, sex and brutality, foolish obedience and mortality—all of it played out in post-apocalyptic 2293. Visually striking, the movie is also windy and pretentious, and if *Zardoz* still fascinates people today, the reason is that disasters are usually interesting to witness.

Sean Connery is Zed, a brutalized warrior-assassin of the Exterminator class who lives to please "Zardoz," the ruler of the film's bleak, primitive landscape. Although Zardoz appears to his followers as a great, floating stone head, the scowling visage obscures the reality that Zardoz is an ordinary man who rules via trickery, after having learned how from the title character from an ancient book, *The Wonderful Wizard of Oz*. In a moment of candor directed only to the audience, Zardoz describes himself as "a fake god by occupation and a magician by inclination. . . . I am the puppet master. I manipulate many of the characters and events you will see. . . . And you, poor creatures, who conjured *you* out of the clay? Is God in show business too?"

Amidst all this posturing is the tale's central conflict: because immortality is possible for the ruling class, the need for sex has nearly vanished. Even more unpromising is that men have grown incapable of sexual arousal, so the future is no future at all. Free will, the love of violence, and an aversion to love are balled up in Boorman's screenplay and then fitted with a dramatic but unimaginative reversal: of all the males on earth, only Zed (as a lot of chilly, expository dialogue explains) is capable of an erection.

When Zed finally realizes that he has been deceived, and that his raison d'etre has been based on lies, he turns against his false god. Zed's violent nature remains, but now he'll turn it to revenge by "inseminating" available females, to begin the task of returning humankind to the kind of natural existence despised by the elite.

Prior to *Zardoz*, John Boorman had effectively guided the Dave Clark Five in their film debut, *Having a Wild Weekend* (1964), and helped to create the iconic Lee Marvin persona in *Point Blank* (1967), a slashingly stylish crime thriller that, like *Zardoz*, explores free will and the byzantine structure of power. Then came *Deliverance* (1972), Boorman's shatteringly effective adaptation of the James Dickey novel about diminished maleness in an affluent, essentially soft society. *Deliverance* turned into a cultural sensation as well as a box-office hit, so—as is often allowed to happen in Hollywood—the tremendous success was followed by a self-indulgent vanity project. Because of the defiantly impenetrable nature of *Zardoz*, and its commercial failure, Boorman's career was derailed and didn't fully recover until thirteen years later, when he wrote and directed *Hope and Glory* (1987), the loosely autobiographical story of a boy during wartime.

Boorman had had no background as a writer of fantasy or science fiction prior to *Zardoz*. He was thrilled with the possibilities of the genre, but stuffed his script with more ideas than he ever could have kept track of, let alone develop sensibly. The film's link to Baum and *Oz* isn't uninteresting, but whatever forcefulness that conceit might have summoned was swept aside by the swirl of other ideas. MGM's *The Wizard of Oz* is a legitimate artifact of late-Depression America; Boorman's *Zardoz* is an encapsulation of the self-indulgence of the 1970s.

Turkish Taffy? No, "Turkish Oz."

Dorothy's heroic quest, particularly as interpreted by MGM, resonates around the world. The makers of a 1971 Turkish *Oz* knockoff, *Aysecik ve Sihirli Cügeler Ruyul Ülkesinde* (*Aysecik and the Bewitched Dwarfs in Dreamland*) unapologetically helped themselves to MGM's costume conceptions and musical format. Shot mostly outdoors by director Tunc Basaran on woodsy natural locations baked by remorseless, unflattering sunlight, *Aysecik* takes numerous liberties with Baum and MGM, including an interlude of mass murder when Munchkin soldiers wipe out a mob of dancing cavemen with cannon fire—and then spend three minutes laughing about it. (The cavemen may be a nod to Baum's Hammerheads.) Pretty, gingham-clad Aysecik (Zeynep Degirmencioglu) is swept to Dreamland by a tornado and devotes herself to staying a step ahead of the Wicked Witch of the South. When the Witch noses around too close for comfort, Aysecik and her friends tear the Scarecrow to shreds so that Dorothy can conceal herself beneath what used to be the Scarecrow's innards. You think: *Well, that was interesting.*

By Western standards, *Aysecik and the Bewitched Dwarfs in Dreamland* lives at the low end of the professional scale, with perfunctory staging, unimaginative lighting, and campy overacting from all but Degirmencioglu; Suna Selen, as the Wicked Witch, is particularly unrestrained. Worse, she's shrill. Special effects are mostly of the mechanical (on-set) variety, with primitive jump cuts that make people and things appear and disappear. The Wizard is suggested by a paltry flame positioned close to the camera, with a forlorn-looking human skull behind. (Over the years, numberless American films have been adapted by Turkish filmmakers, with jaw-dropping results. Aysecik herself appeared in a variant of *Snow White*. If that's too tame to suit you, try "Turkish *Star Wars*," "Turkish *Spider-Man*," "Turkish *Exorcist*," or "Turkish *Rambo*.")

There are some small rewards in "Turkish *Oz*." Besides the Hammerheads, Baum is referenced by small girls that live a doll house—a suggestion of the dainty residents of China Country. The score is an intriguing mix of traditional Turkish folk melodies and distinctly American instrumentation driven by guitar and fiddles. The melodies, and the dancing that go with them, are sprightly fun. The film gets points, too, for having the boldness—or just plain gall—to use appealing, Saturday-morning-cartoon animation to handle the title credits *and* the twister simultaneously. (The cartoon Aysecik looks very much like Judy Garland.) Alas, everything is ultimately betrayed by the meager budget scrounged by producer Özdemir Birsel for Hisar Film and Birsen.

Between 1960 and 1971, Degirmencioglu (who was seventeen when she went to Oz-in-Istanbul) starred in at least fifteen "Aysecik" adventures, including *Aysecik and the Handsome Devil* (1960), *Aysecik and the Poor Princess* (1963), *Aysecik and the Keepers of the Socket* (1969), and *I Adore Aysecik* (1970). The movies made Degirmencioglu a Turkish media favorite, and as she grew up, magazine and newspaper readers witnessed her transition from pigtails to bikinis. When the actress made "Turkish *Oz*," she was an obviously seasoned performer with a girlish voice and a womanly bust. When she retired in 1974, Degirmencioglu was just twenty years old.

The complete "Turkish *Oz*" floats around the USA on muddy bootleg tapes, and brief segments have been posted to YouTube and other Web sites. During the last ten years, the film has been screened by university theaters, bars, and similarly lively venues. When "Turkish *Oz*" was booked into Vancouver's Blim Art Centre in November 2006, advance poster art said, "'Herbal refreshments' recommended!" (Blim had scheduled "Turkish *Oz*" earlier in 2006, and when the movie went AWOL at the eleventh hour, Blim punted and screened "Filipino *Batman and Robin*" [*Alyas Batman en Robin*].)

The more or less official American release of "Turkish *Oz*" was engineered by Shocking Videos in 2000.

Tom and Jerry Travel to Oz

A superior, hour-long animated cartoon, *Tom and Jerry and the Wizard of Oz* (2011), was produced by Turner Entertainment and Warner Bros. for direct-to-video release. Hapless Tom Cat and ingenious Jerry Mouse (both created for MGM by animators William Hanna and Joseph Barbera in 1939–40) are caught in the twister with

Dorothy and swept to Oz. The lively cartoon animation is as close to the smooth "full animation" of cartoons' golden age as we're likely to see on video these days, and Gene Grillo's script follows the 1939 film with satisfying closeness, while being true to the mutually antagonistic natures of the venerable Tom and Jerry. Elements of the original Herbert Stothart score, and many songs by Arlen and Harburg (some with added lyrics), are heard. The cartoon was directed by Spike Brandt, who followed the colorful 1939 costume and production designs.

The cartoon's splendid voice work is by Grey DeLisle, as Dorothy, and Nikki Yanofsky, as the singing Dorothy. (Although DeLisle is an unusually expressive singer and recording artist, she doesn't do these vocals.) Others in the cast: Michael Gough as the Scarecrow (this Michael Gough is American and is not the well-known British actor of the same name); Rob Paulsen as the Tin Woodman; Todd Stashwick as the Cowardly Lion; Laraine Newman, full of Hamilton-style venom as the Wicked Witch; Joe Alaskey as the Wizard; Frances Conroy as Glinda; and Kath Soucie as a new character, Tuffy the diminutive Munchkin mouse, who hopes the Wizard can make him big.

In an intriguing departure from 1939, Tom and Jerry mime the Wizard and the Tin Woodman in Dorothy's bedroom after everybody's return to Kansas—making clear that the adventure has *not* been a dream!

Oz, the Amusement Park

Throughout the summer of 1970, over four hundred thousand people visited a remote spot on North Carolina's Beech Mountain. They went there to find Oz.

Land of Oz was a 450-acre amusement park that opened on June 15, 1970. This celebration of the MGM version of Oz was created by Grover Robbins, a very successful North Carolina–based developer of coastal properties and resorts in his home state and in the Caribbean. He had already put together Tweetsie Railroad, a handsome Wild West theme park in Blowing Rock, North Carolina, and now he wanted to celebrate Oz. The park was developed as a sequential, walk-through attraction that opened with cyclone effects at the Gale farmhouse and took visitors through the entirety of Dorothy's adventure. Only a limited number of visitors could be accommodated at any one time, so guests were cycled through in groups, with various Dorothys escorting people out of the storm cellar, into a "destroyed" section of the house, and into Munchkinland and beyond.

The park was designed by Jack Pentes and Carolina Caribbean Corporation. One of the more clever features was the Wizard's balloon ride, which was built on a disguised ski lift. The angry apple trees were carved trees augmented with plaster sculpture, and in Oz itself, a puce statue of the Horse of a Different Color waited patiently, with carriage. Pentes and his crew dotted the Yellow Brick Road with gaily painted Munchkins formed in stone and designed the Witch's castle to incorporate impressive concrete parapets.

Local and regional anticipation was high during 1969–70, and guests on opening day included former MGM contract star Debbie Reynolds (who is an Oz collector) and her young daughter, Carrie Fisher. In an unfortunate happenstance, Grover Robbins, just fifty years old, died of cancer six months before his dream park opened.

Business was good for some years, but the mountain's difficult roads eventually became obstacles to visitors. Attendance began a steady slide, and after the park closed in 1980, the place was visited by vandals and thieves who wrecked and stole props and entire buildings.

In 1990, some of the acreage was sold for home development, which galvanized some locals. A significant portion of the acreage was held back from development, and the all-volunteer Project Emerald Mountain began restoration and refurbishment. Work wasn't completed at the time, and the park again fell into serious disrepair.

The Land of Oz was cleaned up and partially restored in 2013. A waterfall and central fountain were restored, and the main entryway—with "O" and "Z" on the large gates—was refurbished. The Yellow Brick Road is a bit of a patchwork, as it had to be dug from beneath the encroaching earth. New, bright yellow bricks were inserted among the weathered originals where needed. The stone figures of the Munchkins have been bleached by the elements.

Although no longer a fully functioning park, Land of Oz is promoted as a self-guided walk-through attraction. An annual, two-day Oz party is mounted on the grounds early each October, with actors dressed as Dorothy and the various residents of Oz. The Gale farmhouse has been restored and is now a rental cottage. No smoking and no pets. Sorry, Toto.

Recordings and Other Performances of "Over the Rainbow" by Unexpected People

Chet Atkins (1976; *Chet Atkins Goes to the Movies*)—America's peerless country guitarist gave "Over the Rainbow" a sophisticated acoustic gloss in this recording. Atkins always made it look easy, but only because he was highly disciplined; he gives the Arlen-Harburg classic the respect it deserves.

Jeff Beck (2006; *Official Bootleg USA '06*, a live album)—A legendary rock guitarist fashions his instrumental version of "Over the Rainbow" with delicate precision, playing well off a backing string section and coaxing a lovely, plaintive voice from his guitar.

Beyoncé (2007; non-album live performance at *Movies Rock* telecast)—A sweet, pleasingly unmannered interpretation backed with orchestra.

Ray Charles (1963; *Ingredients in a Recipe for Soul*)—Although a little overproduced with string orchestra and chorus, Charles's version soars on the singer's assertive, gravelly vocals.

Eric Clapton (2002; *One More Car, One More Rider*, a live album)—A leisurely and sincere live performance of "Over the Rainbow" captures the rock legend in fine and mellow voice.

Papa John Creach (1971; *Papa John Creach*)—Creach was an elegant blues violinist with professional experience going back to the 1930s. His much later electric-violin work with Jefferson Airplane and Hot Tuna made him familiar to rock fans, and he embarked on a solo recording career. Creach's easy, soaring "Over the Rainbow" is from his first solo LP.

The Del-Vikings (1957; *They Sing . . . They Swing*)—One of the greatest of all doo-wop groups of the 1950s, the Del-Vikings will be remembered for "Come Go with Me" and "Whispering Bells." The group's version of "Over the Rainbow," backed by the Carl Stevens Orchestra, is highly melodic and very slow—ideal for close, close dancing.

Plácido Domingo (2000; *Songs of Love*)—Opera stars' forays into pop music can have uneasy outcomes, but the great tenor Domingo dialed back his power for "Over the Rainbow" and seemed perfectly at home with the song, which he has reprised on stage many times.

Maynard Ferguson (1955; *Dimensions*)—Young Maynard Ferguson's trumpet brings a vivid, bell-clear tone to "Over the Rainbow," with minimal vibrato. The horn plays effectively against a backdrop of "sweet" saxophones and segues easily into a lovely patch of improvisation. The song appeared, with a disco backbeat and a heavy phalanx of backup brass, on a 1978 Ferguson LP, *Carnival.*

The Flaming Lips (2004; this is a non-album track that the band performed on the December 19, 2004, taping of *Austin City Limits*)—"Over the Rainbow" has not appeared on any Flaming Lips album to date, but it's frequently performed live (and videotaped) by this ingratiating bunch of psychedelic alt-rock Oklahomans. The Lips are famed for their elaborate stage shows, so "live" is a great way to listen to and see their take on the signature song from *The Wizard of Oz.*

Renée Fleming (the song has not appeared on a Fleming album, but videos of live performances are plentiful)—America's finest living soprano has issued numerous pop albums. Her creamy voice isn't particularly well suited to light material, so although her interpretations of "Over the Rainbow" are technically breathtaking, Fleming's vocal shimmer is a little overpowering.

Merle Haggard and the Strangers (1973; *Totally Instrumental with One Exception*)—This LP was the fifth to showcase the Strangers, Merle Haggard's sterling backup band. Like nearly all of the album's cuts, "Over the Rainbow" is an instrumental. (Voices can actually be heard on two tracks, not just one, as the title denotes.) Haggard may have played guitar or fiddle on the recording; in any case, this countrypolitan version has some pleasing down-home flourishes. And at just 1:50, it's sweetly succinct.

Jimi Hendrix (1975; *Crash Landing*)—The "Over the Rainbow" track on this posthumous LP was recorded by the great guitarist in March 1968. For the 1975 mix, Stephen Stills (bass) and Mitch Mitchell (drums) were over-dubbed by studio players.

Chris Impellitteri (1988; *Stand in Line*)—Metal guitar instrumental brings lively, imaginative riffs to the melody. **NOTE:** This recording is frequently, and erroneously, credited to Queen (or to Queen's guitarist, Brian May), Jimi Hendrix, Guns N' Roses, Steve Vai, Joe Satriani, Yngwie Malmsteen, and others.

Israel Kamakawiwo'ole (1990; *Ka 'Ano'i*)—This sensitive voice-and-ukulele version by one of Hawaii's most highly regarded singers is frequently cited in fan popularity polls as second only to Judy Garland's. **NOTE:** Web videos claiming to be reggae star Bob Marley's version of "Over the Rainbow" invariably play Kamakawiwo'ole's recording. Confusion has arisen probably because Marley recorded a non-album single called "Rainbow Country."

Leftover Cuties (the song is not yet on a Leftover Cuties album or EP, but the group has been videotaped performing it live)—Young four-person L.A. band channels the Great American Songbook through a relaxed indie-pop/lounge sensibility, and sparkles. The Cuties go with (variously) standup bass, drums, ukulele, banjo, piano, accordion, trumpet, French horn, and lead singer Shirli McAllen's mandolin. Their mainly instrumental take on "Over the Rainbow" comes on like tasty martini music.

Jerry Lewis (1960; *Big Songs for Little People*)—Lewis is a gifted comic, writer, actor, and filmmaker—but he nursed a desire to become a serious vocalist, too. His grasp of phrasing and inflection are sophisticated, but he simply hasn't the timbre or pitch to be a satisfying singer. In the manner of the day, this version of "Over the Rainbow" is overproduced, with a full orchestra and a female chorus intended to help Lewis negotiate the melody.

Jerry Lee Lewis (1980; *Killer Country*)—Rock's original bad boy has fun with "Over the Rainbow," combining the Jerry Lee heavy-piano treatment with an easy, reflective pace.

Van McCoy (1977; *Van McCoy and His Magnificent Movie Machine*)—McCoy's 1975 disco hit, "The Hustle," is a monster record that's overshadowed the wide range of his considerable and very sophisticated musical gifts: composer, arranger, conductor, producer, and songwriter. *Magnificent Movie Machine*'s "Over the Rainbow" is marked by McCoy's lush arrangements for strings and female chorus, propelled by a disco beat that seems perfect rather than inappropriate.

Me First and the Gimme Gimmes (1999: *Are a Drag*)—This is a high-energy power punk version from one of the best covers-only bands. Great fun. **NOTE:** On the Web, Me First's "Over the Rainbow" is routinely attributed to the Ramones.

Melanie (2005; *Photograph: Double Exposure*)—The tremulous, folky voice of Woodstock veteran Melanie Safka is nicely suited to "Over the Rainbow." The version on this LP was recorded in 1976.

Mormon Tabernacle Choir (1992; *Greatest Hits: 22 Best-Loved Favorites*)—A slick, sober, and disciplined version that's not likely to get you on your feet.

The Ohio Players (1968; *Observations in Time*)—"Over the Rainbow" is a highlight of the debut album of this funk/R&B band that went on to great success in the 1970s. Lead singer Dutch Robinson gives a heartfelt, powerhouse performance that invokes doo-wop, jazz, and Muscle Shoals–style R&B.

Phish (1996; *Live Phish Vol. 12*)—Ambitious, three-disc live album from these long-form improv rockers has many high points, including "Over the Rainbow" done by Page McConnell on solo Theremin (he was inspired when a rainbow appeared over the venue). The band hasn't recorded "Over the Rainbow" in the studio and rarely performs it live, so this album is the best way to hear a uniquely eerie version.

Louis Prima (1999; *Beepin' and Boppin'*)—Bandleader, trumpeter, and vocalist Louis Prima prospered for decades with jump jazz pounded out to a rock 'n' roll beat. He was a raspy, infectious singer, an enthusiastic trumpeter, and a great showman. The Prima version of "Over the Rainbow" included on this latter-day compilation was recorded between 1949 and 1954.

Procol Harum (1975; *The Last Concert, Live!*)—The classical-rock band's live version of "Over the Rainbow" is incorporated into the midpoint of another song, "Grand Hotel." In its entirety, the cut is ambitious, melodic, and surprisingly playful.

Keith Richards (1977; bootleg LP, *Learning the Game*)—This version of "Rainbow" is leisurely paced and pleasingly lo-fi, with Richards accompanying himself on piano, with Bobby Keys on alto sax.

Leon Russell & New Grass Revival (1981 studio-version single release; and 2007 live version; *The Live Album*)—Already a legendary guitarist by 1981, Russell also was a soulful vocalist. His live version of "Over the Rainbow" is elegant and intimate, sung against Russell's own lush piano.

Sandy Hook Elementary Students, with Ingrid Michaelson (2013; iTunes, Amazon mp3, and other outlets)—Just a month after twenty children and six adults were killed by gunfire at a Connecticut grade school, a choral group of twenty-one of the victims' classmates recorded "Over the Rainbow," a song that's heartbreaking in its aptness. Proceeds from the recording went to the Newtown Youth Academy and the United Way of Western Connecticut.

Ray Stevens (1975; *Misty*)—Stevens achieved commercial success in the 1960s with novelty tunes the likes of "Ahab the Arab" and "Gitarzan." Beginning around 1970, he shifted to emphasize his lightly pleasing "straight" vocal style. Stevens's "Over the Rainbow" is unadventurous but enjoyable.

Sonny Stitt (1968; *Soul Electricity*)—The great acid-bop saxophonist included "Over the Rainbow" on this album of Great American Songbook standards. Stitt recorded the LP with a Varitone amplifier mounted to his alto and tenor sax. Stitt's tenor tone on "Over the Rainbow" is rich, with a laid-back pace. Others in the quartet: Billy James (drums), Billy Butler (guitar), and Don Patterson (organ).

Straight No Chaser (2010; *With a Twist*)—This highly disciplined, smartly amusing a cappella group paired a reggae-influenced "Over the Rainbow" with "I'm Yours" on *With a Twist*, the group's first non-holiday album.

Sun Ra and His Arkestra (1977; *Somewhere Over the Rainbow*, recorded live)— Mystical free-jazz exponent Sun Ra's piano-dominated take on "Over the Rainbow" is remarkable—it's at once grave, dissonant, and beautiful, with an unexpected dash of jauntiness at the midpoint.

Taco (1991; *Puttin' on the Ritz*)—Taco (Ockerse) broke across America in 1982 with his synth-pop version of "Puttin' on the Ritz." He faded quickly from American radar but has maintained a very successful career across Europe (particularly Germany and Austria) as a singer and as an actor in film, television, and theater. Taco's "Over the Rainbow" has only vague synth elements; it's a competent and straightforward interpretation.

Connie Talbot (2007; *Over the Rainbow*)—Talbot was just six years old when she sang "Over the Rainbow" on a popular TV show, *Britain's Got Talent*, in 2007. *Over the Rainbow* was her first album; the child's talent is precocious and undeniable, with a naïve sweetness that's well suited to the album's title song.

Tiny Tim (1996; *Girl*)—In 1968, this falsetto vocalist with a fondness for very old songs was one of the most talked-about people in America. With his ukulele, peculiar looks, and carefully cultivated image as an eccentric, Tiny Tim (real name: Herbert Khaury) achieved major pop stardom that had nearly evaporated by 1970. Tim's version of "Over the Rainbow" was released the year of his death. The recording is odd—and quite lovely.

Gene Vincent (1960; 45 rpm single, b/w "Who's Pushing Your Swing")—Rock 'n' roll/rockabilly giant Gene Vincent is best remembered for "Be-Bop-A-Lula," one of the most celebrated records of the early rock era. He performed his slow and tender version of "Over the Rainbow" in Los Angeles on KTTV's *Town Hall Party* in November 1959; the single was released early the following year. That recording was finally issued on an LP, *Gene Vincent's Greatest Hits*, in 1969.

Oz Fan Fiction

Fan fiction (sometimes called fanfiction or FF) is a worldwide cultural phenomenon by which people create and disseminate unauthorized fictionalizations based on favorite movies and TV shows. (Fan fiction inspired by books and plays exists, as well, but in far lower numbers than TV and movie pieces.) Some fan fiction is novel-length (often presented in serial installments); most is considerably shorter.

The phenomenon dates to the Conan Doyle "Sherlock Holmes" stories of the 19th century, but didn't gain wide notice until the mid-1960s, when amateur writers responded enthusiastically to the original *Star Trek* television show. Over the subsequent years, numberless films and television series have inspired amateur fiction. Today, much of what moves the authors is adventurous (*Pirates of the Caribbean, Lost*), fantastical (*Star Wars, Game of Thrones, Twilight*), teen oriented (*Glee, High School Musical*), romantic (*Titanic, Moulin Rouge*), humorous (*The Big Bang Theory, Toy Story*), or violent (*Fast and the Furious, Criminal Minds*). Even the soap operas *General Hospital* and *The Young and the Restless* are reflected in fan fiction.

Vital to a proper appreciation of fan fiction is that the aficionados have a shared body of knowledge—a deep background in particular shows and movies, characters, and tropes. The writers are thus free to honor or contravene their inspiration, assured that everybody else in the community will "get it."

Technology has greatly expanded fan fiction's reach. What was shared among a very few via mimeograph or ditto forty years ago now fills the Internet, where it can conceivably be seen by millions.

Whatever the inspiration, fan fiction ranges from intriguing to awful, with an undeniable bias toward awful and with a dollop of "calculated to offend almost everybody" tossed in for spice. Sex and violence can figure strongly in these tales.

It's easy enough to dismiss fan fiction for its naiveté, fractured syntax, and sentimentality; and you needn't be a sophisticate to be wearied by the material's failed attempts at thrills or humor, or depressed by its sometimes anxious journeys into eros. But this prose (and occasional verse) is obviously important to the people that write and read it. The writers, by definition, are creating something—which, in a day of passive, prefabricated fun, is rare. Readers, in turn, connect with the writer, and with each other. Now, with fan-fiction sites that include "Comments" sections, writer-reader connections can be specific and immediate.

Virtually all of the fan fiction inspired by *The Wizard of Oz* is based on the 1939 film, because the movie provides the fullest shared experience and thus (in theory) the most satisfaction for all. The original Baum novels, with the exception of the first, are read only by zealots, and even the first one doesn't spark fannish interest like the MGM movie. And if any fan fiction out there has been spun off from Larry Semon's 1925 movie, I haven't found it. (Much of the best *Oz* fan fiction is collected annually in *Oziana*, the publication of the International Wizard of Oz Club. The club also publishes *The Baum Bugle*.)

Naturally enough, fan-fiction characters often function as avatars of the writers. Sometimes, contrary to their established personas, familiar *Oz* characters explode with aggression, grapple with their sexual identities, or struggle to negotiate miserable family situations. Tellingly, many characters in *Oz* fan fiction are isolated and lonely.

Given all of this, many *Oz* stories written by enthusiasts provoke smiles, sympathy—or shudders. In a story posted on the Net in 2013, Dorothy blithely tosses a bucket of gasoline on the already-burning Scarecrow.

"AAAAAAAAA!" cries the Scarecrow. Meanwhile, the Winged Monkeys shout, "Yo!"

A great proportion of the pieces reflect the writers' own anxieties, as in a 2013 short story about a boy, "Dorian Gale," who is upset about his parents' divorce, and his subsequent exile to his aunt and uncle's farm.

Frequently, though, *Oz* fan fiction is just plain sweet. In a 2012 piece of just some ninety words, the Tin Woodman makes a gift of a dandelion to the Cowardly Lion. The Tin Woodman explains that he thought of the Lion the moment he saw the flower. The Lion is delighted with the sentiment and envelops the Tin Woodman in a hug. And so that the Scarecrow won't feel left out, the Tin Woodman pulls him into the hug, too.

And there, gracefully, the tale ends.

Gay Fandom

There is a legend in gay circles that Judy Garland inspired the Saturday, June 28, 1969, uprising at the Stonewall Inn, a Greenwich Village gay bar that had been invaded by police many more times than was reasonable. Across New York City, similar bars and clubs were regularly harassed, too, so when the cops showed up at the Stonewall to roust gays on that June night, the patrons fought back, igniting a dustup that spilled into the street and led to three days of protests and demonstrations. Thus was born, many will say, the LGBT movement. The "Judy legend" exists because the events at Stonewall took place a day after the star's funeral, and because Judy is special to a generation of men whose sexuality put them at odds with the mores of their day.

The fondness of gay audiences for *The Wizard of Oz* is inextricably linked to gay interest in Judy Garland. Some of that fondness relates to the fantastical nature of the movie; cultural historian David J. Skal has characterized Halloween as a "gay high holy day," and it's not a stretch to surmise that Judy's participation in the Halloweenish fun of *Oz* is a big attractor of gay fans. On the more drearily clinical side, an undergrad psych student might say that adolescent gay males, caught in a particularly difficult search for validation and identity, may gravitate to larger-than-life women from pop culture—big-personality women that combine explosive talent with a willingness to reject criticism and crises of faith. Refinery29.com blogger Hayden Manders has written, "Judy Garland is, by and large, the definition of gay icon. She was woman who didn't fit the script of A-list beauty, but became the darling of Hollywood." The blog goes on to quote Heather Love, a professor of English at the University of Pennsylvania: "[W]omen are marginalized, so gay men identify."

Many current gay icons (Manders cites Lady Gaga, Kylie Minogue, and Madonna) are activists for gay causes. According to Manders, these people "work to raise awareness and promote acceptance (not just tolerance)." Because they have defied often-vitriolic disapproval, and stared down illness and other personal challenges, they define themselves, on their own terms.

Judy Garland was aware of her gay fan base, which cheerfully celebrated her during the swingin' '60s (when, perhaps not coincidentally, Judy's concert vocals were at their most brilliantly raw and emotional). But despite that Judy had made herself a sort of silent advocate for sexual rights by marrying bisexual director Vincente Minnelli (in 1945), she had come of age in a constrained time very different from the 1960s. Also, she remained mindful of the conservatism of the greater portion of her fans and felt inhibited about acknowledging the fondness she felt for her gay fans. Indeed, when pressed by the boobish Chicago TV host Irv Kupcinet during a September 1967 broadcast, a plainly uncomfortable Judy protested herself right into the landscape of the reactionary. Kupcinet had the temerity to ask Judy to define "fag hag" and then mentioned a *Time* magazine review of a Garland concert in which the female writer noted that a lot of the audience's enthusiasm was generated by its gay members. Kupcinet found this sinister and didn't want to let it go.

KUPCINET
This is an unusual charge I've never heard leveled in describing an audience. *Time* magazine, in a recent story, said that Judy Garland, for some reason, which was not clear to me—

JUDY
Ewww ...

KUPCINET
... attracts a lot of ...

JUDY
Ewww.

KUPCINET
... of homosexuals in her audience.

Judy retorted that the entire notion was "ridiculous" and added that her live audiences always include children.

At that point, Kupcinet goaded Judy into suggesting that the journalist is a lesbian, and then he chuckled, saying, "She's a jolly good fellow."

Finally, Judy seemed to be at her wit's end: "Well, I, I don't mind, you know, for so many years, uh, uh, uh, uh, I've been misguided and uh, rather brutally, uh, uh, treated by the press, but I'll be damned if I like to have my audience mistreated."

The video clip makes for uneasy viewing, not least because Judy is miserably defensive when she has no reason to be. Her discomfiture is very obvious, and you realize that Kupcinet took relish in pushing her into a blind alley.

Regardless, Judy was forgiven. Kupcinet's talk show was syndicated, but Kup didn't have nearly the reach of Johnny Carson, or even Mike Douglas. People who saw his interview with Judy had no way to see it again or share it with others—no VCRs, no YouTube. Judy's star continued to glow for gay fans.

As America's Baby Boomer gay population has continued to age along with everybody else (and as AIDS took its awful toll in the 1980s and '90s), the shared memory of Judy-as-icon has diminished. It's likely that most gay men younger than forty are aware of her mainly as the gifted young star of *The Wizard of Oz*. The powerhouse quality of Judy's later vocals, and her exertions to keep a grip on her existence, were galvanizing to gay men when to be gay was to be vulnerable and closeted. Today, young gay men may view her as too fragile for their tastes. If that's the case, it's a mark not of any lack in Judy but of the great evolution that was encouraged by her presence.

Dark Side of the Rainbow

Other than the "hanging munchkin" fable, the most widespread bit of folklore pertaining to MGM's *The Wizard of Oz* is that Pink Floyd's 1973 rock album, *The Dark Side of the Moon*, was carefully written and timed to correspond to—and comment on—selected sequences of the movie. It's all about synchronization: start the movie and wait until the second or third roar of the MGM lion, or after the lion has *finished* roaring (suggestions vary), and then hit PLAY on your CD (or drop the needle). Allow the forty-three-minute record to play through. Proponents insist you'll be astonished by the uncanny relationship of Pink Floyd's lyrics and melodies to MGM's images.

Pink Floyd was one of the most ambitious psychedelic rock groups and rock-soundtrack composers of the 1960s and '70s. The band was founded in London in 1965 by Syd Barrett, Richard Wright, Roger Waters, and Nick Mason. The early Pink Floyd albums (the first was released in 1967) were well-wrought acid rock, but the band's ambitions (particularly as exemplified by Waters) grew quickly. *The Dark Side of the Moon* was Floyd's eighth studio album and was immediately popular. (By this time, Barrett had left the band, and David Gilmour had joined.) The record went to number one on *Billboard's* albums chart and became a cultural sensation. Many fans were smitten by its gloomily existentialist ruminations on death, alienation, futility, greed, and other standard adolescent and post-adolescent preoccupations. For the musically sophisticated, *Dark Side* was an elegant monument of art rock, with lushly played minimalist melodies, hypnotic beats, jazz flourishes, and flirtations with classical forms. Vocals were shared, variously by Gilmour, Wright, Waters, and session singer Clare Torry. R&B singer-songwriter Doris Troy (famed for "Just One Look") also sang backup. The elegant, jazz-inflected saxophone heard on "Money" and other cuts was played by session musician Dick Parry. The record was produced and engineered by Alan Parsons (later of the Alan Parsons Project) and smartly mixed by Chris Thomas (who went on to produce Badfinger, Procol Harum, the Sex Pistols, the Pretenders, and INXS).

The Dark Side of the Moon is one of the best-selling albums in recording history. Although officially certified by the Recording Industry Association of America as platinum 15x (15 million units sold), the true number is considerably higher. U.S. sales alone top 20 million, and total worldwide sales are somewhere between 35 million and 40 million. The album first appeared on *Billboard*'s Top 200 album chart in March 1973, entering at number 95. It eventually spent a week at number one and didn't fall off the chart until July 1988—an astonishing 736 weeks. *Dark Side* shortly returned to the chart, where it remained for another five weeks. Total Top 200 chart run: 741 weeks. Since then, *The Dark Side of the Moon* has been a fixture on *Billboard*'s Catalog Albums chart, which tracks older LPs that continue to rack up significant weekly sales. Today, about 8,500 copies of *Dark Side* are purchased every week, a tally that outpaces the low end of the Top 200 chart.

In 2011, the original *Dark Side of the Moon* Capitol recording was remastered and released on CD. It is a rock evergreen.

But why, of all rock albums, was *Dark Side* selected for intense, *Oz*-centric scrutiny? The answer literally stares us in the face: the album sleeve (by Storm Thorgerson and Aubrey Powell's Hipgnosis design group) depicts a narrow beam of white light piercing a triangle (presumably, a pyramidal prism) and emerging from the other side as a fanned spectrum of color—a rainbow, if you care to see it that way. (The illustration was executed by George Hardie.) Because there was no way to compare the LP to the movie until the advent of home video in the late 1970s, there was no talk of an *Oz/Dark Side* relationship for some years after the LP's release. (In other words, before Beta and VHS, nothing in the album's lyrics or melodies caused anybody to recall *The Wizard of Oz*.) Nothing, in fact, was heard of a thematic relationship until the early 1990s, when the Web-based Usenet

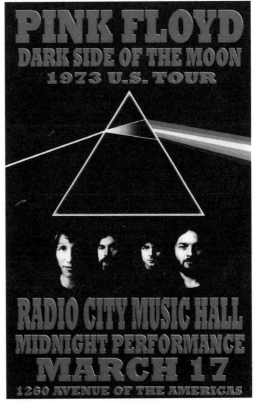

Many years after Pink Floyd toured in support of *The Dark Side of the Moon*, some of the band's fans claimed incredible connections between the album and *The Wizard of Oz*.

discussion group posted a bit of chatter about Floyd and *Oz*. Charles Savage, a reporter with Fort Wayne's *Journal Gazette*, picked up on the claim and contacted the International Wizard of Oz Club for reaction and additional information. The person who responded to Savage's query had never heard of Pink Floyd, which may have suggested to Savage that the Usenet notion was baloney. Well, a story was fashioned anyway and ran in the *Journal Gazette*'s August 1, 1995, edition. Other journalists were intrigued enough to perpetuate the tale, and when MTV "broke" the story in the late 1990s, the idea became a sensation with Floyd fans, and with people who'd assumed there was nothing left to discover about *The Wizard of Oz*.

Various Web sites now enumerate—sometimes at tedious length—the presumed interplay of *The Dark Side of the Moon*, track by track, with *The Wizard of Oz*. Of the many supposed links, here are just a few:

- A lyric from the seamlessly blended Track 1 and Track 2, "Speak to Me/ Breathe," refers to being "Balanced on the biggest wave," which synchs with Dorothy's attempt to keep her balance on the top rail of the pigpen.
- The title of Track 3, "On the Run," has the same acronym, OTR, as "Over the Rainbow," the soundtrack tune that's heard during the Floyd cut. Also, the Floyd sound effect of an airplane takeoff synchs with Toto's wagging tail; and the sound of a helicopter takeoff synchs with Toto's leap onto a piece of farm equipment.
- Track 4, "Time," includes the sounds of an alarm clock and clocks ticking the hour. Because this synchs up with our glimpse of Miss Gulch/Wicked Witch on the bicycle, the sound effects foreshadow the Witch's death, because her time eventually runs out. A bit later in the song, slow guitar chords sound in counterpoint to a rapidly ticking clock. These oppositional sounds metaphorically cancel each other out, suggesting balance and life energy. And that's significant, because on-screen, Toto's life is in the balance. Fortunately, the life energy of the guitar/clock foreshadows that Toto will emerge in one piece.
- Track 5, "The Great Gig in the Sky," is dominated by the soaring, wordless vocals of Clare Torry. To some listeners, Torry's vocal suggests an Irish dirge, a wailed reaction to death. (Actually, Torry's vocal is pure R&B/soul, to such a degree, in fact, that many listeners have assumed that Torry, who is white, is black.) At the moment the song's tempo changes, Dorothy is struck on the head by the windblown window. "Great Gig" ends just as the house lands on the Wicked Witch of the East, killing her.
- "[T]hink I'll buy me a football team" is a lyric phrase from Track 6, "Money." This Floyd cut is heard as Dorothy begins to explore Munchkinland, a place that isn't likely to produce many football stars. So, naturally enough, the lyric must refer to another sport. How about horseracing? MGM production chief Louis Mayer bred racehorses. Who rides racehorses? Jockeys. And jockeys are small—like Munchkins.

- Track 7, "Us and Them," says, "Haven't you heard/It's a battle of words," just as Glinda and the Wicked Witch exchange dialogue.
- Track 8, "Any Colour You Like," begins as Dorothy happens upon the Scarecrow and the puzzling fork in the road. Assuming that the title of the song comes from Henry Ford's frequently misquoted remark regarding his Model T—"Any customer can have a car painted any color that he wants so long as it is black"—the song suggests the concept of choice. (Ford's comment is in his 1922 autobiography. Whether or not he ever said it out loud is open to debate.) At the cornfield, Dorothy has some important choices: to engage the Scarecrow in conversation; to remove him from his peg; to listen to his fractured advice; to accept him as a traveling companion; and to select which part of the road to take. "Any Colour You Like" plays on as Dorothy and the Scarecrow are escorted through the Emerald City in the carriage pulled by the Horse of a Different Color. The MGM carriage (some people have claimed) had been owned by Abraham Lincoln, who freed America's slaves, who were people of color.
- "You shout and no one seems to hear" is a lyric line from Track 9, "Brain Damage." The apple tree gives Dorothy an angry lecture because she's picked one of his apples (the tree "shouts"), while no one on the *Oz* set has noticed ("no one seems to hear") that a Munchkin has hanged himself. (For more on this particular madness, see "Merry Old Land of Rumors," chapter 18.)
- In the album's concluding cut, "Eclipse" (Track 10), the lyric phrase "everything under the sun is in tune" is mirrored on-screen by the curtains in the Tin Woodman's cottage, which match Dorothy's gingham dress.

One *Oz*–Floyd Web site throws out dozens more examples, track by track, connecting the dots in unconvincing detail, invoking Joan of Arc, the gold standard, communism, Eve's Tree of Knowledge, the War of the Roses, Occupied France, the Society for Psychical Research, Socrates, the etymology of the word "lunatic," Shakespeare's Romeo, and (inevitably) Carl Jung.

There's more: when *The Dark Side of the Moon* ends, you're supposed to cue it up again and discover *additional* clear-as-glass connections to *The Wizard of Oz.*

Once discussion of the supposed *Oz* links had gathered a good head of steam, members of Pink Floyd flatly stated that *Dark Side* has nothing at all to do with the movie. They have insisted that as they worked on the LP, *The Wizard of Oz* wasn't on their radar, in their minds, or on their TV screens.

During a 2003 interview published in *Rolling Stone*, the album's producer, Alan Parsons, discussed the technical difficulty of synchronizing original audio to an existing film and remarked on the nature of coincidence:

> One of the things any audio professional will tell you is that the scope for the drift between the video and the record is enormous; it could be anything up to twenty seconds by the time the record's finished [playing]. And anyway, if you play any record with the sound turned down on the TV, you will find things that work.

If that's not clear enough, consider this: "Us and Them," which supposedly mates with Munchkinland, the Wicked Witch, and the ruby slippers, was written in 1970, as part of Pink Floyd's soundtrack for *Zabriskie Point* (1970). That elliptical Michelangelo Antonioni film is about student activism, pot, love, and a stolen airplane. When Antonioni rejected "Us and Them," Floyd picked up the melody three years later for *The Dark Side of the Moon*.

You may be relieved to learn that thematic links between *Oz* and *Zabriskie Point* have yet to be explored.

Follow the Yellow Brick Road

A Selected Oz Timeline, 1939 and After

Because Baum's *Oz* and the MGM movie are indelible parts of the international popular imagination, they have been referenced, alluded to, adapted, and spoofed more times than can probably be counted. Here, then, is a timeline of some particularly unusual and otherwise intriguing *Oz*-related creations and events. For even more *Oz* timeline minutiae, see ozclub.org.

1939: Bandleaders Glenn Miller and Bob Crosby have #1 and #2 hits, respectively, with recordings of "Over the Rainbow."

August 15, 1939: *The Wizard of Oz* has its Hollywood premiere. • The movie is released in Greece.

August 17, 1939: *The Wizard of Oz* has its New York City premiere.

August 21, 1939: *The Wizard of Oz* opens in Canada.

August 25, 1939: *The Wizard of Oz* goes into general release across the USA.

September 18, 1939: *The Wizard of Oz* opens in Brazil.

November 1939: *The Wizard of Oz* is released in Great Britain.

November 17, 1939: *The Wizard of Oz* is released in Central and South America.

December 1939: Department stores around the USA feature *Oz* window displays.

January 1, 1940: *The Wizard of Oz* opens across Mexico.

January 2, 1940: *The Wizard of Oz* is released in Sweden.

February 24, 1940: Roberta Jeffries, 16, of Memphis wins a national Oz contest and receives a pair of MGM ruby slippers.

March 18, 1940: *The Wizard of Oz* opens in Estonia.

March 21, 1940: *The Wizard of Oz* is released in Hungary.

March 26, 1940: *The Wizard of Oz* opens in Denmark.

April 9, 1940: *The Wizard of Oz* opens in Ireland.

April 18, 1940: *The Wizard of Oz* is released in Australia.

December 13, 1940: *The Wizard of Oz* is released in Portugal.

December 1942: A *Wizard of Oz* stage production opens in Britain at the Grand Theatre, Croyden.

1943: An *Oz*-inspired superhero adventure, "The Wizard of Wisstark," is the cover story of DC-National's *Leading Comics* #7. Cover art by Jon Small. Story by Joe Samachson; interior art by Pierce Rice. Featured stars are the Seven Soldiers of Victory: Crimson Avenger, Green Arrow, Shining Knight, Speedy, Star-Spangled Kid, Stripesy, Vigilante, and Wing.

November 21, 1943: *The Wizard of Oz* opens in Finland.

March 5, 1944: Judy Garland returns to Oz for a broadcast of radio's *Command Performance* program. She trades comic jibes with Bob Hope and sings "Over the Rainbow." Her performance is filmed and is made available on laser disc in 1995.

March 1, 1945: *The Wizard of Oz* is released in Spain.

1946: New York's Nomix introduces Oz Ice Cream ("a Wiz of an Ice Cream").

June 26, 1946: *The Wizard of Oz* opens in France.

August 8, 1946: *The Wizard of Oz* opens in Belgium and the Netherlands

February 6, 1947: *The Wizard of Oz* is released in Hong Kong.

December 4, 1947: *The Wizard of Oz* opens in Italy. This is the picture's first release in a formerly Axis nation.

June 1, 1949: *The Wizard of Oz* is re-released in the USA.

1950: The Winter-Spring 1950 issue of *The Magazine of Fantasy and Science Fiction* publishes "The Exiles," a science-fiction/fantasy short story by Ray Bradbury. On Mars, Edgar Allan Poe, Charles Dickens, Ambrose Bierce, Algernon Blackwood, and other deceased authors grow alarmed when an Earth rocketship carrying the last 200 extant copies of purposely burned books approaches the Red Planet. The crewmembers are insane, and the famous authors on Mars worry about the fate of their work and the work of other writers whose books are on board. The rocket touches down, and although the authors summon their imaginative powers to frighten the travelers off, the crewmen manage to unload the books and burn them. One crewman claims to have glimpsed the beautiful Emerald City of Oz on the Martian horizon, looking as it did in a story he'd once read. But as the books are torched, the crewman witnesses the great spires crumble to the ground. "The Exiles" was originally published, in different form, as "The Mad Wizards of Mars," in the September 15, 1949, issue of *Maclean's* magazine. "The Exiles" was adapted into comic book form by writer-artist Tom Sutton in 1986 for *Alien Encounters* #10.

May 22, 1950: Puppeteer Burr Tillstrom mounts *The Land of Oz* as an NBC-TV special; singer-actress Fran Allison reads from the book as the puppets act out the story. Unlike the hand puppets Tillstrom and Allison interact with on *Kukla, Fran and Ollie*, the *Oz* puppets are marionettes.

September 28, 1950: Judy Garland is released from her contract with MGM.

October 6, 1950: *The Wizard of Oz* is released in Austria.

December 25, 1950: Judy Garland reprises her role as Dorothy for a sixty-minute Christmas Day broadcast of *Lux Radio Theatre*. Daughter Liza Minnelli, just four years old, is in the CBS-radio studio audience and is heard briefly as herself. Of the movie's original cast, Judy is the only one to return. Key supporting roles are filled by Hans Conried as the Scarecrow, Herb Vigran as the Tin Woodman, Ed Max as the Cowardly Lion, Herb Butterfield as the Wizard, Noreen Gammill as the Wicked Witch of the West, Betty Lou Gerson as Glinda, and David Light as Toto.

April 19, 1951: *The Wizard of Oz* opens in West Germany.

January 6, 1952: *The Wizard of Oz* is released in India.

January 15, 1953: *The Wizard of Oz* is released in the Philippines.

March 6, 1953: Maud Baum dies. The Baum family home is torn down soon after.

1954: Chicago-based Swift introduces Oz Peanut Butter. The product is packed in five-inch illustrated jars that double as collectible drinking glasses. The jar art (there were at least nine different designs) is in the angular cartoon style of the mid-1950s. The peanut butter also is packaged in an illustrated tin jar, with screw-off top, that doubles as a sand pail. A *Wizard of Oz* coloring book is issued as a premium in 1955. This artwork shows a faint nod to W. W. Denslow, although the Swift Dorothy is blonde. Illustrated Swift Oz Peanut Butter advertising-promotion ball-point pens were issued as well, probably for use by sales reps. • 1954: The Checkers record what is probably the first doo-wop version of "Over the Rainbow"; the cover is released on the King label as a 45 rpm single (#4719).

November 16, 1954: Disney Studio purchases the rights to eleven *Oz* books.

December 25, 1954: *The Wizard of Oz* is released in Japan.

June 17, 1955: *The Wizard of Oz* is given its second big-screen re-release.

1956: *Dell Junior Treasury* #5 adapts Baum's *The Wonderful Wizard of Oz* to comic book form, with adaptation by Gaylord DuBois and art by Mel Crawford. • Disney purchases the rights to another twenty *Oz* books.

August 2, 1956: MGM and CBS-TV sign an agreement allowing four telecasts of *The Wizard of Oz*.

1957: The International Wizard of Oz Fan Club is founded in New York, with sixteen members, by thirteen-year-old Justin Schiller. • Baum's Oz books are removed from the children's collections at the Detroit public library system, because of inappropriate messages to young readers. The *Detroit Times* responds with a serialized publication of *The Wonderful Wizard of Oz*. • View-Master issues *Wizard of Oz* reels; the characters are portrayed by puppets.

September 11, 1957: The second half hour of *Disneyland*'s "Fourth Anniversary Show" features the Mouseketeers, who ask Mr. Disney about future projects. One of those is *The Rainbow Road to Oz*, Disney's first live-action musical. It would star, among others, some of the Mouseketeers. In a special *Disneyland* preview, the Mouseketeers sing and dance to Buddy Baker–Tom Adair tunes from the project. The segment features Darlene Gillespie as Dorothy, Bobby Burgess as the Scarecrow, Annette Funicello as Ozma, and Doreen Tracey as the Patchwork Girl of Oz. By the spring of 1958, Walt Disney has abandoned the Mouseketeer *Rainbow Road to Oz*, which is never made.

1959: Walt Disney announces a Land of Oz attraction for Disneyland. It is never built. • Henry Regnery publishing company returns all of the *Oz* books to print. • The first Japanese translation of Baum's *The Wonderful Wizard of Oz* is issued as *Oz Mako Tzukai.*

1960: The Rankin-Bass animation studio releases 105 five-minute TV cartoons comprising *Tales of the Wizard of Oz.* The cartoons fiddle with Dorothy's friends, calling them Socrates the Scarecrow, Rusty the Tin Man, and Dandy the Lion. • Working with the Film Maker's Cooperative, American experimental filmmaker Harry Smith completes his "film number 13," *Oz,* a 108-minute, avant-garde take on Baum's *Oz.* The movie is in 35mm and widescreen. As prints make the rounds during the next few years, the film is variously titled *The Approach to Emerald City* and *The Magic Mushroom People of Oz.* Contrary to some sources, Smith's *Fragments of a Fate Forgotten* is a discrete film (from 1981), and not a retitled version of *Oz.* • Baum's *The Wonderful Wizard of Oz* is translated into Chinese as *Le Yeh Sien Tsung.* • The Vibrations' doo-wop version of "Over the Rainbow" is released on Checker (#1002). The recording has a lively R&B "shout" lead vocal, but may be more notable for its songwriting credits, which misspell Harold Arlen's name as "Arlan."

September 18, 1960: "The Land of Oz," an episode of *Shirley Temple Theatre,* is broadcast on NBC-TV. Temple takes two roles, Princess Ozma and Tip.

1961: MGM announces a *Wizard of Oz* cartoon show for television; the idea is stillborn. • Project Ozma, a project of the National Radio Observatory, searches for extraterrestrial life.

1963: Chicago's Dramatic Publishing issues *The Wizard of Oz,* a two-act play by Anne Coulter Marten. • An episode of *Discovery '63,* ABC's intelligent show for kids, features Margaret Hamilton, who discusses L. Frank Baum with hosts Frank Buxton and Virginia Gibson.

February 9, 1964: NBC broadcasts an animated feature by Rankin-Bass, *Return to Oz.* The film is a spin-off from the 1960 Rankin-Bass *Tales of the Wizard of Oz* short cartoons. Dorothy is played by cartoon voice artist Susan Conway.

March 1, 1964: On this evening's episode of CBS-TV's *The Judy Garland Show,* the star is joined by Ray Bolger. Judy, Bolger, and Jane Powell perform the abandoned "Jitterbug" number from *The Wizard of Oz.*

Spring 1964: *American Quarterly* magazine publishes Henry M. Littlefield's "The Wizard of Oz: Parable on Populism." The much-debated essay suggests that L. Frank Baum's first Oz book has a Populist political subtext.

November 27, 1964: Official groundbreaking for Land of Oz theme park is done in Van Nuys, CA.

1965: To tie in with its sponsorship of this year's annual telecast of *The Wizard of Oz,* Procter & Gamble offers plastic *Oz* hand puppets as premiums with laundry products Zest, Downy, and Top Job. • Disneyland Records releases *Walt Disney Presents the Scarecrow of Oz,* a twelve-inch, 33⅓ LP with Ray Bolger acting as audio host as well as giving voice to the Scarecrow. • American General Pictures releases *The Wizard of Mars,* a budget-challenged science-fiction oddity about four astronauts (including a young woman named Dorothy) that travel to Mars, follow a battered yellow road, and discover a great, gleaming city ruled by a wizard, who manifests himself as the great, disembodied head of actor John Carradine. Directed, written, and produced by David L. Hewitt.

January 26, 1965: On their 25th anniversary, Bert Lahr's wife, Mildred, surprises her husband with a first edition of Baum's *The Wonderful Wizard of Oz*, which Mildred has found at auction.

Spring 1965: The cover story for DC's *The Adventures of Jerry Lewis* #89 is "The Wizard of Ooze." Story by Arnold Drake (probable); art by Bob Oksner.

February 13, 1966: Fourteen *Wizard of Oz* floats appear in this year's New Orleans Mardi Gras parade.

April 1966: Gold Key's *Walt Disney's Comics and Stories* #307 features "The Wizard of Bahs," with Daisy Duck and Pluto filling in for Dorothy and Toto. Story: Vic Lockman. Art: Tony Strobl (pencils) and Mike Royer (inks).

September 8, 1967: ABC-TV premiere of *We're Off to See the Wizard*, a weekly cartoon-and-film series for children. Dorothy and her friends, and the Wizard himself, are hosts, and appear in wraparounds to relatively recent live-action feature films from the MGM library. The films, which include *Lili* and *Huckleberry Finn*, are not related to Oz and are telecast over the course of two or three episodes. The program is produced by MGM and supervised by animator Chuck Jones. The voice-over cast includes four legendary voice actors: Mel Blanc, June Foray, Don Messick, and Daws Butler. *We're Off to See the Wizard* completes its network run on September 20, 1968.

October 1, 1967: A yearlong "Wizard of Oz" underwater show opens at Weeki Wachee Springs, Brookville, Florida.

1968: Baum's *The Wizard of Oz* is translated into Tamil, as *Mantiravatiyin Katai.*

January 1968: A new book by Alice Payne Hackett, *70 Years of Best Sellers*, selects Baum's *The Wonderful Wizard of Oz* as the world's number-one favorite children's book.

1969: Land of Oz theme park opens at Banner Elk, North Carolina. • Procter & Gamble repeats its 1965 *Wizard of Oz* puppet promotion. • Disneyland Records releases a series of twelve-inch, 33⅓ LPs paired with storybooks: *The Wizard of Oz* (with forty-four-year-old Disneyland Records veteran Robie Lester as Dorothy), *The Cowardly Lion of Oz*, and *The Tin Woodman of Oz*. Narration is by Sam Edwards.

Spring 1969: *MAD* magazine #128 (cover-dated July 1969) publishes a counterculture musical spoof, "The Guru of Ours," written by Frank Jacobs and illustrated by Mort Drucker.

June 22, 1969: Judy Garland dies in London.

October 31, 1969: Writer-director Barry Mahon's low-budget film musical *The Wonderful Land of Oz* opens in a few American theaters. The seventy-two-minute feature is loosely based on Baum's second Oz book, *The Marvelous*

Land of Oz. Mahon is an exploitation filmmaker responsible for *1,000 Shapes of a Female, International Smorgas-Broad, Nudes on Tiger Reef,* and dozens more.

November 1969: Knopf publishes *Notes on a Cowardly Lion,* John Lahr's biographical memoir of his father, Bert Lahr. The book is acclaimed and remains a milestone of its genre.

December 25, 1969: Chicago's WGN-TV airs Larry Semon's *The Wizard of Oz* (1925).

c. 1970: The American Heart Association airs a cartoon-animated public service announcement featuring the Tin Woodman, who urges everybody to eat healthy foods.

1970: MGM employee Kent Warner discovers four pairs of ruby slippers in a studio costume warehouse. He sells the unused "Arabian Test" pair to actress Debbie Reynolds; sells a pair to collector Michael Shaw; puts one up for auction; and keeps the nicest pair for himself. • First Greek translation of Baum's *The Wizard of Oz.* • First Afrikaans translation of Baum's *The Wizard of Oz,* as *Die Ongelooflike Towenaar van Oz.*

January 17, 1970: "The Wizard of Aberdeen," a loose biography of L. Frank Baum, airs on the popular syndicated TV series *Death Valley Days.* Written and directed by Stephen Lord, with Conlan Carter as Baum.

May 3, 1970: At an auction of material purchased from MGM, and displayed at what remains of the studio, a pair of Judy Garland's ruby slippers (at least four were made in 1938–39) is purchased by a Beverly Hills haberdasher for $15,000. • At the same auction, one of Bert Lahr's Cowardly Lion costumes (two were made) is purchased by an L.A.-area physician for $2,400.

Spring 1970: DC's *Adventure Comics* #394 includes "The Mysterious Motr of Doov," in which Supergirl and her super-cat, Streaky, travel into the past and unknowingly inspire L. Frank Baum to write *The Wizard of Oz.* Written by Cary Bates and illustrated by Win Mortimer (pencils) and Jack Abel (inks).

December 30, 1970: Jack Haley sings "If I Only Had a Heart" on TV's *The Mike Douglas Show.*

February 7, 1971: Sixteen *Wizard of Oz*–themed floats appear in the New Orleans Mardi Gras parade.

1972: The Dunkin' Donuts restaurant chain introduces Munchkins donut holes, described by the company as "Little Pops of Pleasure." A serving is defined as a single Munchkin, which suggests that a real aficionado should enjoy ten or twelve servings at a clip.

Spring 1972: North Carolina–based Custom-Craft Furniture introduces *Oz*-themed bedroom furniture for children.

c. 1973: Veteran special-effects technician Kenneth Strickfaden sells the Wicked Witch's hand-blown crystal ball to Maxwell Smith's Vectrex Corporation, a Santa Monica prop house.

1973: Baum's *The Wizard of Oz* is translated into Turkish, as *Billur Kosk.* • Michael Patrick Hearn's *The Annotated Wizard of Oz* is published by New York's Clarkson N. Potter. More extravagant later editions are published by Norton.

- Pioneer Drama Service publishes *The Wizard of Oz in the Wild West*, a play by Willard Simms in which the *Oz* characters meet Annie Oakley and other historical figures.

January 1, 1973: An *Oz*-themed float in Pasadena's Tournament of Roses parade wins the Governor's Trophy. Large, mechanical heads of the Scarecrow, Tin Woodman, and Cowardly Lion dominate the float, which also carries original Munchkin players Billy Curtis, Hazel Resmondo, and Jerry Maren.

1974: A heart-health short inspired by *Oz* and the Tin Woodman, *It's a Heart*, becomes available to schools and other institutions. • Mego toy company issues an MGM-based *Wizard of Oz* playset.

February 6, 1974: Writer-director John Boorman's *Oz*-inspired *Zardoz* is released in the United States. (See the "Dorothy Has a Hairy Chest" sidebar in chapter 19.)

December 5, 1974: A Filmation cartoon feature, *Journey Back to Oz*, is released to U.S. theaters following a 1971 television airing. Liza Minnelli (who recorded her part in the 1960s, as the producers looked for funding) is Dorothy. Others in the voice cast: Mickey Rooney as the Scarecrow, Danny Thomas as the Tin Woodman, Milton Berle as the Cowardly Lion, and Margaret Hamilton as Aunt Em. Also with Ethel Merman, Paul Ford, Herschel Bernardi, Mel Blanc, Larry Storch, Paul Lynde, Jack E. Leonard, and soprano Risë Stevens. Songs are by Jimmy Van Heusen (music) and Sammy Cahn (lyrics).

1975: A *Wizard of Oz* reunion at New York's Waldorf Astoria hotel is highlighted with appearances by Margaret Hamilton, Ray Bolger, and Jack Haley. • A touring show starring the Hudson Brothers performs a comic version of *Oz*, with twenty-two-year-old singer Karen Wyman as Dorothy. While a teenager, Wyman had early breaks on *The Dean Martin Show* and *The Ed Sullivan Show*, where she displayed a precociously big voice and superb confidence.

December 28, 1975: Following a fire, an original Judy Garland/Dorothy gingham dress is stolen from North Carolina's Land of Oz theme park.

1976: Margaret Hamilton reprises her Wicked Witch role for an appearance on TV's *Sesame Street*. • *Journey Back to Oz* is telecast on ABC, with Bill Cosby as host. • Writer-director Chris Löfvén's *20th Century Oz* is released in Australia; the film concerns the adventures of rock groupie Dorothy (Joy Dunstan) in an Oz-like dream world with peculiar, and ominous, parallels to Baum and MGM. In this variant of the tale, the Wizard (Graham Matters) is a legendary rock star about to perform his farewell concert.

1977: Aljean Harmetz's *The Making of The Wizard of Oz* is published by Knopf. • Popular mystery novelist Stuart Kaminsky publishes *Murder on the Yellow Brick Road*, a whodunit in which the on-set murder of a Munchkin brings PI Toby Peters to MGM, where he labors to see that Judy Garland isn't the next victim. • *Wizard of Oz* collector plates based on the MGM movie are issued by Knowles China Company. • *The Brady Bunch Hour*, a live-action musical variety show starring the original cast of *The Brady Bunch*, does the impossible by placing the *Oz* characters in a production number based on the disco hit "Car Wash." Ann B. Davis is the Wicked Witch; guest star Rip Taylor is the Cowardly Lion. • A BBC-TV spoof of *The Wizard of Oz* makes light of Great Britain's budget woes.

November 1977: MGM's *The Wizard of Oz* is named the third-best American movie by the American Film Institute, trailing only *Casablanca* and *Gone With the Wind.*

1978: Ray Bolger contributes an introduction to Doubleday's 1978 hardcover reissue of Baum's *The Wizard of Oz.* • Pre-production begins on *The Wonderful Wizard of Oz,* a feature-length cartoon that is never made. Producer: Rob Roy Madleigh. • Millennium Records releases *Meco: The Wizard of Oz,* a disco LP of songs from the MGM film, produced by Meco Monardo; arranged by Harold Wheeler.

Fall 1978: Cleveland native Margaret Hamilton returns to her hometown to star in the Cleveland Playhouse production of *Night Must Fall.*

October 28, 1978: "Race Through Oz," an episode of NBC-TV's *Yogi's Space Race* cartoon show, sends Yogi, Jabberjaw, and Huckleberry Hound on "the yellow brick spaceway" to "disco Oz." If this strikes you as a complete contravention of *Oz* and Yogi Bear, you're not alone.

November 2, 1978: The *Oz* collection of Justin Schiller is auctioned by Swann Galleries. The catalogue of items owned by the founder of the International Wizard of Oz Club is a hefty 144 pages.

November 6, 1978: *Rainbow,* a TV-movie about the early life and career of Frances Gumm/Judy Garland, airs on NBC. Former child star Jackie Cooper directs; cast members include Broadway veteran Andrea McArdle as Dorothy and Martin Balsam as Louis B. Mayer.

1979: PBS produces *The Making of the Wizard of Oz,* a documentary written by Oz historian Aljean Harmetz and featuring Ray Bolger, Jack Haley, and Margaret Hamilton. The host is Angela Lansbury.

April 9, 1979: Jack Haley and Ray Bolger appear together on the annual Oscar Awards telecast and perform "We're Off to See the Wizard."

May 12, 1979: Los Angeles celebrates Wizard of Oz Day with appearances by Ray Bolger, Jack Haley, Margaret Hamilton, Mervyn LeRoy, Billy Curtis, Jerry Maren, and Hazel Resmondo.

November 10, 1979: In "The Planet of Oz," an episode of TV's animated *The World's Greatest Super Friends,* Superman, Aquaman, and Wonder Woman are transformed by mischievous Mr. Mxyzptlk into Dorothy's companions.

1980: MGM's *The Wizard of Oz* is released to home video on VHS and Beta. • Land of Oz theme park at Beech Mountain, North Carolina, closes. • General Mills sponsors a Crispy Wheats 'n Raisins cereal commercial starring Dorothy and her friends.

November 25, 1980: Muller-Rosen Productions releases *Thanksgiving in Oz,* a half-hour animated cartoon intended for syndication to TV. The cartoon puts Dorothy and her friends in a Thanksgiving setting, but *Dorothy in the*

Land of Oz, an alternate version that has no reference to the holiday, is also made available to prolong syndication sales. Notables among the voice cast include Sid Caesar as the Wizard and Lurene Tuttle as Aunt Em.

1981: A filmed Minneapolis stage production, *The Marvelous Land of Oz*, airs on cable-TV network HBO. • Monica Bayley's *The Wonderful Wizard of Oz Cookbook* is published by Macmillan. The illustrations are reprints of pieces by the original *Oz* artist, W. W. Denslow. Find recipes for Scarecrow Survival Snacks, Aunt Em's Chicken and Dumplings, and Toto's Chocolate Almond Bark.

January 17, 1981: One segment of this broadcast of *The Richie Rich/Scooby-Doo Show and Scrappy Too!* is "Scooby's Trip to Ahz." Wonder-dog Scooby conks his head and dreams that he and human friend Shaggy travel to Ahz, where Scooby becomes a lion, Shaggy a scarecrow, and dog-pal Scrappy Doo a tin dog.

April–May 1981: A large sand sculpture of Emerald City is displayed at San Diego's Mission Valley Shopping Center.

June 11, 1981: A tourist attraction, Dorothy's House, opens at Liberal, Kansas. The site includes a gift shop, guided tour, and the story of Oz compressed into about fifteen minutes.

July 31, 1981: *Under the Rainbow*, a movie comedy based very loosely on the Hollywood experiences of the Munchkin players during 1938–39, opens across America. (For more, see chapter 5.)

October 1, 1981: Christie's auctions a pair of the MGM ruby slippers for $12,000.

1982: *A Barnstormer in Oz*, by noted fantasy author Philip José Farmer, is published by Phantasia Press. In this alternate-Oz tale, the son of Dorothy Gale, a flier named Hank Stover, becomes lost in a green cloud and emerges in Oz. Farmer's premise is that the first Baum novel is the only Oz novel; the Scarecrow still rules Oz, but the land is on the verge of civil war.

1983: Schocken Books's Critical Heritage series publishes *The Wizard of Oz*, a collection of analytical essays by Gore Vidal, Ray Bradbury, James Thurber, and others. • Buffalo-based QRS Music Rolls releases a player-piano roll with songs from the 1939 *Oz* movie.

February 24, 1983: Doris (Valerie Landsburg) hits her head and dreams she's in Oz, in the "Not in Kansas Anymore" episode of NBC's *Fame*. Also features series regulars Debbie Allen (as the Good Witch of the South) and Albert Hague (as the Wizard of Shorofsky).

May 1983: The Academy of Motion Picture Arts and Sciences hosts a special tribute to MGM's *Wizard of Oz*. Among the guests are Margaret Hamilton, Ray Bolger, Jerry Maren, Mervyn LeRoy, makeup artist William Tuttle, and *Oz* historian Aljean Harmetz.

1984: Eldridge Publishing issues *A Recall to Oz*, a new play by Michelle Van Loon. The play is a sequel to the MGM movie and features Dorothy in old age.

January 1, 1984: The Burbank, California, float in the Tournament of Roses Parade has a *Wizard of Oz* theme. Jerry Maren, Buddy Douglas, and Nels Nelson appear as Munchkins.

January 14, 1984: In the "Games People Play" segment of this broadcast of ABC's *Fantasy Island*, one young woman longs for love, another seeks courage, and the third wants to be appreciated for her mind. With guest stars Berlinda Tolbert, Lynda Day George, and Jenilee Harrison.

May 1984: Ten minutes of episode 9,413 of the popular CBS soap, *The Guiding Light*, consist of an elaborate and charming Oz dream sequence involving Nola (Lisa Brown), who can't decide on a name for her unborn baby. Bluescreen technology and other video effects create an ornate vision of Oz; in a touch that's right out of the first Baum book, Nola and her friends don green glasses before entering the Emerald City.

1985: A live-action Disney feature, *Return to Oz*, premieres at New York's Radio City Music Hall. Actress Fairuza Balk, age ten, is Dorothy. The film adapts *The Wonderful Wizard of Oz* and portions of *Ozma of Oz*. Others in the cast are Nicol Williamson, Jean Marsh, and Piper Laurie. Directed by Walter Murch. • Ray Bolger writes an introduction for a new *Oz* novel by "Onyx Madden" (James Fitch), *The Mysterious Chronicles of Oz or The Travels of Ozma and the Sawhorse.*

December 16, 1985: "The Improbable Dream" episode of the syndicated sitcom *What's Happening Now!!* sends Carolyn (Reina King) to Oz, where she meets peculiar variations of her real-life friends.

1986: Conservative Christians in Tennessee seek to remove L. Frank Baum's *The Wonderful Wizard of Oz* from schools and other tax-supported libraries, because the book includes among its characters *good* witches—creatures that are, of course, an impossibility. When the ban gets no traction, supporters urge Tennessee parents to remove their children from public schools.

Spring 1986: A traveling Smithsonian exhibition features an original pair of ruby slippers, Ray Bolger's Scarecrow costume, and a matte painting of the Emerald City.

June 28, 1986: A gingham dress worn by Judy Garland in 1938–39 sells at Sotheby's for $20,000.

November 1986: Ornate *Oz*-themed topiaries are exhibited at the Chrysanthemum Festival and Wonderful Garden of Oz, at Longwood Gardens, Kenneth Square, Pennsylvania.

1987: Franklin Heirloom Dolls issues a seventeen-inch limited-edition Dorothy Gale doll. Retail price is $135. • Britain's Club Biscuits (chocolate-covered cookies) re-creates the approach to the Emerald City in a sophisticated television commercial based on the MGM *Oz* movie. Some twenty years later, the intricate matte painting of the Emerald City created for the commercial is auctioned by Profiles in History.

September 1987: The Smithsonian acquires an original 1938–39 MGM *Oz* script.

November 18, 1987: Lorimar Home Video releases *Dorothy Meets Ozma of Oz*, a thirty-minute direct-to-video animated cartoon hosted by actor Michael Gross.

1988: *The Marvelous Land of Oz*, a ninety-minute television cartoon by Cinar Films of Canada, is released. This is unrelated to the live-action feature of the same title that aired on cable TV in 1981. The Cinar version is narrated by Canadian actress Margot Kidder. • A *Wizard of Oz* poster drawn in adolescence by singer Janis Joplin is displayed at the Janis Joplin Memorial in Joplin's hometown, Port Arthur, Texas. • Hawaiian vocalist Israel Kamakawiwo'ole records "Over the Rainbow," accompanying himself on ukulele. When the recording is finally issued in 1993, it becomes an enormous hit and helps establish Kamakawiwo'ole as a leading figure in Hawaiian music.

February 28, 1988: MGM's *The Wizard of Oz* is one of forty American films screened in the USSR as part of a bid to thaw U.S.-Soviet relations.

June 21, 1988: The ruby slippers won by Roberta Jeffries in 1940 are auctioned at Christie's for $165,000. The buyer is Anthony Landini. The same auction brings $20,000 for the Lion's bug sprayer (seen at the beginning of the excised "Jitterbug" sequence), $19,000 for an early edition of the first Baum novel signed by all principal members of the MGM cast (Toto included), and $10,000 for two Munchkin costume sketches by Gilbert Adrian.

August 9, 1988: The Kent Warner slippers, which Warner had liberated from MGM in 1970, sell at a Christie's auction for $165,000. The slippers (which are distinct from the pair auctioned six weeks earlier) are purchased by Philip Samuels.

September 22, 1988: The government of Montserrat issues a commemorative set of MGM *Oz* postal stamps. The set of four features bust images of Dorothy, the Scarecrow, the Tin Woodman, and the Cowardly Lion. In an interesting decision made by the issuer, the Lion is depicted in shades of tan and green.

December 16, 1988: A Witch's hat worn by Margaret Hamilton is auctioned by Sotheby's for $33,000.

1989: The 50th anniversary of the MGM film encourages a product-licensing blitz that incorporates promotion by surviving Munchkin players. • A Downy fabric softener commercial promises a five-dollar rebate to purchasers of the anniversary MGM/UA VHS release of *The Wizard of Oz*. The spot is a mix of new footage and snippets from Frank Morgan's performance as the Gatekeeper. • *The Wizard of Oz* is one of the first twenty-five films selected by the United States National Film Preservation Board for preservation in the Library of Congress. The selection places the movie in the National Film Registry, marking it as not simply a superior film but a significant part of the American experience. *Oz* enters the Registry amidst good company; other 1989 inductees include *High Noon*, *Singin' in the Rain*, *Vertigo*, *Casablanca*, *Gone With the Wind*, *Sunrise*, *Some Like It Hot*, and the movie that convinced

MGM to go ahead with *Oz*, *Snow White and the Seven Dwarfs*. • *Trouble in Oz*, a thirty-five-minute anti-drug film, is co-produced by the Orange County Sheriff's Department, The Center for Drug-Free Living, and General Mills. • An eminent jewelry concern, the House of Harry Winston, creates a pair of ruby slippers studded with 4,600 rubies and 50 carats of diamonds.

March 22, 1989: *The Wizard of Oz Live!*, produced and directed by Michel Grilikhes, opens at New York's Radio City Music Hall. More than forty actors lip-synch dialogue and music from the 1939 film. Five different dogs play Toto. Product-placement signage is visible on the stage, and *Oz* souvenirs are hawked at intermission. Grilikhes, a former producer at NBC-TV, has already staged popular, giant-scale "arena" versions of *Disney on Parade* and *Peter Pan*; *The Wizard of Oz Live!* eventually tours seventy cities over a span of eighteen months.

May 1, 1989: A Disney-MGM theme park opens at Orlando, Florida. One attraction, the Great Movie Ride, finishes in the Land of Oz. Animatronic Munchkins lend additional color, and ruby slippers owned by Anthony Landini are on display.

May 31, 1989: The 1939 *Wizard of Oz*, with all TV cuts and other edits restored, is released by MGM/UA Home Video.

July 1, 1989: The 1939 Langley/Ryerson/Woolf script is published by Dell as *The Wizard of Oz: The Screenplay*.

August 1989: The Macy's department store in New York's Herald Square mounts a 50th-anniversary *Oz* promotion with decorated show windows and Oz attractions located in customer areas. • A non-fiction book by Rhys Thomas, *The Ruby Slippers of Oz*, traces the provenance and other aspects of the ruby slipper saga. Publisher: Tale Weaver.

August 19, 1989: Jack Haley Jr. and Lorna Luft (daughter of Judy Garland) appear in Culver City, California, to promote the MGM/UA Home Video release of *The Wizard of Oz*.

September 1989: The Library of Congress selects MGM's *The Wizard of Oz* to be one of twenty-five American movies placed on a National Film Registry. Under tenets of the National Film Preservation Act of 1988, the 1939 *Oz* will be henceforth protected, with no edits or other alterations allowed.

September 15–17, 1989: Chesterton, Indiana, mounts a two-day Oz Festival on the film's 50th anniversary.

1990: A Tin Woodman/Jack Haley lookalike is featured in a Pfizer commercial about treatment for arthritis.

February 20, 1990: Jack Haley Jr. and Turner Entertainment produce *The Wonderful Wizard of Oz: 50 Years of Magic*, a documentary examining the 1939 MGM movie.

March 23, 1990: The United States Postal Service issues stamps commemorating four great Hollywood movies of 1939: *The Wizard of Oz*, *Gone With the Wind*, *Beau Geste*, and *Stagecoach*. The *Oz* stamp is a close-up portrait of Dorothy, with Toto.

March 31–April 1, 1990: At an auction held in Los Angeles by Camden House, a matte painting of the Emerald City brings $44,000.

June 1990: Thirteen surviving Munchkin players appear at the Judy Garland Festival in Grand Rapids, Minnesota (not Michigan).

June–August 1990: Turner Enterprises produces *The Wizard of Oz*, thirteen 23-minute cartoons based on the 1939 movie. • Charlton Heston narrates a 25-minute documentary, *The Hollywood Road to Oz*, which runs continuously as part of "The Road to Oz: The Life of L. Frank Baum," an exhibit sponsored by the Samuel Goldwyn Foundation and mounted at the Frances Howard Goldwyn branch of the L.A. public library.

July 1990: Sudan, Kansas, inaugurates its Wizard of Oz Festival.

August 17, 1990: U.S. release of David Lynch's *Wild at Heart*, a provocatively nightmarish, and queerly funny, "kids on the run" satire with repeated references to *The Wizard of Oz*. Dialogue exchanged by Sailor (Nicolas Cage) and Lula (Laura Dern) frequently invokes *Oz*, particularly references to what *New York Times* writer Caryn James astutely described as the "road movie" aspect of the 1939 classic. Here, the lovers travel across a violent, dangerous landscape, some of it engineered by Lula's "witch" of a mother (Diane Ladd, Laura Dern's real-life mom). Yet amidst flight and outrageous violence, the lovers are protected by a latter-day Glinda (Sheryl Lee), who comes to them from the sky, inside a bubble.

October 1990: Fifteen Munchkin players are reunited at Oztoberfest, in Liberal, Kansas.

December 1990: Neiman Marcus department store offers gemstone ruby slippers, made by House of Harry Winston, for $3 million.

December 10, 1990: A biographical TV-movie about L. Frank Baum, *The Dreamer of Oz*, airs on NBC. John Ritter is Baum; Annette O'Toole is Maud Baum.

Late 1990: *MAD* magazine #300 runs "The Wizard of Odds," in which a cyclone transports Dorothy (caricatured to look like Judy Garland) into the 1990s, where she meets Donald Trump, Vanna White, Tammy Faye Baker, and other luminaries. Written by Frank Jacobs; illustrated by Sam Viviano.

1990–91: As the ratings of ABC-TV's quirky *Twin Peaks* begin to slip late in 1990, the network repeatedly shifts the show's time slot and frequently preempts it. In a network spot designed to let fans know the show airs on Thursday nights, the Log Lady, the Man from Somewhere Else, and other *Peaks* characters reenact Dorothy's bedside scene from the 1939 movie.

1991: Paul Nathanson's academic study *Over the Rainbow: The Wizard of Oz as a Secular Myth of America* is published by the State University of New York Press. The book discusses the MGM movie not in aesthetic terms, but as a confirmation of an American yearning for security, certitude, and other elements of a largely mythical past that can be codified in quasi-religious terms. • Vass Records issues a CD of NBC's 1939 *Maxwell House Good News* "Wizard of Oz" radio broadcast.

October 1991: Groundbreaking ceremony is made in Las Vegas for the MGM Grand Hotel. Plans are to fill the lobby and other common areas with memorabilia from the 1939 *Wizard of Oz*.

1992: Plans for a $300 million Kansas City theme park, The Wonderful Wizard of Oz, are announced. Funding falls apart, and the park is never built.

October 27–November 8, 1992: *Oz*, an original ballet by the Paul Taylor Dance Company, is performed at New York's City Center. Writer and choreographer: Paul Taylor.

1993: Film historian John Fricke's documentary *We're Off to See the Munchkins* is released by Cinema Video Productions. • Sega's *Wizard of Oz* video game is introduced for Super Nintendo. • A very elaborate Energizer Battery commercial pits the Energizer Bunny against the Wicked Witch of the West. Stage actress Denise Moses is remarkably like Margaret Hamilton.

December 18, 1993: The MGM Grand Hotel opens in Las Vegas. The entryway is dominated by life-size animatronic figures of Dorothy, the Scarecrow, the Tin Woodman, the Cowardly Lion, and the Wicked Witch of the West.

1994: In *Volshebnik Izumrudnogo Goroda*, a Russian film version of Baum's *The Wizard of Oz* and a novel by Aleksandr Volkov, heroine Elli and dog Totoshka run afoul of the Wicked Witch and are beset by ogres, tigers, and other fantastic creatures. Scripted by Vadim Korostylyov; directed by Pavel Arsyonov. Katya Mikhajlovskaya is Elli. • Singer Marusha has a top ten German hit with a dance version of "Over the Rainbow."

June 27–28, 1994: Guests at screenings of the MGM *Wizard of Oz* at Glendale, California's Alex Fuil Society include surviving Munchkin players, Baum family members, and the movie's assistant choreographer, Dona Massin.

Summer 1995: The Columbian Museum in Wamego, Kansas, hosts a "Century of Oz" exhibit of three thousand items from the collection of Tod Machin.

June 1995: The Judy Garland Museum in Grand Rapids, Minnesota, acquires a treasure: the original MGM carriage pulled by the Horse of a Different Color.

September 1995: *The Wizard of Oz on Ice* opens in Florida and goes on national tour. The $9 million show is produced by Kenneth Field. The skating Dorothy is Jeri Campbell; Dorothy's voice is provided by singer-actress Laurnea Wilkerson.

October 1995: A sculpture of the Tin Woodman is unveiled at Chicago's Oz Park in Lincoln Park. The nine-foot-tall piece by John Kearney is sculpted from chrome car bumpers and weighs nine hundred pounds. The Tin Woodman is joined in Oz Park by Kearney's Cowardly Lion in 2001 and Kearney's Scarecrow in 2005.

November 1995: Hudson's department store sponsors a *Wizard of Oz* float in the Detroit Thanksgiving Day Parade. The float is thirty-five-feet long. Inside the flagship Hudson's, visitors enjoy twenty-one scenes from the *Oz* story.

1996: The United States Postal Service issues four commemorative songwriter stamps, including one honoring *Oz* songwriter Harold Arlen. •

Film-memorabilia collector James Comisar, owner of one of two Bert Lahr Lion costumes, works with the Los Angeles County Museum of Art to begin a two-year restoration of the costume and skins. A steel-armature mount, and a reconstructed face sculpted in Lahr's likeness (based on a new mold made from the face of one of Lahr's sons, Herbert), are prepared. • As part of a renovation of the three-year-old MGM Grand Hotel in Las Vegas, an elaborate animatronic *Oz* attraction is permanently dismantled. • A *Wizard of Oz* exhibit in support of the latest home-video release tours the USA in a Greyhound bus decorated outside with *Oz* graphics and displaying artifacts and replica items inside. • Godly virtues are expressed by Dorothy and her friends in *The Gifts Are Divine, the Plan Is Awesome*, a twenty-one-minute short produced by the Presbyterian Church (U.S.A.) and filmed at Purdue University.

February 1996: A Smithsonian exhibit, America's Smithsonian, tours the USA. A pair of ruby slippers finds favor with the public, but a section of the exhibit dealing with L. Frank Baum's supposed Populist agenda isn't well received, and is shortly eliminated.

February 27, 1996: *The Wizard of Oz on Ice* is broadcast by CBS-TV. Skating star Oksana Baiul is Dorothy, with the character's voice provided by singer-actress Shanice (Wilson). Others in the cast: Victor Petrenko (Scarecrow), Bob Frank (Tin Woodman), Mark Richard Farrington (Cowardly Lion), and Bobby McFerrin (the Wizard).

September 28, 1996: Nickelodeon network's comedy-music show *All That* does "The Wizard of Cos," with series regular Kenan Thompson impersonating Bill Cosby.

November 1996: The New York Public Library mounts an exhibit honoring *Wizard of Oz* lyricist E. Y. "Yip" Harburg.

1997: Sirocco Productions releases *Oz: The American Fairyland*, a documentary look at L. Frank Baum and the continuing popularity of all things Oz. The film is directed by Gayle O'Neal and Leonard A. Swann Jr.

1998: Film director Tim Burton is linked to a television drama, *Lost in Oz*. The project is later abandoned. • Actor Rod Steiger says he's at work on a sequel to the 1939 *Oz*, featuring Dorothy at sixty. Although Elizabeth Taylor expresses interest, the script is never produced.

March 28, 1998: Fashion designer Isaac Mizrahi shows an MGM *Oz*-themed collection during New York Fashion Week.

April 4, 1998: Readers of *USA Today* vote "There's no place like home" as the most-quotable line of movie dialogue.

June 1998: The American Film Institute ranks *The Wizard of Oz* at #6 on its all-time list, behind *Citizen Kane* (#1), *Casablanca*, *The Godfather*, *Gone With the Wind*, and *Lawrence of Arabia*.

September 12, 1998: Jack Dawn, William Tuttle, and other *Wizard of Oz* makeup artists are honored with "A Tribute to the Wizard of Oz," an exhibit curated in Los Angeles by Scott Essman.

1999: Monkeys in Silk presents *The Oz Witch Project*, a nine-minute live-action spoof of the "found-footage" hit *The Blair Witch Project* and *The Wizard of Oz*. Meredith Salenger (Dorothy) and Curtis Eames (the Cowardly Lion) are perky and appealing, but even at nine minutes, the spoof wears out its welcome. It's written by Michael Rotman and M. J. Butler and directed by Rotman. • Hopelessly Incompetent Productions completes *The Wicked Witch Project*, a twenty-six-minute live-action spoof of *The Blair Witch Project* and *The Wizard of Oz*, directed by Joe Barlow; written by Barlow and Kevin Darbro. Darbro is amusing as the *oilaholic* Tin Man, but twenty-six minutes (twenty minutes of story plus six minutes of unfunny outtakes) just feels like a hammer to the head.

January 1, 1999: A Munchkinland float wins the Grand Marshal's trophy at the Tournament of Roses Parade.

June 9, 1999: A musical revue, *Over the Rainbow: Yip Harburg's America*, opens in Philadelphia.

June 16, 1999: The American Film Institute ranks Judy Garland as the number-eight female screen legend.

October 19, 1999: A digitally restored *The Wizard of Oz* is released on DVD by Warner Bros. Home Video.

December 10, 1999: At a Christie's auction in London, a Judy Garland gingham dress is sold for $324,000 to collector Michael Benson.

2000: The Children's Museum of Los Angeles produces an audio adaptation of *The Wonderful Wizard of Oz*, on the book's 100th anniversary. Ambitious at three hours and forty minutes, the production is adapted and directed by David Ossman, and features the voices of Michelle Trachtenberg (Dorothy), Rene Auberjonois (the Scarecrow), Nestor Serrano (the Tin Woodman), Robert Guillaume (the Cowardly Lion), Phyllis Diller (the Wicked Witch), Harry Anderson (the Wizard), and Annette Bening (as Glinda). Others in the cast: John Goodman, Mark Hammill, Michael Learned, Mako, Norman Corwin, Edie McClurg, and the Firesign Theatre (as the Hammerheads). The adaptation is syndicated to public radio as an installment broadcast and is heard on many NPR stations late in the year. The performance is also released on audiocassette and CD. • Colonial Radio Theatre issues a ten-cassette, 11½-hour audio adaptation of the first five *Oz* novels. • Tips for effective use of the Web at public libraries are offered in a short film, *The Wizard of the Web*. • Wizard of Biz CEO Jeff Slutsky stages and videotapes a slick, professionally performed "motivational, Broadway-style production," *The Wizard of Sales*. Songs (with the original Harold Arlen melodies) include "Somewhere Over My Sales Goals," "Ding! Dong! The Product Pitch Is Dead," and "If I Only Had Some Leads." Dorothy's sales secret?—the ruby sales manual! Wizard of Biz customizes the show's content to suit discrete clients. • Mattel's "Dorothy" Barbie is advertised in television commercials.

January 30, 2000: During the Super Bowl telecast, FedEx airs a whimsical commercial in which the service makes a successful delivery, by truck, to Munchkinland.

February 2000: HarperCollins publishes *Oz, the Hundredth Anniversary Celebration: 30 Favorite Artists and Writers Celebrate 100 Years of Oz.* Contributors assembled by editor Peter Glassman include Chris Van Allsburg, Jules Feiffer, Madeleine L'Engle, Leo and Diane Dillon, and Maurice Sendak.

May 15, 2000: The 100th anniversary of the publication of L. Frank Baum's first Oz book, *The Wonderful Wizard of Oz.*

May 24, 2000: *Oz* collector David Elkouby purchases a pair of ruby slippers for $666,000 at a Christie's auction.

June 29, 2000: A judge prohibits West Coast autograph dealer Nate Sanders from selling the special Oscar awarded to teenage Judy Garland for her work in *The Wizard of Oz.* Sanders had listed the statuette for $3 million.

July 19, 2000: An early edition of Baum's *The Wonderful Wizard of Oz,* signed by the principal cast members of the MGM movie, sells at auction for $49,300.

October–November 2000: Focus on the Family produces a radio program for children, *Adventures in Odyssey: The Great Wishy Woz.* The series of broadcasts links a thinly disguised Land of Oz with Jesus. Key characters are Dotty, Manny Kin, Metal Guy, Mystical Mountain Lion, and the Great Wishy Woz, and a villain called Wicked and Mean and Generally Not Very Nice Woman.

November 4, 2000: Los Angeles Central Library opens "A Century of Oz" exhibit featuring some five hundred items from the collection of Willard Carroll.

2001: The National Endowment for the Arts, the Recording Industry Association of America (RIAA), and Scholastic Inc. designate "Over the Rainbow" as "The Song of the Century." Because the complete list of twenty-five songs notes particular recordings, the award is more accurately the song and recording of the century. Judy Garland's version of "Over the Rainbow" is chosen, naturally enough. Rounding out the top five, in descending order, are "White Christmas" by Bing Crosby, "This Land Is Your Land" by Woody Guthrie, "Respect" by Aretha Franklin, and "American Pie" by Don McLean. • Tabori & Chang publishes Willard Carroll's charming *I, Toto: The Autobiography of Terry, the Dog Who Was "Toto."* The book is reissued by Abrams in 2013.

January 2001: A shimmering 1994 recording of "Over the Rainbow" by American singer Eva Cassidy is released as a single in 2001 and becomes a hit in Great Britain, five years after Cassidy's death.

February 25, 2001: Judy Davis and Tammy Blanchard play mature/young Judy Garland in an acclaimed ABC-TV-movie, *Life with Judy Garland: Me and My Shadows.* In 2002, Davis's performance brings her an Emmy, a Golden Globe, a Screen Actors Guild Award, and the AFI Award. Tammy Blanchard is awarded an Emmy (as best supporting actress).

2002: Colonial Radio Theatre adapts *The Emerald City of Oz* for children's radio and later issues the broadcast on audiocassette. • Screenwriter Zach Helm completes a film script called *Surrender Dorothy* as a possible star vehicle for actress Drew Barrymore as the great, great granddaughter of Dorothy. The project soon passes from discussion.

May 2002: The Metropolitan Museum of Art mounts a major exhibition of work by *Wizard of Oz* costume designer (Gilbert) Adrian, "Adrian: American Glamour."

May 16, 2002: New York's Swann Galleries auctions the impressive *Oz* collection belonging to Irene Fisher.

June–September 2002: The Hollywood Entertainment Museum mounts a successful exhibition, "Judy Garland: Princess of Oz."

July 4, 2002: Cable network Turner Classic Movies airs the MGM *Wizard of Oz* as a sing-along.

April 2003: Ruby-encrusted sandals that are not related to the *Oz* books or 1939 movie are offered for sale, for $1.6 million, by Harrods department store in London.

June 3, 2003: The American Film Institute cites Margaret Hamilton's Wicked Witch of the West as the fourth most awful villain in screen history.

November 2003: The Oz Museum opens in Wamego, Kansas.

2004: Fundamentalist leaders Jerry Falwell and Pat Robertson take a stab at encouraging a ban on television showings of the 1939 *Wizard of Oz*, because, they say, the film corrupts the morals of youth. When Robertson is asked how he knew this, he answers, "The Almighty told me." Scheduled broadcasts of *Oz* go on as before. • OZsome Enterprises releases *Adventures in Oz with Cheryl*, a children's fitness video featuring muscular health advocate Cheryl Ann Silich as Dorothy. (In a geographic impossibility, the Gales' Kansas farm is depicted as sitting atop a towering plateau surrounded by great peaks and waterfalls.)

January 2004: In an impressive bit of technical trickery in a TV commercial, M&M's combines footage of Judy Garland in *The Wizard of Oz* with talking, computer-generated M&M candies that gather around her bedside. Because the gist of the spot is new colors for M&M's, the entire commercial is in sepiatone. Animation directed by Chris Johnson. A later spoof on *MAD TV* cast Nicole Parker as Dorothy. The message: "Good candy, bad commercial."

January 30, 2004: During the annual Super Bowl telecast, FedEx airs a commercial in which the Lollipop Guild Munchkins lose their high voices in the middle of their song welcoming Dorothy. When a FedEx truck drops in (literally, squashing the Wicked Witch of the East) to make a delivery of helium-filled balloons, the relieved Munchkins inhale the gas and continue their greeting. Impeccably made-up actors portray the Lollipop Guild in this very successful mix of original *Wizard of Oz* footage, new live-action, and computer-generated images. Unfortunately for FedEx, the commercial is skewered by the National Inhalant Prevention Council because it supposedly endorses the inhalation of helium. On February 14, FedEx announces that the commercial has been pulled.

February 25, 2004: PBS broadcasts *Judy Garland: By Myself* as an installment of its *American Experience* series. The Garland documentary is produced by *Oz* historian John Fricke.

June 22, 2004: The key tune from *The Wizard of Oz*, "Over the Rainbow," is chosen by the American Film Institute as the #1 film song in American movie history. "Ding! Dong! The Witch Is Dead," another song from the MGM classic, comes in at number eighty-two. For the record, others in the AFI's top five are "As Time Goes By" (#2; *Casablanca*), "Singin' in the Rain" (#3; *Singin' in the Rain*), "Moon River" (#4; *Breakfast at Tiffany's*), and "White Christmas" (#5; *Holiday Inn*).

October 10, 2004: In a NASCAR Nextel Cup race at Kansas (City) Speedway, four cars are decorated with *Wizard of Oz* themes. The drivers running *Oz* livery are Brendan Gaughan (the Scarecrow), Jeff Gordon (the Cowardly Lion), Scott Riggs (the Tin Man), and Elliott Sadler (Toto). The event is merchandised via miniature die-cast cars manufactured by Action.

2005: One of ten checked pinafores made for Judy Garland (as of 2014, six were known to survive) sells at auction in London for $252,000.

April 1, 2005: A Profiles in History auction brings $54,600 for Margaret Hamilton's Witch hat and $14,900 for a winged monkey figurine "study" made for reference at MGM.

April 27, 2005: The Bonhams & Butterfield auction house sells a Judy Garland gingham dress for $252,000.

April 28, 2005: The United States Postal Service issues a stamp commemorating *Wizard of Oz* lyricist E. Y. "Yip" Harburg.

May 20, 2005: ABC airs *The Muppets Wizard of Oz* TV special, featuring Ashanti as Dorothy, Jeffrey Tambor as the Wizard, Queen Latifah as Aunt Em, and David Alan Grier as Uncle Henry. Key voice work is done by Steve Whitmire (Kermit, the Scarecrow), Dave Golez (Gonzo, Tin Thing), Eric Jacobson (Miss Piggy, Lion, Witches), and Bill Barretta (Pepe the Prawn, Toto).

August 27–28, 2005: Thieves break through a rear emergency door and make off with a pair of ruby slippers on exhibit at the Judy Garland Museum in Grand Rapids, Minnesota. The shoes are insured for $1 million and have been on loan from Los Angeles collector Michael Shaw.

October 2005: Warner Home Video releases *The Wizard of Oz Three-Disc Collector's Edition* DVD set.

December 2005: Singer Kylie Minogue's live version of "Over the Rainbow" is released as a digital single.

2006: Vocalist Katharine McPhee has a #12 hit with her recording of "Over the Rainbow." • In a television commercial, the Tin Woodman (an actor outfitted like Jack Haley) is chased hither and yon by mobs of screaming children. Reason: a Chef Boyardee Ravioli logo is on his back. Canned ravioli, get it? • *Apocalypse Oz*, a thirty-minute movie short blending Baum's *The Wonderful*

Sydney Symphony & Sydney Opera House present

THE WIZARD OF OZ WITH THE SYDNEY SYMPHONY

Restored original cinematic masterpiece with orchestrations played live by Sydney Symphony

The Wizard of Oz was screened at the Sydney (Australia) Opera House in 2006, with Herbert Stothart's score performed live by the Sydney Symphony. The presentation was part of the touring "Symphonic Night at the Movies" series, conceived by the American television and stage producer John Goberman.

Wizard of Oz and Conrad's *Heart of Darkness*, follows Amerasian teen Dorothy, who's sick and tired of Kansas and accepts an assignment to execute her father. Dad is a former army man who returned insane from Vietnam and is now ensconced in the American desert, where he calls himself the Wizard. The short's cleverest touch is that nearly all the dialogue is taken, word for word, from MGM's *Wizard of Oz* and *Apocalypse Now*.

June 10, 2006: The United States Postal Service's new Legends of Hollywood stamp series issues one commemorating Judy Garland.

September 2006: The American Film Institute ranks *The Wizard of Oz* as the third-greatest movie musical, behind *Singin' in the Rain* (#1) and *West Side Story*.

2007: The American Film Institute (AFI) designates *The Wizard of Oz* as the tenth-greatest film ever made. • Warner Bros. uses clips from the MGM *Oz* movie in a TV spot warning against DVD piracy. The message: "MELTING THE WICKED WITCH: GOOD. PIRATING DVDS: BAD." • In a Trina Tea commercial made for TV viewers in Spain, a mild alt-rock version of "We're Off to See the Wizard" plays over various city folk who hop, skip, and leap along polka-dotted streets and a pedestrian mall.

March 9, 2007: Orange Park Florida kicks off its Southeast Wizard of Oz Festival.

April 6, 2007: A 1939 Winkie costume sells for $115,000 at a Hollywood auction held by Profiles in History. The costume is complete except for boots; none of those are known to have survived from any of the Winkie outfits.

May 7, 2007: "The Wonderful Wizard of Song," a musical revue celebrating *Oz* songwriter Harold Arlen, begins a nationwide tour.

December 2–4, 2007: The Sci Fi cable network airs a three-part, 4½-hour miniseries, *Tin Man*. According to one of the show's producers, the Tin Man character (established here as a bitter peace officer) is a rugged and determined antihero in the mold of Clint Eastwood. Heavy science fiction elements and dark visual and thematic tones take the characters and plot further still from the traditional concept of Oz. Although *Tin Man* is a cable-ratings smash, *Variety*'s reviewer complains about its mashup of pop-culture influences and its struggle to appeal to "fanboys and their imaginary girlfriends." With Zooey Deschanel as DG (Dorothy), Neal McDonough as Wyatt Cain (the Tin Man), Alan Cumming as Glitch (loosely based on the Scarecrow), Raoul Trujillo as Raw (loosely based on the Cowardly Lion), Kathleen Robertson as Azkadellia (a beautiful villainess possessed by an evil witch), and Richard Dreyfuss as the Mystic Man (a deposed ruler with echoes of the Wizard).

2008: An AFI list places MGM's *Wizard of Oz* at number one in the fantasy category. • After twenty-seven years, the Wizard of Oz Festival in Chesterton, Indiana, is canceled because of lack of interest and the travel difficulties of the film's few surviving players. • The statute of limitations for theft runs out on the August 2005 burglary of a pair of original ruby slippers from the Judy Garland Museum in Grand Rapids, Minnesota. If the thief were now to be unmasked, he or she could be prosecuted only for possession. • *The Spectator* magazine describes management consultant Charles Leadbeater as "the Wizard of the Web."

July 2008: Following a ho-hum audience reaction to *The Wizard of Oz* musical presentation at London's Southbank Centre and tepid reviews, Southbank personnel were outed as the writers of positive comments posted to Whatsonstage.com.

October 2008: Anti–mind control zealots at the Kassandra Project claim that traumatized mind slaves were programmed with story elements from Baum and MGM's *The Wizard of Oz*, as a way to control behavior.

Late 2008: Marvel Comics kicks off an eight-issue miniseries, *The Wonderful Wizard of Oz*, adapting Baum's first Oz novel. The series is written by Eric Shanower and illustrated by Skottie Young. A hardcover edition collecting all eight issues is released late in 2009.

2009: Warner Home Video releases a two-disc *Wizard of Oz* DVD set, comprised of the print upgrade from 2005 and extras. • *The Secret of Oz*, a documentary about the international monetary crisis, returns to the venerable Populist/gold standard point of view about Baum's first *Oz* novel to suggest that all the clues to international financial salvation are in the book. Directed by William T. Still. • Hallmark releases a commemorative set of MGM-*Oz*-themed Christmas ornaments. • "Vicky and the Wicked Witch," an *Oz*-parody ad (with licensed content) for the Orange cinema chain's "two-for-one Wednesday" promotion, airs in Britain. In the spot, regular-gal Vicky and the Witch are unlikely best friends who hang out, shop, and go to the movies together. • A computer-animated television commercial for Chips Ahoy cookies casts a cookie as Dorothy. Moments after the tornado deposits him in Munchkinland, the cookie is grabbed by a gigantic hand that reaches down from the top of the frame—presumably to eat him. The spot is in sepiatone and color. • In a live-action commercial for iParty party stores, Dorothy sits up in bed to tell her friends that "there's no place like iParty!" The commercial is in black and white (not sepia) and color.

February 1, 2009: In a General Electric commercial aired during the Super Bowl, a computer-generated Scarecrow sings "If I Only Had a Brain" while dancing high on a power tower. Although that kind of high-voltage location is probably the last place a man made of straw should be, the Scarecrow is nevertheless a pleasing spokesman for GE's "smart grid technology."

September 23, 2009: Select movie theaters around the USA show MGM's *The Wizard of Oz* for one night only, in high definition. The showings are produced by Fathom Events, in connection with Turner Classic Movies, to note the film's 70th anniversary. A documentary, *To Oz! The Making of a Classic*, accompanies the feature.

2010: *Surrender Dorothy*, a Zack Helm script written in 2002 as a possible star vehicle for Drew Barrymore (as Dorothy's great-great granddaughter), is resurrected, with Barrymore now attached as director; whether she would take the Dorothy role is up in the air. As in 2002, however, discussion of *Surrender Dorothy* shortly diminishes.

March 2010: Two new Oz feature films are in development at Warner Bros: *Oz*, from the people behind the Twilight film series; and *The Wizard of Oz*, in which Dorothy's granddaughter travels to Oz to fight evil. To date, neither film has been made.

March–May 2010: The BBC's *Over the Rainbow* TV talent show searches for a young vocalist to play Dorothy in the upcoming Andrew Lloyd Webber stage adaptation of MGM's *The Wizard of Oz*.

May 2010: British vocalist Danielle Hope, winner of the BBC's *Over the Rainbow* TV talent contest, releases a popular version of "Over the Rainbow."

June 2010: BBC *Over the Rainbow* TV talent show runner-up vocalists Sophie Evans and Lauren Samuels release separate versions of "Over the Rainbow."

September 10, 2010: Fish Fry & a Flick, staged at the Discovery World waterfront in Milwaukee, screens MGM's *The Wizard of Oz* simultaneously with Pink Floyd's *Dark Side of the Moon* LP. The show is called Dark Side of the Rainbow.

October 2010: Actor Robert Downey Jr. is attached to Disney's *Oz the Great and Powerful*, to be directed by (according to various rumors and reports) Guillermo del Toro, Timur Bekmambetov, Adam Shankman, Sam Mendes, or Sam Raimi. When the film is made (for 2013 release), Raimi is the director and James Franco stars.

November 2010: Warner Bros., which now owns the rights to the 1939 movie, announces a remake of *Oz*, to be directed by Robert Zemeckis from the original 1939 script. To date, the film has not been made.

2011: British sculptor Mike Hill creates a full-size, costumed Margaret Hamilton Wicked Witch of the West. Fantasy-film director Peter Jackson commissions

Hill to sculpt and dress a full-size Winged Monkey for his private collection. • The publish-it-yourself outfit called Xlibris issues a novel called *Adolf Hitler in Oz: A Children's Book for Adults*. Author Sam Sackett's tale revolves around late-breaking Nazi technology, which propels Hitler from the certain doom of the *Führerbunker* to Oz—where he schemes to make himself leader and master. He fails, and goes to jail, because of his fundamental misunderstanding of Baum's Oz ethos. • In *The Witches of Oz*, a syndicated TV miniseries, best-selling author Dorothy Gale has an epiphany: her Oz novels are based on her own repressed memories of her adventures in that magical—and dangerous—land. Cheap production values and a penchant for the dark side help kill the film's entertainment value. Directed by Leigh Scott, with Paulie Rojas as Dorothy and Christopher Lloyd as the Wizard. • Aberdeen, South Dakota, promotes itself with a series of slick TV commercials featuring Dorothy (as a happy shopper), the Tin Woodman (as a happy tourist), the Cowardly Lion (as a frightened moviegoer), and the Scarecrow (as a museumgoer and high-end shopper). The typography of "There's no place like Aberdeen" mimics the style of the main titles of the MGM movie.

May 15, 2011: The Wicked Witch's hand-blown crystal ball sells at a Profiles in History auction for $129,800.

March 3–31, 2012: An exhibition, Visions of Oz: A Celebration of Art from Over the Rainbow, is mounted at Heritage Square Museum in Los Angeles. The works encompass illustration, sculpture, paintings, and Baum first editions and other Baum-related rarities.

July 2012: The sepia-tinted music video for Carrie Underwood's "Blown Away" places the singer in a farmyard as a tornado brews in the distance.

August 7, 2012: An independent feature film called *After the Wizard* is released directly to DVD by Breaking Glass Pictures. The story concerns a Kansas orphan girl who travels to Oz to recruit the Scarecrow and the Tin Woodman to follow her back to Oz, to locate Dorothy. The film is written and directed by Hugh Gross.

2013: The Wicked Witch of the West is ranked fourth on the AFI's best-villains list, behind Hannibal Lecter (*The Silence of the Lambs*), Norman Bates (*Psycho*), and Darth Vader (*Star Wars*). • A McDonald's commercial dresses a little girl in gingham and ruby slippers, stuffs her with fast food, and hands her stubby *Wizard of Oz* Happy Meal toys. Presented in sepia and color. • In promotions to coincide with the "event" re-release, *The Wizard of Oz 3D*, Warner Bros. teams with a smorgasbord of other businesses: Macy's (2013 Thanksgiving Day parade hot-air balloon and "balloonheads" of Oz characters); QVC (jewelry, toys, beauty products and other collectibles and gift items); McDonald's (Happy Meals with *Oz* toy figures); and the Food Network (a *Cupcake Wars* competition, judged by film historian Leonard Maltin). Other corporate partners—some of which were a little unlikely— were Amtrak (an in-station and on-train adventure sweepstakes); Langer Juice Company (commemorative badging on packaging); One Kings Lane (movie memorabilia); Simon Malls (*Oz*-themed Kidgets Club events); and Gourmet Trading Company (*Oz* tags on bunches of asparagus). Even the National Highway Traffic Safety Administration and the Ad Council get Ozified, with TV, radio, print, and digital public service announcements focused on child safety. • Warner sells product-license rights to Mattel, Steiff, Jazwares, PaperStyle, the Noble Collection, Madame Tussaud's, and some eighty other high-profile companies that produce toys, clothing, stationery, jewelry, games, and personal care items. • *I Will Kiss These Walls*, a play mounted by Chicago's Albany Park Theater Project, invokes MGM's *The Wizard of Oz* to underscore the devastating effects on children and young adults of home foreclosure—simply, the loss of home. Music and direction by David Feiner, Maggie Popadiak, and Rossana Rodríguez Sánchez.

January 13, 2013: After noting in the day's blog posting that global warming is a "media fraud," americanthinker.com likens President Obama to the sham who calls himself the Wizard of Oz.

February 14, 2013: *Oz the Great and Powerful*, a splashy prequel to the 1939 film, is released and becomes a big hit for Walt Disney Pictures, grossing $493 million worldwide on a budget of $215 million. (Because rights to the 1939 movie are now owned by Warner Bros., Disney has been obliged to create a fresh story, with no relation to proprietary elements from the MGM film.) The story focuses on the arrival in Oz of magician Oscar Diggs, who is proclaimed the Wizard, and what happens when he's embroiled in a conflict involving three witches. Written by Mitchell Kapner and David Lindsay-Abaire, from a story by Kapner; directed by Sam Raimi. In the cast: James Franco (Diggs/the Wizard), Mila Kunis (Theodora), Rachel Weisz (Evanora), and Michelle Williams (Annie/Glinda). The film is large, expansive, and entertaining, but seems a little long at 130 minutes, and bows a bit beneath the weight of its opulent computer-generated effects.

February 22, 2013: CreateSpace publishes Horace Martin Woodhouse's *The Essential Wizard of Oz: 101 Things You Didn't Know About the Most-Watched Movie in Film History*.

March 2013: Disney announces that a sequel to its current hit, *Oz the Great and Powerful*, will be produced, with same cast, probably for release in 2015. • The Pittsburgh Symphony orchestra plays the Herbert Stothart *Wizard of Oz* score, and songs by Arlen and Harburg, during five screenings of the 1939 movie. The venue is Pittsburgh's Heinz Hall, a concert hall built as a movie palace in the 1920s.

April 2013: The April 8, 2013, death of former British prime minister Margaret Thatcher—always a controversial and divisive figure—inspires some mean-spirited rejoicing in Britain, and even a revival of "Ding! Dong! The Witch Is Dead."

Summer 2013: The Judy Garland Museum in Grand Rapids, Minnesota, hires Minneapolis investigators Alexander & Associates to look into the 2005 burglary theft from the museum of an original pair of Judy Garland ruby slippers. • CBS-TV announces development of *Dorothy*, a proposed medical drama with characters loosely based on Dorothy and other familiar *Oz* figures.

July 2013: Word leaks that cable TV's Syfy (formerly Sci Fi Channel) network, apparently encouraged by the success of its 2007 miniseries *Tin Man*, plans a post-apocalyptic miniseries called *Warriors of Oz*. As imagined by producer Timur Bekmambetov, a soldier from present-day Earth is transported to a war-ravaged future Oz, and teams with Heartless, Brainless, and Coward to topple a despotic wizard. • The blue-and-polka-dot dress worn by Judy Garland during the discarded Richard Thorpe shoot is auctioned for $300,000 by L.A.-based Profiles in History auction house. Bay Area resident Barry Barsamian had owned the dress for more than thirty years.

September 2013: Show-business blogs report that the CW television network is negotiating for the rights to *Dorothy Must Die*, a 2014 young-adult novel by Danielle Paige. The book posits that another girl from Kansas, Amy Gumm (the surname is, of course, the real one of Judy Garland), is recruited by witches to journey to Oz and steal the Scarecrow's brains, the Tin Woodman's Heart, and the Lion's courage—and then kill Dorothy. Like nearly every other recent *Oz*-inspired project, *Dorothy Must Die* is widely described as "edgy." (A digital-only setup story called *No Place Like Oz: A Dorothy Must Die Prequel Novella*, was published in November 2013.) The story's follow-the-red-brick-road idea saw print as early as 1989, in "Follow the Other Brick Road," fan fiction by Frederick E. Otto, published in the 1989 edition of *Oziana*, the annual publication of the International Wizard of Oz Club. • NHTSA and the Ad Council join Warner Bros. to promote safety-belt use in a PSA featuring clips from the 1939 movie.

September 12, 2013: Price Stern Sloan publishes *The Wizard of Oz Mad Libs*, a licensed book perpetuating the wildly successful Mad Libs concept created by Roger Price and Leonard Stone.

September 20, 2013: With completely restored visual and audio elements, the 1939 *Wizard of Oz* is tweaked with well-handled 3-D effects and released to IMAX screens. What has been planned as a one-week national engagement finds enthusiastic audiences and plays for four weeks. (See chapter 16.)

October 2013: Lifetime cable channel announces it's developing *Red Brick Road*, a reportedly edgy take on Dorothy and the character's exploration of those red bricks amidst the yellow that we see in the 1939 film. (The red bricks, an invention of MGM's production department, are allowed because a division of Warner Bros. is a *Red Brick Road* co-producer.) Like Syfy channel's *Warriors of Oz*, *Red Brick Road* takes inspiration from the dark fantasy of the very successful HBO series *Game of Thrones*. • Sketchy information is leaked about *The Land of Oz*, a feature film that may be scheduled for 2014 release. Madisyn Wright has been cast as Dorothy.

October 30, 2013: The estate of Jack Haley Jr. sues Warner Bros. over "fiduciary rights" to a documentary produced by Haley's production company in 1989.

The original understanding had been a 50-50 split of revenue, which the Haley estate feels has not been honored. The documentary, *The Wonderful Wizard of Oz: The Making of a Movie Classic*, has been included as an extra on various Warner Home Video issues of *The Wizard of Oz* for more than twenty years and has produced considerable revenue. The Haley estate asks for equitable distribution of profits to date and a broader release for the doc. Warner, on the other hand, wants full ownership of the documentary and offers the Haley estate $150,000 to purchase it outright.

October 2013 through March 2014: The Farnsworth Art Museum in Rockland, Maine, hosts a *Wizard of Oz* exhibit of original props, posters, first-edition Baum books, and other rarities co-owned by filmmaker and longtime *Oz* collector Willard Carroll. From a collection of more than 100,000 *Oz*-related items, Carroll and the Farnsworth's chief curator, Michael Komanecky, have selected 107 for the exhibit. Carroll's collection of all things Oz is thought to be the world's largest. Items from it had been publicly exhibited only once before, at the Los Angeles Public Library in 2000. Carroll curated a 1999 book, *100 Years of Oz*, and masterminded a charming "autobiography," *I, Toto*, in 2001.

November 1, 2013: The Chuck Jones Gallery of San Diego hosts "We're Off to See the Wizard," an exhibition of new artworks inspired by MGM's *The Wizard of Oz*. A portion of the show's proceeds is donated to Habitat for Humanity.

January 2014: Post-production is complete on *L. Frank Baum's The Wonderful Wizard of Oz*, a modestly budgeted adaptation of the first L. Frank Baum *Oz* novel. Written by Sean Gates; directed by Clayton Spinney. Cast: Mariellen Kemp (Dorothy), Steven Lowry (Scarecrow voice; the character is a CGI creation), Nick Chopper (the Tin Woodman), Marie Rizza (Wicked Witch of the West), and the Cowardly Lion playing himself (whether a costumed actor or CGI is unclear at this writing). Because the official trailer suggests a well-intentioned semi-professional effort, the film is likely to be released directly to DVD. • NBC-TV orders ten episodes of *Emerald City*, a purported "reimagining" of Baum's *Oz* that revolves around a feisty, twenty-year-old Dorothy.

January 16, 2014: Ruth Robinson Duccini, the last of the female Munchkin players, dies in Las Vegas at ninety-five.

January 24, 2014: Popular PBS program *Antiques Roadshow* announces that professional appraiser Simeon Lipman has valued Bert Lahr's working script for *The Wizard of Oz* at $150,000. The script was brought to *Antiques Roadshow* by Lahr's great-grandson when the program was shooting in Detroit in the summer of 2013. The episode airs January 27, 2014.

January 28, 2014: Oscar telecast producers Craig Zadan and Neil Maron announce that the March 2, 2014, broadcast will include a celebration of the 75th anniversary of *The Wizard of Oz*.

March 3, 2014: Video surveillance captures a woman thought to have stolen replica ruby slippers from a display at a Staten Island hotel.

May 9, 2014: U.S. theatrical release of *Legends of Oz: Dorothy's Return*, a visually imaginative computer-animated musical sequel to Dorothy's first adventure in Oz. (The film was announced in 2012 as *Dorothy of Oz*.) This time, the Kansas girl is reunited with her friends, makes new ones, and faces a fresh adversary, the Jester. Directed by Will Finn and Dan St. Pierre, with voices by Lea Michele (Dorothy), Dan Aykroyd (the Scarecrow), Kelsey Grammer (the Tin Man), James Belushi (the Cowardly Lion), and Martin Short (the Jester). Also with Patrick Stewart, Oliver Platt, and Bernadette Peters. Songs by Bryan Adams.

August 8–10, 2014: Winkie Con 50, the fiftieth Oz Con International, is held in San Diego.

Epilogue
Disney and Warner at War in Oz

This is how it stood in 2014: If Warner Bros. could have beaten Disney Pictures to death with a pair of ruby slippers, it would have done that. And if Disney could have strangled Warner Bros. with the strings of the China Girl marionette, they'd have done so in a heartbeat. Hollywood studios are naturally competitive, but when two entertainment giants lay simultaneous claim to intimately related properties—well, no studio lawyers are apt to starve anytime soon. Warner owns the rights to the 1939 MGM *Wizard of Oz* movie and to key elements of that movie, including (according to Warner) Dorothy. Disney, on the other hand, has linked itself to Oz creator L. Frank Baum and to the Oz novels that came after the first.

Warner and Disney employ wondrous storytellers, but the companies' argument is about commerce rather than art. Let's be clear: there's a lot of potential commerce at stake here—hundreds of millions of dollars. Each studio wants to make money without any infringement or other interference from the other. Warner jealously guards what it owns and has aggressively laid claim to Oziana that it may not own at all. Disney has been very careful not to offend its rival by straying into territory that Warner has already marked.

The feud became public in 2011, when Disney was well into development of the movie that became *Oz the Great and Powerful* (2013) and Warner was readying its home-video and merchandising arms for the 75th anniversary of the beloved Judy Garland film, as well as a splashy 3-D IMAX re-release. (Warner acquired the rights to the 1939 classic in 1996, when it merged with Turner Entertainment, which had acquired the MGM film library some ten years before that.)

But the 1939 *Wizard of Oz* wasn't Warner's only card. To the contrary, as Disney developed its *Oz* feature, Warner had *three* in development: a sequel entitled *Oz: The Return to the Emerald City*; a modern-day riff called *Surrender Dorothy*; and a non-musical epic called *The Wizard of Oz*. The last was to be directed by Guillermo del Toro and produced to very high (and expensive) standards. Warner also wanted to push *Oz* properties into television, beginning with a punky fantasy concept called *Red Brick Road*.

Because Warner viewed the 1939 movie as the wellspring of all things Oz, the studio frankly resented Disney's plans. Warner wanted gravy too, so in 2010 Warner president Alan Horn gave the del Toro *Oz* the green light.

Over at Disney, the project that became *Oz the Great and Powerful* was so secret that it was referred to only by a code name: *Brick*. Like Warner, Disney planned to sink a lot of money into an *Oz* movie and didn't want to be bullied or dissuaded. Disney went on the offensive by insisting that Warner's designation of the 1939 film as *the* Oz source was nonsense. The true source of Oz, they said, is the most obvious one: the books by L. Frank Baum. Even though the books are in public domain and can be adapted by anybody, any which way, Disney paid for the rights to Baum *Oz* novels that were published after the first. The company felt its claim was legally sound as well as clear.

In 2011, Warner Bros. won a big round in the 8th Circuit Court of Appeals when it was granted "character protection" based on its holding of copyright to the 1939 *Wizard of Oz*. Warner was happy to interpret this to mean that Disney couldn't even have a *character* named Dorothy in its movie, no matter what she did or what she looked like. Likewise, the presence of a Disney Scarecrow, Cowardly Lion, or other principal characters wouldn't be tolerated.

Disney didn't wish to test every particle of Warner's reasoning, but felt it was on solid legal ground with its conception of the Wizard as a young man with no *specific* relationship to Frank Morgan's Wizard. Similarly, *Oz the Great and Powerful* includes among its characters Glinda, flying monkeys, Winkies, Munchkins, residents of Emerald City, and people from Kansas. And for some legal protection, perhaps, *Great and Powerful* features Baum characters, such as China Girl and various Quadlings, which are not part of the MGM adaptation.

In 2011, the year of the Circuit Court ruling, something even more interesting happened: Alan Horn was fired from his post as president of Warner Bros.

Very shortly, Horn was the chief of film production at Disney, responsible for shepherding *Oz the Great and Powerful* to its completion.

Because Horn knew that Warner was going to go very big into toys and other 1939-related merchandise, he encouraged Disney to spin off the characters from its *Oz* adventure. (This tack was taken, but Disney realized that its brand-new characters didn't have the heft or appeal of the long-established favorites from 1939. Although China Girl dolls and a few other pieces were very well received, Disney didn't find the toy bonanza it had hoped for.)

In 2012 (by which time the studio had taken a big loss on a mega-budget fantasy, *John Carter*), Disney protected the wording of its *Oz*-movie title by filing for trademark registration of "Oz the Great and Powerful." A week later, Warner filed for trademark of "The Great and Powerful Oz." This seemed silly—and it was—but those hundreds of millions of dollars were still up for grabs. Each studio would do whatever it could to get a leg up on the other.

It was at about this time that Warner Bros. took another look at its proposed slate of new *Oz* movies. Rather unexpectedly, two of the three, *Surrender Dorothy* and *The Wizard of Oz*, were shelved (or put into turnaround or sent to limbo or exiled to nowheresville, or however else you might characterize what happens to movies that are probably never going to be made). The only new Warner-Oz project left standing was *Oz: The Return to the Emerald City*, the sequel to the 1939 adventure. It was made as a computer-animated feature slated for release in March 2013; the date was later pushed back to May 2014.

Despite the pullback, Warner continued to protect what it felt was its property: the publisher of a neuroscience book called *If I Only Had a Brain* received a letter written by lawyers, and the people behind a clothing line called the Wizard of Azz got one, too. Warner has pursued dozens of perceived infringements since 2010 and probably won't stop any time soon.

Well, let the corporations quarrel. The rest of us will visit Oz, again and again, enjoying what neither attorneys nor time can diminish.

Appendix
The Wizard of Oz Cast and Credits

The Wizard of Oz

Cast and credits, as seen on screen

Opening Credits

NOTE: The credits that follow faithfully reproduce the use of capitalization and punctuation seen on screen, except for the lengths of ellipses, which vary depending on the length of job titles and persons' names.

Metro Goldwyn Mayer Presents

The WIZARD of OZ

PRODUCED BY LOEW'S INCORPORATED

A VICTOR FLEMING PRODUCTION

with
JUDY GARLAND
FRANK MORGAN
RAY BOLGER
BERT LAHR
JACK HALEY
BILLIE BURKE
MARGARET HAMILTON
CHARLEY GRAPEWIN
AND THE MUNCHKINS

Screen Play by NOEL LANGLEY, FLORENCE RYERSON
and EDGAR ALLAN WOOLF

Adaptation by NOEL LANGLEY

From the Book by L. FRANK BAUM

MUSICAL PROGRAM
Musical Adaptation by HERBERT STOTHART
Lyrics by E. Y. HARBURG
Music by HAROLD ARLEN

Associate Conductor . . . . .GEORGE STOLL
Orchestral and Vocal Arrangements. . . .GEORGE BASSMAN
MURRAY CUTTER
PAUL MARQUARDT
KEN DARBY
Musical Numbers Staged by BOBBY CONNOLLY

Photographed in Technicolor

Photographed in Technicolor by. . . . . . .HAROLD ROSSON, A.S.C.
Technicolor Color Director . . . . .NATALIE KALMUS
Associate . . . . .HENRI JAFFA

Recording Director . . . . .DOUGLAS SHEARER
Art Director. . . . . .CEDRIC GIBBONS
Associate . . . . .WILLIAM A. HORNING
Set Decorations. . . . . .EDWIN B. WILLIS
Special Effects. .ARNOLD GILLESPIE
Costumes by . . . . .ADRIAN
Character Make-Ups Created by . . . . . . .JACK DAWN
Film Editor . . . . .BLANCHE SEWELL

Western Electric SOUND SYSTEM

Produced by MERVYN LeROY

Directed by VICTOR FLEMING

For nearly forty years this story has given faithful service to the Young in Heart; and Time has been powerless to put its kindly philosophy out of fashion.

To those of you who have been faithful to it in return

. . . and to the Young in Heart . . . we dedicate this picture.

End Credits

The End

CAST

Dorothy . . . . JUDY GARLAND
Professor Marvel. . . . . . . FRANK MORGAN
"Hunk". . . . . RAY BOLGER
"Zeke". . . . . BERT LAHR
"Hickory". . . . . JACK HALEY
Glinda . . . . BILLIE BURKE
Miss Gulch. . . . . MARGARET HAMILTON
Uncle Henry . . . . CHARLEY GRAPEWIN
Nikko . . . . PAT WALSHE
Auntie Em . . . . CLARA BLANDICK
Toto. . . . . TOTO
The Singer Midgets As The Munchkins

Some Who Received No Screen Credit

NOTE: This is a selected list. To note all personnel would create a list of prohibitive length. Also, some names have been lost over the years. For example, the actress cast as the old woman in the rocking chair that flies past Dorothy's window inside the twister is unknown; likewise, the names of the two fellows in the rowboat and the farmer milking his cow. Of the dozens of extras in the Emerald City sequence, the names of only a handful are known today.

Only key Munchkin players are noted.

More extensive cast-and-credits lists are available on the Web.

Associate producer: Arthur Freed

Director, conceptualizations only: Norman Taurog
Director, dismissed after shooting for two weeks; footage discarded: Richard Thorpe
Director, conceptualizations only: George Cukor
Director, deleted Scarecrow dance sequence: Busby Berkeley
Director, Kansas sequences only: King Vidor

Camera operators: Sam Cohen, Val O'Malley, Ray Ramsey
Technicolor associate: Allen M. Davey
Technicolor assistant: Cliff Shirpser

Music supervisor: Nat W. Finston

Supervising editor: Margaret Booth

Assistant director: Al Shenberg
Assistant director: Wallace Worsley

Production design: Jack Martin Smith
Construction coordinator: Gerald F. Rocket
Head sculptor: Henry Greutert

Special effects supervisor: Edwin Bloomfield
Miniatures: Marcel Delgado, Donald Jahraus
Director of photography, visual effects: Max Fabian

Director of matte paintings: Warren Newcombe
Matte painter: Candelario Rivas
Sound designer: O. O. Ceccarini
Sound editor: T. B. Hoffman
Sound effects editor: James Graham
Special sound effects: Franklin Milton

Character make-up: Sydney Guilaroff, Emile LaVigne, Norbert A. Myles, Web Overlander, Charles H. Schram, Lee Stanfield, Jack H. Young

Stunts: George Bruggeman

Kodachrome still photographer: Eric Carpenter

Wardrobe supervisor: Sam Kress

Animal trainer: Carl Spitz

Technical adviser: Maud Gage Baum

Additional Cast

Jimmy the Crow: Scarecrow's tormentor

Buddy Ebsen: Tin Woodman (voice only, heard in some musical sequences)

Lorraine Bridges: Glinda (singing voice)

Charles Becker: Munchkin mayor
Harry Earles: Lollipop Guild greeter (right)
Jackie Gerlich: Lollipop Guild greeter (left)
Nita Krebs: Lullaby League greeter (left); Munchkin lady in green
Mitchell Lewis: Captain of the Winkie guard
Jerry Maren: Lollipop Guild greeter (middle)
Yvonne Moray: Lullaby League greeter (right)
Olga Nardone: Lullaby League greeter (center)
Meinhardt Raabe: Munchkin coroner
Matthew Raia: Munchkin city father
"Little Billy" Rhodes: Munchkin barrister

Nick Angelo, Billy Bletcher, Robert Bradford, Lorraine Bridges, Lois Clements, Pinto Colvig, Ken Darby, Abe Dinovitch, Jon Dodson, Zari Elmassian, J. D. Jewkes, Lois Johansen, The King's Men, Rad Robinson, Betty Rome, Harry Stanton, Carol Tevis: Munchkin voices (various)

Helen Seamon: Emerald City woman with Siamese cat
Lois January: Emerald City beautician

Mitchell Lewis: Captain of the Winkie guard

Selected Bibliography

Books

Auxier, Randall E., and Phillip S. Seng, eds. *The Wizard of Oz and Philosophy: Wicked Wisdom of the West.* Open Court. Chicago: 2008.

Bennett, Colin. *The Guide to Kinematography.* E. T. Herron & Co. London: 1917.

Bingen, Steven, Stephen X. Sylvester, and Michael Troyan. *M-G-M: Hollywood's Greatest Backlot.* Santa Monica Press. Santa Monica, CA: 2011.

Bloom, Ken, *The American Songbook: The Singers, the Songwriters, and the Songs.* Black Dog & Leventhal. New York: 2005.

Bordman, Gerald. *American Musical Comedy.* Oxford University Press USA. New York: 1982.

Carey, Gary. *All the Stars in Heaven: Louis B. Mayer's M-G-M.* E. P. Dutton. New York: 1981.

Carroll, Willard. *I, Toto: The Autobiography of Terry, the Dog Who Was Toto.* Stewart, Tabori & Chang. New York: 2001.

Clarke, Gerald. *Get Happy: The Life of Judy Garland.* Random House. New York: 2000.

Cohen, Mitchell, ed. *Heart of the Tin Man: The Collected Writings of Jack Haley.* tinmanonline.com. [No place of publication given]: 2000.

Conover, David, and Philip J. Riley. *War Eagles: The Unmaking of an Epic.* BearManor. Duncan, OK: 2011.

Cox, Stephen. *The Munchkins Remember: The Wizard of Oz and Beyond.* E. P. Dutton. New York: 1989.

Daniel, Noel. *The Circus: 1870s–1950s.* Taschen. Cologne: 2012.

Dictionary of National Biography, Volume 24. Macmillan. New York: 1890.

DuPré, Michelle, Marilyn Fu, and Amy Lennard Goehner. *The Wizard of Oz: 75 Years Along the Yellow Brick Road.* LIFE Books. New York: 2013.

Ebsen, Buddy. *The Other Side of Oz.* Donovan Publishing. Newport Beach, CA: 1983.

Eliot, Marc. *Walt Disney: Hollywood's Dark Prince.* Birch Lane. New York: 1993.

Epstein, Daniel Mark. *Sister Aimee.* Harcourt Brace Jovanovich. New York: 1993.

Flamini, Roland. *Scarlett, Rhett, and a Cast of Thousands.* Collier Books. New York: 1975.

Fordin, Hugh. *The World of Entertainment: The Arthur Freed Unit.* Doubleday. New York: 1975.

Frank, Gerold. *Judy.* Harper & Row. New York: 1975.

Fricke, John. *Judy: A Legendary Film Career.* Running Press. Philadelphia: 2010.

Fricke, John, Jay Scarfone, and William Stillman. *The Wizard of Oz: The Official 50th Anniversary Pictorial History.* Warner Books. New York: 1989.

Gillespie, A. Arnold, Philip J. Riley, and Robert A. Welch, eds. *The Wizard of MGM.* BearManor. Duncan, OK: 2011.

Harmetz, Aljean. *The Making of The Wizard of Oz.* Knopf. New York: 1977.

Hartzman, Marc. *American Sideshow.* Tarcher/Penguin. New York: 2005.

Haver, Ronald. *A Star Is Born: The Making of the 1954 Movie and Its 1983 Restoration.* Applause. New York: 2002.

Higham, Charles. *Merchant of Dreams: Louis B. Mayer, M.G.M. and the Secret Hollywood.* Donald I. Fine. New York: 1993.

Jablonski, Edward. *Harold Arlen: Happy with the Blues.* Da Capo. New York: 1986.

Katz, Ephraim. *The Film Encyclopedia, Second Edition.* HarperPerennial. New York: 1994.

Lahr, John. *Notes on a Cowardly Lion.* Knopf. New York: 1969.

Langley, Noel, Florence Ryerson, and Edgar Allan Woolf. *Production #10160: The Wizard of Oz* [March 15, 1939, continuity script]. Turner Entertainment/ MGM/UA Home Video. [No place of publication given]: 1993.

LeRoy, Mervyn, and Dick Kleiner. *Mervyn LeRoy: Take One.* Hawthorn Books. New York: 1974.

Mank, Gregory William. *Women in Horror Films, 1940s.* McFarland. Jefferson, NC: 1999.

Manvell, Roger. *The International Encyclopedia of Film.* Crown. New York: 1972.

McElwee, John. *Showmen, Sell It Hot!* GoodKnight Books. Pittsburgh: 2013.

Merriam Webster's Collegiate Dictionary Eleventh Edition. Merriam-Webster. Springfield, MA: 2003.

Meyerson, Harold, and Ernie Harburg. *Who Put the Rainbow in The Wizard of Oz? Yip Harburg, Lyricist.* University of Michigan Press. Ann Arbor: 1995.

Rosner, Bruce Charles, ed. *Unseen Cinema: Early American Avant-garde Film 1893–1941.* Black Thistle Press/Anthology Film Archives. New York: 2001.

Royle, Nicholas. *The Uncanny.* Manchester University Press. Manchester, UK: 2003.

Rushdie, Salman. *The Wizard of Oz.* British Film Institute. London: 1992.

Schickel, Richard. *The Men Who Made the Movies.* Atheneum. New York: 1975.

Sherman, Fraser A. *The Wizard of Oz Catalog.* McFarland. Jefferson, NC: 2005.

Skal, David J. *Death Makes a Holiday: A Cultural History of Halloween.* Bloomsbury. New York: 2003.

Spivak, Jeffrey. *Buzz: The Life and Art of Busby Berkeley.* The University Press of Kentucky. Lexington: 2011.

Taylor, Al, and Sue Roy. *Making a Monster.* Crown. New York: 1980.

Temple, Shirley. *Child Star.* McGraw Hill. New York: 1988.

Williams, Esther, with Digby Diehl. *The Million Dollar Mermaid.* Simon & Schuster. New York: 1999.

Periodicals

Bell, Allison. "Inland Empire Cities Were Once 'In' with Hollywood for Movie Previews." *Los Angeles Times.* June 25, 2010.

Catsos, Gregory. "The Wonderful Witch: A Lost Interview with Margaret Hamilton." *Filmfax.* October–November 1993.

Crowe, Jerry. "Ambrose Schindler Followed His Own Road to Success at USC and Beyond." *Los Angeles Times.* July 10, 2011.

Denby, David. "Books: Hitler in Hollywood." *The New Yorker.* September 16, 2013.

Dennis, Ken. "Frank Morgan, the Merriest Man." *Films of the Golden Age.* [date unknown].

Gardner, Eriq. "Disney, Warner Bros. Fighting Over 'Wizard of Oz' Trademarks." *The Hollywood Reporter.* February 13, 2012.

Greenspun, Hank. "Ornate and Entertaining: Spectacular Sahara Opens." *Las Vegas Sun.* October 8, 1952.

Guzman, Rafer. "'The Wizard of Oz' review: 3-D Adds Little to a Classic." *Newsday.* September 17, 2013.

James, Caryn. "Today's Yellow Brick Road Leads Straight to Hell." *The New York Times.* August 19, 1990.

King, Susan. "'Wizard of Oz' Cowardly Lion Costume Could Be Yours (for a Price)." *Los Angeles Times.* March 8, 2013.

Krebs, Albin. "Beatrice Lillie, Comedienne and Lovable Eccentric, 94." *The New York Times.* January 21, 1989.

Leleux, Robert. "The Road Gets Rougher for Judyism's Faithful." *The New York Times.* April 5, 2012.

Lumenick, Lou. "First Review: 'The Wizard of Oz' in 3-D." *New York Post.* September 15, 2013.

McCann, Matt. "Kodachrome's Lasting Color and Memory." *The New York Times.* August 12, 2013.

"Mike Hill: Sculptor of Scares." *Famous Monsters of Filmland.* March–April 2013.

Neill, Michael, and Bonnie Bell. "Now a Half Century Down the Yellow Brick Road, Six Munchkins Remember Oz." *People.* June 26, 1989.

Nelson, Valerie J. "Shirley Temple Black, Iconic Child Star, Dies at 85." *Los Angeles* Times. February 11, 2014.

Puig, Claudia. "For 'The Wizard of Oz,' There's No Place Like IMAX." *USA Today.* September 19, 2013.

"Rivals in Beauty Contest." *The Milwaukee Journal.* September 12, 1934.

"Romance of the Lady Bouncer, the Midget and the Jilted Midgetess." *The Milwaukee Sentinel.* February 27, 1938.

Rothenberg, Fred. "NBC Wins Week's Ratings." Associated Press. February 18, 1986.

Rudolph, Kalie. "The Golden Era of Hollywood: The Making of *The Wizard of Oz* and *Gone With the Wind.*" *Voces Novae.* (*Chapman University Historical Review*), Vol. 2, No. 2. 2011.

"Sea Trip Brought No Cure, Just Change of Symptoms." *Pittsburgh Post-Gazette.* October 20, 1931.

Shirshekan, Jonathan. "Jack Dawn: One of the Real Wizards of Oz." *Famous Monsters of Filmland* #266. March–April 2013.

Taylor, Quentin P. "Money and Politics in the Land of Oz." *The Independent Review.* Winter 2005.

Thistle, Franklin L. "The Off-Stage Shenanigans of Strippers." *Adam.* February 1959.

Torgerson, Dial. "Dreams Auctioned." *Los Angeles Times.* May 4, 1970.

"Yes, Tall Girls Do Marry, Says 6-Foot-2 Lois De Fee." *St. Petersburg Times.* July 29, 1941.

Zeitchik, Steven, and Daniel Miller. "Clash of 'Oz' Titans." *Los Angeles Times.* March 11, 2013.

Paper

Parker, David B. "Oz: L. Frank Baum's Theosophical Utopia." Kennesaw Academic Forum. 1996.

Web Sites

www.boxoffice.com
casinogambling.about.com
www.cinematographers.nl
classiq.me
collections.oscars.org
www.dark-side-of-the-rainbow.com
www.davemanuel.com/inflation-calculator.php
dawnschickflicks.blogspot.com
www.deadline.com/hollywood/
www.fandango.com
www.geni.com/documents
www.haroldarlen.com
www.hiddenhistoryofoz.wordpress.com
www.ilab.org
www.javasbachelorpad.com
www.jgdb.com (Judy Garland Database)
www.loc.gov
www.lucyfan.com
www.matildajoslyngage.org
michaelstvtray.tumblr.com
www.mikeclinesthenplaying.com
www.themoneymasters.com
www.noahs-ark.org

www.otrcat.com

ozclub.org

oz.wikia.com

www.pachofaunfinished.wordpress.com

press.princeton.edu

www.psychotronicpaul.blogspot.com/cult-cartoons

www.scpr.org

screendeco.wordpress.com

www.snopes.com

www.thebioscope.net

www.thejudyroom.com

www.lucyfan.com

mgmbacklot.info

theozenthusiast.blogspot.com

www.refinery29.com

www.simplypawsomeblog.wordpress.com

www.songwritershalloffame.org

www.tralfaz.blogspot.com

www.usagold.com

www.vanityfair.com

www.waltdisneysreturntooz.com

www.widescreenmuseum.com

wiki.answers.com

Index

Page numbers in **boldface** indicate photos or other images.

THE FAQ SERIES